Fifth Edition

Children's Literature, Briefly

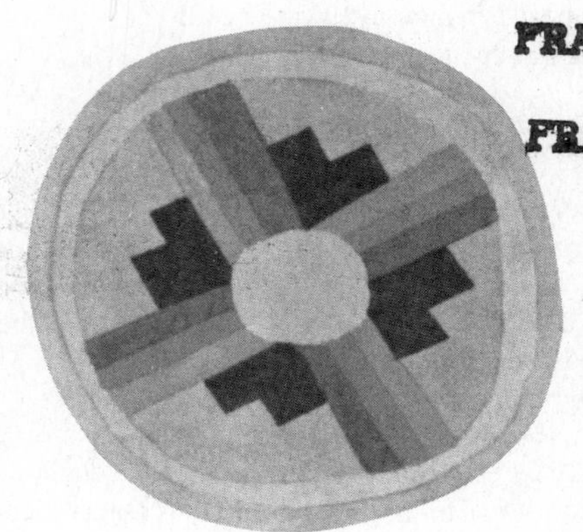

Michael O. Tunnell
Brigham Young University

James S. Jacobs
Brigham Young University

Terrell A. Young
Washington State University

Gregory Bryan
University of Manitoba

Boston Columbus Indianapolis New York San Francisco Upper Saddle River
Amsterdam Cape Town Dubai London Madrid Milan Munich Paris Montreal Toronto
Delhi Mexico City Sao Paulo Sydney Hong Kong Seoul Singapore Taipei Tokyo

Vice President, Editor-in-Chief: Aurora Martínez Ramos
Development Editor: Hope Madden
Editor: Erin K. L. Grelak
Editorial Assistant: Michelle Hochberg
Vice President, Director of Marketing: Margaret Waples
Executive Marketing Manager: Krista Clark
Production Editor: Annette Joseph
Editorial Production Service: Omegatype Typography, Inc.
Manufacturing Buyer: Megan Cochran
Electronic Composition: Omegatype Typography, Inc.
Interior Design: Omegatype Typography, Inc.
Art Director: Linda Knowles
Cover Designer: Susan Paradise

Credits and acknowledgments borrowed from other sources and reproduced, with permission, in this textbook appear on appropriate page within text or on pages xvii–xx.

Library of Congress Cataloging-in-Publication Data

Children's literature, briefly.—5th ed. / Michael O. Tunnell . . . [et al.].
p. cm.
Rev. ed. of: Children's literature, briefly / Michael O. Tunnell, James S. Jacobs. 4th ed. c2012.
Includes bibliographical references and index.
ISBN-13: 978-0-13-248056-7 (pbk.)
ISBN-10: 0-13-248056-5 (pbk.)
1. Children's literature—Study and teaching. 2. Children's literature—History and criticism. 3. Children—Books and reading. I. Tunnell, Michael O. Children's literature, briefly.
PN1008.8.J33 2012
809'.89282—dc22

2010034285

10 9 8 7 6 5 4 RRD-VA 15 14 13 12

www.pearsonhighered.com

ISBN-10: 0-13-248056-5
ISBN-13: 978-0-13-248056-7

About the Authors

Michael O. Tunnell teaches children's literature at Brigham Young University. He has published several professional books, including *The Story of Ourselves: Teaching History through Children's Literature* (with Richard Ammon), as well as a variety of journal articles about children's books and reading. He also writes for young readers. Some of his titles include *The Children of Topaz*, *Mailing May*, *Wishing Moon*, and *Candy Bomber: The Story of the Berlin Airlift's "Chocolate Pilot."* He has twice served on the award selection committee for the John Newbery Medal, the oldest and most prestigious children's book prize.

James S. Jacobs began his career happily teaching English in grades 7 through 12. Next he taught at a junior college where, to his dismay, he was assigned to teach a children's literature course. He discovered a new love and life path and returned to graduate school for a degree in children's literature. Since then he has taught it at Brigham Young University. He interrupted his university life to gain experience in an elementary classroom, teaching fourth grade for two years at a U.S. Army school in Germany. His academic writing focuses on Lloyd Alexander and he has written one picture book for children.

Terrell A. Young teaches courses in children's literature and reading at Washington State University. He also serves as a member of the Board of Directors of the International Reading Association and has served on numerous book award committees. Terry has published many articles and books about reading and children's literature. His most recent books are *Creating Lifelong Readers through Independent Reading* (with Barbara Moss) and *Matching Books and Readers: Helping English Learners in Grades K–6* (with Nancy Hadaway). He was the 2006 recipient of the International Reading Association Outstanding Teacher Educator in Reading Award.

Gregory Bryan is a member of the faculty of education at the University of Manitoba, Canada. He teaches children's literature and early and middle years literacy courses. His research interests revolve around notions of reading engagement. In 2009, he completed his Ph.D. from the University of British Columbia, having previously completed his undergraduate and master's degrees at Brigham Young University. Greg was born and raised in Australia and returns home as often as possible.

Contents

Part Two The Books Themselves

Preface

When the first edition of this book was published in 1996, we stated in the preface that we felt the subtitle should be "A children's literature textbook for people who don't like children's literature textbooks." Until that time, we had taught children's literature at the university without using a textbook because virtually all the ones available were too expensive and too extensive for an introductory course. We owned and regularly consulted the available texts, but they seemed more like reference books. Our biggest concern, though, was neither the cost nor the length but the hours stolen from students when they could be reading actual children's books. The focus of a children's literature course should be on those marvelous children's titles. They are more important than any text, including this one, and we originally wrote this book on that assumption.

Though the massive children's literature tomes are still around today, a variety of shorter texts are now available. As with the authors of competing textbooks, we have written our book as an overview to shed light on children's literature and its use with young readers. However, one way in which ours may differ is in its conversational rather than academic voice. We have made an effort to make the reading as enjoyable as possible, while still providing all the pertinent information and ideas relating to the field of children's literature.

Our job as teachers, whether university or elementary, is to introduce children's books and illuminate them for our students. These books can offer insight and pleasure without having to be explained, analyzed, or used as objects of study. Yet appropriate commentary, if it is secondary to the books and doesn't become too self-important, can help both teachers and children find their own ways to the rewards of reading.

The goal of this text, then, is to provide a practical overview of children's books, offering a framework and background information while keeping the spotlight on the books themselves. That's why we kept the textbook itself and each chapter short.

And that's why we limited the book lists. The world of children's literature offers only one completely dependable book list—your own. Throughout the following chapters, we present ours, absolutely trustworthy in every way—to us. You are allowed to harbor serious doubts about our choices, but the value of the lists is that they may save you time wandering up and down library aisles.

We organized our book lists at the end of the chapters under four different headings. It is important to note that the titles we suggest are mostly for young readers up through eighth grade (age 14).

1. *Fifteen of Our Favorites.* The 15 books listed at the ends of Chapters 7–14 are terrific reading. These lists are very short, the result of much negotiating, often emotional, but largely friendly. The purpose of the 15 is to provide solid suggestions for those who wonder where to find a good book. Each title is annotated to give a brief idea of the content.

2. *Others We Like.* These titles (generally around 30) are also annotated. Each is a book we like very much. Don't be surprised if you find some of them more appealing than our 15 favorites.
3. *Easier to Read.* Next, we have added 10 to 15 titles that are shorter and appeal to children who are struggling to make reading a rewarding pastime.
4. *Picture Books.* In most genre chapters, we have included 15 to 20 picture books we consider excellent. Not all of these titles are for use exclusively in the lower grades; many are appropriate for the upper grades as well.

New to This Edition

In revising the previous edition of *Children's Literature, Briefly,* we concentrated on recasting many of the chapters to achieve more clarity. This required reexamining our views on literature, reading education, and education in general. Though our philosophies have remained mostly unchanged, we believe that we understand them better than before and therefore have been able to communicate them more clearly and effectively—our major goal with this new edition. To achieve this goal, we invited two colleagues on board to help with the revision: Dr. Terrell Young from Washington State University and Dr. Gregory Bryan from the University of Manitoba. Their perspectives and expertise have added greatly to the fifth edition of *Children's Literature, Briefly.*

Besides the changes mentioned above, we have made a number of other alterations, including the following:

- We added five children's book titles to "Ten of Our Favorites," a list of our top picks found at the conclusion of the chapters in Part Two. Now, we offer "Fifteen of Our Favorites."
- Instead of annotating only the books in the "Fifteen of Our Favorites" list, as in the past, we have added annotations to the 30 to 40 books in the list titled "Others We Like."
- We have changed Appendix A from "Guidelines for Building a Classroom Library" to "Guidelines for Building and Using a Classroom Library." Obtaining books now comprises only half the content. The other half focuses on maximizing student access to classroom libraries and to the research related to the use and effectiveness of those collections.
- We have reworked Appendix B ("Book Selection Aids"), which covered print sources, to now include 60% print sources and 40% online resources.
- Chapter 18 ("Teaching with Children's Books") has been largely recast, with an updated and enlarged review of the research that supports the use of children's books in homes and schools. You will also find that Chapter 17 has been heavily reworked, with a fresh and updated look at what has come to light recently in the area of student reading motivation.
- The Database of Children's Literature appears on the MyEducationKit Web site for this text. The database includes more than 22,000 children's titles searchable by author, illustrator, awards won, publication date, and topic.

Prepare with the Power of Classroom Practice

MyEducationKit's easy-to-assign homework and activities will engage your students and ensure that they come to class more prepared. It saves you the class time would otherwise be spent reviewing the basics and lets you devote that time to higher-level learning experiences. Informed by evidence-based practice, MyEducationKit connects your course content to real classrooms with interactive exercises and activities that enhance students' learning and give them a deeper understanding of teaching.

- Prepare your students to analyze, reflect, and respond to **real classroom situations** with assignments that provide them with video, case studies, and authentic student and teacher artifacts.
- Search through more than **22,000 exemplary titles of children's literature** on the Database of Children's Literature.
- Reflect on the craftsmanship behind quality children's literature using the **podcasts and conversations** with many of today's top writers and illustrators.
- Use the **lesson planning software** to develop high-quality lesson plans. The software also makes it easy to integrate your state's content standards into all of your lesson plans.
- Prepare your students to pass their teacher licensure exams by familiarizing them with **teacher certification test** requirements. This module includes descriptions of what is covered on each exam and opportunities to answer sample test questions.

Acknowledgments

We would like to thank the reviewers of our manuscript for their valuable insights and comments: Diane Barone, University of Nevada, Reno; Lisa L. Sandoval, Joliet Junior College; Jean Stringam, Missouri State University; and Rhonda L. Truitt, Ed. D., Catawba College.

Thanks also go to our research assistants: Rebecca Maxfield, Jennifer Elison, Courtney Cook, Mallory Keith, Camille Elison, and Jessica McClellan for their help with the textbook and particularly with assembling and entering data for the children's literature database. To you, we are especially grateful.

Credits

Color Illustrations

1. Reprinted with the permission of Atheneum Books for Young Readers, an imprint of Simon and Schuster Children's Publishing Division, from *The Relatives Came* by Cynthia Rylant, illustrated by Stephen Gammell. Illustrations copyright © 1985 Stephen Gammell.

2. From *The Fortune Tellers* by Lloyd Alexander, illustrated by Trina Schart Hyman, copyright © 1992 by Trina Schart Hyman, illustrations. Used by permission of Dutton Children's Books, a division of Penguin Young Readers Group, a member of Penguin Group (USA) Inc., 345 Hudson Street, New York, NY 10014. All rights reserved.

3. From *The Friend* by Sarah Stewart, pictures by David Small. Pictures copyright © 2004 by David Small. Reprinted by permission of Farrar, Straus and Giroux, LLC.

4. From *Frog Goes to Dinner* by Mercer Mayer, copyright © 1974, renewed 2002 by Mercer Mayer. Used by permission of Dial Books for Young Readers, a division of Penguin Young Readers Group, a member of Penguin Group (USA) Inc., 345 Hudson Street, New York, NY 10014. All rights reserved.

5. From *Blueberries for Sal* by Robert McCloskey, copyright 1948, renewed 1976 by Robert McCloskey. Used by permission of Viking Penguin, a division of Penguin Young Readers Group, a member of Penguin Group (USA), Inc., 345 Hudson Street, New York, NY 10014. All rights reserved.

6. Reprinted with the permission of Simon and Schuster Books for Young Readers, an imprint of Simon and Schuster Children's Publishing Division, from *Rosie's Walk* by Pat Hutchins. Copyright © 1968 Patricia Hutchins.

7. Illustration from *The Polar Express* by Chris Van Allsburg. Copyright © 1985 by Chris Van Allsburg. Reprinted by permission of Houghton Mifflin Harcourt Publishing Company. All rights reserved.

8. From *Rapunzel* by Paul O. Zelinsky, copyright © 1997 by Paul O. Zelinsky. Used by permission of Dutton Children's Books, a division of Penguin Young Readers Group, a member of Penguin Group (USA) Inc., 345 Hudson Street, New York, NY 10014. All rights reserved.

9. From *The Voice of the Wood* by Claude Clément, illustrated by Frédéric Clément, translated by Lenny Hort, copyright © 1988 by l'ecole des loisirs. Translation copyright © 1989 by Dial Books for Young Readers. Used by permission of Dial Books for Young Readers, a division of Penguin Young Readers Group, a member of Penguin Group (USA) Inc., 345 Hudson Street, New York, NY 10014. All rights reserved.

10. From *A Chair for My Mother.* Copyright © 1982 by Vera B. Williams. Used by permission of HarperCollins Publishers.

11. Reprinted with the permission of Atheneum Books for Young Readers, an imprint of Simon and Schuster Children's Publishing Division, from *Freedom Summer* by Deborah Wiles, illustrated by Jerome Lagarrigue. Illustrations copyright © 2001 Jerome Lagarrigue.

12. From *Will Moses Mother Goose* by Will Moses, copyright © 2003 by Will Moses, illustrations. Used by permission of Philomel Books, a division of Penguin Young Readers Group, a member of Penguin Group (USA) Inc., 345 Hudson Street, New York, NY 10014. All rights reserved.

13. From *Flying Feet: A Mud Flat Story.* Illustrations © 2004 by James Stevenson. Used by permission of HarperCollins Publishers.

14. Illustration from *Zathura: A Space Adventure* by Chris Van Allsburg. Copyright © 2002 by Chris Van Allsburg. Reprinted by permission of Houghton Mifflin Harcourt Publishing Company. All rights reserved.

15. From *Ben's Trumpet.* Copyright © 1979 by Rachel Isadora Majorano. Used by permission of HarperCollins Publishers.

16. Reprinted with permission of Atheneum Books for Young Readers, an imprint of Simon and Schuster Children's Publishing Division, from *Once a Mouse . . .* by Marcia Brown. Copyright © 1961 Marcia Brown, copyright renewed 1989 Marcia Brown.

17. From *Bernard the Angry Rooster* by Mary Wormell. Copyright © 2001 by Mary Wormell. Reprinted by permission of Farrar, Straus and Giroux, LLC.

18. From *One Night in the Coral Sea.* Illustrations copyright © 2005 by Robin Brickman. Used with permission by Charlesbridge Publishing, Inc. All rights reserved.

19. Illustration from *Golem* by David Wisniewski. Copyright © 1996 by David Wisniewski. Reprinted by permission of Clarion Books, an imprint of Houghton Mifflin Harcourt Publishing Company. All rights reserved.

20. From *Abraham Lincoln* by Ingri and Edgar Parin d'Aulaire, copyright 1939, 1957 by Doubleday, a division of Random House, Inc. Used by permission of Random House Children's Books, a division of Random House, Inc.

21. From Andrea Pinkney's *Ella Fitzgerald: The Tale of a Vocal Virtuosa* © 2002, illustrated by Brian Pinkney. Reprinted by permission of Disney/Hyperion, an imprint of Disney Book Group LLC. All rights reserved.

22. Copyright © 1993 by Bruce McMillan, from *Mouse Views: What the Class Pet Saw.* Used by permission of Holiday House, Inc. All rights reserved.

23. From *The Paper Crane.* Copyright © 1985 by Molly Bang. Used with the permission of Greenwillow Books/HarperCollins Publishers.

24. From *Heartland,* © 1989 by Wendell Minor. Reprinted by permission.

25. Reprinted with the permission of Simon and Schuster Books for Young Readers, an imprint of Simon and Schuster Children's Publishing Division, from *Thorn Rose* by the Brothers Grimm, retold and illustrated by Errol Le Cain. Copyright © 1975 Errol Le Cain.

26. From *Round Trip.* Illustrations © 1983 by Ann Jonas. Used by permission of HarperCollins Publishers.

27. From *Saint George and the Dragon* by Margaret Hodges, illustrated by Trina Schart Hyman. Text copyright © 1984 by Margaret Hodges; illustrations copyright © 1984 by Trina Schart Hyman. Reprinted by permission of Little, Brown and Company.

28. Illustration from *Tuesday* by David Wiesner. Copyright © 1991 by David Wiesner. Reprinted by permission of Clarion Books, an imprint of Houghton Mifflin Harcourt Publishing Company. All rights reserved.

29. From *Deep in the Forest* by Brinton Turkle, copyright © 1976 by Brinton Turkle. Used by permission of Dutton Children's Books, a division of Penguin Young Readers Group, a member of Penguin Group (USA) Inc., 345 Hudson Street, New York, NY 10014. All rights reserved.

30. From *Snow-White and the Seven Dwarfs: A Tale from the Brothers Grimm* translated by Randall Jarrell, illustrated by Nancy Ekholm Burkert. Illustrations © 1972 by Nancy Ekholm Burkert. Reprinted by permission of Farrar, Straus and Giroux, LLC.

31, 32. Reprinted with the permission of Simon and Schuster Books for Young Readers, an imprint of Simon and Schuster Children's Publishing Division, from *Thorn Rose* by the Brothers Grimm, retold and illustrated by Errol Le Cain. Copyright © 1975 Errol Le Cain.

33. Copyright © 1992 by Glen Rounds, from *Three Little Pigs and the Big Bad Wolf.* Used by permission of Holiday House, Inc. All rights reserved.

34. From *Arrow to the Sun* by Gerald McDermott, copyright © 1974 by Gerald McDermott. Used by permission of Viking Penguin, a division of Penguin Young Readers Group, a member of Penguin Group (USA) Inc., 345 Hudson Street, New York, NY 10014. All rights reserved.

Text

p. 2: From *The Body and How It Works* by Steve Parker. Copyright © Dorling Kindersley 1987, 1998. Reproduced by permission of Penguin Books Ltd.

p. 12: From *Halloween Pie,* reprinted by permission of Michael Tunnell.

p. 19: From *The Amazing Bone* by William Steig. Copyright © 1976 by William Steig. Reprinted by permission of Farrar, Straus and Giroux, LLC.

p. 21: From *Ira Sleeps Over* by Bernard Waber. Copyright © 1972 by Bernard Waber. Reprinted by permission of Houghton Mifflin Harcourt Publishing Company.

p. 22: *From Millions of Cats* by Wanda Gag, copyright 1928 by Wanda Gag, renewed © 1956 by Robert Janssen. Used by permission of Coward-McCann, a division of Penguin Young Readers Group, a member of Penguin Group (USA) Inc., 345 Hudson Street, New York, NY 10014. All rights reserved.

p. 22: *Goodnight Moon* © 1947 by Harper & Row. Text © renewed 1975 by Roberta Brown Rauch. Illustrations © renewed 1975 by Edith Hurd, Clement Hurd, John Thacher Hurd, and George Hellyer, as trustees of the Edith and Clement Hurd 1982 Trust. Used by permission of HarperCollins Publishers.

p. 22: Excerpt from *Buford the Little Bighorn* by Bill Peet. Copyright © 1967, renewed 1991 by William B. Peet. Reprinted by permission of Houghton Mifflin Harcourt Publishing Company. All rights reserved.

p. 22: From Walt Disney's *Snow White and the Seven Dwarfs* published by Random House © 1973 Walt Disney Productions, used by permission from Disney Enterprises, Inc.

p. 22: From *Snow-White and the Seven Dwarfs: A Tale from the Brothers Grimm* translated by Randall Jarrell, illustrated by Nancy Ekholm Burkert. Illustrations © 1972 by Nancy Ekholm Burkert. Reprinted by permission of Farrar, Straus and Giroux, LLC.

p. 32: Text copyright © 1993 by David Schwartz. Used by permission of HarperCollins Publishers.

p. 32: Reprinted with the permission of Simon and Schuster Books for Young Readers, an imprint of Simon and Schuster Children's Publishing Division from *Rosie's Walk* by Pat Hutchins. Copyright © 1968 Patricia Hutchins.

p. 33: From *Never Spit on Your Shoes* by Denys Cazet. Reprinted by permission of Scholastic.

p. 41: Photo reprinted courtesy of The Horn Book, Inc. www.hbook.com

p. 54: Used by permission of HarperCollins Publishers.

p. 64: Text copyright © 1995 by George Shannon. Used by permission of HarperCollins Publishers.

p. 65: From *If You Hopped Like a Frog* by David Schwartz. Reprinted by permission of Scholastic.

p. 67: Excerpt from *Brown Bear, Brown Bear, What Do You See?* by Bill Martin, Jr. Copyright © 1967 by Holt, Rinehart and Winston; renewed 1995 by Bill Martin, Jr. Copyright © 2004 by the Estate of Bill Martin, Jr. Reprinted by arrangement with Henry Holt and Company, LLC.

p. 68: From *Sheep in a Jeep* by Nancy Shaw, illustrated by Margot Apple. Text copyright © 1986 by Nancy Shaw. Reprinted by permission of Houghton Mifflin Harcourt Publishing Company. All rights reserved.

p. 70: From *Max's First Word* by Rosemary Wells, copyright © 1979 by Rosemary Wells. Used by permission of Dial Books for Young Readers, a division of Penguin Young Readers Group, a member of Penguin Group (USA) Inc., 345 Hudson Street, New York, NY 10014. All rights reserved.

p. 85: "Take the Butterfly" from *One at a Time* by David TW McCord Trust. Copyright © 1961, 1962, 1965, 1966, 1968, 1970, 1971, 1972, 1973, 1974. Reprinted by permission of Little, Brown and Company.

p. 87: "New Kid on the Block." Text copyright © 1984 by Jack Prelutsky. Used by permission of HarperCollins Publishers.

p. 89: "Song of the Train" from *One at a Time* by David TW McCord Trust. Copyright © 1961, 1962, 1965, 1966, 1968, 1970, 1971, 1972, 1973, 1974. Reprinted by permission of Little, Brown and Company.

p. 90: "I Like It When It's Mizzly" by Aileen Fisher. From *I Like Weather* © 1991. Reprinted by permission of Marian Reiner.

p. 91: "Full of the Moon." Copyright © 1959, renewed 1986 by Karla Kuskin. Used by permission of Scott Treimel NY.

p. 91: "My Box" by Myra Cohn Livingston. From *The Way Things Are and Other Poems* © 1974. Reprinted by permission of Marian Reiner.

p. 91: "Teevee" by Eve Merriam. From *Jamboree Rhymes for All Times* © 1981. Reprinted by permission of Marian Reiner.

p. 92: "How to Tell the Top of a Hill." Reprinted by permission of the Ciardi Family Publishing Trust.

p. 92: "Pigeons" by Lillian Moore. From *I Thought I Heard the City* © 1997. Reprinted by permission of Marian Reiner.

p. 93: "Love Song." Copyright © 2011 by The Arnold Adoff Revocable Living Trust.

p. 94: "Stockings." Copyright © 1992 by Valerie Worth. Used by permission of HarperCollins Publishers.

p. 94: "Pencils." Copyright © 1992 by Barbara Juster Esbensen. Used by permission of HarperCollins Publishers.

p. 95: "Keepsake" from *Honey, I Love and Other Poems* by Eloise Greenfield. Text copyright © 1978 by Eloise Greenfield. Used by permission of HarperCollins Publishers.

p. 95: "The Kite That Braved Old Orchard Beach." Copyright © 1991 by X. J. Kennedy. Reprinted by permission of Curtis Brown, Ltd.

p. 95: "Night." Reprinted by permission of The Gina Maccoby Literary Agency. Copyright © 1959, renewed 1987 by Mary Ann Hoberman.

p. 96: "Music Lesson" from *A Dime a Dozen* by Nikki Grimes, copyright © 1998 by Nikki Grimes. Used by permission of Dial Books for Young Readers, a division of Penguin Young Readers Group, a member of Penguin Group (USA) Inc., 345 Hudson Street, New York, NY 10014. All rights reserved.

p. 96: "When I Dance." Copyright © 1977 by Lee Bennett Hopkins. Reprinted by permission of Curtis Brown, Ltd.

p. 98: "A Flamingo Is" © J. Patrick Lewis, 1990.

p. 100: "Things" from *Honey, I Love and Other Poems* by Eloise Greenfield. Text copyright © 1978 by Eloise Greenfield. Used by permission of HarperCollins Publishers.

p. 109: From "Wishful Thinking—or Hopeful Dreaming" by Lloyd Alexander. Children's Literature Research Collection, Free Library of Pennsylvania. Reprinted by permission.

p. 178: From *Amazing Mammals* by Dr. Alexandra Parsons. Copyright © Dorling Kindersley 1990, 1998. Reproduced by permission of Penguin Books Ltd.

p. 178: From *The Mysterious Universe* by Ellen Jackson. Text copyright © 2008 by Ellen Jackson. Reprinted by permission of Houghton Mifflin Harcourt Publishing Company. All rights reserved.

p. 180: Text copyright © 1985 by Seymour Simon. Used by permission of HarperCollins Publishers.

Chapter 1

Why Read?

Like most important questions, "Why read?" seems embarrassingly obvious. Reading simply *is* important. Period. We know that, and we assume everyone else knows that. Even in today's climate of constant controversy and limitless lawsuits, where no one appears to agree with anyone on anything, reading receives unanimous support. An antireading position has no voice, claims no champion, and gets no press. No magazine or newspaper prints an article about the evils of the reading act or how time spent with print is wasted. The push is always toward more reading. So why is reading universally acclaimed?

Engaged and Unengaged Reading

Engaged Reading—Immediate Rewards

Engaged reading, like eating, is one of life's activities that simultaneously yields both pleasure and benefit. When we chomp down on a three-way chimichanga, the sensations of texture, temperature, and taste reward us right then. No one needs to confirm the results; from our own personal taste buds, we know immediately that the bite is satisfying. In addition, our digestive system now turns the agreeable mixture of beans, beef, lettuce, onions, and tortilla into nutrients that keep us going. Benefits—energy and good health—automatically follow the pleasing meal, but the primary reason for lifting a fork is the immediate reward of tasting.

Immediate is the operative word. At the very moment their eyes pass over the words, engaged readers are personally motivated, focused, and involved. They have their reward as soon as they are drawn into the subject, thinking of nothing beyond those sentences, paragraphs, and pages, even the reading process itself. Engaged readers don't even see words after the first line or two. In a story, they see scenes, people, and action. In nonfiction, they test theories or think of applications or chew on the facts.

Visit the MyEducationKit for this course to enhance your understanding of chapter concepts with activities, weblinks, podcasts, and a searchable database of more than 22,000 children's literature titles.

When we already have an interest in what we read, engaged reading comes naturally. No one wonders if the instructions to assemble a swing set for a much-loved but impatient 3-year-old will make good reading. The purpose is determined, and the reading engages immediately. Before the first word is read, we know the instructions are worth it. At a bookstore sale table, a Civil War buff picks up a book on Stonewall Jackson and is likely to buy it. A child with an interest in dinosaurs is drawn to a book on the subject. Even when a book is not particularly well written, the person who is interested in the topic becomes an engaged reader without persuasion or effort.

If a reader does not display a specific interest, some books create that interest. The first paragraph of *The Ruby in the Smoke* (Philip Pullman, 1985) often entices readers to turn the next page.

> On a cold, fretful afternoon in early October, 1872, a hansom cab drew up outside the offices of Lockhart and Selby, Shipping Agents, in the financial heart of London, and a young girl got out and paid the driver.
>
> She was a person of sixteen or so—alone, and uncommonly pretty. She was slender and pale, and dressed in mourning, with a black bonnet under which she tucked back a straying twist of blond hair that the wind had teased loose. She had unusually dark brown eyes for one so fair. Her name was Sally Lockhart; and within fifteen minutes, she was going to kill a man. (p. 3)

Nonfiction can have the same immediate attraction. In *The Body: And How It Works,* by Steve Parker (1998), a double-page spread focuses on the skin. The first paragraph reads:

> On the outside, you are dead. Your hair and the surface of your skin are made of dead cells. But less than a millimeter away under the surface of your skin are some of the busiest cells in your body. They are continually dividing to make new layers of skin cells which harden and die, to replace the top layer of skin as it is worn away. Every day millions of dead skin cells rub off as you wash, dry yourself with a towel, get dressed and move about. Much of the "dust" in a house is dead skin which has rubbed off the bodies of people. (1998, p. 10)

Immediate reward, a dependable criterion for determining why people choose to read, is difficult for others to predict. Yes, we can choose books that reflect the interests of a reader, and yes, we can recommend books that are pleasing to us. But only the individual reader knows what is personally attractive and satisfying and to what degree. Sometimes their choices surprise us. Consider the following actual incidents:

- Conventional wisdom says that a reader must comprehend a certain percentage of written material for reading to be successful, yet 3-year-old Bobby Morgan, whose parents read to him regularly, got up early to spend time with issues of *National Geographic,* which he preferred to picture books. His parents knew that he was comprehending only a fraction of the material, but he continued to spend hour after hour with the magazine.

- Common sense indicates that we seek comfortable surroundings when engaging in a long activity such as extended reading, yet Sean, a college student, drove to the bookstore on a snowy day to buy a new book and decided to spend a few minutes looking it over in his car before heading home. Time passed, and the sun set. To continue reading, Sean had to hold the book to the window so the lights from the parking lot would shine onto the page. Four hours later, he started his chilled car for the drive to his apartment.

- Educational practice says that the difficulty of a text should be matched to individual reading abilities, yet Bill, a junior high student with second-grade reading skills, chose a book far beyond his tested level. A part of his school day was spent in intensified reading instruction in a lab setting, with the last half-hour devoted to uninterrupted individual reading. Educator Dan Fader watched Bill during his 30 minutes of reading time until the bell sounded. "Still absorbed in his reading, Bill closed the book, glanced at the cover, placed the book in his bag, and started for the door. Intrigued by this 13-year-old second-grade reader, I crossed his path at the door and walked with him as I asked, 'What are you reading?' *'Jaws.'* 'Is it good?' 'Yeah!' 'But isn't it hard?' 'Sure it's hard, but it's worth it!'" (Fader, 1976, p. 236).

"It's worth it!" When seeking satisfaction from print, only the individual reader can judge what "is worth it." When we look only for specific information—the sodium content in a frozen lasagna, the definition of *arcadian,* or what Jason's teacher said in the note he brought home—it is essential that we get the facts but not essential that we read them ourselves. Seeking information from print indeed can be engaging, but if someone else reads and tells us what we want to know, we generally can be satisfied. In her transactional theory of literature and reading, Louise Rosenblatt (1978) calls this reading for facts *efferent* reading. We are engaged and motivated to acquire that knowledge, but it is not imperative that we discover it with our own eyes.

Esthetic reading is different from efferent reading because the goal is not to acquire facts but to participate in something new. In esthetic reading, readers focus on what they are experiencing as their eyes pass over the words. This kind of reading cannot be summarized by another but must be done personally because it is not centered on data. The facts are not the most important part; engagement with the experience is. Knowing the plot of *Tuck Everlasting* (Babbitt, 1975) is not the same as experiencing with Winnie Foster her difficult choice between following a natural life span or living forever as a young girl. Being told that the protagonist in *Stargirl* (Spinelli, 2000) shakes up the social structure at school with her honest but unorthodox views of life comes nowhere close to being with her as she brings her ukulele and white rat to class. Reading for experience—esthetic reading—can no more be done by someone else and then reported to us than our eating can be done by another. We don't want information on food flavors; we want those flavors to flow over our own taste buds. When we read for experience, we aren't satisfied simply by knowing where the book ends up. We want to make that journey to the final page ourselves because when we have lived in a really good book, we are never quite the same again.

In short, engaged readers—those who read for personal reasons—know the satisfying feeling of finding pleasure in print and being rewarded in two areas: locating information and gaining experience.

Engaged Reading—Long-Term Benefits

In addition to the immediate rewards offered by engaged reading, a stunning number of benefits accumulate over time as by-products of reading for personal pleasure. Those who read satisfying books of their own choosing with some regularity can expect the following to happen to them. These benefits do not comprise a comprehensive list but are only some of the results of personal reading over months and years.

- Increase automaticity and speed at the word recognition level. We simply learn to read faster. (Cunningham and Stanovich, 1998)
- Greatly expand vocabulary. (Anderson, Wilson, & Fielding, 1988)
- Develop reading comprehension abilities. (Juel, Griffith, & Gough, 1986)
- Experience gains in reading achievement. (Taylor, Frye, and Maruyama, 1990)
- Increase verbal fluency. (Cullinan, 2000)

- Score higher on achievement tests in all subject areas. (Krashen, 2004)
- Acquire greater insight into human nature and decision-making. (Bruner, 1996)
- Gain a better understanding of other cultures. (Meek, 1991)
- Score higher on general knowledge exams. (Cunningham & Stanovich, 1998)

Remember that all these benefits arrive naturally as we continue to read self-selected, personally pleasing books and materials. The focus of that reading is still on the immediate rewards—we pick up books because they are interesting and satisfying—but unmistakable growth and development comes automatically as we spend time with those books we like. And over years, all those skills we develop and knowledge we acquire result in our becoming educated people. It is possible to get a diploma without getting an education, and conversely, it is possible to become educated without earning a diploma. But educated people, with or without diplomas, are always readers.

Besides the increased academic strengths that come from engaged reading, Jim Trelease (2006, p. xxv) identifies other personal benefits that await those who welcome books into their lives.

> One can arguably state: reading is the single most important social factor in American life today. Here's a formula to support that. It sounds simplistic, but all its parts can be documented, and while not 100 percent universal, it holds true far more often than not.
>
> 1. The more you read, the more you know. (Foertsch, 1992)
> 2. The more you know, the smarter you grow. (Anderson, Hiebert, Scott, & Wilkinson, 1985; Ravitch & Finn, 1987)
> 3. The smarter you are, the longer you stay in school. (Associated Press, 1994)
> 4. The longer you stay in school, the more diplomas you earn and the longer you are employed—thus the more money you earn in a lifetime. (Lee, 1994; Day & Newburger, 2002)
> 5. The more diplomas you earn, the higher your children's grades will be in school. (ACT, 2004; Perie, Moran, & Lutkus, 2005)
> 6. The more diplomas you earn, the longer you live. (Rogot, Sorlie, & Johnson, 1992; Marmot, 2005)

Still other long-term benefits of engaged reading can be viewed through the lens of bibliotherapy. In its broadest definition, *bibliotherapy* is any kind of emotional healing that comes from reading books. Therapy derived from books falls into at least three different categories: (1) the broad therapeutic feelings of recreation and gratification experienced by an individual reader, (2) the sense of connectedness felt by members of a group who read and share books together, and (3) the particular information and insight books can provide in dealing with specific personal problems (Chatton, 1988).

The first two categories, recreation and connectedness, result naturally from reading. Those who have found compelling titles experience the first category as they discover the deep satisfaction, stimulation, and comfort that books can bring. The second category—connectedness—occurs when readers experience a book along with others, a new dimension to the group relationship. A teacher and classroom of children who read a book together are able to connect with one another in new ways when laughing, crying, or simply talking about their mutual experience.

The third category—dealing with specific and often deep-seated personal problems—is, of course, best reserved for trained psychologists and psychotherapists, who can and do use books successfully in their practices. Other adults can serve children simply by reading and recommending good books and allowing personal insight, comfort, and the answering of troubling questions to come in their own natural and timely ways. Bibliotherapy, whatever the level, promises parents, teachers, and children personal rewards as a result of time spent with books.

Unengaged Reading

Unengaged reading is the reading of necessity, the reading required by others or forced on us. Unengaged reading is the reading we do not like, the reading we do for others, the reading we have to do, that we would not do if not required. Classic unengaged reading is largely associated with school. In the classroom setting, with its emphasis on instruction and mastery, it is easy for the teacher to focus on the peripherals instead of the book itself. Students are given stories or passages to read not for the places the words take them or thoughts they present but as underbrush where the secret skills of reading or the elements of literature hide out. The sentences and paragraphs are camouflage for initial consonant blends, prediction questions, comprehension checks, vocabulary words, theme, tone, symbolism, and the objects of a multitude of other skills lessons.

This is not to say that the skills of reading are unimportant. The skills need to be learned, and students need the confidence that comes from understanding how language works and from an awareness that they are becoming skilled and competent readers. The problem comes when students are given a good story to read but the primary goal is not involvement with that story but rather to hunt down or explain peripheral matters. This emphasis is a bit like sitting down to Thanksgiving dinner and seeing only vitamins and minerals on your plate or, worse yet, being served a pile of pills instead of the steaming turkey and trimmings because, after all, those nutritional elements are what is important for fueling our bodily furnaces.

In short, engaged reading is personal and unengaged reading is not. Few immediate or lasting benefits come from unengaged reading. If the reader is not involved with the text—not engaged in the information or experience—the reading remains empty and unproductive, speaking neither to our hearts nor our heads.

Does this mean that any assigned book will be unengaged reading and therefore automatically suffers the kiss of death? Of course not. An assigned book may begin as unengaged, uninteresting reading yet become important, even invaluable, to the reader. For that to occur, however, it must receive the reader's personal stamp of approval. Somewhere between the covers, even with the full knowledge that the book is required reading and a part of the final grade, the reader may become personally involved in the text. At that point, the book moves from assigned reading to personal reading—from unengaged to engaged. If the book doesn't make that switch, though, it never develops the power to influence or affect the reader. (See Figure 1.1.)

Other Considerations

How the Role of Teacher Expectations Affects Reading Behavior

The expectations a teacher sets for a reading often contribute to engagement and unengagement. If teachers respect the book as an experience that recreates the very texture of life, and encourage students to make their own discoveries while reading, the result often is engagement. If teacher expectations highlight the peripherals, unengaged reading is frequently the outcome. People generally do not turn to books because they want to study the author's use of vocabulary or have a desire to describe the major and minor characters any more than people attend movies to examine the cinematographer's use of the long shot or analyze the kinds of background music. We read fiction and go to the movies to get lost in the story, to see through eyes other than our own. Almost magically, participating in these vicarious experiences sheds light on our own lives. We compare, test, experience, and come away with new thoughts and visions, wondering how we would have

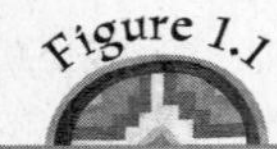

Figure 1.1 Unengaged and Engaged Reading

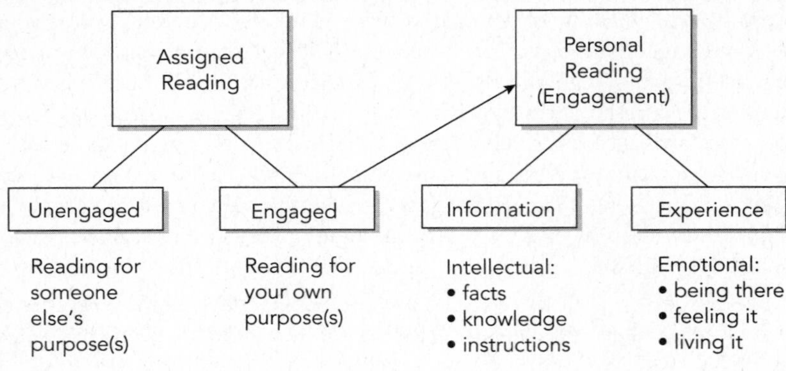

responded in similar situations. The same idea of engagement holds true for nonfiction as well as fiction. When we are engaged in reading informational books, it is largely not the facts that rivet us but the thoughts and insights that come as we read. In *Shipwreck at the Bottom of the World* (Armstrong, 1998), we marvel at Shackleton's courage in leading his men across Antarctica after their ship was crushed by ice. We also ponder the achievements of those visionaries who defied convention in *Seven Wonders of the Ancient World* (Curlee, 2002).

If someone forces us to shift all our concentration from the experience to the externals—the form, the theme, the use of language, or simply the facts in nonfiction—the focus on these elements may make reading the book or attending the movie no more than tedious labor. When teachers provide a purpose for reading that ignores or overshadows the story, they misuse the book. With the best of intentions, they can weaken the power of reading in a variety of ways. In an effort to improve vocabulary, for example, teachers ask students to find the nine examples of onomatopoeia in the first chapter of *Island of the Blue Dolphins* (O'Dell, 1960). Or before having students read a chapter, teachers introduce the difficult vocabulary and ask students to locate the words, define them, and use them in sentences. Or when students know that a traditional book report (plot, setting, theme, characterization, style, point of view) is expected, they tend to focus on the task instead of the experience and come away less fulfilled.

Would our experience with a good movie be enhanced if the manager of the theater passed out mandatory study guides to be completed while we watched the film? We would look over the questions, and our purpose for viewing the movie would shift from living the film to ferreting out the correct responses. At the end, we would not have seen the movie at all. We would have witnessed a collection of facts we needed to identify and isolate. If such were the case, we would likely stop going to movie theaters altogether.

At times, teacher expectations can actually change how a student responds to a book. Lloyd Alexander, an author who attributed his writing success to childhood reading, discovered *Treasure Island* at home as a child and loved it—pure engaged reading. He lived with Jim, he pondered the story when he was away from the book, and he longed to return to the people and events of the tale. Years later, he was assigned the same novel in a high school English class. This time, the reading did not yield the same involvement. Class discussion centered on elements he found uninteresting, assignments interfered with his experience, and he failed the final test "because I couldn't remember the construction of that damned blockhouse" (Alexander, 1993). The teacher held "discussions" with the class but asked only factual questions, gave assignments that did not include Lloyd's focus, and based success on a test of specific and unimportant details. Instead of helping Lloyd get deeper into the story, the teacher's approach actually kept him from the book, turning an earlier engaged reading experience into an unengaged one.

Some readers have spent so many years reading for others that they never learned how to read for themselves and actually have difficulty identifying their own responses to a book. Even some good students respond automatically to "What did you think about the book?" with thoughts like "What does the teacher want?" "What should I have thought about the book?" and "What am I supposed to think about the book?" They have been taught to look for teacher answers and have difficulty seeing that the act of reading can't serve two masters.

We read either for ourselves or for some other purpose. When anything comes between the reader and the printed page, such as a teacher's expectation or an assignment, the reading tends to be unengaged and remain artificial.

Why Do So Few People Choose to Read?

After consulting the National Institute for Literacy, the National Center for Adult Literacy, and the U.S. Census Bureau, Hedges (2009, p. 44) reported: "A third of high school graduates never read another book for the rest of their lives, and neither do 42 percent of college graduates. In 2007, 80% of the families in the United States did not buy or read a book."

One possible reason so many people quit reading after graduation is that they seldom went beyond assigned reading during their time in school. Despite having completed the required reading that marks the path to a diploma, a surprising number of supposedly educated graduates have rarely, if ever, known the sustaining thrill of reading a book that speaks directly and personally to them. The reading they did was for someone else, according to someone else's expectations, and thus life was never breathed into the books they completed for their classes. In short, the books never happened.

These unengaged readers, the ones who can read but don't, are sometimes called *aliterate*. The aliterate person has all the necessary know-how to unlock the meaning in print but chooses not to pick up books. And, as the sign over a small school library reminds us, "The person who can read, and doesn't, is no better off than the person who can't read."

Recognizing Engaged Readers

How do we know if a reader is engaged or unengaged? An engaged reader is not aware of the reading process. Engaged readers don't even see words after the first sentence or two. In a story, they see scenes, people, action. In nonfiction, they test theories or think of applications or chew on the facts. But in neither instance do they focus on the skills of reading. They are unaware of how many pages they have read or how long they have been at the book. They pace themselves accordingly, gulping down great whacking passages quickly or dawdling over a line that gives them particular delight. They never say, "Look at me. I have chosen the correct sound of *y* at the end of *happy*—long *e*. I didn't confuse it with the long *i* sound, like at the end of *fly*. I am comprehending this paragraph with 80 percent accuracy and can pick out the topic sentence." During engaged reading, there is no focus on skill, decoding, or vocabulary. When engaged readers come to a word they can't pronounce or define, they skip right over it without hesitation or guilt. A real reader engaged in a book is no more aware of reading skills than a running back threading his way through the defensive team is aware of his ability to run. He is not saying, "Right foot, then left foot, now pivot 45 degrees on the next step." His focus is on the game, and he simply uses his body to get where he wants to go. When something gets in the way, both the athlete and the reader improvise—self-correct—so the goal is still in sight and the action is uninterrupted.

The Rewards of Reading

So, why do we read? For personal and immediate reward. We read what already interests us. We also read to discover new interests through a skillfully written account that takes us places we never have been before. And we can experience the genuine pleasure of having an assigned book work its way under our skin and become part of us. Author Gary Paulsen, whose early years in Minnesota were largely spent in the library, suggests we should "read like a wolf eats" (1987)—in great hulking bites, with vigor, as often and much as possible. In the middle of this enthusiastic sampling of print, we will find those things that personally are worth it, while allowing the rest to slough off naturally. All the while, we increase our range of reading skills, build our general knowledge, and strengthen our education without being aware of our growth. The very real benefits come predictably and automatically.

Occasionally, we even stumble onto a benefit that defies expectation. For instance, actor Walter Matthau may have discovered the ultimate bonus of engaged reading. In response to the question "What book made the greatest difference in your life?" he wrote:

> The book that made the greatest difference in my life was *The Secret in the Daisy,* by Carol Grace, Random House, published 1955.
>
> The difference it made was enormous. It took me from a miserable, unhappy wretch to a joyful, glad-to-be-alive human. I fell so in love with the book that I searched out and married the girl who wrote it.
>
> Most sincerely,
> Walter Matthau (Sabine & Sabine, 1983, p. 29)

PEARSON myeducationkit™

Go to the MyEducationKit for this text, where you can:

- Search the Database of Children's Literature, housing more than 22,000 titles searchable in every genre by authors or illustrators, by awards won, by year published, and by topic and description.
- Explore genre-related Assignments and Activities, assignable exercises showing concepts in action through database use, video, cases, and student and teacher artifacts.
- Listen to podcasts and read interviews from some of the brightest and most enduring stars of children's literature in the Conversations.
- Discover weblinks that will lead you to sites representing the authors you learn about in these pages, classrooms with powerful children's literature connections, and literature awards.

Chapter 2

What Is a Good Book?

When we select books for children, we want to pick good ones. The trouble is, we're not always sure what "good book" means. Left to our own choosing, we thumb through titles, trying to find something that seems beneficial and desirable for young readers. We forge ahead, sometimes oblivious of the criteria we use to determine what is good. But criteria we have.

Choosing Children's Books

All adults choose children's books according to some kind of standard, even though we may be unaware of exactly why we pick one book over another. Our first responsibility when selecting books, then, is to determine what guides our choices. For instance:

1. The lessons they teach. We want children to learn the correct lessons about life. If a book teaches what we want taught, we call it a good book.
2. Large, colorful illustrations. Young eyes need stimulation, and color provides it better than black and white. Also, the pictures need to be large enough for children to see clearly.
3. Absence of harshness. Children will run into difficulty soon enough. Let them enjoy childhood. Protect them from the tough side of life as long as possible.
4. Absence of scariness. We don't want to invite fears or nightmares.
5. Absence of swearing. We don't want books to model inappropriate behavior.
6. Short. Keep the reading easy.
7. Simple vocabulary. We don't want to frustrate or overpower children.
8. Familiar content. We think our child will respond to a book about zoos because we go to one often. If a book connects with a child's experience, it will be a better book.
9. Personal and/or social preference. We want the values and social views represented in the book to be what we consider appropriate.

Visit the MyEducationKit for this course to enhance your understanding of chapter concepts with activities, weblinks, podcasts, and a searchable database of more than 22,000 children's literature titles.

A problem with the reasons just listed is that they are narrow and sometimes misguided; they focus on only a tree and miss the forest. If we want to help create lifelong readers by choosing books that appeal to the greatest range and number of children, we need to view the book as a whole instead of focusing on only a small element of it. And the most trustworthy standard for viewing the whole book is to look at the experience it offers. Titles of lasting value can almost be defined as experiences that re-create the very texture of life.

Problems can arise, however, in trying to convince others of the power of that experience. It is largely human nature to think others will respond the way we do. When books please us, we think they are well written or have other measurable literary value that ought to be recognized by our friends. Works that leave us cold are somehow lacking in merit for most everyone. Note the following two cases that illustrate this point.

Case 1: "*The Wind in the Willows* (Grahame, 1908) is a classic," he said. "It has received critical acclaim for a century, and I loved it. If you want a wonderful experience, take it now and read it." So she did. Her response was different, however: total boredom. How do we explain that a book of acknowledged literary merit can excite one person while the friend he recommends it to finds the title definitely ho-hum?

Case 2: The librarian held up a book between thumb and forefinger like a five-day-old fish. "The Nancy Drew books lack quality and merit. This series is predictable and weak." Maria, fifth grade, reads the beginning of a newly released Nancy Drew mystery and can't put it down until she finishes. A trained librarian judges a title to be substandard literature, yet Maria considers it a good book. How can this be?

People often don't see eye-to-eye when it comes to judging whether a book is worthwhile because *good book* is a common phrase with two different definitions, one based on quality and the other on taste.

Judging a Book: Literary Quality versus Personal Taste

Quality

A good book is one created by a knowledgeable and skilled author in which the elements of literature measure up under critical analysis. Quality has nothing to do with how old or new a book is. Books from decades or centuries past are not necessarily better works—even some so-called classics may not be well written. Some people may be inclined to feel current books are stronger while not realizing their reactions may be determined by a variety of factors having little effect on the quality of writing. Modern themes, language, and/or societal issues may trump the author's writing skill for some individuals—even if they don't realize it. For instance, a novel that deals with an issue a person feels strongly about (child abuse, destruction of the rainforests, autism) may lead readers to confuse subject matter with quality writing. But it is, of course, not the issue or topic that makes for a well-written story but rather the craft with which it is told.

However, the exact recipe for solid writing does not exist—if it did, anyone privy to the formula could predictably crank out an award winner. As W. Somerset Maugham once said, "There are three rules for writing a good novel. Unfortunately, no one knows what they are" (Stephens,

1990). What we do know is that all writers draw from the same words found in the dictionary, make use of the same rules of grammar, and apply the same elements of literature (see below). Yet it remains a mystery how one author can blend the identical raw materials into a veritable literary feast while what another concocts is run-of-the-mill. The simple truth is: Some books *are* better written than others.

While most of us are unable to create fiction like the masters of literature, we are still able to acquire the experience and skills necessary to recognize great writing. We have long used a variety of accepted rubrics to evaluate the written word, and while the evaluation process is still subjective, operating within the purview of these critical elements gives us common ground for making sounder literary judgments. For instance, style and language, character, plot, pacing, setting, tension, mood, tone, point of view, theme, and accuracy are the literary elements most commonly examined in judging excellence.

1. *Style and Language.* How a story is told is as important as the story itself. Style is the way a writer manipulates all the facets of language—such as word choice, syntax, and sentence length—to tell that story (see Chapter 3). The author's style can even reinforce a part of the story, as in Spinelli's (1990) *Maniac Magee,* where the short chapters and short sentences mirror the constant running and rapid movements of the main character.

2. *Character.* Good books must have characters that are unique and believable. People who live between the covers of a book must be as real as people who live across the street. It is impossible to identify with or have feelings for a person unless we know the individual, and it is the author's job to show us the character's personality in such a way that we can become involved with that life.

3. *Plot.* A good plot shows what happens to the characters in such a way that the reader cares about the outcome. Every plot must have a conflict, and how that conflict is resolved carries the book to its conclusion. Well-defined plots, according to author Pam Conrad, introduce a question early on that will be answered yes or no by the end of the story. She calls this the "major dramatic question" (MDQ) and cautions that the MDQ is not asked outright but is clearly evident. The plot, then, is the series of events that lead to the yes or no answer. The MDQ of *Make Way for Ducklings* (McCloskey, 1941) is "Will the ducks make the trip safely from the Charles River to the Boston Public Garden?" In the 2009 Newbery winner, *The Graveyard Book* (Gaiman, 2008), the toddler, who comes to be known as Nobody, survives the brutal murder of his family, though he is the assassin's chief target. When the murderer, Jack Frost, realizes the child is out of his grasp, he sees it as temporary: "He had not failed. Not yet. Not for years to come. There was plenty of time. Time to tie up this last piece of unfinished business. Time to cut the final thread" (pp. 32–33). At the onset, the author leads his readers to wonder, "Will Jack eventually kill Nobody Owens?" and thereby creates the major dramatic question that drives the plot. The development of and growth in Nobody's character comes in part from facing the conflict (survival) implicit in the MDQ.

4. *Pacing.* How quickly or slowly a story moves is pacing. While most books tell their stories at a relatively constant rate, pacing can vary according to the author's desire to linger over the content or move the story along.

5. *Setting.* Where and when the book takes place is the setting. The place can be as vast as a planet or as small as one room. The time may be in the past, the present, or the future, or in imaginary worlds it may be unspecified. When detailed and fleshed out, the physical surroundings add credibility and depth to the story.

6. *Tension.* Fiction without tension is bland. Tension makes the reader want to read on to see how the conflict is resolved and what happens to the people involved in the problem. Even in picture books, tension—a close relative of suspense—is what piques and sustains interest.

7. *Mood.* The atmosphere evoked in the writing is the mood: spooky, hilarious, innocent, understated, exaggerated, caustic, and the like.

8. *Tone.* The tone is the author's attitude toward the subject or audience in a particular book. Tone can reflect the range of human emotion: reverential, sarcastic, condescending, enthusiastic, and so on.

9. *Point of View.* The point of view is the position taken by the narrator. Most stories are told in first person ("I") or third person ("he/she").

10. *Theme.* The central idea of the story is the theme: friendship, coming of age, sibling rivalry, coping with the death of a pet, and adjusting to a new town, to name a few.

11. *Accuracy.* Whenever books deal with real facts, whether centering on them in nonfiction or using them as background in fiction, they must be true. Writers need to do their homework to gain and keep readers' trust.

To this point, we have focused on the written word. However, it is important to note that in judging a title's overall quality, especially illustrated books, we must go beyond the words by considering the illustrations, as well as the design and layout.

12. *Illustrations.* The art or photography in a book can strengthen and extend the content beyond the words. The marriage of illustration and text can yield an experience more powerful than either alone. (See Chapter 4.)

13. *Design and Layout.* All visual elements of a book—such as the cover, the colors, the margins, the spacing, the font style and size, and the positions of page numbers—are a part of the design and layout. Although word order is not affected by the design and layout, word placement on the page is—particularly in picture books. In Tunnell's (1999) *Halloween Pie,* for instance, the words shown below undulate within a snaking current of steam carried by the wind. The steam—laden with the scent of freshly baked pie—and the text lead readers from the witch's cottage to the cemetery, where graveyard creatures are roused by the tantalizing smells.

Soon the wind began to blow. It blew down the chimney.
It blew out the window.

The visual appeal of a book can determine if a potential reader will pick it up or march right on by, and the look of a page can affect the reader's desire to get into the content.

Of the 13 elements listed, 3 provide most of the information for judging the quality of fiction: style and language, character, and plot. When a book reveals its story in powerful language, contains memorable characters, and follows a compelling plot, the fiction generally can be said to have quality.

One additional characteristic of a quality book is worth noting: believability. The key to creating a good book is to make everything believable. We know that fiction is the product of an imagination. The people never lived. The story is made up. The setting often is invented. So why do we care about these people who never were, doing things that never happened, in a place that may not exist? Because the emotional reality is absolutely true. Because their imagined lives reflect the actual lives of living, breathing people. Because we can get genuine experience through living side by side with fictional characters while they endure their trials and enjoy their successes. We participate, we enjoy, and we learn—all simultaneously. Yet if anything in the book reminds us that what we read is invented, the story loses its power, much in the same way that the spell of a movie is broken when we notice a boom microphone hanging over the head of the police chief. All the elements in a story must be logical, sensible, and consistent.

Authors can disrupt the magic of their storytelling by becoming too enamored of their words or their ideas. The use of figurative and descriptive speech, for instance, should meld seamlessly into the narrative. A passage can be beautifully written yet be overwritten. The best of descriptive prose never points to itself as if to say, "Look how ingeniously crafted I am." Such writing interrupts the reader, breaks the spell, and is considered by many to be a writer's self-indulgence. An author ought to stay out of sight, so to speak, when storytelling.

Yet a writer can pay careful attention to all the elements of fiction, skillfully and unobtrusively weaving together a praiseworthy book, and still not win the reader's heart. Why?

Taste

The second definition of a good book is simply "a book the reader likes," quality or not. For instance, *The Wind in the Willows* is judged to be quality literature for children. This prototype of modern animal fantasy skillfully delineates the four main characters, contains satisfying action sequences, and is told in rich and varied language. But some children do not become engrossed in the story when they try to read it, nor do they particularly like to have it read aloud to them. The book has definite literary merit—it is critically a good book—yet for those who are not taken by the story, it has no appeal. Conversely, the Nancy Drew books win no literary awards, yet they continue to be read by many who find pleasure in reading these tales of a young, independent woman who can always solve the mystery. Thousands of children sail through the series, reporting that each Nancy Drew title is a good book. Some adults may think that children who read such formulaic, shallow stories should feel shame for doing so, but so far, no guilt has been detected in those who move quickly from one volume to the next.

So, when determining which books are good, a problem surfaces: The positive feelings a reader has about a book are the same whether they come from a quality book or one of low literary merit. As long as a reader likes a book, quality or not, it is called "good." Were we able to identify precisely the sources of our positive responses, we would more accurately say, "I like this book because the author's skill took me places and showed me things I have not previously thought about or experienced." If the book is well crafted, believable, and supplies all the elements needed for a rewarding new experience, the author should take a bow. What the writer of the book brought to the work creates this "good" response. On the other hand, if we like a book because it serves as a link to something already a part of us, we might say, "I like this book because it connects me with something important in my life." When the book presents us with a view or situation we are hardwired to like—reliving my summer with Grandma, supporting my view that society undervalues females, or illustrating how a selfish child learns kindness—credit for positive feelings toward the book belongs largely to the reader. When we like a book, we usually don't examine the source of our responses. We don't ask if the book takes us new places or connects us with the old. We just say it is a "good" book. We gain some insight by asking ourselves, "Does the 'good' feeling come because of the author's skill, or does it come because of my background and expectations?" Figure 2.1 depicts the roles and meaning of "good" in book quality and reader response.

A book can be written well or badly, and a reader can respond well or badly to both strong and weak books. Quadrant 1 of Figure 2.1 shows that an author has written a book with literary merit, and the reader likes it. We have no problem with a reader who responds positively to quality writing. A well-crafted book deserves no less. Similarly, quadrant 4 presents no difficulty. The author displays little skill in producing a book of minimal merit, and the reader does not respond well to this flawed product. These two unshaded quadrants pose little problem for the teacher and student.

But problems may occur when a quality book is not well received. Quadrant 2 shows that an author has written a good book, but the reader doesn't care for it. Teachers who recognize quality may have a tendency to feel they are shirking their duty if children don't respond favorably to a quality book. Teachers who redouble their efforts to convince the unbeliever that something wonderful is being missed usually drive the unbelieving student further from the book. In quadrant 3, the reader accepts a weak book with open arms. This scenario is often played out as a teacher tries to show the young reader just how poor the book really is. These sincere efforts are generally as successful as trying to dam the Mississippi River using a teaspoon. Attempting to convince enthusiastic young readers that a book is not worthy of devotion is foolish and often counterproductive. They have tried it and liked it. All we can do, and should do, is continue to mention and offer different titles that may appeal to those readers. Allowing individual response is wisest in the long run. (See the discussion of "engaged reading," Chapter 1.) After all, if children read nothing, then our opportunity to broaden their taste and judgment about books is nonexistent.

Evaluating Books: Four Possible Outcomes

	Literary Merit of Book	Reader Response	Literary Merit of Book	Reader Response	
1	+	+	+	–	2
3	–	+	–	–	4

In both quadrants 2 and 3, the teacher needs to accept the honest feelings of the reader, misguided as they might be in the adult eye, and continue to provide and introduce better books. Doing so carries no guarantee that young readers will like them, but it does increase the chances that this may happen. Direct attacks on positive responses to poor-quality books, however, almost guarantee that a rift will develop between teacher and student and, in the case of quadrant 2, between a student and a genuinely good book.

Understanding that a positive response can be a result of either the author's skill or the reader's individual taste can help in solving some mysteries about how readers respond to books. A British reviewer of children's books was surprised when her daughter, Alison, chose as her favorite book one that was far inferior to the many quality titles in their home. The story tells of Peppermint, a pale kitten, who is last in a litter and alone after the others are matched with new families. Eventually, she is given to a girl who loves her, fusses over her, and prepares her so well for the cat show that Peppermint wins first prize. Alison's mother finally realized the appeal of Peppermint's story.

> Alison is an adopted child; her hair is pale straw, her eyes are blue; she was taken home, like Peppermint, to be loved and cared for and treasured. It was a matter of identification not just for the duration of the story, but at a deep, warm, comforting and enduring level. . . . The artistically worthless book—hack-written and poorly illustrated—may, if the emotional content is sound, hold a message of supreme significance for a particular child. (Moss, 1977, pp. 141–142)

When a class of 30 college students read a not-very-good biography about Maria Tallchief, an Osage ballerina who captured the attention of the dancing world in the early 20th century, all the students, except for five women, pronounced the book "mediocre." That enthusiastic handful loved the book and couldn't understand why the others were not impressed by this story that had meant so much to them. During the short discussion, the fact surfaced that all of the five young women had taken and loved ballet as children. When they read about Maria Tallchief, they were reading their own stories. For them, the book served as a link to a meaningful personal experience. The others, without ballet backgrounds, did not find enough to interest them in the shallow way the author presented Tailchief's story.

As adults working with children, we spend our time more productively in quadrants 1 and 2 for two reasons. First, the more a book has to offer readers, the greater the chance the reader will respond. In *Julius, the Baby of the World,* Kevin Henkes (1990) identifies precisely an only child's reaction to the arrival of a new sibling. The reader participates in Lilly's jealousy, as well as shares her outrage when Cousin Garland dares to criticize her baby brother. The author's range of emotion and humor is so broad that readers at a variety of age levels are able to respond. The second reason is that judging literary merit is easier than identifying specific reader idiosyncrasies that predict positive responses to books. We can identify a good plot and pick out a compelling character. But we have no way of knowing that Alison will find comfort in Peppermint or that five students will be linked by their ballet lessons to Maria Tallchief.

This whole evaluative process is somewhat like examining two new couches, both with fabric upholstery and polished wooden trim. From a distance, they appear identical, but one reflects the true value of $2,200 while the other carries an honest price tag of $500. However, if allowed to inspect the couches at close range, even the nonprofessional should be able to determine which couch is of real quality and which is of lesser worth. We can determine the more expensive by examining the stitching, which should be close and even; the fabric, which should be tight and finely woven; the hardwood, which should be joined perfectly, well stained, and flawlessly finished; the padding, which should be thick and firm; the weight, which should be heavy; and the comfort, which should be evident upon sitting. Once identified, however, the quality piece will not necessarily be welcomed into every living room. If its style—say Scandinavian Contemporary or Colonial—does not appeal to me, it is of no importance that I now have the $2,200 couch. I can recognize its fine craftsmanship and can see that its less expensive counterpart is lacking in quality, but that does not make me want to own the fine couch if my taste runs counter to its appearance. Ultimately, the piece must please me before it gets my stamp of approval.

George Woods, the late and longtime children's book critic for the *New York Times,* addressed the topic of evaluating children's books in a speech to an auditorium of college students. "How do we know a good book?" he asked his audience. Pens came to the ready for the scholar's definition. "We know a good book . . . (pause) . . . because it hits us in the gut" (Woods, 1977).

Taste and personal response often determine an individual's decision about the worth of a book. However, there are some generally accepted guidelines about quality writing. Some books simply are better constructed than others, offering a clearer understanding of the human experience and a deeper sense of pleasure. These quality books are the ones we need to introduce to children because they generally have more power to stir up interest and, over time, will provide readers with a more enlarging experience than will mediocre books. Yet we can't force these quality titles on children; we can only offer by enthusiastically sharing them. To become truly engaged readers, children must have the freedom to accept or reject a title. Just as we can't insist on a positive response to a book of quality, we can't erase a positive response to a poorly written book.

In the end, the question of what makes a "good book" is one of respect: respect for the truly fine work of authors who pay their dues and create works of lasting value, and also respect for the response of individual readers who cast the deciding vote on a book's personal appeal. There is, after all, only one list of good books that is completely dependable—your own. However, though your list may have books of both lower and higher literary merit, the quality titles will end up taking you further.

PEARSON
myeducationkit™

Go to the topic Evaluating Children's Literature on the MyEducationKit for this text, where you can:

- Search the Database of Children's Literature, housing more than 22,000 titles searchable in every genre by authors or illustrators, by awards won, by year published, and by topic and description.
- Explore genre-related Assignments and Activities, assignable exercises showing concepts in action through database use, video, cases, and student and teacher artifacts.
- Listen to podcasts and read interviews from some of the brightest and most enduring stars of children's literature in the Conversations.
- Discover weblinks that will lead you to sites representing the authors you learn about in these pages, classrooms with powerful children's literature connections, and literature awards.

Chapter 3

How to Recognize a Well-Written Book

To evaluate the literary merit of a book is to make a judgment about how well the author uses words. "This book is well written" is a common badge of praise. What does *well written* mean? Often, it is nothing more than the speaker's way of saying the book is pleasing. If it pleases me, it must be well written. As evidence supporting a positive response to a book, the phrase "well written" has become a generalized catchall.

Choosing the Right Words

If a book is truly well written, the words between its covers are arranged in almost magical patterns that stir deep emotional responses in readers. The words do far more than relate the events of the story. The words make the book by defining character, moving the plot along, identifying the setting, isolating the theme, creating the tone, identifying the point of view, developing the mood, establishing the pace, making the story believable, and reporting information accurately.

Identifying how words create each literary element, however, does not give us a clear picture of exactly what makes a book so memorable. Certainly, plot must be well structured, but it cannot be separated from the major characters who are living the story. Conversely, well-defined characters lose their appeal if they are not involved in a compelling plot. The elements of writing are integrated, worked into a well-orchestrated whole, by a talented writer.

Visit the MyEducationKit for this course to enhance your understanding of chapter concepts with activities, weblinks, podcasts, and a searchable database of more than 22,000 children's literature titles.

Talented writers create works that are clear, believable, and interesting, and the rules for good writing are essentially the same for children's books and adult books. It is not as if a children's writer is in training to become an author of books for grown-ups. That would be like asking a pediatrician when he will at last get around to the important business of treating adults. Children deserve the best in books geared for them.

Once again (see Chapter 2), a story is not good because it is for a certain audience, about a particular topic, or peopled with certain characters; it is good because of the way it is presented. A work of nonfiction is not good because of the subject matter; it is good because of the way it views and reveals the subject. For example, note the difference in the following reports of the same event:

Case 1: The college football coach finished his 20th successful season and was honored at a banquet where his praises were sung loudly and long. As dishes were being cleared and tables taken down after the festivities, the coach talked with his friend, the college president. At one point, the coach paused and then asked, "President, I appreciate this evening more than you'll ever know. Yet sometimes I find a nagging question in my mind: Would all of you still love me if I lost football games instead of won them?"

"Oh, Coach, we'd love you just as much," the president said as he reached out his arm, pulled the coach in close, and looked him right in the eye. "And we'd miss you."

Case 2: A college student said to his classmate, "Did you hear that last night after the banquet honoring the football coach, the president said he'd be fired if he started losing?"

In case 2, the reader gets all the pertinent information: the banquet in the coach's honor, the president and coach's conversation afterward, and the gist of their exchange. In the first example, the reader gets to participate in the event, discovering the point of the story and its subtle humor simultaneously with the characters.

Human beings can't draw conclusions without information, and we gain information only through the five senses. If data can't enter through one of the holes in the head (sight, sound, taste, or smell) or through the skin (touch), they can't be processed. Good writers know readers need specific information—details that enter through the senses—and take the trouble to provide it. Lesser writers generalize. The difference between providing sensory detail and generalizing is the difference between showing and telling. Where lesser writing *tells* by summarizing (as in case 2), quality writing *shows* us what is going on by providing enough sensory detail to allow us to make personal discoveries and come to personal conclusions (as in case 1). Consider, for instance, the opening paragraph of *The Illyrian Adventure:*

> Miss Vesper Holly has the digestive talents of a goat and the mind of a chess master. She is familiar with half a dozen languages and can swear fluently in all of them. She understands the use of a slide rule but prefers doing calculations in her head. She does not hesitate to risk life and limb—mine as well as her own. No doubt she has other qualities as yet undiscovered. I hope not. (Alexander, 1986, p. 3)

The reader is solidly introduced to Vesper Holly. Alexander reveals Vesper's particular personality by *showing* her skills, accomplishments, abilities, and interests. Had Alexander begun by *telling* us about Vesper, he may have summarized her character by saying, "Miss Vesper Holly is courageous, intelligent, daring, a skilled linguist, delightfully irreverent, and headstrong." We would then know what to expect of her, but we wouldn't know her as well.

The "showing" we need from the printed page comes to us in various forms: precise vocabulary, figurative language, dialogue, music in language, understatement, and unexpected insights. Though not a comprehensive list, these six characteristics identify some of the ways words create interest and personalize content.

Precise Vocabulary

By age 4, children have acquired most of the elements of fully developed language, including sentence structure, word order, subject–verb agreement, verb tenses, and so on (Morrow, 2005). The only additional refinements take place in acquiring more complex structures and in semantics—learning new words and their meanings. Semantic development continues for the rest of their lives.

English has the richest vocabulary of the 5,000-plus languages on the planet. According to the Global Language Monitor, there are one million words in the English language (Altman et al., 2009). One of the great pleasures of language is to find in this fertile and varied vocabulary precisely the right word to use in exactly the right place. Mark Twain described the difference between the right word and the almost right word as being like the difference between lightning and the lightning bug. And the only way to learn the fine differences between words and develop a broad personal vocabulary is to be surrounded by precise words used accurately. When Newbery-winning author Elaine Konigsburg writes for children, she tries "to expand the perimeter of their language, to set a wider limit to it, to give them a vocabulary for alternatives" (1970, pp. 731–732).

William Steig is a master of providing those wider limits, largely by using precise vocabulary. In *The Amazing Bone* (1976), Pearl the pig, wearing her flowered dress and sunbonnet, takes her time coming home from school: "On Cobble Road she stopped at Maltby's barn and stood gawking as the old gaffers pitched their ringing horseshoes and spat tobacco juice." (Someone afraid this sentence would not be accessible to the younger reader would write something like "She stopped at the barn and watched the old men play horseshoes.") Naming the road and the barn gives the story depth and credibility—the place seems to exist. "Gawking" identifies exactly the kind of looking she did—wide-eyed, unabashed staring. "Ringing horseshoes" provides a dimension of sound to the game, adding an additional layer to the picture. And "spat tobacco juice" presents a side of the men and their activities that rounds them out. But the genius on this page is the selection of the word *gaffers.* English has a number of specific words for the phrase *old man:* patriarch, ancient, graybeard, Nestor, grandfather, gaffer, geezer, codger, dotard, Methuselah, antediluvian, preadamite, veteran, old-timer, old soldier, old stager, dean, doyen, senior, elder, oldest, first-born, seniority, primogeniture (*The New Roget's Thesaurus in Dictionary Form,* 1991, s.v. "old men"). The only ones general enough to be considered for this setting are codger, dotard, gaffer, geezer, and old-timer. *The Compact Edition of the Oxford English Dictionary* (1996) reports that each carries a specific view of old men:

Codger: "A mean, stingy, or miserly (old) fellow; a testy or crusty (old) man"

Dotard: "One whose intellect is impaired by age; one whose dotage is in his second childhood"

Gaffer: "A term applied originally by country people to an elderly man or one whose position entitled him to respect"

Geezer: "A term of derision applied to elderly persons"
Old-timer: "[O]ne whose experience goes back to old times"

Gaffer is the only term that is neither negative nor neutral. Its positive connotation complements the pleasant, unhurried scene while reflecting a strong image of the elderly.

The right words do not have to be fancy or complex. Even ordinary words can be right. In *Julius, the Baby of the World* (Henkes, 1990), the birth of Julius brings misery to his sister, Lilly. To her friends, and even strangers, this former only child dutifully gives warnings about the perils of newborns. To a very pregnant woman she meets on the sidewalk, Lilly offers this dire prediction: "You will live to regret that bump under your dress!" "Will live to regret" does not mince words. It carries no waffling and allows no possibility that the situation could end well. Calling the baby a "bump" makes it less than human—reduces it to an inanimate, shapeless mass—which reveals the depth of Lilly's negative feelings more powerfully than had she said, "You will be sorry you're pregnant."

In *Temporary Times, Temporary Places* (Robinson, 1972), teenaged Marilyn is stunned when she comes out of the church after an evening social to see her friend Janet walking away with the boy of their dreams, the one they have spent endless hours discussing. He has never spoken to either of them, and here he is leaving with Janet. Carrying her sweater in her hand, Marilyn can only stare: "She was standing on the steps of the church, mouth open, eyes wide, sweater dragging." With those six words—"mouth open, eyes wide, sweater dragging"—astonishment is *shown.* Robinson has thought about what astonishment looks like in this situation and presented it precisely. A lesser writer, who tells instead of shows, would have written something like "She was standing on the steps of the church, a look of astonishment on her face." This sentence tells readers they should feel Marilyn's astonishment, but it does not create the image or the experience. In Robinson's hands, the scene is more specific, more complete, and more believable.

Figurative Language

Simile, metaphor, personification, and imagery are examples of figurative language. All add specificity, clarity, power, and layers of meaning. In addition, figurative language is economical. It conveys meaning quickly and with emotional intensity. For example, in *Maniac Magee,* we are shown that March, supposedly the month of spring and hope, can also be a brute: "During the night, March doubled back and grabbed April by the scruff of the neck and flung it another week or two down the road" (Spinelli, 1990, p. 149). Spinelli's personification of March reminds us vividly that this unpredictable month of spring can also present a sudden nastiness.

From *Tuck Everlasting* comes the lingering image of Mae Tuck, described as a "great potato of a woman" (Babbitt, 1975, p. 7). In five words, Babbitt creates a feeling for Mae's lumpy shape, her absence of pretense, her plainness, her lack of color, her solidness, her accessibility, and other earthy and dependable traits associated with a vegetable that is not spectacular, fragile, or rare but is a nutritional staple.

Figurative language can add power and insight to whole paragraphs. It is one thing to say that Winnie Foster was made to do housework continually, but in *Tuck Everlasting,* the author underscores the seriousness of cleaning in Winnie's household by loading the description with images of war.

> Winnie had grown up with order. She was used to it. Under the pitiless double assaults of her mother and grandmother, the cottage where she lived was always squeaking clean, mopped and swept and

> scoured into limp submission. There was no room for carelessness, no putting things off until later. The Foster women had made a fortress out of duty. Within it, they were indomitable. And Winnie was in training. (Babbitt, 1975, p. 44)

When we read the paragraph, we get the solid impression that housecleaning in the Foster cottage is the focal point of life. Only when we go back and pick out the military terms Babbitt has chosen—"double assaults," "fortress," "duty," "in training"—do we see the image of soldiers in battle that has helped persuade us of the Foster obsession with cleanliness.

Dialogue

Speech reveals character. When a person's mouth opens, truth emerges about personality, motives, desires, prejudices, and feelings. Bernard Waber has an ear for real speech that reveals the nuances, challenges, and bluffing responses of sibling conversation. In *Ira Sleeps Over,* Ira has been invited to spend the night at a friend's house—his first sleepover. When his older sister learns of his plans, she asks:

> "Are you taking your teddy bear along?"
>
> "Taking my teddy bear along!" I said. "To my friend's house? Are you kidding? That's the silliest thing I ever heard! Of course, I'm not taking my teddy bear."
>
> And then she said: "But you never slept without your teddy bear before. How will you feel, sleeping without your teddy bear for the very first time? Hmmmmmmm?" (Waber, 1972, pp. 5–7)

In this brief exchange between brother and sister, Waber shows the older sister's need and ability to control her younger brother with what appears to be an innocent question: "Are you taking your teddy bear along?" What difference does it make to her if he takes it? None, but her job is to make his life miserable, and she performs it well. His reply, a little too quick and laced with false bravado, shows his insecurity. And her final statement is a knockout punch that leaves him no chance to get to his feet, reminding him that he has never slept alone, asking how that would feel, and ending with that taunting "Hmmmmmmm?"

If speech is not natural and not as individual as a particular personality, it depicts the characters as shallow and stiff, distracting from the story and consequently weakening it. There are still children's books being published today that incorporate stilted dialogue which reads like this reworked version of the *Ira Sleeps Over* excerpt from above.

> "Will you take your teddy bear?" she asked.
> "No, I will not take my teddy bear," I said. "I will not take it to my friend's house."
> "You will not like sleeping without a teddy bear," she said. "You will be unhappy."
> "Do not worry. I will not be unhappy. I am not a baby," I said.

This dialogue is written with the primary goal of providing simplified reading, rather than engaging storytelling.

Music in Language

The sounds of words increase the appeal and strength of a story as they blend together, create emphasis, repeat tones, establish patterns, provide a cadence, and add variety. After 80 years, the rhythm in *Millions of Cats* (Gág, 1928) still rings in the ear and burrows into the mind: "Hundreds of cats, Thousands of cats, Millions and billions and trillions of cats." The rhyme in *Goodnight Moon* (Brown, 1947) does the same: "Goodnight stars. Goodnight air. Goodnight noises everywhere."

Buford in *Buford the Little Bighorn* (Peet, 1967) is a small mountain sheep whose horns have grown enormously, way out of proportion to his body. They cause him balancing problems, and he falls from craggy heights but is saved when his horns hook onto a small tree. From then on, his friends have to help him over the rough spots in their high, rocky world. To help him climb a steep ledge, two sheep from above grab his horns in their teeth and pull, while one butts him skyward, giving "Buford a big boost from below" (Peet, 1967, p. 3). Those explosive *b*'s echo the heavy sounds and sudden movements of butting and boosting as well as link the phrase together by repeating the sound.

Because the eye does not detect the fine points of language as accurately as the ear, it is common for authors to submit their writing to a final check by reading it aloud. In two versions of "Snow White," the queen questions the mirror in language that is subtly yet powerfully different. Submit the following two passages to the read-aloud test:

> Mirror, mirror on the wall. Who is the fairest one of all? (Walt Disney Productions, 1973, p. 2)

> Mirror, mirror on the wall, Who is fairest of us all? (Grimm Brothers, 1972, p. 2)

Uneven meter in the first passage makes it more difficult to read aloud; the cadence is rougher and the sound choppier. The language in the second example flows, falling smoothly and effortlessly from the mouth. The result is a more musical reading. The second also echoes an archaic form of speech that matches the "once upon a time" setting of the fairy tale.

Varied sentence length is another feature of language that appeals to the ear. In natural speech patterns, sentences are of differing length. These diverse sentences add variety to the language, creating balance, interest, and appeal. Read aloud the opening passages from the Disney and Grimm versions of "Snow White," paying attention to how they feel coming from the mouth and how they fall upon the ear.

> Long ago there lived a princess named Snow White. She was a beautiful princess. And like all princesses she lived in a castle.
>
> Her stepmother, the queen, also lived in the castle. The queen had a magic mirror. Every day she looked into the mirror and asked the same thing.
>
> "Mirror, mirror on the wall. Who is the fairest one of all?"
>
> The mirror always gave her the same answer. "Oh, queen, YOU are the fairest one of all." (Walt Disney Productions, 1973, p. 2)

> Once it was the middle of winter, and the snowflakes fell from the sky like feathers. At a window with a frame of ebony a queen sat and sewed. And as she sewed and looked out at the snow, she pricked her finger with the needle, and three drops of blood fell in the snow. And in the white snow the red looked so beautiful that she thought to herself: "If only I had a child as white as snow, as red as blood, and as black as the wood in the window frame!" (Grimm Brothers, 1972, pp. 1–2)

For most readers, the many short sentences in the first example interrupt the flow of the story, creating a degree of choppiness. The varied sentence construction in the second helps produce

a smooth and flowing narrative that reads with a musical quality. The first has 10 sentences; the second 4. The first has an average of 7.9 words per sentence; the second 23.5. Having more words per sentence is not necessarily an earmark of good writing, but in this case, the longer sentences help paint stronger, more emotion-laden images.

Understatement

When facts and feelings are presented clearly in writing, readers draw their own conclusions without being told precisely what to think. Readers then participate in the experience instead of being led through it. Part of this participatory process is understatement, which presents minimal but carefully chosen facts and details without any explanatory comment. Understatement is simply very brief "showing."

The opposites of understatement are overstatement and sensationalism. A simple example is found in Appelt's *The Underneath* (2008). The characters, abandoned and mistreated dogs and cats, exhibit their unhappiness or pain through the noises they make. But the author chooses to overstate their misery by frequent repetition of "unhappy" words, such as "Ranger . . . howled and howled and howled" (p. 74). But worse are the sensationalized exclamations: "*Yeeeeeeoooooowwwwwww!,*" "*Aaaaaaarrrrrrrggggghhhhhhh!*" (p. 292). And the incessant use of "sound" words with added letters to approximate onomatopoeia and multiple exclamation marks: "CRRAAACCKKK!!! SPLLIIITTTT!!! BOOOMMMM!!!" (p. 267). Such overstated writing is a cheap way of trying to create excitement and tension but ultimately falls short.

The power of understatement is evident in *Tuck Everlasting* (Babbitt, 1975). Angus Tuck tries to convince young Winnie Foster, whom he has grown to love like his own child, not to drink from the same magical spring that has transformed the Tucks into people who cannot age or die. When the Tuck family is forced to move away, Angus is uncertain of what Winnie will do—let her life follow its natural course, as he counseled, or submit to the enticements of living forever. In the epilogue, Angus and Mae Tuck return to Winnie's town 60 years later and visit the cemetery. When he discovers her tombstone, Angus's throat closes and he briefly salutes the monument, saying, "Good girl." No long discourses with his wife about Winnie's wise decision. No fits of crying or sentimental remembrances. Just "good girl."

In Don Lemna's (2008) *When the Sergeant Came Marching Home,* the author creates a bit of black humor through the use of understatement. Donald's father, newly returned from World War II, moves his family to a remote Montana farm. In the summer, Donald attends the Fourth of July celebration in the small town nearby. He is minding his own business when someone speaks to him.

> "I lost my finger," a small voice behind me said.
>
> I looked around and saw that there was a little girl with large, dark eyes, about five or six years old. She held her hand up, and I saw that it had only three fingers. . . .
>
> "I put it in Father's machine," she said, looking sadly down at it. "It chopped it off."
>
> "That's too bad," I said.
>
> "There was blood all over the place," she said. "My mother fainted."
>
> I imagined her mother falling over, and I nodded at her.
>
> "It didn't hurt at first," she said.
>
> "Well, nice talking to you," I said. "I'm going to get an ice-cream cone." (p. 187)

Donald thinks he's finally escaped the unnerving little girl, but the little voice is suddenly there again.

> "Gears," someone said. It was the little girl. She was sitting beside me.
> "What?"
> "There was a hole in Daddy's machine and I wondered what was in there."
> I didn't reply.
> "There were gears in there," she said. (p. 188)

Though the event the little girl describes is horrific, her deadpan, understated, and rather detached descriptions make for a strangely funny scenario. Donald is new in town and doesn't realize the girl is well known for her dispassionate accounts of her maiming. This becomes clear to him when a friend shows up and instantly responds to the girl's presence. " 'Hello, Joanne,' Rachel said. 'Don't tell me about your finger' " (p. 189).

A final example comes from Lois Lowry's (1977) novel *A Summer to Die.* Meg's family is going through a period of mourning as it becomes clear that leukemia is at last going to take her older sister's life. On the way home from a particularly good hospital visit, the family sings childhood songs, capturing the comforting feelings of what life used to be like before Molly became so ill. After that scene, the next words are, "Two weeks later, she was gone" (Lowry, 1977, p. 108). No jarring telephone brings news of the inevitable. No explicit details describe her last moments. We have lived through the disease, joined in the family's efforts to understand and draw together, and now the inescapable has arrived. That's all we need to know. Understatement gives power to writing because of what is not said and shows that an author trusts readers to make important, personal connections with the story.

Unexpected Insights

Like life, good stories contain occasional small surprises. We live with characters as they work their way through problems but may be delighted suddenly by an eye-opening insight about the human experience that comes from their struggles. For instance, Maniac Magee wonders why the people in East End call themselves black. "He kept looking and looking, and the colors he found were gingersnap and light fudge and dark fudge and acorn and butter rum and cinnamon and burnt orange. But never licorice, which, to him, was real black" (Spinelli, 1990, p. 51). "That's absolutely right," we find ourselves saying. We were aware that differences exist within races but did not see the general truth with such fresh precision until we looked through Maniac's eyes.

Lloyd Alexander is famous for such insights. In the five-book series *The Prydain Chronicles,* the elderly Dwyvach Weaver-Woman presents a beautiful cloak to the girl Eilonwy. "Take this as a gift from a crone to a maiden," says Dwyvach, "and know there is not so much difference between the two. For even a tottering granddam keeps a portion of girlish heart, and the youngest maid a thread of old woman's wisdom" (1968a, p. 115). And in counsel to Taran, who is disappointed that he did not accomplish more while away on his quest, the enchanter Dallben points out, "There are times when the seeking counts more than the finding" (Alexander, 1964, p. 215). These discoveries are not proverbs or maxims tacked onto the story; they surface naturally and appropriately as the characters learn about their own situations.

Even an animal fantasy has the potential of revealing subtle insights about the human condition. In *Masterpiece,* by Elise Broach (2008), an extended family of beetles lives in the walls of a Manhattan apartment. When the young beetle Marvin overhears the apartment's humans talking of divorce, he asks his mother, "Why don't beetles ever get divorced?" His mother's answer:

"Well, our lives are short, darling. What would be the point? We have so little time, we must spend it as happily as possible." She continues to explain that a day not being stepped on, having enough food and a safe place to sleep, and having family and friends close by is—"well, that's a good day, isn't it? In fact, a perfect day." Marvin's mother offers us, the human race, a bit of insight into our petty, self-made troubles that make getting along so difficult. Her parting words as she tucks Marvin into bed: "Also, we have no lawyers" (p. 171).

In *Charlotte's Rose* (Cannon, 2002), a 19th-century Welsh woman has lost four children as babies and is saddened because they died unbaptized and are therefore damned. With another couple and some family members, she agrees to meet with a pair of traveling missionaries, one thin as a pole and the other looking like a mountain with a beard. She starts the conversation.

> "I was told you . . . don't baptize your babies. Is this true?"
> The mountain with the beard nodded.
> "Why not?"
> "Why should we?"
> "So they won't go to hell."
> "Why would babies go to hell?"
> "Because they have not been cleansed of sin."
> Mountain smiled. So did Pole.
> "God deliver us from sinful babies," said Pole.
> "Gambling babies," said Mountain.
> "Drinking babies."
> "Cussing babies."
> "Lying babies."
> "Cheating babies."
> "Thieving babies."
> I laughed, and so did Papa and the Bowens. (pp. 71–72)

And so does the reader. The new perspective—the unexpected insight—simply brings a smile to the lips.

Skilled writers, who pay attention to small details and keep looking until they discover truth, help us to find a freshness and more precise understanding even in familiar things. When Beric, the youthful slave and protagonist in *Outcast,* accidentally cut his hand while in ancient Rome, he instinctively lifted the wound to his mouth. Instantly he tasted the blood, "both salty and sweet" (Sutcliff, 1995, p. 118). Those of us who also have raised a nicked finger to our lips recognize that Sutcliff's "both salty and sweet" describes accurately the unusual taste of our own blood, and we automatically say, "That's it. That's exactly what blood tastes like." Unexpected insights add depth and credibility to the story while providing the reader with recognition and connections.

Elements of Weak Writing

The easiest definition of weak writing is to say it is the opposite of good writing: not clear but fuzzy, not believable but implausible, not interesting but dull. Particularly in children's books, however, some weak elements stand out: didacticism, condescension, and controlled vocabulary.

Didacticism, discussed more fully in Chapter 5, is writing that pretends to be a story but actually is a lesson. Good books can and do provide lessons, but in good books, the stories are primary and the lessons are secondary. They are secrets to be discovered rather than sermons to be suffered. The learning and insights—the lessons—arrive as additional gifts, by-products of experiencing a good story. When the main purpose of fiction is to promote the message instead of to provide an experience, the book has been weakened.

Condescension may be slightly harder to pin down than didacticism. Condescension often results when the author underestimates the reader's abilities, as in labeling the esophagus a "food tube" in a nonfiction book aimed at fourth graders. "Food tube" is an uncommon and babyish term, and 10-year-old children are perfectly capable of saying and reading "esophagus." Condescension doesn't trust the reader to get the point and over-explains the obvious. Evident mostly in books for very young readers, a condescending tone also treats children with a certain wide-eyed amazement bordering on phoniness. In *The Boat Alphabet Book,* for instance, the general, straightforward description of different kinds of boats occasionally slips into a condescending tone. Accompanying a realistic drawing of an ocean-going tanker is this text: "Tankers are ships that carry liquids. Most tankers carry oil products such as crude oil, kerosene, grease, and gasoline." The entry then concludes with, "What else could a tanker be carrying? Maybe chocolate milk?" (Palotta, 2001, p. 22). This question talks down to young readers in a misguided effort by the author to fit in with his audience—to be "one of the kids." Instead, he is pandering to his audience. It's as if he's turning away from the children to wink at other adults in a conspiratorial way, indicating how well he believes he's relating to his young, naïve readers. But by condescending to them, the author destroys the tone he established at the onset—a serious look at both the pleasurable and utilitarian uses of boats and ships.

Controlled vocabulary is based on the idea that children learn to read easy words first and then graduate slowly to more difficult ones to avoid frustration. However, so-called dumbed-down text, which overly controls vocabulary and arranges words in unnatural patterns ("I see the mat. The mat is tan. It is a tan mat."), often has proven to be more difficult for children to read and understand than text with interesting words and language patterns. The dumbed-down text does not correspond with what they have learned about language through the ear (Goodman, 1988). Children can sometimes learn difficult words more easily than seemingly simple ones. If first graders are shown the words *surprise, was,* and *elephant,* the one they will learn to sight read first is *elephant.* Although it is longer and more difficult, it is also more specific. Try drawing a picture of a *surprise* or a *was.* The hardest of the three—the one that takes the most exposures to become included in children's sight vocabulary—is *was.*

In the 1980s, basal companies recognized the power of natural text and began to include excerpts from authentic literature as a part of their reading programs. However, in the 1990s, schools began buying and using sets of controlled-vocabulary paperback books instead of basal textbooks. Therefore, to meet demand, basal companies also began to include with their literature-based reading series sets of controlled-vocabulary paperbacks. Today, teachers must choose wisely because, once again, reading materials available in the elementary schools may focus on particular word patterns, largely ignoring the appeal of natural language and cohesive stories.

In short, the standards for a well-written children's book are no different from the standards for any well-written book. The author treats the audience with respect and writes so that the text is honest and interesting. The literary devices (see Figure 3.1) employed to achieve that honesty and interest operate so smoothly they remain virtually invisible. The story (fiction) and the information (nonfiction) are so compelling that the reader sails along, engaged in the insights and precise language and unaware of the talent and time necessary for making the final product appear so effortless.

An Evaluation Guide for Fiction

Author: ______________________________

Title: ______________________________

Publisher: ______________________________

Summary: ______________________________

Evaluation

Plot:

Believability (absence of coincidence, sentimentality, etc.) 1 2 3 4 5 6 7 8 9 10

Comment:

Major dramatic question (clear early in book?) YES YES (but slow emerging) NO

Comment:

Other considerations (satisfactory conclusion, tension, clear conflict, etc.) 1 2 3 4 5 6 7 8 9 10

Comment:

Style and language (precise vocabulary, figurative language, dialogue, cadence, understatement, unexpected insights, etc.) 1 2 3 4 5 6 7 8 9 10

Comment:

Pacing 1 2 3 4 5 6 7 8 9 10

Comment:

Character (dynamic protagonist, characters "ring true" [including cultural considerations], etc.) 1 2 3 4 5 6 7 8 9 10

Comment:

Setting (detail, texture) 1 2 3 4 5 6 7 8 9 10

Comment:

Theme (absence of overt didacticism?) 1 2 3 4 5 6 7 8 9 10

Comment:

Other considerations (mood, tone, etc.) 1 2 3 4 5 6 7 8 9 10

Comment:

Is it a well-rounded piece? 1 2 3 4 5 6 7 8 9 10

Comment:

OVERALL RATING (10 high; 1 low) 1 2 3 4 5 6 7 8 9 10

Comment:

PEARSON myeducationkit™

Go to the topic Evaluating Children's Literature on the MyEducationKit for this text, where you can:

- Search the Database of Children's Literature, housing more than 22,000 titles searchable in every genre by authors or illustrators, by awards won, by year published, and by topic and description.
- Explore genre-related Assignments and Activities, assignable exercises showing concepts in action through database use, video, cases, and student and teacher artifacts.
- Listen to podcasts and read interviews from some of the brightest and most enduring stars of children's literature in the Conversations.
- Discover weblinks that will lead you to sites representing the authors you learn about in these pages, classrooms with powerful children's literature connections, and literature awards.

An Illustration Guide to Accompany Chapter 4

How to Recognize a Well-Illustrated Book

1. From *The Relatives Came* by Cynthia Rylant, illustrated by Stephen Gammell.

2. From *The Fortune-Tellers* by Lloyd Alexander, illustrated by Trina Schart Hyman.

3. From *The Friend* by Sarah Stewart, illustrated by David Small.

4. From *Frog Goes to Dinner* by Mercer Mayer.

5. From *Blueberries for Sal* by Robert McCloskey.

6. From *Rosie's Walk* by Pat Hutchins.

7. From *The Polar Express* by Chris Van Allsburg.

8. From *Rapunzel* by Paul O. Zelinsky.

9.

From *The Voice of the Wood* by Claude Clément, translated by Lenny Hort, illustrated by Frédéric Clément.

From *A Chair for My Mother* by Vera B. Williams.

10.

11.

From *Freedom Summer* by Deborah Wiles, illustrated by Jerome Lagarrigue.

12.

From *Will Moses Mother Goose* by Will Moses.

From *Flying Feet: A Mud Flat Story* by James Stevenson.

14.

From *Zathura* by Chris Van Allsburg.

From *Ben's Trumpet* by Rachel Isadora.

about to be snatched up by a crow.
He hurried
16.

From *Once a Mouse. . .* by Marcia Brown.

17. From *Bernard the Angry Rooster* by Mary Wormell.

18. From *One Night in the Coral Sea* by Sneed B. Collard, illustrated by Robin Brickman.

19. From *Golem* by David Wisniewski.

20. From *Abraham Lincoln* by Ingri and Edgar Parin d'Aulaire.

21. From *Ella Fitzgerald: The Tale of a Vocal Virtuoso* by Brian Pinkney.

From *Mouse Views: What the Class Pet Saw* by Bruce McMillan.

22.

It happened just as the stranger had said. The owner had only to clap his hands and the paper crane became a living bird, flew down to the floor, and danced.

23.

From *The Paper Crane* by Molly Bang.

24.

From *Heartland* by Diane Siebert, illustrated by Wendell Minor, © 1989.

25.

From *Thorn Rose* by the Brothers Grimm, illustrated by Errol Le Cain.

26.

From *Round Trip* by Ann Jonas.

27. From *Saint George and the Dragon* by Margaret Hodges, illustrated by Trina Schart Hyman.

28. From *Tuesday* by David Wiesner.

29. From *Deep in the Forest* by Brinton Turkle.

30. From *Snow-White and the Seven Dwarfs* by the Brothers Grimm, translated by Randall Jarrell, illustrated by Nancy Ekholm Burkert.

31. From *Thorn Rose* by the Brothers Grimm, illustrated by Errol Le Cain.

32. From *Thorn Rose* by the Brothers Grimm, illustrated by Errol Le Cain.

33. From *Three Little Pigs and the Big Bad Wolf* by Glen Rounds.

34. From *Arrow to the Sun* by Gerald McDermott.

Chapter 4

How to Recognize a Well-Illustrated Book

In this age of visual bombardment—daily overloads of images in magazines, on television, at the movies, on computer screens, and on smart phones and MP3 players—do children need even more images in picture books? The answer is a resounding "Yes!" The problem is not that children have too much to see but that they must learn to be discriminating about what they see. We use the term *visual literacy* to describe this sort of discrimination. More than any other generation, today's children need to develop discretion about what they view. Picture books are a perfect vehicle for opening a child's eyes to the beauty and power of art, because they do not function like other books, where words alone tell a story or convey information.

Illustrations in the better picture books share the function of storytelling or concept teaching. In fact, in wordless picture books, the illustrations do the whole job. So the pictures beg for active participation in their viewing, unlike so many of the random images that are flashed daily in front of us. Text and illustration are woven together to communicate. To get the full measure of meaning and fulfillment from a good picture book, the reader must attend carefully to both (Kiefer, 1995). Through the beautifully crafted picture books available today, young readers not only may become aware of the variety of artistic styles, media, and techniques that artists employ, but they also may develop a sense for judging quality.

Visual Literacy: Developing the Ability to "See"

Adults tend to sell children short when it comes to their abilities to perceive the world visually. We have heard our university students—who are, of course, adults—say such things as, "This

Visit the MyEducationKit for this course to enhance your understanding of chapter concepts with activities, weblinks, podcasts, and a searchable database of more than 22,000 children's literature titles.

artwork is too sophisticated for children. Won't they OD on this?" One woman actually asked, "Why do they waste such great art on kids?"

Truth be known, children are generally more visually aware and alert than most adults (McDermott, 1974b). The older we get, the more our visual awareness is likely to be dulled by overload or by the real or imagined expectations our educational systems have imposed on us that alter the way we view images. Honest responses to art and other visual stimuli are programmed out of most children over time. They begin to ignore their own personal reactions and the fascinating details in art in order to second-guess their teachers' agendas, thus becoming basically less aware. This process is not much different from analyzing poetry with children to the point of beating the beauty out of it.

As we have read to young children over the years, they have shown us detail in picture book illustrations that our supposedly sophisticated adult eyes overlooked. For example, we had read *On Market Street* (Lobel, 1981) many times but had not noticed that the figure representing *T* for toys in this alphabet book had on her hands puppets of the immensely popular Frog and Toad characters. That is, we did not notice them until a child pointed them out. Frog and Toad were made famous in Newbery and Caldecott Honor books created by Arnold Lobel—husband of Anita Lobel, who illustrated *On Market Street.* Children have shown us that the church tower clock in each illustration in *Anno's Counting Book* (Anno, 1977) always points to the hour that corresponds with the number being presented. Gerald McDermott has observed that younger children, when reading *Arrow to the Sun* (McDermott, 1974a), notice the sun symbol on the chest of the Sun God's Pueblo Indian child, an obvious visual link between father and son. However, McDermott (1974b) has pointed out that older children tend not to see the boy's emblem.

We are not suggesting teachers are to blame for dulling children's visual perception as they grow older. If anything, the issue with teachers is a matter of omission rather than commission—spending little if any time addressing visual literacy (even when they share picture books with students). However, it is likely that too much viewing of television shows like SpongeBob and its ilk is a major culprit—along with prolonged video game exposure.

Without taking much time from daily instruction, teachers can combat the dulling of visual perception by simply pointing out the artistic principles found in this chapter whenever reading a picture book aloud to their students (both in the primary and intermediate grades). For example, the following section of this chapter addresses the functions of illustrations in picture books. Teachers might take a moment to point out to students how the pictures in a certain book do most of the job in revealing where the story takes place or that by closely examining a character's facial expressions in the illustrations, we learn more about what the person is thinking or feeling. Even the principles concerning visual elements found in the chapter can readily be shared with young readers. Point out, for instance, that the illustrator of *The Relatives Came* (Rylant, 1985) purposefully angled the path leading to the relative's picket fence. He employed the principle that diagonal or slanted lines suggest movement, thus making the car seem to strike the fence with additional momentum. (See Illustration 1 in the color insert.) In this way, teachers and parents can help children retain their natural awareness and develop increased visually literacy. In the process, the adults will be helping themselves become more aware and therefore more appreciative of the images that surround them.

Illustration in picture books is meant to delight, to capture attention, to tell a story or teach a concept, and to develop appreciation and awareness in children. Of course, appreciation is developed in part by consistent exposure to the wonderful varieties of art that are coupled with pleasing stories in today's picture books. Young children begin to sense something special in good

art when they see lots of it. For example, Quincy had seen many fine picture books in his short six years. When he was listening to a new book, *17 Kings and 42 Elephants* (Mahy, 1987), which has jewel-like paintings by Patricia McCarthy, he suddenly interrupted to say, "Dad, these pictures are marvelous!" "Marvelous" was a bit unexpected coming from such a little body, but more amazing was his evaluative response to the illustrations. Quincy didn't have the understanding or the words to analyze McCarthy's batik-painting-on-silk artwork, but he simply knew it was good stuff. How did he know? Because he'd seen so many picture books that he'd developed a level of appreciation that governed his taste in illustrations.

Taste and appreciation come by experience, by comparing a variety of examples. Taste is broadened and cultivated by exposure; it is narrowed or allowed to lay fallow by restricting experience. Indeed, if all that children see in the world of art are cartoons on television, then such will be the standard of art for them.

Functions of Illustrations in Picture Books

"The function of art is to clarify, intensify, or otherwise enlarge our experience of life" (Canaday, 1980). This statement is as true for picture book illustrations as it is for gallery paintings, but picture book artwork also must operate in a manner unique to its special format. Because picture books are made up of a series of illustrations that typically tell a story, the art may function in one or more of the following ways.

Establish Setting

Art is a natural for creating the setting in an illustrated book. Time periods in historical stories or far-flung cultural settings can be brought to life through illustrations in ways words cannot do. Look at *The Fortune-Tellers* (Alexander, 1992) as an example. Lloyd Alexander originally wrote this tale with a pre-medieval European setting in mind. When the publisher selected Trina Schart Hyman to do the illustrations, she envisioned the story set in the west African country of Cameroon. Lloyd agreed to change the venue, and surprisingly, *The Fortune-Tellers* was such a universal story that only two words in the manuscript had to be changed: forest to savannah and bear to lion. As a result, Hyman's illustrations do almost the entire job of establishing both the place and time, which she describes as "the fantastical present" (Hyman, 1995). The handsome people in rainbow-colored costumes and the crisp, highly detailed surroundings create an idyllic, slightly larger-than-life backdrop for Alexander's literary folktale. (See Illustration 2.)

Define and Develop Characters

Artists can give characters an extra fleshing-out through illustrations. David Small's artwork in *The Friend* (Stewart, 2004) intensifies the loving relationship between little Belle and her family's African American housekeeper, Bea, by showing the girl's emotionally distant mother and father. Belle's wealthy parents are departing on an extended trip, yet her lavishly dressed mother only leans down to extend a powdered cheek to accept her daughter's good-bye kiss—no hugs and certainly no tears. Her father, in his driving gloves and camel-hair coat, is impatiently checking his watch, and as they motor away from the mansion, he doesn't look back. (See Illustration 3.) Another illustration shows Belle clinging to Bea as the automobile recedes in the distance, revealing that Bea is more of a mother to the child than her biological parent. The text does not describe this aspect of Mr. and Mrs. Dodd's personalities.

Frog Goes to Dinner (Mayer, 1974), a wordless picture book, relies completely on illustrations to define and develop the characters. Mayer is a marvel when it comes to using facial expressions to communicate what his characters are feeling. Note the double-page illustration of the angry family driving home after they have been thrown out of Fancy Restaurant. Each family member harbors an individual response to the disaster. (See Illustration 4.)

Reinforce Text

The primary function of some picture book illustrations is to reinforce the text. Nonfiction picture books often fall into this category, with the illustrations and diagrams restating visually what the words say. For instance, Steven Kellogg's illustrations for *How Much Is a Million?* (Schwartz, 1985) reinforce the concept of large numbers. For text that reads, "If a billion kids made a human tower . . . they would stand up past the moon," the accompanying illustration shows the top of a stack of happy children with the lunar landscape in the background. The topmost children are holding a banner that reads "1,000,000,000 KIDS."

Illustrations in a picture storybook also may function primarily to reinforce the story. In the ever-popular *Blueberries for Sal* (McCloskey, 1948), for example, readers see what the text describes—the countryside in Maine as well as the characters who are out picking blueberries—but no major extensions to the text are evident. (See Illustration 5.)

Provide a Differing Viewpoint

One of the most enjoyable ways in which illustrations may function in a picture book is that of telling a story different from the text or even being in opposition to the words. In *Rosie's Walk* (Hutchins, 1968), the text says that Rosie the hen takes a peaceful stroll around the farm and gets "back in time for dinner." However, the illustrations tell another tale: A fox, never mentioned in the narrative, lurks behind Rosie every step of the way but is somehow frustrated each time it pounces forward to make Rosie its dinner. (See Illustration 6.)

Peter Spier's *Oh, Were They Ever Happy* (1978) is an example of words and text that are humorously in opposition to one another. Children inadvertently left alone for the day (the babysitter has her days confused and doesn't show) decide to do something nice for their parents—paint the house. The text, consisting mostly of the children's running commentary about their work, portrays the painting project as a marvelous success, while the illustrations show what a horrible mess the kids are making. They paint the bricks and windowpanes; they finish one color of paint and take up another.

Extend or Develop the Plot

The plot of a story may be advanced by illustrations. In wordless picture books, the whole plot is unfolded through pictures. Sometimes the plot is merely extended or rounded a little by the illustrations, as in Stephen Gammell's art in *The Relatives Came* (Rylant, 1985). Gammell shows that one family's journey to a family reunion is a bit perilous because Dad isn't such a good driver. Although Rylant's words say nothing about the driving, Dad levels the mailbox on the way out, loses suitcases from the car's roof rack, careens around mountain curves, and destroys their relatives' fence upon arrival. (See Illustration 1.)

Provide Interesting Asides

Sometimes picture book illustrations are filled with interesting asides—subplots or details not necessarily related to the main story line. In Denys Cazet's (1990) *Never Spit on Your Shoes,* the little dog Arnie tells his mother about his tiring first day at school. Though the illustrations show the events he mentions, each picture reveals other humorous vignettes taking place concurrently. For example, as Arnie tells about Raymond, who can write his name backward, we see this new kid demonstrating his talent on the chalkboard. However, in a corner of the classroom, several animal children are using glue for an art project. A piglet is eating the glue, the sight of which sickens his classmates. In another area of the room, a child approaches the teacher and says, "Thank you very much for inviting me, but I'll be going home now." On another double-page spread, while Arnie describes having lunch in the cafeteria, a hippo is sticking drinking straws in his nose, pretending to be a centipede. His antics awe some at his table and disgust others.

Establish Mood

Illustrations are extremely effective in determining the mood of a picture storybook. *The Polar Express* (Van Allsburg, 1985) is a Christmas story, and Christmas stories typically use a bright and cheery palette. The mood in Van Allsburg's story, however, is mysterious, and he uses dark colors to establish that mood. With muted reds and blues and even muted yellows along with plenty of black and brown, the artist creates an eerie atmosphere as a young boy watches a magical train steam its way into his front yard late Christmas Eve. The mood is maintained as the train whisks him and other children toward the North Pole, zipping past dark forests filled with wolves. (See Illustration 7.)

Style and Media in Picture Book Illustrations

Artists use a vast array of styles and media to create the illustrations in children's books. In fact, some of the best and most varied art being done today appears in picture books. We know a professional artist who regularly checks the children's section at the public library or local bookstore to see what's new because he believes the best contemporary artwork is to be found there.

Excellent illustrations can, of course, be rendered in various styles, ranging from extremely realistic to abstract. *Realism,* or *representational* style, is a faithful reproduction of nature, people, and objects as they actually appear. The illustrations in Zelinsky's *Rapunzel* (1997) are representational. (See Illustration 8.) *Surrealism* is realism skewed. It represents the workings of the unconscious mind by creating a dreamlike state, as in Clément's *The Voice of the Wood* (1989). (See Illustration 9.) *Expressionism,* which is an attempt to give objective expression to inner experience, often makes use of bright colors and figures that are a bit disproportionate. This stylized form is evident in *A Chair for My Mother* (1982). Emotional and physical fatigue burdens Rosa's mother in Vera B. Williams's story. After an apartment fire destroys everything the family owns, she continues working long days waitressing at the Blue Tile Diner, coming home each evening to their new place with its donated furnishings. In Illustration 10, we see her collapsed onto a kitchen chair. The expressionistic style of the painting allows her body to be splayed in an exaggerated manner in order to accentuate the true depth of her mental and physical exhaustion. Another popular style is *impressionism,* which emphasizes light, movement, and color over detail. A fine example of impressionism is Lagarrigue's art for Wiles's *Freedom Summer* (2001). (See Illustration 11.) *Naïve* is a style that gives the appearance of being childlike, perhaps lacking perspective or a sense of proportion. Will Moses, great-grandson of the famous naïve painter Grandma Moses, used a naïve style in his paintings for *Will Moses Mother Goose* (2003). (See Illustration 12.) There are, of course, other artistic styles, including *cartoon art,* as found in James Stevenson's *Flying Feet* (2004). (See Illustration 13.)

The various styles artists use to create their artwork may be rendered in a variety of artistic media. There are basically two categories of media: painterly and graphic.

Painterly media include the most common art materials, such as paint, pencil, and ink. In *Rapunzel,* Zelinsky used *oil paints,* an opaque layering of colors. (See Illustration 8.) Watercolors, which are translucent, were the medium for Stevenson's paintings in *Flying Feet.* (See Illustration 13.) Van Allsburg used *graphite,* or *pencil,* another painterly medium, in *Zathura* (2002). (See Illustration 14.) Also in this category is *pen and ink,* which Isadora used in *Ben's Trumpet* (1979). (See Illustration 15.) Other painterly media include *colored pencils, pastels* (chalk), *charcoal, crayons, felt-tip markers, gouache* (opaque water-based paints), *tempera* (opaque water-based or egg-yolk-based paints), and *acrylics* (plastic paints).

Artists apply painterly media directly to canvas, paper, or some other surface. But when artists use *graphic media,* they generally create the artwork elsewhere before applying it to the final surface. With *woodcuts,* for instance, the artist carves images in relief into a block of wood. Then inks or paints are applied to the wood and transferred to a surface, such as paper. Marcia Brown's illustrations for *Once a Mouse . . .* (1961) are woodcuts. (See Illustration 16; notice the wood grain.) *Linoleum cuts* are similar in technique to woodcuts, but they produce a cleaner line, as in Mary Wormell's *Bernard the Angry Rooster* (2001). (See Illustration 17.) *Collage,* another popular graphic technique, involves cutting and tearing shapes from paper or fabric and arranging them on the page, as in *One Night in the Coral Sea* (Collard, 2005). (See Illustration 18.) Collage may also include other objects that are attached to the surface, like the breakfast cereal and wire hangers in Diaz's illustrations for Bunting's *Smoky Night* (1994). David Wisniewski's dramatic illustrations in *Golem* (1996), created by overlaying intricate paper cutouts, are a sophisticated form of collage. (See Illustration 19.) *Stone lithography* uses a stone printing plate (usually limestone) on which the artist draws with a greasy or waxy medium (wax crayon or special litho paints and pencils). Once the drawing is finished, the artist uses a type of acid that reacts with greasy substances to etch or fix the image onto the stone, readying it to accept ink. Then the stone is moistened with water, which soaks in only where the surface is not etched. The wet stone will not accept oil-based ink, but the greasy substances on the surface will. Thus, when the paper is pressed against the inked stone, only the greasy parts will print. Therefore, the artist must prepare a stone for each color to be added to the illustration. Ingri and Edgar d'Aulaire used stone lithography when creating the artwork for the 1939 edition of their picture book, *Abraham Lincoln.* (See Illustration 20.) A graphic medium that looks a bit like pen-and-ink drawings is called *scratchboard.* A black ink coating is scratched away to show the white surface beneath; color may be added after the "drawing" is complete, as in *Ella Fitzgerald: The Tale of a Vocal Virtuosa* (Pinkney, 2002). (See Illustration 21.) Even *photography* can be considered a graphic technique. Bruce McMillan's *Mouse Views: What the Class Pet Saw* (1993) uses color photography to give children a fresh look at their world. (See Illustration 22.) Also, artists will often mix media, using both graphic and painterly techniques together. A prime example is Molly Bang's *The Paper Crane* (1985), which uses three-dimensional paper cutouts, traditional collage, and painterly techniques. Each page was then photographed to retain its three-dimensional quality. (See Illustration 23.)

Visual Elements

Like all artists, picture book illustrators incorporate several visual elements into the creation of their pictures that subtly affect the way we respond to the art. These elements are line, shape, color, texture, and composition.

Line

Lines in illustrations are either curved or straight. These lines may vary in thickness or length. They may run horizontally, diagonally, or vertically. They may be solid or broken. How line is used often plays an important role in what a picture communicates. For instance, diagonal lines suggest movement (slant of the road in Illustration 1 and of the keyboard in Illustration 15). The dominant vertical lines of the trees in Illustration 7, from Van Allsburg's *The Polar Express,* create a static look, as if this scene were a photograph capturing and arresting a moment in the flow of action. On the other hand, horizontal lines may suggest order or tranquillity, such as the prairie horizon and straight fence lines in Minor's illustration from *Heartland* (Siebert, 1989). (See Illustration 24.)

Artists also use line to direct the viewer's eye. Le Cain's use of line in *Thorn Rose* (1975), the Grimm Brothers' version of "Sleeping Beauty," focuses the eye upon the ominous tower holding the only remaining spinning wheel. The lines created by a balustrade, wall, row of windows, and roof line lead to the upper right-hand corner and seem to converge at the tower that harbors Thorn Rose's fate. Even the fountain and the horizon point the way. In this manner, Le Cain guides our viewing of his painting. (See Illustration 25.)

Shape

Shape is the two-dimensional form representing an object. Shapes may be simple or complex. The objects may be readily identifiable or so abstract as to be difficult to recognize. Curved shapes generally suggest things found in nature, and angular shapes depict objects built by humans. For example, the illustration from *Round Trip* by Ann Jonas (1983) shows from one perspective people sitting in a movie theater. Neither the theater nor the humans are clearly recognizable; they are only suggested by the shapes. The human-made items (seats, lights, screen) are angular forms, while the people are suggested by rounded forms representing heads. (See Illustration 26.)

Color

Color is a visual element with the traits hue, value, and saturation. Hue is simply the color itself (red, blue, yellow), and these hues are often categorized as being either cool (blue, green, violet) or warm (red, yellow, orange). The scene by Le Cain (Illustration 31) predominantly uses reds, yellows, and oranges to create the impression of a hot, bustling kitchen. Value is the lightness or darkness of the color (dark blue, light green), achieved by adding black or white to the hue. As discussed earlier in this chapter, the mood of a picture may be manipulated by value, as in the mysterious mood achieved by the dark palette Van Allsburg used in *The Polar Express* (Illustration 7). Finally, saturation, or chroma, is the brightness or dullness of a color. For example, the brightness of the colors in the picture from *The Fortune-Tellers* (Illustration 2) creates a festive atmosphere, while the muted hues in Illustration 27 add an appropriately ancient feeling to the story of *Saint George and the Dragon* (Hodges, 1984). Illustrations also may be achromatic, rendered in only black, white, and the various shades of gray in between. (See Illustrations 4 and 15.) Monochromatic illustrations use only one hue, such as the all-blue pictures in McCloskey's (1948) *Blueberries for Sal.* (See Illustration 5.)

Texture

Texture is a tactile impression communicated by the artist: rough, smooth, hard, soft, and so on. Collage, as discussed earlier, is the most obvious way of creating texture in illustrations because of its three-dimensional qualities. The cutout crane in Illustration 23, for instance, clearly has the sharp edges of a folded paper bird. However, illustrators most often create a sense of texture on a two-dimensional surface, as with the fabric of the automobile seats in Illustration 4. Mercer Mayer used cross-hatching (the crossing of lines) to produce the coarse texture of the material in both the seats and the boy's suit.

Composition

Composition serves to unify all of the elements in an illustration.

> In arranging the elements on each page, including the printed type, the artist tries to obtain an effective balance between unity and variety and creates visual patterns that may be carried on from page to page. (Kiefer 1995, p. 129)

For example, an artist may balance objects in an illustration, either by distributing them evenly (symmetrically) or irregularly (asymmetrically). In Illustration 28, David Wiesner splits the picture evenly down the center from top to bottom. The backgrounds of both sides are balanced asymmetrically by the careful yet irregular placement of vehicles and people, yet the clouds in the sky (which look like frogs) are symmetric. Another facet of composition concerns object dominance. Artists can ensure that certain shapes are dominant by making them larger or brighter in order to attract the eye. In Illustration 28, the police detective in the foreground is larger than any other individual and thus is the dominant figure. In this way, Wiesner directs the viewer's attention to the detective's actions.

Additional Illustration Criteria: Action and Detail

According to Cianciolo (1976, p. 9), in quality picture book art, "Something of significance is said." In inferior picture books, the art all begins to look the same—flat line and color washes, as in books like the SpongeBob and Dora the Explorer titles. In other words, quality picture book art is individual and unique. Stereotypical artwork denies individuality, both in the artistic rendering and in the characters and settings represented. It is more difficult to relate to the human experience and to get involved with the story when the art depicts generic or stereotypical people and places. In better picture book illustrations, two basic elements tend to give individuality to the illustrations: action and detail.

Depicting Action

Action is important in picture storybooks in particular because the artwork moves the story along. Note the illustration from *Deep in the Forest* (Turkle, 1976), a role-reversal version of "Gold-

ilocks and the Three Bears." (See Illustration 29.) This scene freezes the action at the climax, but the illustration is by no means static. The tilt of the human forms as they barrel forward in pursuit and the wild-eyed little bear with fully outstretched body and churning legs create for us a true sense of the chaotic, frenzied chase. Sometimes action in illustrations is subtle but suggests a great deal of activity. For example, in *Tuesday* (Wiesner, 1991), the police detective examines a lily pad suspended from a pencil, his quizzical look suggesting his mental activity. "Why and how?" he seems to ask himself, unable to fathom the hundreds of frogs who invaded the nighttime sanctity of his town on flying lily pads. (See Illustration 28.) One of the ways picture book artists create tension in their work is by using illustrations to anticipate or foreshadow action. Look at the illustration from *Rosie's Walk* (Hutchins, 1968). (See Illustration 6.) Rosie, still unaware her life is in danger, is about to inadvertently foil another of the fox's attempts to capture her. The rope coiled about her leg shows us what is to come.

Creating Depth with Detail

Certainly, it is not difficult to see that details in illustrations tend to give the artwork depth and allow artists to assert their individuality. Careful attention to detail often requires extensive research before an artist begins work on the illustrations. Depending on the book, illustrators may spend untold hours investigating details of Ming Dynasty culture, the anatomy of wolves, or rain forest botany, for example. In Jarrell's retelling of *Snow-White and the Seven Dwarfs* (Grimm Brothers, 1972), the artist, Nancy Ekholm Burkert, re-created the time period and cultural setting of the tale with accuracy. Even the illustration showing the evil queen's laboratory is stunning in its detail. The accoutrements of black magic are displayed on a workbench; each herb and root is authentic and poisonous. (See Illustration 30.) Trina Schart Hyman's illustrations for *Saint George and the Dragon* (Hodges, 1984) include drawings, primarily in borders surrounding the text, of plants and flowers indigenous to Britain during those ancient times. In researching his book *Make Way for Ducklings,* Robert McCloskey (1941) filled notebooks with artistic studies of ducks—sketches of wing extensions and so on (Schmidt, 1990). He even had ducks swimming in his bathtub and walking about his apartment to use as ready references. McCloskey (1965) pointed out that when he spent time visualizing all the elements of a tree, from leaf to twig to branch to trunk to root, the effort may not be apparent to the viewer of the artistically rendered tree, but the tree is better for his having thought of it in such detail.

Detail also may be evident in the use of perspective in many quality picture books. In Le Cain's *Thorn Rose* (1975), the artist shows a single scene from two very different perspectives. When everyone in the castle falls asleep, one illustration looks past the cook (who is about to box the kitchen boy's ears), out the kitchen door, and beyond the horses sleeping in a stall. Later, when the prince finally arrives on the castle grounds, we are allowed to look past him, past the horses, and back into the kitchen to where the cook is slumped over a table. (See Illustrations 31 and 32.) This may seem a small thing, but such detail provides the setting with depth and makes it a believable place. Obviously, Le Cain envisioned this world carefully and translated his vision into illustrations that give us a sense of being there.

Le Cain also uses his illustrations in *Thorn Rose* to foreshadow subtly the impending doom connected with the last spinning wheel to be found in the kingdom. (See Illustration 25.) In one painting, the artist shows Thorn Rose, now an adolescent, standing on a balcony walkway with a castle tower in the distance. The left side of the illustration is verdant: Thorn Rose is surrounded by flowering plants and peacocks, and the sky is bright. However, as one's eyes move across the

painting toward the tower, the sky darkens ominously. The gardenlike surroundings of the castle give way to a craggy, foreboding appearance. A great serpent, a symbol of evil, slithers along the roofline toward the tower, which has a rather dragonlike look. Of course, the tower holds the accursed spinning wheel. This visual foreshadowing creates a subconscious feeling of tension in the reader.

Indeed, detail can be incredibly subtle. Even the power of a carefully placed line can make loosely drawn pictures suggest a great deal. Consider the illustration from Glen Rounds's *Three Little Pigs and the Big Bad Wolf* (1992). (See Illustration 33.) Although the wolf is rather scratchily drawn, his raggedy appearance makes him look as if he's fallen on hard times. The flowing lines give the wolf a fluid, slinky sense of movement, which seems to say "vagabond."

Most artistic devices are like cosmetics; they must not be too noticeable, or they are not doing their job. Makeup, for instance, must enhance so that we say, "What a gorgeous face," not "What great eye shadow." A device that Maurice Sendak (1963) used in *Where the Wild Things Are* is so subtle that most readers don't notice they are being influenced by it. As Max's anger grows, so do the illustrations, getting larger and larger until they fill a full double-page spread. Then as Max's anger cools, the illustrations begin to shrink.

Care Given to Bookmaking

Finally, the process of fine bookmaking gives us a few other evaluative considerations. The size and shape of books may match the story line, as in Stevens's (1995) *Tops and Bottoms.* A trickster hare promises to do all the work and split the harvest if his well-to-do bear friend will donate the ground to plant a garden. The bear is even allowed to pick whether he wants the tops or the bottoms of what is grown. But when he picks the tops, the hare plants root vegetables. When he changes the next season to bottoms, the hare plants corn. The book is formatted so that it must be turned sideways to read, thus creating a taller double-page spread that matches the verticality of growing things and gives an extended view of what parts of a plant grow above ground and what parts grow below.

Another example of the thoughtful use of book design is found in Gerald McDermott's Caldecott winner, *Arrow to the Sun* (1974a). The rainbow trail, a significant recurring design on Pueblo Native American pottery and other art forms, becomes a unifying factor that threads its way through this traditional story. In Illustration 34, you can see the Sun Lord's earthly child leaving home, following the stripes of the rainbow trail as he begins his hero's journey. It is a path from which he never deviates as he fulfills his quest. Ann Jonas employs uniquely creative design in her book *Round Trip* (1983). It is to be read literally as a round trip. The illustrations are ingeniously crafted so that when we reach the end of the book, we flip it upside down and read it back to the beginning. All the illustrations suddenly transform into new pictures, an optical illusion of sorts. (See Illustration 26; a movie theater becomes a restaurant.) At the same time, the round-trip theme is a part of the story—a trip into the city and then home again.

Even small details such as decorated endpapers enhance the visual appeal of a picture book. The endpapers inside the cover of a book actually bind book to cover and are traditionally white. However, not only are endpapers often brightly colored in many of today's books, but they may be illustrated, sometimes with original pieces not found inside. Good examples are the two original paintings by Helen Oxenbury on the endpapers of Rosen's retelling of *We're Going on a Bear*

Hunt (1989). A deserted, daytime seashore scene appears on the front endpaper, and a nighttime seashore scene with a bear lumbering along in the surf is on the back. In Jerry Pinkney's *Noah's Ark* (2002), the front endpapers depict land and sea, teeming with newly created life—along with colorfully rendered Biblical words blending into the artwork, including "In the beginning God created the heaven and the earth." The back endpapers show an outer-space view of the finished world, with these words: "Seedtime and harvest, cold and heat, summer and winter, night and day, shall never cease as long as the earth endures."

Other illustration techniques extend art beyond the normal sorts of pictures. Hyman's borders in *Saint George and the Dragon* (Hodges, 1984) give the look of observing the story through an old-fashioned window. (See Illustration 27.) In Christopher Bing's illustrations for Ernest Lawrence Thayer's *Casey at the Bat* (2000), real and created reproductions of newspaper clippings, photographs, and other late-19th-century memorabilia (ticket stubs, coins, medals, baseball cards) are superimposed on bold pen-and-ink drawings resembling the sort appearing in old newspapers. Even the front and back matter, such as the acknowledgments and Library of Congress cataloging information, are hidden away within these reproductions. In fact, the whole book is carefully designed to look as if it is a scrapbook from the year 1888.

All these elements of picture book creation and production are what make the visual storytelling and concept-teaching process so successful. Children have available to them some of the best artwork currently available. As teachers and parents, we have the opportunity to help our children become visually literate through fine picture books, and to curb the numbing effects of mindless television viewing. Our charge is to offer our children the best in picture and in word, to give them an arsenal for making artistic and literary judgments and developing taste.

(For more on picture books, see Chapter 7.)

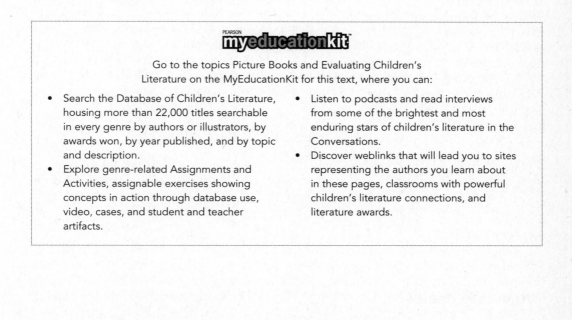

PEARSON **myeducationkit**™

Go to the topics Picture Books and Evaluating Children's Literature on the MyEducationKit for this text, where you can:

- Search the Database of Children's Literature, housing more than 22,000 titles searchable in every genre by authors or illustrators, by awards won, by year published, and by topic and description.
- Explore genre-related Assignments and Activities, assignable exercises showing concepts in action through database use, video, cases, and student and teacher artifacts.
- Listen to podcasts and read interviews from some of the brightest and most enduring stars of children's literature in the Conversations.
- Discover weblinks that will lead you to sites representing the authors you learn about in these pages, classrooms with powerful children's literature connections, and literature awards.

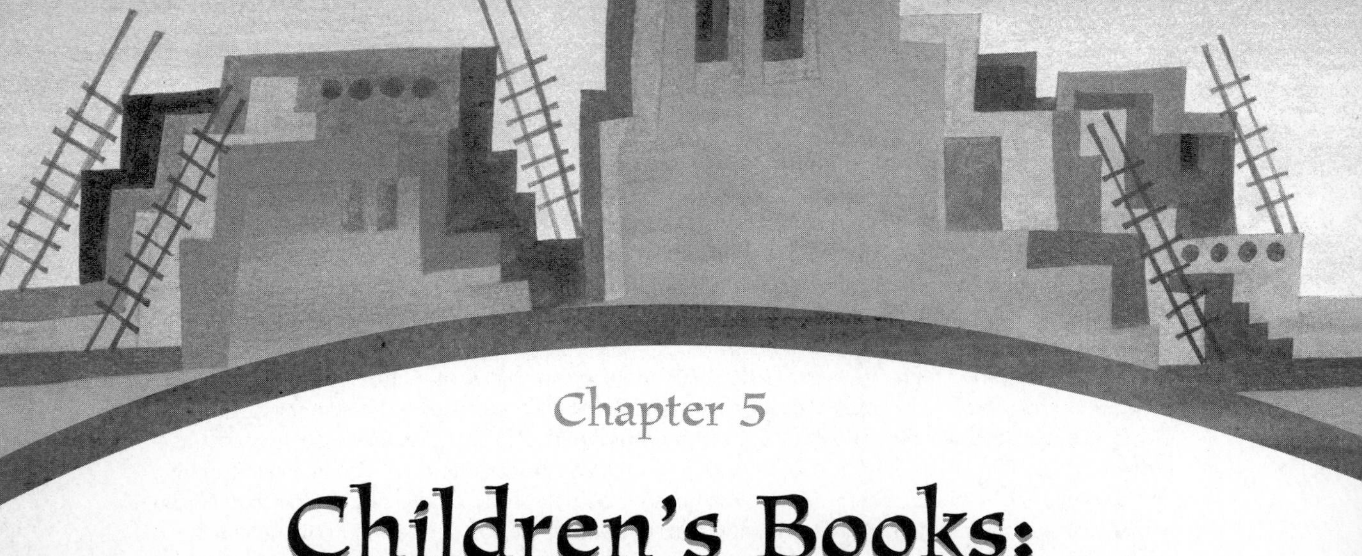

Chapter 5

Children's Books: History and Trends

The notion of childhood dawned late in the history of our Western world, not until the 17th century. The English philosopher John Locke influenced the prevailing attitudes about children as much as anyone in his time. Locke's book *Some Thoughts Concerning Education,* published in 1693, suggested gentler ways of raising children. He even proposed that children's books be made available, books that were easy and pleasant to read. However, *childhood* was a concept only among the affluent until well into the 20th century. As in the days before Locke, many children in both England and the United States continued to be treated as if they were small adults. Consider that child labor laws were not legislated until the early 20th century in both countries. Kids dressed, worked, and lived like their adult counterparts, if that well. Therefore, for the general populace, the idea of special books for children was slow in coming.

Early Books for Children

As far back as the Middle Ages, books intended for youngsters existed in very limited numbers in the form of handwritten texts for the extremely wealthy. However, because literature aimed at young readers has always reflected society's attitudes about children, the stories in these early books were meant to indoctrinate, to provide lessons in proper behavior. The best stories children were exposed to came from storytellers—fairy tales, myths, ballads, epics, and other tales from our oral tradition. Yet these stories were not really meant for children, although they were allowed to listen.

Visit the MyEducationKit for this course to enhance your understanding of chapter concepts with activities, weblinks, podcasts, and a searchable database of more than 22,000 children's literature titles.

Nevertheless, over time these magical tales have become the property of childhood. By the same token, books published in the early days of the printing press, books meant for adults, were also enjoyed and adopted by children. William Caxton, an English businessman and printer, produced several such books, including *Aesop's Fables* (1484), which was decorated with woodcut illustrations. From that time forward, children have claimed many books meant for adult audiences, including such well-known titles as Daniel Defoe's *Robinson Crusoe* (1719), Jonathan Swift's *Gulliver's Travels* (1726), Johann Wyss's *The Swiss Family Robinson* (1814), Walter Scott's *Ivanhoe* (1820), and J. R. R. Tolkien's *The Hobbit* (1937). (See Figure 5.1.)

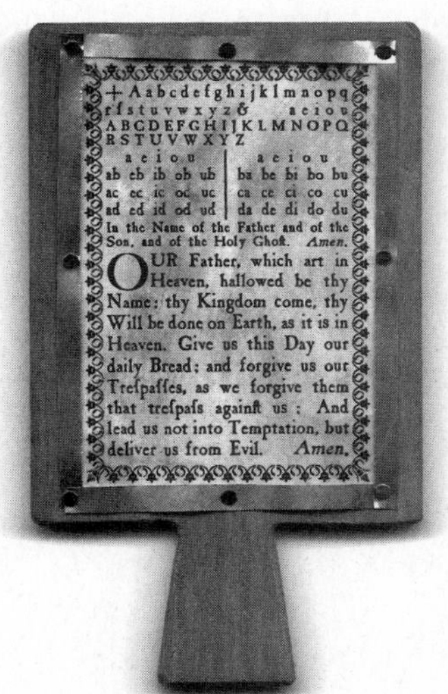

Literature intended specifically for children and published from the 15th through the 17th centuries still was designed to indoctrinate. The so-called hornbooks, or lesson paddles, existed as reading material for children for more than two centuries, beginning in the 1440s. Generally made of wood, these small rectangular paddles (about 3 by 5 inches) had pasted to them pieces of parchment, on which were printed the alphabet, verses from the Bible, or the like. The term *hornbook* comes from the thin, transparent sheet of cow horn that covered and protected the parchment. Hornbooks were particularly popular among the Puritans in colonial America, who believed that children were basically wicked, like adults, and therefore in need of saving. This pious attitude is clearly evident in the first book published for American children, John Cotton's catechism called *Spiritual Milk for Boston Babes in Either England, Drawn from the Breasts of Both Testaments for Their Souls' Nourishment.* First published in England in 1646, it was revised and published in America in 1656.

Despite the preachy, often unpleasant nature of children's literature in the early days of printing, one especially bright spot appeared in 1657. Johann Amos Comenius, a Moravian teacher and bishop, wrote *Orbis Pictus* (The World in Pictures), which is often called the first children's picture book. *Orbis Pictus* is filled with woodcut illustrations that work in harmony with the simple text to describe the wonders of the natural world.

In 1697, Charles Perrault, who had set about collecting the French fairy tales, published his enduring collection, *Tales of Mother Goose,* which included such old favorites as "The Sleeping Beauty" and "Cinderella." Here we find the first mention of Mother Goose, a figure popularized in many subsequent books and stories. Although Perrault's stories were popular with adults in the court of King Louis XIV, his fairy tale collection contains a frontispiece showing an old woman (presumably Mother Goose) telling stories to a group of children.

Even as early as the 16th century, a form of underground reading became popular. Called *chapbooks,* these crudely printed booklets were often sold by peddlers for pennies. Chapbooks became extremely popular in the 17th and 18th centuries and provided the first real break from the oppressive, overly didactic, you-are-a-sinner books for children. The Puritans, of course, decried these tales of Robin Hood, King Arthur, and even an early rendition of "Froggie Went a-Courting." Yet, children and adults reveled in them, though often on the sly.

Chapbooks may have been indirectly responsible for what is arguably the most important development in the history of children's literature—John Newbery's children's book publishing

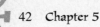

A Chronology of History and Trends in Children's Literature

1400–1800

1440 Introduction of hornbooks. First reading material printed specifically for children.

1484 *Aesop's Fables* published by William Caxton. One of the first books published for adults that was also enjoyed by children.

1580 Introduction of chapbooks. Cheap books offering pleasure reading instead of instruction. Often considered scandalous by many adults.

1646 *Spiritual Milk for Boston Babes in Either England, Drawn from the Breasts of Both Testaments for Their Souls' Nourishment* by John Cotton. Example of a heavily didactic book.

1657 *Orbis Pictus* by Johann Amos Comenius. First illustrated book published specifically for children.

1697 *Tales of Mother Goose* retold by Charles Perrault. Early compilation of oral tradition folk and fairy tales for children.

1719 *Robinson Crusoe* by Daniel Defoe. Island survival story published for adults but popular with children.

1726 *Gulliver's Travels* by Jonathan Swift. Satire and parody published for adults but popular with children because of its wild adventures.

1744 *A Pretty Little Pocket-Book* published by John Newbery. Taught the alphabet with games, rhymes, and fables.

1765 *The History of Little Goody Two Shoes* published by John Newbery. The most famous and enduring of John Newbery's books for children.

1800–1900

1812 *Household Tales* retold by Jacob and Wilhelm Grimm. Popular collection from oral sources of traditional folk and fairy tales.

1814 *The Swiss Family Robinson* by Johann Wyss. Survival story of a shipwrecked family published for adults but popular with children.

1820 *Ivanhoe* by Walter Scott. Adventure novel set in 12th-century England published for adults but popular with children.

1823 *Grimm's Fairy Tales* illustrated by George Cruikshank. Well-known artist commissioned to illustrate book of folk and fairy tales for children.

1835 *Fairy Tales Told for Children* by Hans Christian Andersen. Collection of modern fantasy tales resembling stories from the oral tradition.

1846 *A Book of Nonsense* by Edward Lear. Collection of outrageous and appealing limericks.

1863 *The Water Babies* by Charles Kingsley. Early didactic fantasy novel for children.

1864 *Journey to the Center of the Earth* by Jules Verne. Science fiction novel published for adults but popular with children.

1865 *Alice's Adventures in Wonderland* by Lewis Carroll (Charles Dodgson), illustrated by John Tenniel. Popular fantasy novel that plays with logic in an appealing manner.

1865 *Hans Brinker, or the Silver Skates* by Mary Mapes Dodge. Classic children's novel set in Holland.

1868 *Little Women* by Louisa May Alcott. Trend-setting novel that broke with the tradition of preachy and pious books for children; characters and events reflected honest human experiences.

Continued

1871 *At the Back of the North Wind* by George MacDonald. Serialized in a children's magazine and then published as a popular fantasy novel.

1873 *St. Nicholas Magazine* begins publication. Published 1873–1941; probably the most popular children's magazine of that era.

1876 *The Adventures of Tom Sawyer* by Mark Twain (Samuel Clemens). Adventure story of a 12-year-old boy published for adults but popular with children.

1878 *The Diverting History of John Gilpin* illustrated by Randolph Caldecott. Centerpiece book of English illustrator noted as the first to show action in his illustrations for children.

1878 *Under the Window* illustrated by Kate Greenaway. A collection of verses with accompanying illustrations; first book by one of Britain's most famous illustrators.

1881 *The Adventures of Pinocchio* by Carlo Collodi. Fantasy novel of a wooden puppet who becomes human; one of the early fantasy stories about toys and/or objects coming to life.

1883 *Treasure Island* by Robert Louis Stevenson. A pirates-and-buried-treasure adventure story published for adults but popular with children.

1883 *The Merry Adventures of Robin Hood of Great Renown* written and illustrated by Howard Pyle. Beautifully illustrated classic tale.

1885 *A Child's Garden of Verses* by Robert Louis Stevenson. Early and still-popular collection of poems for children.

1894–95 *The Jungle Books* by Rudyard Kipling. Anthropomorphic animals present lessons for life in interesting tales set in India.

1900–1950

1900 *The Wonderful Wizard of Oz* by L. Frank Baum. First of 14 Oz books written by Baum; the first classic modern fantasy written by an American.

1902 *The Tale of Peter Rabbit* written and illustrated by Beatrix Potter. Beatrix Potter was the mother of the modern picture storybook, and *Peter Rabbit* the firstborn.

1906 *Peter Pan* by J. M. Barrie, illustrated by Arthur Rackham. Became a classic book after first appearing as a play.

1908 *Anne of Green Gables* by Lucy Maud Montgomery. Spunky, likeable Canadian heroine; first in a series.

1908 *The Wind in the Willows* by Kenneth Grahame. Granddaddy of animal fantasies.

1911 *The Secret Garden* by Frances Hodgson Burnett. Classic tale of mystery, friendship, and healing.

1913 *Mother Goose* illustrated by Arthur Rackham. Splendidly illustrated collection of traditional verse.

1922 John Newbery Medal established. The United States' and the world's first prize for children's books. Named for an Englishman.

1926 *Winnie-the-Pooh* by A. A. Milne, illustrated by Ernest Shepard. Gentle animal fantasy that remains a favorite.

1928 *Millions of Cats* written and illustrated by Wanda Gág. First American picture storybook.

1937 *The Hobbit* by J. R. R. Tolkien. High fantasy published for adults but popular with children.

(continued)

Continued

1937 *And To Think That I Saw It on Mulberry Street* written and illustrated by Dr. Seuss (Theodor Geisel). First of Seuss's landscape-changing books for young readers.

1938 Randolph Caldecott Medal established. The United States' prize for illustration in children's books. Named for an Englishman.

1939 *Goodnight Moon* by Margaret Wise Brown, illustrated by Clement Hurd. Classic bedtime read-aloud.

1939 *Madeline* written and illustrated by Ludwig Bemelmans. First of the titles about an irrepressible Parisian girl living in a boarding school.

1941 *Make Way for Ducklings* written and illustrated by Robert McCloskey. Most popular of McCloskey's classic and award-winning titles.

1950–2000

1950 *The Lion, the Witch and the Wardrobe* by C. S. Lewis. First of the classic fantasy series comprising seven titles.

1952 *Charlotte's Web* by E. B. White, illustrated by Garth Williams. Classic Newbery Honor book and animal fantasy; soon overshadowed the year's Newbery winner (*Secret of the Andes*).

1956 Hans Christian Andersen Prize established. International Board on Books for Young People prize honoring an author of international stature.

1957 *Little Bear* by Else Minarik, illustrated by Maurice Sendak. First of the beginning reader picture books.

1957 *The Cat in the Hat* by Dr. Seuss. Along with *Little Bear,* introduced the beginning reader picture book.

1959 *The Lantern Bearers* by Rosemary Sutcliff. Example of fine historical fiction from the 1950s. Winner of the Carnegie award in Great Britain.

1962 *The Snowy Day* written and illustrated by Ezra Jack Keats. First Caldecott Award winner featuring an African American protagonist.

1963 *Where the Wild Things Are* written and illustrated by Maurice Sendak. Controversial picture book that helped usher in the age of new realism. Caldecott winner.

1964 *Harriet the Spy* by Louise Fitzhugh. Groundbreaking novel ushering in the age of new realism.

1964 *The Book of Three* by Lloyd Alexander. Early American challenger to the high fantasy crown long worn exclusively by the British.

1966 Mildred L. Batchelder Award established. American Library Association award for foreign language children's books translated into English.

1967 *A Boy, a Dog, and a Frog* by Mercer Mayer. Often credited with popularizing wordless picture books.

1969 Coretta Scott King Award established. American Library Association award honoring African American writers and illustrators.

1970 *Are You There God? It's Me, Margaret* by Judy Blume. Popular novel dealing with taboos not traditionally addressed in children's books at the time.

1971 *Journey to Topaz* by Yoshiko Uchida. Example of a novel dealing with an unsavory slice of American history.

1972 *Push-Pull, Empty-Full: A Book of Opposites* by Tana Hoban. Early concept book for the very young; Hoban is often cited as popularizing the concept book.

Continued

1974	*My Brother Sam Is Dead* by James Lincoln Collier and Christopher Collier. One of the early historical novels to treat American history from a nontraditional perspective.
1975	*M. C. Higgins, the Great* by Virginia Hamilton. First novel written by an African American to win Newbery Medal.
1975	*Why Mosquitoes Buzz in People's Ears* retold by Verna Aardema, illustrated by Leo and Diane Dillon. First African American to win Caldecott Medal.
1977	NCTE Excellence in Poetry for Children Award established. Given by National Council of Teachers of English; first award in the United States to honor children's poetry.
1981	*A Visit to William Blake's Inn: Poems for Innocent and Experienced Travelers* by Nancy Willard, illustrated by Alice and Martin Provensen. First book of poetry to win Newbery Medal.
1983	*Sugaring Time* by Kathryn Lasky, photographs by Christopher Knight. First photo essay to win Newbery Honor.
1985	*The Polar Express* written and illustrated by Chris Van Allsburg. Instantly popular Caldecott Medal winner that was as much a hit with adults as with children. Has had record-setting sales.
1987	*Lincoln: A Photobiography* by Russell Freedman. First photobiography to win Newbery Medal.
1988	*Joyful Noise: Poems for Two Voices* by Paul Fleischman. First interactive book (choral reading) to win Newbery Medal.
1989	*Color Zoo* by Lois Ehlert. First engineered picture book to win Caldecott Honor.
1990	*Orbis Pictus* Award established. Given by National Council of Teachers of English; first nonfiction book award.
1996	Pura Belpré Award established. American Library Association award for Latino/Latina authors and illustrators.
1998	*Harry Potter and the Sorcerer's Stone* by J. K. Rowling. First book in the all-time bestselling children's series.
2000+	
2000	Michael L. Printz Award established. American Library Association award for young adult literature.
2001	Robert F. Sibert Informational Book Award established. American Library Association award for nonfiction.
2006	Theodor Seuss Geisel Award first presented. American Library Association award for excellence in writing for very young readers (beginning reader books).
2007	*The Invention of Hugo Cabret* by Brian Selznick. Unique combination of picture book and novel; Caldecott winner.

house. Certainly, Newbery was influenced by John Locke, who dared suggest that youngsters should enjoy reading, so it seems likely that he observed the popularity of chapbooks among children and decided there was a market for true children's books. In any case, Newbery ushered in the age of children's books by beginning to publish exclusively for young readers. He released his first title for children in 1744. *A Pretty Little Pocket-Book* taught the alphabet not with catechism but with entertaining games, rhymes, and fables. Newbery published hundreds of books (some of which he may have written himself), the most famous and enduring of which was *The History of Little Goody Two Shoes* (1765). So great was Newbery's contribution to children's publishing that the oldest of the world's children's book prizes bears his name, America's John Newbery Medal, first given in 1922. Still, the moralistic tale continued to dominate much of children's literature, even in many of Newbery's books. Didacticism—emphasizing lesson more than story—ruled well into the 19th century.

Children's Books Come of Age

The 1800s

The onset of the 19th century brought into print some of the most influential, honest, and lasting children's stories. Jacob and Wilhelm Grimm collected from oral sources the German variants of the folk and fairy tales and retold them in their *Household Tales,* which appeared in 1812 and included "Snow White" and "Rumpelstiltskin." Some of Hans Christian Andersen's original fairy tales were published in 1835 in a volume titled *Fairy Tales Told for Children.* The stories of this Danish author, such as "The Ugly Duckling" and "The Emperor's New Clothes," remain popular to this day.

One of the century's greatest contributions to verse for children came from England. Edward Lear's *A Book of Nonsense* (1846), a collection of outrageous limericks, became an immediate bestseller. Lear made the limerick famous, and it remains a favorite verse form among today's children. Robert Louis Stevenson's *A Child's Garden of Verses* (1885) is another poetry collection that many children still love.

A number of noteworthy books surfaced during the second half of the 19th century. Fantasy novels emerged with the publication of such greats as *The Water Babies* by Charles Kingsley in 1863 and, of course, Lewis Carroll's (Charles Dodgson) *Alice's Adventures in Wonderland* in 1865. Other noteworthy titles include *At the Back of the North Wind* by George MacDonald (1871), *The Adventures of Pinocchio* by Carlo Collodi (1881), and the novels of Jules Verne, which mark the advent of the science fiction genre. Beginning with *Journey to the Center of the Earth* in 1864, Jules Verne created stories meant for adults but happily embraced by young readers.

Stories about contemporary life remained preachy and pious until a monumental children's novel made its debut in 1868. *Little Women* by Louisa May Alcott was like a breath of fresh air with its lively characters whose actions, words, and feelings reflected honest human experiences. The character of Jo March, for example, deviated radically from female characters of the past who were docile and certainly inferior to their male counterparts. In fact, Jo was something of a rebel (an early feminist), who railed constantly against what she considered the false set of standards dictated by the Victorian code of behavior. *Little Women* set the course for many realistic novels that immediately followed its publication, including several more from Alcott herself. A few years later came Mark Twain's (Samuel Clemens) *The Adventures of Tom Sawyer* (1876) and Robert Louis Stevenson's *Treasure Island* (first serialized in the magazine *Young Folks,* then published as a book in 1883). The last decade of the 19th century gave us Rudyard Kipling's masterpiece, *The Jungle Books* (1894–1895).

A number of magazines for children began publication during the 19th century. *St. Nicholas Magazine,* published in the United States starting in 1873, set standards of excellence in the world of children's literature. Edited by Mary Mapes Dodge, who wrote *Hans Brinker, or the Silver Skates* (1865), the best-known children's authors and illustrators contributed to *St. Nicholas.* Several novels first appeared in the magazine in serialized form, including *Jo's Boys* by Louisa May Alcott, *Sara Crewe* by Frances Hodgson Burnett, and *The Jungle Books* by Rudyard Kipling.

Children's book illustration also came of age during the 19th century. Illustrators gained status as printing techniques improved and color illustrations became more common. Publishers enticed well-known artists, such as George Cruikshank, who illustrated *Grimm's Fairy Tales* in 1823, to produce work for children's books. The artwork by the immortal Victorian-age illustrators in Great Britain, such as Randolph Caldecott, Kate Greenaway, and Walter Crane, rival the fine work being done today, in spite of comparatively primitive color printing methods. So influential were these artists that two major awards for children's book illustration today bear their names: the Randolph Caldecott Medal, established in 1938 in the United States, and the Kate Greenaway Medal in the United Kingdom, first given in 1956. Randolph Caldecott is often noted as the first illustrator to show action in pictures, as evidenced in *The Diverting History of John Gilpin* (1878), which has perhaps his best-remembered illustrations. In fact, the Caldecott Medal affixed to winning picture books is embossed with the most famous scene, John Gilpin's wild ride. American Howard Pyle also created stunning illustrations for classics like *The Merry Adventures of Robin Hood of Great Renown* (1883), which he also wrote.

1900–1950

And so the domain of children's books was firmly established by the dawning of the 20th century, which began with the birth of the modern picture storybook. Illustrations in books for children, beautiful as they were, functioned primarily as decorations until Beatrix Potter wrote and illustrated her enduring story, *The Tale of Peter Rabbit* (1902). Potter incorporated colored illustration with text, page for page, becoming the first to use pictures as well as words to tell the story. Beatrix Potter was thus the mother of the modern picture storybook, and *Peter Rabbit* the firstborn.

Another first that occurred early in the 20th century was marked by the publication of L. Frank Baum's *The Wonderful Wizard of Oz* in 1900. Modern fantasy had been primarily the domain of the Europeans, especially the British. *The Wonderful Wizard of Oz* was the first classic modern fantasy written by an American.

Many other enduring classics emerged in the first part of the century, such as J. M. Barrie's magical *Peter Pan in Kensington Gardens,* adapted in 1906 into a book from its original form as a play, and Lucy Maud Montgomery's Canadian classic *Anne of Green Gables* (1908), featuring the spunky, red-headed Anne Shirley. Frances Hodgson Burnett's immortal story, *The Secret Garden,* was published in 1911. The granddaddy of animal fantasies appeared in 1908. Kenneth Grahame's *The Wind in the Willows* became the standard for all subsequent animal fantasy stories. Another trend-setting fantasy, A. A. Milne's gentle story of *Winnie-the-Pooh,* was published in 1926.

While talented illustrators such as Arthur Rackham (*Mother Goose,* 1913) were at work in the United Kingdom, the United States produced its counterpart to Beatrix Potter—Wanda Gág. Her *Millions of Cats* (1928) is credited as the first American picture storybook. Its descriptive pictures and rhythmic text have remained unforgettable: "Hundreds of cats, Thousands of cats,

Millions and billions and trillions of cats." Other landmark picture books from the first half of the 20th century include American favorites such as *Goodnight Moon* (1939), a classic bedtime story by Margaret Wise Brown, and *Madeline* (1939), Ludwig Bemelmans's tale of the little, irrepressible Parisian girl who lived in a boarding school. Dr. Seuss (Theodor Geisel), who became the most widely known of American children's book authors and illustrators, released his first book, *And to Think That I Saw It on Mulberry Street,* in 1937. Another immortal name in the history of children's picture books, Robert McCloskey, published *Make Way for Ducklings* in 1941. Today as much as ever, children love this endearing tale of a spunky mother duck and her eight ducklings' dangerous trek through Boston to reach the Public Garden.

Along with the many noteworthy books during the first half of the 20th century, a number of popular but lesser-quality books appeared. The books published by the Stratemeyer Syndicate created a publishing phenomenon that has extended into current times. Beginning in the late 19th century, Edward Stratemeyer saw the potential profit in publishing a quickly produced fiction series for young readers. Certainly, series books had been published and done well before Stratemeyer, but he created a publishing machine that pumped out thousands of titles over the years. Typically, Stratemeyer would outline plots and then turn the writing over to a host of ghostwriters. He published his series books under various pseudonyms, which many children still believe belong to real authors. Some of the Stratemeyer series titles include the Rover Boys, the Bobbsey Twins, Tom Swift, the Hardy Boys, and Nancy Drew. Today series books are commonly the best-selling children's books, despite their sometimes less-than-sterling literary quality (Norris & Pawlowski, 2009; Brooks, Waterman, & Allington, 2003; Chevannes, McEvoy, & Simson, 1997; Greenlee, Monson, & Taylor, 1996; Saltman, 1997; Roback, 2001). Examples include the Amazing Days of Abby Hayes series, the 39 Clues series, the Secrets of Droon books, the Katie Kazoo titles, the Fairy Godmother Academy, the Dragon Slayers' Academy, the Time Surfers books, and the Beast Quest series.

1950–Present

In the latter half of the 20th century, a revolution in the world of children's books occurred. The decade of the 1950s was a stable time for children's publishing. Books still had predictable plots and contained the basic decency and restrained good fun that most adults expected. Some enduring modern classics were born during this period, such as E. B. White's *Charlotte's Web* (1952) and C. S. Lewis's *The Lion, the Witch and the Wardrobe* (1950), not to mention the fine historical fiction of Rosemary Sutcliff (*The Lantern Bearers,* 1959). Another step forward in the world of children's books occurred in 1956, when the International Board on Books for Young People established the major international award for children's writing, the Hans Christian Andersen Prize.

The financial boom of the 1960s, which included large government grants to school libraries, helped make children's publishing big business. More books began to be published and sold, which is reflected by an increase in the number of books chosen as "Notables" each year by the American Library Association. There were 19 Notable titles in 1956 and 62 Notables in 1964.

New Realism

Along with an increase in sales, the 1960s brought a revolution in writing and illustrating: the age of new realism. Long-standing taboos imposed on authors and illustrators began to break

down as the social revolution of the 1960s began to boil. Few books before this time dealt with topics such as death, divorce, alcoholism, and child abuse. In fact, books did not even show children and parents at odds with one another. And there were almost no quality books for children written by and about minorities. Then, in the early 1960s, daring new books began to emerge. A picture book, *Where the Wild Things Are* (1963) by Maurice Sendak, and a novel, *Harriet the Spy* (1964) by Louise Fitzhugh, are often credited with ushering in this age of new realism. Both were mildly controversial, partly because they showed children at odds with their parents. Max's mother in *Wild Things* loses her temper at his unruly behavior and sends him "to bed without eating anything." And Harriet's parents are aloof and too busy to be concerned with her day-to-day activities. Max's psychological fantasy, a vent for his frustration and for the anger he feels toward his mother, and Harriet's eventual need for psychotherapy were unsettling story elements for some adults.

As the 1970s progressed, new realism spread its wings. Shockingly realistic novels and picture books became the mode as authors addressed serious taboos. For example, the novels of Judy Blume, such as her controversial yet extremely popular *Are You There God? It's Me, Margaret* (1970) and her even more explicit *Forever* (1975), treated physical maturation and sex candidly. Authors of historical novels also dared present to young readers varied and often unpopular viewpoints about our past. Books began to look at the American Revolution from perspectives other than that of a righteous rebellion, such as James Lincoln Collier and Christopher Collier's *My Brother Sam Is Dead* (1974). Some regarded these efforts to represent history more accurately as unpatriotic. Embarrassing annals from American history also began to appear more frequently in books for young readers, such as Yoshiko Uchida's book *Journey to Topaz* (1971), a fictionalized autobiographical account of life in the Japanese American internment camps during World War II.

Minority Books

The Snowy Day by Ezra Jack Keats, published in 1962, was the first picture book to show a black child as a protagonist with no vestiges of negative stereotyping. The book won the Caldecott Medal in 1963 and remains a favorite of children. But other than *The Snowy Day,* there were few books with African American characters in the early 1960s (Larrick, 1965), and books written by African Americans about themselves were even scarcer. However, an emphasis in the United States both on international books—many about various races and cultures—and on books written and illustrated by African Americans was encouraged by the establishment of two awards in the 1960s: the Mildred L. Batchelder Award for translated books and the Coretta Scott King Award for African American writers and illustrators. Today, the American Library Association administers both awards.

Still, it was more than a decade before African Americans won Newbery and Caldecott Awards. Finally, in 1975, Virginia Hamilton received the Newbery Medal for *M. C. Higgins, the Great,* and in 1976, illustrator Leo Dillon won the Caldecott Medal (along with his wife, Diane, who is not African American) for *Why Mosquitoes Buzz in People's Ears* (Aardema, 1975). This was indicative of an increase in the number and quality of books created by American minority populations during the rest of that decade.

Although the overall number of books being published steadily increased year by year, titles about minorities in the United States decreased during the 1980s. Between the early 1970s and early 1980s, the number dropped by more than half, according to a list released by the New York Public Library (Rollock, 1989). However, in the 1990s, the negative trend reversed (Micklos,

1996). The estabishment in 1996 of the Pura Belpré Award, a new American Library Association prize for books by Latino/Latina authors and illustrators, reflected a renewed interest in books about minority cultures.

The Changing Trends in Genres and Formats of Children's Books

Strong American high fantasy, rivaling the work of C. S. Lewis, also appeared in the 1960s. Most notable were the five books of The Prydain Chronicles by Lloyd Alexander, beginning with *The Book of Three* (1964).

Historical novels, which waned during the 1970s, began a comeback in the 1980s, and informational books (nonfiction) flourished. Although good informational books were available in earlier decades, an explosion of engaging, well-illustrated, and well-written nonfiction occurred. Informational books, which seldom appeared on Newbery Award lists, began to show up more frequently. Books winning Newbery Honors in the last 30 years include *Homesick: My Own Story* by Jean Fritz (1982); *Sugaring Time* by Kathryn Lasky (1983); *Commodore Perry in the Land of the Shogun* by Rhoda Blumberg (1985); *Volcano* by Patricia Lauber (1986); *The Wright Brothers* (1991), *Eleanor Roosevelt: A Life of Discovery* (1993), and *The Voice That Challenged a Nation: Marian Anderson and the Struggle for Equal Rights* (2004) by Russell Freedman; *The Great Fire* (1995) and *An American Plague: The True and Terrifying Story of the Yellow Fever Epidemic of 1793* (2003) by Jim Murphy; *Hitler Youth: Growing Up in Hitler's Shadow* (2005) by Susan Campbell Bartoletti, and *Claudette Colvin: Twice toward Justice* (2009) by Phillip Hoose. *Lincoln: A Photobiography* by Russell Freedman, published in 1987, was awarded the Newbery Medal. One of the most exciting trends of the 1980s and 1990s undoubtedly was the increase in and emphasis on quality nonfiction for all age levels. Informational books now are better as a whole than ever. (See Chapter 14.) The first national award strictly for nonfiction writing was established by the National Council of Teachers of English in 1990 and appropriately named the *Orbis Pictus* Award in honor of the first nonfiction book published for children. In 2001, the American Library Association also established a nonfiction prize, the Robert F. Sibert Informational Book Award.

Expanding the emphasis placed on books for the very young in the 1970s, an increased number of quality "I can read," or beginning reader, picture books appeared in the 1980s and 1990s. The trendsetters in this area had emerged decades earlier with the 1957 publications of *Little Bear* by Else Minarik and *The Cat in the Hat* by Dr. Seuss. But large numbers of well-written books for fledgling readers were not available until the 1980s. For example, HarperCollins publishes a series called I Can Read Books, of which Minarik's *Little Bear* is a part. Fine authors who often have made a name by writing for older children have contributed to the series, which now offers parents, teachers, and children an exciting array of worthwhile beginning reader books. In 2004, the American Library Association established an award acknowledging excellence in writing for very young readers, the Theodor Seuss Geisel Award. It was first presented in 2006 to Cynthia Rylant (2005) for *Henry and Mudge and the Great Grandpas.*

Poetry also received more attention during the 1980s and 1990s. Two books of poetry won Newbery Medals during this time: *A Visit to William Blake's Inn: Poems for Innocent and Experienced Travelers* by Nancy Willard (1981) and *Joyful Noise: Poems for Two Voices* by Paul Fleischman (1988). In 1977, the National Council of Teachers of English established the Excellence in Poetry for Children Award, a lifetime achievement award honoring poets who write for young readers. Also, novels in poetic form made a mark in the 1990s when *Out of the Dust*

by Karen Hesse (1997) was published. Since that time the number of novels in poetic form has increased substantially and includes the 2009 Newbery Honor book, *The Surrender Tree* (Engle, 2008).

A Changing Marketplace

As the bookselling marketplace changes, publishing automatically changes with it. For instance, federal monies for school libraries in the United States dwindled in the 1970s, and the market for children's books shifted toward a consumer, or bookstore, market. According to Melanie Donovan (2006) of HarperCollins Publishers, retail sales command more than half the children's book market, a significant rise over the 5% to 10% common before 1970. For companies that publish top-selling series paperbacks, 70% or more of sales may derive from retail markets (Donovan, 2006).

This change in marketplace brought about a change in books. In an effort to attract adult retail consumers of children's books, editors shifted some of their emphasis to more lavishly illustrated books as well as to titles for younger audiences. New printing technologies allowed for more affordable yet extremely sophisticated, full-color, camera-separated reproductions. (Picture book art is now scanned and manipulated with computers.) As a result, picture books became more colorful and the renderings increasingly showy, a draw for bookstore patrons. For example, *The Polar Express* by Chris Van Allsburg (1985), with its stunning, Caldecott-winning illustrations, became a popular Christmas gift for adults to give not only to children but also to other adults. Sales skyrocketed, and 500,000 copies were printed within the first two years.

Nonfiction concept picture books and wordless picture books also became popular with consumers. Illustrated with photographs, Tana Hoban's concept books, such as *Push-Pull, Empty-Full: A Book of Opposites* (1972), led the way in this category. Mercer Mayer (1967) popularized the wordless picture book beginning with *A Boy, a Dog, and a Frog.* Baby/board books, virtually indestructible little books for babies and toddlers, invaded bookstores as well. So-called toy (engineered) books also proliferated—pop-up, scratch-and-sniff, texture (touchy/feely) books—which are typically too fragile for library and school markets. Toy books in the 1990s often emphasized the toy more than the book. A book might be packaged with a stuffed animal, an inflatable globe, or even a full-blown kit for building a pyramid or planting a terrarium. An engineered/toy book, Lois Ehlert's *Color Zoo* (1989), was the first of its type to win a Caldecott Honor.

In the 1970s, picture books first became available in paperback, making them cheaper for young readers to own. Publishers further realized that the cheaper series chapter books, published only in paperback, would sell quickly in bookstores. Books like the Hardy Boys made a mammoth resurgence in the 1970s, and other paperback series, such as teenage romance books, began to appear on store shelves. The 1990s brought a proliferation of new paperback series titles—Goosebumps, Fear Street, Animorphs, Saddle Club, American Girls, Bailey School Kids, and so on—as well as the repackaging of older series such as the Boxcar Children and the Nancy Drew mysteries. Also, starting in the 1990s, consumers began to find these books and other children's titles in stores not traditionally connected with bookselling: Walmart, Target, T. J. Maxx, Sam's Club, Costco, and supermarket chains such as Stop & Shop (Rosen, 1997).

In the 1980s and 1990s, children's publishers were doing well financially. Even Wall Street had to pay attention when illustrator Chris Van Allsburg negotiated an $800,000 advance for the book *Swan Lake* (Helprin, 1989). Though this sort of remuneration is not the rule, $1 million advances, especially for multiple-book contracts, are not unheard of today. For example, Putnam

paid Michael Hoeye $1.8 million for the rights to publish his previously self-published novel, *Time Stops for No Mouse* (2002), and two other titles (Baker, 2001). In 2003, Michelle Paver received a £1.5 million advance for her novel *Wolf Brother* (2004), the first of a six-book series set in the Stone Age. Her total international advances totaled around £3 million (Brown, 2004).

The 1980s saw the formation of publishing conglomerates. Larger corporations, often businesses having no relation to books, began purchasing publishing houses. Many long-standing U.S. publishers became imprints of so-called umbrella companies or disappeared altogether. For example, the Macmillan Publishing Company purchased Atheneum, along with other publishing houses, until its children's book division comprised 11 hardcover imprints. Then Macmillan was purchased by Simon & Schuster, which was then acquired by Paramount. Soon Paramount was snapped up by the media conglomerate Viacom. So children's book publishing became even bigger business. At that time, Simon & Schuster's many hardcover children's book imprints were consolidated under three names: Simon & Schuster Books for Young Readers, Atheneum Books for Young Readers, and Margaret K. McElderry Books.

Today, Simon and Schuster is owned by the CBS Corporation (Columbia Broadcasting System), formerly Viacom. At this writing, its number of imprints has expanded to twelve: Aladdin, Atheneum Books for Young Readers, Beach Lane Books, Libros Para Niña, Little Simon, Little Simon Inspirations, Margaret K. McElderry Books, Paula Wiseman Books, Simon & Schuster Books for Young Readers, Simon Pulse, Simon Scribbles, and Simon Spotlight.

One consequence resulting from the advent of mega-publishers is that a bigger corporate structure dictates an even stronger focus on profits. The explosion of products like toy books and celebrity titles help pad the bottom line in an era where most books are now sold in bookstores and other retail outlets, rather than to schools and libraries. Today, some of the large publishing houses include representatives from the bookstore chains, such as Barnes and Noble, in their marketing meetings, and if Barnes and Noble determines it will not purchase a title being considered for publication, then the publisher will likely not produce that book. This means editors no longer have the luxury of saying, as they once did, "This wonderful book will probably not sell many copies, but we will publish it because it deserves to be in print."

As children's books became more profitable, the number of titles published annually in the United States rose from approximately 2,500 in 1975 (Miele & Prakken, 1975, p. 163) to about 4,500 in the mid-1990s (Bogart, 1997) and then up to 5,000 in 1999 (Bogart, 2001). Though retail sales were mostly responsible for such growth, a rise in institutional purchases of books in the mid-1980s into the 1990s had some effect as well. As teachers began to embrace literature-based reading philosophies and methodologies, schools began to purchase more and more trade books (books other than textbooks or reference books) for use in the classroom. Some school systems began to allot a percentage of the textbook budget for the acquisition of children's books, and sales from school paperback book clubs (e.g., Trumpet Club, Scholastic, Troll, Weekly Reader) leaped into the hundreds of millions of dollars.

But in 2001, a shift in educational philosophy, as evidenced by the passage of the No Child Left Behind Act, negatively affected institutional trade book sales. A strict administrative emphasis on "teach and test" deemphasized trade books in the literacy curriculum. This is reflected in the publication *Put Reading First* (Armbruster, Lehr, & Osborn, 2001), which was funded through the U.S. Office of Education. The authors focus on direct instruction and downplay the application of individual reading in the classroom setting. Concerning silent, independent reading (sustained silent reading), the authors say, "Rather than allocating time for independent reading in

the classroom, encourage your students to read more outside of school" (p. 29). But encouraging students to read at home amounts to empty words when engendering a love for books and story is not a part of the equation. (See Chapter 1.)

The 21st Century

As the new millennium dawned, the number of children's trade books published in the United States grew. Though it is always difficult to determine the exact number of juvenile books published in a year—varying sources give varying statistics—the market research company Simba Information (Norris & Pawlowski, 2009) reported the publishing of 13,967 hardcover children's and young adult books in 2008. Interesting trends and events also occurred, such as the industry's love of old titles. Books from 25, 50, even 100 years ago (often long out of print) were being resurrected and rereleased, such as the delightful Freddy the Pig books from the 1930s, 1940s, and 1950s, written by Walter R. Brooks (*Freddy the Detective,* 1932). Other examples include picture books by Newbery-winning author Lois Lenski (*The Little Fire Engine,* 1946), the Newbery Honor book *Enchantress from the Stars* (1970) by Sylvia Louise Engdahl, and Walter Farley's *Black Stallion* (1941).

Since the year 2000, the acquisition of one publisher by another has continued to create larger mega-publishers. For example, Houghton Mifflin purchased Harcourt, another giant in the field, and is now known as the Houghton Mifflin Harcourt Publishing Company. Also, in the first decade of the new millennium, Scholastic Books purchased all of the other major school book clubs: Trumpet Club, Troll, and Weekly Reader.

In 2000, young adult literature was finally recognized with its own American Library Association award, the Michael L. Printz Award. Newbery committee members had long wondered whether to include young adult books with mature themes and older protagonists in their award deliberations. The Printz Award could have alleviated this dilemma, but since the award's inception, the same title has appeared on both award lists more than once.

The American Library Association established two other important children's book awards in the 21st century. The Robert F. Sibert Informational Book Award was first presented in 2001 and the Theodor Seuss Geisel Award, given to books written for beginning readers, in 2006.

The biggest publishing news that started in the 1990s and extended into the 21st century had to be the stunning success of the Harry Potter books. *Harry Potter and the Sorcerer's Stone* by J. K. Rowling (1998) traveled from the United Kingdom to the United States, taking the country by storm. Not only kids but adults, too, were hooked on Harry, and it was not unusual to see air travelers in business suits reading the book. The Harry Potter books are the first children's titles to appear simultaneously on both the adult and children's bestseller lists, and as of this writing, they have sold over 400 million copies worldwide (Schuker, 2009).

Fantasy literature in general increased in popularity with the publication of Harry Potter. The multibook fantasy series, which may include a dozen titles or more, has become a publishing mainstay. Examples include the Children of the Lamp series (P. B. Kerr) published by Scholastic, the Edge Chronicles (Paul Steward and Chris Riddell) from Random House, and the Septimus Heap series (Angie Sage) published by HarperCollins. In this category, the vampire books by Stephenie Meyers, beginning with *Twilight* (2005), have sold millions of copies.

The publishing success of graphic novels is another new trend. Despite a comic-book-like format, these illustrated novels have had an almost cult-like following in the past among adult and teenaged readers. Today, these books have entered the mainstream of publishing and are aimed at both younger and older audiences.

Authors and illustrators of children's books continue to experiment with form and content. The rewards of this experimentation outweigh the obvious risks; many fine books are being published as a result. For example, *The Invention of Hugo Cabret* by Brian Selznick—a unique combination of picture book and novel—won the Caldecott Medal in 2008. However, these risks require that we accept the fact that many more weak books are being published, too. For instance, since the 1990s, we have been in an age of politically correct standards for evaluating books. Children's literature watchdogs—of which there are many from all walks of adult life—are today scrutinizing books for what they deem to be material inappropriate for young readers. However, former school librarian Cynthia DeFelice (2002, p. 21), now a well-known children's book author, points out that "political correctness is the antithesis of honesty and truth, and writing is about nothing so much as trying to capture what is true in words. And the truth, unfortunately, includes some 'upsetting parts.'"

Didacticism before the age of new realism in children's books was mostly concerned with preaching the accepted standards of morality and behavior. However, as DeFelice points out, there is a new sort of didacticism that often focuses on politically correct attitudes and/or causes. A novel can be strengthened by its insights into issues and problems, but not when the book's major purpose is to promote an agenda. Then the message becomes more important than the story, and the book suffers.

In many books today, it is often politically expedient to be artificially evenhanded, as in Rosemary Wells's (2000) *Emily's First 100 Days of School.* Emily is baking cookies with her grandmother when she exclaims joyfully that they are making 72 cookies for Christmas, Hanukkah, Solstice, and Kwanza—exactly the words that would come out of a normal kindergartner! Instead of keeping the story believable, Wells diminishes her usual fine writing style by making certain, at all cost, that every group celebrating a December holiday is included. Using a story as a soapbox interferes with the impact of the reading experience. Chris Van Allsburg's *Just a Dream* (1990), for instance, is an obvious, rather preachy lesson on ecology. Today, many books receiving stellar reviews suffer from this type of didacticism, which often means that, from a literary standpoint, weaker books receive acclaim because of subject matter.

But good old-fashioned didacticism still exists, too—mostly in books written by celebrities whose star status seems to allow them to get away with it. In *Growing Up Is Hard* by Dr. Laura Schlessinger, kindergartner Sammy feels that his life is awful—his teacher wants him to do better, his friend plays with another boy, and he forgets to take out the trash and now can't watch his favorite TV show. His dad, seeing that Sammy is discouraged, talks with him about his problems. After their discussion, Sammy says, "Daddy, I think I get it. I was looking at everything as bad. You made those things look like they could also be good. Let me try now" (Schlessinger, 2001, p. 28). Sammy then puts his life neatly together. The lesson is preached at the reader instead of emerging naturally from the story. Another example is John Lithgow's *Marsupial Sue* (2000), which in greeting-card style sacrifices story to hammer home its message: You should be happy being yourself.

Publishers realize that name recognition associated with celebrity status usually translates into profits, thus the recent wave of picture books by film, music, or radio/television figures such

as Will Smith, Katie Couric, Jamie Lee Curtis, John Lithgow, Maria Shriver, Bill Cosby, Dr. Laura (Laura Schlessinger), Madonna, Billy Joel, Billy Crystal, Leann Rimes, Jerry Seinfeld, Jay Leno, Brooke Shields, and so on. One of the great storytellers of our age, Nobel Prize winner Isaac Bashevis Singer (1992), warned us about the emphasis on message or name recognition rather than story: "In our epoch, when storytelling has become a forgotten art and has been replaced by amateurish sociology and hackneyed psychology, the child is still the independent reader who relies on nothing but his own taste. Names and authorities mean nothing to him."

In some instances, children's literature watchdogs demand that books address in an uncompromising manner any number of "hot" issues: child abuse, sexual orientation, abortion, and so on. Of course, all critics expect the topic to be handled in the certain way they believe it should be addressed. In this vein, an unsettling trend in young adult fiction is the idea that being edgy is desirable. Edginess means pushing the limits of the age of new realism to extremes, and so it is not uncommon to see well-reviewed young adult books focusing on blatant sex and using the foulest of language. Examples include *Teach Me* by R. A. Nelson (2005), which is about a high school girl who sleeps with her teacher, and *Doing It* by Melvin Burgess (2004), which needs no further explanation. Many reviewers and critics believe that edgy means "real" and that "real" means the book is better. However, a book's worth cannot be determined by the presence or absence of edginess.

Considering the changes in books and publishing, including some of the current problematic trends, children's literature is still a testament to John Newbery's vision of providing books for young readers.

PEARSON **myeducationkit**™

Go to the MyEducationKit for this text, where you can:

- Search the Database of Children's Literature, housing more than 22,000 titles searchable in every genre by authors or illustrators, by awards won, by year published, and by topic and description.
- Explore genre-related Assignments and Activities, assignable exercises showing concepts in action through database use, video, cases, and student and teacher artifacts.
- Listen to podcasts and read interviews from some of the brightest and most enduring stars of children's literature in the Conversations.
- Discover weblinks that will lead you to sites representing the authors you learn about in these pages, classrooms with powerful children's literature connections, and literature awards.

Chapter 6

Organizing Children's Literature by Genre

The difficulty in covering the field of children's literature in one course is perhaps best understood by looking at a common undergraduate class for English majors, Shakespeare's Tragedies. The course focuses on one author and only on a part of what he wrote, at that. On the other hand, the content of an introductory course in children's literature comprises all authors of children's books and all the titles they have written. Considering the content, a solitary children's literature course makes only the briefest of introductions to the subject matter—one thread in the whole cloth.

Naturally, the teacher of children's literature must find an organized and digestible way of presenting such massive subject matter—about 250,000 children's books in print in the United States. The most common method of cutting children's literature into smaller bites is to group books by *genre,* a French word meaning "type" or "kind." Genre is a familiar term in many artistic areas: the genres of motion pictures (film noir, documentary, comedy, horror, and so on), or the genres of adult literature (novel, novella, short story, play, and poem).

The Genres

In children's literature, genre identifies books according to content (see Figure 6.1). Beginning at the left of the genre tree, we see that all literature is either *prose or poetry.* To define *poetry,* the initial impulse might be to identify it as rhyming, or condensed, or rhythmic. Yet these obvious elements of poetry are not true distinctions. Some poetry does not rhyme. Some poetry is longer than some prose. Some poetry is less rhythmic than some prose. With all the forms poetry can take—haiku, sonnet, couplet, blank verse, limerick, narrative, cinquain, and free verse, to name

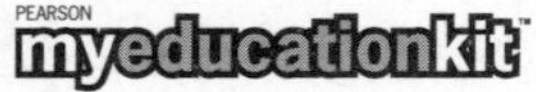

Visit the MyEducationKit for this course to enhance your understanding of chapter concepts with activities, weblinks, podcasts, and a searchable database of more than 22,000 children's literature titles.

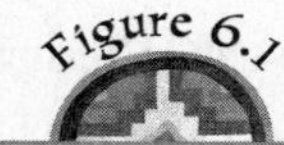

Genres of Children's Literature

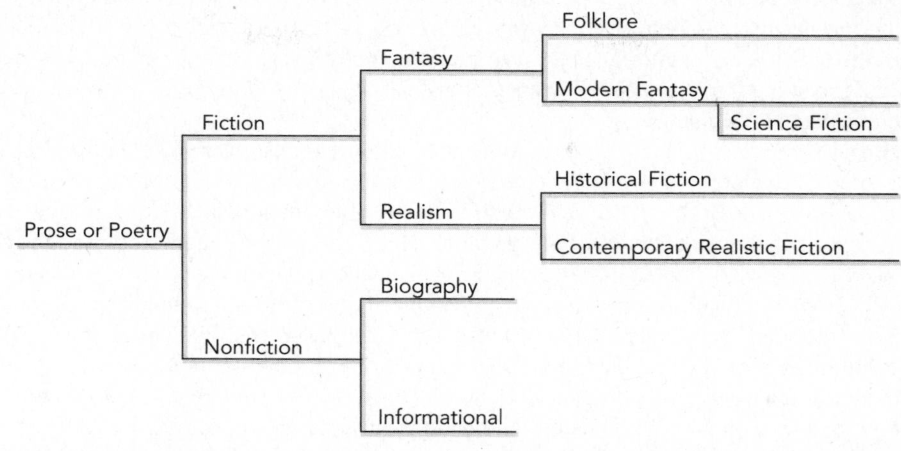

a few—finding a definition that both identifies them all and distinguishes them from prose is next to impossible. It is easier and more practical to define poetry by saying what it is not. The most obvious "not" is that poetry is not written in paragraphs. Poetry may appear on the page as a single line, a thin column, or in the shape of a tree but not in a paragraph. Prose, on the other hand, is always written in paragraphs. Beyond that difference in format, the function of the two literary forms is identical: Both poetry and prose thoughtfully explore the world, give insight into the human condition and experience, and bring pleasure to the reader.

The difference between fiction and nonfiction is verifiability. *Fiction* springs largely from the author's imagination. An idea, question, or incident from the real world may give rise to a work of fiction, and the setting and even many details may be verifiable, but the plot comes from the workings of the mind. In Staple's (2005) *Under the Persimmon Tree,* the setting and story involve the actual events in and accurate cultural trappings of Afghanistan in the days after the attack on the World Trade Center in New York City, including the U.S. counterstrike, the Taliban's repression of women, and the careful descriptions of Afghani cities and villages. However, the plot revolves around two *fictional* characters who eventually meet in a refugee camp. If this book were nonfiction, it would be wholly factual—no fictional elements. *All* the evidence and facts presented in nonfiction books can be verified. The distinction between fiction and nonfiction is similar to determining which answer is correct on a true-false test: If any part of the statement is false, the answer is false. If any part of the book is fiction, the whole book is categorized as fiction.

Nonfiction books are classified as biography and informational. *Biography* (and *autobiography*) tells the story, or at least part of the story, of an actual person's life. As with all nonfiction, reliable sources and documentation are imperative and provide verifiability.

Informational books are called *nonfiction* in adult publishing. Children's libraries classify all books in one of ten categories (ranging by 100s from 000 to 900) in the Dewey Decimal System. All except the 800s (literature—fiction and poetry) are informational books. Anything in the world is grist for the nonfiction mill: building a violin, life in China, the history of the ball bearing, animals that hibernate, how governments work, and so on. In the last part of the 20th century, the informational book genre began to improve and has continued to add compelling titles and appealing formats in the years since. No area of children's literature has changed so dramatically in recent times. Although some excellent informational books were written decades ago, subject matter has broadened, the quality of writing and illustration has improved, and the number of books published has increased.

Realistic fiction and *fantastic fiction* have much in common. Both are invented stories, often with invented characters, and they may take place in invented settings. Even when the setting is real, such as Boston or Berlin, the exact neighborhood is often imagined. The difference between realism and fantasy lies in the laws of our universe. If an invented story takes place in the world exactly as we know it—where dogs bark, trees are green, and gravity is everywhere—it is realistic fiction. If a story has one or more elements not found in our world—if animals speak, magic is present, or time travel is involved—it is called fantasy. The rest of the story might be absolutely realistic, but it is called fantasy if it contains any deviation from natural physical law.

The aim of both *contemporary realistic fiction* and *historical fiction* is to tell an interesting story about people in our world. The definitions are clear in the names of the genres. *Contemporary* identifies a story that takes place in today's world; *historical* indicates a tale that happened earlier, as in pioneer America or medieval England. At times, though, the difference between the two genres depends on the age of the reader. Adults would classify as contemporary a story that happened during the time the World Trade Center in New York was destroyed; to third graders, it would be historical.

Like historical and contemporary fiction, the division between *folklore* (fantasy stories passed down by word of mouth) and *modern fantasy* relates to antiquity. Some stories are as old as humanity. These ancient stories are called traditional because they are part of our human tradition. Their origin is oral; their authors are unknown. Although they are now preserved in print, those who first wrote them down, such as the Brothers Grimm, were not authors but collectors. If a fantasy story has an identifiable author and therefore originated in print, it is called *modern fantasy.* Thus, the tales of Hans Christian Andersen are classified as modern fantasy because we know he created them, even though the tales read like traditional stories. Novels like the Harry Potter books are a more common form of modern fantasy.

Science fiction, included with modern fantasy, deals with scientific possibilities. Both modern fantasy and science fiction contain story elements not found in the known universe, such as being able to change shapes or read another character's thoughts. In fantasy, those abilities just *are* or come about by magic—no questions asked. In science fiction, they result from an injection of distilled fluids discovered in the mucous membranes of a poisonous tree frog or from altering a person's brain chemistry using microlaser bursts. The otherworldly elements in science fiction are based on extrapolated scientific fact pushed into logical but unproven possibilities, such as creating a bionic being that is a perfect reproduction of an existing woman. Modern fantasy needs no such justifications: The character's double appears by magic.

While knowing the different genres can offer understanding in the field of children's literature, none of the definitions is watertight. The categories are not to be slavishly followed. It is possible to make a solid case that some books belong in more than one genre. For example, Livia Bitton-Jackson's *I Have Lived a Thousand Years: Growing Up in the Holocaust* (1997), a

compelling tale of young Livia and her Jewish family being taken from their native Hungary to Auschwitz during World War II, can be classified as both biography and historical fiction. Ruth Heller's series of informational books about the parts of speech, including *Mine, All Mine: A Book About Pronouns* (1997) and *Fantastic! Wow! And Unreal! A Book About Interjections* (1998), are, at the same time, also books of poetry. The correct category for some titles depends not on immutable definition, but on personal decision.

Although genre lines at times may blur, these designations are used most often by adults to organize the field of children's literature. These categories are less important to children, however. Young readers usually do not care if a book belongs to a certain genre. What they want is a good book, regardless of the classification. But adults can use the six genres to help understand the field of children's literature more clearly, to draw on a framework for discussing books, and to provide a yardstick for determining what holes exist in their own particular reading backgrounds. If a teacher has never read modern fantasy or science fiction, for instance, that becomes immediately apparent when considering each of the genres in light of her own reading experience, history, or previous choices. The genres of children's literature (Chapters 9–14) provide a way for us to evaluate where we have sufficient background and where we might strengthen our book knowledge, ultimately helping us serve students better.

Before moving on to the six genre chapters following this one, the reader of this textbook will find two chapters that address book formats important in children's literature. The two formats are so closely associated with categorizing books for children they have become pseudo-genres and, indeed, have their own separate chapters in this book. The picture book (Chapter 7), still a mainstay of beginning reading and the primary-grade classroom, has extended its appeal to include older children and also to offer expanded information in nonfiction picture books. Poetry (Chapter 8), like prose, includes all the genres of literature. However, we choose to treat poetry as a separate genre because too few poems are available to study them under the same classifications we use for prose. If we were absolutely accurate, we would study "biographical prose" and also "biographical poetry," "modern fantasy prose" as well as "modern fantasy poetry," and so on. Because of the relatively small number of published poems, we look at poetry as a whole instead of concentrating on the content of the poems as we do with the other genres.

An additional topic follows the genre chapters: multicultural and international books (Chapter 15). Those titles currently receive close attention because of their importance in helping us build human bridges among groups and nations.

The Book Lists

The world of children's literature offers only one completely dependable book list—your own. Throughout the following chapters, we present ours, absolutely trustworthy in every way—to us. You are allowed to be skeptical about our choices, but their value lies in saving you time wandering up and down library aisles. Please note that we have included a mix of titles from several decades—listing only brand-new books makes no more sense than ignoring Shakespeare because it's "old." Many of the best books have been around for years. John Brunner, science fiction author, points out that only a fool says "This is new, and therefore better" (Talwar, 2005). And so, we list our favorite titles without regard to publication date.

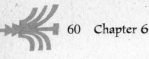

We organized our book lists at the end of the chapters under four different headings.

1. *Fifteen of Our Favorites.* The 15 books listed after each genre chapter in Part 2 are terrific reading. These lists are very short, the result of much negotiating between us, often emotional but largely friendly. The purpose of the 15 is to provide solid suggestions for those who wonder where to find a good book. Each title is annotated to give a brief idea of the content.
2. *Others We Like.* These titles (generally around 30) also are annotated. Although they are the second level of recommendations, each is a book we like very much. Don't be surprised if you find some of them more appealing than the *Fifteen of Our Favorites.*
3. *Easier to Read.* Next we have added 10 to 15 titles of shorter, generally popular books. These help the teacher find inviting titles for children struggling to make reading a rewarding pastime.
4. *Picture Books.* In most genre chapters, we have included 15 to 20 picture books we consider representative and outstanding. Not all of these titles are for use exclusively in the lower grades; many are appropriate for the upper grades as well.

The biggest list we offer you is in the children's literature database to be found on the MyEducationKit for this book—well over 20,000 titles.

PEARSON **myeducationkit**™

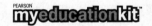

Go to the topics Poetry, Contemporary Realistic Fiction, and Nonfiction on the MyEducationKit for this text, where you can:

- Search the Database of Children's Literature, housing more than 22,000 titles searchable in every genre by authors or illustrators, by awards won, by year published, and by topic and description.
- Explore genre-related Assignments and Activities, assignable exercises showing concepts in action through database use, video, cases, and student and teacher artifacts.
- Listen to podcasts and read interviews from some of the brightest and most enduring stars of children's literature in the Conversations.
- Discover weblinks that will lead you to sites representing the authors you learn about in these pages, classrooms with powerful children's literature connections, and literature awards.

Chapter 7

Picture Books

The picture book is a format of children's literature rather than a genre. Picture books may be of any genre, including poetry. They are unique because illustrations and text share the job of telling the story or teaching content. No other type of literature works in the same manner.

Picture books often are considered to be only for the very young. Yet picture books—from rugged board books for babies to the mysterious tales of Chris Van Allsburg, which adults appreciate wholeheartedly—exist for a wide a range of readers. (See Figure 7.1 for the names of notable authors and illustrators of picture books.) In today's publishing world, the picture book has ascended to a true art form. As full-color printing processes have improved and the demand for quality picture books has increased, some of our best artists and authors spend at least part of their creative lives expressing themselves in the picture book form. (See Chapters 4 and 5 for details about picture book art and about the history and trends in picture book publishing.)

Categories of Picture Books

Several of the following categories serve as a vehicle for discussing the variety of picture books available. Once again, it is important to remember that these divisions are not mutually exclusive. A single book may fall into several categories.

ABC Books

Alphabet books were one of the earliest varieties of illustrated books for children. The most common purpose of the early ABC books was to teach and reinforce the letters of the alphabet—a

Visit the MyEducationKit for this course to enhance your understanding of chapter concepts with activities, weblinks, podcasts, and a searchable database of more than 22,000 children's literature titles.

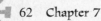

Notable Authors and Illustrators of Picture Books

Anno, Mitsumasa: Wordless concept books.

Brown, Marcia: Appears on the Caldecott list nine times; illustrates in a variety of artistic styles.

Brown, Margaret Wise: Author of gentle picture book stories; best known for *Goodnight Moon.*

Bunting, Eve: Writes picture book texts about social issues.

Burton, Virginia Lee: Author and illustrator of picture books in the 1930s and 1940s; perhaps best known for *Mike Mulligan and His Steam Shovel.*

Carle, Eric: Colorful illustrations rendered in a simplified, naïve style that mostly features animals; best known for *The Very Hungry Caterpillar.*

Cooney, Barbara: Varied subject matter, including picture book biographies, folktales, realistic and historical fiction.

Crews, Donald: Concept books rendered in graphic arts style.

dePaola, Tomie: Prolific illustrator of more than 200 books; trademark style using pastel colors.

Dillon, Leo, and Diane Dillon: Many books on African themes.

Ehlert, Lois: Engineered concept books.

Fox, Mem: Australian author of highly original picture storybooks.

Gammel, Stephen: Airy illustration style created with colored pencil and graphite.

Goble, Paul: Native American themes.

Henkes, Kevin: Family and school stories with talking animals as characters.

Hoban, Russell: Family and school stories with talking animals as characters.

Hyman, Trina Schart: Lavish illustrations accompanying classic fairy tale retellings.

Jeffers, Susan: Best known for illustrated folktales.

Keats, Ezra Jack: Stories of the inner city for primary grades.

Kellogg, Steven: Humorous stories often involving animals; tall-tale retellings.

Lionni, Leo: Modern fables often illustrated with collage.

Lobel, Arnold: Popularized beginning reader picture books with the Frog and Toad series.

Lynch, P. J.: British illustrator, folk/fairy tales and historical stories.

Martin, Bill Jr.: Author noted for his pattern and predictable picture books, such as *Brown Bear, Brown Bear, What Do You See?*

Mayer, Mercer: Popularized the wordless picture book with titles such as *Frog Goes to Dinner.*

Macaulay, David: Best known for award-winning pencil drawings about the construction of historical structures.

McCloskey, Robert: Picture books set in New England, mostly on the coast of Maine.

McDermott, Gerald: Folktales and myths rendered in an abstract artistic style.

Oxenbury, Helen: British illustrator who popularized the baby/board book.

Peet, Bill: Animal fantasies written in lively prose and verse; former Disney animator.

Pinkney, Brian: Scratchboard specialist, mostly African American themes.

Pinkney, Jerry: Watercolor specialist; mostly African American themes.

Polacco, Patricia: Historical and contemporary fiction, often drawn from her own family.

Potter, Beatrix: Mother of the modern picture storybook in English, *The Tale of Peter Rabbit.*

Rand, Ted: Colorful, realistic style paintings.

Rylant, Cynthia: Newbery Award–winning author who also writes quality beginning reader picture books.

Sabuda, Robert: A master of pop-up books.

Say, Allen: Asian American stories reflecting family themes.

Selznick, Brian: Caldecott winner for *The Invention of Hugo Cabret,* a hybrid novel/picture book.

Sendak, Maurice: Fantasy stories, most notably *Where the Wild Things Are.*

Seuss, Dr. (Theodor Geisel): Pioneered the beginning reader picture book with his zany, nonsensical stories.

Continued

Shulevitz, Uri: American illustrator with Israeli roots who won the 1969 Caldecott Medal and thereafter was awarded three Caldecott Honors, the last in 2009.
Small, David: A variety of topics, including zany stories and historical subjects.
Steig, William: Sketchy artistic style and Newbery Award–winning picture book prose.
Stevens, Janet: Animal fantasy.
Stevenson, James: Loose, cartoon-style illustrations.
Van Allsburg, Chris: Fantasy stories for older readers.
Wells, Rosemary: Family and school stories with talking animals as characters.
Wiesner, David: Wordless fantasy stories.
Williams, Vera: Most often paints in an award-winning expressionistic style.
Wisniewski, David: Folktales illustrated with intricate paper cutouts.
Young, Ed: Mostly Chinese folktale variants.
Zelinsky, Paul O.: Traditional tales in classical artistic style.

purpose shared by a smaller number of alphabet books today. Some people assume that this variety of picture books is also meant to introduce the phonic generalizations that correspond with the ABCs. However, alphabet books, for the most part, are not well suited to and generally not intended for this purpose. But if teachers or parents insist on using an ABC book as a medium for teaching the letters and their sounds, then they must take care to find some of the extremely rare books that conform to this task. Three criteria help define this type of ABC book (Criscoe, 1988, p. 233).

1. Words used to represent each letter must begin with the common sound generally associated with that letter. In other words, blends, digraphs, and silent letters should be avoided. MacDonald's *Alphabatics* (1986) violates this principle in its use of *ark* for *A, elephant* for *E,* and *owl* for *O*.
2. Illustrations must represent each letter using only one or two objects that are easily identifiable by and meaningful to young children. Once again, *Alphabatics* often violates this rule. For instance, the word *insect* is used for the letter *I,* and the illustration shows an insect along with a large, bright yellow flower. A young child's attention may be drawn to the flower, associating *I* with *flower.*
3. Illustrations must represent objects that do not have several correct names, thus confusing young readers. *Alphabatics* uses *quail* for *Q,* which would certainly be identified as *bird* by a child. Even the insect in the preceding example would likely be called a bee, a fly, or a bug.

Today, ABC books are largely created as a way in which to enrich children in a variety of imaginative ways. Sometimes they are created as a vehicle for presenting alphabetically arranged information about the world, and artists and authors continue to devise inventive methods of presenting the ABCs to both younger and older readers. For instance, Suse MacDonald's Caldecott Honor book *Alphabatics* (MacDonald,1986) shows each letter going through an amazing acrobatic metamorphosis: *E* tips and turns and mutates until it becomes the legs of an elephant. Stephen Johnson's *Alphabet City* (1995) is as much a look at cities as it is an alphabet book. A series of 26 paintings, so realistic that they are sometimes mistaken for photographs, shows the letters of the alphabet formed by objects found in a cityscape. For example, the letter *G* is located within the wrought iron decorations on a lamppost and *Q* in the wheel assembly of a railroad car.

One of the most inventive ABC books is Cathi Hepworth's *Antics! An Alphabetical Anthology* (1992). Hepworth paints humanlike ants, whose personality traits represent words that begin with each letter of the alphabet and have the letters *ant* embedded in them. For the letter *B,* Hepworth shows an Albert Einstein–type ant labeled "Brilli**ant,**" and for *I,* the illustration shows forlorn, turn-of-the-century "Immigr**ant**s" huddled nervously on the deck of a ship.

Another example of a creative approach to the ABC book is *Tomorrow's Alphabet* by George Shannon (1996). It works this way: "A is for seed—tomorrow's apple. B is for eggs—tomorrow's birds. C is for milk—tomorrow's cheese."

The alphabet may also be used as a vehicle to introduce or categorize information and concepts—even for older readers—or enrich vocabulary with fresh and interesting words. For example, the Caldecott Honor book *Gone Wild* (McLimans, 2006) is a look at endangered species: **X**enopus gilli (cape clawed frog), wild **Y**ak, Gervy's **Z**ebra. *Beastiary: An Illuminated Alphabet of Medieval Beasts* by Jonathan Hunt (1998) is an ABC introduction to the mythical creatures people feared during the Middle Ages: *A* is for amphisbaena, *B* is for basilisk, *C* is for catoblepas, and so on (with a paragraph of explanation for each animal).

Both children and adults find clever ABC books appealing and entertaining, and almost any subject can be the focus. *An Alphabet of Dinosaurs* (Dodson, 1995) identifies 26 dinosaurs, each beginning with a different letter. *M Is for Music* (Krull, 2003) introduces musical terms from allegro to zarzuela. Some titles are self-explanatory: *My First Buddhist Alphabet* (Bates & Bates 2004), *The Gardener's Alphabet* (Azarian, 2000), *Jazz A·B·Z: An A to Z Collection of Jazz Portraits* (Marsalis, 2005), *C is for Cowboy: A Wyoming Alphabet* (Gagliano, 2003), and *C Is for Caboose: Riding the Rails from A to Z* (Todd, Gillingham, & Vance, 2007). Alphabet books can also introduce the unusual. *Candle Time ABC* (Gillis, 2002) features various holidays that use candles as a part of their celebration, and *The Butterfly Alphabet* (Sandved, 1996) shows each letter appearing naturally on the wing design of a butterfly or moth, a task that took the author 25 years to complete.

Counting

Counting books were also one of the earlier types of picture books for children. Numbers and letters have always been considered the rudiments of early education. However, unlike ABC books, counting books usually do help children learn basic numbers and give them practice counting, typically from 1 to 10.

The simplest form of the counting book provides a printed Arabic number accompanied by the same number of like objects:

5 =

However, the better counting books allow for personal discovery and are beautifully illustrated. *Anno's Counting Book* by Mitsumasa Anno (1977) is the classic example and remains one of the best-conceived and -designed of counting books to date.

Anno begins with an important concept generally ignored in counting books: zero. Teachers who work with older elementary children can attest that many of them do not understand how zero works and therefore have problems with place value. So, Anno wisely introduces the idea of zero to children just beginning to learn numbers. The first double-page spread shows a barren,

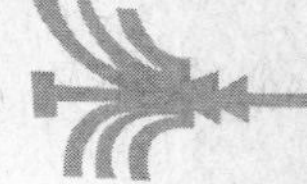

snow-covered landscape. The Arabic number 0 is on the right side of the book, and an empty counting stick partitioned into 10 squares is on the left.

Each succeeding double-page spread shows the same scene, only buildings, people, trees, animals, and other objects are added. For example, on the spread for seven, Anno has the Arabic numeral on the right and seven different-colored cubes stacked in front of the counting stick on the left. Also, the once-barren landscape now has sets of seven of a variety of objects: seven buildings, seven children, seven adults, seven evergreen trees, seven deciduous trees, seven colors in the rainbow, seven windows in one of the houses, seven pieces of laundry on the line, and so on. So much can be discovered in each scene that older children who have mastered counting long ago still search the pictures to find all the sets of one, two, three, and so on. Even the clock in the church tower always shows the hour of the number in question!

Besides variety and opportunity for discovery, Anno also offers fledgling mathematicians one final boon: He does not stop at 10. Anno wisely chooses to go on to 11 and 12, two transitional numbers that do not conform to the usual pattern (oneteen and twoteen?). Anno also has applied the 12 numbers to other concepts. The seasons change throughout the scenes and correspond to the 12 months of the year. Twelve hours are, of course, on the face of the clock. As a whole package, *Anno's Counting Book* is a marvel: beautiful, naïve-style paintings, sound-teaching processes, and pure entertainment. See the booklists at the end of the chapter for other noteworthy counting book titles.

Concept Books and Informational Books

Concept books introduce single, focused concepts to young children. Some typical topics include colors, the idea of opposites (over, under; outside, inside), and basic geometric shapes. ABC and counting books are usually considered concept books as well.

Tana Hoban is well known for her classic concept books that are usually wordless and are illustrated with crisp, clear photographs. *Is It Red? Is It Yellow? Is It Blue?* (1978) has become a concept book classic that reinforces a child's knowledge of colors. Quality concept books tend to help children think about ideas, and Hoban accomplishes this by providing a brilliant color photograph of a city or home scene and then placing colored circles below each photo. The young reader is drawn back and forth between circles and photographs to find the matching colors. Other Hoban titles include *Exactly the Opposite* (1990) and *Cubes, Cones, Cylinders & Spheres* (2000). Other well-known creators of concept books include Anne Rockwell (*Clouds,* 2008), Lois Ehlert (*Lots of Spots,* 2010), Donald Crews (*Cloudy Day, Sunny Day,* 1999), Ellen Stoll Walsh (*Mouse Shapes,* 2007), Byron Barton (*My Car,* 2001), and Gail Gibbons (*Alligators and Crocodiles,* 2010).

Picture books that deal with concepts in greater depth are *informational picture books,* although the lines between concept and informational picture books may blur. For instance, *How Much Is a Million?* by David Schwartz (1985) deals with the concept of large numbers, but this more complex idea may not be ideal for younger children. Another Schwartz book, *If You Hopped Like a Frog* (1999), introduces the concept of ratio by comparing what humans could do if they had particular animal bodies: "If you hopped like a frog . . . you could jump from home plate to first base in one mighty leap!" And his 2009 title, *Where Else in the Wild: More Camouflaged Creatures Concealed—and Revealed,* asks young readers to locate several disguised animals, thus presenting this concept about nature.

Informational picture books for older readers are usually text heavy in comparison to books for the primary and middle grades. The picture book biographies by Diane Stanley are examples (*Michelangelo,* 2000; *Saladin: Noble Prince of Islam,* 2002; and others). They are no different in outward appearance from a standard picture book, but inside, each double-page spread has a full-page illustration on one side and a full page of text on the other. However, *We Are the Ship: The Story of Negro Baseball* by Kadir Nelson (2008) is slightly thicker than most picture books but otherwise the same general shape and size. The difference is that it also has several short chapters and could be considered either chapter book or informational picture book—or both. Nelson's stunning artwork and insightful prose earned a 2009 Sibert Informational Book Award from the American Library Association. Other titles may be so extensive in their coverage of a topic that they do not resemble a picture book once you open their covers. Text is by far predominant, and many of the illustrations—often photographs—are tucked in among the words on a page, such as with the Newbery Honor book *Round Buildings, Square Buildings & Buildings That Wiggle Like a Fish* (Isaacson, 2001). Rather than picture books, these are informational chapter books. (See Chapter 14 for more on informational picture and chapter books.)

Participation Books

A number of picture books are designed to involve children in a physical activity that goes beyond the reading of the text, such as finding hidden objects in an illustration (*Where's Waldo? The Great Picture Hunt* by Martin Handford, 2006), manipulating the flaps and tabs of a pop-up book (*The Wheels on the Bus* by Paul Zelinsky, 1990), or chiming in with a refrain ("Hundreds of cats, Thousands of cats, Millions and billions and trillions of cats" from *Millions of Cats* by Wanda Gág (1928). *Anno's Counting Book* (Anno, 1977) becomes a participation book when children search for and discover the sets of objects representing each number. Another classic participation book is Janet and Allan Ahlberg's *Each Peach Pear Plum* (1979), a marvelous romp through the land of fairy tales and nursery rhymes. It is an "I spy" book, wherein small children search for familiar characters hidden in the illustrations. For instance, one page shows the busy interiors of a cottage. The jumble and activity in the room make it all the more difficult to spot the Three Bears peeking in through a small window. Tana Hoban's *Just Look* (1996) invites participation in the form of a guessing game. Children peer through a page with a die-cut hole that allows them to see only part of a familiar object. After guessing what it is, they lift the page to discover whether they are correct.

Of course, participation books also typically fall into other concept book categories. For instance, Lucy Micklethwait also employs an "I spy" technique to introduce famous art while at the same time teaching concepts, such as in her books *I Spy Colors in Art* (2007) and *I Spy Shapes in Art* (2004). Counting books frequently demand a child's physical participation, and refrains that invite listeners to chime in often appear in picture storybooks.

Wordless Picture Books

Books without words may seem a contradiction in terms to some parents and teachers. "How can kids learn to read by just looking at pictures?" they ask. But young children discover much of what they know about books as they "read" by themselves (left-to-right/top-to-bottom orienta-

tions, the grammar of story, personal pleasure of reading). Also, teachers may find that wordless picture books are a vehicle for practicing the language experience approach. For example, children may create their own text for an action-packed wordless book, such as *Frog Goes to Dinner* by Mercer Mayer (1974) or *Sector 7* by David Wiesner (1999). The teacher records the students' dictated text, and the children then read and reread their new, worded version of the picture book. Or children may try their hand at writing the words for a wordless picture book as a creative and meaningful writing experience.

Wordless picture books are meant, above all, to be enjoyed like all other books. They may tell stories or teach concepts, and many of today's offerings are stunning lessons in art. Mercer Mayer is credited with popularizing the wordless picture book, beginning in 1967 with the publication of *A Boy, a Dog, and a Frog.* Mayer's skill at telling a story and creating characters through illustrations is remarkable: Facial expressions speak with the power of words, visual actions foreshadow events, and the story line flows seamlessly as he focuses the reader's eye with details, visual transitions, and artful composition. On the other hand, the wordless concept books of Tana Hoban (*Is It Red? Is It Yellow? Is It Blue?,* 1978; *Exactly the Opposite,* 1990; *Shapes, Shapes, Shapes,* 1986) teach with economy and clarity. Wordless picture books also may be geared for older readers, such as Shaun Tan's (2007) complex story titled *The Arrival.*

Indeed, wordless picture books have much to offer and have often been noted for excellence. For example, David Wiesner's work has been awarded the most prestigious U.S. prize for picture book art: Caldecott Honors in 1989 for *Free Fall* (1988) and 2000 for *Sector 7* (1999) and Caldecott Medals in 1992 for *Tuesday* (1991) and 2007 for *Flotsam* (2006).

Predictable Books

As young children begin to read, predictable books, sometimes called *pattern books,* often can be their bridge into the world of independent reading. These picture books are characterized by repeated language patterns, story patterns, or other familiar sequences. However, creating a lifeless, stilted, and uninteresting predictable book is an easy trap to fall into if an author focuses on pattern at the expense of good writing and good story. The best of the predictable books are lively, use interesting words, and invite children to chime in. Bill Martin's classic *Brown Bear, Brown Bear, What Do You See?* (1967) is still a favorite in kindergartens everywhere:

> Brown Bear, Brown Bear, what do you see?
> I see a redbird looking at me.
> Redbird, redbird, what do you see?
> I see a yellow duck looking at me.
> Yellow duck . . .

(See other titles in Martin's books making use of the "what do you" sequence: *Polar Bear, Polar Bear, What Do You Hear?* ([1991], *Panda Bear, Panda Bear, What Do You See?* [2003)]; and *Baby Bear, Baby Bear, What Do You See?* [2007].)

Predictable books may use a repeated story pattern, often found in fairy tales and folktales such as "The Three Billy Goats Gruff" and "The Little Red Hen"—and in modern stories such as *Monkey See, Monkey Do.* In Adeney's (2010) reworking of Slobodkina's (1940) enduring tale, *Caps for Sale,* monkeys repeatedly outwit a peddler. Though without a tightly patterned structure,

Laura Numeroff's (2008) *If You Give a Cat a Cupcake* employs a circular plotline, ending where it began, to provide a modicum of predictability. It recounts a series of events—one causing the next—that might occur if someone were to give a feline a cupcake. (Also see the other titles, beginning with *If You Give a Mouse a Cookie* [1985], in Numeroff's "If You Give . . ." series.)

Cumulative tales provide even greater repetition, as in "The House That Jack Built." Sometimes a song or verse is predictable because of its familiarity as well as its repetitive language patterns, such as "There Was an Old Lady Who Swallowed a Fly," which has appeared variously in picture book form (see Simms Taback's [1997] Caldecott Honor book version). Even familiar sequences, such as numbers or days of the week, can make for easily recognized patterns. Eric Carle's *The Very Hungry Caterpillar* (1969) follows an unconventional caterpillar through each day of the week as he eats one, then two, then three of certain foods not meant for caterpillar consumption. The familiarity of numbers and days helps children "read" this well-loved predictable picture book. Nancy Shaw's "Sheep" books (*Sheep Out to Eat,* 1992; *Sheep Trick or Treat,* 1997; *Sheep Blast Off,* 2008; and others) make use of repetitive text and rhyming words to create a predictable text: "Beep! Beep! Sheep in a jeep on a hill that's steep" (*Sheep in a Jeep,* 1986).

Beginning Reader Picture Books

The beginning reader picture book is designed to give fledgling independent readers well-written yet easy-to-read materials. Both Dr. Seuss (Theodor Geisel) and Else Minarik put the beginning reader picture book on the map in 1957 with the publication of Seuss's *The Cat in the Hat* and Minarik's *Little Bear.* Minarik's several Little Bear titles became part of HarperCollins's I Can Read Book series, which continues to be one of the best collections of beginning reader picture books. The series represents all genres, including poetry, and often the books are written and illustrated by some of the best-known names in children's publishing, such as Arnold Lobel, who created the Frog and Toad books. In fact, *Frog and Toad Are Friends* (1970) was chosen as a Caldecott Honor book and *Frog and Toad Together* (1972) as a Newbery Honor book. HarperCollins also publishes the My First I Can Read Book series, with books that have few words yet tell compelling stories. Usually, the HarperCollins I Can Read Books are divided into three to five short chapters to give young readers an early introduction to the format of longer books. However, each page is illustrated so that the look of a picture book is maintained. During the last few years, HarperCollins has begun assigning a difficulty level to these easier readers (Level 1, Level 2, Level 3).

A variety of publishers have developed other beginning reader series in recent years, but no matter the company who issues them, these books are generally of the same size and shape—more like a chapter book rather than a typical picture book. Of course, they are much thinner, each consisting of about 40 pages of illustration and brief text. Examples of beginning reader picture book series besides those from HarperCollins include Simon & Schuster's Ready-to-Read series, Penguin's Easy To Read books, Scholastic's Hello Reader! series, Harcourt's Green Light Readers, and Random House's Step Into Reading series. Newbery winner Cynthia Rylant has created a series of easy-to-read picture books featuring Henry and his dog, Mudge (such as *Henry and Mudge and Annie's Perfect Pet,* 2000; *Henry and Mudge and the Great Grandpas,* 2005; and *Henry and Mudge and the Big Sleepover,* 2006). Rylant has written several other easy reader series, including stories about Mr. Putter and Tabby (*Mr. Putter and Tabby Clear the Decks,* 2010c), Annie and Snowball (*Annie and Snowball and the Magical House,* 2010a), Brownie

and Pearl (*Brownie and Pearl See the Sights,* 2010b) and the guinea pig, Little Whistle (*Little Whistle's Medicine,* 2007). Another popular series of easy readers is Marjorie Sharmat's Nate the Great mysteries (*Nate the Great,* 1972; *Nate the Great on the Owl Express,* 2003; *Nate the Great and the Hungry Book Club,* 2009, and others). However, not all beginning reader picture books are part of a series. Excellent individual titles pop up on many publishers' lists.

Adults often will choose any controlled-vocabulary picture book for their children merely because the words are overly simplified and seem easy to read. However, many of these titles offer little more than vocabulary practice and are of limited interest to children (see Chapter 3). A strong story and a fresh and lively writing style coupled with a wise control of vocabulary make for easier reading. Beginning-reader picture books that are stilted and contrived—that follow the unnatural language patterns evident in basal reading programs that use overly controlled vocabulary—are actually more difficult for young readers (Goodman, 1988).

Picture Storybooks

The origin of the picture storybook goes back to the publication in 1902 of Beatrix Potter's *The Tale of Peter Rabbit* (see Chapter 5). What set Potter's book apart from other illustrated books of the time, including books illustrated by Randolph Caldecott and Kate Greenaway, was the true marriage of illustration and story (see Chapter 4). The hallmark of the picture storybook is that text and illustrations work together to tell a story.

Picture storybooks are the most plentiful and the most popular variety of picture book. Most of the Caldecott winners are picture storybooks, and picture storybooks are the most likely choice for parents and children who read together before bedtime. Such books are read to young children long before they are able to read on their own and are often the best-loved stories from childhood, such as *Make Way for Ducklings* (McCloskey, 1941), *Where the Wild Things Are* (Sendak, 1963), and *The Polar Express* (Van Allsburg, 1985). Picture storybooks are the foundation of literacy training. Children typically learn their favorite books by heart, thus beginning a process that eventually becomes full-fledged reading. The rich vocabulary and sparkling illustrations help broaden language horizons and develop taste in art. See the booklist at chapter's end for noteworthy picture storybook titles.

Engineered Books

The category of engineered books is one of physical structure. Paper engineering involves the cutting, folding, or otherwise restructuring of the normal printed or illustrated page. Pop-up books are likely the best-known variety of the engineered book. Jan Piénkowski has a long-standing reputation for unique pop-up books, such as *Dinnertime* (Carter, 1981), *Haunted House* (1979), *ABC Dinosaurs* (1993), and *The First Noël* (2004). Today, Robert Sabuda's pop-up books set the standard (*The Christmas Alphabet,* 1994; *Dinosaurs: Encyclopedia Prehistorica,* 2005; *Gods and Heroes,* 2010 [with Matthew Reinhart]).

Often pop-ups include pull-tabs, cardboard wheels to be turned, or flaps to be lifted, thus allowing children to manipulate the pages. In *Haunted House,* for example, pull-tabs cause ducks in a wallpaper pattern to come to life and flap their wings and a skeleton to jump from a wardrobe. Paul Zelinsky's *The Wheels on the Bus* (1990) animates the familiar song with the use of similar manipulatives: Bus doors swing open and a rider steps out, riders bounce as the bus goes over bumps, windshield wipers swish back and forth, and babies' mouths open and close as they bawl. Sabuda's pop-up illustrations for Baum's (2000) *The Wonderful Wizard of Oz: A Commemorative Pop-Up* include a tornado that leaps from the page, spinning as you open the book, and green-colored glasses through which to view the Emerald City. In Sabuda's (Barrie, 2008) *Peter Pan: A Pop-Up Adaptation of J. M. Barrie's Original Tale,* readers peer deep into the tangled roots of the Lost Boys' hideout, and Captain Hook's pirate ship springs fully formed from a double-page spread.

Some engineered books rely completely on lifting flaps to reveal concept or story elements. Others provide a tactile experience, such as the classic *Pat the Bunny* by Dorothy Kunhardt (1940), which allows children to pet a fuzzy little rabbit, and *Fuzzy Yellow Ducklings* by Van Fleet (1995), which offers children a variety of textures to feel, as does Sandra Boynton's (2003) *Fuzzy, Fuzzy, Fuzzy! Touch, Skritch, and Tickle Book.*

The die-cut book, with pages that have shapes cut away, became the first type of engineered book to be recognized by a Caldecott committee, when *Color Zoo* by Lois Ehlert (1989) received a Caldecott Honor in 1990. Ehlert incorporates die-cuts to teach geometric shapes while creating the figures of animals (see Chapter 14). Later, in 2000, another die-cut book, *Joseph Had a Little Overcoat* (Taback, 1999), won the Caldecott Award.

A comparatively new variety of engineered book is the electronic book. By embedding a microchip in thicker cardboard pages or covers, readers can make a book play music, make animal noises, create the sounds of a flushing toilet, flash lights, and so on. For example, Eric Carle's *The Very Quiet Cricket* (1997) tells the story of a mute cricket who finally, as the reader turns the last page, finds his "voice"—an authentic-sounding chirp powered by a watch battery.

Engineered books—and the baby/board books discussed next—are distinctions of physical structure, not content. When considering the content, every engineered and baby/board book belongs also in at least one of the picture book categories previously listed.

Baby/Board Books

Baby/board books were firmly established as a distinct type of picture book in 1981 with the publication of Helen Oxenbury's titles *(Dressing; Family; Friends; Playing; Working).* These comparatively armor-clad books are made from thick cardboard with clear plasticized coatings. They are meant to withstand the buffetings, dunkings, and suckings of babies and toddlers. Some of these baby books are wordless, each page depicting a single object, such as a shoe or a spoon, that is common in a baby's environment. Sometimes single words or short phrases accompany illustrations. However, Rosemary Wells's Max books, which were published about the same time as Oxenbury's titles, are a bit more sophisticated. For example, in *Max's First Word* (1979), big sister Ruby is trying to teach her little bunny brother how to talk, but Max's only word is "BANG!" No matter how she prompts him, "bang" is his only response—that is, until Ruby gives him an apple and says, "APPLE, Max. Say, APPLE." Max's final response: "Delicious." Other noteworthy examples of board books include Rosemary Wells's Bunny Reads Back series (*Bingo,* 1999), Janet and Allan Ahlberg's Baby's Catalogue books (*See the Rabbit,* 1998), Jane Simmons's First Daisy Books (*Quack, Daisy, Quack!,* 2002), Joy Cowley's Mrs. Wishy-Washy titles (*Mrs. Wishy-Washy's Splishy-Sploshy Day,* 2005), Michel Blake's Easy-Open Board Books

(*Baby's Day,* 2007), Judy Schachner's Skippyjon Jones series (*Skippyjon Jones Shape Up,* 2008), and Eric Hill's books about the dog Spot (*Spot's Hide and Seek,* 2010).

A current trend in picture book publishing is releasing regular-format picture books in smaller, board book form. Examples include *Prayer for a Child* (Field, 2005 [1944]), *The Snowy Day* (Keats, 1996 [1962]), *Freight Train* (Crews, 1996 [1978]), *Olivia* (Falconer, 2004 [2000]), and *Ella Sarah Gets Dressed* (Chodos-Irvine, 2008 [2003])—all Caldecott or Caldecott Honor titles. Other examples include David McPhail's *Fix-it* (2002 [1984]), Rick Walton's *One More Bunny* (2001 [2000]), and Mark and Caralyn Buehner's *Snowmen at Night* (2004 [2002]). Even Eric Carle's electronic book, *The Very Quiet Cricket* (1997 [1990]), and the classic bedtime story *Goodnight Moon* (Brown, 1991 [1947]), have found their way into the board book format.

Picture books are an abundant resource for initiating children into the worlds of literacy and image. Parents, teachers, and librarians must make a dedicated effort to share with children the best picture books, whether new titles or old, for it is the best books that make the most profound impressions on young minds.

Picture Books Available in Audiovisual Formats

Many picture books are available in nonprint media. Two companies that produce excellent DVDs and CDs are Live Oak Media (www.liveoakmedia.com) and Weston Woods (http://teacher.scholastic.com/products/westonwoods). Consult their Web sites for the latest catalogs and offerings.

The American Library Association honors the most distinguished American video for children with an annual award, the Carnegie Medal for Excellence in Children's Video. Most of the winners are based on children's books. The winners, since its inception in 1991, are found in Figure 7.2.

Picture Book Reading Lists

Fifteen of Our Favorites

Alexander, Lloyd. 1992. *The Fortune-Tellers.* Illustrated by Trina Schart Hyman. Dutton. (Picture story.) A carpenter goes to a fortune-teller and finds that the predictions about his future come true in an unusual way.

Anno, Mitsumasa. 1977. *Anno's Counting Book.* Crowell. (Counting.) A counting book depicting the growth in a village and surrounding countryside during 12 months.

Crews, Donald. 1978. *Freight Train.* Greenwillow. (Concept.) Colors and the names of the cars on a freight train are introduced with sparse but rhythmic text and brilliantly colored illustrations. A Caldecott Honor book.

Henkes, Kevin. 1990. *Julius, the Baby of the World.* Greenwillow. (Picture story.) Lilly is convinced that the arrival of her new baby brother is the worst thing that has happened in their house, until Cousin Garland comes to visit.

Hepworth, Cathi. 1992. *Antics! An Alphabetical Anthology.* Putnam. (ABC.) Alphabet entries from A to Z all have an "ant" somewhere in the word, such as *E* for Ench*ant*er, *I* for immigr*ant*s, *P* for P*ant*aloons, *S* for S*ant*a Claus.

Mayer, Mercer. 1974. *Frog Goes to Dinner.* Dial. (Wordless.) Having stowed away in a pocket,

Figure 7.2

Winners of the Carnegie Medal for Excellence in Children's Video

1991 *Ralph S. Mouse* by George McQuilkin and John Matthews (Churchill Films)
1992 *Harry Comes Home* by Peter Matulavich (Barr Films)
1993 *The Pool Party* by John Kelly and Gary Soto (Distributed by Gary Soto)
1994 *Eric Carle: Picture Writer* by Rawn Fulton (Searchlight Films)
1995 *Whitewash* by Michael Sporn (Churchill Media)
1996 *Owen* by Paul R. Gagne (Weston Woods)
1997 *Notes Alive! On the Day You Were Born* by Tacy Mangan (What a Gal Productions)
1998 *Willa: An American Snow White* by Tom Davenport (Davenport Films)
1999 *The First Christmas* by Frank Moynihan (Billy Budd Films)
2000 *Miss Nelson Has a Field Day* by Paul R. Gagne (Weston Woods Studio)
2001 *Antarctic Antics* by Paul R. Gagne (Weston Woods Studios)
2002 *My Louisiana Sky* by Dante Di Loreto and Anthony Edwards (Aviator Films) and Willard Carroll and Tom Wilhite (Hyperion Studio)
2003 *So You Want to Be President* by Paul Gagne and Melissa Reilly (Weston Woods Studios)
2004 *Giggle, Giggle, Quack* by Paul Gagne and Melissa Reilly (Weston Woods Studios)
2005 *The Dot* by Paul Gagne and Melissa Reilly (Weston Woods Studios)
2006 *The Man Who Walked between the Towers* by Michael Sporn, Paul Gagne, and Melissa Reilly (Weston Woods Studios)
2007 *Knuffle Bunny* by Mo Willems (Weston Woods Studios)
2008 *Jump In! Freestyle Edition* by John Davis, Amy Palmer Robertson, and Danielle Sterling (Kevin Lafferty)
2009 *March On! The Day My Brother Martin Changed the World* by Paul R. Gagne and Melissa Reilly (Weston Woods Studios)
2010 *Don't Let the Pigeon Drive the Bus* by Paul Gagne and Mo Willems (Weston Woods Studios)
2011 *The Curious Garden* by Paul Gagne and Melissa Reilly Ellard (Weston Woods Studios)

Frog wreaks havoc and disgraces his human family at the posh restaurant where they go for dinner.

Parish, Peggy. 1963. *Amelia Bedelia.* Illustrated by Fritz Siebel. Harper. (Beginning reader.) A literal-minded housekeeper causes a ruckus in the household when she attempts to make sense of some instructions.

Peet, Bill. 1982. *Big Bad Bruce.* Houghton Mifflin. (Picture story.) Bruce, a bear bully, never picks on anyone his own size until he is diminished in more ways than one by a small but very independent witch.

Sendak, Maurice. 1963. *Where the Wild Things Are.* Harper. (Picture story.) A naughty little boy, sent to bed without his supper, sails to the land of the Wild Things, where he becomes their king. Winner of the Caldecott Medal.

Steig, William. 1982. *Doctor DeSoto.* Farrar. (Picture story.) A clever mouse dentist outwits his wicked fox patient. A Newbery Honor book.

Turkle, Brinton. 1981. *Do Not Open.* Dutton. (Picture story.) Following a storm, Miss Moody and her cat find an intriguing bottle washed up on the beach. Should they ignore its "Do not open" warning?

Van Allsburg, Chris. 1981. *Jumanji.* Houghton Mifflin. (Picture story.) Left on their own for an afternoon, two bored and restless children find more excitement than they bargain for in a mysterious and mystical jungle adventure board game. Winner of the Caldecott Medal.

Waber, Bernard. 1972. *Ira Sleeps Over.* Houghton Mifflin. (Picture story.) A little boy is excited at the prospect of spending the night at his friend's house but worries about how he will get along without his teddy bear.

Wells, Rosemary. 1979. *Max's First Word.* Dial. (Baby/board.) It seems Max can say only one word, no matter how hard his older sister tries to teach him others.

Wiesner, David. 2006. *Flotsam.* (Wordless.) A boy spots a mysterious old camera that washes up on the beach and discovers a fantasy-filled mystery waiting for him on the roll of film inside.

Others We Like

ABC

Aylesworth, Jim. 1992. *Old Black Fly.* Illustrated by Stephen Gammell. Holt. Rhyming text and illustrations follow a mischievous old black fly through the alphabet as he has a very busy bad day landing where he should not be.

Beccia, Carlyn. 2007. *Who Put the B in the Ballyhoo?* Houghton Mifflin. A rhyming alphabetical description of Big Top life and attractions, interspersed with facts about particular circus acts and personalities of the past.

Brown, Margaret Wise. 2010. *Goodnight Moon ABC: An Alphabet Book.* Harper. Illustrated by Clement Hurd. This ABC book is based on Brown's classic bedtime story.

Dodson, Peter. 1995. *An Alphabet of Dinosaurs.* Illustrated by Wayne D. Barlowe. Scholastic. Colorful illustrations of dinosaurs whose names begin with each of the 26 letters fill the pages of this alphabet book.

Ehlert, Lois. 1989. *Eating the Alphabet.* Harcourt. An alphabetical tour of the world of fruits and vegetables, from apricot and artichoke to yam and zucchini.

Ernst, Lisa Campbell. 2004. *The Turn-Around, Upside-Down Alphabet Book.* Simon and Schuster. An alphabet book in which each letter becomes three different objects as the book is turned different directions, as when *A* becomes a bird's beak, a drippy ice cream cone, and the point of a star.

Howell, Will C. 2002. *Zoo Flakes ABC.* Walker. Snowflake-style cutouts present a different animal for each letter of the alphabet. Includes instructions.

Johnson, Stephen T. 1995. *Alphabet City.* Viking. Paintings of objects in an urban setting present the letters of the alphabet.

Jonas, Ann. 1990. *Aardvarks, Disembark!* Greenwillow. After the flood, Noah calls out of the ark a variety of little-known animals, many of which are now endangered.

Lester, Mike. 2000. *A Is for Salad.* Putnam. Each letter of the alphabet is presented in an unusual way. For example, A is used for salad because the illustration shows an alligator eating a bowl of greens.

Lobel, Arnold. 1981. *On Market Street.* Illustrated by Anita Lobel. Greenwillow. A child buys presents from A to Z in the shops along Market Street.

MacDonald, Suse. 1986. *Alphabatics.* Bradbury. The letters of the alphabet are transformed and incorporated into 26 illustrations, so that the hole in *b* becomes a balloon and *y* turns into the head of a yak.

Martin, Bill, Jr., and John Archambault. 1989. *Chicka Chicka Boom Boom.* Illustrated by Lois Ehlert. Holt. An alphabet rhyme/chant that relates what happens when the whole alphabet tries to climb a coconut tree.

McLimans, David. 2006. *Gone Wild.* Walker. This stampede of wild animals, from Chinese Alligator to Grevy's Zebra, are so rare, they are all endangered.

Melmed, Laura Krauss. 2005. *New York, New York! The Big Apple from A to Z.* Illustrated by Frané Lessac. Harper. New York City has something to offer everyone, from A to Z: in the **A**merican Museum of Natural History see prehistoric **A**nimals, get a **B**ird's-eye view of the **B**rooklyn **B**ridge, and **C**heck out **C**entral Park.

Minor, Wendell. 2006. *Yankee Doodle America.* Putnam. An A to Z of the American Revolution.

Sandved, Kjell. 1995. *The Butterfly Alphabet.* Scholastic. Introduces the letters of the alphabet through rhyming text and close-up examinations of letterlike markings on the wings of various species of butterflies.

Schnur, Steven. 2002. *Winter: An Alphabet Acrostic.* Illustrated by Leslie Evans. Clarion. Contains 26 alphabetically arranged acrostic poems about cold-weather delights (Animals burrowing in the snow, Sledding, etc.).

Shannon, George. 1996. *Tomorrow's Alphabet.* Illustrated by Donald Crews. Greenwillow. *A* is for seed, *B* is for eggs, *C* is for milk. The seed is tomorrow's Apple, the eggs are tomorrow's Birds, the milk is tomorrow's Cheese.

Spirin, Gennady. 2005. *An Apple Pie.* Philomel. Introduces the letters *A* to *Z* while following the fortunes of an apple pie.

Todd, Traci N., Sara Gillingham, and Steve Vance. 2007. *C Is for Caboose: Riding the Rails from A to Z.* Chronicle. With a mix of vintage illustrations and contemporary photos, this book about trains contains simple information about everything from the transcontinental railroad to model trains.

Van Allsburg, Chris. 1987. *The Z Was Zapped: A Play in Twenty-Six Acts.* Houghton Mifflin. Depicts how *A* was in an avalanche, *B* was badly bitten, *C* was cut to ribbons, and the other letters of the alphabet suffered similar mishaps.

Counting

Andreasen, Dan. 2007. *The Baker's Dozen.* Holt. The reader is invited to count from 1 to 13 as a jolly baker makes delectable treats, from one mouth-watering eclair to 12 luscious cupcakes, and serves them to invited guests.

Anno, Mitsumasa. 1982. *Anno's Counting House.* Philomel. A counting book depicting the growth in a village and surrounding countryside during 12 months.

Base, Graeme. 2001. *The Water Hole.* Abrams. As ever-growing numbers of animals visit a watering hole, introducing the numbers from 1 to 10, the water dwindles.

Bond, Michael. 2009. *Paddington at the Beach.* Harper. While at the beach, Paddington Bear is joined by hungry (and sneaky!) seagulls—one after the other. A counting adventure.

Cronin, Doreen. 2005. *Click, Clack, Splish, Splash.* Illustrated by Betsy Lewin. Atheneum. While Farmer Brown sleeps, some of the animals who live on the farm attempt to rescue fish from a tank in the house, releasing 10 fish in 10 buckets while the farmer slumbers.

Dobson, Christina. 2003. *Pizza Counting.* Illustrated by Matthew Holmes. Charlesbridge. Decorated pizzas are used to introduce counting and fractions. Includes facts about pizza.

Fleming, Denise. 1992. *Count!* Holt. The antics of lively and colorful animals present the numbers 1 to 10, 20, 30, 40, and 50.

Geisert, Arthur. 1992. *Pigs from 1 to 10.* Houghton Mifflin. Ten pigs go on an adventurous quest. The reader is asked to find all of them, and the numerals from 0 to 9, in each picture.

Giganti, Paul, Jr. 2005. *How Many Blue Birds Flew Away? A Counting Book with a Difference.* Illustrated by Donald Crews. Greenwillow. Throughout the day, a child notices, counts, and compares numbers of items, such as how many boys and girls are on the playground and how many more girls there are than boys.

Herzog, Brad. 2009. *Full Count: A Baseball Number Book.* Illustrated by Bruce Langton. Sleeping Bear. Baseball stories and facts arranged in a numbered format.

Hutchins, Pat. 1982. *1 Hunter.* Greenwillow. One hunter walks through the forest observed first by two elephants, then by three giraffes, and so on.

Jay, Alison. 2007. *1-2-3: A Child's First Counting Book.* Dutton. A little girl awakens to scenes from fairy tales in which she can count familiar characters or objects from 1 to 10 and back again.

Johnson, Stephen T. 1998. *City by Numbers.* Viking. Paintings of various sites around New York City—from a shadow on a building to a wrought iron gate to the Brooklyn Bridge—depict the numbers from 1 to 21.

Markle, Sandra. 2009. *How Many Baby Pandas?* Walker. Looks at the eight panda pairs that were born at China's Wolong Giant Panda Breeding and Research Center in 2005, examining how they live, grow, and play and the steps that are being taken to prepare them for their release into the wild.

Martin, Bill, Jr., Michael Sampson, and Lois Ehlert. 2004. *Chicka Chicka 1, 2, 3.* Simon & Schuster. Numbers from 1 to 100 climb to the top of an apple tree in this rhyming chant.

Merriam, Eve. 1993. *12 Ways to Get to 11.* Illustrated by Bernie Karlin. Simon & Schuster. Uses ordinary experiences to present 12 combinations of numbers that add up to 11. Example: At the circus, six peanut shells and five pieces of popcorn.

Pinto, Sara. 2009. *The Number Garden.* Bloomsbury. A resourceful pair of rabbits plant carrot seeds and celebrate in a garden that grows as the numbers add up. Twelve elements—one sun, two rabbits, three garden chairs, through 12 stars at night—all add up to 78 items.

Reiser, Lynn. 2006. *Hardworking Puppies.* Harcourt. One by one, 10 energetic puppies find important jobs as dogs who help people in different ways, including by pulling sleds and saving swimmers.

Rose, Deborah Lee. 2009. *The Twelve Days of Springtime: A School Counting Book.* Abrams. Spring means field trips, planting seeds, and discovering new friends for this adventurous class as their teacher introduces them to the season one gift at a time.

Sloat, Teri. 1991. *From One to One Hundred.* Dutton. Illustrations of people and animals introduce the numbers 1 through 10 and then, counting by tens, move on up to 100.

Taback, Simms. 2009. *1-2-3.* Blue Apple Books. Simms Taback's bright colors and bold illustrations bring a fresh look to beginning concept board books.

Tang, Greg. 2007. *Math Fables Too: Making Science Count.* Scholastic. Tang offers 10 rhymes about animals that teach science concepts as well as basic arithmetic (counting and grouping numbers).

Walsh, Ellen Stoll. 1991. *Mouse Count.* Harcourt. Count along with 10 mice as they outsmart a hungry snake.

Concept

Barton, Byron. 1986. *Trains.* Crowell. Brief text and illustrations present a variety of trains and what they do.

Ehlert, Lois. 1989. *Color Zoo.* Lippincott. Introduces colors and shapes with illustrations of shapes on die-cut pages that form animal faces when placed on top of one another.

Ehlert, Lois. 2010. *Lots of Spots.* Beach Lane Books. Introduces the concept of animal camouflage.

Fisher, Valerie. 2006. *How High Can a Dinosaur Count? And Other Math Mysteries.* Schwartz & Wade. Presents fifteen miniature worlds, each showcasing a math problem.

Franco, Betsy. 2008. *Bee, Snails, & Peacock Tails: Shapes Naturally.* Illustrated by Steve Jenkins. McElderry. Shapes are introduced through geometric forms found in nature.

Hoban, Tana. 1978. *Is It Red? Is It Yellow? Is It Blue?* Greenwillow. Young readers match colored dots at the bottom of each page to the colors found in photographs.

Hoban, Tana. 1997. *Look Book.* Greenwillow. Objects in full-color nature photographs are viewed through a die-cut hole in an overlay. Readers guess what the objects are and then discover the truth by lifting the overlay to see the entire picture.

Krebs, Laurie. 2005. *We're Sailing to Galapagos.* Illustrated by Grazia Restelli. Barefoot Books. Rhyming text introduces the wildlife of the Galapagos Islands, such as giant tortoises, black iguanas, and brightly colored lava crabs. Includes facts about the islands and a variety of unusual animals found there.

McMillan, Bruce. 1991. *Eating Fractions.* Scholastic. Food is cut into halves, quarters, and thirds to illustrate how parts make a whole. Simple recipes included.

Micklethwait, Lucy. 2004. *I Spy Shapes in Art.* Greenwillow. Presents objects with the shape of a heart, a triangle, a square and other shapes through paintings by such artists as Magritte, Escher, and Matisse.

Park, Linda Sue. 2005. *What Does Bunny See: A Book of Colors and Flowers.* Illustrated by Maggie Smith. Clarion. A rabbit wanders through the various flowers and colors of a cottage garden.

Payne, Nina. 2001. *Four in All.* Illustrated by Adam Payne. Front Street. Illustrations are accompanied by rhyming lists of things that come in fours, such as "eyes, ears, nose, mouth" and "east, west, north, south."

Schwartz, David M. 1999. *If You Hopped Like a Frog.* Illustrated by James Warhola. Scholastic. Introduces the concept of ratio by comparing what humans would be able to do if they had bodies like different animals.

Schwartz, David M., and Yael Schy. 2009. *Where Else in the Wild: More Camouflaged Creatures Concealed—and Revealed.* Tricycle Press. Poetry and photography work together to present camouflaged animals. Discover why geckos have a spooky reputation; why it pays for a mouse to have a dark-colored back and light-colored belly; and why you wouldn't want to be fooled by a scorpion fish.

Serfozo, Mary. 1988. *Who Said Red?* Illustrated by Keiko Narahashi. McElderry. A little girl and her brother introduce red, green, blue, yellow, and other colors as they wander about their farm.

Walsh, Ellen Stoll. 2007. *Mouse Shapes.* Harcourt. (See also *Mouse Paint* [1995] and *Mouse Magic* [2000].) Three mice make a variety of things out of different shapes as they hide from a scary cat.

Participation

Ahlberg, Janet, and Allan Ahlberg. 1979. *Each Peach Pear Plum.* Viking. Rhymed text and illustrations invite the reader to play "I spy" with a variety of Mother Goose and other folklore characters.

Anno, Mitsumasa. 1977. *Anno's Journey.* Collins. Shows a traveler's journey through historic northern Europe. Fairy tale characters and other interesting figures are hidden within crowds of people, landscapes, and buildings

Boynton, Sandra. 2005. *Dog Train: A Wild Ride on the Rock-and-Roll Side.* Michael Ford, Collaborator. Workman. This full-color songbook features original lyrics and stories that incorporate portions of each song. Boynton's irresistible hippos, cows, and dogs fill the illustrations.

Carlstrom, Nancy. 1986. *Jesse Bear, What Will You Wear?* Illustrated by Bruce Degen. Macmillan. Rhymed text that begs to be recited and colorful illustrations describe Jesse Bear's activities from morning to bedtime.

Cressy, Judith. 2004. *Can You Find It, Too?* The Metropolitan Museum of Art/Abrams. Young readers view many of the world's painting masterpieces through art-based "I spy" puzzlers.

Gág, Wanda. 1928. *Millions of Cats.* Putnam. An old man and his wife must select one cat from a vast horde. Children will want to chime in too repeating the refrain: "Hundred of cats, thousands of cats, millions and billions and trillions of cats."

Handford, Martin. 1987. *Where's Waldo?* Little, Brown. (See the other books in the Where's Waldo series.) The reader follows Waldo as he hikes around the world and must try to find him in the illustrations of some of the crowded places he visits.

Hill, Eric. 2005 (1980). *Where's Spot?* Putnam. A mother dog finds eight other animals hiding around the house before finding her lost puppy. Flaps conceal the hidden animals.

Ljungkvist, Laura. 2007. *Follow the Line through the House.* Viking. Rhyming text invites the reader to search different rooms of a house to find hidden objects.

Martin, Bill, Jr. 1993. *Old Devil Wind.* Illustrated by Barry Root. Harcourt. On a dark and stormy night, one object after another joins in making eerie noises in the old house.

Marzollo, Jean. 2005. *I Spy a Pumpkin.* Photographs by Walter Wick. Scholastic. Easy-to-read riddles are paired with fun, gently spooky photographs.

Micklethwaite, Lucy. 2007. *I Spy Colors in Art.* Greenwillow. Invites young readers to find and identify colors while at the same time introducing them to works of art by Picasso, Magritte, and others.

Munro, Roxie. 2005. *Amazement Park: 12 Wild Mazes.* Chronicle. As readers work their way through the mazes of Amazement Park, they can watch for the blue balloon, follow Mrs. McCourt and her school class, or create and play their own games.

Yolen, Jane. 2009. *How Do Dinosaurs Say I Love You?* Illustrated by Mark Teague. Blue Sky/Scholastic. (See other books in the How Do Dinosaurs series.) Illustrations and rhyming text present some of the different ways dinosaurs (people) can express their love, from cleaning up after making a mess to smiling sweetly instead of roaring.

Wordless

Baker, Jeannie. 2004. *Belonging.* Walker. Observed through the window of a house, a city street gradually becomes a place to call home as the inhabitants begin to rescue their street by planting grass and trees in the empty spaces.

Briggs, Raymond. 1978. *The Snowman.* Random. When his snowman comes to life, a little boy invites him home and in return is taken on a flight high above the countryside.

Day, Alexandra. 2009. *Carl's Snowy Afternoon*. Farrar. After getting all bundled up, the Rottweiler Carl and the baby Madeleine sneak off to go sledding, build a snowman, and slide on the ice at the pond.

Faller, Régis. 2002. *The Adventures of Polo*. Roaring Brook. Polo the dog sets out from his home and enjoys many adventures, including sailing his boat on top of a whale, roasting hot dogs over a volcano, and taking a ride in a spaceship built from a mushroom.

Geisert, Arthur. 2008. *Hogwash*. Houghton Mifflin. The little piggies are dirty, muddy, and covered in paint, but their mamas have just the machine to clean them up.

Goodall, John. 1988. *Little Red Riding Hood*. McElderry. A wordless retelling of the fairy tale about the little girl who meets a hungry wolf in the forest.

Hutchins, Pat. 1971. *Changes, Changes*. Macmillan. Two wooden dolls rearrange wooden building blocks to form various objects.

Lehman, Barbara. 2006. *Museum Trip*. Houghton Mifflin. In this wordless picture book, a boy imagines himself inside some of the exhibits when he goes on a field trip to a museum.

Mayer, Mercer. 1976. *Ah-choo*. Dial. Relates the consequences of an elephant's sneeze.

McCully, Emily Arnold. 2004. *First Snow*. Harper. The first snow has fallen, and the mice children spend the day ice skating and sledding with their grandma and grandpa.

Rohmann, Eric. 1994. *Time Flies*. Crown. A wordless tale in which a bird flying around the dinosaur exhibit in a museum has an unsettling experience when it finds itself back in the time of living dinosaurs.

Schories, Pat. 2006. *Jack and the Night Visitors*. Front Street. After seeing a strange light through the bedroom window, Jack the dog and his boy discover that a little spaceship has landed on the roof outside their window.

Spier, Peter. 1977. *Noah's Ark*. Doubleday. Retells in pictures how a pair of every manner of creature climbed on board Noah's ark and thereby survived the flood.

Spier, Peter. 1982. *Peter Spier's Rain*. Doubleday. Two children play in their backyard during a rainy day.

Tan, Shaun. 2007. *The Arrival*. Arthur A. Levine. A man leaves his homeland and sets off for a new country, where he must build a new life for himself and his family.

Varon, Sara. 2008. *Chicken and Cat Clean Up*. Scholastic. Chicken and Cat run a housekeeping service; Cat fouls up the cleaning but saves the day by catching a purse-snatching mouse.

Wiesner, David. 1991. *Tuesday*. Clarion. Frogs rise on their lily pads, float through the air, and explore the nearby houses while their inhabitants sleep.

Wiesner, David. 1999. *Sector 7*. Clarion. While on a school trip to the Empire State Building, a boy is taken by a friendly cloud to visit Sector 7, where he discovers how clouds are shaped and channeled throughout the country.

Predictable

Adeney, Anne. 2010. *Monkey See, Monkey Do*. Illustrated by Christina Bretschneider. Sea-to-Sea Publications. The monkeys continue to outwit the peddler in this version of Slobodkina's *Caps for Sale*.

Brown, Margaret Wise. 1947. *Goodnight Moon*. Harper. Goodnight to each of the objects in the great green room: the chairs, a comb, and the air.

Christelow, Eileen. 2004. *Five Little Monkeys Play Hide-and-Seek*. Clarion. The five little monkeys try to avoid going to bed by playing hide and seek with the babysitter.

Cowley, Joy. 2005. *Mrs. Wishy-Washy's Splishy-Sploshy Day*. Illustrated by Elizabeth Fuller. Philomel. The meanies are even messier than Mrs. Wishy-Washy's farmyard friends. Can she wash those meanies up and hang them out to dry?

Emberley, Barbara. 1967. *Drummer Hoff*. Illustrated by Ed Emberley. Prentice Hall. A cumulative folk song in which seven soldiers build a magnificent cannon, but Drummer Hoff fires it off.

Hoberman, Mary Ann. 2002. *Bill Grogan's Goat*. Illustrated by Nadine Bernard Westcott. Little, Brown. Hoberman presents the familiar rhyme about a pesky goat that gets in trouble for eating shirts off the clothesline.

Martin, Bill, Jr. 1964. *Brown Bear, Brown Bear, What Do You See?* Illustrated by Eric Carle. Holt. Children see a variety of animals, each one a different color, and a mother looking at them.

Martin, Bill, Jr. 2007. *Baby Bear, Baby Bear, What Do You See?* Illustrated by Eric Carle. Holt. Illustrations and rhyming text portray a young bear searching for its mother and meeting many North American animals along the way.

Numeroff, Laura Joffe. 2008. *If You Give a Cat a Cupcake.* Illustrated by Felicia Bond. Harper. (See other books in the If You Give series.) A series of increasingly far-fetched events might occur if someone were to give a cupcake to a cat.

Rosen, Michael. 2009 (1989). *We're Going on a Bear Hunt.* Illustrated by Helen Oxenbury. McElderry. Brave bear hunters go through grass, a river, mud, and other obstacles before the inevitable encounter with the bear forces a headlong retreat.

Sendak, Maurice. 1991 (1962). *Chicken Soup with Rice.* Harper. This is a look at the months of the year: "Each month is gay, each season nice, when eating chicken soup with rice."

Shaw, Nancy. 2008. *Sheep Blast Off.* Illustrated by Margot Apple. Houghton Mifflin. (See the other books in the Sheep series.) Upon finding a spaceship, sheep climb aboard and bumble around until they blast off into orbit.

Taback, Simms. 2002. *This Is the House That Jack Built.* Putnam. This is a picture rendition of the traditional cumulative tale.

Waddell, Martin. 1992. *Farmer Duck.* Illustrated by Helen Oxenbury. Candlewick. When a kind and hardworking duck nearly collapses from overwork on a lazy farmer's farm, the rest of the animals get together and chase the man out of town.

Wood, Audrey. 2000 (1984). *The Napping House.* Illustrated by Don Wood. Harcourt. In this cumulative tale, a wakeful flea atop a number of sleeping creatures causes a commotion, with just one bite.

Yolen, Jane. 2000. *Off We Go!* Illustrated by Laura Molk. Little, Brown. One by one, baby woodland creatures leave home and sing their way to visit grandma.

Beginning Reader

Arnold, Tedd. 2010. *Super Fly Guy and Buzz Boy.* Cartwheel. (See others in the Super Fly Guy series.) Buzz creates a comic book that features Buzz Boy and Fly Guy as the superheroes.

Bulla, Clyde Robert. 1987. *The Chalk Box Kid.* Illustrated by Thomas B. Allen. Random. Nine-year-old Gregory's house does not have room for a garden, but he creates a surprising and very different garden in an unusual place.

Byars, Betsy. 1994. *The Golly Sisters Ride Again.* Illustrated by Sue Truesdell. Harper. The Golly Sisters, May-May and Rose, share further adventures as they take their traveling show through the West.

Cazet, Denys. 2006. *Minnie and Moo, Wanted Dead or Alive.* Harper. (See others in the Minnie and Moo series.) Trying to help Mr. Farmer with his finances, Minnie and Moo go to the bank to ask for money and are mistaken for the Bazooka sisters, dangerous outlaws.

Cohen, Miriam. 2006 (1990). *First Grade Takes a Test.* Illustrated by Ronald Himler. Star Bright Books. The first grade is distressed by an intelligence test that fails to measure true aptitude.

Howe, James. 2009. *Houndsley and Catina Plink and Plunk.* Illustrated by Marie-Louise Gay. Candlewick. Houndsley likes canoeing and his friend Catina likes bicycling, but each has to help the other learn to enjoy these activities in order to do them together.

Lobel, Arnold. 1970. *Frog and Toad Are Friends.* Harper. (See others in the Frog and Toad series.) Five short tales recounting the adventures of two best friends, Frog and Toad.

Lobel, Arnold. 1981. *Uncle Elephant.* Harper. Uncle Elephant comes to the rescue when his nephew's parents are lost at sea and cares for him until they are found again.

Minarik, Else. 1957. *Little Bear.* Illustrated by Maurice Sendak. Harper. (See others in the Little Bear series.) Little Bear's four adventures include taking a trip to the moon and having a birthday party.

Rylant, Cynthia. 2005. *Henry and Mudge and the Great Grandpas.* Illustrated by Suçie Stevenson. Simon & Schuster. (See others in the Henry and Mudge series.) When Henry and his dog Mudge go with Henry's parents to visit Great-Grandpa Bill in the home with lots of other grandpas, they lead them all on a wonderful adventure.

Rylant, Cynthia. 2010. *Annie and Snowball and the Magical House.* Illustrated by Suçie Stevenson. Aladdin. (See others in the Annie and Snowball series). Annie takes her rabbit to the home of her new friend, Sarah, to play and enjoys seeing the pretty house full of frilly things, walking in the beautiful garden, and making a tiny garden house for a fairy tea party.

Rylant, Cynthia. 2010. *Mr. Putter and Tabby Clear the Decks.* Illustrated by Arthur Howard. Harcourt. (See others in the Mr. Putter and Tabby series.) To relieve the boredom of a long, hot summer, Mr. Putter and his cat Tabby join their fun-loving neighbor, Mrs. Teaberry, and her mischievous dog, Zeke, on an adventurous sightseeing boat cruise.

Seuss, Dr. 1957. *The Cat in the Hat.* Random. Two children sitting at home on a rainy day are visited by the Cat in the Hat, who shows them some tricks and games.

Sharmat, Marjorie Weinman. 2009. *Nate the Great and the Hungry Book Club.* Illustrated by Jody Wheeler. Delacorte. (See others in the Nate the Great series.) Nate and his dog, Sludge, help Rosamond discover who has been tearing pages out of her books.

Van Leeuwen, Jean. 2008. *Amanda Pig and the Wiggly Tooth.* Illustrated by Ann Schweninger. Dial. (See others in the Amanda Pig series.) When Amanda Pig has her first loose tooth, she is reluctant to pull it.

Picture Story

Ackerman, Karen. 1988. *Song and Dance Man.* Illustrated by Stephen Gammell. Knopf. Grandpa demonstrates for his visiting grandchildren some of the songs, dances, and jokes he performed when he was a vaudeville entertainer.

Agee, Jon. 2001. *Milo's Hat Trick.* Hyperion. A failed magician's routine is saved by a bear who can disappear into a top hat.

Allard, Harry. 1977. *Miss Nelson Is Missing!* Illustrated by James Marshall. Houghton Mifflin. The kids in Room 207 take advantage of their teacher's good nature until she disappears and they are faced with a vile substitute.

Arnold, Tedd. 2004. *Even More Parts.* Dial. A young boy is worried about what will happen to his body when he hears such expressions as "I'm tongue-tied," "Don't give me any of your lip," and "I put my foot in my mouth."

Cooney, Barbara. 1982. *Miss Rumphius.* Viking. As a child, Great-Aunt Alice Rumphius resolved that when she grew up, she would go to faraway places, live by the sea in her old age, and do something to make the world more beautiful—and she does all those things, the last being the most difficult of all.

Cronin, Doreen. 2000. *Click, Clack, Moo: Cows That Type.* Illustrated by Betsy Lewin. Simon & Schuster. When Farmer Brown's cows find a typewriter in the barn, they start making demands and go on strike when the farmer refuses to give them what they want.

Demi. 1997. *One Grain of Rice: A Mathematical Folktale.* Scholastic. A reward of one grain of rice doubles day by day into millions of grains of rice when a selfish raja is outwitted by a clever village girl.

dePaola, Tomie. 1975. *Strega Nona.* Prentice Hall. When Strega Nona leaves him alone with her magic pasta pot, Big Anthony is determined to show the townspeople how it works.

Dickens, Charles. 2009. *A Christmas Carol.* Illustrated by Brett Helquist. Harper. Helquist adds new illustrations to the story of a miser who learns the true meaning of Christmas when three ghostly visitors review his past and foretell his future.

Falconer, Ian. 2006. *Olivia Forms a Band.* Atheneum. When Olivia learns that there will be no band at the evening's fireworks display, she decides to form one of her own, with herself as the only musician playing some rather unusual instruments.

Fox, Mem. 2009. *The Goblin and the Empty Chair.* Illustrated by Leo and Diane Dillon. Beach Lane Books. A goblin who for many years has been hiding himself so that he does not frighten anyone finally finds a family.

Frazee, Marla. 2008. *A Couple of Boys Have the Best Weekend Ever.* Harcourt. Friends James and Eamon enjoy a wonderful week at the home of Eamon's grandparents during summer vacation.

Helquist, Brett. 2010. *Bedtime for Bear.* Harper. Just after the first snowfall, Bear is ready to go to sleep until spring, but his friends encourage him to spend one last day playing with them.

Henkes, Kevin. 2006. *Lilly's Big Day.* Greenwillow. When her teacher announces that he is getting married, Lilly the mouse sets her heart on being the flower girl at his wedding.

Hoban, Russell. 1964. *Bread and Jam for Frances.* Illustrated by Lillian Hoban. Harper. (See others in the Frances series.) "Jam on toast," sings Frances about the food she likes most—until she has it for the sixth meal in two days.

Howitt, Mary. 2002. *The Spider and the Fly.* Illustrated by Tony DiTerlizzi. Simon & Schuster. An illustrated version of the well-known poem about a wily spider who preys on the vanity and innocence of a little fly.

Isaacs, Anne. 2010. *Dust Devil.* Illustrated by Paul O. Zelinsky. Schartz & Wade. Having moved to Montana from Tennessee in the 1830s, fearless Angelica Longrider—also known as Swamp Angel—changes the state's landscape, tames a wild horse, and captures some desperadoes.

Keats, Ezra Jack. 1971. *Apt. 3.* Macmillan. On a rainy day two brothers try to discover who is playing the harmonica they hear in their apartment building.

Kellogg, Steven. 1979. *Pinkerton, Behave!* Dial. His behavior may be rather unconventional, but Pinkerton the dog proves it doesn't really matter.

Mayer, Mercer. 1968. *There's a Nightmare in My Closet.* Dial. At bedtime, a boy confronts the nightmare in his closet and finds him not so terrifying after all.

McCloskey, Robert. 1948. *Blueberries for Sal.* Viking. Little Sal and Little Bear both lose their mothers while eating blueberries and almost end up with the other's mother.

Meddaugh, Susan. 2004. *Perfectly Martha.* Houghton Mifflin. (See also other titles in the Martha series.) Martha discovers how the Perfect Pup Institute turns dogs into obedient robots and then does something about it.

Muth, Jon. 2010. *Zen Ghosts.* Scholastic. On Halloween night, Stillwater the giant panda tells Karl, Addy, and Michael a spooky and unusual story.

Peet, Bill. 1983. *Buford the Little Bighorn.* Houghton Mifflin. An awkward and scrawny mountain sheep with oversized horns escapes the hunters to become the sensation of a ski resort.

Polacco, Patricia. 2010. *Junkyard Wonders.* Philomel. Inspired by a teacher who believes each of them is a genius, a class of special-needs students invents something that could convince the whole school they are justifiably proud to be "Junkyard Wonders."

Rohmann, Eric. 2005. *Clara and Asha.* Roaring Brook Press. Young Clara would rather play with her imaginary giant fish, Asha, than settle down to sleep.

Rylant, Cynthia. 1985. *The Relatives Came.* Illustrated by Stephen Gammell. Bradbury. The relatives come to visit from Virginia, and everyone has a wonderful time.

Salley, Coleen. 2009. *Epossumondas Plays Possum.* Illustrated by Janet Stevens. Harcourt. Forgetting his mother's warnings, Epossumondas goes into the swamp alone and then must pretend to be dead again and again as he hears frightening sounds and fears they are being made by the dreaded loup garou.

Scanlon, Liz Garton. 2009. *All the World.* Illustrated by Marla Frazee. Beach Lane Books. Scanlon's words and Frazee's illustrations invite children to explore a variety of settings, starting with a beach where a young interracial family plays.

Seuss, Dr. (Theodor Geisel). 1990 (1938). *The 500 Hats of Bartholomew Cubbins.* Random House. At first, Bartholomew Cubbins has just one hat, but when the King orders him to take it off, he finds that he cannot—each time there is another on his head.

Shulevitz, Uri. 2008. *How I Learned Geography.* Farrar, Straus & Giroux. As he spends hours studying his father's world map, a young boy escapes the hunger and misery of refugee life. Based on the author's childhood in Kazakhstan, where he lived as a Polish refugee during World War II.

Shulevitz, Uri. 2009. *When I Wore My Sailor Suit.* Farrar, Straus & Giroux. A young child spends the day imagining himself to be a sailor on a grand adventure.

Small, David. 1985. *Imogene's Antlers.* Crown. One Thursday, Imogene wakes up with a pair of antlers growing out of her head and causes a sensation wherever she goes.

Stains, Bill. 2009. *All God's Critters.* Illustrated by Kadir Nelson. Simon & Schuster. Stains celebrates how all the animals in the world make their own music in their own way, some singing low and some singing higher.

Steig, William. 1976. *The Amazing Bone.* Farrar. On her way home from school, Pearl finds an unusual bone that has unexpected powers.

Van Allsburg, Chris. 1979. *The Garden of Abdul Gasazi.* Houghton Mifflin. When the dog he is caring for runs away from Alan into the forbidden garden of a retired dog-hating magician, a spell seems to be cast over the contrary canine.

Viorst, Judith. 2009 (1972). *Alexander and the Terrible, Horrible, No Good, Very Bad Day.* Illustrated by Ray Cruz. Atheneum. On a day when everything goes wrong for him, Alexander is consoled by the thought that other people have bad days, too.

Wisniewski, David. 2007 (1996). *Golem.* Clarion. A saintly rabbi miraculously brings to life a clay giant, who helps him watch over the Jews of 16th-century Prague.

Wong, Janet. 2009. *Homegrown House.* Illustrated by E. B. Lewis. McElderry. A young girl describes her grandmother's comfortable, long-time home and wishes that she and her parents could stay in the same house instead of moving so often.

Yolen, Jane. 1987. *Owl Moon.* Illustrated by John Schoenherr. Putnam. On a winter's night under a full moon, a father and daughter trek into the woods to see the Great Horned Owl.

Engineered

Ahlberg, Janet, and Allan Ahlberg. 1986. *The Jolly Postman or Other People's Letters.* Little, Brown. A Jolly Postman delivers letters to several famous fairy tale characters, such as the Big Bad Wolf, Cinderella, and the Three Bears. Each letter may be removed from its envelope page and read separately.

Barrie, James. 2008. *Peter Pan: A Pop-Up Adaptation of J. M. Barrie's Original Tale.* Illustrated by Robert Sabuda. Little Simon. The classic tale of the three Darling children in Never-Never Land with Peter Pan, the boy who would not grow up, illustrated with elaborate pop-ups. The original text is printed on fold-out booklets attached to the pages.

Carle, Eric. 1995. *The Very Lonely Firefly.* Philomel. A lonely firefly goes out into the night searching for other fireflies. A battery inserted in the back cover provides the fireflies' light.

Carle, Eric. 2009. *The Very Hungry Caterpillar Pop-Up Book.* Philomel. In a pop-up edition of the 1969 classic, the hungry little caterpillar literally pops out of the book—crawling along branches, munching through food, and finally rising from the page as a three-dimensional, beautiful butterfly.

Ehlert, Lois. 1990. *Color Farm.* Lippincott. The rooster, dog, sheep, cow, pig, and other animals on a farm are made up of colorful shapes, such as square, circle, rectangle, and triangle. Features die-cut pages.

Hill, Eric. 2005. *Who's There, Spot?* Putnam. The puppy Spot goes around the house and yard, looking in various places to see who's there. By lifting cardboard flaps, for example, young readers discover (along with Spot) a mouse in the cupboard and a frog beneath the grass.

Lee, Jeanie. 2006. *When I Grow Up.* Simon & Schuster. Pull the bottom of each page and watch the images magically transform. A firefighter saves a kitten, a veterinarian treats a puppy, an astronaut flies through outer space, and so on.

Pelham, David. 2007. *Trail: Paper Poetry.* Little Simon. Follow the silvery trail through an enchanting maze of stunning pop-up landscapes, which range from tranquil to mysterious to magical.

Piénkowski, Jan. 2005 (1979). *Haunted House.* Candlewick. The reader is invited to tour a spooky old house. Features pop-up scenes with lift-flaps and pull-tabs.

Piénkowski, Jan. 2003. *The Animals Went in Two by Two: A Noah's Ark Pop-up.* Candlewick. "The animals went in two by two/The elephant and the kangaroo." A traditional rhyme comes to life in a rollicking ark full of flitting bumblebees, swimming pigs, dawdling tortoises, and so on.

Reinhart, Matthew. 2006. *The Jungle Book: A Pop-Up Adventure.* Little Simon. True to Rudyard Kipling's original story, tree branches literally draw the reader in to this tale of Mowgli the Man Cub exploring the pop-up ruins of the Lost City, riding atop three-dimensional thundering elephants, and facing a fierce tiger leaping from the page.

Reinhart, Matthew, and Robert Sabuda. 2010. *Gods and Heroes.* Candlewick. A pop-up encyclopedia of the gods and heroes of mythology.

Sabuda, Robert. 1994. *The Christmas Alphabet.* Orchard. Pristine white paper sculptures pop-up on each page to alphabetically celebrate the Christmas season.

Sabuda, Robert. 2007. *Winter in White.* Little Simon. A brief rhyming tale about winter is illustrated with elaborate pop-up figures.

Sabuda, Robert, and Matthew Reinhart. 2008. *Fairies and Magical Creatures.* Candlewick. Showing mythical beings from household brownies to merfolk lurking deep below the sea, this three-dimensional book brims with facts and fancy.

Taback, Simms. 1999. *Joseph Had a Little Overcoat.* Viking. A very old overcoat is recycled numerous times into a variety of garments. Die-cuts are ingeniously utilized to make the garment shrink from page to page.

Taback, Simms. 2009. *Simms Taback's City Animals.* Blue Apple Books. The reader is invited to guess which animal is hiding beneath fold-outs that reveal a succession of clues.

Van Fleet, Matthew. 1995. *Fuzzy Yellow Ducklings.* Dial. Van Fleet uses fold-out illustrations and simple text to introduce different textures, colors, shapes, and animals.

Van Fleet, Matthew. 2009. *Cat.* Simon & Schuster. Twenty-two breeds of frolicking felines demonstrate synonyms, action words, opposites, and more. Cleverly designed pull tabs and flaps, plus seven textures to pet and a push-button squeaker, offer interactive treats.

Willems, Mo. 2009. *Big Frog Can't Fit In: A Pop-Out Book.* Hyperion. Big Frog, the main character, can't fit into the book, until her friends suggest making a bigger book.

Zelinsky, Paul O. 1990. *The Wheels on the Bus.* Paper engineering by Rodger Smith. Dutton. The wheels on the bus go round, the wipers go swish, the doors open and close, and the people go in and out in this movable book version of the classic song.

Baby/Board

Alborough, Jez. 2007. *Fix-It Duck.* Kane/Miller. When Duck's roof starts leaking, he enlists the help of his friends but then finds more things that need fixing.

Boynton, Sandra, 2006. *Your Personal Penguin.* Workman. Penguin wants nothing more than to be Hippo's friend.

Boynton, Sandra. 2009. *Night-Night, Little Pookie.* Robin Corey/Random House. It's evening, and Mom patiently eases Pookie toward bed.

Buehner, Caralyn. 2004. *Snowmen at Night.* Illustrated by Mark Buehner. Dial. Snowmen play games at night when no one is watching.

Buehner, Caralyn. 2007. *The Escape of Marvin the Ape.* Illustrated by Mark Buehner. Dial. Marvin the Ape slips out of the zoo and finds he likes it on the outside, where he easily blends into city lifestyles.

Chodos-Irvine, Margaret. 2008. *Ella Sarah Gets Dressed.* Red Wagon/Harcourt. Despite the advice of others in her family, Ella Sarah persists in wearing the striking and unusual outfit of her own choosing.

Cowley, Joy. 2005. *Mrs. Wishy-Washy's Scrubbing Machine.* Philomel. Mrs. Wishy-Washy has a new scrubbing machine to help her keep everything clean, including her animals.

Harper, Jamie. 2009. *Yum Yum, Baby Bundt: A Recipe for Mealtime.* Candlewick. An adorable baby and his creative big sister offer their unique "recipes" for a foolproof mealtime.

Hill, Eric. 2009. *Spot Loves His Teacher.* Putnam. Spot loves school. His teacher, Miss Bear, is always there to help out, whether the class is learning to paint, reading a story, or going on a nature walk.

Hoban, Tana. 2007. *Black & White.* Greenwillow. White illustrations appear against a black background, alternating with black illustrations against a white background, depicting objects such as an elephant, butterfly, leaf, horse, baby bottle, and sailboat.

Merberg, Julie, and Suzanne Bober. 2007. *Dreaming with Rousseau.* Chronicle. Set against the backdrop of well-known works by the artist Henri Rousseau, rhyming text reveals a dream of the jungle and its inhabitants.

Newgarden, Mark, and Megan Montague Cash. 2009. *Bow-Wow's Colorful Life.* Harcourt. Bow-Wow pulls sock after sock off his master, each one a different color.

Oxenbury, Helen. 1981. *Dressing.* Simon & Schuster. Baby appears wearing his diaper, undershirt, sock, shoe, shirt, overalls, and hat.

Schachner, Judy. 2008. *Skippyjon Jones Shape Up.* Dutton. Skippyjon the cat does an exercise routine featuring items of various shapes.

Searcy, John, editor. 2006. *My First Tractor Board Book.* DK Publishing. Colorful, labeled pictures introduce children to tractors and the words associated with them, as well as the many jobs tractors are used to perform.

Simmons, Jane. 2002. *Daisy Says, If You're Happy and You Know It.* Little, Brown. Duckling Daisy knows the secret to true happiness: "If you're happy and you know it, oink like a pig" (or buzz like a bee, squeak like a mouse, or even quack like a duck).

Slobodkina, Esphyr. 2008 (1940). *Caps for Sale Board Book.* Harper. A band of mischievous monkeys steals every one of a peddler's caps while he takes a nap under a tree.

Teitelbaum, Michael. 2009. *On the Move!* Characters and environment developed by Design Garage: David Shannon, Loren Long, and David Gordon. Little Simon. Rita, Dan, Max, and Ted are on the move in Trucktown. (See others in Jon Scieszka's Trucktown series.)

Walton, Rick. 2001. *One More Bunny.* Illustrated by Paige Miglio. HarperFestival. Bunnies frolicking at the playground introduce the numbers one through ten and the principles of simple addition.

Traditional fantasy picture books are, for the most part, found in Chapter 9.

PEARSON

myeducationkit

Go to the topic Picture Books on the MyEducationKit for this text, where you can:

- Search the Database of Children's Literature, housing more than 22,000 titles searchable in every genre by authors or illustrators, by awards won, by year published, and by topic and description.
- Explore genre-related Assignments and Activities, assignable exercises showing concepts in action through database use, video, cases, and student and teacher artifacts.
- Listen to podcasts and read interviews from some of the brightest and most enduring stars of children's literature in the Conversations.
- Discover weblinks that will lead you to sites representing the authors you learn about in these pages, classrooms with powerful children's literature connections, and literature awards.

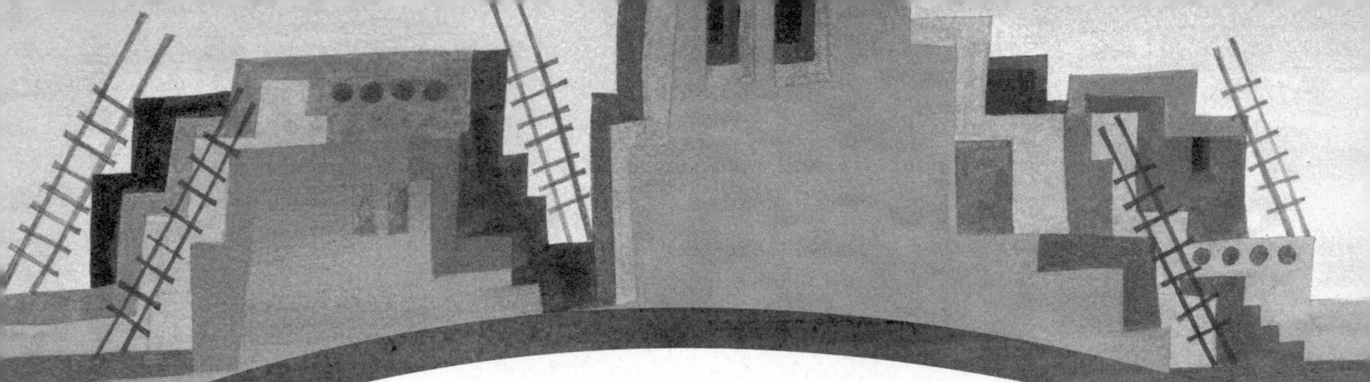

Chapter 8

Poetry

Unfortunately, poetry does not receive the same attention in our elementary and secondary schools as do other literary forms. Several years of informal polls of our undergraduate preservice elementary teachers continue to affirm that a sizable percentage of these students enter teacher training with either an ambivalence toward or a distinct dislike for poetry. From one- to two-thirds of each class admit such negative attitudes.

Is the alarming frequency of these attitudes due to teaching practices that alienate children from poetry or simply due to the absence of poetry in the curriculum? Whatever the reason, the fact remains that if many of our young teachers enter the field with an ambivalence toward poetry—or worse—then it is likely that a similar feeling will be passed to our children.

Why Children May Learn to Dislike Poetry

Children have a natural affinity for poetry, which is exhibited before they enter school by their love for Mother Goose and other nursery rhymes, jingles, and childhood songs. Sometime during the course of their schooling, a great number of these children seem to change their minds about the appeal of poetry. Indeed, some of our teaching practices may be responsible. When asked what sorts of poetry-related school activities they found distasteful, our undergraduate students invariably listed these: memorizing and reciting, writing poetry, and heavy-duty analyzing of a poem's structure and meaning. Many students reported a distaste for playing the "I know the true meaning of this poem; it's your job to discover it" game with their teachers.

Visit the MyEducationKit for this course to enhance your understanding of chapter concepts with activities, weblinks, podcasts, and a searchable database of more than 22,000 children's literature titles.

PEANUTS® by Charles M. Schultz

Teachers who don't appreciate poetry tend to ignore it in their daily routine. They may spend time with a poetry unit—teaching a few forms, giving practice in those forms by having the students write some poems (which are illustrated and posted on the bulletin board), memorizing and reciting some poetry—and then will move on, leaving poetry behind for good.

Haiku, a Japanese poetry form, is commonly the form most abused in this manner. It is a seemingly quick and simple form to teach and write, having only 17 syllables (a line of 5 syllables, a line of 7 syllables, and another line of 5 syllables) that traditionally express something about nature:

> Take the butterfly:
> Nature works to produce him.
> Why doesn't he last?
>
> *David McCord*

Haiku may be short, but it is not simple. Because it is a rather abstract form, children actually require some experience and maturity to understand and appreciate haiku. Thus, as studies of children's poetry preferences indicate, generations of children have been taught to despise haiku (Fisher & Natarella, 1982; Kutiper & Wilson, 1993; Terry, 1974). With proper instructional techniques, however, children can and do learn to appreciate this elegant verse form.

Obviously, teachers who dislike poetry may have negative effects on children's poetry attitudes. However, the overzealous teacher who dearly loves poetry may cause problems, too, by rushing headlong into the sophisticated poems rendered by the traditional poets. Children may be overwhelmed by the complicated structures and intense imagery and figurative language. When pushed at an early age to analyze and discover deeply couched meanings, their excitement about poetry wanes.

Studies of children's poetry preferences reveal children's common dislikes about poetry. Kutiper and Wilson (1993) have summarized the results of several of the best-known studies:

1. The narrative form of poetry [and limericks] was popular with readers of all ages, while free verse and haiku were the most disliked forms.
2. Students preferred poems that contain rhyme, rhythm, and sound.
3. Children most enjoyed poetry that contained humor, familiar experiences, and animals. [Disliked poems about nature.]

4. Younger students (elementary and middle school/junior high age) preferred contemporary poems.
5. Students disliked poems that contained visual imagery or figurative language. (p. 29)

What students like about poetry relates to their early childhood love for poems that are heavily rhymed and straightforward in meaning. What they dislike is frequently associated with teaching practices: the abuse of haiku (which also surfaces in a dislike of nature poems), a lack of connection with the more abstract form of free verse, and the distaste for figurative language. Sometimes in elementary schools and middle schools, we seem to know and teach only simile, metaphor, and personification. After innumerable exercises wherein students are asked to find, circle, and label in a poem (or story) examples of simile, metaphor, and personification, it is little wonder that figurative language seems a burden. So, it is not figurative language they dislike but rather the worksheets they associate with it.

Bernard Lonsdale and Helen Mackintosh (1973) best express how we should approach poetry in the elementary schools:

> Experiences with poetry should be pleasurable and should never be associated with work. Teachers defeat their own purpose if they attempt to analyze the structure or form of the poem other than to show whether it rhymes; what the verse pattern is; and whether it is a ballad, a limerick, a lyric poem, or perhaps haiku. Children in elementary schools should be asked questions of preference and of feeling rather than of knowing. (p. 213)

Children have less opportunity to express preference and feeling when the teacher makes all the decisions about poetry and its use in the classroom. If the teacher selects one poem for the entire class to memorize, fewer children will respond positively than if each is allowed to choose a favorite poem for memorization. If the teacher presents one form of poetry and afterward insists that everyone write a poem in that style, the overall response will be less enthusiastic than if the teacher waits until two or three forms have been introduced and permits students to select the type they wish to write. Insightful teachers can help students see that their poems may be free of form yet extremely personal and powerful. (See *A Celebration of Bees: Helping Children Write Poetry* by Barbara Juster Esbensen, 1995.) The principle of allowing children to make choices whenever possible is closely associated with success in presenting poetry in the elementary classroom. Galda, Cullinan, and Sipe (2010) have reviewed studies (McClure, 1985; Hansen, 2004) indicating that positive school experiences with poetry may bring about changes in children's poetry preferences, building appreciation for formerly disliked poetic elements.

Building Appreciation for Poetry

Children who have learned a dislike for poetry can be lured back by teachers who capitalize on the winning power of light, humorous verse. No collection of light verse has done more to attract children to poetry than Shel Silverstein's *Where the Sidewalk Ends* (1974). Young readers hungrily latch onto Silverstein's lighthearted, sometimes irreverent poems about contemporary childhood. Jack Prelutsky's poems are similar to Silverstein's, but they are more numerous and more varied in theme. Prelutsky's collection *The New Kid on the Block* (1984) actually edged out *Where the Sidewalk Ends* as the most circulated poetry book in the school libraries selected for a poetry preference study (Kutiper & Wilson, 1993). Here is the poem that opens the collection:

The New Kid on the Block

There's a new kid on the block,
and boy, that kid is tough,
that new kid punches hard,
that new kid plays real rough,
that new kid's big and strong,
with muscles everywhere,
that new kid tweaked my arm,
that new kid pulled my hair.
That new kid likes to fight,
and picks on all the guys,
that new kid scares me some,
(that new kid's twice my size),
that new kid stomped my toes,
that new kid swiped my ball,
that new kid's really bad,
I don't care for her at all.

As Kutiper and Wilson (1993) point out, the light verse that children tend to prefer must not remain their only poetry diet. Wise teachers will use the rhythmic, humorous verse to build appreciation for poetry in general and use it as a bridge to more sophisticated contemporary and traditional poetry written for children and adults. Teachers who share poems daily, with no ulterior motive other than to build appreciation, help create students (and future teachers) who will have a lifelong interest in poetry. Share a poem as children wait in the lunch line, sit down after recess, or as a way to begin each school day. One teacher simply wrote a new poem on the chalkboard each day without reading or referring to it. Soon students were commenting on the poems, and some began writing down the ones they liked. Poetry may fit nicely into a social studies (*Got Geography! Poems;* Hopkins, 2006) or science unit (*Scien-trickery: Riddles in Science;* Lewis, 2004)—in fact, into any area of the curriculum. In language study, Ruth Heller's beautifully illustrated poems present the parts of speech (*Kites Sail High: A Book about Verbs,* 1988; *Mine, All Mine: A Book about Pronouns,* 1997; *Fantastic! Wow! and Unreal! A Book about Interjections and Conjunctions,* 1998; and others). The key is consistent, unfettered exposure to poetry by an enthusiastic teacher who begins mixing light verse and more artistic poetry.

Because rhythm is an inherent part of poetry, it is more effective to read poems aloud. Therefore, the avenue to poetry appreciation for many students is the oral highway. Teachers should read poems aloud—fresh selections as well as old favorites—on a regular, even daily basis. And for older, hardcore poetry haters, music is often the road to recovery. Students tend not to associate the lyrics of songs they know and love with poetry. Teachers of older children have changed students' negative attitudes toward poetry by duplicating the lyrics of popular tunes and distributing them as poems. Often barriers will tumble down, clearing the way for sharing other sorts of poetry.

Choral speaking is another oral/aural method for sharing poetry. Through choral speaking, children get the opportunity to play with words and their sounds—to both hear and manipulate the language. For example, free verse (noted by children as one of their least favorite forms) can spring to life when performed as a choral reading. Here is a free-verse poem by Harold Munro, divided into speaking parts by a teacher, that has proven to be an icebreaker with upper elementary students:

Overheard on a Salt Marsh
by Harold Munro

(May also be divided as light voices and dark voices, or switch the boys to water nymphs and the girls to goblins.)

Boys: NYMPH, NYMPH, WHAT ARE YOUR BEADS?
Girls: Green glass, goblin. Why do you stare at them?
Boys: GIVE THEM ME.
Girls: NO.
Boys: GIVE THEM ME.
GIVE THEM ME.
Girls: NO.
Boys: THEN I WILL HOWL ALL NIGHT IN THE REEDS, LIE IN THE MUD AND HOWL FOR THEM.
Girls: Goblin, why do you love them so?
Boys: THEY ARE BETTER THAN STARS OR WATER,
BETTER THAN VOICES OF WINDS THAT SING,
BETTER THAN ANY MAN'S FAIR DAUGHTER,
YOUR GREEN GLASS BEADS ON A SILVER STRING.
Girls: Hush, I stole them out of the moon.
Boys: GIVE ME YOUR BEADS, I WANT THEM.
Girls: NO.
Boys: I WILL HOWL IN A DEEP LAGOON
FOR YOUR GREEN GLASS BEADS,
I LOVE THEM SO.
GIVE THEM ME. GIVE THEM.
Girls: NO.

Sometimes teachers can be intimidated by poetry. "Poetry phobia" often results from a lack of knowledge and usually disappears with increased understanding. Those with poetry phobia can develop confidence when learning about poetry from two children's books: Avis Harley's *Fly with Poetry: an ABC of Poetry* (2000) and *Leap into Poetry: More ABCs of Poetry* (2001). These simple, clever picture books illuminate poetry forms and terms with poetic examples and straightforward definitions. For instance, in *Fly with Poetry,* "Acrostic" is the poetry form for the letter "A," and Harley (2000, p. 11) explains that in such a poem, "the first letters of the lines form a word or sentence when read downward." Then she gives an example of her own making:

Editing the Chrysalis
"At last," cried Butterfly,

Poised
Over its
Empty chrysalis,
"My final draft!"*

Teachers do much to convince children of the worth of poetry when they share what is personally delightful. They are always more successful when presenting poems they honestly like. A folder with readily accessible favorite poems or a shelf holding favorite poetry volumes makes the job easier. If teachers do not have personal favorites, it is only because they have not read enough poems. The pleasure of writing poetry should be modeled in a similar way. We recall a sixth-grade teacher who genuinely enjoyed writing limericks for his students, who soon became so enamored with limericks they chose to stay in during recess to write poems!

The NCTE Poetry Award

To encourage the sharing of poetry with children and to raise the awareness of teachers about the quality of the poetry available, the National Council of Teachers of English (NCTE) established an award to recognize a living poet whose body of work for children ages 3 to 13 is deemed exceptional.

The works of the poets who have won the NCTE Award for Excellence in Poetry for Children are certainly not as well known among children as the poems of Silverstein and Prelutsky, but they provide teachers a reservoir of fine poetry that is both very accessible to children and of better artistic quality than the popular lighter verse. (See *A Jar of Tiny Stars: Poems by NCTE Award–Winning Poets* edited by Bernice E. Cullinan, 1996, and Figure 8.1, which lists additional noteworthy poets.) Here are the names of the award-winning poets, the dates of their awards, and a sample of their poetry. Try reading each selection aloud for full effect.

David McCord, 1977

Song of the Train
Clickety-clack,
Wheels on the track,
This is the way
They begin the attack:
Click-ety-clack,
Click-ety-clack,
Click-ety, *clack*-ety,
Click-ety
Clack.

---

*From *Fly with Poetry* by Avis Harley. Copyright © 2000 by Avis Harley. Published by Wordsong, an imprint of Boyds Mills Press. Reprinted by permission.

Figure 8.1

Notable Children's Poets

Adoff, Arnold
Baylor, Byrd
Ciardi, John
Esbensen, Barbara Juster
Fisher, Aileen
Fleischman, Paul
Florian, Douglas
Giovanni, Nikki
Greenfield, Eloise
Grimes, Nikki
Hoberman, Mary Ann
Hopkins, Lee Bennett
Janeczko, Paul B.
Kennedy, X. J.
Kuskin, Karla
Lewis, J. Patrick
Livingston, Myra Cohn
McCord, David
Merriam, Eve
Moore, Lilian
Nye, Naomi Shihab
Prelutsky, Jack
Schertle, Alice
Siebert, Diane
Silverstein, Shel
Willard, Nancy
Worth, Valerie
Yolen, Jane

Clickety-clack,
Over the crack,
Faster and faster
The song of the track:
Clickety-clack,
Clickety-clack
Clickety, clackety,
Clackety
Clack.

Riding in front,
Riding in back,
Everyone hears
The song of the track:
Clickety-clack,
Clickety-clack,
Clickety, *clickety,*
Clackety
Clack.

Aileen Fisher, 1978

I Like It When It's Mizzly

I like it when it's mizzly
and just a little drizzly
so everything looks far away
and make-believe and frizzly.

I like it when it's foggy
and sounding very froggy.
I even like it when it rains
on streets and weepy windowpanes
and catkins in the poplar tree
and *me.*

Karla Kuskin, 1979

Full of the Moon

It's full of the moon
The dogs dance out
Through brush and bush and bramble.
They howl and yowl
And growl and prowl.
They amble, ramble, scramble.
They rush through brush.
They push through bush.
They yip and yap and hurr.
They lark around and bark around
With prickles in their fur.
They two-step in the meadow.
They polka on the lawn.
Tonight's the night
The dogs dance out
And chase their tails till dawn.

Myra Cohn Livingston, 1980

My Box

Nobody knows what's there but me,
knows where I keep my silver key
and my baseball cards
and my water gun
and my wind-up car that doesn't run,
and a stone I found with a hole clear through
and a blue-jay feather that's *mostly* blue,
and a note that I wrote to the guy next door
and never gave him—and lots, lots more
of important things that I'll never show
to anyone, *anyone* else I know.

Eve Merriam, 1981

Teevee

In the house
of Mr. and Mrs. Spouse
he and she

would watch TV
and never a word
between them spoken
until the day
the set was broken.

Then "How do you do?"
said he to she.
"I don't believe
that we've
met
yet.
Spouse is my name.
What's yours?" he asked.

"Why, mine's the same!"
said she to he,
"Do you suppose that we could be—?"

But the set came suddenly right about,
and so they never did find out.

John Ciardi ("*Char*-dee"), 1982

How to Tell the Top of a Hill

The top of a hill
Is not until
The bottom is below.
And you have to stop
When you reach the top
For there's no more UP to go.
To make it plain
Let me explain:
The one *most* reason why
You have to stop
When you reach the top—is:
The next step up is sky.

Lilian Moore, 1985

Pigeons

Pigeons are city folk
content
to live with concrete
and cement.

They seldom
try
the sky.

A pigeon never sings
of hill
and flowering hedge,
but busily commutes
from sidewalk
to his ledge.
Oh pigeon, what a waste of wings!

Arnold Adoff, 1988

Love Song

great goblets of pudding   powder in milk
hot with marshmallows on a winter afternoon
syrup on vanilla ice cream   frosting on cake
a kind of cake   dripping to dry on warm
doughnuts fresh from the oven   candy
candy bars
bars   chunks   thick and broken pieces   squares
spoons and pots   and lots
before brushing
fudge and milk
and german and sour cream
light and dark and bitter sweet and
even
white
you are no good
for me
you are no good

you are so good

Chocolate
Chocolate
i
love
you so
i
want
to
marry
you

                and
live
    forever
            in the
            flavor
of your
    brown

Valerie Worth, 1991

Stockings (from *At Christmastime*)

Long ago, we
Hung up my
Mother's old

Nylons, and
Woke to find
Them swollen

With beige
Unnatural bulges,
Thigh to toe.

Nowadays, there
Are velvety
Crimson boots,

Brighter, and
Shapelier—but
A lot shorter.

Barbara Esbensen, 1994

Pencils

The rooms in a pencil
are narrow
but elephants   castles and watermelons
fit in

In a pencil
noisy words yell for attention
and quiet words wait their turn

How did they slip
into such a tight place?
Who
gives them their
lunch?

From a broken pencil
an unbroken poem will come!
There is a long story living
in the shortest pencil

Every word in your
pencil
is fearless ready to walk
the blue tightrope lines
Ready
to teeter and smile
down Ready to come right out
and show you
thinking!

Eloise Greenfield, 1997

Keepsake

Before Mrs. Williams died
She told Mr. Williams
When he gets home
To get a nickel out of her
Navy blue pocketbook
And give it to her
Sweet little gingerbread girl
That's me

I ain't never going to spend it

X. J. Kennedy, 2000

The Kite That Braved Old Orchard Beach

The kite that braved Old Orchard Beach
    But fell and snapped its spine
Hangs in our attic out of reach,
    All tangled in its twine.
My father says, "Let's throw it out,"
    But I won't let him. No,
There has to be some quiet spot
    Where cracked-up heroes go.

Mary Ann Hoberman, 2003

Night

The night is coming softly, slowly;
Look, it's getting hard to see.
    Through the windows,

Through the door,
Pussyfooting
On the floor,
Dragging shadows,
Crawling,
Creeping,
Pull down the shades.
Turn on the light.
Let's pretend it isn't night.

Nikki Grimes, 2006

Music Lesson

The choir paints
the sanctuary walls
with bands of sound
more glorious than gold
And all around
the altar, voices raise
In matchless harmonies
of perfect praise—

Perfect, except
for Mom, who tonelessly
expands the meaning of
the phrase "off-key."

She swears I'll miss
her singing when she's gone.
Says she, "Not all folks get
the gift of song."

That may be true,
But miss her singing? *Wrong.*

Lee Bennett Hopkins, 2009

When I Dance

When I dance
caterpillars boogie
into butterflies
wild geese disco
lighting up
skies

the worn-down moon
taps
till it's new
millions of stars

twirl
into view

When I dance
winters
pirouette
to springs—

When I dance
the
whole
wide
world

whirls—
and
sings.

Just before publication of this edition it was announced that J. Patrick Lewis won the 2011 NCTE Poetry Award. Unfortunately it was too late for us to include one of his poems in this edition.

Forms of Poetry

Poetry is distinguishable from prose primarily because of its distinct patterns or forms. The variety of patterns, in turn, distinguishes one form of poetry from another. Of the many forms of poetry, here are a few teachers commonly use in elementary school.

- **Narrative poems.** Narrative poems tell stories. Children usually enjoy narrative poetry because they are naturally attuned to stories and because it is easy to understand. A classic example is Henry Wadsworth Longfellow's "The Midnight Ride of Paul Revere," available in a picture book version (2001) handsomely illustrated by Christopher Bing. Ballads are narrative poems adapted for singing or for creating a musical effect, such as the popular American ballad "On Top of Old Smoky."
- **Lyric poems.** Lyric poetry is melodic or songlike. Generally, it is descriptive, focusing on personal moments or feelings or image-laden scenes. John Ciardi's poem "How to Tell the Top of a Hill" (1982) is an example of a lyric poem (see p. 92).
- **Limericks.** Limericks are humorous poems that were popularized with the publication of Edward Lear's *Book of Nonsense* in 1846 (1863 American edition). The rhyming scheme and verse pattern of limericks are familiar to most children:

A thrifty young fellow of Shoreham
Made brown paper trousers and woreham;
He looked nice and neat
Till he bent in the street
To pick up a pin; then he toreham.

Anonymous

- **Haiku.** As described earlier in this chapter, haiku has a total of 17 syllables (a line of 5 syllables, a line of 7 syllables, and another line of 5 syllables). Refer to "Why Children May Learn to Dislike Poetry," earlier in this chapter, for an example and further description.
- **Concrete poems.** A concrete poem is written or printed on the page in a shape representing the poem's subject. It is a form of poetry that is meant to be seen even more than heard and often does not have a rhyming scheme or a particular rhythm:

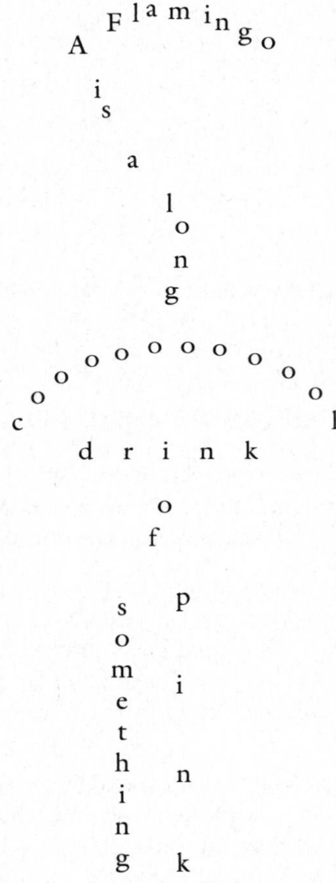

J. Patrick Lewis

- **Free verse.** Free verse, though relying on rhythm and cadence for its poetic form, is mostly unrhymed and lacks a consistent rhythm. Its topics are typically quite philosophical or abstract but intriguing. The poems presented in this chapter by Harold Munro (p. 88) and Valerie Worth (pp. 94) are examples of free verse.

• **Additional poetic forms.** For child-friendly information about 52 forms and/or elements of poetry, see the Avis Harley books mentioned earlier. Also, see Paul Janeczko's picture book, *A Kick in the Head: An Everyday Guide to Poetic Forms* (2005).

Building a Poetry Collection

A poetry collection should include poems that meet the needs of children who are in the process of developing an appreciation of poetry. This means building a collection filled with a variety of poems to match differing tastes and levels of sophistication: light and humorous verse, poems that create vivid images or express hard-to-communicate feelings, story poems, or poetry that plays with the sounds of language.

Do not rely on textbooks to supply poetry for your classroom. Because poems (and other literary works) are protected by copyright laws for the author's lifetime plus 70 years, textbook companies and other anthologizers may choose poems that are old enough to be in the public domain and therefore can be obtained at no cost. Although some old poems appeal to modern children, more contemporary works generally have a stronger draw for today's young reader. A second reason not to rely on textbooks is that some of today's texts may include little or no poetry (Roe, Cuellar, & Fickle, 2004).

The world of children's books offers teachers an almost endless supply of poetry. The reading list at the end of this chapter is representative of the excellent collections available that provide a broad range of poetry to meet every need. Many books of poetry are collections of a single poet's work. (Note collections by the NCTE Poetry Award winners.) However, some fine general anthologies are also listed, such as *The Random House Book of Poetry* (compiled by Jack Prelutsky, 1983) and *Poetry by Heart* (compiled by Liz Attenborough, 2001). Both books have themed sections, such as a collection of scary poems or animal poems, and provide a balance of modern and traditional poets. *The Random House Book of Poetry* contains 579 poems, and although *Poetry by Heart* has considerably fewer poems, it is illustrated by a variety of talented artists. Other useful anthologies include Jack Prelutsky's *The Twentieth Century Children's Poetry Treasury* (1999), Ivan and Mal Jones's *Good Night, Sleep Tight* (2000), Belinda Hollyer's *The Kingfisher Book of Family Poems* (2003), Jane Yolen and Andrew Peters's *Here's a Little Poem: A Very First Book of Poetry* (2007), and *Julie Andrews' Collection of Poems, Songs, and Lullabies* (with Emma Walton Hamilton) (2009).

A number of specialized anthologies appear in the reading list as well. These collections contain poems about a particular topic, written by a variety of poets. Myra Cohn Livingston has created perhaps more specialized poetry collections than anyone else. Examples of her titles include *Cat Poems* (1987a), *Poems for Mothers* (1988), *Birthday Poems* (1989a), *Halloween Poems* (1989b), *Valentine Poems* (1987b), *Poems for Jewish Holidays* (1986), *Animal, Vegetable, Mineral: Poems about Small Things* (1994), and *Cricket Never Does: A Collection of Haiku and Tanka* (1997). Jane Yolen, Lee Bennett Hopkins, and Jack Prelutsky also have compiled many specialized anthologies. Some of the Hopkins collections, for instance, align with the public school curricula: *Marvelous Math: A Book of Poems* (1997), *Spectacular Science: A Book of Poems* (1999), *Got Geography! Poems* (2006), *America at War* (2008), and so on.

The single-poem picture book is another variety of poetry book that is particularly useful for giving children a taste of the more traditional and sometimes more sophisticated poet. For example, Susan Jeffers has illustrated a stunning picture book version of *Stopping by Woods on a Snowy Evening* by Robert Frost (1978), which will attract the most reluctant poetry reader. Other examples include *The Tyger* (1993) by William Blake (illustrated by Neil Waldman), *The Rime of the Ancient Mariner* (1992) by Samuel Taylor Coleridge (illustrated by Ed Young), and *My People* (2009) by Langston Hughes (photographs by Charles R. Smith).

Teachers who do not know the world of children's poetry have a responsibility not only to discover the bounty that awaits them but also to use it to help stem the tide of ambivalence toward poetry among their students. A well-rounded classroom and school library poetry collection will have something for everyone. By sharing and enjoying poetry frequently, teachers and children together will build a lifelong appreciation, as the following poem by Eloise Greenfield expresses.

Things

Went to the corner
Walked in the store
Bought me some candy
Ain't got it no more
Ain't got it no more

Went to the beach
Played on the shore
Built me a sandhouse
Ain't got it no more
Ain't got it no more

Went to the kitchen
Lay down on the floor
Made me a poem
Still got it
Still got it

Poetry Reading Lists

Fifteen of Our Favorites

Ciardi, John. 1962. *You Read to Me, I'll Read to You.* Illustrated by Edward Gorey. Lippincott. Designed so that the child reads the poem on one page and the adult reads the poem on the next page. A collection mostly of humorous verse.

de Regniers, Beatrice Schenk, Eva Moore, Mary Michaels White, and Jean Carr, compilers. 1988. *Sing a Song of Popcorn.* Illustrated by nine Caldecott Award–winning artists. Scholastic. A collection of poems by a variety of well-known poets with illustrations by nine Caldecott medalists.

Esbensen, Barbara. 1992. *Who Shrank My Grandmother's House?* Illustrated by Eric Beddows. Harper. A collection of poems about childhood discoveries concerning everyday objects and things.

Fleischman, Paul. 1988. *Joyful Noise: Poems for Two Voices.* Illustrated by Eric Beddows. Harper. A collection of poems (divided into two columns to be read together by two people) describing the characteristics and activities of a variety of insects. Winner of the Newbery Medal.

Harley, Avis. 2000. *Fly with Poetry: An ABC of Poetry.* Wordsong/Boyds Mills Press. Harley

defines and provides examples of 26 poetry forms, one for each letter of the alphabet: acrostic, blank verse, cinquain, and so on.

Hopkins, Lee Bennett, compiler. 2009. *Incredible Inventions.* Illustrated by Julia Sarcone-Roach. Greenwillow. Sixteen inventions—such as the roller coaster, blue jeans, and Popsicles—are highlighted in 16 poems penned mostly by well-known contemporary children's poets.

Lewis, J. Patrick. 2006. *Once Upon a Tomb: Gravely Humorous Verses.* Illustrated by Simon Bartram. Candlewick. This volume contains darkly humorous poems about death.

Merriam, Eve. 2002. (1987). *Spooky ABC.* Illustrated by Lane Smith. Macmillan. Each letter of the alphabet introduces a different spooky aspect of Halloween.

Nelson, Marilyn. 2009. *Sweethearts of Rhythm: The Story of the Greatest All-Girl Swing Band in the World.* Illustrated by Jerry Pinkney. Dial. In the 1940s, as the world was at war, a remarkable female, African American jazz band performed on the American home front. Their story is told in thought-provoking poems and arresting images.

Prelutsky, Jack. 1984. *The New Kid on the Block.* Illustrated by James Stevenson. Greenwillow. Humorous poems about such strange creatures and people as Baloney Belly Billy and the Gloopy Gloopers.

Schertle, Alice. 1996. *Keepers.* Illustrated by Ted Rand. Lothrop. A collection of poems about personal mementos that bring to mind special moments and feelings.

Siebert, Diane. 2006. *Tour America: A Journey Through Poems and Art.* Illustrated by Stephen T. Johnson. Chronicle Books. Mixed-media artwork and poems evoke familiar and unfamiliar places throughout the United States, including Kentucky's famed Derby, Florida's Everglades, and the Oregon vortex.

Singer, Marilyn. 2010. *Mirror Mirror: A Book of Reversible Verse.* Illustrated by Josée Massee. Dutton. A collection of short poems that when reversed provide new perspectives on the fairy tale characters they feature.

Thayer, Ernest Lawrence. 2000. *Casey at the Bat: A Ballad of the Republic Sung in the Year 1888.* Illustrated by Christopher Bing. Handprint. This rendition of Thayer's immortal poem about baseball hero Casey, who strikes out and loses the big game, is illustrated with reproductions of artifacts, newspaper clippings, photographs, and other late-19th-century memorabilia (ticket stubs, coins, medals, baseball cards).

Yolen, Jane, & Andrew Fusek Peters. 2007. *Here's a Little Poem: A Very First Book of Poetry.* Illustrated by Polly Dunbar. Candlewick. These poems for the very young, one per page, are arranged in four categories: "Me, Myself, and I," "Who Lives in My House?," "I Go Outside," and "Time for Bed."

Others We Like

Andrews, Julie, and Emma Walton Hamilton. 2009. *Julie Andrews' Collection of Poems, Songs, and Lullabies.* Illustrated by James McMullan. Little, Brown. Julie Andrews and Emma Walton Hamilton have selected a mix of their most cherished poems, songs, and lullabies in this diverse poetry collection containing nearly 150 works.

Attenborough, Liz. 2001. *Poetry by Heart: A Child's Book of Poems to Remember.* Scholastic. The more than 100 poems are arranged thematically into nine sections, and each one is illustrated by a different artist.

Cullinan, Bernice E., ed. 1996. *A Jar of Tiny Stars: Poems by NCTE Award–Winning Poets.* Illustrated by Andi MacLeod and Marc Nadel. Wordsong/Boyds Mills. A collection of poems by the winners of the National Council of Teachers of English Award for Poetry for Children, including David McCord, Aileen Fisher, Karla Kuskin, Myra Cohn Livingston, Eve Merriam, John Ciardi, Lilian Moore, Arnold Adoff, Valerie Worth, and Barbara Esbensen.

de la Mare, Walter. 2002 (1947). *Rhymes and Verse: Collected Poems for Young People.* Illustrated by Elinore Blaisdell. Holt. "Only the rarest kind of best in anything can be good enough for the young," wrote Walter de la Mare, and this handsome reissue of an anthology of all his poems for children offers the "rarest kind of best" to a new generation of young people.

Dotlich, Rebecca Kai. 2004. *Over in the Pink House: New Jump Rope Rhymes.* Illustrated by Melanie Hall. Wordsong/Boyds Mills. Appropriate for

reading or chanting aloud while jumping rope, each poem has a lighthearted, whimsical quality.

Esbensen, Barbara Juster. 1995. *Dance with Me.* Illustrated by Megan Lloyd. Harper. A collection of poems depicting the dance of nature.

Fisher, Aileen. 2002. *I Heard a Bluebird Sing.* Illustrated by Jennifer Emery. Wordsong/Boyds Mills. Children selected their favorite Fisher poems to be included in this anthology. Sometimes funny, sometimes poignant, the selections speak from a child's perspective.

Florian, Douglas. 2009. *Dinothesaurus.* Atheneum. Accompanied with appropriately primitive-style dinosaur art, these 20 tongue-in-cheek paleontological poems also provide readers with information about dinosaurs.

Fox, Dan, ed. 2003. *A Treasury of Children's Songs: Forty Favorites to Sings and Play.* The Metropolitan Museum of Art/Holt. In this songbook, 40 classic childhood songs are imaginatively illustrated with treasures from the Metropolitan Museum of Art.

Greenfield, Eloise. 1978. *Honey, I Love and Other Poems.* Illustrated by Leo and Diane Dillon. Harper. To one young narrator, it's the simple things that mean the most, like sharing laughter with a friend, taking family rides in the country, and kissing her mama's arm.

Holbrook, Sara. 2002. *Wham! It's a Poetry Jam: Discovering Performance Poetry.* Wordsong/Boyds Mills. Using over 30 of her own poems as a guide, Sara Holbrook teaches readers how to present poetry with rhythm, movement, and a strong voice.

Hopkins, Lee Bennett. 2006. *Got Geography: Poems.* Illustrated by Philip Stanton. Greenwillow. Vivid poems by 16 poets show that geography isn't just about finding your way. It's the jumping-off point for dreams and imagination.

Janeczko, Paul B., ed. 2001. *A Poke in the I: A Collection of Concrete Poems.* Illustrated by Christopher Raschka. Candlewick. Concrete poems startle and delight the eye and mind, such as when the words form the shape of crows that fly off the page.

Janeczko, Paul B., and J. Patrick Lewis. 2006. *Wing Nuts: Screwy Haiku.* Illustrated by Tricia Tusa. Little, Brown. This hilarious collection of offbeat poetry introduces senryu, a cousin of haiku, and features poems that tackle a range of child-friendly subjects.

Kennedy, X. J. 1986. *Brats.* Illustrated by James Watt. Atheneum. Forty-two poems describe a variety of particularly unpleasant brats.

Kuskin, Karla. 2003. *Moon, Have You Met My Mother?* Illustrated by Sergio Ruzzier. Harper. This comprehensive collection by acclaimed poet Karla Kuskin contains her most celebrated poems as well as new works never before published.

Lewis, J. Patrick. 2005. *Please Bury Me in the Library.* Illustrated by Kyle M. Stone. Harcourt. This collection of original poems about books and reading ranges from sweet to silly to laugh-out-loud funny.

Lewis, J. Patrick. 2009. *The Underwear Salesman: Jobs for Better or Verse.* Illustrated by Serge Bloch. Atheneum. This pun-filled, rhyming survey of jobs, along with its collage illustrations, includes such laborers as the butcher named Sloppy Joe to the underwear salesman, whose sales pitch includes instructions to wear his garments "briefly."

McCord, David. 1977. *One at a Time.* Illustrated by Henry B. Kane. Little, Brown. This collection of poems includes topics such as nature, animals, favorite places, and colors.

Moore, Lilian. 2005. *Mural on Second Avenue and Other City Poems.* Illustrated by Roma Karas. Greenwillow. This collection of poems captures various aspects of life in the city.

Morrison, Lillian. 2001. *More Spice Than Sugar: Poems About Feisty Females.* Illustrated by Ann Boyajian. Houghton. In this collection of poems celebrating high-spirited girls and women, you will meet independent spirits—young rebels, hardy pioneers, mavericks, athletes, and heroines—who dared difficult tasks and who show the strength of the human spirit in the face of hardship.

Moses, Will. 2003. *Will Moses Mother Goose.* Philomel. Folk art paintings accompany this compilation of over 60 of the best-loved Mother Goose rhymes.

Nye, Naomi Shihab, ed. 2000. *Salting the Ocean: 100 Poems by Young Poets.* Illustrated by Ashley Bryan. Greenwillow. These poems were written by young people in grades 1 through 12.

Prelutsky, Jack. 1976. *Nightmares: Poems to Trouble Your Sleep.* Illustrated by Arnold Lobel.

Greenwillow. Here are 12 poems featuring the likes of a vampire, a werewolf, a ghoul, and other monsters.

Prelutsky, Jack, ed. 1999. *The Twentieth Century Children's Poetry Treasury.* Illustrated by Meilo So. Random House. Jack Prelutsky has collected 211 of his favorite poems by 137 poets, representing the best of children's verse from each decade of the 20th century.

Prelutsky, Jack. 2010. *The Carnival of the Animals by Camille Saint-Saëns: New Verses by Jack Prelutsky.* Illustrated by Mary GrandPré. Knopf. Prelutsky's verses, inspired by Camille Saint-Saëns' *The Carnival of the Animals,* are accompanied by an orchestral recording of the musical suite.

Rosen, Michael, ed. 1998. *Classic Poetry: An Illustrated Collection.* Illustrated by Paul Howard. Candlewick. A collection of favorite poems by such writers as William Shakespeare, Emily Dickinson, Edward Lear, Walt Whitman, and Langston Hughes includes a portrait and a brief biographical background of each poet.

Silverstein, Shel. 2009. *A Light in the Attic: Special Edition.* Silverstein's funny, sometimes irreverent poetry in this collection is augmented with 12 new, never-before-published poems.

Stevenson, Robert Louis. 2004. *A Child's Garden of Verses.* Compiled by Cooper Edens. Chronicle. A selection of eight poems from the famous collection illustrated with antique pictures by well-known illustrators of the late-19th and early-20th centuries.

Volavkova, H., ed. 1994. . . . *I Never Saw Another Butterfly: Children's Drawings and Poems from Terezin Concentration Camp, 1942–1944.* Random. In these poems and pictures written and drawn by the young inmates of Terezin concentration camp, we see the daily misery of these uprooted children, as well as their hopes and fears, their courage and optimism.

Worth, Valerie. 2002. *Peacock and Other Poems.* Illustrated by Natalie Babbitt. Farrar. Accompanied by Natalie Babbitt's fine pencil drawings, "Peacock" is joined by 26 other elegant poems by Worth about things as various as pandas and steam engines and icicles.

Worth, Valerie. 2007. *Animal Poems.* Illustrated by Steve Jenkins. Farrar. In this posthumously published collection are 23 animals poems accompanied with masterful cut-paper collages.

Easier to Read

Dakos, Kalli. 2003. *Put Your Eyes Up Here and Other School Poems.* Illustrated by G. Brian Karas. Simon and Schuster.

Hopkins, Lee Bennett, ed. 1987. *More Surprises.* Illustrated by Megan Lloyd. Harper.

Hopkins, Lee Bennett, ed. 1999. *Sports! Sports! Sports! A Poetry Collection.* Illustrated by Brian Floca. Harper.

Hopkins, Lee Bennett, ed. 2003. *A Pet for Me: Poems.* Illustrated by Jane Manning. Harper.

James, Simon. 2000. *Days Like This.* Candlewick.

Katz, Alan. 2008. *Oops!* McElderry.

Kuskin, Karla. 1992. *Soap Soup and Other Verses.* Harper.

Kuskin, Karla. 2004. *Under My Hood I Have a Hat.* Illustrated by Fumi Kosaka. Harper.

Lewis, J. Patrick. 2007. *Big Is Big (And Little, Little): A Book of Contrasts.* Illustrated by Bob Barner. Holiday House.

Livingston, Myra Cohn. 1990. *My Head Is Red and Other Riddle Rhymes.* Illustrated by Tere LoPrete. Dutton.

Lobel, Arnold. 2009. *Odd Owls & Stout Pigs: A Book of Nonsense.* Color by Adrianne Lobel. Harper.

Prelutsky, Jack. 2007. *Me I Am.* Illustrated by Christine Davenier. Farrar.

Prelutsky, Jack, compiler. 2009 (1983). *It's Valentine's Day.* Illustrated by Marilyn Hafner. Greenwillow/Harper.

Wilson, Karma. 2009. *What's the Weather Inside.* McElderry.

Zolotow, Charlotte. 2002. *Seasons: A Book of Poems.* Illustrated by Eric Blegvad. Harper.

Picture Books

Adoff, Arnold. 1973. *Black Is Brown Is Tan.* Illustrated by Emily Arnold McCully. Harper.

Baylor, Byrd. 1986. *I'm in Charge of Celebrations.* Illustrated by Peter Parnall. Scribner's.

Blake, William. 1993. *The Tyger.* Illustrated by Neil Waldman. Harcourt.

Ehlert, Lois. 2010. *Lots of Spots.* New York: Beach Lane.

Fehler, Gene. 2009. *Change-Up: Baseball Poems.* Illustrated by Donald Wu. Clarion.

Frost, Robert. 1978. *Stopping by Woods on a Snowy Evening.* Illustrated by Susan Jeffers. Dutton.

Gliori, Debi. 2009. *Stormy Weather.* Walker.

Kuskin, Karla. 2002. *The Animals and the Ark.* Illustrated by Michael Grejniec. Atheneum.

Lewis, J. Patrick. 2003. *The Snowflake Sisters.* Illustrated by Lisa Desimini. Atheneum.

Lewis, J. Patrick. 2009. *The House.* Illustrated by Roberto Innocenti. Creative Editions.

Longfellow, Henry Wadsworth. 1983. *Song of Hiawatha.* Illustrated by Susan Jeffers. Dial.

Longfellow, Henry Wadsworth. 2001. *The Midnight Ride of Paul Revere.* Illustrated by Christopher Bing. Handprint.

Nye, Naomi Shihab. 2003. *Baby Radar.* Illustrated by Nancy Carpenter. Greenwillow.

Prelutsky, Jack. 2001. *Awful Ogre's Awful Day.* Illustrated by Paul O. Zelinsky. Greenwillow.

Prelutsky, Jack. 2007. *Me I Am!* Illustrated by Christine Davenier. Farrar.

Schertle, Alice. 2004. *All You Need for a Beach.* Illustrated by Barbara Lavallee. Harcourt.

Service, Robert W. 1987. *The Cremation of Sam McGee.* Illustrated by Ted Harrison. Greenwillow.

Siebert, Diane. 1989. *Heartland.* Illustrated by Wendell Minor. Crowell.

Yolen, Jane. 2009. *The Scarecrow's Dance.* Illustrated by Bagram Ibatoulline. Simon and Schuster Children's Publishing.

PEARSON **myeducationkit**™

Go to the topic Poetry on the MyEducationKit for this text, where you can:

- Search the Database of Children's Literature, housing more than 22,000 titles searchable in every genre by authors or illustrators, by awards won, by year published, and by topic and description.
- Explore genre-related Assignments and Activities, assignable exercises showing concepts in action through database use, video, cases, and student and teacher artifacts.
- Listen to podcasts and read interviews from some of the brightest and most enduring stars of children's literature in the Conversations.
- Discover weblinks that will lead you to sites representing the authors you learn about in these pages, classrooms with powerful children's literature connections, and literature awards.

Chapter 9

Folklore: Stories from the Oral Tradition

Stories from the oral tradition had their beginnings around hearthside and campfire. These tales were almost always fantastic in nature, involving magic or talking animals. Originally, they provided entertainment for adults, who freely altered details as they told and retold the stories. As adults shared these stories with one another, children surely lounged about the fringes and listened. In modern times, many of the tales have shifted to being identified with children.

Folklore: A Part of Every Culture

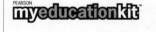

Because these stories were born in the oral tradition, no one knows who first told each tale and which version is the original. Therefore, folklore may be defined as stories that originated orally and have no authors. Given these qualities, we often associate these tales with a collector or reteller. Jacob and Wilhelm Grimm collected, retold, and recorded in print the European variants of some of the best-known traditional tales in our Western cultures, such as "Cinderella," "Sleeping Beauty," and "Little Red Riding Hood." Other collectors include Charles Perrault, who preceded the Brothers Grimm in collecting many of the European tales. He filed off the hard edges of the tales so that they would be more acceptable to the genteel folk of the French court of Louis XIV. Joseph Jacobs collected the British tales loved by young children, such as "The Three Little Pigs" and "The Little Red Hen." Peter Asbjørnsen and Jorgen Moe gathered the Scandinavian tales into a volume titled *East of the Sun and West of the Moon,* which included "The Three Billy Goats Gruff." (See Figure 9.1 for current retellers of traditional stories for children.)

Tales from the oral tradition are part of the fabric of every culture. *The 1001 Arabian Nights,* including the story of Aladdin, is a collection of the Scheherazade tales from the Middle East. Other collections of traditional tales from the Middle East include the Hodja stories from Turkey that tell of the wisdom of Nasreddin Hodja and the Jataka stories from India that are centered on the lives of Buddha. The masterful storytelling of Isaac Bashevis Singer has preserved much of the folklore of Jewish tradition. Tales of Asian, African, and Native American tradition abound and are available to children, most often in stunning picture book versions. (See the list of picture books at the conclusion of this chapter.)

Stories written by modern authors and patterned after traditional tales—such as the work of Hans Christian Andersen and Rudyard Kipling's collection of *Just-So Stories*—are often confused with traditional tales that have no known authors. However, these literary tales are *modern fantasy* stories, for they originated in written form.

Peculiarities of Folklore

Traditional stories differ in various ways from more modern writings and therefore are held to a different critical standard. For example, characters must be well developed in modern stories,

Notable Retellers and Illustrators of Traditional Stories

The names in this list include influential retellers and illustrators of traditional stories other than the pioneers who first preserved these tales in print (Brothers Grimm, Joseph Jacobs, Charles Perrault, and others).

Aardema, Verna (reteller): African folktales.
Bierhorst, John (reteller): Native American folktales.
Brown, Marcia (reteller and illustrator): Folktales from a variety of cultures.
Bruchac, Joseph (reteller): Native American folktales.
Demi (reteller and illustrator): Folk and fairy tales from eastern Europe and Asia.
Dillon, Leo, and Diane Dillon (illustrators): African folktales.
Evslin, Bernard (reteller): Greek myths.
Fisher, Leonard Everett (reteller and illustrator): Greek myths.
Hamilton, Virginia (reteller): Folktale collections, primarily African American.
Hutton, Warwick (reteller and illustrator): Bible stories.
Hyman, Trina Schart (illustrator): European fairy tales.
Kimmel, Eric (reteller): Folktales from around the world.
Martin, Rafe (reteller): Traditional tales from various cultures.
McDermott, Gerald (reteller and illustrator): Myths and folktales from various cultures.
San Souci, Robert D. (reteller): Myths and folktales from various cultures.
Singer, Isaac Bashevis (reteller): Jewish traditional tales.
Sutcliff, Rosemary (reteller): Arthurian and Greek myths and legends.
Yolen, Jane (reteller): Mostly European myths, legends, and fairy tales.
Young, Ed (reteller and illustrator): Asian folklore.
Zelinsky, Paul O. (reteller and illustrator): European fairy tales.
Zwerger, Lisbeth (illustrator): European fairy tales.

but in traditional tales character development is lean and spare. Think of Cinderella, for example. How rounded is her character? We know very little about her. How does she feel about her ill treatment? About her change in fortune? What are her interests? We don't even know much about her physical appearance. If listeners and readers are told about her personality or thoughts, it is only in general terms: "She wept at her mother's grave."

Characters in traditional stories generally are archetypes; they are meant to be symbolic of certain basic human traits, such as good and evil. So, instead of the gradations of character in modern stories, where a character may reveal the mix of good and bad in all of us, in traditional tales we find single-faceted characters who typically do not change during the course of the story. Traditional tales, then, are stories of the human experience told in primary colors, the nuances of life stripped away to reveal the basic component parts: love, fear, greed, jealousy, mercy, and so on. Therefore, traditional stories from around the world are basically alike because fundamental human characteristics and motivations are universal.

Plots are also simple and direct in folklore. And because the tales generally were told by and among the common folk, they are often success stories that show the underdog making good—the youngest son or daughter, the little tailor, unwanted children, and so on. And success is often obtained against overwhelming odds, such as accomplishing an impossible task (spinning straw into gold, slaying invincible monsters).

These story lines are accompanied by typical themes, such as the rewards of mercy, kindness, and perseverance; justice, particularly the punishment of evil; and the power of love. Settings are quickly established and always in the distant past ("Once upon a time . . ."), and time passes quickly (Sleeping Beauty's 100 years of rest pass in a flash). Another hallmark of traditional stories is repeated patterns or elements. The magical number three appears frequently in tales: Rumpelstiltskin's three evenings of spinning straw into gold, Cinderella's three visits to the ball, Jack's three trips up the beanstalk. Or a refrain is repeated throughout the story: "Fee, fi, fo, fum. I smell the blood of an Englishman."

The Universal Nature of Folklore

Although tales certainly vary from culture to culture, it is amazing how alike in form they are—how the basic sorts of literary elements are similar in Chinese stories, in stories from Native American tribes, and in stories from Europe (Frye, 1964). Because traditional tales deal with such basic human experiences, stories like "Cinderella" have surfaced in nearly every part of the world. The variants are different in setting and detail, but a fascinating sameness still exists. "Cinderella" variants include *Yeh-Shen* (1990; Chinese) retold by Ai-Ling Louie, *The Egyptian Cinderella* (1989; Egyptian) by Shirley Climo, *The Rough-Face Girl* (1992; Native American) by Rafe Martin, *Mufaro's Beautiful Daughters* (1987; African) by John Steptoe, *The Gift of the Crocodile* (2000; Indonesian) by Judy Sierra, and *Cinderella* (2005; French) by Barbara McClintock, to mention a few.

Another example of the pervasiveness of traditional stories in modern literature (and conversation) is the almost constant use of allusions to traditional literature. Often we speak and write using a sort of old-tale shorthand. It is a part of the cultural cement that binds us together. We nod knowingly when someone says or writes "Misery loves company" or "You are judged by the company you keep." Both maxims come from Aesop, who either collected most of his fables from more ancient oral sources or, as some scholars believe, did not exist at all. The Greek myths and European variants of the fairy tales are alluded to continually in novels written by authors from Western cultures. Note the distinct part Red Riding Hood plays in Lois Lowry's Newbery-winning historical novel, *Number the Stars* (1989), which takes place during World War II. As Anna makes her way through the woods with a basket of food containing a hidden packet of chemicals designed to disarm the wolf's, or rather the guard dogs', ability to smell the Danish escapees, she suddenly feels as if she's walked this way before.

> The handle of the straw basket scratched her arm through her sweater. She shifted it and tried to run. She thought of a story she had often told to Kirsti as they cuddled in bed at night. "Once upon a time there was a little girl," she told herself silently, "who had a beautiful red cloak." (pp. 106–107)

In fact, we are surrounded by such allusions. We write with Venus pencils; clean with Ajax cleanser; drive on Atlas tires; use words like *volcano, furious, cereal, music;* describe the human body and mind with terms like *Achilles tendon* and *Narcissus complex;* name the planets, the days of the week, and the cities of the world (*Mars, Saturday, Atlanta*)—all from Greek and Roman myths. Perhaps one of the clearest examples of the way the old tales provide a cultural cement is evident in newspaper and magazine cartoons. The political cartoon shown in Figure 9.2 was published in the *Chicago Tribune* when a number of day-care centers in the Chicago area were charged with child abuse and molestation. Because "Hansel and Gretel" is basic to our literary culture, the cartoon needs no caption.

Without Our Common Knowledge of Folktales, This Cartoon Has No Meaning

However simple and straightforward folklore may seem, it is the mother of all literature. There are literally no character types, basic plots, or themes that have not been explored in the oral tradition. Indeed, noted child psychologist Bruno Bettelheim (1977) believed that no other literature better prepares children to meet the complexities of adult life. Folklore is a wonderful metaphor for human existence, and because of its rich imagery and dreamlike quality, it speaks to us deeply. And unless these stories have been dumbed down for printing in educational reading materials or oversimplified picture books, traditional tales are a blueprint for rich, masterful language. (See the example from Randall Jarrell's translation of the Grimm Brothers' *Snow-White and the Seven Dwarfs* in Chapter 3.)

The Values of Fantasy

Besides giving us modern readers a common ground for communicating, folklore—in fact, fantasy literature in general—offers us certain benefits that realistic fiction cannot supply with quite the same power. Lloyd Alexander (1968b), who has drawn liberally from the well of ancient stories to write his modern high-fantasy books, encapsulates these benefits into four notable points:

> First, on the very surface of it, the sheer delight of "let's pretend" and the eager suspension of disbelief; excitement, wonder, astonishment. There is an exuberance in good fantasy quite unlike the most exalted moments of realistic fiction. Both forms have similar goals; but realism walks where fantasy dances. . . .
>
> [Second, fantasy has the] ability to work on our emotions with the same vividness as a dream. The fantasy adventure seems always on a larger scale, the deeds bolder, the people brighter. Reading a fantasy, we never get disinterested bystanders. To get the most from it, we have to, in the best sense of the phrase, "lose our cool. . . ."
>
> Another value of fantasy [is its ability to develop a capacity for belief]. . . . In dealing with delinquency—I do not mean the delinquency that poverty breeds, but the kind of cold-hearted emptiness and apathy of "well-to-do," solid middle-class delinquents—one of the heart-breaking problems is interesting these young people in something. In anything. They value nothing because they have never had the experience of valuing anything. They have developed no *capacity* for believing anything to be really worthwhile.
>
> I emphasize the word *capacity* because, in a sense, the capacity to value, to believe, is separate from the values or beliefs themselves. Our values and beliefs can change. The capacity remains.
>
> Whether the object of value is Santa Claus or Sunday school, the Prophet Elijah or Arthur, the Once and Future King, does not make too much difference. Having once believed wholeheartedly in something, we seldom lose the ability to believe. . . .
>
> Perhaps, finally, the ability to hope is more important than the ability to believe. . . . Hope is one of the most precious human values fantasy can offer us—and offer us in abundance. Whatever the hardships of the journey, the days of despair, fantasy implicitly promises to lead us through them. Hope is an essential thread in the fabric of all fantasies, an Ariadne's thread to guide us out of the labyrinth, the last treasure in Pandora's box.

Types of Folklore

Categories of any genre of literature are never cast in concrete. People will never agree on category names or on whether certain stories belong under certain category headings. Folklore is no different in this respect. However, we will present our view of what constitutes traditional stories, keeping in mind that this list is mostly a tool for introducing you to the stories themselves.

Folktales

Quite rightly, all traditional stories could be called *folktales* or *stories of the people.* We will use this heading to encompass a number of stories that are the most general or universal in nature. The most common kinds of folktales follow.

- *Cumulative tales.* These stories are "added upon" as the telling unfolds. Typically, the story is told up to a certain point, then begun again from near the beginning and told until a new segment is added. Then the teller starts again and again, each time adding a new wrinkle to the story, expanding a chain of events or a list of participants. Probably the best-known examples are the reasonably simple cumulative tale "The House That Jack Built" and the folk song "I Know an Old Lady Who Swallowed a Fly."
- *Pourquoi tales. Pourquoi* means "why" in French. These folktales answer questions or give explanations for the way things are, particularly in nature. Examples are "Why the Bear Is Stumpy-Tailed" and *Why Mosquitoes Buzz in People's Ears* (1975), as retold by Verna Aardema.
- *Beast tales.* Their distinction is simple: Beast tales are stories with animals as the principal players. The animals typically represent humans and are therefore anthropomorphized, such as the animals in "The Three Little Pigs" and "The Three Billy Goats Gruff."
- *Trickster tales.* Often a variety of beast tale, the trickster tale features a character who outsmarts everyone else in the story. Sometimes the trickster is sly and mischievous (Br'er Rabbit from the Uncle Remus stories). In other stories, the trickster is wise and helpful, as with some of the Anansi the Spider folktales from Africa (see the Caldecott-winning *A Story, a Story* by Gail Haley, 1970). Other examples include Gerald McDermott's Native American trickster tales, such as *Raven* (1993), *Jabuti the Tortoise* (2001), and *Pig-Boy: A Trickster Tale from Hawai'i* (2009).
- *Noodlehead, or numbskull, tales.* These humorous stories center on the escapades of characters who are not too bright. Sometimes they really make a mess of things with their incredibly stupid mistakes, as in the story "Epaminondas," in which a silly boy nearly destroys a number of items placed in his charge because he follows the wrong instructions for their care. For example, he is told to wrap butter in leaves and dip it in cool water to keep it in good shape. But then he uses those instructions with a puppy. In other stories, such as the Grimms' "Hans in Luck," the simpleton stumbles merrily through life, coming out on top only because of providence.
- *Realistic tales.* Realistic tales seem to have their basis in an actual historical event or to feature an actual figure from history. These folktales have few, if any, elements of fantasy. An example is "Dick Whittington's Cat," the story of a country boy who goes to London during the reign of King Edward III. Dick, who makes his fortune because his cat is such a fine mouser, later goes on to become the mayor of London. Though the tale is likely fictional, the real Dick Whittington did, indeed, become London's mayor, as well as the town's sheriff.
- *Fairy tales.* Of all the folktales, the fairy tale, or wonder tale, is the most magical. In fairy tales, we see enchantments that go beyond talking animals to fairy godmothers, wicked witches, magical objects (mirrors, cloaks, swords, rings), and the like. (See Chapter 10 for a discussion

of fantasy motifs.) Fairy tales are extremely popular with young listeners and readers. "Snow White," "Cinderella," "Sleeping Beauty," "Beauty and the Beast," and "Aladdin and His Wonderful Lamp" are a few examples of well-known fairy tales.

Tall Tales

Exaggeration is the major stylistic element in tall tales. Many tall tales grew out of the push to open the North American continent to settlement. Tall-tale characters—such as Paul Bunyan, Pecos Bill, Johnny Appleseed, John Henry, and Old Stormalong—were based either on actual people or on a composite of rough-and-tumble lumberjacks, sailors, or cowboys. Tall tales, of course, exist beyond our American culture. For instance, the Chinese tale "The Seven [or Five] Chinese Brothers" tells of several brothers who use amazing talents, such as the ability to swallow an entire sea, to ward off the conquests of an evil emperor.

Fables

Fables are brief stories meant to teach a lesson, and they usually conclude with a moral, such as "A bird in the hand is worth two in the bush" or "Haste makes waste." Besides the well-known collection of Aesop's fables from Greece, there are fables in ancient Egyptian culture, in the *Panchatantra* and the Jataka stories from India, plus a collection of fables by French poet Jean de La Fontaine. John Bierhorst (1987) presents a collection of Native American fables in his picture book titled *Doctor Coyote: A Native American Aesop's Fables.*

Myths

Myths grew out of early people's need to understand and explain the world around them and their own existence; they therefore recount the creation of the world and tell of the gods and goddesses who control the fate of humans. Many myths are similar to pourquoi folktales because they explain nature. For example, the Greek myth of Apollo explains how and why the sun travels across the sky each day. Gerald McDermott's *Musicians of the Sun* (1997), a retelling of an Aztec myth, explains how music and color came into the world. Every culture has its myths, although the Greek myths are perhaps the best known in Western cultures. The international flavor of mythology is evident in Virginia Hamilton's Newbery Honor–winning collection of creation myths, *In the Beginning: Creation Stories from around the World* (1988).

One variety of myth focuses on the heroic quest rather than on the mysteries of planet Earth. The hero myth, such as the story "Jason and the Argonauts," is a grand adventure that usually involves the intervention of heavenly beings. The hero myth is related to the epic.

Epics, Ballads, and Legends

The lines separating epics, ballads, and legends tend to blur. The unifying feature is the hero tale, including hero myths, but epics, ballads, and legends also have distinguishing qualities.

- Epics are lengthy hero tales or even a series of tales focusing on a hero. Examples are the tales of the Trojan War (*The Iliad*) and the return of Odysseus (Ulysses) from Troy to his home in Ithaca (*The Odyssey*). Both of these epics are also steeped in the mythology of ancient Greece. *Beowulf,* the most famous piece of Old English literature, is another well-known epic.

- Ballads are typically hero stories in poetic form. Both *The Iliad* and *The Odyssey* are epic poems supposedly composed by the blind poet Homer, whose existence is doubted by some scholars, although others regard him as the recorder of a much-retold set of tales. In Europe, the bards of old traveled from stronghold to stronghold, entertaining the people by singing ballads about local mythological and legendary heroes.
- The heroes in legends are rooted a bit more firmly in history. So *The Iliad* could be considered an epic and a legendary ballad, since the Greeks actually laid seige to Troy. King Arthur also lives in epic, ballad, and legend. There are mythic stories of Arthur as well as historical accounts that indicate that he indeed existed and unified the British tribes around 500 C.E. Robin Hood, though probably more thief than hero, is a character from ballad and legend. Of course, legendary characters also appear in the tall tales of North America (Mike Fink, Davy Crockett, Johnny Appleseed, John Henry, Casey Jones) and in realistic folktales.

Religious Stories

Classifying religious stories as folklore or myth may bother many people, but *myth* in this sense can be broadly defined as the human quest to discover and share truth concerning the spiritual aspects of existence. However, we tend to label religious beliefs no longer practiced in modern society (worship of the ancient Greek pantheon) as myths, while using the term *religious stories* for tales derived from currently practiced faiths (stories from the sacred writings of Buddhism, Christianity, Hinduism, Islam, and so on).

Books and stories in this category include parables and Old Testament stories, as well as any number of legends or apocryphal tales with religious connections, such as Ruth Robbins's Caldecott-winning *Baboushka and the Three Kings* (1960) and Tomie dePaola's *The Legend of Old Befana* (1980)—both variants of a Christmas story about an old woman too busy to follow the Three Wise Men. Other examples of religious stories include *Buddha Stories* (1997), the Jataka tales retold by Demi; *And the Earth Trembled* (1996), an Islamic version of the creation of Adam and Eve by Shulamith Levey Oppenheim; *Rama: A Legend* (1994) by Jamake Highwater, a novel based on a Hindu epic; *Creation* (2003) by Gerald McDermott; and *The Miracle of Hanukkah* (2006) by Seymour Chwast.

In Defense of Folk and Fairy Tales

"About once every hundred years some wiseacre gets up and tries to banish the fairy tale. Perhaps I had better say a few words in its defence, as reading for children" (Lewis, 1980, p. 213). These words by C. S. Lewis, who is known for his enduring fantasy series, the Chronicles of Narnia, were written as part of his defense of traditional tales in 1952. Yet in far less than 100 years—in fact, on a regular basis—"wiseacres" have been attempting to censor traditional stories. We have already discussed the importance of fairy and folktales but now wish to provide some responses to the major complaints voiced against traditional literature. These objections, as addressed by

Lewis, mainly fall into four categories: psychological fantasy, violence, frightening for young children, and waste of time (Tunnell, 1994).

Psychological Fantasy

Some adults fear that fantasy stories will lead children to be somehow out of touch with reality—to suffer from fantasy in the clinical, psychological sense of the word. Psychological fantasy—the inability of the mind to distinguish what is real—does not result from reading literary fantasy. In fact, children who read stories that contain unrealistic elements—animals that talk, magical events, time travel—are actually less at risk of losing touch with the realities of daily life. Bruno Bettelheim (1977) confirmed this position when he said that fairy stories are not only safe for children but also necessary and that children deprived of a rich fantasy life (which traditional tales provide) are more likely to seek a psychological escape through avenues such as black magic, drugs, and astrology. Through fairy tales and folktales, children may vicariously vent the frustrations of being a child controlled by an adult world, for they subconsciously identify with the heroes of the stories, who are often the youngest, smallest, least powerful characters (Hansel and Gretel, Cinderella, Aladdin). They also are given a sense of hope about their ultimate abilities to succeed in the world.

C. S. Lewis goes a step further, believing that certain realistic stories are far more likely to cause problems than good fantasy stories. He points to adult reading as an example:

> The dangerous fantasy is always superficially realistic. The real victim of wishful reverie . . . prefers stories about millionaires, irresistible beauties, posh hotels, palm beaches, and bedroom scenes—things that really might happen, that ought to happen, that would have happened if the reader had had a fair chance. . . . [T]here are two kinds of longing. The one is an askesis, a spiritual exercise, and the other is a disease. (1980, p. 215)

Violence

Critics suggest that violent acts in some traditional tales will breed violence in young children. The work of psychologist Ephraim Biblow shows how wrong-minded this sort of thinking is. In his experimental study, Biblow (1973) showed that children with rich fantasy lives responded to aggressive films with a significant decrease in aggressive behavior, while low-fantasy children showed a tendency toward increased aggression.

> The low-fantasy child, as observed during play, presented himself as more motorically oriented, revealed much action and little thought in play activities. The high-fantasy child in contrast was more highly structured and creative and tended to be verbally rather than physically aggressive. (p. 128)

Much of the violence in fairy and folktales involves the punishment of truly evil villains. Children are concerned from an early age with the ramifications of good and bad behavior, which is represented in fundamental, archetypal ways in traditional stories. Lawrence Kohlberg's stages of moral development describe the young child as being in the premoral stage (up to about 8 years), which basically means that "the child believes that evil behavior is likely to be punished and good behavior is based on obedience or avoidance of evil implicit in disobedience" (Lefrancois 1986, p. 446). According to Bettelheim (1977), the evil person in fairy tales who meets a well-deserved fate satisfies a child's deep need for justice to prevail. Sometimes this requires destroying the evil altogether.

Violence in movies and many books cannot be equated with the violence in fairy and folktales. Even in the Grimms' version of "Cinderella," one of the bloodiest of fairy stories, the violent acts are surprisingly understated. Both truly wicked stepsisters mutilate themselves (a trimmed heel and a cut-off toe) to make the slipper fit and are revealed by the blood. Later, birds peck out their eyes as punishment for their treachery. Yet the tale simply, compactly states the fact of each violent act. We don't read of viscous fluid streaming down faces or blood spurting on walls and floors. That's the stuff of slasher horror movies and violent video games, sensationalism designed to shock or titillate, but not a careful comment on justice.

Frightening for Young Children

Many adults worry that some of the traditional tales will frighten children, causing nightmares and other sorts of distress. However, because dangerous story elements, such as wicked witches and dragons, are far removed in both time and place from the lives of children, they prove much less frightening than realistic stories of danger that focus on real-life fears (Smith, 1989). C. S. Lewis (1982, p. 39) shared with us his greatest real-life fear as a child—the irrational, nightmare-inducing fear of insects. But he also went on to say that there was little his parents could have done (or undone) to save him "from the pincers, mandibles, and eyes of those many-legged abominations." He believed that it is impossible to predict what will frighten one child in this sort of phobic manner as compared to another, but he was certain that insulating a child completely from fear is a disservice.

> Those who say children must not be frightened may mean two things. They may mean (1) that we must not do anything likely to give the child those haunting, disabling, pathological fears against which ordinary courage is helpless: in fact, *phobias.* His mind must, if possible, be kept clear of things he can't bear to think of. Or they may mean (2) that we must try to keep out of his mind the knowledge that he is born into a world of death, violence, wounds, adventure, heroism and cowardice, good and evil. If they mean the first, I agree with them: but not if they mean the second. The second would indeed be to give children a false impression and feed them on escapism in the bad sense. . . . Since it is so likely they will meet cruel enemies, let them at least have heard of brave knights and heroic courage. Otherwise you are making their destiny not bright but darker. (Lewis, 1982, p. 39)

Fairy and folktales provide children a message of hope. No matter how bleak the outlook or how dark the path, these stories promise children that it is possible to make it through and come out on top. In fact, children who recoil from strong images of danger in fairy tales have the most to gain from the exposure (Smith, 1989).

Some adults feel they can circumvent the problem of frightening children by choosing softened versions of fairy and folktales. This approach may have the opposite effect, causing children to become more distressed. Trousdale (1989) tells the story of a mother who used only the softened version of "The Three Little Pigs" with her young daughter. In this version, the pigs are not eaten, and the wolf is not killed in boiling water. Instead, he comes down the chimney, burns his derriere, rockets up the chimney, and disappears into the sunset, never to be seen again. The little girl said, "He's gonna come back" and began to have nightmares. Trousdale (p. 77) advised the child's mother to read the Joseph Jacobs version, in which the wolf dies; Trousdale soon received a letter that said, "Well, we put the Big Bad Wolf to rest." The evil was destroyed and thus the threat eliminated. The nightmares stopped. As G. K. Chesterton once said, "Fairy tales do not

tell children that dragons exist. Children already know dragons exist. Fairy tales tell children that dragons can be killed" (Dosani & Cross, 2007, p. 38).

Waste of Time

Perhaps the most insidious complaint is that folk and fairy tales are a waste of time. Some adults simply bypass fairy or folktales when making selections to use with children in favor of "more substantial" stories and books about the real world. However, no genre of literature better fosters creativity than fantasy (both modern and traditional). Recall that Biblow's study showed high-fantasy children to be "more highly structured and creative." Russian poet Kornei Chukovsky (1968) claims that fantasy is "the most valuable attribute of the human mind and should be diligently nurtured from the earliest age" (p. 17). He even points out that great scientists have acknowledged this fact and quotes eminent British physicist John Tindale:

> Without the participation of fantasy . . . all our knowledge about nature would have been limited merely to the classification of obvious facts. The relation between cause and effect and their interaction would have gone unnoticed, thus stemming the progress of science itself, because it is the main function of science to establish the link between the different manifestations of nature, since creative fantasy is the ability to perceive more and more such links. (Chukovsky, 1968, p. 124)

As the story goes, a woman with a mathematically gifted son asked Albert Einstein how she should best foster his talent. After a moment of thought, Einstein answered, "Read him the great myths of the past—stretch his imagination" (Huck, 1982, p. 316). Teachers bemoan the lack of creative and critical thinking in today's students. How can we then not promote the very books and stories that cultivate imaginative thought?

Folklore Reading Lists

Fifteen of Our Favorites

Collections and Chapter Books

Hamilton, Virginia. 1988. *In the Beginning: Creation Stories from around the World.* Illustrated by Barry Moser. Harcourt. An illustrated collection of 25 myths from various cultures explaining the creation of the world. A Newbery Honor book.

Lester, Julius. 2006. *Cupid.* Harcourt. Cupid, the spoiled and mischievous god of love, is attracted to and marries the beautiful mortal Psyche, and both learn many lessons about the nature of love.

Lester, Julius. 2006 (1987). *The Tales of Uncle Remus: The Adventures of Brer Rabbit.* Puffin. Lester retells the African American traditional tales about the adventures and misadventures of Brer Rabbit and his friends and enemies.

Manushkin, Fran. 2001. *Daughters of Fire: Heroines of the Bible.* Illustrated by Uri Shulevitz. Silver Whistle/Harcourt. Eleven stories about women of the Hebrew Bible who influenced the course of Jewish history through their courageous actions.

Osborne, Mary Pope. 1998. *Favorite Medieval Tales.* Illustrated by Troy Howell. Scholastic. A collection of well-known tales from medieval Europe, including "Beowulf," "The Sword in the Stone," "The Song of Roland," and "Gudren and the Island of the Lost Children."

Soifer, Margaret, and Irwin Shapiro. 1957 (reissued 2003). *Golden Tales from the Arabian Nights.* Illustrated by Gustaf Tenggren. Random House. Illustrated retellings of 10 stories of Scheherazade, along with the legend of how they came to be told.

Sutcliff, Rosemary. 1994 (1981). *The Sword and the Circle: King Arthur and the Knights of the Round Table.* Puffin. (See Sutcliff's other two Arthur retellings: *The Light Beyond the Forest:*

The Quest for the Holy Grail and *The Road to Camlann: The Death of King Arthur*). A retelling of the classic Arthurian legend follows the adventures of the boy who became a king, his counselor Merlin, his beloved Guinevere, and the Knights of the Round Table.

Sutcliff, Rosemary. 1996. *The Wanderings of Odysseus: The Story of the Odyssey.* Illustrated by Alan Lee. Delacorte. A retelling of the adventures of Odysseus on his long voyage home from the Trojan War.

Picture Books

Dillon, Leo, and Diane Dillon. 1998. *To Every Thing There Is a Season: From Ecclesiastes.* Scholastic. The text is taken from the King James version of the Bible (Ecclesiastes chapter 3, verses 1–8), and each verse is illustrated in the traditional artistic style of a different ancient culture.

Grimm Brothers (translated by Randall Jarrell). 1972. *Snow-White and the Seven Dwarfs.* Illustrated by Nancy Ekholm Burkert. Farrar. A beautifully illustrated rendition of the classic fairy tale. A Caldecott Honor book.

Hasting, Selina. 1985. *Sir Gawain and the Loathly Lady.* Illustrated by Juan Wijngaard. Lothrop. After a horrible hag saves King Arthur's life by answering a riddle, Sir Gawain agrees to marry her and thus releases her from an evil enchantment.

Pinkney, Jerry. 2009. *The Lion and the Mouse.* Little, Brown. In this wordless retelling of an Aesop fable set in the African Serengeti, an adventuresome mouse proves that even small creatures are capable of great deeds when she rescues the King of the Jungle.

San Souci, Robert D. 2010. *Robin Hood and the Golden Arrow.* Orchard. Retells, in easy text, of the Sheriff of Nottingham's plot to hold an archery contest in order to capture the outlaw Robin Hood, but Robin and his band of merry men arrive in disguise with a plan of their own.

Steptoe, John. 1987. *Mufaro's Beautiful Daughters: An African Tale.* Lothrop. Mufaro's two beautiful daughters—one bad-tempered, one kind and sweet—go before the king, who is choosing a wife. An African variant of Cinderella. A Caldecott Honor book.

Zelinsky, Paul O. 1997. *Rapunzel.* Dutton. The author melded several versions of the Rapunzel story in creating this unique telling. Winner of the Caldecott Medal.

Others We Like

Chapter Books and Collections

Doherty, Berlie. 1997. *Tales of Wonder and Magic.* Illustrated by Juan Wijngaard. Candlewick. This collection includes fairy tales, such as "The Girl from Llyn y Fan Fach," "The People Could Fly," "The Bogles and the Moon," "The Boy of the Red Twilight Sky," and "The Black Bull of Norroway."

Fleischman, Paul. 2007. *Glass Slipper, Gold Sandal: A Worldwide Cinderella.* Illustrated by Julie Paschkis. Holt. The author draws from a variety of folk traditions to put together this version of Cinderella, including elements from Mexico, Iran, Korea, Russia, Appalachia, and more.

Garland, Sherry. 2001. *Children of the Dragon: Selected Tales from Vietnam.* Illustrated by Trina Schart Hyman. Harcourt. An illustrated collection of Vietnamese folktales with explanatory notes following each story.

Harris, Joel Chandler (adapted by Van Dyke Parks and Malcolm Jones). 1986. *Jump! The Adventures of Brer Rabbit.* Illustrated by Barry Moser. Harcourt. A retelling of five folktales in which crafty Brer Rabbit tries to outsmart all the other creatures in the animal community.

Heaney, Marie. 2000. *The Names upon the Harp.* Illustrated by P. J. Lynch. Scholastic. The Celtic folk and fairy tales in this collection include "The Children of Lir," "The Birth of Cuchulainn," "Finn and the Salmon of Knowledge," "The Enchanted Deer," and "Oisin in the Land of Youth."

Lively, Penelope. 2001. *In Search of a Homeland: The Story of the Aeneid.* Illustrated by Ian Andrew. Delacorte. Inspired by the ancient masterpiece *The Aeneid* by Roman poet Virgil, modern-day author Penelope Lively pens a poignant retelling of the arduous journeys of Trojan warrior Aeneas.

McKissack, Patricia C. 1992. *The Dark-Thirty.* Illustrated by Brian Pinkney. Knopf. A collection of ghost stories with African American themes,

designed to be told during the Dark Thirty—the half hour before sunset—when ghosts seem all too believable.

Mitchell, Stephen. 2007. *Genies, Meanies, and Magic Rings: Three Tales from the Arabian Nights.* Illustrated by Tom Pohrt. Walker. A retelling of three tales from the *Arabian Nights,* including "Ali Baba and the 40 Thieves," "Abu Keer and Abu Seer," and "Aladdin and the Magic Lamp."

Osborne, Mary Pope. 1996. *Favorite Norse Myths.* Illustrated by Troy Howell. Scholastic. A collection of rarely retold tales come from the "Elder Edda" and the "Younger Edda," two 600-year-old Norse manuscripts.

Osborne, Mary Pope, and Natalie Pope Boyce. 2009. *The Random House Book of Bible Stories.* Illustrated by Michael Welply. Random House. More than 50 stories from the Old and New Testaments come to vivid life. Each story is crafted for reading aloud, so the whole family can share the experience.

Pinkney, Jerry. 2000. *Aesop's Fables.* SeaStar. A collection of nearly 60 fables from Aesop, including such familiar ones as "The Grasshopper and the Ants," "The North Wind and the Sun," "Androcles and the Lion," "The Troublesome Dog," and "The Fox and the Stork."

Sutcliff, Rosemary. 1981. *Tristan and Iseult.* Dutton. Tristan defeats Ireland's greatest warrior and gains the friendship of his uncle, the King of Cornwall, who entrusts him with a very special mission: to sail the seas in search of a queen.

Vinge, Joan D. 1999. *The Random House Book of Greek Myths.* Illustrated by Oren Sherman. Random House. Retells some of the most famous Greek myths about gods, goddesses, humans, heroes, and monsters, explaining the background of the tales and how they have survived.

Yolen, Jane. 2003. *Mightier Than the Sword: World Folktales for Strong Boys.* Illustrated by Raul Colón. Harcourt. A collection of folktales from around the world that demonstrate the triumph of brains over brawn.

Picture Books

Aardema, Verna. 1975. *Why Mosquitoes Buzz in People's Ears.* Illustrated by Leo and Diane Dillon. Dial. A retelling of a traditional west African tale that reveals how the mosquito developed its annoying habit.

Curlee, Lynn. 2008. *Mythological Creatures: A Classical Bestiary.* Atheneum. This bestiary features 16 brief tales introducing classical Greek mythical animals, such as the gryphon and the chimera.

Goble, Paul. 1978. *The Girl Who Loved Wild Horses.* Bradbury. Though she is fond of her people, a girl prefers to live among the wild horses, where she is truly happy and free.

Goble, Paul. 2009. *The Earth Made New: Plains Indian Stories of Creation.* World Wisdom Publishing. This beautifully illustrated Plains Indian creation story celebrates a new Earth after the flood and narrates the making of the buffaloes, mountains, plants, colorful horses, and thunderbirds, among others.

Grimm Brothers. 1975. *Thorn Rose.* Illustrated by Errol Le Cain. Bradbury. Enraged at not being invited to the princess's christening, the wicked fairy casts a spell that dooms the princess to sleep for 100 years.

Grimm Brothers. 1983. *Little Red Riding Hood.* Illustrated by Trina Schart Hyman. Holiday House. On her way to deliver a basket of food to her sick grandmother, Elisabeth encounters a sly wolf.

Grimm Brothers. 2008. *The Fisherman and His Wife.* Illustrated by Rachel Isadora. Putnam. The fisherman's greedy wife is never satisfied with the wishes granted her by an enchanted fish.

Hamilton, Virginia. 2000. *The Girl Who Spun Gold.* Illustrated by Leo and Diane Dillon. Scholastic. In this version of Rumpelstiltskin from the West Indies, Lit'mahn spins thread into gold cloth for the king's new bride.

Hodges, Margaret. 2004. *Merlin and the Making of a King.* Illustrated by Trina Schart Hyman. Holiday. A retelling of four Arthurian legends: "The Sword in the Stone," "Excalibur," "The Lady of the Lake," and "The Last Great Battle."

Hofmeyr, Dianne. 2001. *The Star-Bearer: A Creation Story from Ancient Egypt.* Illustrated by Jude Daly. Farrar. Atum, the creator, brings to life the god of air and goddess of dew and rain, but the closeness of their two children, Geb and Nut, stops him from creating the world.

Isaacs, Anne. 1994. *Swamp Angel.* Illustrated by Paul O. Zelinsky. Dutton. Along with other amazing feats, Angelica Longrider, also known as Swamp Angel, wrestles a huge bear, known as Thundering Tarnation, to save the winter supplies of the settlers in Tennessee.

Johnson-Davies, Denys. 2005. *Goha the Wise Fool.* Illustrated by Hag Hamdy and Hany. Philomel. A collection of 14 tales about the folk hero Nasreddin Hoca, also known as Goha, a man with a reputation for being able to answer difficult questions in a clever way.

Kellogg, Steven. 1986. *Pecos Bill.* Morrow. (See other Steven Kellogg tall tales.) Incidents from the life of Pecos Bill, from his childhood among the coyotes to his unusual wedding day.

Kimmel, Eric. 2010. *The Story of Esther.* Illustrated by Jill Weber. Holiday House. Kimmel retells the Old Testament story of Esther, the queen of Persia.

Lester, Julius. 1994. *John Henry.* Illustrated by Jerry Pinkney. Dial. Retells the life of the legendary African American hero who raced against a steam drill to cut through a mountain.

Louie, Ai-Ling. 1982. *Yeh-Shen: A Cinderella Story from China.* Illustrated by Ed Young. Philomel. This version of the Cinderella story is based on ancient Chinese manuscripts written 1,000 years before the earliest European version.

Martin, Rafe. 1992. *The Rough-Face Girl.* Illustrated by David Shannon. Putnam. In this Algonquin Indian version of the Cinderella story, the Rough-Face Girl and her two beautiful but heartless sisters compete for the affections of the Invisible Being.

Mayer, Marianna. 2000 (1978). *Beauty and the Beast.* Illustrated by Mercer Mayer. SeaStar. Through her great capacity to love, a kind and beautiful maid releases a handsome prince from the spell that has made him an ugly beast.

Mayer, Marianna. 2006. *Legendary Creatures of Myth and Magic.* Illustrated by Michael Hague. Madison Park Press. Introduces a variety of legendary creatures from ancient deities to monsters and supernatural beings that were once either feared or accepted as real.

McDermott, Gerald. 1974. *Arrow to the Sun.* Viking. An adaptation of the Pueblo Indian myth that explains how the spirit of the Lord of the Sun was brought to the world of men.

McDermott, Gerald. 2010. *Monkey: A Trickster Tale from India.* Houghton Mifflin. Crocodile wants to feast on Monkey's heart, and Monkey must outsmart him if he is to enjoy eating mangoes all day.

Moser, Barry. 2001. *The Three Little Pigs.* Little, Brown. A humorous retelling of the fatal episodes in the lives of two foolish pigs and how the third pig manages to avoid the same fate.

Moses, Will. 2006. *Hansel & Gretel.* Philomel. Grandma Moses's folk-artist grandson offers a well-crafted and illustrated retelling of a favorite tale that is as faithful to its source as it is lengthy.

Perrault, Charles (translated by Malcolm Arthur). 1990. *Puss in Boots.* Illustrated by Fred Marcellino. Farrar. A retelling of the French fairy tale, in which a clever cat wins his master a fortune and the hand of a princess.

Pinkney, Jerry. 2006. *The Little Red Hen.* Dial. An illustrated edition of the classic fable of the hen that is forced to do all the work of baking bread and of the animals that learn a bitter lesson from it.

Pinkney, Jerry. 2007. *Little Red Riding Hood.* Little Brown. A sweet little girl meets a hungry wolf in the forest while on her way to visit her grandmother.

Rumford, James. 2007. *Beowulf: A Hero's Tale Retold.* Houghton Mifflin. A simplified and illustrated retelling of the exploits of the Anglo-Saxon warrior Beowulf, and how he came to defeat the monster Grendel, Grendel's mother, and a dragon that threatened the kingdom.

San Souci, Robert. 2004. *The Well at the End of the World.* Illustrated by Rebecca Walsh. Chronicle. Princess Rosamond, who prefers good books to good looks, risks her throne and all her wealth to save her father's life.

San Souci, Robert. 2008. *As Luck Would Have It: From the Brothers Grimm.* Illustrated by Daniel San Souci. August House. Left to take care of the family farm and fortune while their parents are away, twin bear cubs Juniper and Jonas have a series of mishaps before outwitting three thieves, in spite of themselves.

Shannon, Mark. 1994. *Gawain and the Green Knight.* Illustrated by David Shannon. Putnam. Young Gawain proves himself a worthy knight

when he accepts the challenge of a mysterious visitor from the North Country.

Shepard, Aaron. 2003. *The Princess and the Mouse: A Tale of Finland.* Illustrated by Leonid Gore. Atheneum. A retelling of a Finnish folktale about a young man who plans to marry his mouse sweetheart.

Wiesner, David, and Kim Kahng. 2005. *The Loathsome Dragon.* Illustrated by David Wiesner. Clarion. A wicked queen casts a spell over her beautiful stepdaughter, turning her into a loathsome dragon until such time as her wandering brother shall return and kiss her three times.

Wisniewski, David. 1996. *Golem.* Clarion. A saintly rabbi miraculously brings to life a clay giant who helps him watch over the Jews of 16th-century Prague.

PEARSON myeducationkit™

Go to the topic Traditional Literature on the MyEducationKit for this text, where you can:

- Search the Database of Children's Literature, housing more than 22,000 titles searchable in every genre by authors or illustrators, by awards won, by year published, and by topic and description.
- Explore genre-related Assignments and Activities, assignable exercises showing concepts in action through database use, video, cases, and student and teacher artifacts.
- Listen to podcasts and read interviews from some of the brightest and most enduring stars of children's literature in the Conversations.
- Discover weblinks that will lead you to sites representing the authors you learn about in these pages, classrooms with powerful children's literature connections, and literature awards.

Chapter 10

Modern Fantasy

> And so they lived many happy years, and the promised tasks were accomplished. Yet long afterward, when all had passed away into distant memory, there were many who wondered whether King Taran, Queen Eilonwy, and their companions had indeed walked the earth, or whether they had been no more than dreams in a tale set down to beguile children. And, in time, only the bards knew the truth of it. (Alexander 1968a, p. 285)

Lloyd Alexander's epic five-book fantasy series called the Prydain Chronicles ends with these words in *The High King*. Those who have lived vicariously in the imaginary kingdom of Prydain and survived its trials with Taran and Eilonwy yearn to hold on to those golden, mythical times as surely as we reach out longingly to hold onto a pleasant dream. This is the legacy traditional fantasy gives to modern fantasy—a sense of the magical that extends back to our ancient roots. "Magic had its feet under the earth and its hair above the clouds. . . . [In] the beginning, Magic was everywhere and nowhere" (Colwell, 1968, p. 178).

A Definition of Modern Fantasy

As with traditional fantasy, modern fantasy is distinguished from other genres by story elements that violate the natural, physical laws of our known world—events akin to magic. However, modern fantasy has known authors (see Figure 10.1).

The application of these miraculous elements varies greatly in modern fantasy stories: talking animals, imaginary worlds, fanciful characters (hobbits, dwarves, giants), magical beings (witches, sorcerers, genies), and so on. However, quality fantasy stories do not employ fantastic elements casually. In fact, fantasy is probably the most difficult genre to write because an author

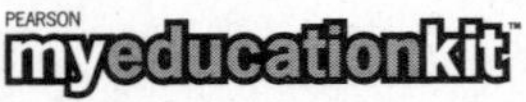

Visit the MyEducationKit for this course to enhance your understanding of chapter concepts with activities, weblinks, podcasts, and a searchable database of more than 22,000 children's literature titles.

Notable Authors of Modern Fantasy

Avi: Supernatural, animal fantasy.
Alexander, Lloyd: High fantasy.
Barron, T. A.: High fantasy.
Bellairs, John: Supernatural.
Christopher, John: Science fiction.
Collins, Suzanne: Science fiction; high fantasy.
Cooper, Susan: High fantasy.
Dahl, Roald: Peculiar characters/preposterous situations.
Dickinson, Peter: Science fiction; high fantasy.
Duncan, Lois: Supernatural.
Engdahl, Sylvia Louise: Science fiction.
Farmer, Nancy: Science fiction.
Funke, Cornelia: Magical powers.
Gaiman, Neil: Magical powers; supernatural.
Haddix, Margaret: Science fiction.
Hahn, Mary Downing: Supernatural.
Hughes, Monica: Science fiction.
Hunter, Mollie: Magical powers; supernatural.
Jacques, Brian: Animal fantasy.
Jones, Diana Wynne: Magical powers.
King-Smith, Dick: Animal fantasy.
Le Guin, Ursula: High fantasy; science fiction.
L'Engle, Madeleine: Science fantasy.
Lewis, C. S.: High fantasy.
McKinley, Robin: High fantasy.
Nix, Garth: High fantasy.
Norton, Mary: Tiny humans; magical powers.
Oppel, Kenneth: Animal fantasy; science fiction.
Pierce, Tamora: High fantasy.
Pullman, Philip: High fantasy.
Riordan, Rick: High fantasy based on Greek and Egyptian mythology.
Rowling, J. K.: Magical powers; high fantasy.
Sleator, William: Science fiction.
Van Allsburg, Chris: Peculiar characters/preposterous situations; magical powers.
White, E. B.: Animal fantasy.
Wright, Betty Ren: Supernatural.
Yolen, Jane: High fantasy; literary folk and fairy tales.

must create a new set of physical laws and then conform unerringly to them. A tiny slip can destroy the credibility of a story. Lloyd Alexander recognizes the need for this sort of specialized internal consistency:

> Once committed to his imaginary kingdom, the writer is not a monarch but a subject. Characters must appear plausible in their own setting, and the writer must go along with the inner logic. Happenings should have logical implications. Details should be tested for consistency. Shall animals speak? If so, do *all* animals speak? If not, then which—and how? Is it essential to the story, or lamely cute? Are there enchantments? How powerful? If an enchanter can perform such-and-such, can he not also do so-and-so? (1965, pp. 143–144)

Modern fantasy stories are not merely a matter of make-believe. Critics hold this genre to the same basic critical standards as they do other genres. For instance, modern fantasy must have strong, believable characters; a strong, credible plot; and should examine issues of the human condition—the universal truths found in all well-written books.

Categories of Modern Fantasy

Modern fantasy stories are sometimes categorized by the type of fantastic story element employed. *Animal fantasy,* for example, is the tag given to stories that depart from reality exclusively because

of talking animals, such as E. B. White's (1952) immortal *Charlotte's Web.* High fantasy, on the other hand, has all the fantasy motifs of a traditional fairy tale yet is a new and original story, such as Tolkien's (1937) *The Hobbit.* Modern high fantasy often includes novelized versions of traditional fairy tales, wherein the plots are expanded and the characters are fully developed, but we have chosen to categorize these stories separately. Therefore, Robin McKinley's (1978) *Beauty,* a novel-length version of "Beauty and the Beast," is listed below under "Novelized traditional tales."

The modern fantasy categories, and titles that exemplify each, follow:

- Animal fantasy: *The Wind in the Willows* by Kenneth Grahame (1908), *Masterpiece* by Elise Broach (2008).
- Toys and objects imbued with life: *Pinocchio* by Carlo Collodi (1904), *The Miraculous Journey of Edward Tulane* by Kate DiCamillo (2006).
- Tiny humans: *The Borrowers* by Mary Norton (1953), *Winter Wood* by Steve Augarde (2009).
- Peculiar characters and situations: *Mary Poppins* by P. L. Travers (1934), *The Graveyard Book* by Neil Gaiman (2008).
- Imaginary worlds: *Alice's Adventures in Wonderland* by Lewis Carroll (1865), *The Celestial Globe* by Marie Rutkoski (2009).
- Magical powers: *The Chocolate Touch* by Patrick Catling (1979), *The Magic Thief* by Sarah Phineas (2008).
- Supernatural tales: *Wait Till Helen Comes: A Ghost Story* by Mary Downing Hahn (1985), *The Seer of Shadows* by Avi (2008).
- Time-warp fantasies: *King of Shadows* by Susan Cooper (1999), *The Gate of Days* by Guillaume Prévost (2008).
- High fantasy: *The Lion, the Witch and the Wardrobe* by C. S. Lewis (1950), *Harry Potter and the Deathly Hallows* by J. K. Rowling (2007).
- Novelized traditional tales: *Beauty* by Robin McKinley (1978); *East* by Edith Pattou (2003).

Modern fairy and folktales, or literary tales, round out this list. As discussed in the last chapter, modern fairy and folktales are written in the form of the ageless traditional tales, which were passed from generation to generation by word of mouth. Although a number of authors have written modern folktales—Oscar Wilde, George MacDonald, Rudyard Kipling, and Jane Yolen, to name a few—the stories of Hans Christian Andersen are perhaps the best known, such as "The Little Mermaid" and "The Steadfast Tin Soldier." Fractured folktales and fairy tales, such as *The True Story of the 3 Little Pigs!* by Jon Scieszka (1989) and *The Giant and the Beanstalk* by Diane Stanley (2004), also fall into this category.

Six Basic Fantasy Motifs

Even though all modern fantasy stories contain some sort of magical element, some stories have a higher fantasy quotient than others. Madsen (1976) identified six basic fantasy motifs; if a story contains all six, it is either a classic fairy tale or an example of modern high fantasy. However, if a story contains fantasy's one necessary ingredient, the motif of magic or the violation of our world's physical laws, it is still classified as fantasy literature.

1. *Magic.* Magic is fantasy literature's most basic element. In fact, each of the other five motifs is tinged by magic to some degree. Magic is often a part of the setting, explaining otherwise inexplicable events. In Lloyd Alexander's *The High King* (1968a), magic is evident in the very fabric of the mythical land of Prydain. Powerful wizards are able to harness the magic in Prydain's atmosphere, an oracular pig can foretell the future, and people try to use magical objects to manipulate their destinies. However, in White's *Charlotte's Web* (1952), the only hint of magic is the ability of the barnyard animals to think and speak like humans. In fact, magic is the only one of the six motifs that appears in that book.

2. *Other worlds (secondary worlds).* In much of fantasy, a special geography or universe is established, a place wherein magic may freely operate. Sometimes these worlds are, as in the fairy tales, simply long, long ago. Alexander's Prydain is just this sort of place, almost recognizable as the world we know but governed by a different set of rules. Authors employ three common methods of incorporating a secondary world into their stories:

- The first and most common is simply setting the entire tale in an imaginary place, as with the lands of Prydain (*The Book of Three* by Lloyd Alexander, 1964) and Middle Earth (*The Hobbit* by J. R. R. Tolkien, 1937).
- The second method takes characters from our primary world into a secondary world through some sort of portal. Classic examples include the tornado whisking Dorothy to the land of Oz (*The Wonderful Wizard of Oz* by L. Frank Baum, 1900), the Pevensie children's passage through the wardrobe into Narnia (*The Lion, the Witch and the Wardrobe* by C. S. Lewis, 1950), and Wendy and her siblings' magic flight to Neverland (*Peter Pan* by J. M. Barrie, 1906). Yet another example is when Harry Potter walks through a solid barrier onto Platform Nine and Three-Quarters, thus entering the magical world of Hogwarts School (*Harry Potter and the Sorcerer's Stone* by J. K. Rowling, 1998).
- The third method involves the secondary world invading our primary world. The magical realms of wizards and witches in the Harry Potter books are places not accessible to Muggles (normal humans)—readers never see a Muggle wandering into Hogswarts or nearby Hogsmeade. But wizards can and do enter the world of humans. In *Harry Potter and the Goblet of Fire* (Rowling, 2000), for example, the wizardry world's biggest sporting event, the Quidditch World Cup, occurs on a Muggle farmstead, as there is no spot large enough in magicdom. In order to protect both wizards and people, anti-Muggle security is employed, such as altering Muggles' memories using memory charms. But when the Deatheaters, followers of the evil Voldemort, attack the World Cup attendees, Muggles and wizards alike suffer from their powerful and deadly spells. The secondary world breaches the primary world, thus affecting the lives of ordinary people.

3. *Good versus evil.* The ancient, archetypal theme of good versus evil is what myth is all about, and modern fantasy stories often have a strong mythological base. "Fantasies are concerned with how good and evil manifest themselves in individuals" (Madsen, 1976, p. 49). This basic theme, of course, gives rise to the conflict in a story, and once again, without conflict there is no story. Fantasy readers usually have no trouble aligning characters on the sides of light or dark, as fantasy characters typically are not fence-sitters.

4. *Heroism.* Natalie Babbitt (1987), drawing on the writings of mythologist Joseph Campbell (1968), explains that the hero's quest will always follow an age-old pattern that is the backbone

of many of today's fantasy stories. This so-called hero's round is a circular journey, ending where it began. It is a time-honored template for various types of stories, though the hero's quest originated in traditional fantasy. The following six elements, drawn from Babbitt (1987), most commonly structure the hero's quest:

- *The hero is called to adventure by some sort of herald.* Taran, in the Prydain Chronicles (see Alexander, 1964), is lured to adventure by Hen Wen, a magical pig whom he follows on a wild chase much the same way Alice follows the white rabbit (*Alice's Adventures in Wonderland*). Heralds from other stories include Gandalf (*The Hobbit*), Toto (*The Wonderful Wizard of Oz*), Mr. Tumnus (*The Lion, the Witch and the Wardrobe*), and Hagrid (*Harry Potter and the Sorcerer's Stone*).
- *The hero crosses the threshold into the other world or into a place that is no longer safe and secure.* The hero leaves a place of relative safety and enters a world of danger. Sometimes he or she passes from the familiar modern world into a forbidding secondary world, as when the children pass through the magical wardrobe into the land of Narnia (*The Lion, the Witch and the Wardrobe*) and when Dorothy is whisked from Kansas to Oz (*The Wonderful Wizard of Oz*). In some stories, the hero already lives in an imaginary kingdom, as Bilbo Baggins does in *The Hobbit,* and is compelled to leave hearth and home to undertake a perilous journey.
- *The hero must survive various trials in the new environment.* Heroes often face both physical hardship and emotional setbacks. They may suffer the misery of long treks through bitter winter weather or the pain of having dear friends relinquish their lives for a noble cause, both of which occur in Alexander's (1968) *The High King.* Often they will be driven to examine their own hearts, as in *Taran Wanderer* (Alexander, 1967). At a time of great personal crisis, Taran seriously considers giving in to his baser instincts by leaving a man to die—a man whose death would greatly uncomplicate his life—but suddenly he faces himself and is filled with dark terror at the thoughts whispering in his head. "Then, as if his heart would burst with [the horror and shame] of it, he cried out in terrible rage, 'What man am I?'" (Alexander, 1967, pp. 152–153). The quest becomes the hero's refining fire.
- *The hero is assisted by a protective figure.* Protective figures provide a sense of security in a tension-filled world. Older, wiser, and sometimes more powerful, the protective figure may serve as the hero's mentor. Readers will identify Dallben (the Prydain Chronicles); Gandalf (*The Hobbit*)*;* Glinda, the Good Witch of the North (*The Wonderful Wizard of Oz*); Aslan (*The Lion, the Witch and the Wardrobe*); and Professor Dumbledore (*Harry Potter and the Sorcerer's Stone*) as protective figures.
- *The hero matures, becoming a whole person.* Did Edmund change in *The Lion, the Witch and the Wardrobe*? How about Dorothy in *The Wonderful Wizard of Oz*? Both of these characters matured significantly during the course of their quests. Taran, from the Prydain books, grows from a foolish boy to a man worthy of ascending to the High Kingship of Prydain. The hero motif involves the age-old rite-of-passage theme, wherein the young are initiated into the ranks of adulthood.
- *The hero returns home.* This step completes the hero's round. In each Prydain book, Taran returns to his home on Dallben's farm; he then symbolically finds home when he discovers his true destiny in the final book, *The High King.* In the high-fantasy novels discussed in this section, all the young heroes return home as their quests draw to an end.

5. *Special character types.* Fantasies may include characters who come from either our legendary past or an author's vivid imagination. These characters are rarely typical humans. Characters from our legendary past are those from traditional tales: fairies, pixies, giants, wicked witches, ogres, vampires, wizards, dwarves, elves, and so on. Some special character types created in recent years by fantasy authors have become almost as well known, such as Tolkien's hobbits, which appear in *The Hobbit* and the Lord of the Rings trilogy.

6. *Fantastic objects.* Characters in fantasy stories often employ magical props in accomplishing their heroic or evil deeds. These objects—such as magic cloaks, swords, staffs, cauldrons, mirrors—are imbued with power. Some well-known props are Dorothy's silver slippers (*The Wonderful Wizard of Oz*), the White Witch's wand (*The Lion, the Witch and the Wardrobe*), the dreadful ring that falls into Bilbo's hands (*The Hobbit*), and Harry Potter's flying broom, the Nimbus Two Thousand (*Harry Potter and the Sorcerer's Stone*).

Some books operate strongly in only one of these six motifs, such as *The Wind in the Willows* by Kenneth Grahame (1908) and White's *Charlotte's Web* (1952), where talking animals qualify as magic. *Tuck Everlasting* (Babbitt, 1975) arguably incorporates four of the six motifs: magic, good versus evil, the hero's round, and fantastic objects. Baum's *The Wonderful Wizard of Oz* operates in all six of the motifs and is thus classified as a high fantasy.

Science Fiction

Science fiction generally appears in chapters about modern fantasy. However, it differs from the stories described to this point. "Science fiction differs from fantasy not in subject matter but in aim, and its unique aim is to suggest real hypotheses about mankind's future or about the nature of the universe" (Engdahl, 1971, p. 450). Science fiction also concerns the way in which scientific possibilities might affect societies of human or alien beings or both. Therefore, it is sometimes called *futuristic fiction.* This combination of scientific fact and scientific possibility is evident in such works as Nancy Farmer's *The House of the Scorpion* (2002), wherein she imagines the consequences of human cloning.

Futuristic fiction sometimes focuses on dystopia—an imaginary place where people live dehumanized and often fearful lives. Examples include the Newbery-winning *The Giver* (Lowry, 1993), the story of a community of people largely devoid of human emotion, and *The Hunger Games* (Collins, 2008), which tells of a suppressed and decaying society forced by its conquerors to partake in a yearly lottery. Each district must choose two of its teenagers to participate in a gladiatorial game, the winner of which is the last one remaining alive.

There is a brand of science fiction, however, that would be better labeled *science fantasy.* These stories play loosely with scientific fact, and the plots are often mixed with magical occurrences. The original *Star Wars* films are examples of science fantasy and even incorporate the six fantasy motifs. The Bionicle titles by Greg Farshtey are also science fantasy. In several mass-market paperback series not to be considered quality literature (Bionicle, Bionicle Chronicles, Bionicle Legends, Bionicle Adventures, Bionicle Graphic Novels, and so on), six biomechanical beings that command elemental powers band together to fight a variety of evil villains.

The magic in fantasy cannot be explained; it is just *there,* without source or reason. But the magic in true science fiction is rooted more firmly in scientific fact. Because "Cinderella" is fantasy, the fairy godmother simply has the power to turn the pumpkin into a coach. If it were science fiction, she would zap the pumpkin with a molecular rearranger (Alexander, 1973).

The Truth in Fantasy

Some adults dismiss all fantasy—traditional fantasy, modern fantasy, even science fiction—as peripheral fluff. It is simply too whimsical for those who want reading for young people to be grounded firmly in reality. Yet these adults miss the point that good fantasy actually tells the truth about life. It clarifies the human condition and captures the essence of our deepest emotions, dreams, hopes, and fears. If fantasy does not do these things, it fails.

Fantasy casts light on the realities of life much as a metaphor illustrates truth in general communication. On the evening news and in daily papers, fantasy language in the form of metaphor is common. Consider the italicized parts of the following: "County medics *see light at the end of the tunnel.*" "Lawmakers *torpedo* peace plan." "During the inquiry, the congressman *played his cards close to his vest.*" How can news writers get away with such wild statements when no tunnel was anywhere near the county medics, the lawmakers did not use a torpedo on the peace plan, and no cards were evident at the congressional inquiry? Because metaphor is an acceptable way of enhancing communication.

In its broad definition, metaphor is figurative language and strengthens writing in at least three ways:

1. *Metaphor speeds understanding.* Metaphor makes the abstract become concrete by introducing an image, resulting in quicker comprehension of a situation. "County medics are confident their current troubles will be resolved in the near future" describes the situation adequately, but using the metaphor of the tunnel introduces the idea more quickly and with more power.
2. *Metaphor creates interest.* No one misunderstands "Lawmakers vote against peace plan," but "Lawmakers torpedo peace plan" is richer and more interesting. The warlike image of a *torpedo* makes the action more deliberate and more vigorous, as well as being ironically juxtaposed to peacemaking.
3. *Metaphor adds emotional appeal.* With the additional layer of meaning introduced by metaphor, the message goes beyond the intellect to act on the emotions. Without the metaphor, we know the congressman involved in the inquiry was secretive and careful in his responses. The metaphor stirs the emotions with suggestions of game playing, calculating, and intense personal interest.

Yet metaphor is more than the sum of these parts. It simply involves the reader more with the story or message, allowing for quicker learning, more precise understanding, and longer retention because of the image. And fantasy, which is a large, worked-out metaphor, illuminates the truths about life in the same ways. As Lloyd Alexander (1968b, p. 387) observes, "There is an exuberance in good fantasy quite unlike the most exalted moments of realistic fiction. Both forms have similar goals, but realism walks where fantasy dances."

Children can read directly about friendship, sacrifice, selfishness, the fear of death, and death itself, but the insight is somehow more meaningful when shown metaphorically through the lives of Wilbur the pig, Templeton the rat, and Charlotte the spider in *Charlotte's Web* (White, 1952).

Because Charlotte is a spider, she can embody all selflessness without losing credibility. On the other hand, if she were a character in realistic fiction dedicated completely to doing good and had no flaw or foible, she would not be believable.

Compared with fantasy, straightforward informational writing does not create the same emotional impact when dealing with topics such as the need for death. Although direct arguments certainly can be made—everyone has a time and season that must end; the Earth would fill if death were to cease; living forever would hold unforeseen difficulties—such intellectual points do not convince the emotions that death ultimately is desirable. This issue is hard to explore even in realistic fiction. No human can honestly present the alternate view because all people from this world, including those in realistic fiction, are destined to die. Yet the fantasy story of Winnie Foster and the Tuck family in *Tuck Everlasting* (Babbitt, 1975) allows probing of this difficult concept. By listening to a family who has lost the ability to age or die, new light is shed on the appropriateness of an eventual death. Understanding the place of death, one of real life's greatest fears and challenges, is seen most clearly in the metaphor of fantasy.

The power of fantasy is reflected in the fact that many of the classic children's stories, those that have withstood the test of time, are fantasies: *Peter Pan* (Barrie, 1906), *Winnie-the-Pooh* (Milne, 1926), *The Wonderful Wizard of Oz* (Baum, 1900), *The Wind in the Willows* (Grahame, 1908), and *Mary Poppins* (Travers, 1934). Certainly, good fantasy stories speak clearly and convincingly about real life, as author Lloyd Alexander observed (1968b, p. 386): "I suppose you might define realism as fantasy pretending to be true; and fantasy as reality pretending to be a dream."

Modern Fantasy Reading Lists

Fifteen of Our Favorites

Alexander, Lloyd. 1999 (1964). *The Book of Three.* Holt. In the first book of the Prydain Chronicles, Taran, assistant pig keeper at Caer Dallben, searches for the oracular pig Hen Wen while the forces of evil gather. (See the other four books in the Prydain Chronicles.) (High fantasy.)

Babbitt, Natalie. 1975. *Tuck Everlasting.* Farrar. The Tuck family is confronted with an agonizing situation when they discover that a 10-year-old girl and a malicious stranger now share their secret about the water from a spring that prevents people from ever growing any older. (Magical powers.)

Broach, Elise. 2008. *Masterpiece.* Holt. After Marvin, a beetle, makes a miniature drawing as an eleventh birthday gift for James, a human with whom he shares a house, the two new friends work together to help recover a Durer drawing stolen from the Metropolitan Museum of Art. (Animal fantasy.)

Christopher, John. 2003 (1967). *The White Mountains.* Simon and Schuster (Macmillan). A young boy and his companions make a perilous journey toward an outpost of freedom, where they hope to escape from the ruling tripod creatures who "cap" adult human beings with implanted metal skull plates that turn them into docile, obedient servants. (See the other three books in the White Mountains series.) (Science fiction.)

Collins, Suzanne. 2008. *The Hunger Games.* Scholastic. In a future North America, where the rulers of Panem maintain control through an annual televised survival competition pitting young people from each of the 12 districts against one another, 16-year-old Katniss's skills are put to the test when she voluntarily takes her younger sister's place. (Science fiction.)

Cooper, Susan. 2007 (1973). *The Dark Is Rising.* Simon Pulse (Atheneum). On his eleventh birthday, Will Stanton discovers that he is the last of the Old Ones, destined to seek the six magical Signs that will enable the Old Ones to triumph over the evil forces of the Dark. A Newbery Honor book. (See the other four books in the Dark Is Rising series.) (High fantasy.)

Engdahl, Sylvia Louise. 2001 (1970). *Enchantress from the Stars.* Walker (Atheneum). When young Elana unexpectedly joins the team leaving the spaceship to study the planet Andrecia, she becomes an integral part of an adventure involving three very different civilizations, each one centered on the third planet from the star in its own solar system. A Newbery Honor book. (Science fiction.)

Farmer, Nancy. 2002. *The House of the Scorpion.* Atheneum. In a future where humans despise clones, Matt enjoys special status as the young clone of El Patrón, the 142-year-old leader of a corrupt drug empire nestled between Mexico and the United States. A Newbery Honor book. (Science fiction.)

Gaiman, Neil. 2008. *The Graveyard Book.* Harper. Nobody Owens, a child marked for death by an ancient league of assassins, escapes into an abandoned graveyard, where he is reared and protected by its spirit denizens. A Newbery Award winner. (Supernatural tales.)

Hale, Shannon. 2003. *The Goose Girl.* Bloomsbury. On her way to marry a prince she's never met, Princess Anidori is betrayed by her guards and her lady-in-waiting and must become a goose girl to survive until she can reveal her true identity and reclaim the crown that is rightfully hers. (Novelized traditional tale.)

Hunter, Mollie. 1975. *A Stranger Came Ashore.* Harper. Twelve-year-old Robbie becomes convinced that the stranger befriended by his family is one of the Selkie Folk and tries to get help against his magical powers from the local wizard. (Magical powers.)

McKinley, Robin. 2005 (1978). *Beauty: A Retelling of the Story of Beauty and the Beast.* Harper. Kind Beauty grows to love the Beast, at whose castle she is compelled to stay. Through her love, she releases him from the spell that had turned him from a handsome prince into an ugly creature. (Novelized traditional tale.)

Pattou, Edith. 2003. *East.* Harcourt. A young woman journeys to a distant castle on the back of a great white bear who is the victim of a cruel enchantment. A novelization of the classic fairy tale "East of the Sun, West of the Moon." (Novelized traditional tale.)

Rowling, J. K. 2007. *Harry Potter and the Deathly Hallows.* Scholastic. Burdened with the dark, dangerous, and seemingly impossible task of locating and destroying Voldemort's remaining Horcruxes, Harry, feeling alone and uncertain about his future, struggles to find the inner strength he needs to follow the path set out before him. (See others in the Harry Potter series.) (High fantasy.)

White, E. B. 2006 (1952). *Charlotte's Web.* Harper. Wilbur the pig discovers that he is destined to be the farmer's Christmas dinner and is desolate until his spider friend, Charlotte, decides to help him. A Newbery Honor book. (Animal fantasy.)

Others We Like

Alexander, Lloyd. 1997. *The Iron Ring.* Dutton. Driven by his sense of *dharma,* or honor, young King Tamar sets off on a perilous journey, with significance greater than he can imagine, during which he meets talking animals, villainous and noble kings, demons, and the love of his life.

Armstrong, Alan W. 2005. *Whittington.* Illustrated by S. D. Schindler. Random House. Whittington, a feline descendant of Dick Whittington's famous cat of English folklore, appears at a rundown barnyard plagued by rats and restores harmony while telling his ancestor's story. A Newbery Honor book.

Avi. 2008. *The Seer of Shadows.* Harper. In New York City in 1872, 14-year-old Horace, a photographer's apprentice, becomes entangled in a plot to create fraudulent spirit photographs, but when Horace accidentally frees the real ghost of a dead girl bent on revenge, his life takes a frightening turn.

Balliett, Blue. 2006. *The Wright 3.* Illustrated by Brett Helquist. Scholastic. (Also see *Chasing Vermeer.*) In the midst of a series of unexplained accidents and mysterious coincidences, sixth graders Calder, Petra, and Tommy lead their classmates in an attempt to keep Frank Lloyd Wright's famous Robie House from being demolished.

Banks, Lynne Reid. 1981. *The Indian in the Cupboard.* Doubleday. (See others in the Indian in the Cupboard series.) A 9-year-old boy receives a plastic Indian, a cupboard, and a little key for his

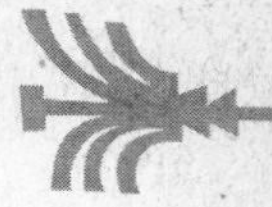

birthday and finds himself involved in adventure when the Indian comes to life in the cupboard and befriends him.

Barron, T. A. 2000. *The Wings of Merlin.* Philomel. (See others in the Merlin series.) Merlin's fragile home on the isle of Fincayra is threatened by the attack of a mysterious warrior with swords for arms and by the escape of Stangmar from his imprisonment, as Merlin continues to move toward his ultimate destiny.

Bellairs, John. 1973. *The House with a Clock in Its Walls.* Dial. (See others in the Lewis Barnavelt series, also written by Brad Strickland after Bellairs's death.) In the bowels of Uncle Jonathan's mansion, an evil wizard has hidden a doomsday clock that will destroy the world unless Lewis can find and destroy it.

Bunce, Elizabeth. 2008. *A Curse As Dark As Gold.* Arthur A. Levine/Scholastic. Upon the death of her father, 17-year-old Charlotte struggles to keep the family's woolen mill running in the face of an overwhelming mortgage, but when a man capable of spinning straw into gold appears on the scene, she must decide if his help is worth the price.

Conrad, Pam. 1990. *Stonewords.* Harper. Zoe discovers that her house is occupied by the ghost of an 11-year-old girl, who carries her back to the day of her death in 1870 to try to alter that tragic event.

Cornish, D. M. 2008. *The Monster Blood Tattoo: Lamplighter.* Putnam. (See others in the Monster Blood Tattoo series.) As Rosamund starts his life as a lamplighter on the Wormway, he continues his fight against monsters, but questions about his origins continue to plague him.

Dahl, Roald. 1988. *Matilda.* Viking Kestrel. Matilda applies her untapped mental powers to rid the school of the evil, child-hating headmistress, Miss Trunchbull, and restore her nice teacher, Miss Honey, to financial security.

DiCamillo, Kate. 2006. *The Miraculous Journey of Edward Tulane.* Illustrated by Bagram Ibatoulline. Candlewick. Edward Tulane, a cold-hearted and proud toy rabbit, loves only himself until he is separated from the little girl who adores him and travels across the country, acquiring a series of new owners.

Dickinson, Peter. 1989. *Eva.* Delacorte. After a terrible accident, a young girl wakes up to discover that she has been given the body of a chimpanzee.

Duncan, Lois. 1976. *Summer of Fear.* Little, Brown. Soon after the arrival of Cousin Julia, insidious occurrences begin that convince Rachel she is a witch and must be stopped before her total monstrous plan can be effected.

DuPrau, Jeanne. 2008. *The Diamond of Darkhold.* Random House. (See others in the Books of Ember series.) Lina and Doon return to the subterranean city of Ember to find a machine described in an ancient book—a machine that may help their town survive the winter.

Fleischman, Sid. 2008. *The Entertainer and the Dybbuk.* Greenwillow. A struggling American ventriloquist in post–World War II Europe is possessed by the mischievous spirit of a young Jewish boy killed in the Holocaust.

Fletcher, Susan. 1989. *Dragon's Milk.* Atheneum. (See others in the Dragon Chronicles series.) Kaeldra possesses the power to understand dragons and uses this power to try to save her younger sister, who needs dragon's milk to recover from an illness.

George, Jessica Day. 2009. *Princess of the Midnight Ball.* Bloomsbury. A retelling of the tale of 12 princesses who wear out their shoes dancing every night and of Galen, a former soldier turned gardener, who follows them in hopes of breaking the curse.

Hahn, Mary Downing. 2008 (1986). *Wait Till Helen Comes: A Ghost Story.* Houghton Mifflin. Molly and Michael dislike their spooky new stepsister Heather but realize that they must try to save her when she seems ready to follow a ghost child to her doom.

Jacques, Brian. 1997 (1987). *Redwall.* Philomel. (See others in the Redwall series.) When the peaceful life of ancient Redwall Abbey is shattered by the arrival of the evil rat Cluny and his villainous hordes, Matthias, a young mouse, determines to find the legendary sword of Martin the Warrior in order to destroy the enemy.

Law, Ingrid. 2008. *Savvy.* Dial. Mibs Beaumont's thirteenth birthday has revealed her "savvy"—a magical power unique to each member of her family. A Newbery Honor book.

Le Guin, Ursula K. 2004 (1968). *A Wizard of Earthsea.* Bantam (Parnassus). (See others in the

Earthsea series.) A boy grows to manhood while attempting to subdue the evil he unleashed on the world as an apprentice to the Master Wizard.

L'Engle, Madeleine. 2007 (1962). *A Wrinkle in Time.* Square Fish (Farrar). (See others in the Time series.) Meg Murry and her friends become involved with unearthly strangers and a search for Meg's father, who has disappeared while engaged in secret work for the government. A Newbery Award winner.

Levitin, Sonia. 2005. *The Goodness Gene.* Dutton. As son of the Compassionate Director of the Dominion of the Americas, Will has been groomed for leadership in a society that values genetic fitness, but he encounters information that causes him to question his society as well as his identity.

Lewis, C. S. 2005 (1950). *The Lion, the Witch and the Wardrobe.* HarperFestival (Macmillan). (See the other six books in the Narnia series.) Four English school children find their way through the back of a wardrobe into the magic land of Narnia and assist Aslan, the golden lion, to triumph over the White Witch, who has cursed the land with eternal winter.

Lowry, Lois. 1993. *The Giver.* Houghton. Given his lifetime assignment at the Ceremony of Twelve, Jonas becomes the receiver of memories shared by only one other in his community and discovers the terrible truth about the society in which he lives. A Newbery Award winner.

Lowry, Lois. 2008. *The Willoughbys.* Houghton. In this nonsensical and fantasy-filled parody of the classic orphan story, the self-centered parents of the four Willoughby children desert them to embark on a treacherous around-the-world adventure, leaving them in the care of an odious nanny.

McAllister, M. I. 2008. *Urchin and the Raven War.* Hyperion. (See others in the Mistmantle Chronicles.) When vicious ravens attack the swans of Swan Isle, Urchin the squirrel and the inhabitants of Mistmantle rush to their aid.

Nix, Garth. 2001. *Lirael.* Harper. (See other titles in the trilogy.) When a dangerous necromancer threatens to unleash a long-buried evil, Lirael and Prince Sameth are drawn into a battle to save the Old Kingdom.

Norton, Mary. 2003 (1953). *The Borrowers.* Harcourt. (See others in the Borrowers series.) Miniature people who live in an old country house by borrowing things from the humans are forced to emigrate from their home under the clock.

O'Brien, Robert C. 2007 (1975). *Z for Zachariah.* Simon Pulse (Atheneum). Seemingly the only person left alive after the holocaust of a war, a young girl is relieved to see a man arrive in her valley—until she realizes that he is a tyrant and she must somehow escape.

Oppel, Kenneth. 2009. *Starclimber.* Eos/Harper. As members of the first crew of astralnauts, Matt Cruse and Kate De Vries journey into outer space on the *Starclimber* and face a series of catastrophes that threaten the survival of all on board. Sequel to *Airborn* and *Skybreaker.*

Prineas, Sarah. 2008. *The Magic Thief.* Harper. (See other in the Magic Thief series.) A young thief is drawn into a life of magic and adventure after picking the pocket of the powerful wizard Nevery Flinglas.

Pullman, Philip. 1995. *The Golden Compass.* Knopf. (See others in the His Dark Materials series.) Accompanied by her daemon, Lyra Belacqua sets out to prevent her best friend and other kidnapped children from becoming the subject of gruesome experiments in the Far North.

Rutkoski, Marie. 2008. *The Cabinet of Wonders.* Farrar. (See the sequel, *The Celestial Globe* [2009], and others to follow.) Twelve-year-old Petra, accompanied by her magical tin spider, goes to Prague hoping to retrieve the enchanted eyes the Prince of Bohemia took from her father and is aided in her quest by a Roma boy and his sister.

Ryan, Carrie. 2009. *The Forest of Hands and Teeth.* Delacorte. Through twists and turns of fate, orphaned Mary seeks knowledge of life, love, and especially what lies beyond her walled village and the surrounding forest, where dwell the Unconsecrated, aggressive flesh-eating people who were once dead.

Shusterman, Neal. 2004. *The Schwa Was Here.* Dutton. A Brooklyn eighth grader nicknamed Antsy befriends the Schwa, an "invisible-ish" boy who is tired of blending into his surroundings and going unnoticed by nearly everyone.

Springer, Nancy. 2001. *I Am Morgan le Fay: A Tale from Camelot.* Philomel. In a war-torn England where her half-brother Arthur will eventually become king, the young Morgan le Fay comes to

realize that she has magic powers and links to the faerie world. Winner of the Newbery Medal.

Stead, Rebecca. 2009. *When You Reach Me.* Wendy Lamb Books/Random House. As her mother prepares to be a contestant on the 1970s television game show *The $20,000 Pyramid,* a 12-year-old New York City girl tries to make sense of a series of mysterious notes received from an anonymous source that seem to defy the laws of time and space.

Tunnell, Michael O. 2009. *Wishes on the Moon.* Speak/Penguin. After a young orphan named Aminah comes to possess a magic lamp, the wishes granted her by the genie inside it allow her to alter her life. Then the magic lamp is stolen, and the primary suspect is her friend, Idris the storyteller.

Vande Velde, Vivian. 2002. *Heir Apparent.* Harcourt. While playing a total immersion virtual reality game of kings and intrigue, 14-year-old Giannine learns that demonstrators have damaged the equipment to which she is connected, and she must win the game quickly or be damaged herself.

Yolen, Jane. 2009. *Dragon's Heart.* Harcourt. (See others in the Pit Dragon Chronicles.) Having been presumed dead, Jakkin and Akki finally return to Austar IV with newfound skills, and the knowledge that what they have learned could either transform their planet or destroy it.

Easier to Read

Bauer, Marion Dane. 2008. *The Green Ghost.* Random House.

Brooks, Walter R. 1932 (reissued 1997). *Freddy the Detective.* Overlook Press. (See others in the Freddy the Pig series.)

Brown, Jeff. 2003. *Stanley, Flat Again.* Illustrated by Steve Björkman. Harper. (Also see *Flat Stanley* and others in the Stanley series.)

Cameron, Ann. 2002. *Gloria Rising.* Illustrated by Lis Toft. Farrar.

Catling, Patrick. 1979 (1952). *The Chocolate Touch.* Morrow.

Cleary, Beverly. 1965. *The Mouse and the Motorcycle.* Morrow. (Also see *Runaway Ralph.*)

Cooper, Susan. 2005. *The Magician's Boy.* Illustrated by Serena Riglietti. McElderry Books.

Coville, Bruce. 2005. *The Weeping Werewolf.* Illustrated by Katherine Coville. Simon & Schuster.

Fleischman, Sid. 1992. *Here Comes McBroom.* Greenwillow. (See others in the McBroom series.)

Gaiman, Neil. 2009. *Odd and the Frost Giants.* Illustrated by Brett Helquist. Harper.

Griffin, Adele. 2001. *Witch Twins.* Hyperion.

Howe, Deborah, and James Howe. 1983. *Bunnicula.* Atheneum. (See others in the Bunnicula series.)

King-Smith, Dick. 1985. *Babe: The Gallant Pig.* Crown.

Krulik, Nancy. 2006. *Witch Switch!* Grosset & Dunlap. (See others in the Katie Kazoo series.)

Osborne, Mary Pope. 2009. *A Good Night for Ghosts.* Random House. (See others in the Magic Tree House series.)

Scieszka, Jon. 2005. *Oh Say, I Can't See.* Illustrated by Adam McCauley. Viking. (See others in the Time Warp Trio series.)

Watts, Irene N. 2009. *Clay Man: The Golem of Prague.* Illustrated by Kathyrn E. Shoemaker. Tundra Books.

Wright, Betty Ren. 1998. *The Ghost in Room 11.* Holiday House.

Picture Books

Agee, Jon. 2001. *Milo's Hat Trick.* Hyperion.

Alexander, Lloyd. 2005. *Dream-of-Jade: The Emperor's Cat.* Illustrated by D. Brent Burkett. Cricket Books.

Bannerman, Helen. 2003. *The Story of Little Black Sambo.* Illustrated by Christopher Bing. Handprint.

Cronin, Doreen. 2000. *Click, Clack, Moo: Cows That Type.* Illustrated by Betsy Lewin. Simon & Schuster.

DiTerlizzi, Tony. 2002. *The Spider and the Fly.* Simon & Schuster.

Henkes, Kevin. 2006. *Lily's Big Day.* Greenwillow.

Kellogg, Steven. 2004 (1977). *The Mysterious Tadpole.* Puffin (Dial).

McKissack, Patricia, and Onawumi Jean Moss. *Precious and the Boo Hag.* Illustrated by Kyrsten Brooker. Atheneum.

Meddaugh, Susan. 2004. *Perfectly Martha.* Houghton. (See others in the Martha series.)

O'Malley, Kevin. 2010. *Animal Crackers Fly the Coop.* Walker.

Peet, Bill. 1977. *Big Bad Bruce.* Houghton.

Rosenberg, Liz. 1993. *Monster Mama.* Illustrated by Stephen Gammell. Putnam.

Small, David. 1986. *Imogene's Antlers.* Crown.

Stanley, Diane. 2004. *The Giant and the Beanstalk.* Harper.

Steig, William. 2007. *The One and Only Shrek! Plus 5 Other Stories.* Square Fish/Farrar.

Stockton, Frank. 2003. *The Bee-Man of Orn.* Illustrated by P. J. Lynch. Candlewick.

Van Allsburg, Chris. 1979. *The Garden of Abdul Gasazi.* Houghton.

Van Allsburg, Chris. 2002. *Zathura.* Houghton Mifflin.

Wiesner, David. 1999. *Sector 7.* Clarion.

Wiesner, David. 2006. *Flotsam.* Clarion.

Yolen, Jane. 1997 (1989). *Dove Isabeau.* Illustrated by Dennis Nolan. Voyager (Harcourt).

Yolen, Jane. 2009. *Come to the Fairies' Ball.* Wordsong.

PEARSON myeducationkit

Go to the topic Modern Fantasy on the MyEducationKit for this text, where you can:

- Search the Database of Children's Literature, housing more than 22,000 titles searchable in every genre by authors or illustrators, by awards won, by year published, and by topic and description.
- Explore genre-related Assignments and Activities, assignable exercises showing concepts in action through database use, video, cases, and student and teacher artifacts.
- Listen to podcasts and read interviews from some of the brightest and most enduring stars of children's literature in the Conversations.
- Discover weblinks that will lead you to sites representing the authors you learn about in these pages, classrooms with powerful children's literature connections, and literature awards.

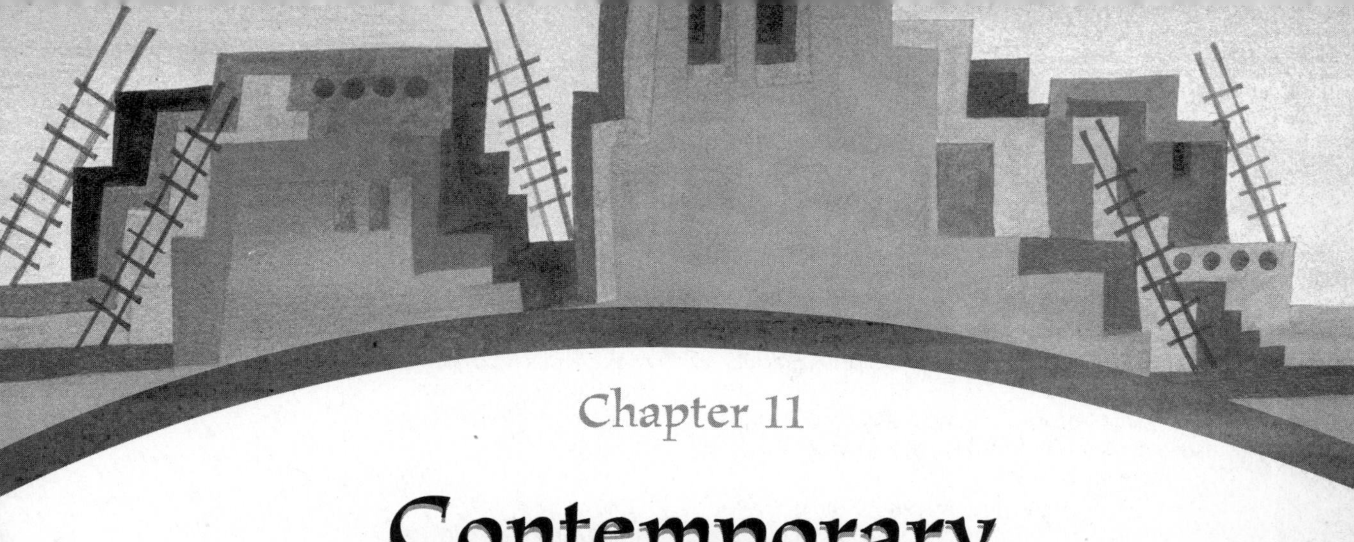

Chapter 11

Contemporary Realistic Fiction

Contemporary realistic fiction tells a story that never happened but *could* have happened. The events and characters of contemporary realistic fiction flow from the author's imagination, just as they do in fantasy. Unlike fantasy, which includes at least one element not found in this world, everything in contemporary realistic fiction is possible on planet Earth. Writers of contemporary realistic fiction (see Figure 11.1) observe life around them to tell their stories, often drawing on their own backgrounds.

Identifying with Contemporary Realistic Fiction

Of all the genres in children's literature, contemporary realistic fiction is perhaps the most popular because it is the most familiar—the most accessible. *This story takes place in my world. This is how I live. This book is about a girl like me.* People are interested in their own lives, and this genre is about "my life." Because the characters in contemporary realistic fiction are similar to people in my town, I get to know them quickly and feel as if I've known them a long time. The main character, in particular, becomes a kindred spirit. She experiences the same disappointments and hopes, rejections and joys as the reader, who is amazed and thrilled to find someone who sees the world through similar glasses. Certainly, the reader can connect with the lives of those who lived in the past and also with fantasy characters, but something about the immediacy of the here-and-now seems to pack an additional emotional punch.

Visit the MyEducationKit for this course to enhance your understanding of chapter concepts with activities, weblinks, podcasts, and a searchable database of more than 22,000 children's literature titles.

Notable Authors of Contemporary Realistic Fiction

Bauer, Joan: Teen problem novels.
Blume, Judy: Teen and preteen problem novels.
Byars, Betsy: Preteen problem novels.
Cleary, Beverly: Primary- and middle-grade humor.
Clements, Andrew: Elementary school stories.
Creech, Sharon: Middle-grade problem novels.
Danziger, Paula: Primary- and middle-grade humor.
George, Jean Craighead: Ecological fiction.
Giff, Patricia Reilly: Primary- and middle-grade humor; problem novels.
Hamilton, Virginia: African American experience.
Henry, Marguerite: Horse stories.
Hobbs, Will: Outdoor adventure stories.
Holt, Kimberly: Preteen problem novels.
Horvath, Polly: Humorous fiction.
Konigsburg, Elaine L.: Humorous childhood experiences; problem novels.
Korman, Gordon: Humorous school and family stories; action series.
Lowry, Lois: Teen and preteen problem novels; middle-grade humor.
Lupica, Mike: Sports fiction.
Martin, Ann: Teen and preteen modern problem novels.
Myers, Walter Dean: African American experience.
Naylor, Phyllis R.: Mysteries; adolescent humor; animal stories.
Park, Barbara: Primary- and middle-grade humor.
Paterson, Katherine: Teen and preteen problem novels.
Paulsen, Gary: Survival and adventure fiction.
Peck, Richard: Teen problem novels; middle-grade family stories.
Sachar, Louis: Middle-grade humor.
Spinelli, Jerry: Teen and preteen problem novels.
Staples, Suzanne Fisher: Problem novels set in Pakistan, India, Afghanistan, and the United States.
Van Draanen, Wendelin: Mysteries and humor.
Voigt, Cynthia: Teen and preteen problem novels.
Williams, Carol Lynch: Teen and preteen problem novels.
Woodsen, Jacqueline: African American experience.
Yep, Laurence: Chinese American experience.

While "my world" is familiar and appealing to readers, it actually remains a limited concept for all of us. No matter where I live or what my life is like, my peers across the country, across town, and even across the backyard fence are experiencing things unknown to me. If I live with both my parents, I do not understand what my classmate Paul is going through now that his father has moved out and he is alone with his mother. But Beverly Cleary's *Dear Mr. Henshaw* (1983) shows me a divorced home and gives me some understanding of a boy who lives in my world but is experiencing it differently. If I live in rural Maine, I benefit by reading about kids in inner-city Chicago and vice versa. In this genre are the experiences in my world that I do not yet have—books dealing with specific regions, cultures, nationalities, minorities, and subgroups that provide an expanded understanding of "my world."

The importance of identifying with one's own life is a key reason that children's books have children as protagonists. The age of the main character is approximately the age of the reader. For this reason, *The Endless Steppe* (1968), Esther Hautzig's memoir about her childhood in World War II Poland and Russia, eventually was published as a children's book, even though she did not have a child audience in mind when she wrote it. Because the main character is a young girl, the

book's market and audience are the same—young readers. The rule of thumb is that children will read about characters who are slightly older than they are but are hesitant about reading books with characters who are younger.

A small but important type of contemporary realistic fiction does not fit the pattern of having children as the main characters, but these books still offer enough humor, adventure, or entertainment to draw young readers. Examples are Peggy Parish's Amelia Bedelia stories about the maid who takes too literally her employer's instructions (told to "ice the cake," she puts ice cubes on its top and sticks the cake in the freezer); Cynthia Rylant's books presenting the day-to-day adventures of an old man and his cat, Mr. Putter and Tabby; and Patricia Polacco's *Someone for Mr. Sussman* (2008), in which Jerome's matchmaker grandmother has a difficult time finding a wife for old Mr. Sussman. Sometimes the main character isn't even human, as in Sheila Burnford's Newbery Honor winner *The Incredible Journey* (1961), the story of two dogs and a cat as they travel 250 miles through the Canadian wilderness to reach their home.

Familiarity may help explain why many children who have not yet discovered the pleasure of books often find their first successful reading experiences with contemporary realistic fiction. Trying out a new book is a risk for the reader, and one who is not steeped in personal reading is less likely to take big chances. Contemporary realistic fiction offers less of a gamble because the book contains elements familiar to the reader. Much of the groundwork already exists for a relationship, or even a friendship, to develop between child and character.

Contemporary Realistic Fiction and Society

Contemporary realism presents a snapshot of society and the child's place in it. Before the mid-1960s, children's fiction typically presented a world without negative or earthy aspects because children generally were kept distant from those parts of life. Geoffrey Trease (1983) lists some of the generally accepted restrictions that applied to the writing of children's books before 1960: no budding love affairs, no liquor, no supernatural phenomena, no undermining of authority, no parents with serious human weaknesses, and no realistic working-class speech (including the mildest cursing). But then in the 1960s, the face of American society took on a new look because of upheavals such as the civil rights movement, the Vietnam War, and large cracks in the traditional family structure. Evidence of the changes appeared on the front pages of newspapers, harsh realities were broadcast into the living rooms of the world on television newscasts, and no neighborhood was free from divorce.

As society changed, books for young readers began to reflect those shifting views. Louise Fitzhugh's *Harriet the Spy* was a pivotal book when it appeared in 1964. The protagonist, Harriet, was a nontraditional girl who dressed in a sweatshirt, spied on neighbors, was neglected by her well-to-do parents, and underwent psychotherapy. All of these plot elements signaled a shift in the acceptable literary content of the early 1960s, which featured children in protected and positive situations.

Controversy over the realities in these and other books spread widely. These changes, beginning in the 1960s and flourishing in the 1970s, came to be called *new realism* (see Chapter 5). The harsher parts of life simply had not been given center stage in books for young readers until then. When the taboos lifted, new books spewed forth problems and realities previously unseen in children's publishing. Topics such as death, divorce, drugs, abuse, profanity, nontraditional lifestyles, and single-parent families not only were mentioned in the books, but they also became major themes.

Society continued to change. A new generation of problems popped up in headlines and public consciousness, such as inner-city survival, teen suicide, gang life, AIDS, random shootings, anorexia nervosa, white supremacy, self-mutilation, and terrorism. As those issues took root in society, they sprouted in contemporary books for children, and that cycle continues as ever-newer concerns surface in both society and writing for young readers.

Because of the immediacy of the problems in realistic fiction, it is most often the genre in which the taboos of literature are tested and traditionally has been the genre that attracts the most controversy. When a book deals with the issue of cocaine in a modern middle school, the emotional impact of the problem tends to be stronger than in a story treating the consequences of opium addiction in 18th-century China. Society was also affected drastically by drugs 200 years ago, but the middle school setting is closer to home both emotionally and physically. That books for children acknowledge such problems is seen as relevant and helpful by some people and abhorred as too stark and unnecessary by others, and thus the debate begins. (For more on controversy and censorship, see Chapter 16.)

Common Categories of Contemporary Realistic Fiction

Children do not ask a librarian, "Do you have another good book of contemporary realistic fiction?" But a child will zero in on a particular type of book found within that genre, wanting another good title about animals. Or sports. Or survival. Or a good humorous book.

Stories in these areas have proven appeal, and teachers who wish to help the variety of students in an average classroom find books of interest would do well to become familiar with some titles from each of the popular reading categories in contemporary realistic fiction: animals, humor, mysteries, problem novels/family stories, series, sports, and survival/adventure. It is important to remember, however, that these categories are neither rigid nor exclusive. A single title may fall into more than one category, such as a sports book that is also humorous. And some types of books may jump genre lines. When young readers have a fondness for mysteries, for instance, they are less concerned if the genre is realistic fiction or fantasy. For this reason, our examples of mysteries in this chapter include titles from genres other than contemporary realistic fiction.

Animals

A mainstay of contemporary realistic fiction is the animal story. The bond between humans and animals is as satisfying as it is ancient, and stories about that relationship continue to reward readers. Marguerite Henry wrote more than 50 stories about animals, beginning at age 11 with a tale about a collie and a group of children, which she sold to a magazine for $12 (Murray, 1997). She wrote about dogs, cats, foxes, birds, and even a burro, but she always came back to horses, winning Newbery Honors for *Justin Morgan Had a Horse* (1945) and *Misty of Chincoteague* (1947) before receiving the Newbery Medal for *King of the Wind* (1948), the story of how an Arabian stallion was brought to England and became one of the founding sires of the Thoroughbred breed. Also popular are books about children and their horses, such as Susan Saunders's *Lucky Lady* (2000) and K. M. Peyton's *Blind Beauty* (2001).

Famous and readable dog books from the past include the incomparable *Lassie, Come Home* by Eric Knight (1940), the guaranteed-to-make-you-cry *Where the Red Fern Grows* by Wilson Rawls (1961), Fred Gipson's *Savage Sam* (1962), and the short and gripping *Stone Fox* (1980) by John Gardiner. Other dog books worth reading are *Beauty* (1988) by Bill Wallace; Phyllis Naylor's Newbery Award–winning *Shiloh* (1991), where a boy rescues an abused beagle and finds the courage to confront its owner; *Because of Winn-Dixie* by Kate DiCamillo (2000), a Newbery Medal winner that shows the delight of a young girl who finds a stray dog; Ann Martin's *A Dog's Life: The Autobiography of a Stray* (2005), and Jim Kjelgaard's immortal *Big Red* (1945).

Humor

It is impossible to have too many humorous books in a classroom or school library. Books that make people laugh appeal to a broad range of students, plus books with healthy doses of humor are often short, an additional attraction for the hard-to-convince. Beverly Cleary's Ramona books continue to find readers in each new generation of elementary students, and Gordon Korman's long string of humorous novels such as *Zoobreak* (2009) are especially popular with boys. Daniel Pinkwater is famous for his peculiar characters and zany situations in both picture books (*The Wuggie Norpel Story,* 1980) and novels (*Fat Camp Commandos,* 2002, plus *The Neddiad,* 2007, and *The Yggyssey,* 2009, which are contemporary offshoots of *The Iliad* and *The Odyssey*). Humor also is able to reach across age lines, as in Janette Rallison's *It's a Mall World After All* (2006), where the characters are teens but the situations will bring smiles to the lips of readers in the upper-elementary grades. In addition to humorous picture books and novels, teachers also should remember the irresistible pull of riddle and joke books on young readers.

Mysteries

Mysteries have been at the top of children's preference lists since the 1920s, regardless of the children's sex, ethnicity, or IQ (Haynes, 1988; Tomlinson & Tunnell, 1994). Because almost everyone likes mysteries, choosing one as a read-aloud at the beginning of a school year will almost guarantee a captive audience.

Sammy Keyes and the Cold Hard Cash (2008) is Wendelin Van Draanen's fourteenth mystery featuring Sammy Keyes, the 13-year-old super sleuth who lives with her grandmother in a seniors-only residence in California. Tony Abbott won the 2009 Edgar Allan Poe Award for the best juvenile mystery with *The Postcard* (2008), a double-layered mystery about Jason and what he discovers when he helps clean out his grandmother's house after her death. *Shakespeare's Secret* (2005) centers on the tale of a missing diamond thought to be owned by Anne Boleyn and supposedly hidden in the house where Hero Shakespeare has just moved with her family. Blue Balliett's *Wright 3* (2006) is a tale of three friends who face intrigue, suspense, and danger in their quest to save a decaying house built by the famous architect Frank Lloyd Wright.

Like many of the categories in this chapter, mysteries are found in genres other than contemporary realistic fiction. For instance, some of Betty Ren Wright's books (*The Dollhouse Murders,* 1983; *Moonlight Man,* 2000; *Crandall's Castle,* 2003) have contemporary settings and deal with contemporary problems, but the mystery often revolves around a supernatural occurrence, which would suggest modern fantasy. In the same way, Pullman's (1985) *Ruby in the Smoke* and Dowell's (2000) *Dovey Coe* are mysteries of another genre—historical fiction, set in 1872 and 1928, respectively.

Problem Novels

Because all novels have a problem—without one, there is no story—all novels technically can be called problem novels. But the term *problem novel* grew out of the age of new realism, when taboo topics became acceptable fare for juvenile books. Most of those topics focus on coping with serious problems of the human condition, including physical and mental disabilities, mental illness, death, peer-group pressure, bigotry, abuse, divorce, terrorism, sibling rivalry, and loneliness—to name but a few. In the problem novel, the problem controls the plot. For example, in Ann Martin's (2003) *A Corner of the Universe,* 12-year-old Hattie's life is turned upside down when her mentally challenged uncle arrives to live with her family. The book then centers on how her life and the lives of those in her family are affected by his presence. Problem novels tend not to be humorous or lighthearted, largely because they deal with serious issues.

Well-crafted problem novels include Irene Hunt's *The Lottery Rose* (2002), the story of a 7-year-old who eventually overcomes the emotional scars of child abuse; *Waiting for Normal* (2008), by Leslie Connor, which shows us a persuasively optimistic Addie, who has parents recently divorced, lives in a trailer with her dysfunctional mother, and is completely believable; and Carol Lynch Williams's *The Chosen One* (2009), the unusually sparse and understated story of 13-year-old Kyra, who lives in an isolated and ruthlessly governed polygamist compound, where she is scheduled soon to become the seventh wife of her 60-year-old uncle.

Life's heavy challenges can appear in a book without that title being classified as a problem novel if the problem is not the major thrust of the story, even though it is present and must be faced. In Betty Ren Wright's *The Dollhouse Murders,* Amy struggles with the love/hate feelings she has for her mentally challenged sister. Nevertheless, that struggle remains a subplot while the ghostly mystery of the dollhouse's connection to the long-ago murders of her grandparents takes center stage. When the problem is not the focus, the book generally is not a problem novel.

School and Family Novels

The problems in school and family stories tend to be less severe than those in problem novels, and the tone generally is lighter. Andrew Clements's *Frindle* (1996) is a humorous tale of the intellectual battle between a wise and seasoned teacher and a bright but very determined fifth-grade boy. In *The Penderwicks on Gardam Street* (2008), Jeanne Birdsall tells of the various plots hatched by four young girls to keep their widowed father from remarrying. The Chinese year of the rat is a year of change, and Taiwanese American Pacy experiences change in spades in Grace Lin's *The Year of the Rat* (2008): Pacy's best friend moves away, a new boy shows up at school, she must find a way to pursue her dream of becoming a writer and illustrator, plus she must learn how to find beauty in new things.

Series Books

Books in series vary greatly in quality. Some find acceptance in the literary mainstream, like Lois Lowry's Anastasia Krupnik stories and Phyllis Reynolds Naylor's titles featuring Alice. These books have a memorable main character, appear first in hardcover, and evolve into a series as the character experiences more adventures. At the other end of the series spectrum are the books

viewed unfavorably by many literary critics. Most are mass-market paperbacks, which seldom appear first as hardbacks and tend to be written according to a formula with a predictable plot, relatively flat characters, and a writing style that leans toward the unimaginative (Tunnell & Jacobs, 2005).

Nevertheless, whatever the content or quality, series books are important to literacy development because of two characteristics: comfort and story. First, series are comfortable because they are familiar and predictable. Readers know the characters—after the first book, they become friends—and readers can make successful guesses about what is going to happen. Second, readers know that they are getting a real story with a clear problem and a satisfying solution. "Young readers frequently complain about the difficulty of getting started in a new book. In a familiar series, this difficulty is averted. This 'instant start' instead of frustration plays a large role in luring that student into regular reading" (Ross, 1995).

Some old series of realistic fiction are still popular, most notably the Hardy Boys and Nancy Drew, which have been reissued in paperback. Since those series first appeared on the scene, other series have captured thousands of devoted readers. Examples include titles appropriate for the early grades, such as the Kids of Polk Street School (Patricia Reilly Giff) and the Pee-Wee Scouts (Judy Delton). Series for grades 2–5 include Junie B. Jones (Barbara Park), Adventures of the Bailey School Kids (Debbie Daly and Marsha Thornton Jones), Cam Jansen (David Jansen and Susanna Natti), Encyclopedia Brown (Donald Sobol), Judy Moody (Megan McDonald), Horse Crazy (Alison Lester), Sassy (Sharon Draper), 39 Clues (variety of authors, including Rick Riordan, Jude Watson, Gordon Korman, Linda Sue Park, and Margaret Peterson Haddix), and Undercover Girl (Christine Harris). Older, action-seeking readers around ages 11–12 will be rewarded with the James Bond–like adventures of 14-year-old Alex Rider (*Eagle Strike,* 2004) by Anthony Horowitz; the brother–sister espionage team in Gordon Korman's On the Run series, beginning with *Chasing the Falconers* (2005); and Beacon Street Girls (Annie Bryant). Of course, not all series books are strictly contemporary realism. For example, the Magic Tree House series (Mary Pope Osborne), the Katie Kazoo books (Nancy Krulik), the Dragonslayers' Academy series (Kate McMullan), and the 43 Old Cemetery Road books (Kate Klise) are modern fantasy.

Whatever the genre, readers tend to immerse themselves in a particular series only until they reach a self-determined level of saturation or until they finish all the titles. As much as some teachers and librarians believe the weaker of the series books are somehow bad for a reader's literary health, if not their overall character, no evidence exists to indicate that those who have indulged in series books, even to extremes, will come to a bad end (Tunnell & Jacobs, 2005). However, the jury seems to still be out on romance books. Romance series appear under dozens of different imprints and names, each with its own label that usually identifies the degree of sexual specificity. Young readers of romance stories often make the easy transition from the limited romance tales for older children and adolescents to the endless number of romance books written for adults.

Sports

Sports stories tend to fall into two groups: game focused and problem focused. Game-focused books are interested in the score and who wins the game. The major dramatic question always centers on victory: "Will the Panthers win the city championship?" Whether the sport is football or ice hockey, soccer or snowboarding, Matt Christopher has titles to offer all sports enthusiasts who like to see the right team win.

Problem-focused sports books have a sports setting, but the major dramatic question always goes beyond the final score. John Tunis, who wrote about baseball in the mid-20th century and whose books recently have been republished, captured so accurately the genuine feel of both real life and baseball that his stories remain fresh many decades later. Each of Alfred Slote's sports novels shows a complex character devoted to sports but centers on an issue other than the game, like leukemia, parental pressure, and personal sacrifice. Mike Lupica, in addition to writing individual novels for both middle school and elementary sports fans, adds two sports books each year to a series for grades 4–6 called Comeback Kids. Sports books for girls? It is becoming easier to find solid and interesting titles with female protagonists, like *The Girl Who Threw Butterflies* (2009) by Mick Cochrane.

Other well-known sports writers include John Ritter (*The Desperado Who Stole Baseball,* 2009), Thomas Dygard (*Second Stringer,* 1998 [football]), Rich Wallace (*Kickers: Benched,* 2010 [soccer]), and Dan Gutman, whose Baseball Card Adventures meld fantasy, historical fiction, and contemporary realistic fiction as 13-year-old Joe travels back in time to the days of famous ball players. Titles include *Jim and Me* (2009), *Ray and Me* (2009), and *Roberto and Me* (2010). Not many sports titles make the Newbery list, but Bruce Brooks won a Newbery Honor for his basketball story *The Moves Make the Man* (1984).

Survival and Adventure

Stories of survival and adventure are most often set in the wilderness. Classic novels of this type include the Newbery Honor books *My Side of the Mountain* (Jean George, 1959) and *Hatchet* (Gary Paulsen, 1987), plus the Newbery-winning *Holes* (Louis Sachar, 1998). Characters sometimes are faced with urban survival, as well. In Felice Holman's *Slake's Limbo* (1974), 13-year-old Aremis Slake, hounded by his fears and misfortunes, flees into New York City's subway tunnels. There he manages to survive, believing he never again will emerge above ground.

Often adventure stories combine survival with discovery, such as in Michael Morpurgo's *Kensuke's Kingdom* (2003), wherein the young protagonist is swept off his family's yacht and washes up on a desert island. Adventure comes when he discovers an old Japanese soldier stranded there more than four decades following World War II. Other tales of adventure involve a trek or a quest, as in Will Hobbs's *The Big Wander* (1992), in which Clay searches the rugged Southwest canyon country for his lost uncle, and *Crossing the Wire* (2006), the story of young Victor Flores's journey north and his eventual attempt at crossing the Mexican border at Arizona to enter the United States. But no matter the reason for the adventure, the draw for young readers is the excitement and danger offered by this type of story.

The offerings of contemporary realistic fiction are as wide as life, helping explore today's people, problems, and places. In this popular genre, young readers can find their own lives, recognize friends, and meet strangers who can show them different ways of living and thinking. Whether the appeal of a book lies in a skillful re-creation of current lifestyles or a comfortable pattern found in a series, the best of contemporary realistic fiction examines human beings facing and overcoming the challenges of living in today's world.

Contemporary Realistic Fiction Reading Lists

Fifteen of Our Favorites

Birdsall, Jeanne. 2008. *The Penderwicks on Gardam Street.* Knopf. The four Penderwick sisters are faced with the unimaginable prospect of their widowed father dating, and they hatch a plot to stop him. (School and family story.)

Clements, Andrew. 1996. *Frindle.* Simon & Schuster. When he decides to turn his fifth-grade teacher's love of the dictionary around on her, clever Nick Allen invents a new word and begins a chain of events that quickly moves beyond his control. (School and family story.)

Connor, Leslie. 2008. *Waiting for Normal.* Katherine Tegen Books/HarperCollins. Twelve-year-old Addie tries to cope with her mother's erratic behavior and being separated from her beloved stepfather and half-sisters when she and her mother go to live in a small trailer by the railroad tracks on the outskirts of Schenectady, New York. (Problem novel.)

DiCamillo, Kate. 2000. *Because of Winn-Dixie.* Candlewick. Ten-year-old India Opal Buloni describes her first summer in the town of Naomi, Florida, and all the good things that happen to her because of her big ugly dog, Winn-Dixie. A Newbery Honor book. (School and family story.)

Hunt, Irene. 2002 (1976). *Lottery Rose.* Berkley (Scribner's). A young victim of child abuse gradually overcomes his fears and suspicions when placed in a home with other boys. (Problem novel.)

Konigsburg, E. L. 2007 (1967). *From the Mixed-Up Files of Mrs. Basil E. Frankweiler.* Atheneum. Twelve-year-old Claudia is tired of her life of responsibility, so she and her little brother run away from home and hide in the Metropolitan Museum of Art. Winner of the Newbery Medal. (School and family story; mystery.)

Martin, Ann. 2002. *A Corner of the Universe.* Scholastic. The summer that Hattie turns 12, she meets the childlike uncle she never knew and becomes friends with a girl who works at the carnival that comes to Hattie's small town. A Newbery Honor book. (Problem novel.)

Naylor, Phyllis Reynolds. 2007 (1989). *Alice in Rapture, Sort Of.* Atheneum. The summer before she enters the seventh grade becomes the summer of Alice's first boyfriend, and she discovers that love is about the most mixed-up thing that can possibly happen to you, especially since she has no mother to go to for advice. (See others in the Alice series.) (School and family story, humor.)

Paterson, Katherine. 1978. *The Great Gilly Hopkins.* Crowell. An 11-year-old foster child tries to cope with her longings and fears as she schemes against everyone who tries to be friendly. A Newbery Honor book. (Problem novel.)

Paulsen, Gary. 2007 (1987). *Hatchet.* Simon & Schuster (Bradbury). After a plane crash, 13-year-old Brian spends 54 days in the wilderness, learning to survive with only the aid of a hatchet given him by his mother and also learning to survive his parents' divorce. A Newbery Honor book. (Animal story.)

Rawls, Wilson. 1961. *Where the Red Fern Grows.* Doubleday. A young boy living in the Ozarks achieves his heart's desire when he becomes the owner of two redbone hounds and teaches them to be hunters. (Animal story.)

Robinson, Barbara. 1972. *The Best Christmas Pageant Ever.* Harper. The six mean Herdman kids lie, steal, smoke cigars (even the girls), and then become involved in the community Christmas pageant. (School and family story.)

Sachar, Louis. 1998. *Holes.* Farrar. As further evidence of his family's bad fortune, which they attribute to a curse on a distant relative, Stanley Yelnats is sent to a hellish correctional camp in the Texas desert, where he finds his first real friend, a treasure, and a new sense of himself. Winner of the Newbery Medal. (Problem novel.)

Spinelli, Jerry. 1990. *Maniac Magee.* Little, Brown. After his parents die, Jeffrey Lionel Magee's life becomes legendary, as he accomplishes athletic and other feats that awe his contemporaries. At the same time he searches in anguish for a place to call home. Winner of the Newbery Medal. (Problem novel.)

Williams, Carol Lynch. 2009. *The Chosen One*. St. Martin's Griffin. In a polygamous cult in the desert, Kyra, not yet 14, sees being chosen to be the seventh wife of her uncle as just punishment for having read books and kissed a boy, in violation of Prophet Child's teachings, and is torn between facing her fate and running away from all that she knows and loves.

Others We Like

Animals

Cleary, Beverly. 1991. *Strider.* Morrow. In a series of diary entries, Leigh tells how he comes to terms with his parents' divorce, acquires joint custody of an abandoned dog, and joins the track team at school.

Farley, Walter. 2008 (1941). *The Black Stallion.* Random House. Pulled to a desert island by a wild black stallion he has freed during a shipwreck at sea and then rescued by a southbound freighter, a 17-year-old boy befriends the horse, trains him by night, and rides him to victory in a match race.

Henry, Marguerite. 2006 (1947). *King of the Wind.* Aladdin (Rand McNally). This story follows the adventures of the Arabian stallion brought to England to become one of the founding sires of the Thoroughbred breed and the mute Arab stable boy who tended him with loyalty and devotion all his life.

Kjelgaard, Jim. 1992 (1945). *Big Red.* Yearling (Grosset). The story of the friendship between a champion Irish setter and a trapper's son, who together face many dangers in the harsh Wintapi wilderness they call home.

Morpurgo, Michael. 2006. *The Amazing Story of Adolphus Tips.* Scholastic. When Boowie reads the diary that his grandmother sends him, he learns of her childhood in World War II England, when American and British soldiers practiced for D-Day's invasion in the area of her home, and about her beloved cat, Adolphus Tip, and the cat's namesake.

Mowat, Farley. 1996 (1961). *Owls in the Family.* Yearling (Little, Brown). When a boy gets two owls as pets, they turn the house topsy-turvy and shake up the whole neighborhood.

Naylor, Phyllis R. 1991. *Shiloh.* Atheneum. (See other Shiloh titles.) When he finds a lost beagle in the hills behind his West Virginia home, Marty tries to hide it from his family and the dog's real owner, a mean-spirited man known to shoot deer out of season and mistreat his dogs.

North, Sterling. 2004 (1963). *Rascal.* Puffin (Dutton). The author recalls his carefree life in a small midwestern town at the close of World War I and his adventures with his pet raccoon, Rascal.

Staples, Suzanne Fisher. 2003. *The Green Dog.* Farrar. During the summer before fifth grade, Suzanne, a daydreaming loner who likes to fish and walk through the woods, acquires a canine companion. Based on the author's childhood in northeastern Pennsylvania.

Wallace, Bill. 2005. *The Pick of the Litter.* Holiday House. Twelve-year-old Tom learns firsthand about honor—first when he is wrongly accused of lying at school and then when he faces the risk of losing a puppy he has come to love while helping his grandfather train hunting dogs. But writing to a new friend helps him sort through his feelings and do the right thing.

Wedekind, Annie. 2009. *Little Prince.* Feiwell and Friends/Macmillan. (See other Breyer Horse Collection titles.) Phin, a Shetland pony, has loved leaving the carnival to become a show pony in the big city, but when his owner loses interest in him, he is sent to a farm for unwanted animals and must find a way to make a home there.

Humor

Blume, Judy. 2003 (1972). *Tales of a Fourth Grade Nothing.* Dutton. Peter finds his demanding 2-and-a-half-year-old brother an ever increasing problem.

Cleary, Beverly. 2007 (1968). *Ramona the Pest.* Morrow. Ramona meets lots of interesting people in kindergarten class, like Davy, whom she keeps trying to kiss, and Susan, whose springy curls seem to ask to be pulled. (See others in the Ramona series.)

Gutman, Dan. 2004. *The Million Dollar Strike.* Hyperion. Best friends Ouchie and Squishy—who love bowling and horror movies, respectively—meet the eccentric owner of a local bowling alley and try to help him save Bowl-A-Rama from the wrecking ball and a destructive psychotic lunatic.

Korman, Gordon. 2004 (1991). *I Want to Go Home.* Scholastic. Rudy is sent to Camp Algonkian Island for the summer and hates it, so he devotes all his energies toward escaping.

Mowat, Farley. 1993 (1953). *The Dog Who Wouldn't Be.* McClelland and Stewart (Little Brown). Based on his boyhood experiences on the Canadian prairies, Mowat tells of his unusual dog who climbed trees and ladders, rode passenger in an open car wearing goggles, and displayed hunting skills that bordered on sheer genius.

Naylor, Phyllis Reynolds. 2008 (1993). *Alice in April.* Atheneum (Aladdin). While trying to survive seventh grade, Alice discovers that turning 13 will make her the Woman of the House at home, so she starts a campaign to get more appreciated for taking care of her father and older brother.

Park, Barbara. 2006 (1988). *Skinnybones.* Knopf. Irrepressible 12-year-old Alex is convinced that he will be a star and impress his schoolmates when, as the winner of a cat food essay contest, he is asked to make a commercial for national television. (See other Skinnybones books.)

Paulsen, Gary. 2007. *Lawn Boy.* Wendy Lamb Books/Random House. Things get out of hand for a 12-year-old boy when a neighbor convinces him to expand his summer lawn-mowing business.

Wiles, Deborah. 2007. *The Aurora County All-Stars.* Harcourt. Every year the boys in a small Mississippi town worry whether their annual July 4 baseball game will be canceled due to their county's anniversary pageant, but one of them uncovers secrets that will fix everything.

See also riddle books and collections of jokes on the children's shelves at libraries and bookstores.

Mysteries

Alphin, Elaine Marie. 2000. *Counterfeit Son.* Harcourt. When serial killer Hank Miller is killed in a shoot-out with police, his abused son Cameron adopts the identity of one of his father's victims in order to find a better life.

Avi. 2009. *Murder at Midnight.* Scholastic. Falsely accused of plotting to overthrow King Claudio, scholarly Mangus the magician, along with his street-smart servant boy, Fabrizio, face deadly consequences unless they can track down the real traitor by the stroke of midnight.

Balliett, Blue. 2004. *Chasing Vermeer.* Illustrated by Brett Helquist. Scholastic. When strange and seemingly unrelated events start to happen and a precious Vermeer painting disappears, 11-year-olds Petra and Calder combine their talents to solve an international art scandal.

Broach, Elise. 2005. *Shakespeare's Secret.* Holt. Named after a character in a Shakespeare play, misfit sixth grader Hero becomes interested in exploring this unusual connection because of a valuable diamond supposedly hidden in her new house, an intriguing neighbor, and the unexpected attention of the most popular boy in school.

Duncan, Lois. 1981. *Stranger with My Face.* Little, Brown. A 17-year-old senses she is being spied on and probably impersonated, but when she discovers what actually is occurring, it is more unbelievable than she ever imagined.

Horowitz, Anthony. 2008. *Snakehead.* Philomel. While working with the Australian Secret Service on a dangerous mission, teenaged spy Alex Rider uncovers information about his parents. (See others in the Alex Rider series.)

Nixon, Joan Lowery. 1986. *The Other Side of Dark.* Delacorte. Seventeen-year-old Stacy awakens from a four-year coma ready to identify, locate, and prosecute the young man who murdered her mother and wounded her.

Raskin, Ellen. 2007 (1978). *The Westing Game.* Novel Units (Dutton). The mysterious death of an eccentric millionaire brings together an unlikely assortment of heirs who must uncover the circumstances of his death before they can claim their inheritance.

Smith, Roland. 2001. *Zach's Lie.* Hyperion. When Jack Osborne is befriended by his school's custodian and a Basque girl, he begins to adjust to his family's sudden move to Elko, Nevada, after entering the Witness Security Program, but the drug cartel against which his father will testify is determined to track them down.

Van Draanen, Wendelin. 2008. *Sammy Keyes and the Cold Hard Cash.* Knopf. Thirteen-year-old Sammy meets a mysterious man who dies of a heart attack after telling her to get rid of the large amount of money he is carrying, leading her to investigate who the man was and how he came

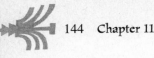

to be carrying so much cash. (See others in the Sammy Keyes series.)

Wright, Betty Ren. 2008 (1983). *The Dollhouse Murders.* Holiday. A dollhouse filled with a ghostly light in the middle of the night and dolls that have moved from where she last left them lead Amy and her retarded sister to unravel the mystery surrounding grisly murders that took place years ago.

Problem Novels

Bauer, Joan. 2000. *Hope Was Here.* Putnam. When 16-year-old Hope and the aunt who has raised her move from Brooklyn to Mulhoney, Wisconsin, to work as waitress and cook in the Welcome Stairways diner, they become involved with the diner owner's political campaign to oust the town's corrupt mayor.

Beaty, Andrea. 2008. *Cicada Summer.* Amulet/ Abrams. Twelve-year-old Lily mourns her brother and has not spoken since the accident she feels she could have prevented, but the summer Tinny comes to town, she is the only one who realizes Lily's secret.

Blume, Judy. 1970. *Are You There God? It's Me, Margaret.* Bradbury. Faced with the difficulties of growing up and choosing a religion, a 12-year-old girl talks over her problems with her own private God.

Byars, Betsy. 1977. *The Pinballs.* Harper. Three lonely foster children learn to care about themselves and each other.

Galante, Cecelia. 2008. *The Patron Saint of Butterflies.* Bloomsbury. When her grandmother takes 14-year-old Agnes, her younger brother, and best friend Honey and escapes Mount Blessing, a Connecticut religious commune, Agnes clings to the faith she loves while Honey looks toward a future free of control, cruelty, and preferential treatment.

Gifaldi, David. 2008. *Listening for Crickets.* Holt. With parents who fight all the time, 10-year-old Jake finds comfort and escape in the stories he creates for himself and his little sister.

Holt, Kimberly Willis. 1998. *My Louisiana Sky.* Holt. Growing up in Saitter, Louisiana, in the 1950s, 12-year-old Tiger Ann struggles with her feelings about her stern but loving grandmother, her mentally slow parents, and her good friend and neighbor, Jesse.

Lowry, Lois. 2007 (1977). *A Summer to Die.* Delacorte (Houghton Mifflin). When their family moved from the city to the country, Molly and Meg face new challenges, but the greatest is when Molly is diagnosed with leukemia.

Philbrick, Rodman. 1993. *Freak the Mighty.* Scholastic. At the beginning of eighth grade, learning-disabled Max and his new friend Freak, whose birth defect has affected his body but not his brilliant mind, find that when they combine forces, they make a powerful team.

Slepian, Jan. 1990. *Risk n' Roses.* Philomel. In 1948, newly moved to the Bronx, 11-year-old Skip longs to shed her responsibility for her mentally handicapped older sister and to give her whole attention to her new friendship with the bold and daring girl who sems to run the neighborhood.

Spinelli, Jerry. 2000. *Stargirl.* Knopf. In this story about the perils of popularity, the courage of nonconformity, and the thrill of first love, an eccentric student named Stargirl changes Mica High School forever.

Whelan, Gloria. 2000. *Homeless Bird.* HarperCollins. When 13-year-old Koly enters into an ill-fated arranged marriage, she must either suffer a destiny dictated by India's tradition or find the courage to oppose it.

Williams, Carol Lynch. 1997. *The True Colors of Caitlynne Jackson.* Delacorte. Twelve-year-old Caity and her younger sister Cara must fend for themselves when their abusive mother storms out of the house with a suitcase and does not come back.

School and Family Novels

Barrows, Annie. 2009. *Ivy & Bea Doomed to Dance.* Chronicle. Second-grade best friends Ivy and Bean beg for ballet lessons. Then, when they are cast as squids in their first recital, they scheme to find a way out of what seems to be boring, hard, and potentially embarrassing.

Birdsall, Jeanne. 2005. *The Penderwicks: A Summer Tale of Four Sisters, Two Rabbits, and a Very Interesting Boy.* Knopf. While vacationing with their widowed father in the Berkshire Mountains, four young sisters, ages 4 through 12, share

adventures with a local boy, much to the dismay of his snobbish mother.

Blume, Judy. 2009. *Friend or Fiend? with the Pain and the Great One.* Delacorte. First grader Jake "The Pain" and his sister, third grader Abigail "The Great One," have more adventures, including visiting their cousins in New York and celebrating their cat Fluzzy's birthday. (See others in the Pain and the Great One series.)

Cleary, Beverly. 2006 (1981). *Ramona Quimby, Age 8.* HarperCollins (Morrow). The further adventures of the Quimby family, as Ramona enters the third grade.

Clements, Andrew. 1999. *The Landry News.* Simon & Schuster. A fifth grader starts a newspaper with an editorial that prompts her burned-out classroom teacher to really begin teaching again, but he is later threatened with disciplinary action as a result.

Fletcher, Ralph. 1995. *Fig Pudding.* Clarion. Cliff describes the excitement, conflict, and sudden tragedy experienced by his large and boisterous family during his eleventh year.

Gilson, Jamie. 2008. *Chess! I Love It, I Love It, I Love It!* Clarion. When second grader Richard and three other members of the Sumac School Chess Club compete in their first tournament, they each learn something about luck, concentration, and teamwork.

Korman, Gordon. 1998. *The 6th Grade Nickname Game.* Hyperion. Eleven-year-old best friends Jeff and Wiley, who like to give nicknames to their classmates, try to find the right one for the new girl, Cassandra, while adjusting to the football coach who has become their new teacher.

Lowry, Lois. 1995 (1979). *Anastasia Krupnik.* Houghton. Anastasia's tenth year has some good things, like falling in love and really getting to know her grandmother, and some bad things, like finding out about an impending baby brother. (See other Anastasia Krupnik titles.)

McGhee, Alison. 2009. *Julia Gillian (and the Quest for Joy).* Scholastic. Ten-year-old Julia Gillian's best friend is keeping secrets, their beloved lunch lady has been replaced by a tyrant, and trumpet lessons prove difficult, making it hard for her to follow the music teacher's advice to "look for the joy."

Williams, Carol Lynch. 2008. *Pretty Like Us.* Peachtree. A shy, small-town girl learns the true meaning of loyalty, love, and beauty through her friendship with a classmate who is suffering from a rare, life-threatening illness.

Sports

Brooks, Bruce. 1984. *The Moves Make the Man.* Harper. A black boy and an emotionally troubled white boy in North Carolina form a precarious friendship.

Christopher, Matt. 2010. *The Home Run Kid Races On.* Little, Brown. Sylvester improves his baseball skills while being coached by a man who bears a striking resemblance to baseball great Ty Cobb.

Cochrane, Mick. 2009. *The Girl Who Threw Butterflies.* Knopf. Eighth grader Molly's ability to throw a knuckleball earns her a spot on the baseball team, which not only helps her feel connected to her recently deceased father, who loved baseball, but also helps in other aspects of her life.

Dygard, Thomas. 1998. *Second Stringer.* Morrow. When Kevin replaces the quarterback and football hero, who has suffered a knee injury, the second stringer needs to prove that he can do the job and is not just a substitute.

Lupica, Mike. 2009. *Shoot-Out: A Comeback Kids Novel.* Philomel. Twelve-year-old Jake must leave his championship soccer team to play on a team with a losing record when his family moves to a neighboring town.

Ritter, John. 2009. *The Desperado Who Stole Baseball.* Philomel. In 1881, the scrappy, rough-and-tumble baseball team in a California mining town enlists the help of a quick-witted 12-year-old orphan and the notorious outlaw Billy the Kid to win a big game against the National League Champion Chicago White Stockings. Prequel to *The Boy Who Saved Baseball.*

Slote, Alfred. 1973. *Hang Tough, Paul Mather.* Harper. A baseball pitcher with an incurable blood disease is determined to get in as much time on the mound as possible.

Spinelli, Jerry. 1996. *Crash.* Knopf. Seventh grader John "Crash" Coogan has always been comfortable with his tough, aggressive behavior, until his relationship with an unusual Quaker boy and his grandfather's stroke make him consider the meaning of friendship and the importance of family.

Tunis, John. 1996 (1940). *The Kid from Tompkinsville.* Sandpiper (Houghton Mifflin). As the

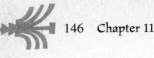

newest addition to the Brooklyn Dodgers, young Roy Tucker's pitching helps pull the team out of a slump, but when a freak accident ends his career as a pitcher, he must try to find another place for himself on the team.

Wallace, Rich. 2010. *Sports Camp.* Knopf. Eleven-year-old Riley Liston tries to fit in at Camp Olympia, a summer sports camp where he is one of the youngest boys.

Survival and Adventure

Blackwood, Gary. 2003 (1987). *Wild Timothy.* Scholastic (Atheneum). Thirteen-year-old Timothy, more interested in reading than in physical activity, reluctantly accompanies his enthusiastic father on a camping trip and, when he accidently becomes lost in the woods, discovers that he is capable of surviving on his own.

Cross, Gillian. 2004. *Dark Ground.* Dutton. Upon waking up naked and alone in a thick jungle, Robert remembers being in a plane with his family but finds no sign of a crash or survivors. Then he discovers he is in an alien place and needs help to make the perilous journey home.

George, Jean Craighead. 2003 (1972). *Julie of the Wolves.* Harper. While running away from home and an unwanted marriage, a 13-year-old Eskimo girl becomes lost on the North Slope of Alaska and is befriended by a wolf pack. (Also see the other Julie books.)

Hobbs, Will. 2006. *Crossing the Wire.* HarperCollins. Fifteen-year-old Victor Flores journeys north in a desperate attempt to cross the Arizona border and find work in the United States to support his family in central Mexico.

Holman, Felice. 1974. *Slake's Limbo.* Scribner's Thirteen year-old Aremis Slake, hounded by his fears and misfortunes, flees them into New York City's subway tunnels, never again—he believes—to emerge.

Napoli, Donna Jo. 2001. *Three Days.* Dutton. When her father suddenly dies while on a business trip, leaving her alone on an Italian highway, 11-year-old Jackie worries what will happen when she is picked up by two men with unknown motives.

Neale, Jonathan. 2004. *Himalaya.* Houghton Mifflin. In alternating chapters, 12-year-old Orrie and her older brother tell the story of a doomed mountain-climbing expedition in which they, their younger brother, their divorced father, and his girlfriend attempt to climb Island Peak in Nepal.

O'Dell, Scott. 2005 (1960). *Island of the Blue Dolphins.* Yearling (Houghton Mifflin). Left alone on a beautiful but isolated island off the coast of California, a young Indian girl spends 18 years not only surviving through her enormous courage and self-reliance but also finding a measure of happiness in her solitary life.

Paulsen, Gary. 1992. *The Haymeadow.* Delacorte. Fourteen-year-old John comes of age and gains self-reliance during the summer he spends up in the Wyoming mountains, tending his father's herd of sheep.

Paulsen, Gary. 1997. *Tucket's Ride.* Delacorte. When 15-year-old Francis and two younger children lose their way in the wilderness of the Southwest, they face capture at the hands of dangerous men.

Sallisbury, Graham. 2007. *Night of the Howling Dogs.* Wendy Lamb Books/Random House. In 1975, 11 Boy Scouts, their leaders, and some new friends camping at Halape, Hawaii, find their survival skills put to the test when a massive earthquake strikes, followed by a tsunami.

Sperry, Armstrong. 2008 (1940). *Call It Courage.* Simon (Macmillan). Sperry relates how Mafatu, a young Polynesian boy whose name means Stout Heart, overcomes his terrible fear of the sea and proves his courage to himself and his people.

White, Robb. 1972. *Deathwatch.* Doubleday. Needing money for school, a college boy accepts a job as a guide on a desert hunting trip and nearly loses his life when he becomes the hunted instead of the hunter.

Easier to Read

Bulla, Clyde Robert. 1975. *Shoeshine Girl.* Crowell. (Problem.)

Byars, Betsy. 2004. *Little Horse on His Own.* Illustrated by David McPhail. Holt. (Animals.)

Christopher, Matt. 1993. *The Dog That Stole Home.* Little, Brown. (Sports; Animals.)

Cleary, Beverly. 1990. *Muggie Maggie.* Morrow. (School and family; Humor.)

Clements, Andrew. 2001. *Jake Drake, Bully Buster.* Simon. (Humor.)

Dahl, Roald. 1992. *The Vicar of Nibbleswicke.* Viking. (Humor.)

Giff, Patricia Reilly. 1996. *Good Luck, Ronald Morgan.* Viking. (Humor. See others in the Ronald Morgan series.)

Joosse, Barbara M. 2006. *Dead Guys Talk.* Clarion. (Mystery.)

MacLachlan, Patricia. 2010. *Word After Word After Word.* Kathryn Tegen/HarperCollins. (School and family.)

Napoli, Donna Jo, and Robert Furrow. 2006. *Sly the Sleuth and the Sports Mysteries.* Dial. (Sports; Mystery.)

Park, Barbara. 2006. *Junie B., First Grader: Aloha-ha-ha!* Illustrated by Denise Brunkus. Random. (Humor. See others in the Junie B. Jones series.)

Peck, Robert Newton. 1974. *Soup.* Knopf. (Humor.)

Roy, Ron. 2010. *March Mischief.* Illustrated by John Steven Gurney. Random House. (Mystery. See others in the Calendar Mysteries series.)

Smith, Doris Buchanan. 1973. *A Taste of Blackberries.* Crowell. (Problem.)

Sobol, Donald. 1963. *Encyclopedia Brown, Boy Detective.* Nelson. (Mystery. See others in the Encyclopedia Brown series.)

Stevenson, James. 1995. *The Bones in the Cliff.* Greenwillow. (Mystery.)

Wright, Betty Ren. 2006. *Princess for a Week.* Holiday House. (Mystery.)

Picture Books

Baylor, Byrd. 1994. *The Table Where Rich People Sit.* Illustrated by Peter Parnall. Scribner's.

Beaumont, Karen. 2005. *I Ain't Gonna Paint No More.* Illustrated by David Catrow. Harcourt.

Bunting, Eve. 1994. *Smoky Night.* Illustrated by David Diaz. Harcourt.

Bunting, Eve. 2000. *The Memory String.* Illustrated by Ted Rand. Clarion.

dePaola, Tomie. 1973. *Nana Upstairs & Nana Downstairs.* Viking.

Hutchins, Pat. 2003. *There's Only One of Me!* Greenwillow.

Juster, Norton. 2005. *The Hello, Goodbye Window.* Illustrated by Chris Raschka. Hyperion.

Polacco, Patricia. 1998. *Thank You, Mr. Falker.* Philomel.

Rosen, Michael. 2005. *Michael Rosen's Sad Book.* Illustrated by Quentin Blake. Candlewick.

Say, Allen. 1997. *Allison.* Houghton Mifflin.

Schertle, Alice. 1995. *Down the Road.* Illustrated by E. B. Lewis. Browndeer/Harcourt.

Seeber, Dorothea. 2000. *A Pup Just for Me: A Boy Just for Me.* Illustrated by Ed Young. Philomel.

Viorst, Judith. 1995. *Alexander, Who's Not (Do You Hear Me? I Mean It!) Going to Move.* Illustrated by Robin Preiss Glasser. Atheneum.

Woodsen, Jacqueline. 2001. *The Other Side.* Illustrated by E. B. Lewis. Putnam.

PEARSON **myeducationkit**™

Go to the topic Contemporary Realistic Fiction on the MyEducationKit for this text, where you can:

- Search the Database of Children's Literature, housing more than 22,000 titles searchable in every genre by authors or illustrators, by awards won, by year published, and by topic and description.
- Explore genre-related Assignments and Activities, assignable exercises showing concepts in action through database use, video, cases, and student and teacher artifacts.
- Listen to podcasts and read interviews from some of the brightest and most enduring stars of children's literature in the Conversations.
- Discover weblinks that will lead you to sites representing the authors you learn about in these pages, classrooms with powerful children's literature connections, and literature awards.

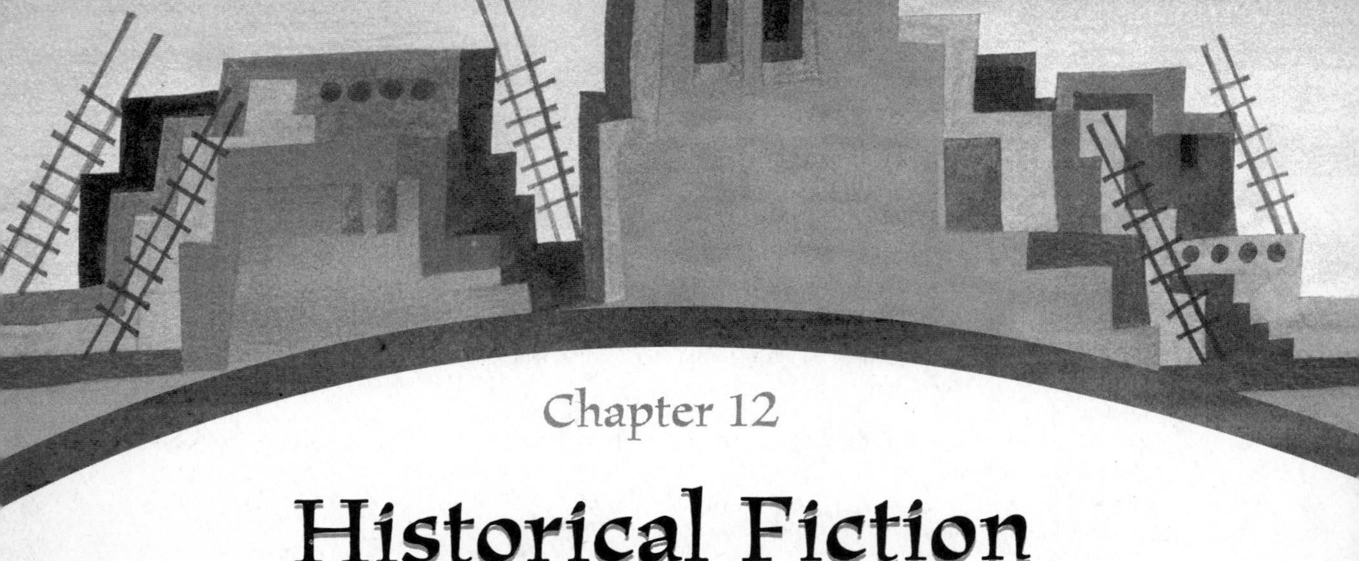

Chapter 12

Historical Fiction

Primary-grade curricula typically have not included the formal study of history because concepts of time develop slowly in children. How can youngsters to whom next week seems like an eternity, or who ask if Grandpa was around when the Pilgrims arrived, possibly gain an appreciation of their historical heritage? However, we have learned that teaching history through narrative, or story, can provide "a temporal scaffolding for historical understanding that is accessible even to quite young children" (Downey & Levstik, 1988, p. 338).

Humans tend to think in terms of narrative structures or story grammars, which basically involve characters formulating goals and then solving problems in order to achieve their goals. Children and adults are more likely to process and remember historical information when it comes in the form of a good story (Armbruster & Anderson, 1984; "Bringing Ancient History Back to Life," 2005; Hidi, Baird, & Hildyard, 1982; Jones, Coombs, & McKinney, 1994; McGowan & Guzzetti, 1991). Therefore, teachers who share and encourage the reading of historical picture books and novels likely are helping students learn historical facts, but more importantly, they are helping students see history as a vital and meaningful subject. Historical fiction can breathe life into what students may have considered irrelevant and dull, thus allowing them to see that their *present* is part of a *living past,* that people as real as themselves struggled with problems similar to their own, and that today's way of life is a result of what these people did in finding solutions.

History Textbooks versus History Trade Books

History textbooks are *not* effective in helping children make meaningful personal connections with the past. Studies report that students at all grade levels name social studies (history) as their most boring class and point to their textbooks as one of the major reasons (Fischer, 1997; Sewall, 1988).

As far back as 1893, the National Education Association declared, "When the facts are chosen with as little discrimination as in many school [history] textbooks, when they are mere lists of lifeless dates, details of military movements . . . [t]hey are repellent" (Ravitch, 1985, p. 13).

The criticism from many historians and educators has not lessened in recent years (American Textbook Council, 2006; Loewen, 1995; Paxton, 1999). "[History] textbooks have relied more and more on broken text and pictorial flash to hold student interest. Efforts to render textbooks 'readable'—at least by the standards of readability formulas—have contributed to their arid prose" (Sewall, 1988, p. 554). A report issued by the American Textbook Council indicates that "the most troubling writing and content are to be found among leading elementary-level social studies textbooks" (Sewall, 2000, p. 12). The report also points out that the most basic change in the books, beginning in the 1990s, has been "the loss of text." There is considerably less print but more illustrations (Sewall, 2000, p. 5).

> Too many topics are covered superficially. Textbooks have trouble building bridges from one subject to another. Language is often choppy, stilted, and impersonal. It is a difficult style to read, understand, or remember. (Sewall, 2000, p. 5)

History Textbooks Cover Too Much

History texts' biggest problems stem from the need to cover so much material that they cannot do justice to many important events, people, and concepts. For instance, Columbus is allowed only six short paragraphs (about 200 words) in the main body of the text in Harcourt's fifth-grade U.S. history text (Berson, Howard, & Salinas, 2007). Then, in a section similar to a sidebar, several entries from Columbus's log are included, amounting to a little less than 500 words—words that do nothing to reveal the cataclysmic consequences of his monumental discovery. In spite of longer coverage for some topics, including Columbus, Macmillan/McGraw-Hill's fifth-grade book (Banks et al., 2009) gives the Holocaust seven sentences (80 words), the Monroe Doctrine six sentences (113 words), and the entire Vietnam War seventeen sentences (290 words). Operation Desert Storm receives no coverage at all. Couple these short offerings with "arid prose," and you often have a formidable product that separates young readers from "the story of ourselves" (Freedman, 1993, p. 41).

The People Are Missing!

If history is indeed the story of ourselves, then another weakness of history textbooks is glaringly evident: The people are missing! The best one-word definition of *history* is, in fact, "people." Without human beings, whose emotions and actions influence the times, there is no history. Ask anyone who has had a memorable history class to describe why it was good, and the reasons always include a focus on people, whether prominent or ordinary.

Jean Fritz (1982), in her autobiographical novel *Homesick,* recalls her first school experience with American history texts:

> Miss Crofts put a bunch of history books on the first desk of each row so they could be passed back, student to student. I was glad to see that we'd be studying the history of Pennsylvania. Since both my mother's and father's families had helped settle Washington County, I was interested to know how they and the other pioneers had fared. Opening the book to the first chapter, "From Forest to Farmland," I skimmed through the pages but I couldn't find any mention of people at all. There was talk about dates

> and square miles and cultivation and population growth and immigration and the Western movement, but it was as if the forest had lain down and given way to farmland without anyone being brave or scared or tired or sad, without babies being born, without people dying. Well, I thought, maybe that would come later. (p. 153)

But it never did.

Not only are people missing in history texts, but so are varying historical perspectives. "To present history in simple, one sided—almost moralistic—terms, is to teach nothing worth learning and to falsify the past in a way that provides worse than no help in understanding the present or in meeting the future" (Collier, 1976, p. 138).

Indeed, history textbooks approach topics from single perspectives; they have space to do little else (Burstein & Hutton, 2005; Foster, Morris, & Davis, 1996; Tunnell & Ammon, 1996). For instance, the American Revolution typically has been reported from the Whig perspective, which depicts "simple, freedom-loving farmers marching in a crusade to fulfill God's plan for a rationally ordered society based on the principles of liberty and equality" (Collier, 1976, p. 133). There are other points of view, however, such as the Imperialist view, which draws attention to the British perspective, and the Progressive view, which promotes economic reasons for the war above ideological or religious reasons. By the same token, Columbus is presented in elementary school textbooks mostly from a Eurocentric perspective. Of course, the Native Americans have a defensible point of view that deglorifies Columbus, but this perspective is covertly censored (Shannon, 1989) from textbook pages simply by not being mentioned. For example, in Macmillan/McGraw-Hill's *The United States: The Early Years* (Berson et al., 2009, p. 63), the Europeans' long history of ill treatment of the native populations is hinted at but sidestepped in only one cryptic sentence: "The [Europeans] may have been friends at first, but a century later, disease and violence destroyed the Taíno."

Historical Fiction: Presenting Multiple Perspectives

"When a textbook is used as the only source of information, students tend to accept the author's statements without question" (Holmes & Ammon, 1985, p. 366). But, once again, history never has a single side to its story, and children's literature in the form of historical fiction (and historical nonfiction) is more likely to invite "the reader to enter into a historical discussion that involves making judgments about issues of morality. . . . What was it like to be a person here? What was the nature of good and evil in that time and place, and with whom shall my sympathies lie?" (Levstik, 1989, p. 137).

This sort of critical thinking about the story of ourselves—which requires students to operate on the highest levels of Bloom's taxonomy of cognitive learning—involves examining conflicting viewpoints and making personal judgments. For example, several pieces of historical fiction for young readers approach the American Revolution from differing perspectives—books such as Esther Forbes's *Johnny Tremain* (1943), a Whig treatment of the Revolution; James and Christopher Collier's *My Brother Sam Is Dead* (1974), a combination of Whig and Progressive treatments; Avi's *The Fighting Ground* (1984), wherein a boy changes from a flaming Patriot to wondering which side (if any) he is on; Scott O'Dell's *Sarah Bishop* (1980), told through the eyes of a girl from a Loyalist, or Tory, family who is brutalized by the war; both the Colliers' *Jump Ship to Freedom* (1981); and Laurie Halse Anderson's *Chains* (2008), African American perspectives of the Revolution that tell of broken promises of liberty and justice for all. Read in

combination, these titles provide the fodder for discussing, debating, and questioning the human motives behind the historical facts. Plus, historical fiction can be an engaging reading experience, which is perhaps the most important reason to involve its use in the classroom.

What Makes Good Historical Fiction?

Historical fiction must, of course, be set in the past. The main characters generally are fictional, though often they rub shoulders with historically prominent people. Sometimes the story's focus is not on events in history but rather on a wholly imaginary plot that is accurately set in a particular period and place from the past. An example is Wilson Rawls's immortal dog story, *Where the Red Fern Grows* (1961), which is set in the Ozarks of Oklahoma in the 1920s. *Where the Red Fern Grows* is perhaps more a dog story than a historical novel. At other times, a story's plot involves the protagonist in famous historical events, such as the fictional Johnny Tremain's involvement in the Boston Tea Party and the battles of Lexington and Concord (Forbes, 1943). Sometimes it is difficult to decide whether certain books are contemporary or historical. Often, the determining factor is the age of the reader; the Gulf War in 1991 may be contemporary for adult readers but ancient history to a fifth grader.

Historical fiction is judged by the same criteria as any other piece of fiction: strength of character development, credibility of plot, quality of writing style, definition of setting, handling of theme. (See Figure 12.1 for a list of skilled authors of historical fiction for young readers.) However, some considerations are peculiar to the genre.

History Should Not Be Sugarcoated

When dealing with historical events, it is important to deal plainly with the truth. Several decades ago, unsettling truths were avoided or even revised in books written for children. The age of new realism in children's literature, which started in the mid-1960s, launched a trend that dictated more honesty in the writing of realistic fiction. Topics that mostly had been avoided or handled gingerly began to appear more frequently and with increased frankness, such as the Japanese American internment camps in the United States during World War II (*Journey to Topaz* by Yoshiko Uchida, 1971), the horrors of slavery (*Nightjohn* by Gary Paulsen, 1993), and the brutality of the Holocaust (*The Devil's Arithmetic* by Jane Yolen, 1988).

Kathryn Lasky (1990) explains that an author of historical fiction has the responsibility to preserve what she calls "the fabric of time" by remaining faithful to the historical context in which a story is set. Lasky (1983a) confronted the difficulty some readers have with that honesty after publication of her book *Beyond the Divide,* a story of traversing the California Trail set in 1849. In her research, she learned that women in the old West were constant targets of crime. They often were left alone and were vulnerable to rape and murder. And if they were raped, the women generally were ostracized, as happened with Serena Billings in *Beyond the Divide.* Lasky received a letter from an adult reader who was angry not so much because Serena was raped but because she was ostracized. The reader said, "[This] account did not set a good example for coping with the hurt and trauma that accompanies rape or for teaching young readers how they might cope with it" (Lasky, 1990, p. 164). Lasky responded by saying, "As a writer of historical fiction, I have an obligation to remain faithful, to remain accountable in my story telling, to the manners and mores and the practices of the period" (1990, p. 165).

Notable Authors of Historical Fiction

Avi: American and European history.
Beatty, Patricia, and John Beatty: American Civil War and westward expansion.
Blackwood, Gary: Alternative American history.
Bruchac, Joseph: Native American history.
Cadnum, Michael: Medieval European history.
Collier, James Lincoln, and Christopher Collier: American Revolution.
Haugaard, Erik Christian: European history.
Hunter, Mollie: British history.
Ibbotson, Eva: European history.
Lasky, Kathryn: American history.
Lester, Julius: African American history.
Meyer, Carolyn: European history.
Morpugo, Michael. World War I; World War II.
O'Dell, Scott: Native American history; American West.
Orlev, Uri: Holocaust.
Park, Linda Sue: Korean history.
Rinaldi, Ann: American history.
Speare, Elizabeth George: Colonial America.
Sutcliff, Rosemary: Early history of Britain.
Taylor, Mildred: African American history.
Uchida, Yoshiko: Japanese American history.
Wilder, Laura Ingalls: Westward expansion.
Yep, Laurence: Chinese American history.

Indeed, much of our history is unsavory. But the lessons history has to teach us will go unlearned if we are forever softening the factual account. Both understanding and being sickened by Serena's treatment help us become more aware of righting the mistakes of the past. In the immortal words of George Santayana, "Those who cannot remember the past are condemned to repeat it."

Historical Accuracy Is Required

Because historical fiction is rooted in history, an infrastructure of accurate historical facts is necessary. When events are documented, they must not be altered. However, when fictionalizing history, authors may take some liberties. For example, they may create dialogue for famous individuals (but should not put words into their mouths that don't fit with their known attitudes and personalities) or may patch in an invented character.

To serve the purpose of storytelling, for instance, Esther Forbes (1943) created conversations between Johnny Tremain and many of the well-known Sons of Liberty. What Paul Revere said to Johnny is certainly not factual, although it reflects what Forbes knew about Revere's attitudes and personal life. The fictional Johnny serves as a vehicle to unite in an efficient way the major people and the complex events of the Boston Revolt, pulling fragmented occurrences together into a cohesive story. On the other hand, if Forbes had invented a surprise appearance of George Washington at the Boston Tea Party for dramatic effect, the reworking of the facts would have destroyed the story's historical credibility.

The Historical Period Should Come to Life

A historical period is brought to life when the author re-creates the physical environment, patterns of daily living, and spirit of the times. What was it like to live from day to day in Boston in 1775? Or London in 1215? What did a servant eat? What diseases were feared? Who went to school and who didn't?

Mollie Hunter (1976, p. 43), winner of Britain's Carnegie Award for her historical novel *The Stronghold* (1974), feels that this sort of realism can best be communicated in writing when authors have come to know the place and time so well that they "could walk undetected in the past," waking in the morning to know the sort of bed they'd be sleeping in or reaching in their pockets to grasp familiar coins. Creating this atmosphere in a novel also depends on avoiding modern terms. Joan Blos (1985), author of the Newbery Award–winning *A Gathering of Days* (1979), points out that authors of historical novels struggle with the compromises that must be made in maintaining strict historical validity and that sometimes the rules require bending to make a story readable. An overabundance of archaic speech in a story of the Middle Ages may derail a young reader. However, she says, "historical material and thought lack validity if expressed in modern phrases, idioms, or linguistic rhythms," as in this example relating to the American Revolution: "Peering out of her bedroom window, Deeny saw bunches of Hessians heading for the green" (1985, p. 39). "Bunches" to describe groups of people is an informal, modern use of the word that is out of place in a colonial American setting. Another example is found in *Tiger* (Stone, 2005), the first novel in a martial arts series set in 17th-century China. It is historically jarring to hear the young protagonists addressing one another with the phrase "Hey, guys."

Re-creating the spirit of the times may be the most important and most difficult challenge an author faces. To understand the motivating factors that led individuals or groups of people to make decisions that altered the patterns of life or the course of political history is not a simple affair. What stirred the winds of change or suppressed them? The spirit of the times fueled the American rebellion against the Crown in the 1770s or encouraged the acceptance of slavery in the 1850s, but not everyone was moved by the spirit in the same way. Some colonists resisted the American Revolution, and some Southerners operated stations on the Underground Railroad. Yet the varying perspectives that often lead to the conflicts that initiate change, both in the past and today, are the very sort of spirit that should permeate good historical stories.

The History Usually Is Revealed through the Eyes of a Young Protagonist

Although young main characters seem a requirement for most children's fiction, historical novels have an especially pressing need for them. Because young readers are accosted with a study of history that generally ignores the people who aren't historically famous—people like themselves—almost no children are ever mentioned. Therefore, the gap between themselves and the dusty past widens. A young protagonist who is inserted into the tumultuous times of the Boston Revolt or the difficult period of the Great Depression allows young readers to experience history through the senses of someone who views life in a similar way—as a child.

Jane Yolen (1989, p. 246) tells of being invited to talk to a group of eighth graders about the Holocaust. Horrified, the students asked her if she made "all that stuff up." The realities of Europe in the 1930s and 1940s were so far outside their realms of experience that they thought this story of such massive human suffering was a joke. People couldn't do such things to one another. Yolen's answer to this problem is found in her novel *The Devil's Arithmetic* (1988), which uses a fantasy technique to transport a 14-year-old American Jewish girl of the 1980s back to World War II Poland. As a youngster disconnected with her own past, Hannah is allowed to experience personally the spirit of the times and ask questions such as "How could you be so dumb as to believe those Nazis when they say you are only being resettled?" Yolen (1989) explains,

> Children are mired in the present. . . . [So, by] taking a [young reader] out of that *today* in a novel, [by introducing] a child protagonist that the reader identifies fully with, and throwing the [protagonist] backwards or forwards in time, the reader too is thrown into the slipstream of yesterday or tomorrow. The reader becomes part of that "living and continuous process," forced to acknowledge that we *are* our past just as we *are* our future. (p. 248)

Whether bringing a modern child back in time or creating a young protagonist who is born to that time, authors of historical fiction thereby are able to give their young audience a sense of connecting with the past.

Avoid Too Much Attention to Historical Detail

Telling a good story is still the essence of historical fiction. Although authors may be tempted to cram in as many details from their historical research as possible, including too much historical detail may make the writing laborious and destroy the sense of story. Joan Blos (1985) notes two common ways an author may give in to this temptation. First, "the overstuffed sentence" (or paragraph or chapter) is loaded with far too many intrusive clauses of historical explanation:

> Zeke was eager to get to the corner. He wanted to be certain that when the procession came by he could see President Abraham Lincoln who, with his running mate, Senator Hannibal Hamlin of Maine . . . (p. 38)

Second, "the privy observed" involves a character who launches into inappropriate descriptions. Blos explains that a good test is to ask whether a contemporary character would carry on about a similar detail and gives this example:

> Sam's mother adjusted one of the four round dials that adorned the front of the white enameled stove, turning it from High to Simmer, and waiting a minute to be sure that the heat had been reduced. (pp. 38–39)

Types of Historical Fiction

Historical fiction generally can be divided into five categories.

1. *A story of historical events happening before the life of the author.* Most historical stories are of the type that are set completely in the past, in a period the author has not personally experienced. This means that the author relies completely on historical research rather than personal experience in creating the story. An example of this common variety of historical novel is Linda Sue Park's Newbery Award–winning tale set in 12th-century Korea, *A Single Shard* (2001).

2. *A contemporary novel that becomes historical fiction with the passage of time.* When Marie McSwigan (1942) wrote *Snow Treasure* during World War II, it was a contemporary novel based on the heroic true story of Norwegian children who smuggled gold bullion past Nazi guards in broad daylight on their sleds. They hid the gold in a snow cave, from which it was later secreted away by the British. All of today's schoolchildren and all of their teachers were not yet born when this event occurred. *Snow Treasure* is now most firmly in the realm of historical fiction.

3. *Authors chronicle their own life stories in a fictional format.* Another variety of historical fiction is unusual because the author recounts episodes from his or her own life. In other words, the story is a fictionalized account of the time period and events experienced by the author but often written about years later. The Little House books by Laura Ingalls Wilder, beginning with *Little House in the Big Woods* (1932), are books of this type.

4. *The protagonist travels back into history.* Time travel, a feature of fantasy rather than realism, has been used as a mechanism to transport contemporary characters into the past and then later return them to their own time. Everything else in this type of historical novel conforms to the realistic nature of the genre. As mentioned earlier, Jane Yolen's *The Devil's Arithmetic* (1988) is an example of this type.

5. *A novel speculates about alternative historical outcomes.* Authors sometimes create "What if?" stories about history. For example, Gary Blackwood's *Year of the Hangman* (2002) postulates about the state of affairs had the American colonists lost the Revolutionary War. George Washington is in prison and other patriots, such as Benjamin Franklin, are hiding in the French-controlled territory around New Orleans. This type of story accentuates the tenuous turning points that could have easily changed the course of events. Also see Blackwood's *Second Sight* (2005), wherein he imagines that John Wilkes Booth is unsuccessful in his attempt to assassinate President Abraham Lincoln.

Reviewing the Value of Historical Fiction

Historical fiction at its best is a good story and can be enjoyed as a read-aloud at home or school or as an exciting individual reading experience. Young readers may be influenced in developing lifelong positive reading behaviors by the power of story found in historical novels and picture books. Of course, historical fiction can quicken dry historical facts and breathe life into the people and events of the past. It may aid young children in developing a sense of time and of how they fit into the scheme of history. Indeed, children may connect, often for the first time, with their own heritage by reading "the story of ourselves," as offered in historical fiction. Plus, they will be better prepared to face their futures. As Winston Churchill once said, "The farther backward you can look, the farther forward you can see."

Historical Fiction Reading Lists

Fifteen of Our Favorites

Banks, Lynne Reid. 2005. *Tiger, Tiger.* Delacorte. Two tiger cub brothers are taken from the jungle to ancient Rome, where one becomes the pampered pet of Caesar's daughter and the other becomes a man-eating "entertainment act" at the Coliseum.

Cannon, A. E. 2002. *Charlotte's Rose.* Wendy Lamb Books/Random House. As a 12-year-old Welsh immigrant carries a motherless baby along the Mormon Trail in 1856, she comes to love the baby as her own and fear the day the baby's father will reclaim her.

Conrad, Pam. 1985. *Prairie Songs.* Harper. Louisa's life in a loving pioneer family on the Nebraska prairie is altered by the arrival of a new doctor and his beautiful but tragically frail wife.

Fleischman, Paul. 1993. *Bull Run.* Harper. Northerners, Southerners, generals, couriers, dreaming boys, and worried sisters describe the glory, the horror, the thrill, and the disillusionment of the first land battle of the Civil War.

Fletcher, Susan. 1998. *Shadow Spinner.* Atheneum. When Marjan, a 13-year-old crippled girl, joins the Sultan's harem in ancient Persia, she gathers for Shahrazad the stories that will save the queen's life.

Lasky, Kathryn. 1996. *True North: A Novel of the Underground Railroad.* Scholastic/Blue Sky Press. Because of the strong influence that her grandfather, an abolitionist, has in her life, 14-year-old Lucy assists a fugitive slave girl in her escape.

Lemna, Don. 2008. *When the Sergeant Came Marching Home.* Holiday House. In 1946, when his father returns from the war, a 10-year-old boy and his family move from the Montana town where they had been living to an old, run-down farm in the middle of nowhere, where they work hard trying to make ends meet.

McCaffrey, Anne. 1996. *Black Horses for the King.* Harcourt. Galwyn, son of a Roman Celt, escapes from his tyrannical uncle and joins Lord Artos, later known as King Arthur, using his talent with languages and his way with horses to help secure and care for the Libyan horses that Artos hopes to use in battle against the Saxons.

Park, Linda Sue. 2001. *A Single Shard.* Clarion. Tree-ear, a 13-year-old orphan in medieval Korea, lives under a bridge in a potters' village and longs to learn how to throw the delicate celadon ceramics himself. Winner of the Newbery Medal.

Speare, Elizabeth George. 1958. *The Witch of Blackbird Pond.* Houghton Mifflin. In 1687 in Connecticut, Kit Tyler—who feels out of place in the Puritan household of her aunt and befriends an old woman the community thinks is a witch—suddenly finds herself standing trial for witchcraft. Winner of the Newbery Medal.

Sutcliff, Rosemary. 1995. *The Outcast.* Farrar, Straus. Exiled from his ancient British tribe, Beric is captured by the Romans and forced into slavery, but he harbors the hope of escaping to return to his homeland.

Taylor, Mildred. 1976. *Roll of Thunder, Hear My Cry.* Dial. A black family living in the South during the 1930s is faced with discrimination. Because the family owns its own land and is uncharacteristically independent for the era, they have an unusually difficult time living with such prejudice. Winner of the Newbery Medal.

Venkatraman, Padma. 2008. *Climbing the Stairs.* Putnam. In India in 1941, when her father becomes brain damaged in a nonviolent protest march, 15-year-old Vidya and her family are forced to move in with her father's extended family and become accustomed to a totally different way of life.

Watkins, Yoko Kawashima. 1986. *So Far from the Bamboo Grove.* Lothrop. A young Japanese girl, her older sister, and her mother struggle to escape the dangers of an angry Korea as World War II ends.

Yolen, Jane. 1988. *The Devil's Arithmetic.* Viking Penguin. Hannah resents the traditions of her Jewish heritage until time travel places her in the middle of a small Jewish village in Nazi-occupied Poland.

Others We Like

Anderson, Laurie Halse. 2008. *Chains.* Atheneum. After being sold to a cruel couple in New York City, a slave named Isabel pays for spying for the rebels during the Revolutionary War. She eventually decides that freedom will come at the hands of neither the Americans or the British and so takes matters into her own hands.

Armstrong, William. 1971. *Sour Land.* Harper. For Anson Stone and his three motherless children, the quiet black man who enters their lives as teacher and friend fills a lonely void but also brings home a tragic reality.

Avi. 2009. *Hard Gold.* Hyperion. Determined to find his 19-year-old uncle and best friend, Jesse, who left for Colorado to find enough gold to pay the mortgage and save the family's Iowa farm, 12-year-old Early Whittcomb joins up with a barber, his wife, and his daughter on a wagon train heading for the gold fields near Pike's Peak in 1858.

Blackwood, Gary. 2005. *Second Sight.* Dutton. In Washington, D.C., during the last days of the Civil War, a teenaged boy who performs in a mind-reading act befriends a clairvoyant girl whose frightening visions foreshadow an assassination plot.

Blundell, Judy. 2008. *What I Saw and How I Lied.* Scholastic. In 1947, with her jovial stepfather Joe back from the war and family life returning to normal, teenaged Evie, smitten by the handsome young ex-GI who seems to have a secret hold on Joe, finds herself caught in a complicated web of lies whose devastating outcome changes her life and that of her family forever. Winner of the National Book Award.

Collier, James Lincoln, and Christopher Collier. 1974. *My Brother Sam Is Dead.* Four Winds. Tragedy strikes the Meeker family during the Revolution when one son joins the rebel forces while the rest of the family tries to stay neutral in a Tory town. A Newbery Honor book.

Crowe, Chris. 2002. *Mississippi Trial, 1955.* Phyllis Fogleman/Penguin. In Mississippi in 1955, a 16-year-old finds himself at odds with his grandfather over issues surrounding the kidnapping and murder of a 14-year-old African American from Chicago.

Erdrich, Louise. 2005. *The Game of Silence.* HarperCollins. Nine-year-old Omakayas, of the Ojibwe tribe, moves west with her family in 1849.

Fletcher, Susan. 2006. *Alphabet of Dreams.* Atheneum. Fourteen-year-old Mitra, of royal Persian lineage, and her 5-year-old brother Babak, whose dreams foretell the future, flee for their lives in the company of the magus Melchoir and two other Zoroastrian priests, traveling through Persia as they follow star signs leading to a newly born king in Bethlehem.

Forbes, Esther. 1943. *Johnny Tremain.* Houghton Mifflin. This Newbery-winning story of Boston during the Revolutionary War, from the Tea Party through the Battle of Lexington, is presented through the eyes of a young apprentice turned dispatch rider for the Committee of Public Safety.

Fox, Paula. 1973. *The Slave Dancer.* Bradbury. Kidnapped by the crew of an Africa-bound ship, a 13-year-old boy discovers to his horror that he is on a slaver and his job is to play music for the exercise periods of the human cargo. Winner of the Newbery Medal.

Greene, Bette. 1973. *The Summer of My German Soldier.* Dial. When German prisoners of war are brought to her Arkansas town during World War II, 12-year-old Patty, a Jewish girl, befriends one of them and must deal with the consequences of that friendship.

Hopkinson, Deborah. 2004. *Hear My Sorrow: The Diary of Angela Denoto, a Shirtwaist Worker.* Scholastic. Forced to drop out of school at the age of 14 to help support her family, Angela, an Italian immigrant, works long hours for low wages in a garment factory and becomes a participant in the shirtwaist worker strikes of 1909. (See other titles in the Dear America series.)

Hunt, Irene. 1964. *Across Five Aprils.* Follett. Young Jethro Creighton grows from a boy to a man when he is left to take care of the family farm in Illinois during the difficult years of the Civil War.

Hunter, Mollie. 1998. *The King's Swift Rider: A Novel on Robert the Bruce.* HarperCollins. Unwilling to fight but feeling a sense of duty, 16-year-old Martin joins Scotland's rebel army as a swift rider and master of espionage for the leader, Robert the Bruce.

Ibbotson, Eva. 2004. *The Star of Kazan.* Dutton. After 12-year-old Annika, a foundling living in late 19th-century Vienna, inherits a trunk of costume jewelry, a woman claiming to be her aristocratic mother arrives and takes her to live in a strangely decrepit mansion in Germany.

Klages, Ellen. 2006. *The Green Glass Sea.* Viking. It is 1943, and 11-year-old Dewey Kerrigan is traveling west on a train to live with her scientist father—but no one will tell her exactly where he is. When she reaches Los Alamos, New Mexico, she learns why: He's working on a top-secret government program.

Lasky, Kathryn. 1994. *Beyond the Burning Time.* Scholastic (Blue Sky). When, in the winter of 1691, accusations of witchcraft surface in her small New England village, 12-year-old Mary Chase fights to save her mother from execution.

Lasky, Kathryn. 2010. *Ashes.* Viking. In 1932 Berlin, 13-year-old Gaby Schramm witnesses the beginning of Hitler's rise to power, as soldiers become ubiquitous, her beloved literature teacher starts wearing a jeweled swastika pin, and the family's dear friend, Albert Einstein, leaves the country while Gaby's parents secretly bury his books and papers in their small yard.

Lasky, Kathryn. 2010. *Hawksmaid: The Untold Story of Robin Hood and Maid Marion.* HarperCollins.

In 12th-century England, Matty grows up to be a master falconer, able to communicate with the devoted birds that later help her and Fynn, also known as Robin Hood, to foil Prince John's plot to steal the crown.

Lester, Julius. 2005. *Day of Tears: A Novel in Dialogue.* Hyperion. March 2 and 3, 1859, were the days of the largest slave auction in American history, which took place in Savannah, Georgia. On the first day of the auction, torrential rain began falling, stopping only when the auction had ended. The simultaneity of the rainstorm with the auction led to these two days being called "the weeping time."

Lester, Julius. 2008. *Guardian.* Harper. In a rural southern town in 1946, a white man and his son witness the lynching of an innocent black man. Includes a historical note on lynching.

Lowry, Lois. 1989. *Number the Stars.* Houghton Mifflin. In 1943, during the German occupation of Denmark, 10-year-old Annemarie learns how to be brave and courageous when she helps shelter her Jewish friend from the Nazis. Winner of the Newbery Medal.

McGraw, Eloise. 1961. *The Golden Goblet.* Coward. Ranofer struggles to thwart the unsavory plans of his evil brother, Gebu, so he can become a master goldsmith like their father in this exciting tale of ancient Egyptian mystery and intrigue. A Newbery Honor book.

Meyer, Carolyn. 2004. *Patience, Princess Catherine.* Harcourt. In 1501, 15-year-old Catharine of Aragon arrives in England to marry Arthur, the eldest son of King Henry VII. But she soon finds her expectations of a happy settled life radically changed when Arthur unexpectedly dies and her future becomes the subject of a bitter dispute between the kingdoms of England and Spain.

Meyer, Carolyn. 2009. *The True Adventures of Charley Darwin.* Harcourt. In 19th-century England, young Charles Darwin rejects the more traditional careers of physician and clergyman, choosing instead to embark on a dangerous five-year journey by ship to explore the natural world.

Morpurgo, Michael. 2006. *The Amazing Story of Adolphus Tips.* Scholastic. When Boowie reads the diary that his grandmother sends him, he learns of her childhood in World War II England, when American and British soldiers practiced for D-Day's invasion in the area of her home, and about her beloved cat, Adolphus Tip, and the cat's namesake.

Napoli, Donna Jo. 2008. *Smile.* Dutton. In Renaissance Italy, Elisabetta longs for romance, and when Leonardo da Vinci introduces her to Guiliano de Medici, whose family rules Florence but is about to be deposed, she has no inkling of the romance—and sorrow—that will ensue.

O'Dell, Scott. 1986. *Streams to the River, River to the Sea: A Novel of Sacagawea.* Houghton Mifflin. A young Indian woman, accompanied by her infant and cruel husband, experiences joy and heartbreak when she joins the Lewis and Clark Expedition seeking a way to the Pacific.

Orlev, Uri. 1984. *The Island on Bird Street.* Houghton Mifflin. During World War II, a Jewish boy is left on his own for months in a ruined house in the Warsaw Ghetto, where he must learn all the tricks of survival under constantly life-threatening conditions.

Paulsen, Gary. 1993. *Nightjohn.* Delacorte. Twelve-year-old Sarny's brutal life as a slave becomes even more dangerous when a newly arrived slave offers to teach her how to read.

Pullman, Philip. 1988. *The Ruby in the Smoke.* Knopf. In 19th-century London, 16-year-old Sally, a recent orphan, becomes involved in a deadly search for a mysterious ruby.

Richter, Hans Peter. 1970. *Friedrich.* Holt. A young German boy recounts the fate of his best friend, a Jew, during the Nazi regime.

Rinaldi, Ann. 2009. *My Vicksburg.* Harcourt. During the siege of Vicksburg, 13-year-old Claire Louise struggles with difficult choices when family and friends join opposing sides of the war.

Rodman, Mary Ann. 2008. *Jimmy's Stars.* Farrar. In 1943, 11-year-old Ellie is her brother Jimmy's "best girl," and when he leaves Pittsburgh just before Thanksgiving to fight in World War II, he promises he will return, asks her to leave the Christmas tree up until he does, and reminds her to "let the joy out."

Speare, Elizabeth George. 1961. *The Bronze Bow.* Houghton Mifflin. After witnessing the crucifixion of his father and subsequent demise of his

mother, Daniel, a young Jewish boy living at the time of Christ, vows revenge on the Romans. Winner of the Newbery Medal.

Springer, Nancy. 2010. *The Case of the Gypsy Goodbye.* Philomel. After 14-year-old Enola Holmes seeks the missing Duquessa Del Campo in the seedy underbelly of 19th-century London, she finally reaches an understanding with her brothers Sherlock and Mycroft. See others in the Enola Holmes Mystery series.

Taylor, Theodore. 1969. *The Cay.* Doubleday. When the freighter on which they are traveling is torpedoed by a German submarine during World War II, an adolescent white boy, blinded by a blow on the head, and an old black man are stranded on a tiny Caribbean island, where the boy acquires a new kind of vision, courage, and love from his old companion.

Uchida, Yoshiko. 1971. *Journey to Topaz.* Creative Arts. After the Pearl Harbor attack, an 11-year-old Japanese American girl and her family are forced to go to an aliens camp in Utah.

Yep, Laurence. 1977. *Dragonwings.* Harper. In the early 20th century, a young Chinese boy joins his father in San Francisco and helps him realize his dream of making a flying machine. A Newbery Honor book.

Easier to Read

Avi. 1979. *Night Journeys.* Morrow.

Bulla, Clyde Robert. 1956. *The Sword in the Tree.* Crowell.

Coerr, Eleanor. 2002 (1977). *Sadako and the Thousand Paper Cranes.* Putnam.

Gardiner, John. 1980. *Stone Fox.* Crowell.

Giblin, James Cross. 2006. *The Boy Who Saved Cleveland.* Holt.

Giblin, James Cross. 2008. *Did Fleming Rescue Churchill? A Research Puzzle.* Holt.

Gregory, Kristiana. 2004. *When Freedom Comes.* Scholastic. (See others in the My America series.)

MacLachlan, Patricia. 1985. *Sarah, Plain and Tall.* Harper.

McKissack, Patricia C. 2008. *The Home-Run King.* Viking. (See other titles in the Scraps of Time series.)

McSwigan, Marie. 1942. *Snow Treasure.* Dutton.

Nixon, Joan Lowery. 2000. *Aggie's Home.* Delacorte. (See other titles in the Orphan Train Children series.)

Turner, Ann. 1985. *Dakota Dugout.* Illustrated by Ronald Himler. Macmillan.

Wilder, Laura Ingalls. 1932. *Little House in the Big Woods.* Harper.

Woods, Brenda. 2003. *The Red Rose Box.* Puffin.

Woods, Brenda. 2006. *My Name Is Sally Little Song.* Putnam.

Wyeth, Sharon. 2003. *Message in the Sky, Corey's Underground Railroad Diary.* Scholastic. (See other titles in the My America series.)

Picture Books

Fletcher, Susan. 2007. *Dadblamed Union Army Cow.* Illustrated by Kimberly Bulcken Root. Candlewick.

Gauch, Sarah. 2009. *Voyage of the Pharos.* Illustrated by Roger Roth. Viking.

Goble, Paul. 1987. *Death of the Iron Horse.* Bradbury.

Hest, Amy. 1997. *When Jessie Came across the Sea.* Illustrated by P. J. Lynch. Candlewick.

Lasky, Kathryn. 1997. *Marven of the Great North Woods.* Illustrated by Kevin Hawkes. Harcourt.

Levine, Ellen. 2007. *Henry's Freedom Box.* Illustrated by Kadir Nelson. Scholastic.

Lorbiecki, Marybeth. 2006. *Jackie's Bat.* Illustrated by Brian Pinkney. Simon & Schuster.

Mochizuki, Ken. 1997. *Passage to Freedom: The Sugihara Story.* Illustrated by Dom Lee. Lee & Low.

Polacco, Patricia. 1994. *Pink and Say.* Philomel.

Provensen, Alice. 2005. *Klondike Gold.* Simon & Schuster.

Reynolds, Aaron. 2009. *Back of the Bus.* Illustrated by Floyd Cooper. Philomel.

Ryan, Pam Muñoz. 1999. *Amelia and Eleanor Go for a Ride.* Scholastic.

Say, Allen. 2002. *Home of the Brave.* Houghton Mifflin.

Thayer, Ernest Lawrence. 2000. *Casey at the Bat: A Ballad of the Republic Sung in the Year 1888.* Illustrated by Christopher Bing. Handprint.

Tsuchiya, Yukio. 1988. *Faithful Elephants: A True Story of Animals, People and War.* Illustrated by Ted Lewin. Houghton Mifflin.

Tunnell, Michael O. 1997. *Mailing May.* Illustrated by Ted Rand. Greenwillow.

Wiles, Deborah. 2001. *Freedom Summer.* Illustrated by Jerome Lagarrigue. Atheneum.

Williams, Marcia. 2007. *Archie's War Scrapbook.* Candlewick.

Winter, Jeanette. 1988. *Follow the Drinking Gourd.* Knopf.

Woodson, Jacqueline. 2005. *Show Way.* Illustrated by Hudson Talbot. Putnam.

Yin. 2001. *Coolies.* Illustrated by Chris K. Soentpiet. Philomel.

Yolen, Jane. 1992. *Encounter.* Illustrated by David Shannon. Harcourt.

PEARSON myeducationkit™

Go to the topic Historical Fiction on the MyEducationKit for this text, where you can:

- Search the Database of Children's Literature, housing more than 22,000 titles searchable in every genre by authors or illustrators, by awards won, by year published, and by topic and description.
- Explore genre-related Assignments and Activities, assignable exercises showing concepts in action through database use, video, cases, and student and teacher artifacts.
- Listen to podcasts and read interviews from some of the brightest and most enduring stars of children's literature in the Conversations.
- Discover weblinks that will lead you to sites representing the authors you learn about in these pages, classrooms with powerful children's literature connections, and literature awards.

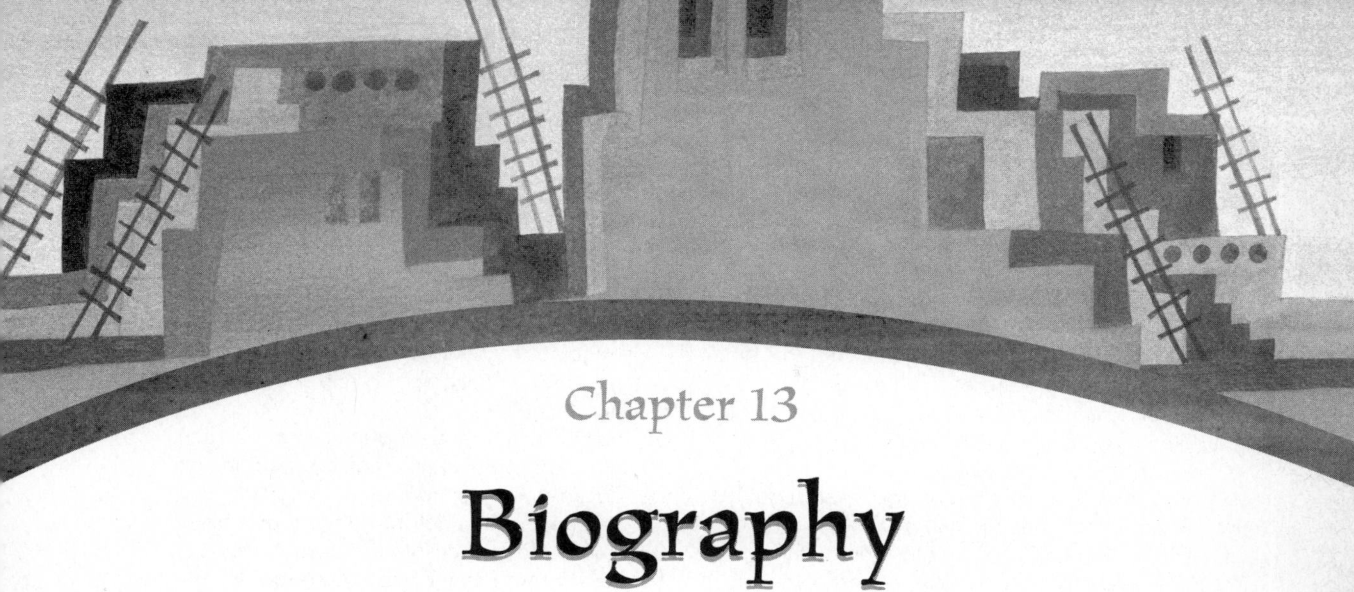

Chapter 13

Biography

"Dear Mr. Freedman," a young boy wrote in a letter, "I read your biography of Abraham Lincoln and liked it very much. Did you take the photographs yourself?" (Freedman, 1993a, p. 41). Russell Freedman, whose book *Lincoln: A Photobiography* (1987) won the Newbery Medal, explains that this fan letter expresses the highest praise a biographer can receive:

> Did you take the pictures yourself? he asks. That youngster came away from my book with the feeling that Abraham Lincoln was a real person who must have lived the day before yesterday. That's exactly the response I'm aiming for. After all, the goal of any biographer, any historian, is to make the past seem real, to breathe life and meaning into people and events that are dead and gone. (1993a, p. 41)

Of course, not all biographies are historical. Contemporary individuals are the topics of biographies and certainly autobiographies. Yet the goal of the biographer ought to be the same: "to breathe life and meaning into people and events" (Freedman, 1993a, p. 41).

The word *biography* renders its own definition: *bio* = life, *graphy* = writing. This specialized variety of nonfiction writing focuses on the lives of human beings—usually, people who are famous. (See Figure 13.1 for a list of notable children's book biographers.)

Typical Personalities in Biographies

Because famous personalities typically are the focus of adult as well as juvenile biographies, it is easy to organize biographies by either the careers of the individuals or some other factor responsible for their fame.

- *Scientists and inventors.* Perhaps Thomas Alva Edison is the most popular inventor in juvenile biographies. Other popular scientists and inventors include Albert Einstein, Stephen

Notable Biographers

Adler, David: Picture book and simplified biographies.
Burleigh, Robert: Picture book biographies.
Demi: Picture book biographies; Far Eastern figures, such as Buddha and Genghis Kahn.
Fisher, Leonard Everett: Picture book biographies.
Fleming, Candace. Complete biographies of famous Americans.
Freedman, Russell: Photobiographies.
Fritz, Jean: American history biographies.
Giblin, James Cross: Picture book and complete biographies; social histories.
Krull, Kathleen: Collective biographies.
Lasky, Kathryn: Partial, complete, and picture book biographies, often of lesser-known subjects.
Marrin, Albert: Biographies for middle school and junior high school readers.
Meltzer, Milton: Biographies and social histories.
Partridge, Elizabeth: Complete biographies.
Pinkney, Andrea: Picture book biographies of African American figures.
St. George, Judith: Picture book biographies.
Severance, John: Complete biographies.
Stanley, Diane: Picture book biographies for older readers.

Hawking, George Washington Carver, the Wright Brothers, Madame Curie, and Alexander Graham Bell.

- *Political leaders.* The category of political leaders includes presidents and senators as well as kings, queens, and other monarchs. The publishing of this type of biography can be influenced by current elections, coups, or other swings in power. On the eve of a presidential election, especially when no incumbent is running, some publishers will have biographies of both candidates ready for printing. When the results are announced, the winner's biography goes into production and the loser's into the recycling bin.

Indeed, publishers may rush to capitalize on someone in the public eye who suddenly makes a mark, such as the first African American U.S. president to be elected (or an Olympic swimmer who wins eight gold medals). However, people like Abraham Lincoln are standard and lasting fare, as exemplified by Carl Sandburg's (1928) *Abe Lincoln Grows Up,* Russell Freedman's (1987) *Lincoln: A Photobiography,* Candace Fleming's (2008) *The Lincolns,* and many, many other biographies written over the years about the 16th U.S. president. Only time will tell whether any current public figure will achieve what it takes to become standard fare for juvenile biographies in the generations to come.

- *Artists, musicians, actors, authors, and other people from the arts.* The category of people in the arts also has a trendy facet. For example, many musicians and actors popular with young people do not really measure up over time and are soon forgotten, such as the rock group Strawberry Alarm Clock from the 1960s. Yet there is a market for quickly done, heavily illustrated with photographs, and reasonably brief biographies of figures in our popular culture. On the other hand, Mozart, the Beatles, and Glenn Miller are musicians who seem to warrant and get serious attention by biographers. Painters and authors are subjects that are less trendy for children. In fact, prior to the 1980s, few biographies of authors were written for young readers. Now, many children's and young adult writers are filling the gap by publishing their autobiographies.

• *Sports personalities.* A few sports figures, such as Babe Ruth, Jim Thorpe, Jackie Robinson, and Babe Didrickson Zaharias, have withstood the test of time and appear in serious biographies for young readers. Others may be well remembered in years to come, and yet others will be forgotten except by the baseball, football, or basketball aficionado. Again, a trendy element exists in sports biography, almost to the point of dominating the subject. Watch for the slick, photograph-laden biographies that immediately appear after each Olympics, such as those for the reigning women's gymnast and figure skater.

• *Explorers and adventurers.* Men and women who take risks to push back the frontiers of science and geography make for interesting reading. Historical figures who line up nicely with the social studies curriculum show up often in biographies for young readers. For example, a spate of Christopher Columbus biographies appeared during the quincentennial commemoration of his monumental voyage. They provided broad coverage and varied perspectives on the motives for and impact of Columbus's mission. Milton Meltzer's *Columbus and the World around Him* (1990) was frank, perhaps even critical, about Columbus's shortcomings, and Kathy Pelta's *Discovering Christopher Columbus: How History Is Invented* (1991), though more complimentary, examined how historian biases and the infusion of myth into history have slanted Columbus's story. Newer titles continue to appear, such as *Columbus: Explorer of the New World* (2001) by Peter Chrisp, *You Wouldn't Want to Sail with Christopher Columbus* (2004) by Fiona MacDonald, and *Christopher Columbus: The Voyage That Changed the World* (2008) by Emma Carlson Berne.

Some intrepid individuals, despite the fact that they aren't common topics in elementary social studies, nevertheless capture young readers' imaginations. Amelia Earhart is an example. Authors continue to write about her, and young readers, especially girls, continue to find this female aviation pioneer fascinating. Titles about Earhart include Szabo's *Sky Pioneer: A Photobiography of Amelia Earhart* (1997), Ryan's *Amelia and Eleanor Go for a Ride* (1999), Winters's *And Fly She Did! The Amazing Childhood Adventures of Amelia Earhart* (2005), Taylor's *Amelia Earhart: This Broad Ocean* (2010), and Fleming's *Amelia Lost* (2011).

Often, we think of explorers as being from the past. Of course, our modern astronauts and oceanographers are no less daring in pushing back the remaining frontiers and are worthy subjects of current biographies.

• *Humanitarians.* Jane Addams, Albert Schweitzer, Florence Nightingale, and Mother Teresa may be interesting subjects for young readers because of their daring and selfless deeds. The heroic qualities of humanitarians add special appeal to their stories.

• *People who overcome tremendous odds.* Biographies of people who overcome tremendous odds focus on a different sort of heroism. Many biographies have been published about Helen Keller (including her autobiography), and her story of struggling to overcome nearly insurmountable physical difficulties continues to be popular reading for children and young adults.

• *Villains.* Is there a place among children's biographies for history's truly wicked? Certainly, most biographies capture the lives of people who have admirable qualities. However, villains' stories provide a contrast and a warning—and are generally interesting. Adolf Hitler is one of the villains many young readers find most horrific yet fascinating, as portrayed in the biography *The Life and Death of Adolf Hitler* by James Cross Giblin (2002).

• *Other interesting people.* A trend in juvenile biography is to write about today's ordinary people who have interesting lifestyles, occupations, or experiences. Examples are Molly Bang's

Nobody in Particular: One Woman's Fight to Save the Bays (2000), the story of a female shrimper's attempt to stop a chemical company from polluting a bay in east Texas, and Kathryn Lasky's *Vision of Beauty: The Story of Sarah Breedlove Walker* (2000), a book about an impoverished black woman who made a fortune creating beauty and hair-care products for African Americans. This category also includes books about lesser-known personalities from history, such as *Charlotte Forten: A Black Teacher in the Civil War* (Burchard, 1995). Other examples are Don Brown's *Uncommon Traveler: Mary Kingsley in Africa* (2000), the biography of a self-educated 19th-century English woman who traveled alone through west Africa to learn about its people; Uri Shulevitz's *The Travels of Benjamin of Tudela: Through Three Continents in the Twelfth Century* (2005), the story of a Jewish man who embarked on a 14-year journey through Italy, Greece, Palestine, Persia, China, and Egypt; and Kathleen Krull's *The Boy Who Invented TV: The Story of Philo Farnsworth* (2009), a look at the little known Utah farm boy who pioneered television. Books like these give children the sense that everyone, not just the big names from history, has a story and can make a contribution.

Types of Biographies

Until the age of new realism began to change the face of children's books in the 1960s (see Chapter 5), juvenile biographies generally were fictionalized, sometimes at the expense of honesty and accuracy. Many publishers, librarians, and educators felt that children would not read a biography unless it looked and read like a novel.

Fictionalized biographies are less common today. Instead, fictional treatments of a real person's life are generally classified as historical fiction. However, a personal narrative—an individual's own, slightly fictionalized story—is still considered a biography. Personal narratives are written in narrative or story form, rather than in pure expository or nonfiction form. An example is the Newbery Honor book *Upon the Head of the Goat* (1981), Aranka Siegal's powerful autobiographical story of her family's Holocaust ordeal.

The *authentic biography,* written as true nonfiction, is today's trend in biographies for young readers. Although crafted in expository form rather than narrative (as with novels), authentic biographies can be as vigorous and entertaining as good fiction. Milton Meltzer, known for his biographies and informational books about history and social change, says, "I think I've used almost every technique fiction writers call on (except to invent the facts) in order to draw readers in, deepen their feeling for people whose lives may be remote from their own, and enrich their understanding of forces that shape the outcome of all our lives" (quoted in Donelson & Nilsen 1989, p. 259).

Note the stylistic flair Russell Freedman gives to these paragraphs in his biography of Lincoln:

> Today it's hard to imagine Lincoln as he really was. And he never cared to reveal much about himself. In company he was witty and talkative, but he rarely betrayed his inner feelings. According to William Herndon, his law partner, he was "the most secretive—reticent—shut-mouthed man that ever lived."
>
> In his own time, Lincoln was never fully understood even by his closest friends. Since then . . . he has become as much a legend as a flesh-and-blood human being. While the legend is based on truth, it is only partly true. And it hides the man behind it like a disguise. (1987, p. 2)

The viewpoints in biographies also vary greatly. Subjectivity can't be avoided totally because authors are humans. For example, if an author is a Holocaust survivor, writing an objective biography of Adolf Hitler would be difficult. Likewise, a civil rights activist might have trouble writing an honest biography about Martin Luther King Jr., an account that would show King's weak points as well as his strong ones. As Newbery-winning author James Daugherty (1972) once said, "When you're writing biography, you're also writing autobiography." In other words, how biographers feel about their subjects affects, at least subtly, how they portray them.

The scope of a biography is often dictated by format, age of intended readers, and purpose, as indicated by the categories that follow.

- *Autobiographies.* When people write about their own lives, the problem with objectivity is even more acute. However, autobiography provides the unique viewpoint of self-revelation. What writing about oneself loses in objectivity it gains in wholeness. No one has as complete a view of a life as the one who lives it. Biographers who write of others' lives can never get inside their subjects' heads and hearts, although this distance may allow for a more balanced and objective view.

  This category historically had few contributors because most famous individuals write their personal stories for an adult audience. Then in the 1980s and 1990s, publishers began to encourage children's authors and illustrators to write autobiographies for young readers. Children are interested in the people who create their books, and this effort proved successful. Notable examples of author/illustrator autobiographies for children include the Newbery Honor book *Homesick, My Own Story* (1982) by Jean Fritz, the Caldecott Honor books *Bill Peet: An Autobiography* (1989) and *How I Learned Geography* (2008) by Uri Shulevitz, and the Pura Belpré Award winner *Under the Royal Palms* (1998) by Alma Flor Ada.

- *Picture book biographies.* Picture book biographies, usually intended for very young readers, are brief and heavily illustrated. Generally 32 pages, the standard length for picture books, such biographies provide an overview, focusing on the highlights of a subject's life. A picture book biography series by David Adler is an example of the authentic biographies in this category. Titles include *A Picture Book of Anne Frank* (1993), *A Picture Book of Sacagawea* (2000), *A Picture Book of John Hancock* (with Michael Adler, 2006), and *A Picture Book of Cesar Chavez* (with Michael Adler, 2010). Picture book biographies for more sophisticated readers (upper elementary, junior high school) include books created by Diane Stanley. Her titles—such as *The Bard of Avon: The Story of William Shakespeare* (with Peter Vennema, 1993), *Cleopatra* (with Peter Vennema, 1994), *Michelangelo* (2000), and *Saladin: Noble Prince of Islam* (2002)—have more text and are enjoyed by children in the middle and upper grades.

- *Simplified biographies.* Simplified biographies are aimed at newly independent readers and appear as picture books or as chapter books, typically with frequent illustrations. Examples include two series published by Grosset and Dunlap: the Who Was books (*Who Was George Washington?* by Roberta Edwards, 2009) and the Smart About Art books about well-known artists (*Pierre-Auguste Renoir: Paintings That Smile* by True Kelley, 2005). Jean Fritz's popular biographies of American Revolutionary War personalities are included in this category. Though heavily illustrated, these books emphasize text rather than illustration. In lively prose, Fritz covers the lives of Paul Revere, Samuel Adams, John Hancock, Benjamin Franklin, Patrick Henry, and King George III.

- *Complete biographies.* Although complete biographies may be in simplified, picture book, or lengthy chapter book format, their purpose is to span the entire life of a subject. Russell Freedman's biographies are excellent examples and include four that appear on the Newbery list: *Lincoln: A Photobiography* (1987), *The Wright Brothers: How They Invented the Airplane* (1991), *Eleanor Roosevelt: A Life of Discovery* (1993b), and *The Voice That Challenged a Nation: Marian Anderson and the Struggle for Equal Rights* (2004). Another of the finest biographers for young readers is Jean Fritz. Besides the shorter books about American Revolutionary War personalities mentioned earlier, she has longer titles, such as *Bully for You, Teddy Roosevelt!* (1991), *Harriet Beecher Stowe and the Beecher Preachers* (1994), *Why Not, Lafayette?* (1999), and so on. Also noteworthy are recent titles by James Cross Giblin (*Good Brother, Bad Brother: The Story of Edwin Booth and John Wilkes Booth* [2005] and *The Rise and Fall of Senator Joe McCarthy* [2009]) and Candace Fleming (*Our Eleanor: A Scrapbook Look at Eleanor Roosevelt* [2005] and *The Great and Only Barnum: The Tremendous, Stupendous Life of Showman P. T. Barnum* [2009]).
- *Partial biographies.* Partial biographies have a more focused purpose than do complete biographies. They cover only a segment of the subject's life, as in Sandburg's *Abe Lincoln Grows Up* (1928), which deals only with Lincoln's childhood, and Golenbock's *Teammates* (1990), which focuses on the years that Jackie Robinson and Pee Wee Reese worked together to break the color barrier in major league baseball. Robert Coles's *The Story of Ruby Bridges* (1995) covers several months in the life of the 6-year-old African American girl confronted by the hostility of white parents trying to keep her out of Frantz Elementary School in New Orleans in 1960. Another notable example is Kathryn Lasky's *Georgia Rises: A Day in the Life of Georgia O'Keeffe* (2009).
- *Collective biographies.* Collective biographies contain a number of short biographical pieces about subjects who have a common trait—for example, Kathleen Krull's books about presidents (*Lives of the Presidents,* 1998), musicians (*Lives of the Musicians,* 1993), sports heroes (*Lives of the Athletes,* 1997), pirates (*Lives of the Pirates,* 2010), and so on. Some collective biographies feature popular current personalities, such as professional athletes, actors, and rock stars. Although this sort of offering may not be well written, the interest level for many children is high. A recent trend has provided excellent material for young readers in the form of picture book collective biographies, such as *So You Want to Be an Explorer* (St. George, 2005), which compares the lives of a variety of these adventurers.

Judging Biographies for Young Readers

Because biography is a brand of nonfiction, good biographies exhibit certain characteristics that vary from those in fiction. Naturally, the need for authenticity cannot be ignored. First and most basic, the facts in a biography must be accurate. Often biographers acknowledge their sources of information somewhere in their books as a way of letting their readers know that a great deal of research went into their writing. Also, authors of authentic biographies must take care with the use of direct quotation. Jean Fritz (1988) makes it clear that she does "not use quotation marks unless I have a source" (p. 759). For instance, in *Can't You Make Them Behave, King George?*

George's mother is quoted as saying, "Stand up straight, George. Kings don't slouch" (1977, p. 8). Although these words may sound fabricated, Fritz found them in *King George III* by John Brooke (1972). Of course, fictionalized biographies take greater liberties with the words spoken by the characters, which is why they often are classified as historical fiction.

Despite striving for accuracy and authenticity, biographers cannot be totally objective. Because they are human, personal perspectives will always color the ways in which they present their subjects. Objectivity may be further compromised because so-called historical facts about people are difficult to nail down, as they are likely to be tinged by the personal perspectives of those who interpreted them in earlier years. Nevertheless, competent biographers work hard to avoid these pitfalls as much as possible. They will undertake exhaustive research that serves to help them recognize bias in their sources. And they regularly take stock of their own attitudes about their subjects to keep their own brand of bias in check.

Therefore, competent biographers will avoid making blatant personal judgments in their books, thus allowing the actions and words of their subjects to speak for themselves. For example, Jean Fritz presents Christopher Columbus as a rather arrogant, egotistical individual in her brief biography *Where Do You Think You're Going, Christopher Columbus?* (1980). However, she does not state, "Christopher Columbus was a self-absorbed egomaniac." Instead, she allows the reader to come to that conclusion through Columbus's words and deeds, as when he robs Rodrigo of the promised prize for spotting land first: "Columbus said no, he had, himself, sighted land when he'd seen a light at ten o'clock. How could it be otherwise? Surely God, who had gone to so much trouble to bring him here, meant him to have the honor" (Fritz, 1980, p. 30).

One of the shortcomings of some juvenile biographies is that they glorify their subjects, turning them into idols or making them larger than life. This is another form of stereotyping that alienates readers from the subject of a biography instead of helping them know that person as a real human being. To present a balanced view means looking at the blemishes as well as the strong points. Instead of conveying the message, for instance, that Abraham Lincoln was born virtually perfect, a more positive and effective message for young readers is that Lincoln had many of the same human weaknesses as the rest of us, but he was able to rise above them to do great things.

Freedman's biography of Lincoln provides a nice blend of blemishes and strong points. We see a Lincoln who was self-effacing, who stood bravely to sign the Emancipation Proclamation (though it was popular with nearly no other politicians), and who wrote the Gettysburg Address. But we also see the Lincoln whose law office was a colossal mess, who argued with his wife, and who suffered from severe depression for much of his life. We like this Lincoln better than the one on a pedestal, because we recognize him as one of us. Note how human and vulnerable Lincoln appears when forced to end his courtship of Mary Todd:

> Early in 1841, Lincoln broke off the engagement. He had known bouts of depression before, but now he plunged into the worst emotional crisis of his life. For a week, he refused to leave his room. People around town said that he had thrown "two cat fits and a duck fit." He had gone "crazy for a week or two." To his law partner Stuart, who was serving a term in Congress, Lincoln wrote: "I am the most miserable man living. If what I feel were equally distributed to the whole human family, there would not be one cheerful face on earth." (Freedman, 1987, pp. 31–32)

Biographies should, of course, conform to the standards of good writing. Facts are not enough; those may be obtained from an encyclopedia or biographical dictionary. Biographies must engage young readers with fresh prose and riveting perspective, bringing the subjects to life.

Biography Reading Lists

Fifteen of Our Favorites

Unless otherwise noted, the books in this list are complete biographies.

Bitton-Jackson, Livia. 1997. *I Have Lived a Thousand Years: Growing Up in the Holocaust.* Simon and Schuster. (Autobiography/personal narrative.) The author describes her experiences during World War II, when she and her family were sent to the Nazi death camp at Auschwitz.

Fleischman, Sid. 2008. *The Trouble Begins at 8: A Life of Mark Twain in the Wild, Wild West.* Greenwillow. (Partial biography.) When Mark Twain first started giving speeches, the poster advertising them read, "Doors open at 7. The trouble begins at 8." However, the seven years that Samuel Clemens spent meandering the Wild West are the focus of this book, and the author tells of Clemens's various bouts of gold fever and get-rich-quick schemes. But he also shows that Clemens always fell back on his newspaper writing for stability.

Fleming, Candace. 2005. *Our Eleanor: A Scrapbook Look at Eleanor Roosevelt's Remarkable Life.* Atheneum. With photographs on every page and special attention given to each important person, place, and project, this biography provides a portrait of a remarkable life.

Fleming, Candace. 2009. *The Great and Only Barnum: The Tremendous, Stupendous Life of Showman P. T. Barnum.* Schwartz & Wade. Readers can visit Barnum's American Museum; meet Tom Thumb, the miniature man (only 39 inches tall), and his tinier bride (32 inches); experience the thrill Barnum must have felt when, at age 60, he joined the circus; and discover Barnum's legacy.

Freedman, Russell. 1987. *Lincoln: A Photobiography.* Clarion. Photographs and text trace the life of the Civil War president. Winner of the Newbery Medal.

Freedman, Russell. 2004. *The Voice That Challenged a Nation: Marian Anderson and the Struggle for Equal Rights.* Clarion. Marian Anderson was a world-renowned African American opera star by the mid-1930s, but because of her race she was often denied the right to perform in her own country—including at Constitution Hall, the largest and finest auditorium in Washington, D.C. A Newbery Honor book.

Fritz, Jean. 1973. *And Then What Happened, Paul Revere?* Illustrated by Margot Tomes. Coward. A short, illustrated biography of this American Revolution hero. (See the other titles in Fritz's series about personalities from the American Revolution: *Can't You Make Them Behave, King George? What's the Big Idea, Ben Franklin? Where Was Patrick Henry on the 29th of May? Why Don't You Get a Horse, Sam Adams?* and *Will You Sign Here, John Hancock?*)

Giblin, James Cross. 2005. *Good Brother, Bad Brother: The Story of Edwin Booth and John Wilkes Booth.* Clarion. Brothers John and Edwin Booth became two of America's finest stage actors, but their opposite political loyalties during the Civil War led them to dramatically different fates.

Giblin, James Cross. 2009. *The Rise and Fall of Senator Joe McCarthy.* Clarion. When Cold War tension was at its height, Joseph McCarthy conducted an anti-Communist crusade endorsed by millions of Americans, despite his unfair and unconstitutional methods.

Hoose, Phillip. 2001. *We Were There, Too! Young People in U.S. History.* Farrar. (Collective biography.) Biographies of dozens of young people who made a mark in history, including explorers, planters, spies, cowpunchers, sweatshop workers, and civil rights workers.

Hoose, Phillip. 2009. *Claudette Colvin: Twice toward Justice.* Melanie Kroupa Books/Farrar. On March 2, 1955, an impassioned African American teenager, fed up with the daily injustices of Jim Crow segregation, refused to give her seat to a white woman on a segregated bus in Montgomery, Alabama. Instead of being celebrated, as Rosa Parks would be just nine months later, 15-year-old Claudette Colvin found herself shunned by her classmates and dismissed by community leaders. A Newbery Honor book.

Krull, Kathleen. 2000. *Lives of Extraordinary Women: Rulers, Rebels (and What the Neighbors Thought).* Harcourt. (Collective biography.) Focuses on the human sides of 20 of history's most influential women: queens, warriors, prime ministers, First Ladies, and revolutionary leaders. (See others in Krull's Lives Of series.)

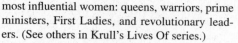

Meltzer, Milton. 2002. *Ten Kings: And the Worlds They Ruled.* Illustrated by Bethanne Andersen. Dutton. (Collective biography.) The author covers the highlights and lowlights of these kings: Hammurabi, David, Alexander the Great, Attila, Charlemagne, Kublai Khan, Mansa Musa, Atahualpa, Louis XIV, and Peter the Great.

Peet, Bill. 1989. *Bill Peet: An Autobiography.* Houghton Mifflin. (Autobiography.) The well-known author and illustrator relates the story of his life and work, including his years at Disney Studios. A Caldecott Honor book.

Stanley, Diane. 1997. *Michelangelo.* Harper. (Picture book biography.) A biography of the Renaissance sculptor, painter, architect, and poet, well-known for his work on the Sistine Chapel and St. Peter's Cathedral in Rome.

Others We Like

Unless otherwise noted, books in this list are complete biographies.

Ada, Alma Flor. 1998. *Under the Royal Palms.* Atheneum. (Autobiography.) The author recalls her life and impressions growing up in Castro's Cuba.

Fleming, Candace. 2003. *Ben Franklin's Almanac: Being a True Account of the Good Gentleman's Life.* Atheneum. Brings together 18th-century etchings, artifacts, and quotations to create the effect of a scrapbook of the life of Benjamin Franklin.

Fleming, Candace. 2008. *The Lincolns: A Scrapbook Look at Abraham and Mary.* Schwartz & Wade. Though Abraham and Mary Todd Lincoln's backgrounds differed considerably, both were intellectuals who shared interests in literature and politics, as well as a great love for each other.

Freedman, Russell. 1990. *Franklin Delano Roosevelt.* Clarion. Photographs and text trace the life of Franklin Delano Roosevelt, from his birth in 1882 through his youth, early political career, and presidency to his death in Warm Springs, Georgia, in 1945.

Freedman, Russell. 1999. *Babe Didrikson Zaharias: The Making of a Champion.* Clarion. A biography of Babe Didrikson, who broke records in golf, track and field, and other sports at a time when female athletes had few opportunities.

Freedman, Russell. 2010. *Lafayette and the American Revolution.* Holiday House. The study of Marquis de Lafayette of France emphasizes his service in the American Revolutionary War.

Fritz, Jean. 1994. *Harriet Beecher Stowe and the Beecher Preachers.* Putnam. The Beecher family was both an influential and a tragic family who shaped many areas of American thinking and politics. Harriet Beecher Stowe is the focus of this book, which chronicles her transformation from a restless young woman too shy to use her own name in print to a confident speaker whom Lincoln once called "the little lady who started the great big war."

Fritz, Jean. 2007. *Who's Saying What in Jamestown, Thomas Savage?* Illustrated by Sally Wern Comport. Putnam. In 1608, 13-year-old Thomas Savage arrives in Jamestown. The ship's captain, Christopher Newport, and John Smith give Thomas to Powhatan and ask the boy to learn the Native American's language and act as an interpreter.

Giblin, James Cross. 2002. *The Life and Death of Adolf Hitler.* New York: Clarion. Giblin explores the forces that shaped Hilter, as well as the social conditions that furthered his rapid rise to power. Giblin traces the arc of the man's life: his childhood, his years as a frustrated artist in Vienna, his extraordinary rise as dictator of Germany, and his final days in an embattled bunker under Berlin.

Golenbock, Peter. 1990. *Teammates.* Illustrated by Paul Bacon. Harcourt. (Picture book; Partial biography.) Golenblock describes the racial prejudice experienced by Jackie Robinson when he joined the Brooklyn Dodgers and became the first black player in Major League Baseball and depicts the acceptance and support he received from his white teammate Pee Wee Reese.

Jiang, Ji Li. 1997. *Red Scarf Girl: A Memoir of the Cultural Revolution.* Harper. (Autobiography/Personal narrative.) The author recounts the repression and fear she experienced growing up in the 1960s during China's Cultural Revolution.

Krull, Kathleen. 2004. *The Boy on Fairfield Street: How Ted Geisel Grew Up to Become Dr. Seuss.* Illustrated by Steve Johnson and Lou Fancher. Random House. (Picture book.) Introduces the life of renowned children's author and illustrator Ted Geisel, popularly known as Dr. Seuss, focusing on his childhood and youth in Springfield, Massachusetts.

Krull, Kathleen. 2010. *A Boy Named FDR: How Franklin D. Roosevelt Grew Up to Change America.* Illustrated by Steve Johnson and Lou Fancher. Random House. (Picture book.) Krull focuses on the childhood of Franklin Roosevelt and how it led to his four terms as president of the United States.

Lewis, J. Patrick. 2005. *Heroes and She-Roes: Poems of Amazing and Everyday Heroes.* Illustrated by Jim Cooke. Dial. (Picture book; Collective biography.) Twenty-one poems celebrate and chronicle the actions of real-life persons (and one dog) who have performed heroic acts in service of others.

Marrin, Albert. 2007. *The Great Adventure: Theodore Roosevelt and the Rise of Modern America.* Dutton. Theodore Roosevelt is one of America's liveliest and most influential figures. He was a scholar, cowboy, war hero, explorer, and brilliant politician. As president, Roosevelt's far-reaching policies abroad and at home forever changed both our nation's place in the world and the life of every modern American.

McClafferty, Carla Killough. 2008. *In Defiance of Hitler: The Secret Mission of Varian Fry.* Farrar. (Partial biography.) At a time when most Americans ignored the atrocities going on in Europe in 1940, American journalist Varian Fry put himself in great danger to save strangers in a foreign land. He was instrumental in the rescue of more than 2,000 refugees, including novelist Heinrich Mann and artist Marc Chagall.

Meltzer, Milton. 1990. *Columbus and the World around Him.* Watts. Describes the voyages of Columbus, the terrible impact of the Spaniards on the Indians, and the ultimate cultural influence of the Native Americans on their white conquerors.

Nelson, Marilyn. 2009. *Sweethearts of Rhythm: The Story of the Greatest All-Girl Swing Band in the World.* Illustrated by Jerry Pinkney. Dial. (Partial biography.) In the 1940s, an all-female band found its way to the most famous ballrooms in the United States, and they dared to be an interracial group. This partial biography is told through poetry.

Parks, Rosa (with Jim Haskins). 1992. *Rosa Parks: My Story.* Dial. (Autobiography.) This well-known civil rights story is considerably refreshed by Parks's personal narrative, punctuated by numerous black-and-white photographs.

Partridge, Elizabeth. 2005. *John Lennon: All I Want Is the Truth.* Viking. Partridge relies heavily on Lennon's own writings and the wealth of interviews he granted to reveal an unflinchingly honest portrait of a troubled, angry, and highly creative individual who was captivated by rock and roll and often used it as a means of expressing his unhappiness and confusion.

Paulsen, Gary. 1990. *Woodsong.* Bradbury. (Autobiography.) For a rugged outdoor man and his family, life in northern Minnesota is a wild experience involving wolves, deer, and the sled dogs that make their way of life possible. Includes an account of the author's first Iditarod, a dogsled race across Alaska.

Reef, Catherine. 2001. *Sigmund Freud: Pioneer of the Mind.* Clarion. Reef explains Freud's groundbreaking theories and methods and shows how Freudian thought has affected our culture, changing the way we think about everything from art and literature to raising children. Archival family photographs round out this intimate look at a fascinating individual.

St. George, Judith. 2000. *So You Want to Be President?* Illustrated by David Small. Philomel. (Caldecott winner; see also *So You Want to Be an Inventor* [2002] and *So You Want to Be an Explorer* [2005]; Collective biography; Picture book.) Presents an assortment of facts about the qualifications and characteristics of U.S. presidents, from George Washington to Bill Clinton.

Sandler, Martin W. 2008. *Lincoln through the Lens: How Photography Revealed and Shaped an Extraordinary Life.* Walker. Sandler offers a complete portrait of this celebrated president through a review of his childhood upbringing, political views and goals, and historic legacy and through an examination of his speeches (including the Gettysburg Address), period photographs, personal statements, and more.

Severance, John. 1999. *Einstein: Visionary Scientist.* Clarion. The author identifies Einstein's complex theories and makes clear why his ideas are still the basis of work by today's top physicists. He also reveals many of Einstein's inner complexities and eccentricities, exploring the personal and

public controversies that followed him throughout his life.

Stanley, Diane. 2002. *Saladin: Noble Prince of Islam.* Harper. (Picture book biography.) Richard the Lionhearted led the armies of the Third Crusade, and the leader of his Islamic foes was Saladin, an extraordinary man who was remarkable for his generous and chivalrous ways. Saladin was also a warrior who longed for peace and was courageous in battle and merciful in victory.

Szabo, Corinne. 1997. *Sky Pioneer: A Photobiography of Amelia Earhart.* National Geographic. A biography, with numerous photographs and quotes from Earhart herself, tracing this determined woman's life and interest in flying.

Collective Biographies

Buller, Jon, et al. 2005. *Smart about the First Ladies.* Grosset & Dunlap. (See others in the Smart About series.)

Colman, Penny. 2006. *Adventurous Women: Eight True Stories about Women Who Made a Difference.* Holt.

Dendy, Leslie. 2005. *Guinea Pig Scientists: Bold Self-Experimenters in Science and Medicine.* Holt.

Fradin, Dennis. 2003. *The Signers: The 56 Stories behind the Declaration of Independence.* Illustrated by Michael McCurdy. Walker.

Freedman, Russell. 1987. *Indian Chiefs.* Holiday House.

Glass, Andrew. 2001. *Mountain Men: True Grit and Tall Tales.* Doubleday. (Picture book.)

Harness, Cheryl. 2001. *Remember the Ladies: 100 Great American Women.* Harper. (Picture book.)

Krull, Kathleen. 1999. *They Saw the Future: Oracles, Psychics, Scientists, Great Thinkers, and Pretty Good Guessers.* Atheneum.

Leiner, Katherine. 1996. *First Children: Growing Up in the White House.* Tambourine.

Lester, Julius. 2001. *The Blues Singers: Ten Who Rocked the World.* Illustrated by Lisa Cohen. Hyperion. (Picture book.)

Meltzer, Milton. 1998. *Ten Queens: Portraits of Women of Power.* Illustrated by Bethanne Andersen. Dutton.

Parker, Nancy Winslow. 2001. *Land Ho! Fifty Glorious Years in the Age of Exploration.* Harper. (Picture book.)

Pinkney, Andrea Davis. 2000. *Let It Shine: Stories of Black Women Freedom Fighters.* Illustrated by Stephen Alcorn. Harcourt.

Provensen, Alice. 1995. *My Fellow Americans: A Family Album.* Browndeer/Harcourt. (Picture book.)

Yolen, Jane. 2008. *Sea Queens: Women Pirates around the World.* Charlesbridge.

Easier to Read

Adler, David A., and Michael S. Adler. 2009. *A Picture Book of Harry Houdini.* Holiday House. (See the other titles in the Picture Book Of series.)

dePaola, Tomie. 2006. *I'm Still Scared.* Putnam. (See other titles in dePaola's autobiographical series that begins with *26 Fairmount Avenue.*)

Eboch, M. M. 2008. *Jesse Owens: Young Record Breaker.* Illustrated by Meryl Henderson. Aladdin. (See other titles in the Childhood of Famous Americans series.)

Freedman, Russell. 1997. *Out of Darkness: The Story of Louis Braille.* Clarion.

Kelley, True. 2005. *Pierre Auguste Renoir: Paintings That Smile.* Grosset & Dunlap. (See other titles in the Smart about Art series.)

Kimmel, Elizabeth Cody. 2003. *As Far as the Eye Can Reach: Lewis and Clark's Westward Quest.* Random House.

Kramer, S. A. 1995. *Ty Cobb: Bad Boy of Baseball.* Random House.

Kraske, Robert. 2005. *Marooned: The Strange but True Adventures of Alexander Selkirk, the Real Robinson Crusoe.* Illustrated by Robert Andrew Parker. Clarion.

Mayo, Margaret. 2000. *Brother Sun, Sister Moon: The Life and Stories of St. Francis.* Little, Brown.

Meaderis, Angela Shelf. 1994. *Little Louis and the Jazz Band.* Lodestar/Dutton.

Meltzer, Milton. 2008. *Albert Einstein: A Biography.* Holiday House.

Osborne, Mary Pope. 1987. *The Story of Christopher Columbus, Admiral of the Ocean Sea.* Dell. (See other books in the Dell Yearling Biography series.)

Stewart, Whitney. 2009. *Who Was Walt Disney?* Illustrated by Nancy Harrison. Grosset & Dunlap. (See other titles in the Who Was series.)

Picture Books

Bridges, Ruby. 1999. *Through My Eyes*. Scholastic.

Burleigh, Robert. 2004. *Seurat and La Grande Jatte: Connecting the Dots*. Abrams.

Corey, Shana. 2000. *You Forgot Your Skirt, Amelia Bloomer!* Illustrated by Chesley McLaren. Scholastic.

Darrow, Sharon. 2003. *Through the Tempests Dark and Wild: A Story of Mary Shelley, Creator of Frankenstein*. Illustrated by Angela Barrett. Candlewick.

Demi. 2008. *Marco Polo*. Marshall Cavendish.

Demi. 2009 (1991). *Genghis Khan*. Marshall Cavendish.

Fisher, Leonard Everett. 1999. *Alexander Graham Bell*. Atheneum.

Giblin, James Cross. 2000. *The Amazing Life of Benjamin Franklin*. Scholastic.

Hurst, Carol Otis. 2001. *Rocks in His Head*. Illustrated by James Stevenson. Greenwillow.

Judge, Lita. 2009. *Yellowstone Moran: Painting the American West*. Viking.

Keating, Frank. 2002. *Will Rogers: An American Legend*. Illustrated by Mike Wimmer. Harcourt.

Kerley, Barbara. 2001. *The Dinosaurs of Waterhouse Hawkins*. Illustrated by Brian Selznick. Scholastic.

Krull, Kathleen. 2005. *Houdini: World's Greatest Mystery Man and Escape King*. Illustrated by Eric Velasquez. Walker.

Krull, Kathleen. 2009. *The Boy Who Invented TV: The Story of Philo Farnsworth*. Illustrated by Greg Crouch. Knopf.

Lasky, Kathryn. 1994. *The Librarian Who Measured the Earth*. Illustrated by Kevin Hawkes. Little, Brown.

McCully, Emily Arnold. 2006. *Marvelous Mattie: How Margaret E. Knight Became an Inventor*. Farrar.

McGinty, Alice B. 2009. *Darwin: With Glimpses into His Private Journal and Letters*. Illustrated by Mary Azarian. Houghton.

Rockwell, Anne. 2009. *Big George: How a Shy Boy Became President Washington*. Illustrated by Matt Phelan. Harcourt.

St. George, Judith. 2008. *Stand Tall, Abe Lincoln*. Illustrated by Matt Faulkner. Philomel.

Shulevitz, Uri. 2005. *The Travels of Benjamin of Tudela: Through Three Continents in the Twelfth Century*. Farrar.

Sis, Peter. 2003. *The Tree of Life: A Book Depicting the Life of Charles Darwin: Naturalist, Geologist & Thinker*. Farrar.

Stanley, Diane. 1998. *Joan of Arc*. Morrow.

Stanley, Diane. 2009. *Mozart, the Wonder Child: A Puppet Play in Three Acts*. HarperCollins.

PEARSON myeducationkit

Go to the topic Nonfiction on the MyEducationKit for this text, where you can:

- Search the Database of Children's Literature, housing more than 22,000 titles searchable in every genre by authors or illustrators, by awards won, by year published, and by topic and description.
- Explore genre-related Assignments and Activities, assignable exercises showing concepts in action through database use, video, cases, and student and teacher artifacts.
- Listen to podcasts and read interviews from some of the brightest and most enduring stars of children's literature in the Conversations.
- Discover weblinks that will lead you to sites representing the authors you learn about in these pages, classrooms with powerful children's literature connections, and literature awards.

Chapter 14

Informational Books

Informational books are nonfiction and present current and accurate knowledge about something found in our universe. The information in them is *verifiable* (the key word in defining nonfiction) in published sources such as books or magazines, in original sources such as letters and journals, or from firsthand, observable facts. Expository writing—the form of language that explains and conveys information—is generally used for creating nonfiction.

The Purpose of Informational Books

The writer of fiction and the writer of nonfiction approach their tasks from different viewpoints. Fiction writers create their stories; nonfiction authors report on the real world.

> With fiction, you start with the embryo and build a person's life. You begin with "What if?" and create a whole world. You work from the inside out. With nonfiction, you start with a complete life—or an invention, or a historical event, or an animal—and take it apart layer by layer to find out what made it happen or what makes it work. You work from the outside in, like peeling away the layers of an onion. (Facklam, 1990, p. 28)

Nonfiction books for children are divided into two main categories: biography (see Chapter 13) and informational books. Traditionally, students choose nonfiction for personal reading with far less frequency than fiction. But if the content of this genre truly includes everything in this interesting and vibrant cosmos, why don't they flock to informational books? At least three factors may help explain their largely negative attitudes.

1. *Informational books traditionally are not used for pleasure reading.* When a baby is born, parents who have learned that books can stimulate the intellect of their children plus provide

bonding experiences begin reading almost immediately to their newborns. Because of the high cost of picture books, they learn early to use the local library, where picture books have been gathered together for easy browsing and selection. What is the subject matter of these thousands of picture books? Almost without exception, they are fiction. All those desirable skills, attitudes, and memories that come from early reading typically are associated with fiction. Reading nonfiction aloud for pleasure is a rarity.

2. *Children's visits to the informational section of the library often are not by choice.* Although some elementary school children discover that reading nonfiction is pleasurable, many of them go to the informational section only when they have been assigned a report requiring use of the library. Most children want to find their information as quickly and with as little pain as possible, remembering to change a word in each paragraph so it doesn't have to be put in quotation marks. They often do not come away from writing that report convinced that informational reading is personally rewarding.

3. *Informational books have a reputation for being boring.* To many college students, the benefit of reading a nonfiction book is to save money on sleeping pills. For 30 years, we have asked majors in elementary education for their immediate personal reaction to the term *informational books.* Only a few students in those three decades have identified nonfiction as desirable or interesting. Author Margery Facklam says many adults share this view: "Nonfiction is utilitarian—like underwear and hot water heaters—the kinds of things you *have* to buy when you'd really like caviar and cruisers. Libraries have to buy nonfiction so kids can write reports" (Facklam, 1990, p. 27).

Today's nonfiction for children is both attractive and appealing. No other genre in children's literature has made such dramatic advances in gaining readers' attention. Authors and publishers have discovered that the purpose of an informational book is not merely to present data but to stir readers' interest in a particular subject. Of course, when readers already have developed an interest in something, virtually any book with new information about that topic will be appealing. If Frank loves motorcycles, he will embrace almost any book about motorcycles. But if readers know nothing about a particular subject, the book must fuel their initial interest with mind-grabbing content. In the hands of a skilled author, any topic is potentially exciting. (The converse is also true: In the wrong hands, any topic can be deadly dull.) Fiction and nonfiction have much in common on this point. Skilled writers, regardless of genre, create interest by the ways they approach their subjects and shape their books. (See Figure 14.1 for a list of notable authors of children's nonfiction.)

Finding Good Informational Books

The writer of compelling nonfiction does not simply collect and display facts but weaves information and details into a vision that reveals the subject in a way readers find irresistible. How do adults recognize nonfiction books that are likely to spark curiosity in elementary students? We often can tell the potential of an informational book by picking it up and thumbing through it for no more than a minute or two. If we are not "caught" before the time is up, the book ordinarily is not one that will grab younger readers who are unfamiliar with the topic. Usually the "catching" comes during the first minute and generally for one of the following five reasons: (1) attractive design, (2) little-known facts, (3) unusual viewpoints, (4) fascinating comparisons, and (5) first-person accounts. (See Figure 14.2 for a nonfiction evaluation form.)

Notable Authors and Illustrators of Informational Books

Aliki: Informational picture books for younger readers.

Ancona, George: Photographer and author of photoessays.

Arnosky, Jim: Illustrator and author of nature books.

Bartoletti, Susan Campbell: Social histories.

Blumberg, Rhoda: History—transcontinental railroad, California gold rush, Louisiana Purchase, Commodore Perry in Japan.

Cobb, Vicki: Hands-on science books.

Cole, Joanna: Science topics—notably, the Magic School Bus series.

Curlee, Lynn: Author and illustrator of picture books about famous structures.

Davis, Kenneth: Best known for his Don't Know Much About series, which covers many topics.

Fisher, Leonard Everett: Illustrator and author of books on a variety of topics—architecture, historical figures and events, social history.

Freedman, Russell: Social histories.

Gibbons, Gail: Informational picture books for preschool and primary grades on a variety of topics.

Giblin, James Cross: Informational chapter books about unique subjects—scarecrows; histories of chairs, windows, and eating utensils; plagues; Rosetta Stone; chimney sweeps.

Heller, Ruth: Illustrator and author of brilliantly colored picture books about the individual parts of speech and about plants and animals.

Jenkins, Steven: Picture books about animals and nature.

Lasky, Kathryn, and Christopher Knight: Wife (author) and husband (photographer) team; photoessays, primarily about nature topics.

Lauber, Patricia: Physical and natural science topics.

Markle, Sandra: Natural science, math, and computer books.

Marrin, Albert: World and American history.

McKissack, Patricia, and Fredrick McKissack: Primarily African American history.

Meltzer, Milton: Social histories; known particularly for presenting history using the words of the people who lived through it.

Micklethwait, Lucy: Picture books about fine art.

Murphy, James: U.S. social histories—immigrant train, Chicago fire, Civil War.

Pringle, Laurence: Natural and physical science books.

Sabuda, Robert: Nonfiction pop-up books.

Sandler, Martin: American history.

Schwartz, Alvin: Specialist in American folk culture; collects superstitions, legends, true stories, scary stories, tongue twisters.

Simon, Seymour: Physical and natural science topics.

Tang, Greg: Picture books about mathematics.

Attractive Design

Conventional wisdom cautions against making hasty decisions about books by their appearance: "Don't judge a book by its cover." Yet children pass over books that appear boring or unrewarding. Beverly Kobrin's motto is "Say NO to ugly books" (Kobrin, 1988, p. 59). An informational book may have solid and thoughtful content, but if it does not have visual appeal—attractive cover, interesting photographs or illustrations, varied page layout—it seldom gets the chance to work on a child unless someone else points out the strengths.

In years past, nonfiction books looked more like textbooks than they do today. Books for older children were built of substantial chapters with information that seemed to drone on and on.

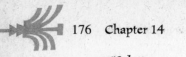

Figure 14.2 An Evaluation Guide for Nonfiction

Author: ______________________

Title: ______________________

Publisher: ______________________

Synopsis: ______________________

Evaluation

Style and language (precise vocabulary, figurative language, strong and clear exposition, personal voice, avoids didacticism and condescension, etc.) Comment:	1 2 3 4 5 6 7 8 9 10
Compelling details (quotations, anecdotes, little-known facts, etc.) Comment:	1 2 3 4 5 6 7 8 9 10
Fascinating comparisons Comment:	1 2 3 4 5 6 7 8 9 10
Unusual subjects or viewpoints Comment:	1 2 3 4 5 6 7 8 9 10
Personalized content (new perspectives, first-person accounts, etc.) Comment:	1 2 3 4 5 6 7 8 9 10
Accuracy (up-to-date research, references, no mixing of fact and fiction or anthropomorphism, etc.) Comment:	1 2 3 4 5 6 7 8 9 10
Attractive design (photos, artwork, etc) Comment:	1 2 3 4 5 6 7 8 9 10
Photo or artwork captions (new information?) Comment:	1 2 3 4 5 6 7 8 9 10
Is it a well-rounded piece? Comment:	1 2 3 4 5 6 7 8 9 10
RATING (10 high; 1 low) Comment:	1 2 3 4 5 6 7 8 9 10

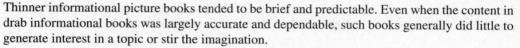

Thinner informational picture books tended to be brief and predictable. Even when the content in drab informational books was largely accurate and dependable, such books generally did little to generate interest in a topic or stir the imagination.

Currently, informational books for children are designed to catch the eye. Careful attention is given to making both the cover and the contents visually appealing. The increased use of illustrations and photographs has resulted in many new titles appearing in picture book format—large, slender volumes that skillfully mix text and illustration to enhance the content. The cover of *Extreme Scientists: Exploring Nature's Mysteries from Perilous Places* (Jackson, 2009) is a photograph of a woman in protective clothing with a coiled rope over her shoulder descending on a long line into the yawning opening of a dark cave. Inside the book, the number and variety of photographs complement the fresh and interesting layouts to entice the reader to explore further. Instead of the traditional front cover, *Charles Darwin and the Beagle Adventure* (Wood & Twist, 2009) looks like an antique document case that opens by lifting a magnetic flap. The interior of the book is replete with facsimilies and transcriptions of Darwin's work that take the reader into the past and offer a feeling of authenticity to the contents.

A company that focuses on attractive book design to entice young readers into nonfiction is DK Publishing. DK's consistent and noteworthy design features are (1) limiting each double-page spread to one topic, (2) using colorful, varied photographs and illustrations contrasted against white backgrounds, and (3) providing clusters of nonsequential text that can be read in any order or skipped entirely. In *The Human Body Q & A* (Walker, 2010), a sampling of topics is What is my body made from? What makes athletes fast and flexible? Do smart people have bigger brains? and Why don't we live forever? A single topic is addressed on a double-page spread. Clusters of text, each working in tandem with an accompanying illustration or photograph, help clarify that topic. The reader is in charge of how much or how little information to engage and finishes when satisfied.

Attractive design is more than cosmetic appeal. The design of a book helps in two ways to capture readers. The first is catching the reader's attention, and the second is keeping it.

Little-Known Facts

Information becomes interesting when details are included. Details in nonfiction make the difference between showing and telling, just as they do in fiction, but in nonfiction, that difference often accounts for a reader's becoming interested in a new subject or ignoring it. Little-known facts are details that create images that stir up interest and provide a starting point for greater understanding.

For example, *Stephen Biesty's Cross-Sections: Man of War* (Platt, 1993) explores the little-known facts of life aboard a British warship during the Napoleonic era, when sailing ships ruled the world's oceans. Men on these vessels were at sea for long periods. With no refrigeration, the kinds of food were limited—salt pork, dried peas, salt beef, oatmeal, beer in sealed barrels, and hard, moldy cheese. Fresh bread was out of the question, but each ship had a store of unleavened bread called hardtack, which was something like very thick crackers. Unfortunately, weevils and black-headed maggots liked hardtack, too, and sailors inadvertently chewed them up in their bites of the hard biscuits. The sailors found "black-headed maggots were fat and cold, but not bitter . . . like weevils" (p. 12). Weevils were impossible to dislodge, but the cook knew how to get rid of the black-headed maggots. He placed a raw fish on a plate on top of the hardtack. When it was completely covered with maggots, he threw the fish into the sea, replacing it as necessary until no more maggots appeared. The hardtack then was easier to eat. These little-known facts help take the reader into the life of an early sailor, providing a platform for expanded learning.

The human face of the Holocaust is presented in *Smoke and Ashes* (Rogasky, 2002). Not only does Rogasky present a broad view of treatment of the Jews by the Nazis, but she also offers unusual insights and explanations, such as how German children were taught to view Jews. The caption next to the photograph of a board game reads:

> Children were taught from the earliest years to stay away from "the evil Jew." Here is a popular children's game called "Get the Jews Out!" By throwing dice, the winner manages to get six Jews out of their homes and businesses—the circles—and on the road to Palestine. The game sold over a million copies in 1938, when Nazi policy was to force Jews to emigrate. (Rogasky, 2002, p. 12)

Little-known facts sometimes allow books written for an adult audience to find their place in the elementary classroom. *Alaska Bear Tales* (Kaniut, 2003) is a collection of more than 100 encounters between bears and humans in Alaska that have been taken from magazines, newspapers, and personal interviews. The variety is enormous—in length, violence, and humor. In these encounters some people were killed, some maimed, and some left unscathed, with the same true for the bears—for example:

> One of the most unusual bear escapes and deaths I've heard about took place near Wainwright. A woman was walking along the beach across the bay from Wainwright. She was gathering coal when she saw a bear approaching. She searched her brain for some means of escape, realizing that she couldn't outrun Nanook. It seemed futile, and as the bear shuffled up to her, it opened its mouth just inches from her. As a last resort, she shoved her fur-mittened fist down its throat and withdrew her arm before it could bite her, leaving the mitten in its throat. The bear instantly started choking, and forgot about its victim. Within minutes it lay suffocated at her feet. (p. 219)

And that is the only incident of a mitten-killed brown bear on record.

Little-known facts create interest in familiar topics as well as in new ones. *Amazing Mammals,* for example, describes a fox's unusual hearing: "A fox's ears are so sensitive it can hear a worm wriggling on the other side of a field" (Parsons, 1990, p. 15). In *The Mysterious Universe,* we visit the summit of Mauna Kea in Hawaii, where the average temperature is below freezing: "Only a few creatures manage to live at the summit [including] the weiku bug. If you pick up a weiku bug, the warmth of your hand will kill it" (Jackson, 2008, p. 29). Another example can be found in *Our White House,* where we discover that Teddy Roosevelt, the 26th president of the United States, not only devoured books—reportedly he read a book per day—but also wrote 35 books, plus more than 150,000 letters (National Children's Book and Literary Alliance, 2008, p. 93).

A regular sprinkling of little-known facts spices up classroom instruction, as well as individual lives in that classroom, by presenting students with specifics to think about and by reminding everyone just how broad and interesting this world is.

Unusual Viewpoints

Like little-known facts, unusual viewpoints also can reach out and grab readers. *Color Zoo,* a Caldecott Honor book (Ehlert, 1989), is a book of shapes aimed at preschoolers—one shape cut from the center of each heavy page. By overlaying three shapes at a time, Ehlert creates the face of an animal, which changes to a new shape and a different animal as each page is lifted. Keeping the same set of eyes, the lion (turn page) becomes a mouse, which (turn page) becomes a fox. The

young reader practices not only identifying the shapes but also seeing how different animal faces contain those shapes. The unusual viewpoint of *Color Zoo,* a book created for the very young, also captures the attention of adults.

Another example is *Arms and Armor* (Byam, 2000), a picture book of selected weapons that humans have developed since earliest times. The photographs and text are simple enough to appeal to children in the middle grades and complete enough to satisfy adults. Stone axes are no surprise, nor is the variety of swords and knives used throughout history. But Byam presents some unusual inventions developed specifically for us to hurt one another. The African throwing knife from Zaire is an odd starlike arrangement of sharp edges and five irregularly placed points with one handle: "When thrown, the knife turns around its center of gravity so that it will inflict a wound on an opponent whatever its point of impact" (Byam, 2000, p. 22). Another unusual weapon is the Apache pistol used around 1900 in Paris. It has a six-shot cylinder but no barrel, so it was accurate only at point-blank range. Instead of a barrel, it sports a folding dagger ideal for stabbing, and the pistol grip is a set of brass knuckles—three weapons in one.

In *Round Buildings, Square Buildings, and Buildings That Wiggle Like a Fish,* Philip Isaacson (2001) looks at the function and particularly the visual appeal of dozens of structures, including the Brooklyn Bridge. After a brief discussion of the French and Egyptian influences in its stone towers, he mentions the thin cables that support the road and how he sees those massive towers and spidery cables contrasting and interacting with each other.

> Most bridges are made of concrete and steel and tell us about the power of engineering. The Brooklyn Bridge is not like them; it tells us about the shapes of grand old buildings. It will always be a wonder because of a friendly game it seems to play. Its designers wove webs of light wires and cables and hung them from the towers to hold the bridge's roadways and paths. The fat towers make the webs look silky, and the silky webs make the towers seem even heavier than they are. This game of tag will go on forever. (p. 14)

The interplay of towers and cables adds to the beauty of the Brooklyn Bridge.

From *Round Buildings, Square Buildings, and Buildings That Wiggle Like a Fish* by Philip M. Isaacson.

David Feldman asks questions about common and often unnoticed things in our everyday world and then tries to find answers:

- Why do women open their mouths when applying mascara?
- Why do some ice cubes come out cloudy and others come out clear?
- Why is an elephant's nose called a *trunk?*
- Since doughnut holes are so popular, why can't we buy bagel holes?
- Why don't birds tip over when they sleep on a telephone wire?
- How does the Campbell Soup Company determine which letters to put in its alphabet soup? Is there an equal number of each letter? Or are the letters randomly inserted in the can?
- Why don't crickets get chapped legs from rubbing their legs together? If crickets' legs are naturally lubricated, how do they make that sound?
- Why do we have to close our eyes when we sneeze?

Although Feldman's 11 books (the latest: *Why Do Pirates Love Parrots?* [2006]) are aimed at an adult audience, they have great appeal for elementary-aged children. In each title, he presents these mysteries he calls "imponderables" and also how he found answers to them. (He is not always successful and then requests assistance from readers.) In his hunt to solve real mysteries, Feldman's books not only show children unusual viewpoints but also teach them naturally and effectively how to observe, question, research, and discover.

Sometimes the unusual viewpoint of a book is revealed in its title, enticing readers to pick it up immediately. Consider these examples:

Belly-Busting Worm Invasions! Parasites That Love Your Insides (Tilden, 2007)
Kids Shenanigans: Great Things to Do That Mom and Dad Will Just Barely Approve Of (Klutz Press Editors, 1992)
The Secret Life of School Supplies (Cobb, 1981)
Gold: The True Story of Why People Search for It, Mine It, Trade It, Steal It, Mint It, Hoard It, Shape It, Wear It, Fight and Kill for It (Meltzer, 1993)
I Wonder What's under There? A Brief History of Underwear (Lattimore, 1998)
What You Never Knew about Tubs, Toilets, and Showers (Lauber, 2001)
Gut-Eating Bugs: Maggots Reveal the Time of Death (Denega, 2007)
How Much Can a Bare Bear Bear: What Are Homonyms and Homophones? (Cleary & Gable, 2007)

In short, the unusual viewpoint, whether on the cover or inside the book itself, is often the spark that ignites reader desire to learn more.

Fascinating Comparisons

Human beings do not communicate well in the abstract or the complex. When we talk about any abstract or complex concept—kindness, the plight of endangered species, divorce, war, digestion, enormous numbers—we understand much more quickly and clearly when comparisons bring the fuzzy areas into sharp focus. Fascinating comparisons create instant and powerful images, communicating clearly in much the same manner as metaphor or simile.

How tough are the threads in a spider web? In *How Strong Is It*? we read that spider strands are five times stronger than any substance human beings have been able to produce. If a spider could make a huge web where each silk strand were as big as a pencil, it would stop a Boeing 747 in midflight (Hillman, 2008, p. 5).

According to Ellen Jackson (2008) in *The Mysterious Universe,* when very large stars burn out, those about 10 times bigger than our sun, they explode and become supernovae. A Type II supernova can leave behind a neutron star with atoms packed so tightly together by gravity that "a teaspoon of material from a neutron star would weigh more than a pile of a billion cars" (Jackson, 2008, p. 22).

Seymour Simon, a former science teacher who has written more than 100 informational books for young readers, frequently uses comparisons to clarify his content. In *Saturn,* he mentions that the ringed planet is much larger than Earth. How much larger? "If Saturn were hollow, about 750 planet Earths could fit inside" (1985, p. 5). Made of gases, Saturn is also lighter than Earth. How much lighter? "If you could find an ocean large enough, Saturn would float on the water" (p. 5). Comparisons make the information instantly clear.

Large numbers can be the focus of an entire book. In *How Much Is a Million?* David Schwartz (1985) uses comparisons to give readers a grasp of how the numbers million, billion, and trillion differ from each other by comparing how long it takes to count to each. To count to a million, saying each number completely and going nonstop, would take 23 days. To reach a billion would consume 95 years, and counting to a trillion, over 200,000 years.

Fascinating comparisons can be found in the illustrations as well as the text. In *Incredible Comparisons,* Russell Ash (1996) looks at 23 separate topics, including the universe, disasters, animal speed, the human body, and big buildings. In addition to showing differences in the text (the same volume of stone found in the Great Pyramid would build 40 Empire State Buildings), he includes a line-up of 15 well-known buildings, each drawn to scale, so the reader can see the relative sizes of some of the world's most famous structures. The Leaning Tower of Pisa, for example, reaches about halfway up the Statue of Liberty.

The digestive process becomes clearer in Linda Allison's *Blood and Guts* (1976) by comparing the intestine to a toothpaste tube. After food leaves the stomach as "a mashed-up, milky liquid," it goes into the small intestine,

> a long, curly tube with a shaggy lining. It is equipped with its own set of digestive juices for final food breakdown. The walls of this tube hug and push the food along in an action called peristalsis (perry STAL sis).
>
> Peristalsis puts the squeeze on food muscles in the intestinal wall. They contract and relax, forcing the food around and through. It's the same way you might squeeze a tube of toothpaste. (p. 76)

First-Person Accounts

When the author has been somewhere or done something and then writes about it, the resulting book often has the feel of a personal tour. It is not a recounting of information but an experience that reader and author seem to discover together. *My Season with Penguins: An Antarctic Journal* (Webb, 2000) shows the power of a personal story. In journal format, Sophie Webb combines scientific and artistic viewpoints in her account of why scientists want to research penguins and she is candid about the messy and smelly work of studying animals. With her attention to detail and humor, the result is a personal journey for the reader that ends up being much more than a compilation of information.

The Boys' War (Murphy, 1990) focuses on the Civil War from the viewpoints of boys age 16 and younger who served in that conflict (estimated between 250,000 and 420,000). Anticipating the glory of battle, young soldiers found instead fear and disillusionment, which resulted in their loss of innocence. This was documented in their journals and letters. Private Henry Graves wrote to his family:

> I saw a body of a man killed the previous day this morning and a horrible sight it was. Such sights do not effect [sic] me as they once did. I can not describe the change nor do I know when it took effect, yet I know that there is a change for I look on the carcass of a man with pretty much the same feeling as I would do were it a horse or dog. (p. 75)

The words of the young soldier put a face on the weariness and desensitization mentioned in a less descriptive way by the author.

The phenomenon of the Dust Bowl is an event that comes clearer to young readers through the eyes of individuals who faced those difficult days. Glenn McMurry, a Kansas farmer, paints a vivid picture of the Dust Bowl's frequent and blinding dust storms. The wind began to blow as he was in the shed milking a cow, and by the time he was finished, the dust in the air was so dense that he couldn't find his way back to the house.

> The wind was blowing so hard by this time and one's voice could barely be heard above it. After walking for a while, I realized I was in danger of . . . wandering aimlessly in the fields. With my hand outstretched I proceeded to walk in what I hoped was the right direction. Suddenly, I felt something and realized it was the corner of the house. As a matter of fact, had I been a few inches further to my right, I would have missed it entirely. I have shuddered many times since. What if I had missed the house! After that incident, I stretched a wire between the house and the milk shed to help me find my way back should another storm overtake me as this one had. (*Years of Dust,* Marrin, 2009, p. 72)

Life was hard for the people living in these dry, dust-choked regions of America during the Great Depression. Poverty and hunger were especially prevalent among these once-fertile but now dessicated farmlands. Martin Sandler (2009) recounts a particularly poignant example in his book *The Dust Bowl through the Lens.* Marguerite Dunmire, "a teacher in the Dust Bowl area of Nebraska," noticed a little girl in her class looking particularly pale and weak. She asked the girl to go home and eat something. " 'Oh, I can't do that,' the child replied. 'Today is my sister's turn to eat' " (Sandler, 2009, p. 72).

During the 1800s in the American South, slaves were kept illiterate by law. Despite that law, some did learn to read and write, as did many blacks who were free. In Milton Meltzer's *The Black Americans: A History in Their Own Words* (1984), we read the words of Solomon Northrup, a free black man who was kidnapped in New York and taken to New Orleans, where he was sold on the auction block. Other blacks were auctioned the same day, including a woman named Eliza who had two children. One, the boy, was sold separately.

> She kept on begging and beseeching them, most piteously, not to separate the three. Over and over again she told them how she loved her boy. A great many times she repeated her former promises—how very faithful and obedient she would be; how hard she would labor day and night, to the last moment of her life; if he would only buy them all together. But it was of no avail; the man could not afford it.

> The bargain was agreed upon, and Randall must go alone. Then Eliza ran to him; embraced him passionately; kissed him again and again; told him to remember her—all the while her tears falling in the boy's face like rain. . . .
>
> The planter from Baton Rouge, with his new purchase, was ready to depart.
>
> "Don't cry, mama. I will be a good boy. Don't cry," said Randall, looking back, as they passed out the door.
>
> What has become of the lad, God knows. It was a mournful scene indeed. I would have cried myself if I had dared. (pp. 49–50)

The human drama in this heartbreaking scene, which must have been repeated thousands of times, has greater impact because it is recounted by one who was a part of it. This authoritative, human touch can't help but increase reader response.

Jim Murphy's (2009) book *Truce* tells the story of the World War I Christmas truce between the British and the Germans in 1914. Against orders, the soldiers met in "No Man's Land," the deadly strip of land between their respective trenches, to celebrate on Christmas Eve—and discovered they rather liked one another. When ordered to fire on the enemy Christmas Day, the soldiers on both sides rebelled. A German officer recalled the startling event:

> When the order to fire was given, the men struck. . . . The officers . . . stormed up and down, and got, as the only result, the answer, "We can't—they are good fellows, and we can't." Finally the officers threatened the men with, "Fire, or we do—and not at the *enemy*!" Not a shot had come from the other side, but at last [we] fired, and an answering fire came back, but not a man fell. We spent that day and the next wasting ammunition in trying to shoot the stars down from the sky. (pp. 86–87)

This and other comments from the men on the frontlines, who on a crisp Christmas Eve recognized their so-called enemies as brothers, most clearly reveal the idiocy of war.

Good informational books are not buckets of facts but personal tours. Authors of compelling nonfiction teach the same way good classroom teachers teach: They examine a subject, make discoveries, think about things, and then share their personal views of what they find interesting.

Accuracy

The basis of all informational books is accuracy. The books exist to introduce the reader to the world or to present something particular about it, so the content must be factual and dependable. Anything that might lead a young reader to assume inaccuracies about factual information must be avoided. This includes anthropomorphism (giving animals and objects human traits or motives) and mixing fact and fiction, such as inserting an imagined story of a boy who survives the destruction of Pompeii in the midst of an informational book on the subject.

Readers often can recognize the accuracy of an informational book by looking at the author's notes, references, acknowledgments, and appendices. However, footnotes generally are not used in the text because they intrude on the reading and learning experience. The truth is that the average reader, even an adult reader, doesn't know if all the facts are correct in a children's informational book. And taking time to check the accuracy with other sources is laborious. We are, after all, reading the book to learn this information.

Today, we trust the author to have done appropriate homework, and we rely on the publisher to have facts checked. Occasionally, mistakes do slip through. Certainly, inaccuracies cannot be excused or overlooked, but we maintain the same position as with books for adults: We take the word of the author until other evidence shows us we should not.

Types of Informational Books

Informational books fall into recognizable categories that generally are determined by format. The following formats make up the typical nonfiction book categories: traditional chapter books, informational picture books, activity books (craft, how-to, experiment), concept books, journals and interviews, photo essays, pop-ups, reference books, and series.

Traditional Chapter Book Format

The bulk of children's informational books introduce or explain one subject in a traditional chapter book format. The depth of detail may vary, depending on the age of the target audience or the length of the book. For example, an accounting of the Shackleton expedition to Antarctica is treated in 48 pages in Connie and Peter Roop's *Escape from the Ice* (2001). The same topic spans 134 pages in Jennifer Armstrong's *Orbis Pictus* Award winner, *Shipwreck at the Bottom of the World* (1998).

Traditional nonfiction chapter books may be a general survey of an enormous topic, such as Mary Pope Osborne's (1996) *One World, Many Religions,* an overview of our varied faiths. Or an informational chapter book may focus on a narrower topic, such as *Children of the Dust Bowl: The True Story of the School at Weedpatch Camp* (Stanley, 1992), an *Orbis Pictus* Award–winning social history that documents the plight of migrant workers who came to California during the Great Depression.

All topics, whether presented in broad strokes or examined under a magnifying glass, are fair game for traditional nonfiction chapter books. Examples include superstitions (*Cross Your Fingers, Spit in Your Hat: Superstitions and Other Beliefs* by Alvin Schwartz, 1974), prehistoric cave paintings (*Painters of the Caves* by Patricia Lauber, 1998), bats (*Creatures of the Dark* by Seymour Simon, 2006), and shipwrecks (*Shipwrecks: Exploring Sunken Cities beneath the Sea* by Mary Cerullo, 2009).

Informational Picture Books

Informational picture books serve the same purposes as informational chapter books: They are to present accurate and appealing content aimed at awakening an interest in the reader. The difference lies only in the format: They are usually taller, thinner, and more heavily illustrated than chapter books. In recent years, the informational picture book has become commonplace, with many being created for readers in the upper-elementary grades as well as in middle school and junior high.

The informational picture book presents an idea in sufficient depth to pique curiosity as it increases understanding. These books can treat large topics, such as Bill Bryson's *A Really Short History of Nearly Everything* (2008), as well as smaller subjects like secret messages and cryptography, which Gary Blackwood addresses in *Mysterious Messages* (2009).

Activity Books

Activity books include any books that invite the reader to engage in a specific activity beyond their reading. Classic types of activity books include science experiments; how-to, craft, and cookbooks; and art activities, such as Joan Irvine's *Easy-to-Make Pop-Ups* (2005). By following clear directions, children are able to create more than 30 three-dimensional pop-ups for cards, toys, or gifts. In *Fun with Hieroglyphs* (Roehrig, 2008), young readers learn about hieroglyphics as they use the book and 24 rubber stamps to write their own names, produce common words, and construct messages. Today's offerings in activity books seem practically unlimited.

Concept Books

Usually, the first type of informational book a child sees is a concept book (discussed at length in Chapter 7), a simplified picture book that presents basic knowledge about one topic in a way both understandable and interesting for a small child beginning to learn about the world. Concept books often invite the young reader to engage in some activity to reinforce the idea being presented, such as picking out which object is small and which is large in Margaret Miller's *Big and Little* (1998), identifying the circles and squares from familiar surroundings in Tana Hoban's *So Many Circles, So Many Squares* (1998), and peering at the sky to identify clouds as guided by Anne Rockwell's book *Clouds* (2008).

Journals and Interviews

Journals and interviews are the two most common kinds of books based on primary sources. *Charles Darwin and the Beagle Adventure* (Wood & Twist, 2009) weaves Darwin's letters and journal notes throughout the text, helping illuminate the man and his monumental voyage of discovery. Interviews, like journals, offer information directly to the reader with only a minimum of author manipulation, such as the books by Jill Krementz. For examples, see *How It Feels to Live with a Physical Disability* (Krementz, 1992) and *A Very Young Writer* (Krementz, 2007).

Photo Essays

Photo essays employ photographs in a journalistic fashion to capture emotion and to verify information. Photographs accompany the text on almost every page in a photo essay. For example, in the Newbery Honor book *Volcano: The Eruption and Healing of Mount St. Helens* (Lauber, 1986), the story of the devastating eruption of the mountain and its recovery from fire, ash, and shifted landmass are documented in stunning photos. But the pictures do more than merely illustrate; they also create in the reader a sense of the massive devastation and then kindle emotions associated with recovery as they show nature healing itself. *Our World of Water: Children and Water around the World* (Hollyer, 2009) shows children, mostly from Third World countries, acquiring and using water. The text and images sensitize readers to the sometimes scarce, sometimes unsanitary sources of this most precious of commodities. *Ellis Island: Coming to the Land of Liberty* by Raymond Bial (2009) employs modern and archival photographs. The old and the new blend seamlessly and highlight the emotions generated over decades of immigration.

Juxtaposing the visions of the immigrants with the current visitors to Ellis Island serves to create a sense of poignancy.

Pop-Ups

Once pop-up books were largely for entertainment, but today, a number of excellent informational books appear in pop-up format. *The Amazing Pop-Up Geography Book* (Petty & Maizels, 2001) uses hidden doors, sliding boats, and pop-up mountains to present facts about the Earth. *Moon Landing* by Richard Platt and David Hawcock (2008) is replete with a launching rocket soaring off the page, a pop-up lunar surface, and a detailed three-dimensional space suit, offering a fresh look at the race to the moon.

Robert Sabuda and Matthew Reinhart are currently the best-known names in pop-up books, both fiction and nonfiction. They often collaborate, and their work is complex and eye popping. Nonfiction titles include *Encyclopedia Prehistorica: Dinosaurs* (Sabuda, 2005), *Encyclopedia Prehistorica: Sharks and Other Sea Monsters* (Sabuda & Reinhart, 2006), and *Mega-Beasts* (Sabuda & Reinhart, 2007). On every double-page spread, a large pop-up leaps up from the book and is often accompanied by smaller pop-ups that reveal additional pertinent information. The three-dimensional examination of the topic allows one to stare down the gullet of a shark or watch the movements of a dinosaur.

Predators by Lucio and Meera Santoro (2008) is constructed in a similar manner to the Sabuda/Reinhart books. It introduces an interesting variety of animal predators from water spiders to bald eagles. As one opens the book, a spider web suspended by branches unfolds, rising to a height of six inches above and covering most of the first double-page spread. Dangling above the web lurks a spider awaiting its prey. Doors with additional pop-ups and further information are located along the perimeters.

Reference Books

Encyclopedias, encyclopedic overviews of specific subjects, dictionaries, and atlases are examples of reference books. Although some children may spend time browsing in reference books or occasionally reading them from beginning to end, young readers generally go to reference books for isolated bits of knowledge. The current trend to make reference books attractive and readable adds a new dimension: reference books as recreational reading. The common reference book offerings—dictionaries, almanacs, atlases, and so on—are more appealing than ever. There are also titles that cover a variety of less-than-usual reference book topics, such as the *Encyclopedia of the End: Mysterious Death in Fact, Fancy, Folklore, and More* (Noyes, 2008).

DK Publishing and Scholastic are two publishers that produce a number of interesting and readable reference books. An example from Scholastic is the *Scholastic Encyclopedia of the Presidents and Their Times* (Rubel, 2009). *The Most Fantastic Atlas of the Whole Wide World . . . By The Brainwaves* is an offering from DK Publishing (2009).

Series

School libraries traditionally have informational books in series, partly because school subjects provide ready-made topics. For example, elementary schools frequently have a series of books

about the United States, one title per state, which students use mostly for doing reports. Although the information in traditional series is generally acceptable, their appeal is usually low. Often, information is neatly stacked in unexciting lines of text that do little to reach out to the reader.

Fortunately, some series have been conceived and executed by those who go beyond simply listing information to seeing inside it. Their views are accurate, and the books convey excitement about the topics. Kenneth C. Davis, for example, has created the upbeat Don't Know Much About series that provides kid-friendly introductions to a broad selection of topics, including interesting approaches to school subjects like *Don't Know Much about American History* (2003): Some other titles are *Don't Know Much about Mummies,* 2005; *Don't Know Much about Anything,* 2007; and *Don't Know Much about Literature,* 2009.

The Come Look with Me series, published by Charlesbridge, is designed to help children examine and understand diverse styles and media in artwork. Titles include *Come Look with Me: Exploring Modern Art* (Wright, 2003), *Come Look with Me: American Indian Art* (Salomon, 2007), and *Come Look with Me: Asian Art* (Lane, 2008).

The Let's-Read-and-Find-Out Science series, published by HarperCollins, is aimed at readers in the primary grades. The titles are in picture book form and come in four levels of reading difficulty. Sample titles are *What Makes a Magnet?* by Franklyn Branley (1996), *Almost Gone: The World's Rarest Animals* by Steve Jenkins (2006), and *What's So Bad about Gasoline? Fossil Fuels and What They Do* by Anne Rockwell (2009).

As never before, informational books are appealing, accurate, and practical for classroom use. Evidence that these books are finding their place in the world of children's literature includes the recent establishment of three awards exclusively for nonfiction books: the *Orbis Pictus* Award, given by the National Council of Teachers of English, and two awards presented by the American Library Association, the Robert F. Sibert Award and the YALSA Award for Excellence in Nonfiction for Young Adults. These awards underscore what teachers and children have already discovered about today's informational books: They not only teach us about the world, but they also make pleasurable reading.

Informational Book Reading Lists

Fifteen of Our Favorites

Armstrong, Jennifer. 1998. *Shipwreck at the Bottom of the World: The Extraordinary True Story of Shackleton and the Endurance.* Crown. Describes the events of the 1914 Shackleton Antarctic expedition, when, after being trapped in a frozen sea for nine months, their ship, *Endurance,* was finally crushed, forcing Shackleton and his men to make a very long and perilous journey across ice and stormy seas to reach inhabited land.

Bartoletti, Susan Campbell. 2005. *Hitler Youth: Growing Up in Hitler's Shadow.* Scholastic. Bartoletti explores how Hitler gained the loyalty, trust, and passion of so many of Germany's young people and includes telling interviews with surviving Hitler Youth members. A Newbery Honor book.

Cobb, Vicki, and Kathy Darling. 1980. *Bet You Can't: Science Impossibilities to Fool You.* Lothrop. (See the companion volume, *Bet You Can.*) Describes more than 60 impossible tricks, each based on scientific principles that are explained in accompanying text.

Curlee, Lynn. 2007. *Skyscraper.* Atheneum. Examines the history of the design of tall buildings. (See also Curlee's other picture books about various famous structures.)

Freedman, Russell. 2005. *Children of the Great Depression.* Clarion. Along with photographs by famous photographers of the Depression era, Freedman's overview clearly covers the causes of the Great Depression, schooling, work life, migrant work, the lives of children who rode the rails, entertainment, and so on.

Freedman, Russell. 2010. *The War to End All Wars: World War I.* Clarion. Freedman recounts the tensions leading up to World War I and then examines not only the technological innovations that made killing more efficient and the major events of the war but also the human stories of soldiers and others impacted by the conflict.

Jenkins, Steve. 2004. *Actual Size.* Houghton Mifflin. Discusses and gives examples of the sizes and weights of various animals and parts of animals.

Macaulay, David. 1998. *The New Way Things Work.* Houghton. Text and numerous detailed illustrations introduce and explain the scientific principles and workings of hundreds of machines.

Meltzer, Milton. 1993. *Gold: The True Story of Why People Search for It, Mine It, Trade It, Steal It, Mint It, Hoard It, Shape It, Wear It, Fight and Kill for It.* Harper. Discusses the value of gold and how it has been sought after and used in countries around the world throughout history.

Micklethwait, Lucy. 1993. *A Child's Book of Art: Great Pictures, First Words.* DK Publishing. Famous paintings are used to introduce basic concepts (seasons, weather, opposites, colors, counting, etc.) to young children.

Murphy, Jim. 1990. *The Boys' War.* Clarion. Documents the lives of the young boys who actually fought in the American Civil War. Illustrated with archival photographs.

Nelson, Kadir. 2008. *We Are the Ship: The Story of Negro League Baseball.* Jump and the Sun/Hyperion. Using an "Everyman" player as his narrator, Kadir Nelson tells the story of Negro League baseball from its beginnings in the 1920s through the decline after Jackie Robinson crossed over to the majors in 1947.

Sabuda, Robert, and Matthew Reinhart. 2007. *Mega-Beasts.* Candlewick. Using pop-up illustrations and fold-out pages, this book introduces some of the largest and smallest prehistoric animals.

Schwartz, Alvin. 1974. *Cross Your Fingers, Spit in Your Hat: Superstitions and Other Beliefs.* Lippincott. Superstitions are collected into 23 categories, such as love and marriage, money, ailments, travel, weather, school, and death.

Stanley, Jerry. 1992. *Children of the Dust Bowl: The True Story of the School at Weedpatch Camp.* Crown. Stanley describes the plight of the migrant workers who traveled from the Dust Bowl to California during the Depression and were forced to live in a federal labor camp. He also focuses on the marvelous school that was built for their children.

Others We Like

Allison, Linda. 1976. *Blood and Guts.* Little, Brown. (See others in the Brown Paper School Book series.) Allison presents and discusses the elements of the human body in a conversational tone and also includes suggestions for related experiments and projects.

Ambrose, Stephen. 2001. *The Good Fight: How World War II Was Won.* Atheneum. In 96 pages of liberal photographs and precise text, Ambrose chronicles World War II from beginning to end.

Bachrach, Susan D. 2000. *The Nazi Olympics: Berlin 1936.* Little, Brown. Bachrach captures the surrounding history and complexities of these worldwide games held in a highly politicized Germany.

Bartoletti, Susan. 2010. *They Called Themselves the K.K.K.: The Birth of an American Terrorist Group.* Houghton Mifflin. Filled with chilling and vivid personal accounts, this is the story of how six young men pulled pillowcases over their heads and began a secret terrorist group that spread across the South and beyond.

Blackwood, Gary. 2008. *The Great Race: The Amazing Round-the-World Auto Race of 1908.* Abrams. In February of 1908, six cars from four countries gathered in Times Square for the pistol shot that began the first around-the-world automobile race.

Blackwood, Gary. 2009. *Mysterious Messages: A History of Codes and Ciphers.* Dutton. From the ingenious ciphers of Italian princes to the spy books of the Civil War to the advanced techniques of the CIA, codes and code breaking have played important roles throughout history.

Blumberg, Rhoda. 2003 (1985). *Commodore Perry in the Land of the Shogun.* Lothrop. One of history's most significant diplomatic achievements was Commodore Matthew Perry's role in opening Japan's closed society to world trade in the 1850s.

Cerullo, Mary M. 2009. *Shipwrecks: Exploring Sunken Cities beneath the Sea.* New York: Dutton. Cerullo examines two strikingly different shipwrecks in the United States separated by 2,000 miles and two centuries.

Cohn, Amy L., compiler. 1993. *From Sea to Shining Sea: A Treasury of American Folklore and Folk Songs.* (Illustrated by 11 Caldecott Medal and 4 Caldecott Honor book artists.) Scholastic. A compilation of more than 140 folk songs, tales, poems, and stories telling the history of the United States and reflecting its multicultural society.

Crowe, Chris. 2003. *Getting Away with Murder: The True Story of the Emmett Till Case.* Phyllis Fogelman/Penguin. Crowe presents the true account of the murder of 14-year-old Emmett Till in Mississippi in 1955.

Curlee, Lynn. 2005. *Ballpark: The Story of America's Baseball Fields.* Atheneum. Filled with anecdotes about these "green cathedrals," *Ballpark* also explores the changing social climate that accompanied baseball's rise from a minor sport to the national pastime.

Dash, Joan. 2000. *The Longitude Prize.* Farrar. John Harrison, inventor of watches and clocks, spent 40 years working on a time machine that could be used to accurately determine longitude at sea.

Davis, Kenneth C. 2003. *Don't Know Much about American History.* Harper. (See others in the Don't Know Much About series.) In question and answer format, Davis presents a history of the United States, from the exploration of Christopher Columbus to the terrorist attacks of September 11, 2001.

Fleischman, John. 2002. *Phineas Gage: A Gruesome but True Story about Brain Science.* Houghton Mifflin. Phineas Gage survived 11 years after a 13-pound iron rod was shot through his brain in 1848, but he was changed. This case astonished doctors then and still fascinates them today.

Freedman, Russell. 2006. *Freedom Walkers: The Story of the Montgomery Bus Boycott.* Holiday House. Freedman covers the events surrounding and including the Montgomery bus boycott, the end of segregation on buses.

Fritz, Jean. 2004. *The Lost Colony of Roanoke.* Illustrated by Hudson Talbott. Putnam. Fritz describes the English colony of Roanoke, which was founded in 1585, and discusses the mystery of its disappearance.

Giblin, James Cross. 1990. *The Riddle of the Rosetta Stone.* Crowell. Giblin describes how the discovery and deciphering of the Rosetta Stone unlocked the secret of Egyptian hieroglyphics.

Henderson, Douglas. 2000. *Asteroid Impact.* Dial. In text and illustrations, Henderson explores the theory that the collision of an asteroid with Earth ended the Cretaceous Period and caused the extinction of the dinosaurs.

Isaacson, Philip M. 2001 (1988). *Round Buildings, Square Buildings, & Buildings That Wiggle Like a Fish.* Knopf. Isaacson explains the function and appeal of various buildings around the world, including churches, fortresses, bridges, air terminals, mills, cliff dwellings, tombs, and lighthouses of particular note.

Jackson, Donna M. 1996. *The Bone Detectives: How Forensic Anthropologists Solve Crimes and Uncover Mysteries of the Dead.* Photographs by Charlie Fellenbaum. Little, Brown. Jackson explores the world of forensic anthropology and its applications in solving crimes.

Jackson, Ellen. 2008. *The Mysterious Universe: Supernovae, Dark Energy, and Black Holes.* Houghton Mifflin. Astonomer Alex Filippenko's explanations of fairly complex celestial matters are clear and generate contagious excitement for our universe.

Jenkins, Martin. 2009. *The Time Book: A Brief History from Lunar Calendars to Atomic Clocks.* Illustrated by Richard Holland. Candlewick. Jenkins delivers on his promise to cover the history of time, from addressing the question of What is time? to explaining Einstein's theory of relativity.

Jones, Charlotte Foltz. 1996. *Accidents May Happen: Fifty Inventions Discovered by Mistake.* Delacorte. Discoveries sometimes result from misunderstandings and quirky or silly mishaps.

Lefkowitz, Arthur S. 2006. *Bushnell's Submarine: The Best Kept Secret of the Revolutionary War.* Scholastic. David Bushnell invented America's first submarine during the Revolutionary War in time to unsuccessfully attack a British warship.

Margulies, Phillip, and Maxine Rosalier. 2008. *The Devil on Trial: Witches, Anarchists, Atheists, Communists, and Terrorists in America's Courtrooms.* Houghton Mifflin. Five high-profile court cases, including the Scopes monkey trial and the Alger Hiss case, show what it means to be impartial and fair in complex situations involving the face of evil.

Marrin, Albert. 2002. *Dr. Jenner and the Speckled Monster: The Search for the Small Pox Vaccine.* Dutton. In 1796, Dr. Edward Jenner developed and administered the world's first vaccine and dramatically influenced the course of history.

McKissack, Patricia, and Fredrick L. McKissack. 1994. *Christmas in the Big House, Christmas in the Quarters.* Illustrated by John Thompson. Scholastic. McKissack describes the customs, recipes, poems, and songs used to celebrate Christmas in the big plantation houses and in the slave quarters just before the Civil War.

Murphy, Jim. 2009. *Truce.* Scholastic. On the first Christmas Eve of World War I, soldiers stopped their shooting and fighting to celebrate together.

Noyes, Deborah. 2008. *Encyclopedia of the End: Mysterious Death in Fact, Fancy, Folklore, and More.* Houghton Mifflin. This A–Z encyclopedic encounter with all things related to death and dying offers a broad illumination of the biological, spiritual, and historical aspects of death.

Pascoe, Elaine. 2005. *Fooled You: Fakes and Hoaxes through the Years.* Illustrated by Laurie Keller. Holt. Pascoe examines famous hoaxes from the 1800s to present times, including why people were so easily fooled.

Rogasky, Barbara. 2002 (1988). *Smoke and Ashes.* Holiday House. Rogasky includes the details of life in Nazi concentration camps and also tackles the larger questions of ethics, values, and history.

Rubin, Susan Goldman. 2001. *There Goes the Neighborhood: Ten Buildings People Loved to Hate.* Holiday House. Brief overviews of 10 buildings in Europe and the United States, including the Eiffel Tower and the Washington Monument, show how they went from initial rejection by the public to becoming beloved icons.

Sandler, Martin W. 2009. *The Dust Bowl through the Lens: How Photography Revealed and Helped Remedy a Natural Disaster.* Walker. This photo essay of archival images from the 1930s illuminates Sandler's explanation of how Americans endured and ultimately triumphed over this disaster.

Sayre, Henry. 2004. *Cave Paintings to Picasso: The Inside Scoop on 50 Art Masterpieces.* Chronicle. Sayre introduces 50 celebrated works of art, including King Tut's sarcophagus and Andy Warhol's paintings of Campbell's Soup cans, providing historical and interpretive information for each piece.

Schwartz, Alvin. 2010 (1981). *Scary Stories to Tell in the Dark.* HarperCollins. These macabre, funny, and fantastic tales are collected from people across the United States.

Simon, Seymour. 1979. *Pets in a Jar.* Puffin. Simon presents a how-to guide for collecting and keeping as pets such small animals as snails, toads, worms, ants, butterflies, and starfish.

Tunnell, Michael O. 2010. *Candy Bomber: The Story of the Berlin Airlift's "Chocolate Pilot."* Charlesbridge. During the massive airlift of food and supplies into war-torn West Berlin just after World War II, U.S. Air Force pilot Lt. Gail Halvorsen dropped candy to sugar-starved children using small parachutes.

Tunnell, Michael O., and George W. Chilcoat. 1996. *The Children of Topaz: The Story of a Japanese-American Internment Camp Based on a Classroom Diary.* Holiday House. This book is centered on the diary of a third-grade class of Japanese American children being held with their families in an internment camp during World War II.

Walker, Barbara M. 1995. *The Little House Cookbook: Frontier Foods from Laura Ingalls Wilder's Classic Stories.* Illustrated by Garth Williams. Harper. These recipes are based on the pioneer food written about in the Little House books of Laura Ingalls Wilder and are accompanied by quotes from the books and descriptions of the food and cooking of pioneer times.

Walker, Sally M. 2005. *Secrets of a Civil War Submarine.* Carolrhoda. The first half of this story of the *Hunley* follows its conception, construction, and one mission; the second tells of the search for, eventual location of, and raising of the only submarine used in the Civil War.

Walker, Sally. 2009. *Written in Bone: Buried Lives of Jamestown and Colonial Maryland.* Carolrhoda. Archaeologists and other scientists can determine not only the details of individual people who lived in early Jamestown but also how life was lived in colonial America.

Easier to Read

Altman, Joyce. 2001. *Lunch at the Zoo: What Zoo Animals Eat and Why.* Illustrated by Rick Chrustowski. Holt.

Bang, Molly, and Penny Chisholm. 2009. *Living Sunlight: How Plants Bring the Earth to Life.* Blue Sky Press.

Bare, Colleen Stanley. 1993. *Never Grab a Deer by the Ear.* Dutton.

Bishop, Nic. 2009. *Butterflies and Moths.* Scholastic.

Fritz, Jean. 1987. *Shh! We're Writing the Constitution.* Illustrated by Tomie dePaola. Putnam.

George, Jean Craighead. 2000. *How to Talk to Your Dog.* Illustrated by Sue Truesdell. Harper.

George, Jean Craighead. 2002. *Summer Moon.* Harper. (See others in the Seasons of the Moon series.)

Getz, David. 1994. *Frozen Man.* Illustrated by Peter McCarty. Holt.

Getz, David. 2000. *Purple Death.* Illustrated by Peter McCarty. Holt.

Grover, Wayne. 1993. *Dolphin Adventure.* Greenwillow.

Hubbell, Patricia. 2009. *Boats: Speeding! Sailing! Cruising!* Illustrated by Megan Halsey and Sean Addy. Marshall Cavendish.

Lavies, Bianca. 1993. *Compost Critters.* Dutton.

Markle, Sandra. 2000. *Outside and inside Dinosaurs.* Atheneum.

Markle, Sandra. 2009. *Animals Marco Polo Saw: An Adventure on the Silk Road.* Illustrated by Daniela Jaglenka Terrazzini. Chronicle. (See others in the Animals . . . Saw series.)

Osborne, Mary Pope, and Natalie Pope Boyce. 2008. *Penguins and Antarctica.* Illustrated by Sal Murdocca. Random House. (See others in the Magic Tree House Research Guide series.).

Rockwell, Anne. 2009. *What's So Bad about Gasoline? Fossil Fuels and What They Do.* Illustrated by Paul Meisel. Collins. (See others in the Let's-Read-and-Find-Out Science series.)

Simon, Seymour. 2006. *Emergency Vehicles.* Chronicle. (See others in the SeeMore Reader series.)

Simon, Seymour. 2009. *Dolphins.* Collins.

Singer, Marilyn. 2008. *Eggs.* Illustrated by Emma Stevenson. Holiday House.

Sobol, Donald J., and Rose Sobol. 1991. *Encyclopedia Brown's Book of Strange but True Crimes.* Illustrated by John Zielinski. Scholastic.

Trumble, Kelly. 1996. *Cat Mummies.* Illustrated by Laszlo Kubinyi. Clarion.

Picture Books

Arnosky, Jim. 2009. *Crocodile Safari.* Scholastic.

Barton, Chris. 2009. *The Day-Glo Brothers.* Illustrated by Tony Persiani. Charlesbridge.

Bass, Hester. 2009. *The Secret World of Walter Anderson.* Illustrated by E.B. Lewis. Candlewick.

Burleigh, Robert. 1991. *Flight: The Journey of Charles Lindbergh.* Illustrated by Mike Wimmer. Philomel.

Burleigh, Robert. 2009. *One Giant Leap.* Illustrated by Mike Wimmer. Philomel.

Celenza, Anna Harwell. 2006. *Gershwin's Rhapsody in Blue.* Illustrated by Joann E. Kitchel. Charlesbridge.

Collard, Sneed B. 2008. *Wings.* Illustrated by Robin Brickman. Charlesbridge.

Curlee, Lynn. 2009. *Trains.* Atheneum.

Floca, Brian. 2007. *Lightship.* Atheneum.

Giblin, James Cross. 2004. *Secrets of the Sphinx.* Illustrated by Bagram Ibatoulline. Scholastic.

Heller, Ruth. 1998. *Fantastic! Wow! and Unreal! A Book about Interjections and Conjunctions.* Grosset & Dunlap. (See others in Heller's English grammar picture book series.)

Hooper, Meredith. 2001. *Who Built the Pyramid?* Illustrated by Robin Heighway-Bury. Candlewick.

Hopkinson, Deborah. 2006. *Sky Boys: How They Built the Empire State Building.* Illustrated by James E. Ransome. Schwartz & Wade.

Jenkins, Steve. 2007. *Living Color.* Houghton Mifflin Harcourt.

Jenkins, Steve, and Robin Page. 2010. *How to Clean a Hippopotamus: A Look at Unusual Animal Partnerships.* Houghton Mifflin.

Kerley, Barbara. 2008. *What to Do about Alice? How Alice Roosevelt Broke the Rules, Charmed the World, and Drove Her Father Teddy Crazy!* Illustrated by Edwin Fotheringham. Scholastic.

Kudlinski, Kathleen V. 2005. *Boy, Were We Wrong about Dinosaurs*! Illustrated by S. D. Schindler. Dutton.

Macaulay, David. 2003. *Mosque.* Houghton. (See also the other Macaulay picture books about architecture, such as *Castle, Cathedral,* and *Pyramid.*)

Prince, April Jones. 2005. *Twenty-One Elephants.* Illustrated by François. Houghton Mifflin.

Swain, Ruth Freeman. 2003. *How Sweet It Is (and Was): The History of Candy.* Illustrated by John O'Brien. Holiday House.

Tang, Greg. 2007. *Math Fables Too: Making Science Count.* Illustrated by Taia Morley. Scholastic.

Weitzman, Jacqueline Preiss. 2002. *You Can't Take a Balloon into the Museum of Fine Arts.* Illustrated by Robin Preiss Glasser. Dial. (See others in the You Can't Take a Balloon series.)

PEARSON **myeducationkit**™

Go to the topic Nonfiction on the MyEducationKit for this text, where you can:

- Search the Database of Children's Literature, housing more than 22,000 titles searchable in every genre by authors or illustrators, by awards won, by year published, and by topic and description.
- Explore genre-related Assignments and Activities, assignable exercises showing concepts in action through database use, video, cases, and student and teacher artifacts.
- Listen to podcasts and read interviews from some of the brightest and most enduring stars of children's literature in the Conversations.
- Discover weblinks that will lead you to sites representing the authors you learn about in these pages, classrooms with powerful children's literature connections, and literature awards.

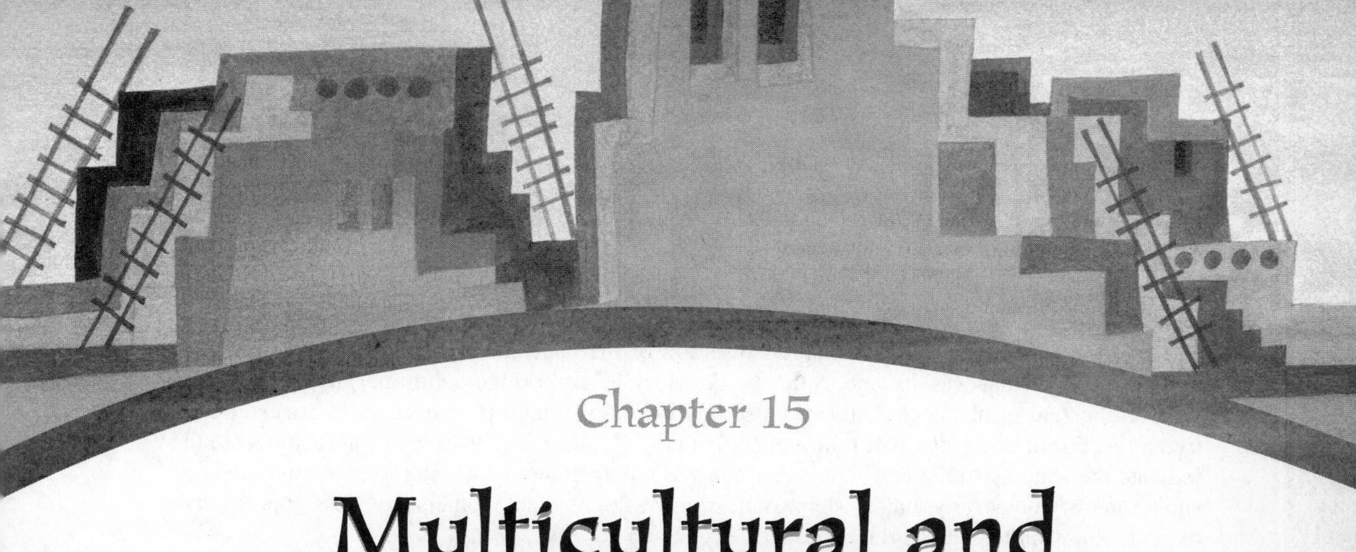

Chapter 15

Multicultural and International Books

Multicultural and international books offer positive experiences to young readers in at least three ways. Books about specific cultures and nations can

- Foster an awareness, understanding, and appreciation of people who seem at first glance different from the reader.
- Present a positive and reassuring representation of a reader's own cultural group.
- Introduce readers to the literary traditions of different world cultures or cultural groups within a specific nation.

Well-written books that express multicultural themes or are international in their origins may have a profound effect on readers, prompting a global outlook as well as an understanding that members of the human family have more similarities than differences.

Multicultural Literature

Today, we have a growing awareness and concern to include all cultures and nationalities as equal members of the world's family. However, we are far from achieving this ideal. Well-written multicultural (diverse culture) children's books may serve to help our new generations see people living in far-flung parts of the globe or even in their own city as equal and valuable citizens.

Multicultural literature has often been equated with books about people of color, especially within the United States and Canada: African Americans, Native Americans, Asian Americans,

Visit the MyEducationKit for this course to enhance your understanding of chapter concepts with activities, weblinks, podcasts, and a searchable database of more than 22,000 children's literature titles.

Latinas/Latinos. However, this definition is far too narrow. Our diverse population includes a variety of cultural groups that often cross color lines, such as religious groups. Jews, Catholics, Muslims, Mormons, and Amish all have their own subcultures and often have been misunderstood and even persecuted for their beliefs. Books can promote understanding among religious factions. For example, many Jewish students have expressed both interest and pleasure in reading Barbara Robinson's *The Best Christmas Pageant Ever* (1972). Some students said they had always wondered about the Christian Christmas tradition of the pageant, and Robinson's book made understandable what was strange to them—the story helped bridge a cultural gap. Individuals with intellectual or physical challenges also deserve books that represent them in honest, positive ways. For instance, the half million people in the United States who are Deaf (capitalized to indicate they belong to the Deaf culture, not just that they do not hear) are represented by only a smattering of books for young readers. With so few titles available, others have less opportunity to get to know and understand the Deaf.

The labels and terms we use to talk about diverse cultures are sometimes self-created and sometimes created by external forces, such as government agencies. As cultural groups continue to create new terms and labels to identify themselves, it can be difficult to keep up with the currently acceptable words to describe or identify cultures. In this chapter, we have tried to employ the terms that are most prevalent in the current literature.

The Need for Multicultural Books

Xenophobia, the mistrust or fear of people who are strangers or foreigners, is in part responsible for our worldwide inability to live together in peace, affording one another equal opportunities. Parents and society may purposely or inadvertently program children to mistrust, fear, or even hate certain groups of people who are unlike them. Teaching children at an early age "about the [positive] differences and similarities between people will not singularly ensure a more gentle and tolerant society, but might act as a prerequisite to one" (Sobol, 1990, p. 30). Candy Dawson Boyd (1990) makes it clear that we cannot begin too early to give our children a multicultural perspective:

> We know that there's a substantial body of research on the development of racial consciousness begun in 1929, and what does it tell us? It tells us that children develop negative attitudes towards other people as they take on the culture of their parents. It tells us that by age three, racial awareness is evident. *Three.* And that by age ten, racial attitudes have crystallized.

Yet children in early adolescence "are not too old for significant attitudinal change. Counteraction is therefore possible" (Sonnenschein, 1988, p. 265).

Literature can be one of the most powerful tools for combating the ignorance that breeds xenophobic and judgmental behaviors. "For decades experienced educators have reported success stories about using children's literature to broaden attitudes toward people from a variety of cultures" (Hansen-Krening, 1992, p. 126). Rudine Sims Bishop, who has long been a champion of the well-written multicultural book, believes that "literature is one of the most powerful components of a multicultural education curriculum, the underlying purpose of which is to help make the society a more equitable one" (Bishop, 1992, p. 40). In support of this view, she quotes James Baldwin: "Literature is indispensable to the world. . . . The world changes according to the way people see it, and if you alter, even by a millimeter, the way a person looks at reality, then you can change it" (Sims, 1982, p. 1). Indeed, studies have indicated that students' prejudices have been reduced because of their involvement with good multicultural books (Pate, 1988; Darigan, 1991; Wan, 2006).

It is the specificity in the books that make them useful, as discovered by Rebecca Bigler of the University of Texas.

> Bigler ran a study in which children read brief biographies of famous African-Americans. For instance, in a biography of Jackie Robinson, they read that he was the first African-American in the major leagues, and how he suffered taunts from white fans. Those facts—in five brief sentences were omitted in the version given to the other children.
>
> After the two-week history class, the children were surveyed on their racial attitudes. White children who got the full story about historical discrimination had significantly better attitudes toward blacks than those who got the neutered version. Explicitness works. "It also made them feel some guilt," Bigler adds. "It knocked down their glorified view of white people." They couldn't justify in-group superiority. (Bronson & Merryman, 2009)

Certainly, children of minority cultural groups need books that bolster self-esteem and pride in their heritage (Nieto, 2000). And children of all groups, especially majority children, need books that sensitize them to people from cultural groups and social conditions different from their own. By the same token, "White people, as the majority in U.S. society, seldom think of themselves as *ethnic*—a term they reserve for the other, more easily identifiable groups. Nevertheless . . . we are all ethnic, whether we choose to identify ourselves in this way or not" (Nieto, 2000, p. 26).

Judging Multicultural Literature

As with all books, multicultural books ought to measure up to the criteria used to judge literature in general (see Chapters 2 to 4). A good book tells a credible, interesting story and is an honest, believable experience, regardless of the content. With multicultural themes and content, however, additional content needs to be considered.

Racial or cultural stereotyping must be avoided. Stereotypes are alienating because they perpetuate a simplified, biased, and often negative view of groups of people: All African Americans are poor, all Mexicans are lazy, all Asians are secretive and sly, all Jews are born entrepreneurs, and all white Americans are arrogant and loud. Though common elements often link the lives and daily practices of members of a cultural group, it is important to communicate that every group is made up of individuals who have their own sets of personal values, attitudes, and beliefs. Books written for children need to represent characters who are members of cultural minorities as true individuals and must present a positive image. However, this still leaves room for showing both positive and negative behaviors in minority-group as well as majority-group characters. For instance, in the Newbery-winning novel *Roll of Thunder, Hear My Cry,* a story of racial prejudice in Mississippi of the 1930s, Mildred Taylor (1976) creates African American characters who represent a broad spectrum of human characteristics. Cassie Logan is proud and honorable, though a bit stubborn. T. J. is weak and dishonest. By the same token, Taylor does not make all whites racial bigots.

Cultural details need to be represented accurately in literature. These may include the use of dialects or idioms; descriptions of ethnic foods, customs, and clothing; and information about

religious beliefs and practices. Of course, sensitivity to subcultures within a group is also important. For example, customs vary among the different factions of Judaism; Hasidic Jews are strictly orthodox, as evidenced by dress codes and other identifiable practices, but Reform Jews are much less bound by religious law. In the same way, customs and lifestyles vary greatly among the many Native American tribes.

Cultural authenticity, a sensitive issue in children's literature today, means that those from within a culture feel that a book has accurately and honestly reflected their experiences and viewpoints. We acknowledge that the idea of cultural authenticity is debatable. Some say that people within a culture vary widely in innumerable ways, making the rigid definition of their culture impossible. However, many people feel that books representing a specific cultural group should not be written by someone who is an outsider. For instance, the Newbery-winning novel *Sounder* by William Armstrong (1969) portrays the lives of a poor family of African American sharecroppers. Armstrong is not African American, and critics charge that there is no way he could understand the nuances of living in this culture. "Someone who does not share the specifics of a culture remains an outsider, no matter how astute a student or how well-meaning their intentions" (Wilson, 1990, p. A25). Some critics even maintain that many multicultural books written by outsiders provide a distorted view because the author is biased or culturally prejudiced.

At the same time, others believe that if outsiders make concentrated efforts not only to understand but also to inhabit a different cultural world, then they may indeed be able to write with accurate voice. Of course, some rare authors seem to have a particular gift for "imagining others' lives" (Horn, 1993, p. 78). For instance, Miriam Horn (1993) makes a case for Eudora Welty's uncanny ability:

> "Miss Eudora" could . . . enter into the stolid, exhausted body of an old black woman or let loose with a bluesy tale as full of tumbles and howls as a Fats Waller jam. Before she was 30, she could feel the frantic loneliness of a middle-aged traveling salesman. . . . She could even, on the hot night in 1963 that civil-rights leader Medgar Evers was killed, transform her own soft, lilting voice into the bitter ranting of a hate-filled assassin. Of the story she wrote that night in the voice of the murderer she says: "You have to give any human being the right to have you use your imagination about them." (p. 78)

Whoever the author, it is of great importance to have books for young readers that are culturally accurate.

Awareness about the types of multicultural books that exist may be helpful in judging and selecting books for libraries and classrooms. Certainly, they include folktales, biographies, historical novels, informational books, fantasy, picture books, and contemporary realistic novels. However, Rudine Sims Bishop (Bishop, 1992) suggests that there are three additional general categories of books about people of color: neutral, generic, and specific. In many instances, these categories can also be applied to other cultural groups:

- *Culturally neutral children's books* include characters from cultural minorities but are essentially about other topics. Bishop says that this variety is made up mostly of picture books and gives the example of a book about medical examinations wherein "a Japanese-American child might be shown visiting the doctor, who might be an African-American female" (1992, p. 46). Neutral books randomly place multicultural faces among the pages in order to make a statement about the value of diversity.

- *Generic books* focus on characters representing a cultural group, but few specific details are included that aid in developing a cultural persona. Instead, the characters are functioning in the books as regular people existing in a large common culture, such as American culture. A classic example is the Caldecott-winning *The Snowy Day* by Ezra Jack Keats (1962), which features an African American family living in an inner city. The book shows a black child enjoying newly fallen snow, just as any child might. Although this book is noted as one of the first picture books to have an African American child as a protagonist, some critics feel that the child's mother is presented as a stereotypical black woman—the large, loving Negro mammy image. Although this variety of multicultural book contains little culturally specific material, readers concerned about multicultural issues still scrutinize these books hoping to find characters with realistic, nonstereotypical qualities.
- *Culturally specific children's books* incorporate specific cultural details that help define characters. Cultural themes are evident, if not prevailing, in fictional plots or nonfiction content. Of course, in picture books the artwork expresses many of these cultural details. In this category of multicultural literature cultural accuracy is particularly important. The recommended reading list at the conclusion of this chapter is organized by cultural divisions and presents books considered by many to be both quality literature and culturally authentic.

The Growth of Multicultural Literature

Children's books in the past generally treated minority groups badly or ignored them completely. However, when African American author Arna Bontemps (1948) won a Newbery Honor in 1949 for *Story of the Negro* and became the first African American to appear on the Newbery list, he ushered in the real beginnings of change for all cultural groups. Though few other minority authors or illustrators appeared on award lists during the next two decades, more of their work was being produced. Also, books by majority-culture authors that presented less stereotypical images of minority cultures appeared and received awards: *Song of the Swallows* by Leo Politi (1949) won the Caldecott Award in 1950 and was the first Caldecott winner with a Latino protagonist. Then *Amos Fortune, Free Man* by Elizabeth Yates (1950; African American protagonist), *Secret of the Andes* by Ann Nolan Clark (1952; Native American protagonist), and . . . *And Now Miguel* by Joseph Krumgold (1953; Latino protagonist) each won the Newbery Award. *The Snowy Day* by Ezra Jack Keats won the Caldecott in 1963 (African American protagonist).

As the civil rights movement gained momentum in the 1960s, awareness of and sensitivity toward minorities increased. In 1965, the literary world was awakened by the publication of a startling article titled "The All White World of Children's Books." Printed in the *Saturday Review* and written by Nancy Larrick, this article reported that almost no African Americans appeared in any of the nation's children's books. The publishing and library worlds took notice, and efforts to include more African Americans in children's books eventually blossomed to include additional racial minorities, people with physical and mental disadvantages, and other groups.

In 1966, the Council on Interracial Books for Children (CIBC) was founded. Its publication pointed to racial stereotypes still appearing in children's books, and its efforts with publishers

helped promote and get into print the works of authors and illustrators of color, particularly African Americans. In fact, for a number of years, the CIBC sponsored an annual contest for unpublished writers and illustrators of color and saw to it that the winners' works were published. The authors and illustrators who were given their start by the CIBC are some of the best known today in the world of multicultural children's literature: African American authors Mildred Taylor and Walter Dean Myers, Native American author Virginia Driving Hawk Sneve, and Asian American writers Ai-Ling Louie and Minfong Ho.

In 1969, the American Library Association (ALA) established the Coretta Scott King Award to recognize the distinguished work of African American writers and illustrators. Soon after, in 1974, the National Council for the Social Studies created the Carter G. Woodson Award for the most distinguished children's books that treat topics related to ethnic minorities and race relations.

As books by minority authors and about diverse cultures began to receive more attention, writers and illustrators of color also began to receive the major U.S. literature awards. In 1975, Virginia Hamilton won the Newbery Award for *M. C. Higgins, the Great* (1974), becoming the first African American to be so honored. The next year, Leo Dillon became the first African American to win the Caldecott Medal, an award he shared with his wife, Diane, for their illustrations in *Why Mosquitoes Buzz in People's Ears,* written by Verna Aardema (1975). More recently, Christopher Paul Curtis (1999) was awarded the 2000 Newbery Medal for *Bud, Not Buddy,* and Jerry Pinkney (2009) received the Caldecott Medal for *The Lion & the Mouse* in 2010.

In 1990, Ed Young became the first Chinese American to win the Caldecott Medal (*Lon Po Po: A Red Riding Hood Story from China,* 1989), and in 1994, Allen Say was the first Japanese American to win the award (*Grandfather's Journey,* 1993). It was not until 1995 that a person of Latina/Latino background was awarded one of the ALA's major children's book prizes. David Diaz won the Caldecott for his illustrations in *Smoky Night,* written by Eve Bunting (1994). Since that time, the ALA has established the Pura Belpré Award (1996) to honor the work of Latina/Latino writers and illustrators. In 2002, Linda Sue Park, who is Korean American, was awarded the Newbery Medal for *A Single Shard* (2001), and in 2005, Cynthia Kadohata, who is Japanese American, won the Newbery for *Kira-Kira* (2004).

Since the 1960s, more authors from minority cultural and racial groups have been writing for children and appear consistently on best-books lists and awards lists. Still, there is much room for growth in this area of publishing. More minority titles and writers are needed—particularly Latina/Latino and Native American writers—as are books representing the intellectually and physically disabled cultures.

International Books

Just as multicultural books dealing with North American societies assist in creating a bridge of understanding, international books can help children gain an appreciation and understanding of global societies. The history and culture of other countries, as well as their literary traditions, are illuminated through books that have their origins outside North America.

The most common international books in the United States and Canada are English-language titles written and published in other English-speaking countries, such as the United Kingdom, Australia, and New Zealand. Because these books need no translation, they can be acquired and marketed readily by U.S. and Canadian publishers. (See Appendix D for the names of foreign English-language book awards.)

Although translated books are less plentiful in North America, this area of publishing is growing. These foreign-language books were originally written and printed in other countries. Companies in the United States and Canada acquire the rights to publish them, and they are translated into English. A very limited number of foreign-language children's books from other countries are released in North America in untranslated form.

One consideration when judging translated books is the quality of the translation. Though the flavor of the country needs to be retained, the English text must be fluent and readable yet not too Americanized. Often, a few foreign words and phrases can provide readers a feel for the culture and language, but too many may be troublesome for some children.

There is an ever-increasing exchange of children's books among countries, but most of the international books published in the United States and Canada come from Europe. Each year since 1966, publishers from around the world have attended an international children's book fair in Bologna, Italy, where they share their books and work out agreements for publishing them in other countries.

Since World War II, a number of organizations, publications, and awards have been established to promote the idea of an international world of children's books. In 1949, the International Youth Library was founded in Munich, Germany. It has become a world center for the study of children's literature. In 1953, the International Board on Books for Young People (IBBY) was established, and soon a fter, in 1956, this organization created the first international children's book award. The Hans Christian Andersen Medal is given every two years to an author whose lifetime contribution to the world of children's literature is considered outstanding. In 1966, a separate award for illustration was added to the Hans Christian Andersen Medal, and IBBY also began publishing *Bookbird,* a journal linking those interested in international children's books. In 1968 in the United States, the ALA first presented the Mildred Batchelder Award to the U.S. publisher of the most noteworthy translated children's book of the year.

With the increased emphasis on well-written multicultural and international children's books, teachers and parents have an additional means by which they may help children avoid the pitfalls of ignorance that breed intolerance, hatred, and conflict. In an atomic age, we certainly cannot afford the increasingly deadly outcomes sparked by xenophobic behaviors.

Multicultural Book Reading Lists

Many fine multicultural and international titles, indeed many of our favorites, have been included in the other reading lists in this book. For the most part, they have not been repeated here.

African American

Bolten, Tonya. 2003. *Wake Up Our Souls: A Celebration of Black American Artists.* Abrams.

Byran, Ashley. 2007. *Let It Shine: Three Favorite Spirituals.* Atheneum.

Clifton, Catherine, ed. 1998. *I, Too, Sing America.* Illustrated by Stephen Alcorn. Houghton.

Cline-Ransome, Lesa. 2000. *Satchel Paige.* Illustrated by James Ransome. Simon & Schuster.

Curtis, Christopher Paul. 1995. *The Watsons Go to Birmingham—1963.* Delacorte.

Curtis, Christopher Paul. 2007. *Elijah of Buxton.* Scholastic.

Draper, Sharon M. 1997. *Forged by Fire.* Atheneum.

Draper, Sharon M. 2006. *Copper Sun.* Atheneum.

Giovanni, Nikki. 2005. *Rosa.* Illustrated by Bryan Collier. Holt.

Hamilton, Virginia. 1995. *Her Stories: African American Folktales, Fairy Tales, and True Tales.* Illustrated by Leo Dillon and Diane Dillon. Blue Sky/Scholastic.

Haskins, James. 2006. *John Lewis in the Lead: A Story of the Civil Rights Movement.* Lee & Low.

Hopkinson, Deborah. 1999. *A Band of Angels: A Story Inspired by the Jubilee Singers.* Illustrated by Raúl Colón. Atheneum.

Hopkinson, Deborah. 2010. *First Family.* Illustrated by A. G. Ford. Katherine Tegen Books.

Johnson, Angela. 2010. *Sweet, Hereafter.* Simon & Schuster.

Lester, Julius. 2005. *The Old African.* Illustrated by Jerry Pinkney. Dial.

Lester, Julius. 2008. *Guardian.* Amistad/Harper.

Lorbiecki, Marybeth. 2006. *Jackie's Bat.* Illustrated by Brian Pinkney. Simon & Schuster.

McKissack, Patricia C., and Fredrick L. McKissack. 2003. *Days of Jubilee: The End of Slavery in the United States.* Scholastic.

Meltzer, Milton. 1984. *The Black Americans: A History in Their Own Words, 1619–1983.* Crowell.

Myers, Walter Dean. 2010. *The Cruisers.* Scholastic.

Nelson, Marilyn. 2005. *A Wreath for Emmett Till.* Illustrated by Philippe Lardy. Houghton Mifflin.

Nelson, Vaunda M. 2009. *Bad News for Outlaws: The Remarkable Life of Bass Reeves, Deputy U.S. Marshal.* Illustrated by R. Gregory Christie. Carolrhoda Books.

Pinkney, Andrea Davis. 2010. *Sit-In.* Illustrated by Brian Pinkney. Little Brown.

Shange, Ntozake. 2009. *We Troubled the Waters.* Illustrated by Rod Brown. Amistad/Harper.

Spires, Elizabeth. 2009. *I Heard God Talking to Me: William Edmondson and His Stone Carvings.* Farrar.

Taylor, Mildred. 2001. *The Land.* Phyllis Fogelman Books.

Woodson, Jacqueline. 2001. *Other Side.* Illustrated by E. B. Lewis. Putnam.

Woodson, Jacqueline. 2008. *After Tupac and D Foster.* Putnam.

Asian American

Choi, Sook Nyul. 1991. *The Year of Impossible Goodbyes.* Houghton.

Ho, Minfong. 2003. *The Stone Goddess.* Orchard.

Kadohata, Cynthia. 2004. *Kira-Kira.* Atheneum.

Kadohata, Cynthia. 2010. *A Million Shades of Gray.* Atheneum.

Kajikawa, Kimiko. 2009. *Tsunami!* Illustrated by Ed Young. Philomel.

Lee, Milly. 2006. *Landed.* Illustrated by Yangsook Choi. Farrar, Straus & Giroux.

Lin, Grace. 2008. *The Year of the Rat.* Little, Brown.

Lin, Grace. 2009. *Where the Mountain Meets the Moon.* Little, Brown.

Lord, Bette Bao. 1984. *In the Year of the Boar and Jackie Robinson.* Harper.

Mochizuki, Ken. 1993. *Baseball Saved Us.* Illustrated by Dom Lee. Lee & Low.

Mochizuki, Ken. 1997. *Passage to Freedom: The Sugihara Story.* Illustrated by Dom Lee. Lee & Low.

Morey, Janet Nomura, and Wendy Dunn. 1992. *Famous Asian Americans.* Dutton.

Mori, Kyoko. 2000. *Stone Field, True Arrow.* Metropolitan.

Park, Linda Sue. 2001. *A Single Shard.* Clarion.

Park, Linda Sue. 2008. *Keeping Score.* Clarion.

Salisbury, Graham. 1994. *Under the Blood-Red Sun.* Delacorte.

Say, Allen. 1993. *Grandfather's Journey.* Houghton Mifflin.

Say, Allen. 2010. *The Boy in the Garden.* Houghton Mifflin.

Uchida, Yoshiko. 1981. *A Jar of Dreams.* McElderry.

Wong, Janet. 2000. *The Trip Back Home.* Illustrated by Bo Jia. Harcourt.

Yee, Paul. 1990. *Tales from Gold Mountain: Stories of the Chinese in the New World.* Macmillan.

Yee, Paul. 2008. *Learning to Fly.* Orca.

Yep, Laurence. 1977. *Child of the Owl.* Harper.

Yep, Laurence. 2008. *Dragon Road.* Harper.

Young, Ed. 2006. *My Mei Mei.* Philomel.

Hispanic American (Latino)

Alvarez, Julia. 2009. *Return to Sender.* Knopf.

Ancona, George, Alma Flor Ada, and F. Isabel Campoy. 2005. *Mi música/My Music.* Children's Press.

Bernier-Grand, Carmen T. 2009. *Diego: Bigger Than Life.* Illustrated by David Diaz. Marshall Cavendish.

Buss, Fran Leeper. 1991. *Journey of the Sparrows.* Lodestar.

Canales, Viola. 2005. *The Tequila Worm.* Wendy Lamb Books/Random House.

Carlson, Lori M., ed. 2005. *Red Hot Salsa: Bilingual Poems on Being Young and Latino in the United States.* Holt.

Cofer, Judith Ortiz. 1995. *An Island Like You: Stories of the Barrio.* Orchard.

Deedy, Armen Agra. 2007. *Martina the Beautiful Cockroach: A Cuban Folktale.* Illustrated by Michael Austin. Peachtree.

Delacre, Lulu. 2000. *Salsa Stories.* Scholastic.

Engle, Margarita. 2008. *The Surrender Tree: Poems of Cuba's Struggle for Freedom.* Holt.

Garza, Xavier. 2005. *Lucha Libre: The Man in the Silver Mask: A Bilingual Cuento.* Cinco Puntos Press.

Gonzáles, Lucía. 2008. *The Storyteller's Candle/La velita de los cuentos.* Illustrated by Lulu Delacre. Children's Book Press.

Jiménez, Francisco. 2008. *Reaching Out.* Houghton Mifflin. (Sequel to *The Circuit: Stories from the Life of a Migrant Child* and *Breaking Through.*)

Johnston, Tony. 2009. *My Abuelita.* Illustrated by Yuyi Morales. Harcourt.

Krumgold, Joseph. 1953. *. . . And Now Miguel.* Crowell.

Martínez, Floyd. 1997. *Spirits of the High Mesa.* Arte Público Press.

Martínez, Reuben. 2010. *Once upon a Time: Traditional Latin American Tales.* Illustrated by Raúl Colón. Rayos/HarperCollins.

Mora, Pat. 2009. *Fiesta! Celebrate Children's Day/Book Day.* Illustrated by Rafael López. Rayos/HarperCollins.

Ryan, Pam Muñoz. 2000. *Esperanza Rising.* Scholastic.

Ryan, Pam Muñoz. 2010. *Neruda: A Novel.* Scholastic.

Soto, Gary. 2000. *Chato and the Party Animals.* Illustrated by Susan Guevara. Putnam.

Soto, Gary. 2005. *Help Wanted: Stories.* Harcourt.

Native American

Begay, Shonto. 1992. *Ma'ii and Cousin Horned Toad: A Traditional Navajo Story.* Scholastic.

Begay, Shonto. 1995. *Navajo: Visions and Voices across the Mesa.* Scholastic.

Bierhorst, John. 1987. *Doctor Coyote: Native American Aesop's Fables.* Illustrated by Wendy Watson. Macmillan.

Bruchac, Joseph. 2006. *The Return of Skeleton Man.* Illustrated by Sally Wern Comport. HarperCollins.

Bruchac, Joseph. 2009. *Night Wings.* Illustrated by Sally Wern Comport. HarperCollins.

Cohen, Carol. 1988. *The Mud Pony.* Illustrated by Shonto Begay. Scholastic.

Dorris, Michael. 1996. *Sees Behind Trees.* Hyperion.

Ekoomiak, Normee. 1988. *Arctic Memories.* Holt.

Erdrich, Louise. 2008. *The Porcupine Year.* HarperCollins. (Sequel to *The Birchbark House* and *The Game of Silence.*)

Freedman, Russell. 1996. *The Life and Death of Crazy Horse.* Drawings by Amos Bad Heart Bull. Holiday House.

Goble, Paul. 2002. *Mystic Horse.* HarperCollins.

Goble, Paul. 2010. *The Boy and His Mud Horses: And Other Stories from the Tipi.* World Wisdom.

Harjo, Joy. 2000. *The Good Luck Cat.* Illustrated by Paul Lee. Harcourt.

Highwater, Jamake. 1977. *Anpao: An American Indian Odyssey.* Lippincott.

Maher, Ramona. 2003. *Alice Yazzie's Year.* Illustrated by Shonto Begay. Tricycle Press.

O'Dell, Scott. 1970. *Sing Down the Moon.* Houghton Mifflin.

Sneve, Virginia Driving Hawk. 2005. *Bad River Boys: A Meeting of the Lakota Sioux with Lewis and Clark.* Illustrated by Bill Farnsworth. Holiday House.

Sneve, Virginia Driving Hawk. 2007. *Lana's Lakota Moons.* Bison Books.

Tingle, Tim. 2006. *Crossing Bok Chitto.* Illustrated by Jeanne Rorex Bridges. Cinco Puntos Press.

Viola, Herman J. 1998. *It Is a Good Day to Die: Indian Eyewitnesses Tell the Story of the Battle of the Little Bighorn.* Crown.

Religious Cultures

Ammon, Richard. 2000. *An Amish Year.* Illustrated by Pamela Patrick. Atheneum. (Christian–Amish.)

Cormier, Robert. 1990. *Other Bells for Us to Ring.* Delacorte. (Christian–Catholic.)

Demi. 1998. *The Dalai Lama.* Holt. (Buddhist.)

Demi. 2003. *Muhammed.* McElderry. (Islam.)

Demi. 2005. *Mary.* McElderry. (Christian.)

Feiler, Bruce. 2004. *Walking the Bible: An Illustrated Journey for Kids through the Greatest Stories Ever Told.* HarperCollins. (Judeo-Christian.)

Galante, Cecilia. 2008. *The Patron Saint of Butterflies.* Bloomsbury. (Religious cults—Christian.)

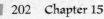

Genari, Anita. 1996. *Out of the Ark: Stories from the World's Religions.* Illustrated by Jackie Morris. Harcourt. (Various religions.)

Ghazi, Sumaib Hamib. 1996. *Ramadan.* Illustrated by Omar Rauuan. Holiday House. (Islam.)

Glossop, Jennifer. 2003. *The Kids Book of World Religions.* Illustrated by John Mantha. Kids Can Press. (Various religions.)

Hartz, Paula R. 2009. *Native American Religions.* Chelsea House. (North American Indians—rites and ceremonies.) (See others in the World Religions series.)

Heuston, Kimberley. 2002. *The Shakeress.* Front Street. (Shakers, Mormons.)

Highwater, Jamake. 1994. *Rama: A Legend.* Holt. (Hindu.)

Kimmel, Eric. 2004. *Wonders and Miracle: A Passover Companion: Illustrated with Art Spanning Three Thousand Years.* Scholastic. (Jewish.)

Kimmel, Eric. 2008. *The Mysterious Guests: A Sukkoth Story.* Illustrated by Katya Krenina. Holiday House. (Jewish.)

Oppenheim, Shulamith Levey. 1994. *Iblis: An Islamic Tale.* Illustrated by Ed Young. Harcourt. (Islam.)

Osborne, Mary Pope. 1996. *One World, Many Religions: The Ways We Worship.* Knopf. (Various religions.)

Rylant, Cynthia. 1986. *A Fine White Dust.* Bradbury. (Christian–Protestant.)

Sturges, Philemon. 2000. *Sacred Places.* Illustrated by Giles Laroche. Putnam. (Various religions.)

Weil, Sylvie. 2009. *Elvina's Mirror.* Jewish Publication Society. (Jewish.)

Williams, Carol Lynch. 2009. *The Chosen One.* Macmillan. (Religious cults—Christian.)

Cultures of the Physically and Mentally Challenged

Bloor, Edward. 1997. *Tangerine.* Harcourt. (Visual impairment.)

Choldenko, Gennifer. 2004. *Al Capone Does My Shirts.* Putnam. (Autism.)

Draper, Sharon. 2010. *Out of My Mind.* Atheneum. (Cerebral palsy.)

Erskine, Kathryn. 2010. *Mockingbird.* Philomel. (Asperger's syndrome.)

Ferris, Jean. 2001. *Of Sound Mind.* Farrar. (Deafness.)

Fraustino, Lisa Rowe. 2001. *The Hickory Chair.* Illustrated by Benny Andrews. Scholastic. (Visual impairment.)

Gantos, Jack. 2000. *Joey Pigza Loses Control.* Farrar. (Attention-deficit hyperactivity disorder.)

Gernis, Meg. 2000. *ABC for You and Me.* Photographs by Shirley Leamon Green. Albert Whitman. (Down syndrome.)

Giff, Patricia Reilly. 2008. *Eleven.* Wendy Lamb Books. (Learning disability.)

Lawlor, Laurie. 2001. *Helen Keller: Rebellious Spirit.* Holiday House. (Deafness, visual impairment.)

Maguire, Gregory. 1994. *Missing Sisters.* McElderry. (Developmental/physical disability.)

Martin, Ann M. 2002. *A Corner of the Universe.* Scholastic. (Autism/emotional disorder.)

McKenzie, Ellen Kindt. 1990. *Stargone John.* Illustrated by William Low. Holt. (Emotional disorder.)

McMahon, Patricia. 2000. *Dancing Wheels.* Photographs by John Godt. Houghton Mifflin. (Developmental/physical disability.)

Miller, Sarah. 2007. *Miss Spitfire: Reaching Helen Keller.* Atheneum. (Deafness, visual impairment.)

Millman, Isaac. 2000. *Moses Goes to School.* Farrar. (Deafness.)

Morpurgo, Michael. 1996. *The Ghost of Grania O'Malley.* Viking. (Cerebral palsy.)

Nazum, K. A. 2008. *The Leanin' Dog.* HarperCollins. (Emotional disorder.)

Rottman, S. L. 1999. *Head above Water.* Peachtree. (Down syndrome.)

Uhlberg, Myron. 2005. *Dad, Jackie, and Me.* Illustrated by Colin Bootman. Peachtree. (Deafness.)

White, Ruth. 2000. *Memories of Summer.* Farrar. (Psychiatric illness.)

Williams, Carol Lynch. 2008. *Pretty Like Us.* Peachtree. (Progeria.)

Winkler, Henry, and Lin Oliver. 2010. *A Brand-New Me.* Grosset & Dunlap. (See others in the Hank Zipzer series.) (Dyslexia/learning disability.)

Wolff, Virginia Euwer. 1988. *Probably Still Nick Swansen.* Holt. (Learning disability)

International Book Reading Lists

English-Language Books

Aiken, Joan. 2007. *Bridle the Wind.* Harcourt. (U.K.)

Almond, David. 2006. *Clay.* Delacorte. (U.K.)

Cowley, Joy. 2008. *Chicken Feathers.* Illustrated by David Elliot. Philomel. (New Zealand.)

Dowd, Sioban. 2009. *Bog Child.* David Fickling. (U.K.)

Fine, Anne. 2008. *The Road of Bones.* Farrar. (U.K.)

Fox, Mem. 1987. *Possum Magic.* Illustrated by Terry Denton. Harcourt. (Australia.)

Fox, Mem. 2010. *Two Little Monkeys.* Illustrated by Jill Barton. Beach Lane Books. (Australia.)

Hughes, Monica. 2000. *Storm Warning.* Harper. (Canada.)

Ibbotson, Eva. 2004. *The Star of Kazan.* Dutton. (U.K.)

Lunn, Janet. 1997. *The Hollow Tree.* Knopf. (Canada.)

Mahy, Margaret. 2009. *The Magician of Hoad.* McElderry. (New Zealand.)

Naidoo, Beverley. 2009. *Burn My Heart.* Amistad. (South Africa.)

Nicholson, William. 2007. *Jango.* Harcourt. (U.K.)

Nix, Garth. 1995. *Abhorsen.* EOS/Harper. (Australia.)

Nix, Garth. 2010. *Lord Sunday.* Scholastic. (See others in The Keys of the Kingdom series.) (Australia.)

Oppel, Kenneth. 2009. *Starclimber.* EOS/Harper.

Park, Ruth. 1980. *Playing Beatie Bow.* Macmillan. (Australia.)

Pullman, Philip. 1985. *Ruby in the Smoke.* Knopf. (U.K.)

Pullman, Philip. 2008. *Once upon a Time in the North.* Illustrated by John Lawrence. David Fickling. (U.K.)

Sutcliff, Rosemary. 1993. *Black Ships before Troy.* Illustrated by Alan Lee. Delacorte. (U.K.)

Tan, Shaun. 2009. *Tales from Outer Suburbia.* Arthur A. Levine. (Australia.)

Valgardson, W. D. 1995. *Winter Rescue.* Illustrated by Ange Zhang. McElderry. (Canada.)

Waugh, Sylvia. 2004. *Who Goes Home?* Delacorte. (U.K.)

Wynne-Jones, Tim. 2010. *Rex Zero: The Great Pretender.* Farrar. (Canada.)

Translated Books

Björk, Christina. 1999. *Vendela in Venice.* Illustrated by Inga-Karin Eriksson. R & S Books. (Swedish.)

Bredsdorff, Bodil. 2009. *Eidi.* Farrar. (Danish.)

Brun-Cosme, Nadine. 2009. *Big Wolf and Little Wolf.* Illustrated by Olivier Tallec. Enchanted Lion Books. (French.)

Carmi, Daniella. 2000. *Samir and Yonatan.* Scholastic. (Hebrew.)

Chotjewitz, David. 2004. *Daniel Half Human: And the Good Nazi.* Richard Jackson/Atheneum. (German.)

Dalokay, Vedat. 1994. *Sister Shako and Kolo the Goat: Memories of My Childhood in Turkey.* Lothrop. (Turkish.)

de Beers, Hans. 2001. *Alexander the Great.* North-South. (German.)

De Mari, Silvana. 2006. *The Last Dragon.* Hyperion. (Italian.)

Duquennoy, Jacques. 1999. *Operation Ghost.* Harcourt. (French.)

Funke, Cornelia. 2008. *Inkdeath.* Chicken House/Scholastic. (German.) (See also *Inkheart* and *Inkspell.*)

Gaarder, Jostein. 1996. *The Solitaire Mystery.* Illustrated by Hilde Kramer. Farrar. (Norwegian.)

Gallaz, Christophe. 1985. *Rose Blanche.* Illustrated by Roberto Innocenti. Creative Education. (French.)

Goscinny, René. 2005. *Nicholas.* Illustrated by Jean-Jacques Sempé. Phaidon Press. (French.)

Gündisch, Karin. 2001. *How I Became an American.* Cricket Books. (German.)

Heine, Helme. 1998. *The Boxer and the Princess.* McElderry. (German.)

Hole, Stain. 2008. *Garmann's Summer.* Eerdmans. (Norwegian.)

Holtwijk, Ineke. 1999. *Asphalt Angels.* Front Street. (Dutch.)

Holub, Josef. 2005. *An Innocent Soldier.* Arthur Levine/Scholastic. (German.)

Lindgren, Astrid. 1983. *Ronia, the Robber's Daughter.* Viking. (Swedish.)

Linevskii, A. 1974. *An Old Tale Carved Out of Stone.* Crown. (Russian.)

Llorente, Molina. 1993. *The Apprentice.* Farrar. (Spanish.)

Maruki, Toshi. 1982. *Hiroshima No Pika.* Lothrop. (Japanese.)

Orlev, Uri. 2003. *Run, Boy, Run.* Houghton Mifflin. (Hebrew.)

Reuter, Bjarne. 1994. *The Boys from St. Petri.* Dutton. (Danish.)

Richter, Hans Peter. 1972. *I Was There.* Holt. (German.)

Stolz, Joëlle. 2004. *The Shadows of Ghadames.* Delacorte. (French.)

Thor, Annika. 2009. *A Faraway Island.* Delacorte. (Swedish.)

Uehashi, Nahoko. 2008. *Moribito: Guardian of the Spirit.* Arthur A. Levine. (Japanese.)

Yumoto, Kazumi. 2002. *The Letters.* Farrar. (Japanese.)

Zei, Aliki. 1979. *The Sound of the Dragon's Feet.* Dutton. (Greek.)

PEARSON **myeducationkit**™

Go to the topic Multicultural Literature on the MyEducationKit for this text, where you can:

- Search the Database of Children's Literature, housing more than 22,000 titles searchable in every genre by authors or illustrators, by awards won, by year published, and by topic and description.
- Explore genre-related Assignments and Activities, assignable exercises showing concepts in action through database use, video, cases, and student and teacher artifacts.
- Listen to podcasts and read interviews from some of the brightest and most enduring stars of children's literature in the Conversations.
- Discover weblinks that will lead you to sites representing the authors you learn about in these pages, classrooms with powerful children's literature connections, and literature awards.

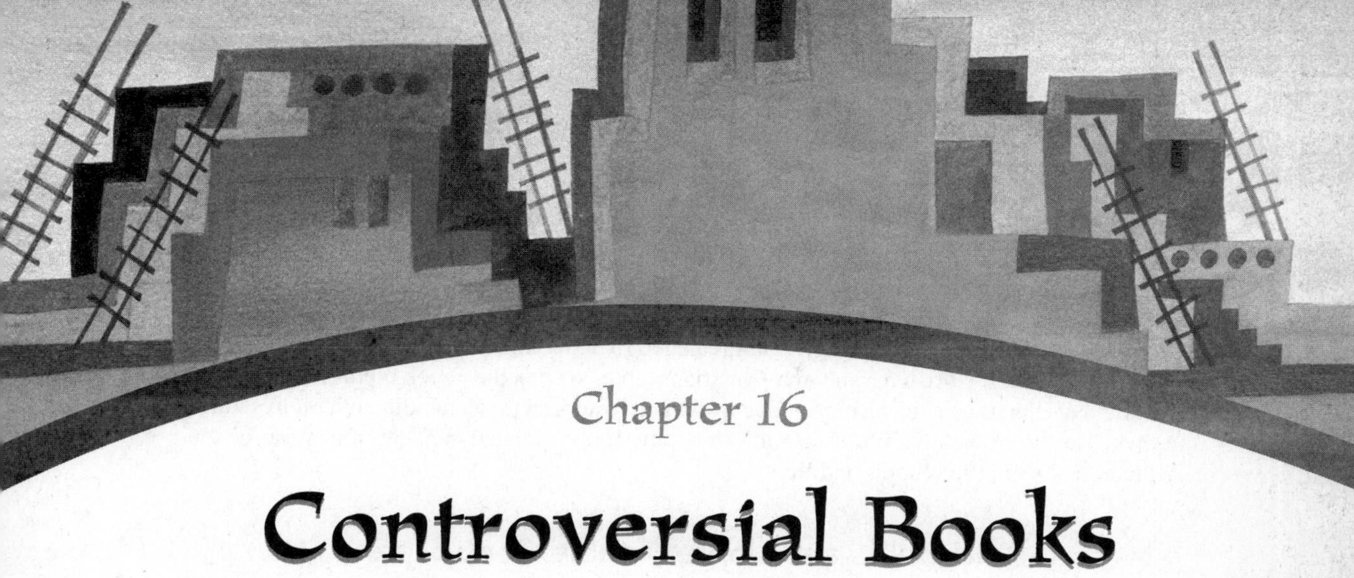

Chapter 16

Controversial Books

Books are dangerous. They can undermine morals, fuel revolutions, and indoctrinate our children. Hitler certainly believed in the power of print and saw to it that publications challenging Nazi policy or written by anyone he deemed an enemy of the state (which, of course, included all books by Jewish authors) were banned, or worse, burned. No doubt there are books that we as individuals would find offensive or that would challenge our way of thinking and make us uncomfortable. But danger exists far less in these books than in the people who would usurp the power and authority to decide for the rest of us what is fit to be read.

The First Amendment

Our First Amendment rights are under constant attack by those who consider paramount their personal agendas, sets of standards, or brands of special interest. The more radical or fanatical the group objecting to certain printed materials—and extremists come from both the political right and the political left—the more control they seek over individual freedom of choice. Give fanatics the power, and they will decide for us what is best, as Hitler, who was so self-aggrandizing, did for his people. Supreme Court Justice William Brennan eloquently expressed this idea when he said, concerning the censorship case *Texas* v. *Johnson,* "If there is a bedrock principle underlying the First Amendment, it is that the Government may not prohibit the expression of an idea simply because society finds the idea itself offensive or disagreeable" (American Library Association, 2009).

This is not to say that individuals should not have the right to make decisions about the personal acceptability of books. Not only have we the right, but we also have the responsibility to make choices for ourselves and to help our children make wise choices. And if we find a book

Visit the MyEducationKit for this course to enhance your understanding of chapter concepts with activities, weblinks, podcasts, and a searchable database of more than 22,000 children's literature titles.

particularly offensive or dangerous, we should express that opinion without seeking to destroy the book.

In today's diverse society, what may seem clearly offensive to one group of people may be viewed as beautiful and uplifting by another. An example of this dichotomy occurred in Rockford, Illinois. Parents of a particular religious sect felt that reading Greek myths in the public schools was an evil practice. Believing strongly in the truth of their Christian convictions, they considered the Greek myths pagan theology that threatened to undermine the faith of their children. Of course, many others, Christians and non-Christians alike, viewed the Greek myths as remarkable literature that illuminates the history of our world and fosters an understanding of cultures unlike our own. The controversy in Illinois is, unfortunately, not an isolated incident of this sort of censorship aimed at public schools and libraries.

Predictable and Unpredictable Controversy

We do not wish to give the impression that any and all books should be available without considering the ages of the children or the prevailing community standards. For example, in virtually every community, excessively pornographic books are unacceptable materials for school and public libraries and even for bookstores. We use the term *excessively* because even pornography does not seem to have clearly defined borders. Some adults consider Judy Blume's *Are You There God? It's Me, Margaret* (1970) to be a form of pornography because it includes sexual topics. Others would consider laughable the labeling of this book as pornographic. Nonetheless, a fine line often must be trod by school librarians and teachers when it comes to preserving intellectual freedoms and students' right to read. In some instances, certain titles are kept in closed areas to be circulated only with parental permission. Sex education books, such as Robie Harris's *It's Not the Stork!* (2006), often are kept on these restricted shelves, especially in elementary schools.

As school and library personnel know, sex and profane language in books for young readers predictably generate controversy anywhere in the country. Other topics may be volatile in particular communities—such as violence, the occult, racism, and religion—but sex and bad language in children's books seem to alienate adults generally. For example, *And Tango Makes Three* (2005), written by Peter Parnell and Justin Richardson, is based on a true story of two male Chinstrap Penguins, Roy and Silo, at New York City's Central Park Zoo. Realizing the couple had pair bonded, a zookeeper gave them a fertilized egg, which they incubated until it hatched; the new penguin chick was named Tango. While many found the book "cute" and "charming," others felt it was "anti-family," promoted homosexuality, and was unsuited to the age group. It quickly became the most challenged book in 2006, 2007, and 2008 and was the second most challenged book in 2009. The so-called gay-themed books continue to spark controversy. Lauren Myracle's *Luv Ya Bunches* (2009) was removed as an elementary book fair selection because one of the four protagonists has same-sex parents. Sarah Brannen's (2008) *Uncle Bobby's Wedding,* a book about a young guinea pig's jealousy when her favorite uncle marries his boyfriend, made the 10-most-challenged list the year it was published.

Language issues extend to more than just profanity. For instance, Susan Patron received the 2007 Newbery Medal for her book *The Higher Power of Lucky* (2006). Teachers and librarians across the country declared on listservs and blogs that they would not have the book in their classrooms and libraries. Why? Because of one word they felt was inappropriate for 9- to 12-year-olds: *scrotum.* Interestingly, many reviewers praised Patron's use of correct terminology and avoidance

of the less acceptable vernacular terms. When it comes to children's reading, adults seem particularly sensitive to this issue.

Because controversies about sexual content, profanity, violence, and gay themes in books are predictable, teachers and librarians know that if they use certain books they must be prepared to weather the inevitable storm of complaints. Unpredictable controversies, on the other hand, take educators by surprise. They can feel extremely vulnerable and even defenseless against unexpected censorship attacks for which they have prepared neither intellectually nor emotionally. Here are several surprising examples of unpredictable controversy occurring within the last few decades:

- Author Rachel Vail was invited to speak at an elementary school in Woodbury, New York, where her picture book *Jibberwillies at Night* (2008) was banned from the library. She was told her book that deals with children's nighttime terrors "might make kids develop fears or worries that they otherwise didn't have" (Whelan, 2009).
- The 1970 Caldecott winner, William Steig's *Sylvester and the Magic Pebble* (1969), seemed an innocuous animal fantasy until someone pointed out that the policemen in the book were depicted as pigs. The book was published during the era of Vietnam War protests, when police officers often were branded as "pigs" by demonstrators. "No wonder that the children and some adults have no respect for the law enforcement officer. . . . We demand the book be removed," said the International Conference of Police Associations (Harvey, 1971).
- A public librarian reported an objection about a children's Halloween book raised by a woman who claimed to be a witch. She "felt the book was anti-witch and presented an unfair and unfavorable picture" (Chu, 1982, p. 7).
- A poem in Shel Silverstein's popular collection *A Light in the Attic* (1981) tells of a girl who tries to make a milkshake by shaking a cow and is accompanied by a pen-and-ink drawing that shows her in action. The Eagle Forum, a politically conservative organization, charged that the illustration was "an example of subliminal suggestion of 'sex with animals'" (Haferd, 1988).
- Dr. Seuss (1971) found his book *The Lorax* in hot water in Laytonville, California, a single-industry lumber town. *The Lorax* tells of a "little creature who loses his forest home when greedy Once-lers cut down all the Truffula trees." Residents saw this as "a flagrant attack on the livelihood" of the town and on the lumber industry in general and demanded that the book be removed from the second-grade required reading list (Arias & McNeil, 1989).
- The Newbery Award–winning book *Bridge to Terabithia* by Katherine Paterson (1977) consistently shows up on the American Library Association's yearly banned-books list. Not surprisingly, many complaints center on the theme of death and the use of bad language, but one 1998 complaint accused the book of creating "an elaborate fantasy world that might lead to confusion."
- Ed Young's 1993 Caldecott Honor book, *Seven Blind Mice* (1992), is a variant of the story of the three blind men and the elephant. Each mouse, a different and brilliant color, incorrectly identifies the object (elephant) it encounters until the white mouse solves the riddle. A host of critics surfaced, complaining that representing the white mouse as the "savior" perpetuates the racist viewpoint of white supremacy.
- BBC News (2001) reported "a bonfire of Harry Potter books" in Alamogordo, New Mexico, started by the congregation of the Christ Community Church. About the book burning, Pastor

Jack Brock said, "Behind that innocent face [Harry Potter] is the power of satanic darkness. Harry Potter is the devil and he is destroying people."

- One school decided to ban *Trouble on Tarragon Island* (Tate, 2005), a book about the preservation of old-growth forests. The book was pulled from the school library after a complaint that the book is not sensitive to aging women, given that reference is made to sagging breasts and uses the word *bazoongas* (Tate, 2007).

Intellectual Freedom and Individual Choice

Controversy about children's books may spring from anywhere, and the challenge may be about almost anything. Often, the prevailing social and political climate will determine what is controversial at a given point in time.

So, how should we as teachers and school librarians proceed in our selection and use of books? First, we need to affirm our personal commitment to individual choice by examining how we view books. If we see them strictly as mirrors that must reflect our particular mores, lifestyles, or standards, then our problem is a difficult one. Whose standards or beliefs are the books to model? The answer could mean the difference between Greek myths or no Greek myths. If, instead, we view books as windows to the world, we have determined that literature is designed to celebrate diversity and that we accept the risks that may accompany such a stance.

The diagram in Figure 16.1 shows an expanding circle encompassing ever-increasing numbers of the population some hope to control when it comes to books. However, attempting to exert control over the reading choices of others is myopic. As we move outward through the concentric

Figure 16.1 Circles of Control

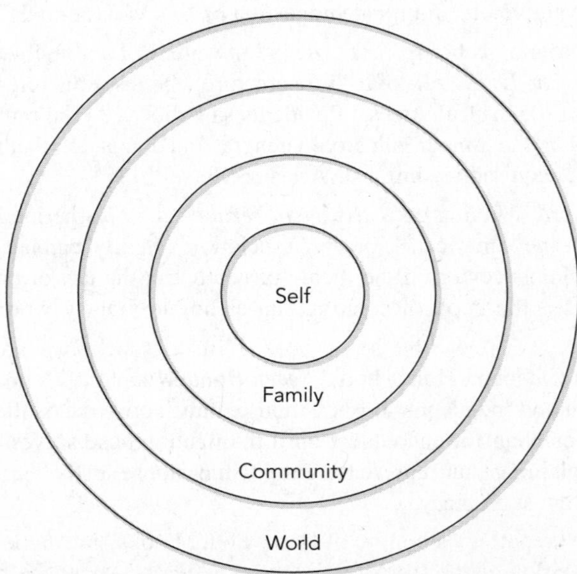

circles in the diagram, it is less probable that the manner in which a book affects us will be the same for other individuals. For example, one who decides a book containing sexual indiscretions should be universally abhorred might be surprised to know the story convinces a teenager across town that sexual abstinence until marriage is the best choice for him.

The smallest circle is "Self." No one would disagree that we each have the responsibility to decide what we personally will or will not read and, as the circle widens, that parents have the right to at least influence the reading of their minor-aged children. It is the people who view books strictly as mirrors who more likely will choose to operate in the expanded circles of control by seeking to censor reading materials in their community or, if they only had the power, in the entire world. The International Conference of Police Associations wished to exercise this sort of far-reaching control by demanding that *Sylvester and the Magic Pebble* (Steig, 1969) be removed from all libraries.

Professional organizations such as the American Library Association (ALA), the International Reading Association (IRA), and the National Council of Teachers of English (NCTE) have adopted statements of philosophy concerning intellectual freedom and our right to read. Organizations that actually assist teachers and librarians who need help in fighting censorship attacks include the ALA's Freedom to Read Foundation (phone: 800-545-2433, ext. 4226; http://www.ftrf.org), the National Coalition against Censorship (phone: 212-807-6222; http://www.ncac.org), and People for the American Way (phone: 800-326-7329; http://www.pfaw.org). But even with this sort of support network, teachers and librarians may wish to exercise some caution, especially in selecting books to read aloud to children or to be required classroom reading. Therefore, a few touchstones may help us decide about potentially controversial books.

Carefully Consider Assigned Books

There is a difference between a book that is assigned reading and a book that is merely available on school or classroom library shelves. When a title is compulsory reading for students, book watchdogs are more strident. Teachers should consider carefully whether a book they plan to assign is one they would be willing to defend.

Recognize That Positive Learning Can Come from Negative Portrayals

It is not unusual for books with negative content to be dismissed out of hand. For example, some adults do not want their children reading a novel that involves drug abuse, because they feel it may plant a suggestion that could lead to trouble. However, if the story illustrates the negative consequences of drug abuse, the book actually may be desirable. That drug use appears in a book does not automatically condemn the title; its presence may serve positive ends.

Even religious literature includes negative episodes for positive purposes. In the Bible, King David's story involves lust, adultery, deceit, and even murder in an illustration of how indulgence and becoming self-serving can lead to undesirable ends.

Avoiding the harsh and often unsavory realities of life does not make them go away. In fact, a child may be more susceptible to the effects of controversial material by being totally unprepared. As Jane Smiley (1994) said, "A child who is protected from all controversial ideas . . . is as vulnerable as a child who is protected from every germ. The infection, when it comes, and it will come, may overwhelm the system, be that the immune system or the belief system."

Judge Books Holistically

It is impossible and unfair to judge a book simply by the subject. All books that deal with sexual topics or contain swear words are not automatically bad. Nor are they automatically good. The way in which these subjects are presented makes the difference. If uncomfortable subject matter offers insight, helps develop attitudes and skills for dealing successfully with life, and fosters resolution or hope, the book may be a worthwhile addition to a recommended list.

In the Newbery Honor book *The Great Gilly Hopkins* (Paterson, 1978), Gilly's actions are reprehensible: stealing, lying, slandering, and swearing. However, she is hurting and hardened because of being abandoned. Finally meeting her mother allows Gilly to relinquish her unrealistic dreams concerning a happy life with this shiftless woman. With this issue resolved, she is able to respond to the people who do care about her, and her behaviors begin to change. Such resolution provides hope. Hopeful books are easier to defend.

Determine When a Book Is Developmentally Appropriate for Children

Some exposure to life's harshness can prepare children for difficult times; too much exposure can traumatize them. With literature, we hope to sensitize children to important issues of the human experience. If details are too explicit, however, children may be traumatized instead of sensitized. The age of the children can make a difference—what may be appropriate for 12-year-olds may not be appropriate for 8-year-olds. Also, individual differences in children of the same age can be significant. Adults need to know both the books and the children to make this judgment call.

An example of a book that sensitizes most 11-year-olds to an issue without an excess of raw detail is Paula Fox's Newbery winner *The Slave Dancer* (1973). She goes just far enough in this story of the American slave trade to show people's inhumanity without becoming too explicit. By comparison, the adult book *Roots* by Alex Haley (1976), published three years earlier, covers the same basic material in far more complete and explicit detail.

However, former school librarian and current children's book author Cynthia DeFelice (2002) wonders if we shouldn't trust children more than we often do. She remembers the powerful experience she had reading *To Kill a Mockingbird* (Lee, 1960) when she was in fifth grade.

> My parents had given it to me, but when I brought it out at school, I was told I had to bring in a note from my parents saying it was okay. As I reread the book . . . [recently], part of me kept thinking, "This would never be given to a fifth grade child today and what a shame."
>
> I thank my parents for having faith that I would be able to take the events of that story, the discussions of rape, the racial and class conflicts, the sometimes cruel actions and crude personalities of the diverse characters, and see them through the eyes of young Scout Finch and come to understand them along with her. (DeFelice, 2002, p. 18)

Handling Book Challenges

Because controversy about books is so unpredictable, almost any book sitting on the library shelf or being shared in the classroom might be challenged by parents and other adults—even the dictionary, as in the case of a southern California school board that pulled the popular *Merriam-Webster* dictionary from school shelves (Kelly, 2010). Therefore, we may find ourselves defending our choices of books. If a parent comes in to complain, remember that reaching an understanding is possible and even probable. Sometimes the problem may be a simple misunderstanding that can be cleared up once teacher and parent communicate. For example, parents may hear about a troublesome book but then discover they have been misinformed. However, if a serious challenge surfaces, teachers and librarians need to have a plan in place to control a potentially explosive situation.

The first rule of thumb when materials are challenged is to deal with *only* one book at a time. Allowing complainants to challenge several books at once or all books by one author makes for an unmanageable situation. To keep things under control, each library system, school, or school district must have policies and procedures to govern censorship cases. Consider the following three guidelines for handling book challenges: (1) materials selection policy, (2) grievance procedure, (3) steps to reduce emotional tension.

Materials Selection Policy

A selection policy will guide the process of choosing books and other media for libraries and classroom use. Often, guidelines and procedures outlined in a selection policy will include the ALA's Library Bill of Rights or other "right to read" statements that confirm the institution's support of the First Amendment and intellectual freedom. Also, selection policies will suggest the use of nationally recognized review journals in helping to make selections. Generally, a selection committee with teacher representatives from various grade levels or disciplines, and sometimes with parent representatives, is named to make final selection recommendations. Policy statements also may specify the standards of all materials used in a school setting, even personal books that a teacher may bring to read to students.

Grievance Procedure

Each library system, school, or school district must have a formal grievance procedure in place, either as a section of the materials selection policy or as a separate document. This procedure dictates the process by which an individual may request that the library or school reconsider a book. It always includes a formal complaint form that must be filled out and signed by the complainant. A sample form is shown in Figure 16.2. With no signature, the school or library does not need to consider the challenge to the book. However, if the form is signed and filed, the grievance procedure dictates further action by the library system or school district. Generally, a committee, which may be the same as the selection committee, is convened to consider the complaint. It is wise to include community representation. The recommendation of the committee is then forwarded to the school or library board, which makes the final decision. It is possible that the censors might take their case to the court system if they are not pleased with a board's decision. However, the fact that the complaint was given a fair and careful hearing can only strengthen a school's or library system's case.

Steps to Reduce Emotional Tension

With policies in place, teachers and librarians can breathe easier. Still, when the time comes to face someone who is challenging a book, two other guidelines are helpful.

First, we must make a supreme effort to keep conversation with an upset parent or library patron on a rational rather than an emotional level. Be sure to *listen to the complaint* without overreacting. This may not be as easy as it sounds, for often teachers and librarians feel attacked and their natural response is to be defensive. If angry words rule, however, chances

Example of Citizen's Request for Reconsideration of a Book

Citizen's Request for Reconsideration of a Book

Paperback ________
Author ________________________ Hardcover ________
Title ________________________
Publisher (if known) ________________________
Request initiated by ________________________
Telephone ________ Address ________________
City ________________________ Zip Code ________

Complainant represents:
________ Himself/herself
________ Organization (Name) ________________
________ Other group (Identify) ________________

1. To what in the book do you object? (Please be specific; cite pages.) ________

2. What do you feel might be the result of reading this book? ________

3. For what age group would you recommend this book? ________

4. Is there anything positive about this book? ________

5. Did you read the entire book? ________ What parts? ________

6. Are you aware of the judgment of this book by literary critics? ________

7. What would you like the library/school to do about this book?
________ Withdraw it.
________ Return it to the selection committee/department for reconsideration.
________ Do not assign or lend it to my child.
________ Other. (Please explain.) ________

8. In its place, what book would you recommend that would convey as valuable a picture and perspective of the subject treated? ________

________________ ________________
Signature of Complainant Date

are the book will not be as big an issue as the escalating distaste for one another. So, we need to hold our tongues and listen, which allows us to determine if the complaint is a product of a misunderstanding or if we need to channel the complainant peacefully into the formal grievance procedure.

Second, along with listening calmly to the complainant, we should also *get someone else to listen:* another librarian, the teacher from across the hall, or the principal. Having someone else present helps keep everyone honest and serves to reduce tension. People are always more careful with their words when others are there to hear. If the complainant remains unsatisfied, the next step is to have that person *fill out the request to reconsider a book* (Figure 16.2) and begin the formal grievance procedure.

Approximately 85% of book challenges go unreported and receive no media attention (Doyle, 2009). Of the top-10 challenged titles of 2008, 9 were young adult or children's books. Also, of the top 10 most challenged authors of 2008, all 10 were young adult or children's writers (American Library Association, 2009). These figures are indicative of the particular attention adult censors give to books for young people. As we have seen earlier in this chapter, these challenges are spawned by a vast variety of special interests that may or may not represent mainstream thought. And even if mainstream opinion is supported by a successful censorship attempt, then certain voices from our pluralistic society will be silenced. Ultimately, those of us who love books and cherish the right to choose must actively stand on the side of individual choice and intellectual freedom. We close with a quote from Lois Lowry, an author whose books have been both highly honored and challenged—including her Newbery Award–winning futuristic story of dystopia, *The Giver* (1993).

> Submitting to censorship is to enter the seductive world of *The Giver:* the world where there are no bad words and no bad deeds. But it is also the world where choice has been taken away and reality distorted. And that is the most dangerous world of all. (Lowry, 2008, p. 55)

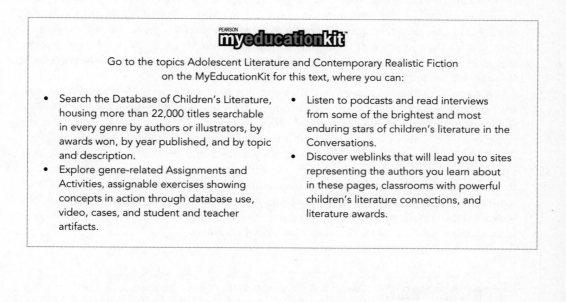

PEARSON **myeducationkit**

Go to the topics Adolescent Literature and Contemporary Realistic Fiction on the MyEducationKit for this text, where you can:

- Search the Database of Children's Literature, housing more than 22,000 titles searchable in every genre by authors or illustrators, by awards won, by year published, and by topic and description.
- Explore genre-related Assignments and Activities, assignable exercises showing concepts in action through database use, video, cases, and student and teacher artifacts.
- Listen to podcasts and read interviews from some of the brightest and most enduring stars of children's literature in the Conversations.
- Discover weblinks that will lead you to sites representing the authors you learn about in these pages, classrooms with powerful children's literature connections, and literature awards.

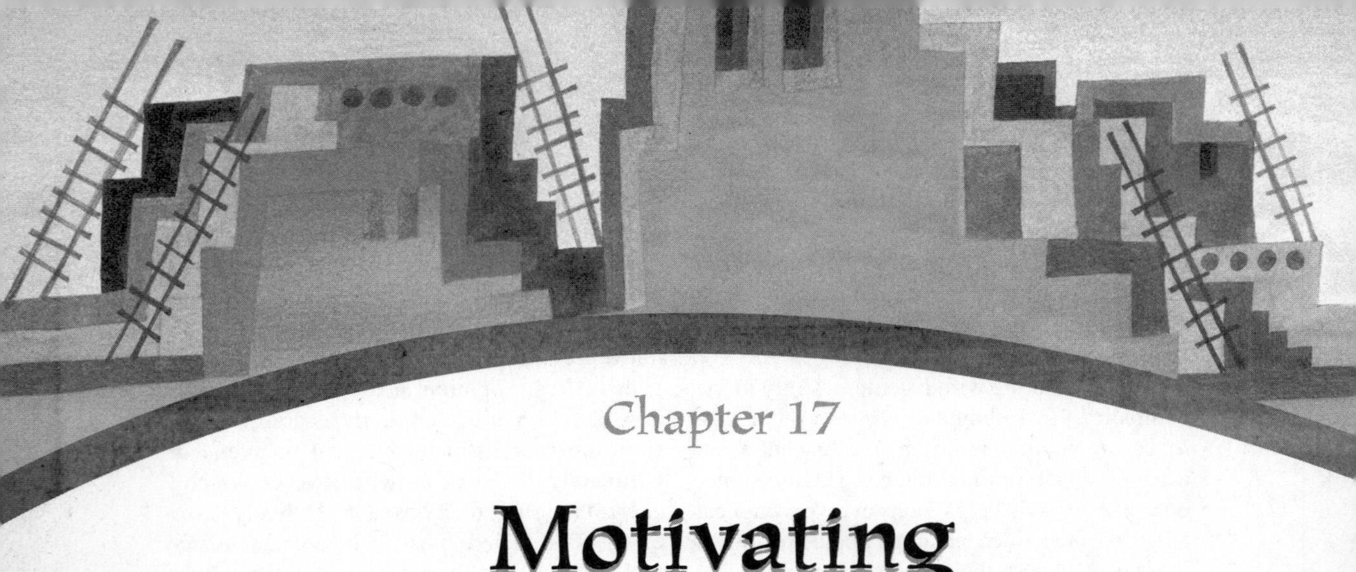

Chapter 17

Motivating Students to Read

Many children spend little time reading. For anyone who has witnessed the vacant look and glazed eyes of a child under the spell of a favorite television program, it is no surprise to learn that television viewing consumes much of children's time. According to parents and guardians of children aged 2 to 17, in the year 2000, American children spent almost two-and-a-half hours (147 minutes) watching television every single day. Television screens, however, are not the only screens to attract children's attention. In 2000, U.S. children reportedly spent almost four-and-a-half hours (281 minutes) each day watching television programs or videotapes, playing video games, using the computer, or surfing the Internet. In an increasingly electronic age, this represented an increase of 21 minutes per day from the time spent in front of screens the previous year (Woodard & Gridina, 2000).

A more recent study (Vandewater, Bickham, & Lee, 2006) reported less television viewing, with children aged 3 to 12 watching, on average, 108 minutes of television per day, although on weekends the number of minutes watched rose to an average of 142 minutes per day. This study, however, reported that the same children averaged fewer than 15 minutes per day reading. On weekends, this average rose but only marginally to 16.5 minutes reading per day. These findings are similar to Wigfield and Guthrie's (1997) findings that children in grades 4 and 5 read for an average of only 10 to 15 minutes per day. It is little wonder that students' lack of reading motivation is a major cause for concern among teachers (O'Flahavan, Gambrell, Guthrie, Stahl, & Alvermann, 1992), while children's television viewing continues to be a concern for parents (Jordan, Hersey, McDivitt, & Heitzler, 2006; redOrbit, 2006).

Visit the MyEducationKit for this course to enhance your understanding of chapter concepts with activities, weblinks, podcasts, and a searchable database of more than 22,000 children's literature titles.

Some argue that schools do a good job of helping children to develop the skills of reading yet fail to adequately develop positive reading attitudes. As Trelease (2001) has said, "We've taught children *how* to read but have forgotten to teach them to *want* to read" (p. 5). Merely teaching children how to read achieves little if children have no desire to do so (Morrow, 2004). After all, as Mark Twain said, "The man who does not read good books has no advantage over the man who cannot." Essentially, the ideal reader is a finely tuned balance of both "skill and will" (Applegate & Applegate, 2004, p. 554). Perhaps schools need to do more to address students' reading will.

While there might be debate about whether teachers are adequately and effectively addressing reading attitudes, there is little doubt that reading attitudes are a concern for teachers. In one large self-report mail survey, 94% of the 1,207 elementary teacher respondents said that one of their teaching goals was to develop motivated young readers (Baumann, Hoffman, Moon, & Duffy-Hester, 1998).

The important role of motivation in school achievement has long been recognized (Krathwohl, Bloom, & Masia, 1964). Teachers' concern with the motivation of their students is well founded, given the established link between motivation and achievement (Baker, Dreher, & Guthrie, 2000). The more motivated children are, the greater the amount and breadth of their reading, even after controlling for previous amount and breadth of reading (Guthrie, Wigfield, Metsala, & Cox, 1999; Wigfield & Guthrie, 1997). A highly motivated, voracious middle school reader might read as many as 50 million words per year, compared to an average for that age level of about one million words per year. The least capable and least motivated middle school readers might read just 100,000 words per year (Nagy & Anderson, 1984).

The more children read, the better readers they become (Cunningham & Stanovich, 1998; Gambrell & Marinak, 2009; Guthrie, Schafer, & Huang, 2001), opening up an ever-increasing reading ability gap over their struggling and unmotivated peers. Stanovich (1986) has described this as the *Matthew effect,* whereby the rich (capable and motivated readers) get richer and the poor (struggling and unmotivated readers) get poorer.

Reading Role Models

One concern is that teachers are not sufficiently strong reading role models. Recognizing the importance of teachers as role models for their students, Applegate and Applegate (2004) coined the term *Peter effect.* In the Christian bible, when a beggar asked Peter for money, he replied that he could not give the beggar what he did not have. Applegate and Applegate contend that a teacher who is not an enthusiastic, engaged, motivated reader cannot model for children reading enthusiasm, engagement, and motivation. In one study, more than half of the 195 preservice teachers were classified as "unenthusiastic" about reading. Only one-quarter (25.2%) of the preservice teacher candidates were classified as reading "enthusiasts," of which only 6.7% were identified as being "avidly enthusiastic" about reading (Applegate & Applegate, 2004).

Figure 17.1 provides a quiz that will help you determine how positive a reading model you are for your students. In addition, the figure offers ways to become a stronger model by suggesting some ways to improve.

There is never a guarantee that our most sincere efforts as teachers will motivate anyone. The best we can do is put forth such efforts, sincerely and continually, and hope that students will resonate with what they see and hear. However, teachers must *be* readers before they can motivate children to *become* readers. If the adults in children's lives love to read—and model that

Figure 17.1

Reading Model Self-Assessment for Teachers

How Good a Reading Model Am I?

Personal Model

1. I read in a book for personal pleasure at least two different days per week. Yes No
2. Two of my favorite authors for children are ____________ and ____________.
3. One of my favorite illustrators of children's books is ____________.
4. The title of a picture book published during the past three years is ____________.
5. The title of a children's chapter book published during the past three years is ____________.
6. I have a personal library of more than 40 children's trade books. Yes No
7. The book I am going to read next is ____________.
8. During the past three months, I found myself showing an interesting book to someone else or mentioning it in conversation. The title is ____________.
9. My favorite genre or type of book is ____________.
10. Two of my favorite authors for adults are ____________.

Classroom Model

1. At least twice weekly, I engage in personal reading where my students can see me with a book. Yes No
2. My students can identify at least one type of book I like or dislike. Yes No
3. I have a growing classroom library of trade books. Yes No
4. I introduce or "book talk" books with my students at least twice a week. Yes No
5. I read aloud a picture book or from a chapter book to my class at least once every day. Yes No
6. I read aloud something other than books to my class daily. Yes No
7. Sustained silent reading (SSR) is a part of our daily schedule. Yes No
8. I always read in my own book during SSR. Yes No
9. I require my children to read regularly on their own outside class. Yes No
10. I run a regular book club program or encourage children to buy books, and I help make that possible. Yes No

Scoring

Personal Model. Each question counts 2 points.

1. Yes = 2 points. If teachers aren't reading, they can't deliver an honest love of books to students.
2. 1 point for each author. Teachers who read children's books will respond more to some authors than others and need to recognize they have favorites.
3. 2 points for completion. Even die-hard upper-elementary teachers need to be familiar with picture books.
4. 2 points for completion. If teachers know only old books, their chances for reaching children will be more limited.
5. 2 points for completion. See number 4.
6. One point for every 20 children's trade books you own (2 points maximum).
7. 2 points for completion. If you don't have an idea of what to read next, chances are you're not reading much.
8. 2 points for completion. If teachers never talk about the books they read, their influence will be limited.

Continued

9. 2 points for completion. Identifying a favorite type of book or genre is important self-knowledge.
10. 1 point for each author. Teachers who are readers generally will have a broader interest than just children's books.

Classroom Model. Each "yes" response receives 2 points.

1. Yes = 2 points. Adults who are most successful in turning children into readers don't hide their own reading. This is as true at home as in the classroom.
2. Yes = 2 points. If you emphasize personal reading with children, they need to learn about your personal reading, which includes the types of books you like and those that are not as appealing to you. Children deserve a teacher with identified favorites.
3. Yes = 2 points. We have a difficult time convincing children that books are worthwhile if none are at hand.
4. Yes = 2 points. Sharing titles consistently will give children needed and welcome ideas of what to read next as well as draw attention to the pleasure and importance of reading.
5. Yes = 2 points. Hearing books read aloud is the most important classroom activity for turning children into readers.
6. Yes = 2 points. The more we immerse students in real reading (see Chapter 1), the better chance we have that they will become readers.
7. Yes = 2 points. SSR is the second most important classroom activity for turning children into readers.
8. Yes = 2 points. The key to a successful SSR program is seeing the teacher read.
9. Yes = 2 points. This is the most important out-of-class activity for turning children into readers.
10. Yes = 2 points. Book ownership is a mark of a truly literate person.

Each quiz has a maximum of 20 points. Scores and ratings for each quiz, and both combined, follow:

Personal or Classroom Score	Total Score	Rating
16–20	32–40	Stupendous. You're a fine model.
12–15	24–31	Very good. You're better than most.
8–11	16–23	Okay, but you need work.
4–7	8–15	Weak. Quick—get books into your life.
0–3	0–7	Don't have children or teach school just yet.

enthusiasm—they can serve as the bedrock of successful literacy education. Indeed, Perez (1986) tells us that nothing in the entire school has a greater impact on convincing children that books are worthwhile than teachers' reading habits:

> Teachers have a choice in motivating children to become lifelong readers. They can either preach on the joys of reading, or they can model for the youngsters what a reader who enjoys reading does. And what teachers do ultimately will depend on how much they truly believe in the importance of reading. (Perez, 1986, p. 11)

Perhaps the most effective way to motivate children to read is to identify their interests and then locate books on those subjects. Although this method generally works well, in many libraries, all the books on a favorite topic are soon exhausted, so the teacher still needs to know how to get children interested in other subjects. Teachers can help create the desire to read when they introduce and read from a variety of children's books they personally like.

While no method is foolproof, choosing personal favorites to recommend to children seems likely to be at least as successful as any other way of selecting titles. Even picking books exclusively from lists of award winners, such as the Caldecott and Newbery, carries no guarantee that children will respond positively to them. But when teachers introduce and read from books they genuinely like, students are more likely to be motivated, for two reasons:

1. Those books generally are better books. They usually are more solidly crafted and contain more levels on which children can make connections.
2. When teachers recommend books that are personally meaningful, a genuine and irresistible enthusiasm accompanies their words. When people talk about books they like, those who listen are often influenced by their sincerity and conviction.

Insofar as reading is concerned, nothing we offer children is more important than an adult who reads. Children end up doing what we do, not what we say, and all the admonitions about the importance of reading in their lives will fall on deaf ears if they view us as people who don't take our own advice. When we speak from experience, however, our words are more honest and persuasive.

Learning from Motivated Readers

A group of college-aged Americans living in Germany was trying to learn German but making slow progress. An old hand offered a piece of advice that made an enormous difference: "If you want to speak like the Germans, listen to the way Germans speak." Embarrassingly simple and obvious, this advice changed the course of the Americans' learning, which until then had been too formal and academic.

We adapt that advice for this chapter: "If we want students to be motivated readers, we must look at how motivated readers read." Teachers sometimes believe that students need careful preparation to read a book or that they have to be bribed or prodded into reading. Yet some children jump right into books, reading without the benefit of preparatory steps or the intervention of either a carrot or a stick. Two principles underlie the motivation of these eager readers: (1) Reading is personal, and (2) reading is a natural process. The following common characteristics of motivated readers reflect these two principles:

1. Motivated readers don't read for others but rather for their own purposes. They read what is important to them and know that real reading isn't done to answer someone else's questions or fill out a worksheet.
2. Motivated readers have personal and identifiable likes and dislikes in books: subject matter, authors, illustrators, formats, styles, and so on.
3. Motivated readers feel rewarded during the reading process. They find immediate pleasure in the book and don't read because they will need the information next year.

4. Motivated readers don't feel trapped by a book. They can put it down without guilt when it no longer meets their needs.
5. Motivated readers aren't hesitant about passing judgment on a book. They have their own viewpoints and don't apologize for them.
6. Motivated readers read at their own rate. They skip, scan, linger, and reread as necessary or desirable.
7. Motivated readers don't feel obligated to remember everything they read. They find reading worthwhile even if they can't recall every concept or idea, and they allow themselves to skip over words they don't know as long as they understand the idea or story.
8. Motivated readers read broadly, narrowly, or in between, depending on how they feel.
9. Motivated readers develop personal attachments to books they like.
10. Motivated readers find time to read regularly.

Motivated readers don't look over their shoulders as they read. They are in charge. We adults shouldn't get excited when students put down books without finishing them, when they devour what we think are worthless books, when their taste does not reflect our own, or when they read very narrowly.

Yet teachers with the best of intentions can interfere with motivated readers. Often, the most difficult hurdle is simply *getting out of their way.* Whatever an adult does that keeps the child from becoming involved with the book is something to be avoided. It is easy to spot mind-numbing exercises that treat the book as merely a repository of facts to be mined, and those practices should be avoided. We should always ask ourselves, "Are the things I am asking my students to do in response to a book adding to their enjoyment and understanding of that book?" Any practice for which the answer is "no" is a practice to be avoided.

Yet even the right principles can be followed with too much fervor, as is evident in the following two examples.

Rose Napoli is an experienced, dedicated teacher who became enthusiastic about trade books and their classroom use during a summer institute. She returned to her teaching inflamed with ideas about allowing students to choose their own books, providing time for them to read, and initiating discussions based on their personal responses. The trouble was that Rose's enthusiasm had become so strong that she simply overpowered the children. She jumped immediately into questions about their involvement with the stories and so peppered them with requests for their feelings that even those children who had initially responded began to keep quiet. Only when Rose began to let students talk from their own perspectives and sincerely listened to them did the children start to respond honestly. In time, their simplistic but honest comments became more complex and perceptive and Rose eventually found the kind of student involvement she earlier had tried to force (Calkins, 1994, pp. 243–249).

Gordon Whiting, a professor at Brigham Young University, prided himself on allowing his 9-year-old daughter adequate rein in selecting the books she would read. He was pleased to see her choose Laura Ingalls Wilder's Little House series and wasn't bothered when she finished them all and began immediately to reread the seven titles in the slipcase. She read them a third time—then a fourth. When she began a fifth reading, Gordon maintained his silence but wondered if she wouldn't be served better by reading something else. As his daughter started the sixth time, he had to hold his tongue. When she picked up the first book to begin a seventh reading, he could keep his peace no longer. He didn't forbid her to read them again but insisted she read one different book before returning to the series. The result? She quit reading altogether. Chances are good that she would have moved to other titles in her own time, but clearly, she was getting something from the series that caused her to read the books again and again.

We simply don't know what goes on in the heads of children when they are immersed in a book. If they are to become motivated readers, we must allow them to be in charge.

Disconnection between In-School and Out-of-School Reading

Some children don't read *outside* school because they have negative experiences with reading *inside* school. At the same time, some children actually *do* read outside school but are considered nonreaders in school because of the types of reading required there (Booth, 2006; Forbes, 2008; Worthy, 2000).

Moje (2009) identifies a disconnection between in-school and out-of-school reading. This disconnection isn't just in the texts children read in school versus out of school. Even with the same texts, the way that children read outside school is different from what is expected and indeed required of them in school. Moje argues that the classroom reading lacks the dynamic, authentic, functional, and social purposes of the reading that young people do outside school. She believes that schools need to do a better job in connecting reading to students' interests and experiences, making reading more authentic and purposeful and thus reforming the schools, rather than attempting to reform the students.

Authentic literacy tasks are the types of activities that are practiced not just within the walls of a schoolroom but also for real-life purposes outside school (Duke, Purcell-Gates, Hall, & Tower, 2006). In many classrooms, however, reading instruction involves the liberal use of things such as worksheets and basal reader textbooks—the types of materials that are used only in schools.

It is important for teachers to be aware that authentic reading and literacy tasks increase students' motivation to read (Gambrell & Marinak, 2009). Teachers need to listen to what their students have to say and to use that information to enhance the appeal and the effectiveness of classroom reading time (Moje, 2000). Teachers should use students' out-of-school experiences to help to shape the in-school experiences that they provide for their students (Moje, 2000; Sanford, 2005–2006). In doing so, more positive readers' identities might be developed.

When we ignore students' interests or negatively judge their reading tastes, we run the risk of turning them away from reading altogether. Author/librarian Patrick Jones (2005) relates a story from his childhood. He was an avid reader of wrestling magazines. On one occasion, the 12-year-old Jones approached the librarian at a public library and nervously asked if the library had any wrestling magazines. Jones says that the look that came across the librarian's face at the "mere mention of wrestling magazines in her library" was so sour that he thinks he might accidentally have asked the librarian to show "what her face would look like if she sucked on a lemon for a hundred years!" Despite the humorous way in which Jones relates the story, there is little humor in his concluding remark: The librarian "made me feel stupid, and I never went back" (p. 127).

Teachers (and librarians) need to ask, "Do the literacy practices of my classroom disempower some and empower others?" (Cairney, 2000, p. 63). Patrick Jones felt decidedly disempowered by

the librarian's reaction to his wrestling magazine enquiry and decided not to go back to the library. We need to be careful not to place negative value judgments on students' out-of-school reading. It is far better for us to embrace children's out-of-school literacies and to welcome them into the classroom. We will not only do our students a favor, but we may be in for some pleasant surprises.

One of the authors of this text, Gregory Bryan, remembers how a student challenged him to read one of Dav Pilkey's Captain Underpants books. Although Greg approached the book with reluctance, he enjoyed the slapstick humor. Another time, Greg turned to Gary Paulsen's (1987) *Hatchet,* thinking, "There is no way this book can be as good as my students say that it is." Ever since, *Hatchet* has been one of Greg's favorites.

Reading Incentive Programs

Teachers sometimes use an incentive program to introduce children to books and to get them involved in reading. Reading incentive programs are of two types: teacher generated and commercially prepared.

Teacher-generated reading incentive programs generally use a chart or other visual record to keep track of each child's reading. Often thematic, the chart may be called "Shoot for the Moon," with a rocket ship for each child lined up at the bottom and a moon at the top. For every book read, the rocket ship advances an inch. Or paper ice-cream cones may line the back wall. Every time a child reads a book, the title is written on a paper scoop of ice cream and placed on the cone. When every cone has 10 scoops, the class has an ice-cream party.

Commercially prepared reading incentive programs are available to schools and school districts. While the specifics differ from program to program, they usually give point values to books, which can then be redeemed for prizes. To be sure that children read the books, a quick evaluation is included as a part of the program—usually, a multiple-choice quiz that requires the child to score within a certain range to get credit for reading the book and often gives more points for a higher score.

Both kinds of programs—teacher generated and commercially sponsored—have the potential to be helpful or harmful. Given this, educators need to carefully consider the potential benefits and risks before they employ reading incentive programs (Fawson & Moore, 1999). Incentive programs are helpful if they actually aid children in finding and getting involved with books. Sometimes the rewards offered in an incentive program will be just what children need to be encouraged to read when they otherwise would not. Once a child has taken the first step, he or she might then find enjoyment in reading and, in turn, develop into a genuinely engaged reader. Yet teachers need to exercise caution about incentive programs. Some research shows that extrinsic rewards actually can hinder the development of intrinsic motivation to read (Krashen, 2004) and that such programs are potentially damaging in terms of their influence on the development of lifelong readers (Fawson & Moore, 1999). Other research reports that extrinsic rewards don't necessarily have a negative impact on intrinsic motivation to read, at least in the areas of attitude, time on task, and performance (Cameron & Pierce, 1994).

Teachers need to be aware that when they offer a prize as a reward for reading, they must be able to determine when the prize overshadows the book. Teachers should ask, "How can I know if the student is reading for the prize or for the love of the book?" If they aren't sure of the answer,

then they should examine the situation more closely to determine whether the reward is getting in the way. If the reading never becomes as important as the prize, then the incentive program is no longer serving the intended purpose and, rather than being helpful, is perhaps being harmful. If teachers are sure students are motivated primarily by the books, then there might be nothing wrong with students' collecting points or receiving prizes.

Recent research by Gambrell and Marinak (2009) suggests that if we are to employ a reading incentive program, one of our important considerations should be the notion of *reward proximity.* If we want children to value pizza, then the reward should be a pizza party. If, however, we want children to value books, then we should give them books as reward for their reading. Unrelated rewards—what might be termed *tokens*—may actually undermine and decrease motivation to read (Gambrell & Marinak, 2009).

An example of an incentive program going awry was given by a university student who told about the contest sponsored by his school when he was in the third grade. Whoever read the most books over three months would win a bicycle. This student burned with the idea of owning that bike and read during every free moment at school and home. He read more than any of the fourth, fifth, or sixth graders. And he won the bicycle. During the schoolwide assembly, when the principal presented him with the prize, his fine example was held up to the rest of the students as stellar and enviable. Finishing the story, the student said, "Since winning the bike, I have not read one book except those required by my classes." The reading champion of the school never was a reader. To win a bicycle, he simply engaged in a competitive activity involving books.

In another instance at another school, empty paper cutout jars were displayed in the halls with the name of each student written on a jar. Each time a student finished a book, a paper jellybean was stapled inside that child's jar. At the end of a month-long reading blitz, prizes were awarded to those students with the most jellybeans inside their jars. Upon closer investigation, it was revealed that the winning student—the one who had completed the most books in the whole school—had restricted her book choices to very thin (and generally uninteresting) books consisting of just a handful of pages each. In this case, the reading blitz severely limited the type of reading that many students were doing. One can imagine that, within such a program, no student would dare approach a long, thick (and interesting) book like one of the Harry Potter volumes.

There are several problems with incentive programs. One is that some competitive students can't stand to lose. Like the boy who won the bike, their compulsion to win often overshadows the pleasures of reading, and they tend to zoom through book after book with little thought about their reading beyond the aim to win. Another problem with incentive programs is that they tend not to help those most in need of help. In the previous example, the jellybean jars of the struggling and unmotivated readers often remained empty, making their reading struggles obvious to everyone in the school. This public showcasing of their struggles was hardly the confidence boost that they needed.

Some concerns also accompany the commercial incentive programs adopted by a district or school. Students who read for points are interested only in books approved by the program. Many terrific books aren't a part of the program, so students skip over them because they don't count in the point total. Since passing the program's test on each book is the mark of a successful reader, some students find other ways to answer the questions, such as viewing a movie based on the book. An additional problem is that the tests themselves are not always accurate. Matthew, a sixth grader uninterested in books, found a title that captivated him. He stayed up several nights in a row to finish it, but when he took the commercial test (Accelerated Reader), he failed.

The fact is, to make such tests discriminating, the questions are often so nitpicky or confusing that they are both meaningless to the reader and useless for evaluation. For example, the first two authors of this book, Mike and Jim, took the Accelerated Reader 10-question quiz for *Tuck Everlasting* (Babbitt, 1975), a book they had each read at least a dozen times. When they scored 80%, they tried again, discussing each test item as they proceeded. Still, they were only able to score 90%. It wasn't that they were unprepared. They simply could not figure out what two of the questions were really asking. If two adults who were very familiar with the book were stymied by some of the test items, how would fifth graders feel? In fact, author Susan Fletcher (2006) took the Accelerated Reader test for her own book, *Dragon's Milk* (1989), and scored only 80%. Roland Smith (2010) suffered the same results for his book *Thunder Cave* (1995).

While concerns exist with individual reading incentive programs, group motivation and group record keeping are largely positive and helpful. The teacher who requires students to keep records of their personal reading can tally each week's reading and then display the increasing total—perhaps in a thermometer where the temperature rises with continued reading. Teachers sometimes use paper footprints, upon which each student records the titles of each book that he or she read. The footsteps are taped to the wall; as soon as the footsteps extend around the room, the students are rewarded with a party or celebration. These visual summaries provide bragging rights to everyone in the class, as opposed to the individual successes offered by the rocket ship or ice-cream charts. When a goal is reached, everyone participates in the victory, even those kids who have read few or no books. No one but the teacher is aware of the amount that each child reads, so no additional stigma is placed on those who are not performing. This system gives the teacher the opportunity to work individually with those students who need extra time and attention.

It is important, however, to remember that one reward—and one reward only—keeps people reading over time: the reading itself. Over the long haul, people turn to books because books are worthwhile, not because they are the means to treats or grades. As Ormrod (1998) says, "Extrinsically motivated students may have to be enticed, cajoled, or prodded [and] are often interested in performing easy tasks and meeting minimal standards" (p. 476). Without an intrinsic motivation to read, students may never reach their full potential as literacy learners (Gambrell & Marinak, 2009).

Organizing the Classroom to Get Children into Books

Teachers desirous of making reading a natural part of the classroom landscape will want to plan so that books fit smoothly and easily into the school day and their students' lives. Six areas to consider when organizing the ideal reading classroom are setting an example, providing access to books, making time for books, creating a reading atmosphere, working with parents, and choosing meaningful activities and assignments.

Set an Example

In motivating children to read, one of the most important elements is a teacher who reads. The power of a teacher's example, as described earlier in this chapter, appears here as a reminder. "The key to developing a personal love of books is a teacher who communicates enthusiasm and an appreciation of literature through his attitudes and examples" (Wilson & Hall, 1972, p. 341). In other words, students need to see their teachers reading and hear them talking about books. During the time when the whole class is reading self-selected books, teachers should often be reading, too. At other times, they should talk with students who are having trouble engaging in reading, helping to motivate them. A teacher also might begin the day by briefly sharing something interesting with the students from his or her personal reading.

Without such overt and honest examples, the power of a teacher's influence is to a great degree lost. A graduate student wondered why her example of being an avid reader didn't rub off on her children. She finally realized that she hadn't provided a reading model for them because she did her reading in the bathtub or after they were asleep. They never saw her with a book.

Provide Access to Books

The love of reading cannot be taught generally; it depends on contact with specific titles, certain subjects, and particular authors. To engage all students, a wide variety of books of different formats and levels of difficulty needs to be available in the elementary classroom. All grades need fiction, nonfiction, and poetry. Every lower grade needs some chapter books. Every upper grade needs some picture books. The most sincere and devoted intentions to help children become readers turn to dust if books are not handy for teachers to read aloud and introduce to the class and for students to pick over for self-selected reading time.

Appendix A suggests specific ways to acquire books and build a classroom library. Appendix C lists some appealing magazines.

Make Time for Books

Put book reading on the agenda. If reading for its own sake doesn't appear on the daily schedule, the message to students is clear: "We do not value personal reading in this classroom." After all, "a student doesn't have to be particularly bright to conclude that reading can't be very important if . . . little time is made for it during the school day" (Smith, Smith, & Mikulecky, 1978, p. 83). Hiebert and Martin (2009) have summarized research that suggests elementary students may only read 7 to 18 minutes a day in school, even when the school dedicates 90 minutes to literacy instruction. "In fact, the mandates for longer reading periods could even, unintentionally, result in lower [amounts of reading opportunities] if students become increasingly disengaged by spending long periods of time in tedious or trivial practice tasks" (p. 5).

Four useful ways to structure time for books are (1) reading aloud, (2) allowing self-selected reading, (3) introducing books to children, and (4) going to the library.

Make Time to Read Aloud

Good experiences with reading aloud don't just happen. They occur when certain principles are followed:

1. Reading aloud at the same time every day has a number of advantages over working it in when convenient. Having a scheduled time
   - Assures the teacher and the class that the reading will happen.

- Legitimizes the activity by making it a regular part of the school day.
- Allows the students to anticipate the experience.

2. Teachers should honestly like the books they read aloud. There is an enormous difference between reading a book aloud only because it's handy and reading a book aloud because it's loved.
3. Teachers should not read aloud unfamiliar books. The temptation is great to discover the contents of a book along with the class, but too many drawbacks can occur:
   - The teacher may not like the book.
   - The book may have unpleasant surprises—words the teacher isn't comfortable saying aloud, a character with negative traits who shares a name with a child in the class, or something in the plot that's inappropriate.
   - The teacher can't dramatize or emphasize highlights because they are unknown ahead of time.
   - Most important, the teacher's enthusiasm for the story will likely be weak because he or she is learning at the same time as the children.
4. Teachers should do the oral reading themselves. Even if a child is skilled enough to read the book aloud, the teacher's participation carries a message: "Our teacher *wants* to be a part of this activity; it must be important." In addition, students get to see a teacher's personal involvement in books that, over time, generally will include both laughter and tears. Children benefit from much more than the story when an adult reads aloud.
5. Teachers should not expect all students to like every book. They should tell the class, "We will read many books in class this year. No one will like them all, but I expect everyone will find some they do like."
6. Teachers should establish rules for read-aloud time. Some teachers allow students to draw; others don't. Some are not concerned when children put their heads down on the desk; others are. If anything bothers a teacher, it must be fixed, or the distraction will weaken the reading experience.
7. Teachers should allow students access to the books they have already shared as read-alouds. After the teacher has read a book aloud, students will often want to read that same book. This allows students to revisit their enjoyment of the book, perhaps discovering details they may have missed during the class read-aloud.

Make Time for Self-Selected Reading

Students need time at school to read books of their own choosing (Krashen, 2004). In one study of 35 sixth-grade language arts teachers in nine different schools, *all* of the 35 teachers agreed that allowing self-selection is a good way to improve reading attitudes and achievement (Worthy, Turner, & Moorman, 1998). Self-selection enables students to develop independence (Fresch, 1995). High interest and involvement in self-selected texts often allows readers to succeed with material that, for all other intents and purposes, would be considered well beyond their capacity (Hunt, 1996–1997).

During self-selected reading time, the number-one rule is simple: For the allotted time, everyone has the opportunity to read material of his or her own choosing. Other things to remember include the following:

1. Anything personally interesting is fair game. Where children are concerned, the important thing is not *what* a child reads but *that* a child reads. When children have positive and enjoyable reading experiences, they will more likely turn to quality literature when the time is right. While children are young, however, it is important to allow them to read the things that they enjoy. When forced to read certain texts, many children will resist the imposition and lose the motivation to read. But given the freedom to make their own reading choices, these children can become avid, deeply engaged readers (Worthy, 2000).
2. If someone starts a book and loses interest, finishing it is *not* required.
3. The teacher makes no written assignments for the books read during self-selected reading time.
4. At the end of the reading period, students may be given the opportunity to discuss what they have been reading during self-selected reading time.
5. The teacher should anticipate possible distractions or interruptions and let students know what to do about them. Fine-tuning the activity is inevitable—no one can consider every possible difficulty beforehand. But being clear on as many points as possible makes for a smoother reading time—for example:
   - What does a student do who finishes a book in the middle of a reading period? (Students should be sure to have at least one additional book in their desks, particularly when they are getting to the end of the one they're reading.)
   - Do children have to stay in their seats during the entire reading time? (Some teachers have trained students to get up quietly and find another book; others don't allow them to wander about for any reason.)
   - What happens if a student took the book home last night and forgot to bring it back today? (A box or plastic carton of short books or magazines might be available so that appealing reading material isn't difficult to locate.)
6. It isn't necessary for self-selected reading to be conducted in absolute silence. A teacher calling out for silence is potentially more distracting and disturbing. Let's not forget that outside school, very little of the reading that people do is completed in a setting in which there is total silence. There is a place for the helpful and motivating influence of reading conversations between students, if the talking is subdued enough not to distract others (Bryan, 2009).

Make Time to Introduce Books to Children

Simply releasing children into a world filled with books does not make them readers. If they have no interest in books, no reading habit, and nothing they are looking for, children can easily ignore a wealth of superb titles. It is up to the teacher to bridge the gap between book and child, and one successful way to do that is for the teacher to introduce new titles to the students.

There are many ways to introduce books. But all that's necessary is holding up the book so students can see what it looks like while telling them something about it. Teachers are most successful when introducing books they have read and liked, but it's possible to introduce books they don't yet know. Reading the blurb on the back of a paperback or on the inside flap of a hardcover usually provides enough information to present the book to the class.

A book-introduction time should be on the daily schedule, but the number of books shown to students can vary. For the first week or two of the school year, teachers may want to introduce as many as five or more per day to ensure that enough books have been presented to get the students

started. After that, a book or two every day is fine. The point is to provide students with some titles they can look forward to trying out.

Make Time for Going to the Library

If the elementary school has a library, teachers should plan to get their children there regularly. Some teachers elect not to sign up the entire class, but after a few introductory visits, they make a schedule for students to use the library singly or in pairs before and after school, at lunch, or during the school day. If the class visits together, the teacher should always stay in the library and circulate among the students, helping them find good books. The more titles they know and the more excitement that's generated for books, the more successful the library visit will be.

Even with the teacher present in the library, students may wander aimlessly and create small disturbances. Giving them specific directions before entering can help eliminate trouble and streamline the process. These three directions from the teacher to the students work as well as any:

1. *Try 'em on.* "Your job is to find books that fit you. One way to pick a good chapter book is to turn somewhere near the middle and start reading. If you read two or three pages and find the story interesting, this could be a good choice."
2. *Check 'em out.* "Check out the books that appeal to you."
3. *Read 'em.* "Sit down and read your books until we all are ready to go back to class."

Create a Reading Atmosphere

In light of the new literacy studies (Barton, Hamilton, & Ivanič, 2000; Cope & Kalantzis, 2000; Gee, 2004; Street, 1995), literacy is now recognized as a situated phenomenon. That is, the ways that people use and understand literacy vary according to the situation. With the new literacy studies, a shift in focus occurred, providing the genesis for an increased awareness and sensitivity toward the social and cultural role of reading and how these social and cultural interactions influence readers. Gee (2000) reasons that literacy makes sense only in terms of the context in which it takes place. A classroom context where reading is valued has an atmosphere that says "Books are important." That message may be delivered in a number of ways:

- Make the emotional climate safe but exciting. Accept students' reactions to books—never belittle them. Hope that students will catch your enthusiasm for books without expecting them to mirror your reading preferences.
- Promote the idea of a community of readers. Focus on developing a group attitude that reading is a pleasurable way of making discoveries about the world. Everyone in the community will have the chance to select reading materials that reflect his or her personal choices and interests.
- Liven up the room. Ask for old displays or posters from bookstores. Tack up children's drawings inspired by books. Display books or book jackets. Write publishers to ask for free, attractive materials—posters, postcards, bookmarks—to decorate the walls. (Check publishers' offerings in the *CBC Features* brochure from the Children's Book Council, mentioned in Appendix B.)
- Keep the classroom library visible, not behind locked cabinet doors. Have books become a part of the classroom's interior decoration scheme.

- As your personality and classroom space permit, allow students to do self-selected reading in places other than at their desks. You may want to set up a reading center—a place designated for pleasure reading that may have pillows, a comfortable chair or couch, and other homey furnishings. But make sure everyone gets to use the reading center. If it becomes the domain of those who finish their work first, those students who need it most will never get the chance.
- Connect students and authors. Children are curious about the people who write their books. Enliven the literary atmosphere in the classroom by encouraging young readers to contact authors through their personal Web sites. Using the e-mail address usually available at each site, students can write to their favorite author. If an author doesn't have a Web address, have students write letters to the author in care of the publisher. Publishers' addresses are available on the Web or can often be found on the back of a book's title page.
- Create an environment in which students have enjoyable, successful reading experiences. Bandura (1986) argues that the greatest single predictor for engagement in school tasks is success. His *cycle of success* suggests that as we enjoy success, we become more engaged. In turn, as we become more engaged, we enjoy more success. This notion is not dissimilar to the *pleasure–practice–proficiency* cycle (see Figure 17.2). Despite struggling with literacy, children can still be guided through positive, pleasurable reading experiences. And the more students derive pleasure from reading, the more likely they are to continue to read and to practice, which will in turn help them to develop into better, more proficient readers. The better we get at reading, the more pleasurable the pursuit becomes, and so the more we practice, and so on. Once students become switched on to reading, they will likely remain so.

Work with Parents

Except at the often painfully polite back-to-school evenings, parents and teachers usually have contact only when there is trouble. As a result, teachers and parents have a natural hesitancy to communicate, much to the delight of many children, who prefer keeping their two worlds sepa-

Pleasure–Practice–Proficiency Cycle

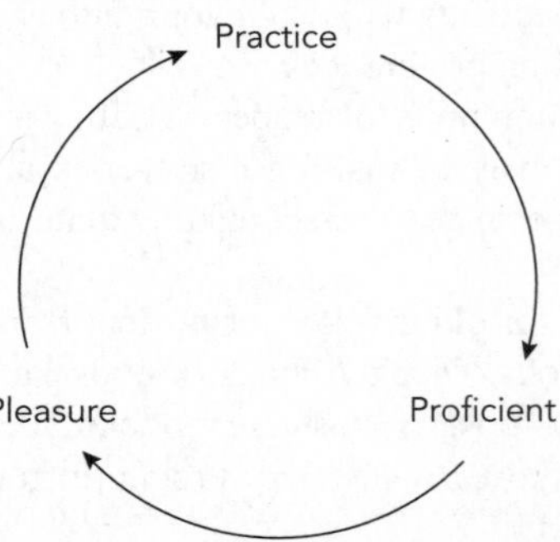

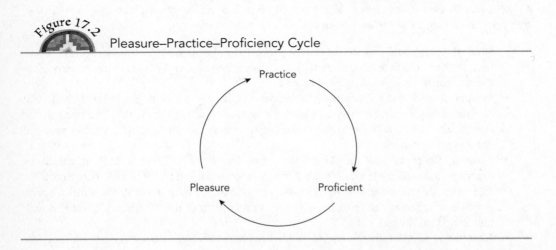

rate. The teacher who decides to bridge this traditional gap between school and home can do so with relative ease and much positive effect on children and their reading.

You need to initiate this contact, either through a letter or a meeting with each child's parents. To gain support for your approach to reading, that contact should make two points: Let parents know about your emphasis on personal reading, and request their support in helping it work.

Communicate with Parents

Communicate to parents the benefits of regular, year-long reading for their child, both in school and at home. Include your own views on the advantages of daily reading, and perhaps also cite research that supports those ideas (see Chapter 18).

Request Parental Support

Request parental support for each child's personal reading at home. Parents can help their child in the following ways:

- Encourage the child to read regularly at home. Setting aside a certain time is helpful. (If you require children to read daily outside school, mention that and ask for parental support.)
- Talk with the child about the books being read.
- Read with and to the child.
- Buy books as gifts for birthdays and holidays, and allow the child to buy from school-sponsored book clubs when possible.
- Help the child create a place in his or her bedroom to keep personal books.
- Read where the child can see you.
- Periodically tell the child about what you are reading.
- Volunteer to come to the classroom and assist children with their reading.

Choose Meaningful Activities and Assignments

The purpose of having children engage in an activity after reading a book is to enhance their experience, not to check their reading or to evaluate their comprehension. Chapter 18 describes activities, but the idea is noted here as one of the six areas to consider when planning instruction to highlight reading.

Remember that not every book a child reads must result in a written report or other learning activity. In fact, most personal reading experiences should *not* be coupled with an assignment. But when a learning activity does center on literature, children should be able to select from a variety of titles.

The ideas in this chapter come from years of classroom experience—both ours and others'. Unfortunately, following these ideas to the letter won't guarantee that every child will become a motivated reader. No reading approach, person, or program has a 100% success rate with children. Simply expect that in every classroom, you will have some tough nuts to crack—children who will not fall in love with books no matter what you do. Implementing these ideas, however, will increase the odds that children will read more and read better.

PEARSON
myeducationkit

Go to the topics Adolescent Literature, Multicultural Literature, and Contemporary Realistic Fiction on the MyEducationKit for this text, where you can:

- Search the Database of Children's Literature, housing more than 22,000 titles searchable in every genre by authors or illustrators, by awards won, by year published, and by topic and description.
- Explore genre-related Assignments and Activities, assignable exercises showing concepts in action through database use, video, cases, and student and teacher artifacts.
- Listen to podcasts and read interviews from some of the brightest and most enduring stars of children's literature in the Conversations.
- Discover weblinks that will lead you to sites representing the authors you learn about in these pages, classrooms with powerful children's literature connections, and literature awards.

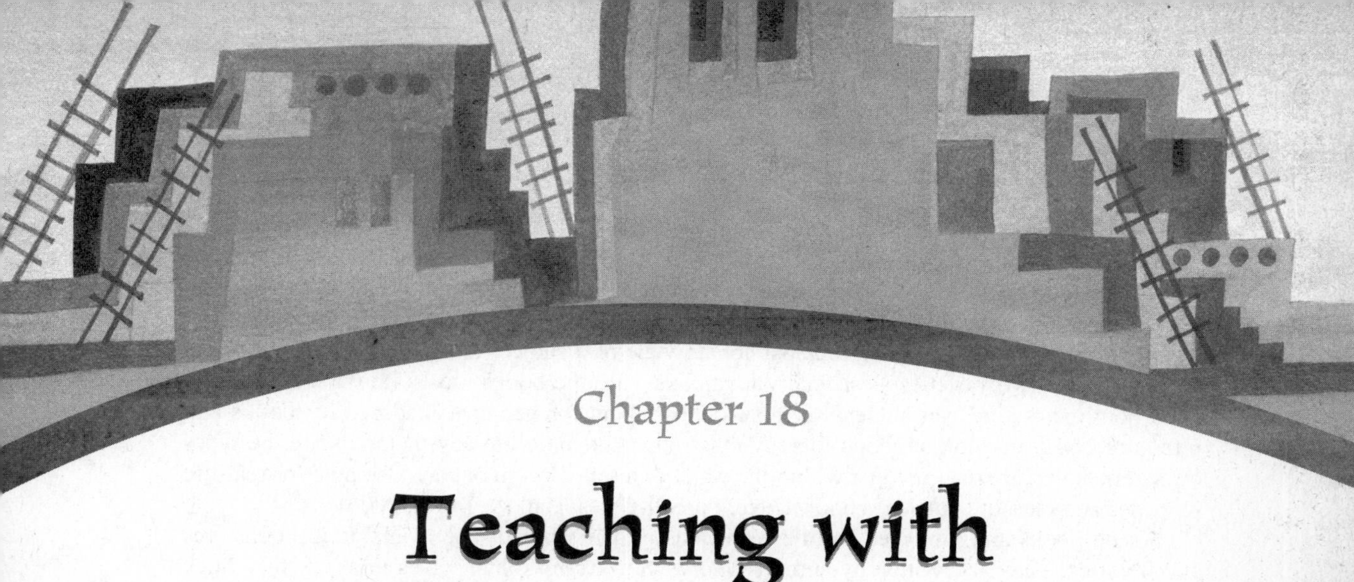

Chapter 18

Teaching with Children's Books

The use of reading textbooks—basal readers—traditionally has been the primary method of teaching reading in North American classrooms. Over one-third of all fourth-grade teachers rely exclusively on basal textbooks for teaching reading (Wade & Moje, 2000, p. 611). Basals are heavily used in more than 90% of elementary school classrooms (Reutzel & Cooter, 2009, p. 240).

With such a heavy reliance on basal materials, children's literature has often been forced to the outer edge of reading instruction. In many instances, the role served by children's literature has been reduced to one of merely serving as enjoyment "when the real work of learning to read was completed" (Martinez & McGee, 2000, p. 158). Such an erroneous and undervalued view of children's literature seems similar to a football coach holding his star quarterback—his most valuable player—in reserve, to be used only during the postgame celebration (Bryan, Tunnell, & Jacobs, 2007). Just as a coach desirous of a Super Bowl victory will not confine his best player to the bench until after the game, a teacher whose goal is to help children become lifelong readers will not restrict access to children's literature until the end-of-school party.

In this chapter, we advocate the use of children's books for instructional purposes—for teaching children how to read and for teaching children across the different subject areas. After all, few discoveries are more valuable to the development of a lifelong learner than finding out there is something personally worthwhile between the covers of a book. Students who are self-motivated readers continue their education throughout their lives.

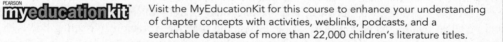

Visit the MyEducationKit for this course to enhance your understanding of chapter concepts with activities, weblinks, podcasts, and a searchable database of more than 22,000 children's literature titles.

Opening Doors with Books

Schools use books as tools of education, and those books fall into three distinct categories: reference, text, and trade. Each type of book is philosophically different and serves a different purpose.

Reference books are those volumes a person consults for an immediate answer to a specific question, such as a dictionary, encyclopedia, atlas, or thesaurus. Textbooks are designed for use in formal instruction, presenting a dispassionate view of a subject in an organized, methodical manner. These two varieties—especially textbooks—are the books most often associated with classroom instruction, yet students seldom choose them for personal reading. Textbooks and reference books are not authentic literacy materials. Authentic literacy materials are the types of materials that are read not just within the walls of a schoolroom but are also read for real-life purposes and pleasure outside school (Duke, Purcell-Gates, Hall, & Tower, 2006).

Trade books are published for the retail market and typically are available in bookstores and libraries. They are written by authors who wish to express themselves in a way they hope will appeal to readers who seek pleasure, insight, and knowledge. However, with the exception of English teachers, educators historically have not considered trade books of much use in the classroom.

Textbooks and reference books both have an important role in education, but trade books should not be dismissed. When children are interested in what they read and read broadly—fiction, nonfiction, or both—they can learn much of value from trade books. People are able to grow and develop intellectually without the carefully structured approach to learning typical of textbooks. In fact, some individuals have gained the bulk of their learning primarily through independent, authentic reading of trade books, as the following examples illustrate:

- Robert Howard Allen has never seen his father. Divorced before he was born, Robert's mother left him at age 6 to be raised by his grandfather, three great-aunts, and a great-uncle, all of whom lived in the same house in rural Tennessee. After his grandfather taught him to read, Robert regularly read the Bible to a blind great-aunt. "From age seven he read thousands of books—from Donald Duck comics to Homer, James Joyce and Shakespeare. . . . He began picking up books at yard sales, and by his early 20s he had some 2000 volumes" (Whittemore, 1991, p. 4). Robert never went to school, not even for a day. He stayed home and helped—and read. At age 30, he easily passed a high school equivalency test, and at age 32, he showed up at Bethel College in McKenzie, Tennessee. Three years later, he graduated summa cum laude (3.92 GPA) and continued his education by enrolling in graduate school at Vanderbilt University. Having earned his Ph.D. in English, he became a visiting lecturer at Murray State University in Kentucky (Whittemore, 1991).
- Roy Daniels was a "very, very slow reader" (Fink, 2006, p. 70) who continued to struggle with reading despite years of assistance from tutors. He didn't develop even basic reading fluency before he was 11. Daniels was confused by lowercase letters that are similar in appearance (such as *b* and *d, m* and *n,* for instance). Although reading continued to present difficulties, Daniels developed a deep interest in science. He began avidly reading whatever books about science that he could find. As time passed, Daniels tackled increasingly difficult science books, relying "to a great extent" on contextual clues whenever he encountered unfamiliar words. Daniels got better and better at reading as he engaged in lots of reading practice, voraciously reading books that slaked his thirst for scientific knowledge. Today, despite years as a struggling reader, Roy Daniels

is a biochemist and professor at the Stanford University School of Medicine. He is one of the world's leading authorities on cystic fibrosis and muscular dystrophy and has written almost 200 scientific articles (Fink, 2006).

- Dale Wasserman makes his living writing for stage and screen. This winner of almost 50 writing awards is perhaps best known for the musical drama *Man of La Mancha.* After an initial five-year run on Broadway, it was revived in 1972, 1977, 1992, and 2002. In addition to the Broadway productions, the musical has been performed across the world in many different languages. When Dale was 14—"undisciplined, secretive, and almost entirely unschooled"—both his parents died, and the Wasserman children were parceled out to relatives and orphanages. Dale lasted a month before running away, hitching a ride to Pierre, South Dakota, and in the middle of the night hopping on his first freight train. For the next five years, he rode the rails, never having a home, going to a school, or working a steady job. While crossing the country on freight trains, however, Dale did not neglect his learning. "In the library of a small town, I would select two books, slip them under my belt at the small of my back, read as I rode, and slip them back into the stacks of another library in another town far down the line, where I would 'borrow' two more. I thus acquired a substantial, if incoherent, fund of knowledge that, together with my experience, became my total education"—an education sufficient for him to become a renowned playwright (Wasserman, 2001, p. 64).

The Strengths of Trade Books

People can and do acquire substantial knowledge beyond the walls of formal education when they read often and broadly. We need to recognize that books can create interest in readers, that people learn better when they are interested, and that many of us can learn a great deal by reading widely on our own. The purpose of both fiction and nonfiction trade books is not so much to inform, which they do very well, as it is to excite, to introduce, to let the reader in on the irresistible secrets of life on Earth.

Consider the following two passages that describe asteroids: one from a textbook and the other from an informational trade book.

Passage 1: Science textbook

Asteroids are rocky or metallic objects that orbit the Sun. They are too small to be considered planets. . . . Some astronomers suggest that asteroids are material that never combined to become a planet. They are found mostly in a belt between the orbits of Mars and Jupiter. They orbit the Sun just like planets. Some asteroids travel out as far as Saturn's orbit. Others have orbits that cross Earth's path.

Space probes have passed by asteroids and obtained much information. On June 2, 1997, the spacecraft NEAR encountered the asteroid Mathilde. This and other flybys by space probes are giving a good picture of the nature of these smaller members of the solar system. The spacecraft *Galileo* has already flown by the asteroids Gaspra and Ida. (Moyer et al., 2002, p. C-55)

Passage 2: Science trade book

Made of stone, or nickel and iron, or a mix of both stone and metal, asteroids are rubble from a planet that never formed. Some asteroids are less than a mile across. Some are much larger. A few are as big as very small planets.

Because of their small size, the asteroids' orbits are easily disturbed. Jupiter is an enormous planet, and its gravity can pull smaller asteroids in new directions. The gravity of larger asteroids can also tug

> on smaller ones that pass close by. And from time to time, asteroids can collide and be nudged into new orbits.
>
> By such events, some asteroids can be pulled or pushed out of the asteroid belt to fall closer to the sun. They can wander in long, elliptical orbits that cross the paths of Mars and the other inner planets, including Earth. These asteroids can hit the planets—and on rare occasions they do. (Henderson, 2000, pp. 7–8)

The following points identify some of the strengths of trade books, as compared to textbooks. Note how these apply to the examples above.

Writing Style

Whereas textbooks are formal and often unappealing to children, trade books are designed to engage young readers. Trade book authors shape and develop their views in individualized language, allowing for a personalized explanation that often results in more meaning and perspective. Textbooks, on the other hand, tend to use a more detached and disjointed style, which can result in puzzling information like that found in the second paragraph of the textbook example. It offers precise information about space probes, including their names and the names of asteroids they pass by. Without background information or perspective, however, the reader has difficulty finding meaning in those facts. In addition, we are told that these probes have garnered "much information" and provide "a good picture of the nature of [asteroids]," but no details are shared with us.

Varied Formats and Structures

Trade books come in all sizes, formats, and lengths. The illustrations in trade books are generally superior, often containing stunning artwork. Textbooks have an industrial appearance and usually have less appealing illustrations and diagrams.

Many Perspectives

Books are available on any subject, providing overviews as well as exhaustive treatments from a variety of viewpoints. For example, dozens of trade books about asteroids are available, rounding out reader knowledge as much as one chooses. Textbooks typically offer one perspective. Because trade books are shorter and more quickly read, one can read many trade books and get many perspectives.

Rich Language

Trade books are written in more interesting and engaging language. They are deliberately written to both entertain and inform. The language in trade books creates images by using more precise, colorful vocabulary. The sentences are varied and read more interestingly. Trade books have the freedom and space to make meaningful comparisons and use more detail to enlarge understanding.

Depth of Content

Trade books can provide the space to bring a subject to life with interesting observations and details, presenting the reader with a richer understanding of the topic. Because textbooks must cover such a large number of topics, they are unable to develop a single idea with any depth.

Therefore, textbooks offer a broad and consequently shallower view of subjects that does not allow for the kind of compelling presentation available in trade books. For example, another passage in the textbook quoted earlier simply mentions that asteroids can hit the Earth. The trade book, however, chronicles the event of an asteroid's entry into atmosphere, its collision with the planet, and the blasting of a crater 25 miles deep and 100 miles across. It describes in fascinating detail the vaporization at the impact point, the earthquakes, the fires, and the debris that caused a worldwide period of intense heat followed by darkness and freezing temperatures. It is difficult to provide readers this kind of detail and insight in the limited space allowed by a textbook.

Currency

Trade books are written and published more often and more quickly than textbooks, offering the latest findings and information. In addition, most school districts can afford a new textbook for each subject only every 5 to 10 years, which is a distinct disadvantage in this information-rich age. Because textbooks are so expensive, some classrooms still use textbooks decades old.

Voice

Trade books allow a personal viewpoint to emerge in the writing. Information has more power to influence others when it is presented through the strong, individual voice of a human being. Textbooks, usually written by committee, have no personal voice; their viewpoint is detached and distant. Whereas trade books often contain a strong individual voice, textbooks generally do not. In striving for objectivity, the viewpoints in textbooks tend to be impersonal and bland.

Reflect Individual Reading Abilities

Different trade books suit different levels of reading ability. A given set of classroom textbooks will be at the reading level of only a select number of students. In a typical classroom, the reading abilities of students vary widely. Because of the number and variety of trade books, students at many levels—even those with reading problems—can locate titles on any subject. They can find books they can read, learn from, and enjoy.

Tools of Lifelong Learning

Trade books are available in all libraries and bookstores. They are the books people use most often to learn about the world after they have graduated from high school. Trade books are the stuff of real-life reading. Textbooks are limited to formal education and can be found only in classrooms and academic bookstores. Regular bookstores have none, and libraries very few, which causes some people to ask, "If schools are to prepare children for lifelong learning, why do they rely so heavily on a tool that is not easily accessible in their actual future?"

Teachers should not think that only informational books can generate interest in school subjects. Historical fiction, for instance, sheds light on history in a way that nonfiction has difficulty duplicating. Introducing historically accurate fiction—complete with its compelling plot and well-developed characters—can, as Cynthia Stokes Brown (1994) says, make history come alive by allowing children more readily to "identify . . . with heroes and heroism and . . . explore their own lives and identity, character and convictions through heroic stories" (p. 5).

Research Support for Using Trade Books to Teach Reading

The mandated use of scripted reading programs like basal series often raises doubts about the place of authentic reading material, including children's trade books, in the classroom (MacGillivray, Ardell, Curwen, & Palma, 2004). Unfortunately, resistance to such mandates can produce dire consequences for teachers—even to the point of costing them their jobs (Jaeger, 2006). Yet there is a wealth of research support for the use of authentic children's literature in teaching children reading.

Neuman's research (Neuman, 1997; 1999; Neuman & Celano, 2001) has focused on the importance of children's access to books. In a project called Books Aloud, Neuman investigated the impact of making books available to economically disadvantaged children in day care facilities in large metropolitan areas in Pennsylvania. Over 300 not-for-profit child care centers, servicing over 17,000 children, were flooded with high-quality, hardcover children's books. The $2.1 million project aimed to provide to each center five books for every child, resulting in a contribution of almost 90,000 books and the bookcases and storage racks to display them. Because collaborative activities were planned between the day care centers and libraries, over 54,000 additional new books were also donated to local libraries. Ten hours of read-aloud and thematic activity instruction were provided to participating child care staff.

Using systematic random sampling, 400 3- and 4-year old children were selected for study participation. As an experimental control, 100 children were also selected from comparable child care centers not involved in the project. The early literacy skills of each child were assessed prior to and after the project. Along with increased physical access to the books, study participants spent more time reading and engaging with books. The Books Aloud children also talked more often about books and reading. The children achieved higher poststudy scores and demonstrated greater improvement than the control group in all six project literacy assessment measures: concepts of print; concepts of writing; concepts of narrative; receptive vocabulary; letter name knowledge; and environmental print knowledge.

The book access studies of Neuman (1997; 1999; Neuman & Celano, 2001) and others (e.g., Dowhower & Beagle, 1998; Morrow, Connor, & Smith, 1990; Robinson, Larsen, & Haupt, 1996) demonstrate the educational and attitudinal benefits of increased access to books. In an alternative study, Duke (2000) revealed the paucity of access to informational books in schools. In the classrooms she observed, Duke found that, on average, first-grade children spend only 3.6 minutes per day with informational books during classroom written language activities. This scarcity of informational text use was even more apparent for children in poorer communities, where the average time spent with informational texts fell to just 1.9 minutes per day. Half of the grade 1 classrooms from poorer schools spent no time *at all* with informational texts during four days of classroom observations. These findings led Duke to challenge the assumption that children struggle to comprehend informational texts because these texts are inherently harder to read. Rather, Duke suggested that the reason many children struggle with informational texts is simply because they don't have enough experience working with them.

Morrow and colleagues (Morrow, Tracey, Woo, & Pressley, 1999) conducted interviews and observations in classrooms identified as providing exemplary instruction. The study involved six first-grade teachers from three different school districts in New Jersey. All of the teachers were

identified by school district supervisors and administrators as exemplary teachers, successfully "educating large proportions of their students to be readers and writers" (p. 463). In addition to two full-day visits, each classroom was observed eight times during language arts instruction, for a total of approximately 25 hours of observations in each classroom. The classroom observations revealed that all of the classrooms provided a literacy-rich environment for the children. Shelves, baskets, and other storage spaces housed many books representing a variety of genres, providing students with a wide range of choices. The classrooms were said to include "elaborate literacy centers" (p. 465). Throughout the school day, each teacher provided opportunities for children to engage in many types of reading experiences. These experiences included read-alouds and children reading books independently, in pairs, and in small groups. Reading skills were taught in context, through the use of children's literature.

In a paper commissioned by the National Reading Conference, Pressley (2001) reiterated the desirability of contextualized reading instruction in classrooms "flooded with literature" (p. 24) when he discussed effective beginning reading instruction. Pressley argued that "excellent" early years classrooms involve children doing "a great deal of actual reading," from books, as opposed to completing activities related to reading, like filling in worksheets (p. 24).

Literature-based instruction has also been effective in helping children to catch up after entering school with limited early literacy experience and exposure. Early reading experiences help children develop interest in books, as well as to gain abilities to comprehend and to connect storybook information to their own lives. While early literacy experiences are important, research has demonstrated that with good teaching, children can make up for lost time when they enter school (Purcell-Gates, McIntyre, & Freppon, 1995). Purcell-Gates's team studied children who started school with relatively little knowledge of books. Observations took place in classrooms that employed literature-based instruction and those that did not. When children were exposed to strong reading instruction, whether skills based or literature based, they were shown to be able to catch up to their peers. Importantly, however, in classrooms that emphasized literature-based instruction, the catch-up students exhibited "significantly greater growth in their knowledge of written language and more extensive breadth of knowledge of written linguistic features" (p. 659).

The idea of using children's literature for classroom instruction isn't new. For many decades now, there has been research support for the practice. In the 1960s, Cohen (1968) demonstrated the benefits of using a literature component for reading instruction. In the 1970s, Fader, Duggins, Finn, and McNeil (1976) achieved success using children's paperbacks in inner-city secondary classrooms. Similarly successful results were achieved using trade paperbacks with boys in a rehabilitative training school for delinquent youth. In the 1980s, a literature-based, developmental program for first graders called the Shared Book Experience achieved success throughout New Zealand (Holdaway, 1982). In the early 1990s, Morrow (1992) investigated the impact of a literature-based program on the literacy achievement of children from U.S. minority backgrounds. In the study, the experimental groups' time spent working with basal materials was reduced so that teachers could introduce more literature-based activities, including independent and self-selected reading. Children in the experimental groups outperformed their counterparts in a range of literacy measures.

Research support for literature-based instruction continues in the new millennium. Recent studies reflect the motivational benefit of access to books. Both Edmunds and Bauserman (2006) and Pachtman and Wilson (2006) interviewed and surveyed children with regard to motivation to read. Pachtman and Wilson reported that having a well-stocked classroom library was the single most important factor influencing children's reading practices. Edmunds and Bauserman similarly found that children's motivation to read is strongly influenced by access to books.

Using Trade Books in the Reading Curriculum

Given the many strengths of trade books and given the research support for literature-based instruction, many teachers use trade books to augment reading instruction and provide children with authentic experiences while teaching students how to read.

Talking about Books

The most natural response to reading is talking about what one has read. Our desire to share with others information about what we read has given rise to the numerous adult book discussion groups—often called *book clubs*—which can now be found from coast to coast. This natural response to reading has an equally important role to play in school.

Grand Conversations

For books or poems everyone has read or has had read to them, discussions can provide opportunities for meaningful responses. Peterson and Eeds (1990) call these discussions "grand conversations." They are characterized by teachers participating fully in the conversations—modeling and sharing their thought processes and personal interpretations about the story. Teachers are not, however, the central focus and need to be careful that their comments don't become pronouncements. The spotlight is on the book and the readers' responses. The teacher is no longer seen as the authority possessing all the answers but is simply a participant with the students (Eeds & Peterson, 1997; Wells, 1995). Teachers allow and encourage students to share their personal responses, providing open-ended prompts when necessary for group discussion: "What did you notice in the story?" "What do you remember from the story?" "What details in the story remind you of your own life?"

Grand conversations can also include the discussion of literary merit and technique. As long as the questions don't have right and wrong answers—so the talk is truly a discussion—children will become involved. Questions might include "What hints did the author drop to prepare us for the ending?" "Are there any facts or details in the book that let us know Josh was not to be trusted?" "Can you find an image—a picture in your mind—put there by the author that helps you to see the castle clearly?"

Teachers must be prepared for discussion that extends beyond their own level of preparation and understanding. In a grand conversation, even a young child can notice something an experienced teacher has missed. For instance, when discussing *Sylvester and the Magic Pebble* (Steig, 1969), 6-year-old Tracy responded to an illustration showing Sylvester using the magic pebble to abruptly stop a rainstorm as ducks in the background peer skyward in confusion. Tracy shared with her teacher examples of things she thought were funny:

Tracy: When Sylvester finds the red pebble—and the ducks are cute . . .
Teacher: The what?
Tracy: The ducks are cute . . .

Teacher: The ducks *are* cute. They've got their bills up in the air like they're just enjoying the sunshine, having a grand time, uh-huh . . .
Tracy: Or else they're thinking, "How'd that happen?"
Teacher: How'd what happen?
Tracy: The rain started, then stopped.
Teacher: Yes! Of course they're thinking that!
Tracy: They go—"It started a little while ago—what happened?" (Peterson & Eeds, 1990, pp. 17–18)

The teacher was looking at the picture but had not noticed the ducks. She was dumbfounded that a 6-year-old had picked up on a subtle point of interpretation that she had overlooked.

Literature Circles

Literature circles (Daniels, 2002; Day, Spiegel, McLellan, & Brown, 2002) provide an opportunity for small groups of children to talk together about a text. Children ask their own questions about a book and help each other answer those questions. Time isn't unstructured, however. Literature circles include discussion of characters and events, personal experiences and observations, and even writing and the writing process.

Certain elements help foster this kind of group learning. The small groups are temporary and linked to readers' book choice. Different groups read different books. Groups meet at scheduled and regular times. Students use written or drawn notes to guide both their reading and their discussion. Topics for discussion come from the students. Group meetings are to be open, natural conversations about the book. The teacher serves as a facilitator, not as a group member or instructor. Any evaluation is by teacher observation and student self-evaluation. When the book is finished and the discussion is over, students form new groups with new books.

Written and Creative Responses

Although literature circles and grand conversations provide for natural and authentic response to books, opportunities for written or otherwise creative responses are also important for children. Before considering specific approaches and activities, it is critical to understand the principles that lead to successful involvement with books so that meaningful responses can occur.

Newbery-winning author Madeleine L'Engle (1980) outlined the main characteristic of involvement teachers want to capitalize on:

> Readers usually underestimate their own importance. If a reader cannot create a book along with the writer, the book will never come to life. Creative involvement: That's the difference between reading a book and watching TV.
>
> In watching TV, we are passive—sponges; we do nothing. In reading we must become creators, imagining the setting of the story, seeing the facial expressions, hearing the inflection of the voices. The author and reader "know" each other; they meet on the bridge of words. (pp. 37–38)

We want readers to "create a book along with the writer." We want them to live in the book—to be active in their experience and response. To keep them from being "sponges," we must provide them with assignments and activities that allow the kind of reading to take place where reader and author "meet on the bridge of words."

If an activity allows and encourages readers to respond in a way that L'Engle calls "creative involvement," the assignment is generally a plus. When used with self-selected books, such an activity is helpful as long as it adheres to three principles: (1) Students choose the books they wish to respond to, (2) students choose the activities, and (3) students read most books without any obligation to respond.

Even when students are enthusiastic about a certain way of responding to books, teachers need to remember that variety is the key to keeping them involved. Figure 18.1 provides a range of alternative ways children might respond to their reading. No one response or activity designed to involve readers with their books works for long. Students may love recording their personal thoughts in a reading journal, but if it is required for every book, the idea wears thin.

Reconsidering the Traditional Book Report

If assigned responses detract from the reading experience and diminish the desire to read, they need to be rethought. Such a response is the traditional book report, which focuses on elements of fiction, including plot, characters, setting, style, and theme. It has been said to have done more to kill the love of reading in Americans aged 9 to 18 than any other idea to come from the schools (Root, 1975), and as an evaluative tool, it often tells a teacher very little.

Traditional book reports are almost universally detested. Although most Americans remember writing traditional book reports in school, very few remember the task with fondness. Book reports continue to be used because some teachers demand tangible evidence that the child has read the book. Of course, it is possible for students to write reports on books they have not read. Any sixth grader can offer a variety of ways. Rent the movie. Read the front flap. Talk to someone about the book. Use someone else's old book report. Or for the daring, invent the book—title, author, plot, characters—the entire thing. The only defense for traditional book reports is that they foster imagination by teaching kids to cheat creatively.

The response options in Figure 18.1 offer alternatives to the traditional book report. It is important to remember, however, that with the worthy and useful goal of having students respond thoughtfully to what they read, asking for a response to every book will likely backfire and turn a positive experience into a negative one. Readers don't want to respond to every book they read any more than viewers want to respond to every movie they see. Most of the books a person reads should be left alone. The reading is sufficient.

But every so often, perhaps once or twice a grading period, teachers can ask students to respond to a book they have read. Allowing students to select the title and giving them some choice in the method of response are essential if the response is to have any real meaning to them.

Reconsidering the Traditional Whole-Class Novel

Just as it is foolhardy to expect all children to complete book reports for all of the books they read, it is also foolish to expect all children to read the same novel. In this textbook, we provide lists containing the titles of many wonderful books. Yet we recognize that, although these books appeal to us and will likely appeal to many children, no one book is guaranteed to work for all children. Despite this, very often in classrooms, teachers select a novel, purchase 30 copies of

Death to the Traditional Book Report

Writing Activities

1. Rewrite part of the story, telling it from the viewpoint of a different character.
2. Write an advertisement for the book. Identify where the advertisement will be displayed.
3. Write a poem based on the book.
4. Make up riddles about the book or any parts of it.
5. Write a rebus of the book's title, a short summary, or a certain scene in the book.
6. Develop a word game based on the book (word scramble, crossword puzzle, acrostic).
7. Write a letter to the author, particularly if you enjoyed the book or have a question about it. (Send the letter to the publisher of the book and it will be forwarded.)
8. Write an imaginary interview with the main character—or any character or object.
9. Make a newspaper that summarizes or presents elements from the book. Include as many regular departments of a newspaper (sports, comics, lovelorn, classified ads, business, and so on) as you desire.
10. Write your own book on the same theme, perhaps writing some text and outlining the rest.
11. Rewrite a section of the book in either radio or stage script.
12. Select a passage or quotation that has special significance for you. Write it down and then tell why it is meaningful.
13. Rewrite the story or part of the story as a news article.
14. Rewrite part of the book in a different time period—space age future, prehistoric days, Wild West, etc.
15. Write some trivia questions to exchange with someone else.
16. Write a chapter that tells what happened before or after the book.
17. If the book were made into a movie, choose who would play the characters. (See if you can select real people familiar to your classmates.)
18. Write a letter from some character to a real or fictitious person not in the story.
19. Write the same scene from three or four different points of view.
20. Write a simplified version of the story in picture book form.
21. Write a review of the book.

Art and Craft Activities

1. Make a diorama of an important scene in the book.
2. Construct a mobile representative of the book or some part of it.
3. Draw portraits of the main character(s).
4. Draw a mural that highlights events from the book or retells the story.
5. Draw a picture in the same style as the illustrator or using the same medium (pen and ink, collage, watercolor, etc.).
6. Cut out words from newspapers and magazines and create a word collage that gives a feeling for the book.
7. Use stitching or liquid embroidery to make a wall hanging or decorate a T-shirt with art related to the story.
8. Draw a coat of arms for a character(s), and explain the significance of each symbol.
9. Draw a silhouette of a person, scene, or object from the book.
10. Design a new dust jacket for the book.
11. Illustrate what you believe is the most important idea or scene from the book.

(continued)

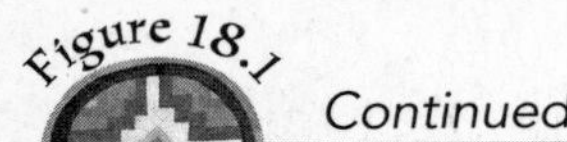

Continued

12. Make a poster advertising the book.
13. Make a time line of the important events in the book.
14. Make a roll movie of the book that can be shown on a TV set made from a box. Use your own illustrations, photographs, or pictures cut from magazines.
15. Retell the story using a flannel board and bits of string, yarn, and felt, or create recognizable characters to use in the retelling.
16. Identify the important places in the book on a map of your own making.
17. Make paper dolls and clothes of the main character(s).
18. Make a travel poster inviting tourists to visit the setting of the book.
19. Construct a scene or character out of clay.
20. Design a costume for a character to wear.
21. Prepare and serve a food that the characters ate or that is representative of the book.

Drama, Music, and Assorted Activities

1. Make puppets—sack masks, socks, or finger—of the characters and produce a puppet show of the book.
2. Dress as a character and present some of the character's feelings, or tell about a part of the book, or summarize very briefly the story.
3. Videotape a dramatized scene from the book.
4. Write a song that tells about the book.
5. Conduct an interview between an informed moderator and character(s) . . . maybe TV news?
6. Research music from the time of the book, and find some songs the characters may have sung.
7. Pantomime a scene from the book.
8. Perform a scene from the book with one person taking all the parts.
9. Choosing a familiar tune, write lyrics that tell about the book.
10. For each character in the book, choose a musical selection that typifies that person.
11. Give a sales pitch to get listeners excited about the book.
12. Give a party for the characters and their friends or for characters from many books. Invite parents and have characters present themselves.
13. Research some real aspect of the book, and present your newly found facts.
14. Bring something from home that reminds you of the book. Explain.
15. Choose a real-life person who reminds you of a character in the book. Explain.
16. Select one passage that is the focal point of the book. Explain.
17. Collect and display a collage of quotes that you like from the book.
18. Make a board game using characters and elements from the book. Have pitfalls (lose a turn, etc.) and rewards (shake again, etc.) reflecting parts of the book.
19. Find other books on the same subject, and set up a display with them.
20. Perform a choral reading from the book, or write something about the book to perform in a choral reading.
21. Emphasize the setting of the book using any or all of the following: (a) objects, (b) food, (c) costumes, (d) culture, (e) music, (f) art.

that novel, and then assign it as required reading for *all* students. Most classes are comprised of a mix of boys and girls, some stronger readers and some less capable readers, and children with interests ranging from ballet to basketball, animals to armies, machines to malls, and horror to history. How is it, then, that educators so often expect that one book—any one book—is going to suit the needs and desires of a classroom full of different people?

In any classroom of approximately 30 students, it seems unlikely that any one book will satisfy the interests of more than, say, half of the children. It is even more unlikely that any one book will be at an appropriate level of difficulty for most of the children assigned to read it. For some children, given their interests and abilities, the assigned book is going to be much too difficult. For others—perhaps those with a well-developed interest and background in the topic—an assigned book could be too simple.

Furthermore, as discussed in the preceding chapter, choice is an important reading motivator. Because we want children to have opportunities to discuss books in class and because we have some specific things that we want students to read and learn about, having all students self-select different texts is perhaps not the best situation. Rather, for activities like novel studies and literature circles, teachers can provide choices while still imposing some limits. For instance, Roald Dahl's *Matilda* (1988) is a wonderful book, but it might not be suitable for all fourth graders. For some, it might be too hard; for others, too simple. For some, it might be just plain boring. Teachers increase their chances of successful classroom reading experiences by providing options for children. Rather than provide 30 copies of *Matilda,* perhaps the teacher could offer six copies of *Matilda* and six copies each of other Dahl books, such as *Charlie and the Chocolate Factory* (1964), *James and the Giant Peach* (1961), *The Witches* (1983), and *Danny: The Champion of the World* (1975). Students could then select from five options, thus increasing the likelihood that they would find a book that appealed to them. This approach would also endow students with the motivating sense of ownership that comes from having chosen the book they are reading. Some boys who might balk at reading about the female protagonist in *Matilda* would be enthusiastic in choosing to read about the boy in *Danny: The Champion of the World.* After all, boys often express reading preferences differing from girls' (Farris, Werderich, Nelson, & Fuhler, 2009).

When we think back on some of our worst reading experiences from school, we recognize that those experiences were often ones in which we were forced to read a book for which we had little interest. Teachers often justify assigning a specific title on the basis that the book will be "good for them." One of the authors of this textbook, Greg, recalls being forced to eat boiled pumpkin when he was a child, presumably because his parents considered it would be "good for him." Greg claims to be "doing quite well, thank you very much," despite completely eliminating boiled pumpkin from his diet as soon as he left home. He suspects, however, that he would be doing considerably less well if being forced to read certain books at school had turned him away from reading forever. In forcing children to read specific books, that is a risk that teachers take. Many of the books that are assigned as class novels—those believed to be good for a child—are those books considered (by adults) to be classics. But what adults consider classics are generally not popular reading choices for children (Ivey & Broaddus, 2001; Worthy, Moorman, & Turner, 1999).

As with the selection of Roald Dahl books mentioned earlier, teachers might provide students with choices around a certain theme. In the previous example, the theme was simply a study of works by Roald Dahl. Another theme that works well in the upper-elementary grades is wilderness survival. Rather than be assigned Gary Paulsen's *Hatchet* (1987), students might choose from books such as *Lost in the Barrens* (Mowat, 1956), *Island of the Blue Dolphins* (O'Dell, 1960), *Julie of the Wolves* (George, 1972), and *Baboon* (Jones, 2007). A theme about problems in school might include *Stargirl* (Spinelli, 2000), *Crash* (Spinelli, 1996), *Vive la Paris* (Codell, 2006), *Schooled* (Korman, 2007), *The 6th Grade Nickname Game* (Korman, 1998), *Me and Rolly Maloo* (Wong, 2010), and *Loser* (Spinelli, 2002). All of these books have enough "big theme" ideas in common that discussion need not be limited only to small groups who have read specific titles. Rather, a whole-class discussion can be conducted based on the similarities contained in the books—issues such as bullying, teasing, and ostracizing schoolmates.

The whole-class novel-reading approach restricts students by exposing them to just one book at a time. Providing choices around a theme offers exposure to many books. As children hear their peers talk about their book choices, they will likely gain enthusiasm and want to read some of the other books, in addition to their own. As Fisher and Ivey (2007) state:

> When students read widely from books they have selected, they are more prepared to discuss the books with their peers and to write complex analyses of the themes and ideas. What's more, they are motivated to read more. (p. 496)

Using Trade Books in the Other Subject Areas

The ways that trade books can be used in the classroom are many and varied. A major strength of trade books compared to many textbooks and reference books is their ability to create interest and encourage reading. This being the case, it is important that, when using trade books for instructional purposes, we choose ways to preserve these books' ability to stimulate and engage readers.

One way for teachers to show students the appeal of trade books in the instructional program is to involve them in the school day. Children won't see how books from the library fit into daily instruction unless teachers include them as a natural part of classroom learning. An easy way to bring these books into lessons is to ask the librarian for titles on the subject to be taught. Teachers can look through the books until they find enough interesting ideas, experiments, or information for a lesson or unit. Then they can present it to the class, showing the books that gave them the information. Teachers' use of these books as read-alouds is particularly important in the lower grades, where children have more limited reading abilities. Middle- and upper-grade children will be able to make more of their own discoveries.

When authors embed mathematical or scientific concepts within a story, they provide contextual information and a level of enjoyment that might otherwise be missing from some math or sciences classes. The increased level of enjoyment adds interest and excitement to the study of a given subject. Contextualizing information—that is, embedding the information within a story—potentially contributes to increased student understanding and helps students to recognize the wonders of the world around them.

What follows are some examples of ways that children's literature trade books can be used for teaching and learning across the curriculum. The possibilities are limited only by the seemingly boundless imaginations of children and the willingness of the teacher to allow students to use those imaginations.

Children's Literature and Mathematics

The professional educational literature contains many reports of teachers successfully teaching mathematical concepts through the use of trade books. One such example is Forbringer's (2004) discussion of the use of *The 13 Days of Halloween* (Greene & Raglin, 2000). The book is a take-off on the traditional song "The Twelve Days of Christmas." A romantic ghoul endeavors to win the favor of his "ghoulfriend" by showering her with gifts, beginning with a vulture in a dead tree. On the second day, the ghoulfriend receives two hissing cats and a vulture in a dead tree. As with the Christmas song, in this Halloween version, each day, the ghoul presents an accumulation of more and more gifts. Forbringer used the book with second-grade children to provide them with practice using multiple representations in problem solving. After discussing the story, the children began figuring out how many of each gift was presented. How many ghosts? How many cooked worms? Many children used a combination of drawings, tally marks, and numerals in their calculations. Patterns were identified, and where appropriate, some children counted by fives. Others started counting by tens. A variety of mathematical discoveries were made in the context provided by the story.

Whitin (2008) reports the use of *How Much Is a Million* (Schwartz & Kellogg, 1985) in classrooms. In each instance, the book was read aloud to the students. Students were then encouraged to think of others ways to investigate the concept of one million. In the second grade, the children were asked if they thought their classroom contained one million of anything. It was suggested that there might be one million loops in the carpet. Using mathematical concepts such as area and averages and the skills of rounding and using a calculator, the children explored the notion of one million. Rather than individually count one million loops (something that *How Much Is a Million* tells us would likely have taken at least 23 days—morning, noon, and night), children counted loops in a two-inch-square piece of carpet. Then they determined an average number of loops for such an area and used that size of square as a measuring unit for working with the whole carpet. Although some university students might balk at the mathematics involved, these grade 2 children were guided through an informative, engaging mathematical exploration that was richly energized by the context provided by Schwartz's text and Steven Kellogg's illustrations. Other classrooms, containing other grades, explored the mathematics of the book in other ways.

Among many other similarly encouraging reports of the use of children's literature to facilitate mathematical learning, Shatzer (2008) discusses the use of *The Wolf's Chicken Stew* (Kasza, 1996) as a gateway for involving students in counting and measuring. Malinsky and McJunkin (2008) discuss the use of Burns's (1994) book *The Greedy Triangle* as a means of helping children to explore angles. Again, so long as the teacher is prepared to allow students to exercise their imaginations, the options for mathematical investigations inspired by trade books seem almost without limit.

Children's Literature and Science and Social Studies

Veronica Carrillo is a Los Angeles teacher with a passion for science. Her third-grade classroom library houses nearly 200 science-related books, including many picture books. One day, a student expressed interest in learning about various inventions, including the origins of everyday items that were once seen as exciting innovations. In her class, Veronica began to read aloud stories about inventors and their discoveries. The books engendered so much excitement that students began borrowing books about inventors to read at home with their families. "My entire class became very excited about trying to create things," Veronica said (Brassell, 2006, p. 339). Soon, the classroom began to fill up with inventions the children had created at home! The skillful use of trade books by a teacher willing to encourage her students to use their imaginations had provided a framework for children to learn about and practice science.

With middle-years students, sets of novels provide a good framework for studying many science topics. For instance, the study of bird life can be enhanced through the use of books like the following: *Hoot* (Hiaasen, 2002); *Blue Heron* (Avi, 1992); *The Very Worst Thing* (Hayden, 2003); *Wringer* (Spinelli, 1997); and *Owls in the Family* (Mowat, 1961). In addition to containing many details about the appearances and behaviors of birds, these books also present conservation themes and are therefore valuable to a class learning about preservation of the environment.

Teachers should use nonfiction—especially in grades 3 and above—to strengthen and update content area curricula, as well as to make the subject matter more lively and interesting. For instance, a teacher could round up informational dinosaur books of varied lengths and levels of difficulty, including such titles as *Outside and Inside Dinosaurs* (Markle, 2000), *Encyclopedia Prehistorica: Dinosaurs* (Sabuda & Reinhardt, 2005), *Boy, Were We Wrong about Dinosaurs!* (Kudlinski, 2005), and *Giant Sea Reptiles of the Dinosaur Age* (Arnold, 2007). Students might work in small groups to research certain aspects of dinosaur life (care of young, food chain, extinction, warm-blooded theory, etc.) and then report their findings in creative ways to the entire class. Or students might work individually, choosing books that match their interests, reading levels, or assigned dinosaur topics. In social studies, teachers could use the same approach to study New World explorers, the American Revolution, or World War II.

Children's Literature and Health Education

A common theme-based unit in elementary classrooms is the five senses. Textbooks containing information about the senses might serve teachers' needs, but trade books dealing with the individual senses might be more effective for children.

For instance, some interesting conversations about smells can be engendered through a classroom read-aloud of books like *Dog Breath* (Pilkey, 1994) and *Skunk Dog* (Jenkins & Pratt, 2008). In response, students might discuss some of their favorite and least-favorite smells. A discussion of the sense of sound might start with students listening to books such as *Night Noises* (Fox & Denton, 1989). Students can create soundscapes to accompany this book. They can produce various sound effects to match all the sounds in the book.

Reading *My Little Sister Ate One Hare* (Grossman & Hawkes, 1996) would offer an interesting way to begin exploring the sense of taste. In this book, using rhyming verse, the narrator tells of all the things that his little sister ate. As she swallows each new thing, the expectation increases that she will surely become sick. It is fun to ask children what they think each thing would taste like. Children might also identify the things in the book they would most and least like to eat. The class can then graph the results, embracing a natural bridge between language activities, health class, and mathematics.

The sense of sight can be discussed around *The Black Book of Colors* (Cottin & Faria, 2008). This title also works well for learning about the sense of touch because it contains braille text. Again, the possibilities are endless.

Important components of health education for older students include such topics as body image and self-concept, as well as the issue of bullying. In the middle school grades, the "problems in school" novels mentioned earlier in this chapter are a useful resource when discussing how people feel about themselves and others. Novels such as Korman's (2007) *Schooled* and Spinelli's (2000) *Stargirl* help middle and high school students to identify some of the ways that they can be better friends and better school citizens. After reading one or both of these books, many students have become committed to be more understanding, more compassionate, and more supportive of their schoolmates.

Three Principles of Using Trade Books to Teach Subject Matter

In any program that uses trade books to spark learning, the following three principles seem to be important keys. They can be implemented in a wide variety of ways. As long as these three principles are followed, good things will likely result.

1. *Students read trade books as they are meant to be read*—as windows to the world that do not cover a subject but, like peeling layers off an onion, uncover it.
2. *Teachers allow students to discover, or uncover, the information.* When teachers know *exactly* what students should find in a given trade book, that book is being misused. Teachers who allow students to select their own evidence are often pleasantly surprised at what they bring back as proof of learning, even when the assignment is fairly specific (for example, "Find evidence of how animals adapt to their environment.").
3. *Students share their discoveries and insights.* Teachers reinforce genuine learning by providing some means for excited students to present new knowledge to an audience or make a personal response to new discoveries—through an oral or written summary, a poster or display, an explanation to a small group, or a diary or story from the perspective of a character in the book.

Trade books even can be used to learn beyond the curriculum. They explore so much more of the world than is covered in traditional school subjects: child labor laws, the development of dynamite, the making of baseball bats, printing paper money, living with a terminal disease, illustrating comic books, and on and on. It is difficult to find a topic in the world that is *not* the focus of a children's book.

After briefly discussing with students how much interesting information exists outside school subjects, teachers may assign them to find books about topics they will not learn about in school yet are appealing to them. After reading these books, students should have a chance to share their new knowledge. Using trade books to learn subject matter provides children freedom to discover while still keeping them accountable.

In helping children to develop intellectually, we make the greatest strides when we concentrate on helping them become curious. Curious people are observant and aware. They ask questions and try to find answers. Being curious is a mindset that's common among people who make new discoveries and solve problems. It is the curious who continue to learn under their own power. As Rabelais reportedly advised us, "Children are not vessels to be filled but fires to be lit." Because trade books reflect the curiosity and humanity of authors who have learned to see and wish to share that vision, they have the spark that can light that flame.

PEARSON myeducationkit™

Go to the topics Picture Books, Poetry, and Nonfiction on the MyEducationKit for this text, where you can:

- Search the Database of Children's Literature, housing more than 22,000 titles searchable in every genre by authors or illustrators, by awards won, by year published, and by topic and description.
- Explore genre-related Assignments and Activities, assignable exercises showing concepts in action through database use, video, cases, and student and teacher artifacts.
- Listen to podcasts and read interviews from some of the brightest and most enduring stars of children's literature in the Conversations.
- Discover weblinks that will lead you to sites representing the authors you learn about in these pages, classrooms with powerful children's literature connections, and literature awards.

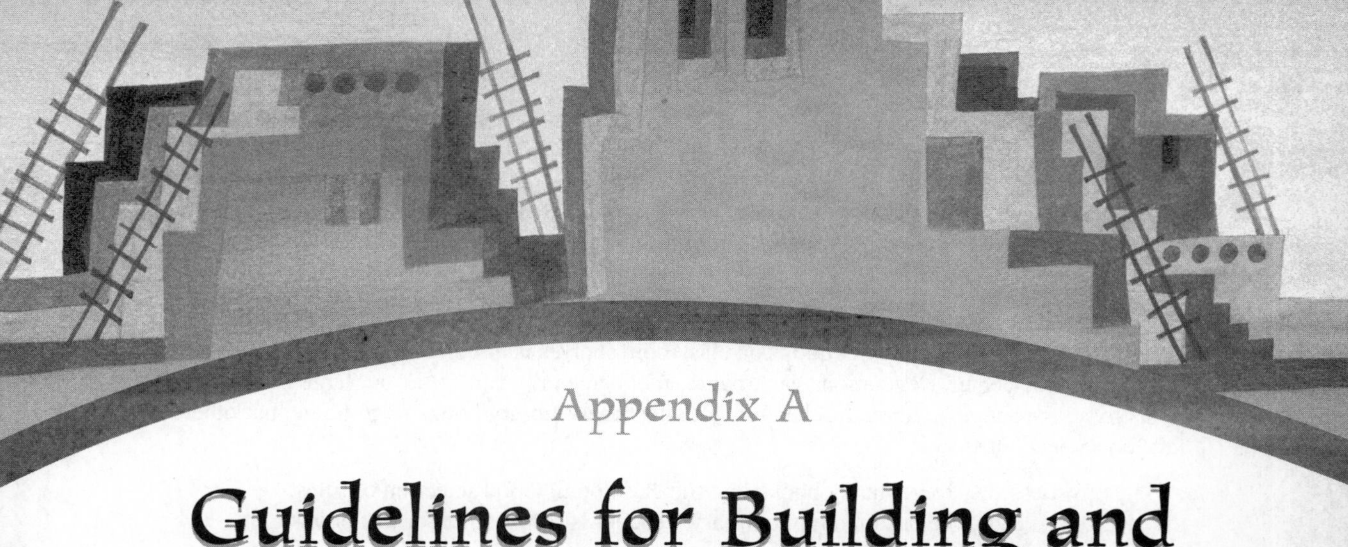

Appendix A

Guidelines for Building and Using a Classroom Library

Every classroom needs its own library. Even if the school has a fine offering of books in an attractive central library or media center, each classroom should have a collection of conspicuously displayed titles, for three main reasons:

1. If books are present and prominent, they can be found easily and used for sustained silent reading, for browsing, and for answering personal questions as well as questions arising from classroom discussions.
2. The presence of trade books in a classroom speaks volumes about their central place in the learning process. Simply by being there, shelves of real books—not textbooks—give evidence to the teacher's commitment to immediate and lifelong learning. If a teacher talks about the importance of reading but only a few books are visible, the message rings hollow to young ears.
3. Children in classrooms with classroom libraries read 50% to 60% more than do children in classrooms without them (Morrow, 2003). Students in classrooms with ready access to a variety of books, magazines, and other materials have better attitudes toward reading, reading achievement, and comprehension (Moss & Young, 2010).

The greatest obstacle to building a classroom library is impatience. Once convinced of the value of having books close at hand, most teachers want their collections to mushroom *right now.* The enthusiasm and desire are understandable but sometimes harmful. It simply takes time, usually years, to get the kinds and numbers of books a teacher wants. The point is to begin building the collection and to resist the natural feeling of discouragement because it isn't growing faster. Concentrate on two areas: finding free books and raising money to buy books. Even in tight economic times, both are possible.

Free Books

With ingenuity and grit, a teacher can bring books into the classroom from a variety of sources, such as the following. Note the pluses (+) and minuses (–) of each.

School Library

The easiest and fastest way to get books on classroom shelves is to borrow them from the school library or media center. Regulations vary, but teachers generally can check out large numbers of books for classroom use. Some teachers do not allow these library books to go home, but others develop a checkout system.

+ Effortless way to get many books into the classroom. Good selection of titles.
– Books need to be returned to the library. Teacher is responsible for lost books.

Public Library

Another quick way to get books on the shelf is to visit the public library and borrow as many titles as allowed. Many libraries have special arrangements for classroom teachers, which often include a longer checkout time and an easier checkout system. If your town has no local library, you are likely served by some other library—in a neighboring town, a county system, a bookmobile, or the state library.

+ Wide selection of materials. Immediate availability.
– Transporting books back and forth. Teacher is responsible for lost books. Limited checkout time.

Asking Students to Bring Books from Home

Many children have books at home that are appropriate for classroom reading. Often, they are willing to share these books with others for the year. Before they bring their personal books, ask students to write their names in the books in at least two places. Tell them to leave treasured books at home because they can be lost or damaged even when students take pains to treat them carefully. During the final week of the school year, these books are to be returned to their owners.

+ Less work for the teacher than any other method. Students feel ownership in their library and like to recommend their personal titles to others.
– Inevitably, some books will be damaged or will disappear.

Bonus Titles from Book Clubs

When students order from a book club, the teacher receives points that can be used to order free books. Ordering regularly from a book club not only helps students by focusing on book reading and ownership but also by adding substantially to the classroom library with the bonus books. Some clubs even have extra teacher catalogs offering Big Books, classroom sets, recommended packages of preselected books, or individual titles for good reading.

+ Bonus books are often attractive and always new.
– Somewhat limited selection.

Birthday Books

If it is a classroom custom for parents to provide a treat on their child's birthday, the teacher can request that a book be donated to the classroom library instead. Inscribing the child's name and birth date inside the front cover helps personalize the gift and make it more noteworthy. Be sure parents do not think they need to spend a great deal. Paperbacks are perfectly acceptable as birthday books. These birthday books might be placed on a special shelf.

+ Encourage parents to participate in building the library. Children leave a legacy for others.
– Can introduce a small degree of competitiveness.

Library Discards

All libraries undergo a periodic weeding process. The titles taken from the shelves are usually sold for a dollar or less. It is possible that a library will donate these discards to a school. Ask the library director.

+ Little or no cost.
– Many titles are discarded for good reasons, including excessive wear, unusual topics, and being outdated. Be selective in your choices.

Raising Money for Books

Teachers have three sources of money to buy trade books: (1) ask, (2) earn, or (3) dip into their own bank accounts. The third is the quickest but should be avoided. The first two can produce adequate funds to keep new books coming to classroom shelves, and the easier of those is simply to ask. All requests for raising money need to be cleared with the principal. Sometimes you may be unaware of conditions or rules that affect your plans. To ensure maximum success, the principal must support your efforts in soliciting funds.

In addition, when you request money to buy trade books for your classroom, you should write some kind of rationale or proposal. Ask about and follow the procedure of each particular benefactor. If a benefactor has no formal procedure, present a clear, attractive, professional-looking, but brief (one page is fine) request at the time you ask for funds. Include a specific dollar amount you are seeking, the kinds and number of books you will buy, and the benefit those books will bring to your students and teaching. Frankly, if you can't make it clear how these books will benefit your students, you don't deserve the money.

Ask for Money

The Principal

Resist the urge to think asking the principal is senseless, even if the faculty was just asked to cut back on copier paper because money is tight this year. Schools are budgeted organizations and have to keep money in reserve for unforeseen problems. Usually, some funds remain near the end of the fiscal year. Because budgeted monies are spent instead of returned, a worthy project has a high chance of getting funding at that time.

To increase the chance for support from the principal, acknowledge that money is short, look at the expenditures made for your classroom, and identify purchases you can do without. Perhaps you can get by without a basal workbook or can commit to using 10 fewer reams of copier paper (and stick to that). Principals often are edgy about requests for money because so many teachers simply ask. When your idea is stated clearly in writing *and* accompanied by your willingness to cut present expenses, your chances of getting the money are greatly improved.

The PTA (or similar organizations)

The PTA (Parent/Teacher Association) is committed to improving the school and generally hosts some kind of fundraiser as a part of its duties. Write a plan that shows how you will strengthen teaching and learning by using more trade books in the curriculum. You are likely to merit closer consideration if you propose the idea along with other teachers, showing how all of you can share or rotate the books to get maximum use from them.

Local Service Clubs

Service organizations such as Rotary, Kiwanis, Sertoma, Lions, Eagles, and B.P.O.E. (Elks) are interested in being a part of and improving the community. Requesting $200 to $300 for a specific improvement in a school is reasonable. Follow the group's specific procedures. If invited to a meeting, prepare the children so that they make the bulk of the presentation.

Grants

It is surprising how many district and state grants are available. Call the school district office to ask about them, and overcome the idea that applying for grants is formidable. The applications for some educational grants can be filled out in half an hour, and the awards are significant. Teachers may also apply for special funding in areas of their interest. For instance, if you are particularly fond of social studies or feel a need to strengthen your social studies instruction, propose a plan that relies more heavily on trade books to involve students and improve their social studies learning.

Earn Money

The following all involve some kind of labor beyond a simple request.

Host a Book Fair

Bringing tables full of new books to the school for student browsing and buying is called a book fair. Usually, book fairs run a number of days and provide an easy way for students to discover and buy appealing titles. An additional advantage is that a percentage of the total sales goes to the school, generally from 20% to 40%. Books are available from local bookstores (it's always nice to have a local bookstore support the project and bring a salesperson), local news distributors (check the Yellow Pages under "Magazines—Distributors" and then select an adult to be in charge), and national companies. A national book fair company is Scholastic Book Fairs. Go online to www.scholastic.com/bookfairs to locate the nearest Scholastic Book Fair office.

Organize a Fundraiser

Avoid commercial programs that prey on schools. Most people feel held hostage by children who ask them to buy overpriced jewelry or very small bars of expensive chocolate. A good fundraiser should enable the children to learn something. For example, one teacher taught students how to make salt-and-pepper centerpieces for picnic tables, which they then constructed and sold.

Have Children Earn Money for Books

Instead of asking children to bring money for books, contact parents and ask for support in having their children work at home doing extra chores for a standard price. All parents pay perhaps a dollar an hour for good, honest labor.

Set up a Student Store

During lunch, your class sells treats to the student body, keeping profits for books. Students help plan and conduct the daily business. Sometimes this gets approval more easily when it is for a specified period of time—say, one month.

Where to Buy Books

Once you have money for books, you want to spend it wisely. Following are some recommended sources, including the pluses (+) and minuses (–) of each.

Book Clubs

The biggest book club is Scholastic: phone 800-724-2424 and online at http://teacher.scholastic.com/clubs. Scholastic has separate clubs according to grade levels and even has a club for books in Spanish (Club Leo).

+ Inexpensive. Relatively quick turnaround time—maximum of 2 weeks if the order is called in or submitted online.
– Limited titles. Some books are a slightly smaller size than regular bookstore editions.

Local Bookstores

Ask about educational discounts. (If you can't get at least 20%, look elsewhere.) Inquire about minimum orders. (Some stores give no discounts on small purchases.) Take the school's tax-exempt number to avoid paying sales tax.

+ Immediate availability.
– Discount is small. Availability limited to stock on hand.

Local Paperback Wholesalers

Cities with populations over 100,000 are likely to have a paperback distributor. Look in the Yellow Pages under "Magazines—Distributors." Those listed generally carry a line of paperbacks, including children's books, and sell them at a substantial discount to teachers who pay with a school check or purchase order. Call first for details.

+ Books available today. Can do your own book club or book fair.
– Paperback wholesalers are found only in metropolitan areas. Limited to stock on hand.

Local Sources for Used Books

Some bookstores specialize in used books and have decent ones for greatly reduced prices. Thrift stores have better prices, but the pickings tend to be slimmer. Garage sales offer even less choice but can provide some great books at bargain prices. Books purchased at garage sales can sometimes be exchanged for other books at used book stores.

+ Very inexpensive.
– Very limited selection. Condition of books varies.

Internet Bookstores (New and Used Books)

Today, the Internet provides schools and individuals the opportunity to find any book, new or used, at discounted prices. For example, Allbookstores.com (http://www.allbookstores.com) speeds up the searching process for buyers by comparing the offerings and prices of the major online booksellers, such as Amazon.com, Barnes & Noble.com, Alibris, Abebooks.com, and Half.com.

+ Selection is endless. New, used, and out-of-print books are available. For orders over $25 or $50, shipping may be free.
– Shipping for inexpensive single titles may exceed the price of the book.

Paperback Books

The Booksource (http://booksource.com) offers paperback titles for a 25% discount on orders of 25 books or more. Shipping is free. In addition, the Booksource offers teachers many additional services. For example, it offers selected lists for struggling readers, suggested classroom libraries by grade level, and specially created lists according to individual teacher need.

+ Wide selection (25,000 titles).
– No discount on orders of 24 books or fewer.

Remaindered Books

When books go out of print, publishers frequently sell the remaining copies in bulk to a remainder house. These books are then available at tremendous savings, often discounted 80% from the original price. Sources for remaindered books can be found online. Two good ones are Book Closeouts (http://www.bookcloseouts.com) and Daedalus Books (http://www.daedalusbooks.com).

+ Enormous savings on new books. Will ship to private as well as institutional addresses.
– Limited to returned and remaindered titles.

Free (or Almost Free) Books for Students: Reading Is Fundamental

Reading Is Fundamental (RIF) will not help build a classroom library, but it will provide books to give to students. RIF is a federally funded nonprofit organization with the goal of increasing book ownership among students, particularly those with special needs (defined as meeting one criterion from a list of 10, including below-average reading skills, eligibility for free or reduced-price lunch, emotional disturbance, no access to a library, or having disabilities). When 80% of the children in a school or special school program meet 1 of the 10 criteria, RIF will give 75% of necessary funds to buy paperback books for all students in the qualifying group (25% of the money must be provided locally). RIF provides 100% of the necessary funds for children of

migrant or seasonal farm workers. Deadlines for submitting applications are January 14 and October 1. Contact: Reading Is Fundamental, Inc., 1825 Connecticut Avenue, Suite 400, Washington, DC 20009. Phone toll-free: 877-RIF-READ (877-743-7323). Web site: http://www.rif.org. E-mail: contactus@rif.org.

Planning and Evaluating the Classroom Library

Good classroom libraries are more than just books on shelves. That said, the books on the shelves do matter a great deal. Often, classroom libraries are filled with books that are too difficult for the struggling readers in the classroom to read (Allington & Cunningham, 2007). Teachers need to be very intentional about the books in their classroom collections. Here are some goals to work toward (Moss & Young, 2010). The classroom library should have:

- At least 7 books per child
- A 50/50 balance of fiction and nonfiction
- A range of nonfiction text with lots of expository text
- A range of fiction including contemporary realistic fiction, historical fiction, folk literature, fantasy, and science fiction
- An assortment of poetry
- Plenty of magazines
- Popular series books
- A balance of "boy" and "girl" books
- Varied cultural representations in books
- New books added regularly
- At least one-third of the books below grade level so all children find easy books to read

Using the Classroom Library

Once a classroom has a library, the teacher has to make some decisions about its use. Should those books be limited to reading in the classroom, or can students take them home? Are students on their honor to return the books, or should there be some kind of checkout system? How many books is each child allowed to check out? How long may children keep the books? Does the teacher serve as class librarian, or can children handle the job?

Each teacher has to devise a system that is personally comfortable. One fact every teacher can count on: If children borrow books from a classroom library, some titles will be lost. Period. The only way not to lose books is to keep students from touching them. Accepting this inevitability is essential. Yet few titles are lost to calculated theft. Most missing books are due to students misplacing them or simply forgetting to return them. Some kind of system is recommended to help students remember they have a book from the classroom library. The easiest system is to have the students themselves write their names, dates, and book titles on a form attached to a clipboard or filed in a folder. As students return books, they draw lines through their names and the other information. Appointing one or more students as librarians also works well.

No matter how small the school budget, it is possible for a teacher to find free books and money for books. With perseverance and patience, any teacher can build an enviable library that will help turn kids into readers.

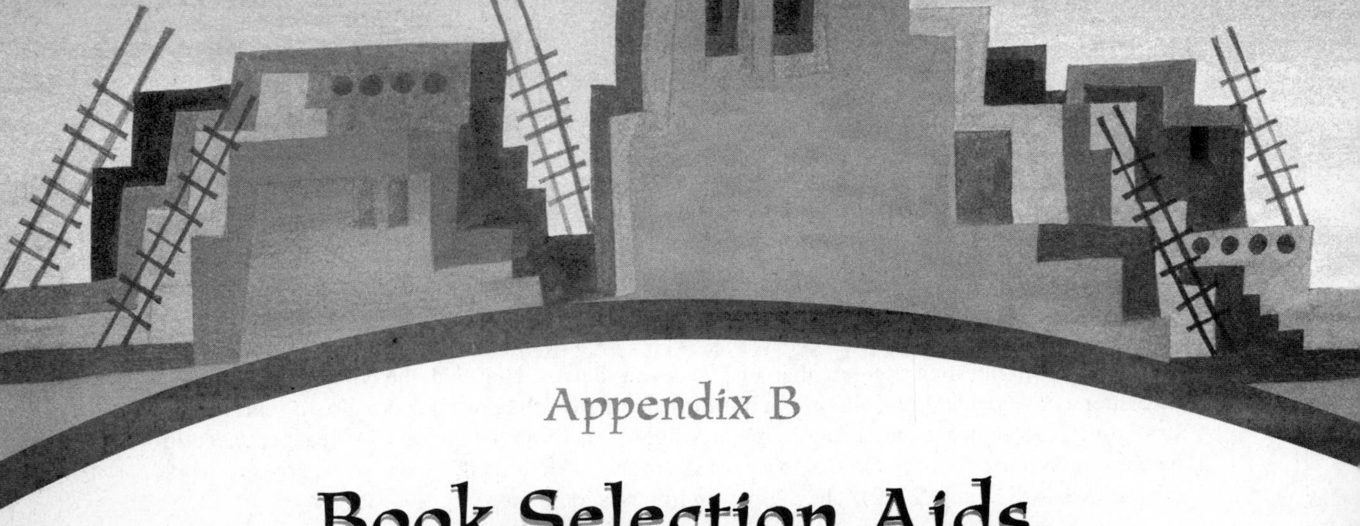

Appendix B

Book Selection Aids

Professional Organizations

American Library Association (ALA)

http://www.ala.org

Founded in 1876, the ALA is the oldest and largest national library association in the world. It works to maintain the highest quality of library and informational services in institutions available to the public. The ALA publishes *Booklist,* one of the most respected book review journals.

- ***Association for Library Service to Children (ALSC).*** ALSC, a branch of the ALA, evaluates and selects print and nonprint materials to use in libraries for children. Awards sponsored by ALSC include the John Newbery and Randolph Caldecott Medals, the Mildred L. Batchelder Award, the Laura Ingalls Wilder Award, the Pura Belpré Award, and the Robert F. Sibert Award.
- ***Young Adult Library Services Association (YALSA).*** YALSA's special focus is on library services for older youth beyond the elementary level. Awards granted by YALSA include the Michael L. Printz Award and the Margaret A. Edwards Award.

The Children's Book Council (CBC)

http://www.cbcbooks.org

The CBC sponsors National Children's Book Week in November and Young People's Poetry Week in April. Each year, the council cosponsors the selection of outstanding trade books through its participation in the following: Children's Choices (with the International Reading Association), Outstanding Science Trade Books for Children (with the National Science Teachers Association), and Notable Children's Trade Books in the Field of Social Studies (with the National Council for the Social Studies). The CBC publishes a twice-yearly newsletter, *CBC Features.*

International Reading Association (IRA)

http://www.reading.org

The IRA seeks to improve the quality of reading instruction at all educational levels and to promote a lifelong love of reading. The IRA also promotes children's literature through its annual book awards (IRA Children's Book Awards), its Teachers' Choices list of 30 books that children

might not discover without the help of a teacher, and through its cooperation with the Children's Book Council in administering Children's Choices, an annual booklist chosen by young readers. The IRA also publishes *The Reading Teacher,* a journal for elementary-level teachers interested in reading education. *The Reading Teacher* focuses on the theory and practice of teaching reading to elementary-age children. Features include children's and professional book reviews, research reports, and practical teaching ideas. It is published eight times a year.

- ***Children's Literature and Reading.*** This IRA special interest group sponsors the Notable Books for a Global Society annual book list of 25 of the best multicultural books for students K–12. The SIG publishes *The Dragon Lode,* which features articles about children's book authors and illustrators and other aspects of children's literature. It is published twice a year.

National Council of Teachers of English (NCTE)

http://www.ncte.org

The NCTE works to increase the effectiveness of instruction in English language and literature. Children's literature is promoted through award programs for nonfiction writing (*Orbis Pictus* Award) and poetry (NCTE Excellence in Poetry for Children Award). NCTE publishes *Language Arts,* a journal for elementary-level teachers interested in language education. *Language Arts* includes themed issues on topics relating to the teaching of English and language arts as well as practical teaching ideas, reviews of children's books, and reviews of professional resources.

- ***Children's Literature Assembly (CLA).*** A branch of the NCTE, the CLA also sponsors the NCTE Notable Children's Books in the Language Arts. The CLA also publishes *The Journal of Children's Literature,* which contains articles and features on all aspects of children's literature, including news and other items of interest to members. It is published twice each year. The CLA website contains book lists, related links, and information about the assembly and its projects. http://www.childrensliteratureassembly.org

The United States Board on Books for Young People (USBBY)

http://www.usbby.org

The United States Board on Books for Young People (USBBY) serves as the U.S. national section of the International Board on Books for Young People (IBBY), which was founded to promote international understanding and goodwill through books for children and teenagers. USBBY selects an annual list of Outstanding International Books. IBBY publishes *Bookbird: A Journal of International Children's Literature,* a quarterly journal containing articles examining children's book authors, illustrators, titles, and publishing trends from around the world.

Publications About Children's Literature

Review Sources

Booklist

http://www.ala.org

This review journal from the American Library Association describes its purpose as "to provide a guide to current print and nonprint materials worthy of consideration for purchase by small and medium-sized public libraries and school library media centers." Printed biweekly, *Booklist* publishes annually a list of best books titled "Editor's Choice," as well as the ALA Notable Children's Books and Best Books for Young Adults. *Book Links: A Quarterly Supplement to Booklist* is an added benefit to a *Booklist* subscription. *Book Links* features author profiles and interviews, thematic classroom connections bibliographies, and practical classroom ideas.

Horn Book Magazine

http://www.hbook.com

Published six times per year, *Horn Book* magazine contains reviews of books, articles about literature, and interviews with authors. *Horn Book* cosponsors the Boston Globe/Horn Book Awards and publishes a list of best books called "Fanfare." The July/August issue includes the acceptance speeches for Newbery and Caldecott Awards.

Kirkus Reviews

http://www.kirkusreviews.com

Kirkus is published twice monthly. It makes an effort to review a book two months before its official publication date.

School Library Journal

http://www.slj.com

This monthly journal is one of the most complete providers of news, information, and reviews for librarians and media specialists. A special issue in December includes an index and a "Best Books" section.

Publishers Weekly

http://www.publishersweekly.com

In addition to providing weekly reviews of titles for both adults and children, *Publishers Weekly* offers spring and fall special editions on books for young readers. Regular features include interviews with authors, illustrators, and publishers.

Children's Literature Blogs

Many books are available that offer bibliographies of children's books, yet these books quickly become dated. Teachers and librarians now often look on blogs (web logs, which are updated regularly) to find current children's books.

Big A little a

http://www.kidslitinformation.blogspot.com

This blog includes children's book news and a weekly gathering of children's book reviews from American and English newspapers.

Blue Rose Girls

http://bluerosegirls.blogspot.com

A group of children's book illustrators began this collective blog with a fresh take on the bookmaking process, publishing business, and children's literature field.

Book Ends: A Booklist Blog

http://bookends.booklistonline.com

Middle school librarians Cindy Dobrez and Lynn Rutan show that two heads are better than one as they review children's and young adult books in a Siskel-and-Ebert fashion.

Chicken Spaghetti

http://www.chickenspaghetti.typepad.com/chicken_spaghetti

Susan Thomsen provides reviews and news on children's literature.

The Children's Book Compass

http://www.marilyncarpenter.wordpress.com

Marilyn Carpenter not only reviews books for children and teens, but she also highlights ways of sharing books in classrooms.

Cynsations

http://www.cynthialeitichsmith.blogspot.com

Author Cynthia Leitich Smith offers a range of up-to-the-moment news, interviews, reviews, booklists, and more.

Fuse #8

http://www.schoollibraryjournal.com/blog/1790000379.html

Formerly an independent blogger, Betsy Bird was so successful that her blog is now hosted at *School Library Journal*'s blog site. She is a children's librarian at the well-known Donnell Branch of the New York City Public Library.

INK: Interesting Nonfiction for Kids

http://inkrethink.blogspot.com

The goal of this blog is to encourage children's reading of nonfiction. The postings, which are by some of today's greatest nonfiction authors, provide insight into authors' craft, how photos and illustrations are integrated into the text, and subjects that flood the market.

JacketFlap

http://www.jacketflap.com/index.asp

This blog provides interesting statistics and publisher information, and also serves as a clearinghouse for many different blogs related to children's literature in one mega blog.

The PlanetEsme Plan: The Best New Books from Esme's Shelf

http://planetesme.blogspot.com

This blog, by Esmé Raji Codell, provides brief reviews of current books that are often thematically linked to older books.

Poetry for Children: About Finding and Sharing Poetry with Young People

http://poetryforchildren.blogspot.com

Sylvia Vardell regularly posts reviews, interviews, podcasts, resources, and links to help teachers and librarians connect children to poetry and poets.

ReadRoger

http://www.hbook.com/blog

Horn Book Magazine's editor, Roger Sutton, maintains a regular blog with children's literature–related information, opinions, interviews, and more.

Selected Web Sites for Finding Books

The Library of Congress Online Catalog

http://catalog.loc.gov

This site allows users to search the entire holdings of the Library of Congress in a number of ways: by author, title, subject, notes, publisher, category, date, collection, ISBN, and Dewey Decimal or Library of Congress call number. Specialized searches are also possible. Among other possibilities, users can locate the complete output of one author (all titles appear here, even out-of-print), check the exact wording of the title, determine the correct date of publication, find out which books are on the library shelf next to a certain title, and see how many different editions of a title have been published.

BookFinder

http://www.bookfinder.com

Locating out-of-print books was a frustrating pursuit until the advent of the Internet. BookFinder brings together a worldwide inventory of millions of volumes from thousands of individual book dealers who specialize in used, hard-to-find, and rare books. Simply type in the title or author, and a list of available books appears on the screen. After looking at price and a detailed description of the condition, the user selects the desired copy and then is given all the necessary ordering information.

Amazon.com

http://www.amazon.com

This site needs no explanation. Amazon.com, the largest online bookstore, is also an exhaustive source for finding both in-print and out-of-print titles.

Appendix C

Magazines for Children

A broad variety of magazines is available to match the interests of almost any young reader: *Clavier's Piano Explorer* for young music lovers, *School Mates* for chess fans, *Junior Baseball* for little league baseball players, *Disney's Princess* for young fans of the animated princesses in Disney's films, and more. Successful magazines can and do have circulations from 100 (*Acorn Magazine*) to three million (*Highlights*).

A selection of children's magazines belongs in every elementary school because magazines

- Offer the latest, freshest information about many subjects.
- Present a variety of viewpoints on a specific topic.
- Draw the attention and interest of young readers with appealing layouts and photography.
- Are not imposing, thus attracting readers who hesitate to open a book.
- Support and strengthen the elementary school curriculum.
- Help children see that different texts can and should be read in different ways.

Following are magazine titles selected for their quality, energy, curricular applications, and/or general appeal. Because subscription rates frequently change, as may addresses and phone numbers, we have provided the Web site address for each magazine, which will provide the most current information.

Appleseeds (Ages 8–11). *Appleseeds* is a history and culture magazine for children in grades 3 through 5. Authors integrate the social studies with the language arts as carefully researched articles are told in story format. In addition to articles, each issue features puzzles, games, and recipes. Web site: http://cobblestonepub.com.

Ask (Ages 7–10). A Smithsonian magazine for younger readers, *Ask* is a science and discovery magazine for elementary-age children. The magazine features the best in science, history, technology, and the arts. Young readers investigate the world with inventors, artists, thinkers, and scientists of the past and present. Web site: http://www.cobblestonepub.com.

Babybug (6 Months–2 Years). This board-book magazine designed for small hands (cardboard pages, 6 ¼ by 7 inches with rounded edges and no staples). *Babybug* contains simple stories, rhymes, and colorful pictures. Web site: http://www.cricketmag.com.

Boy's Life (Ages 7–17). Published by Boy Scouts of America, this magazine covers electronics, cartoon features, sports, hobbies and crafts, careers, history and science, and scouting projects and programs. Fiction is also included. Web site: http://www.scouting.org.

Boys' Quest (Ages 6–12). In addition to fiction and nonfiction pieces, *Boys' Quest* has many exploratory, investigative, and problem-solving pages. This publication "emphasizes wholesome, innocent, childhood interests" and is designed "to inspire boys to develop interest in reading at an early age." Web site: http://www.boysquest.com.

Calliope (Ages 8–15). World history and archaeology are presented to young readers through fiction and nonfiction, time lines, maps, activities, and historical photographs, demonstrating that history is a continuation of events, not a series of isolated, unrelated occurrences. Web site: http://www.cobblestonepub.com.

Chickadee (Ages 6–9). *Chickadee* is a science and nature magazine from Canada for younger children. Illustrated with drawings and color photographs, each issue contains a short story or poem, an easy-to-read animal story, puzzles, a science experiment, and a pull-out poster. Web site: http://www.owlkids.com.

Childart (Ages 6–14). Published by the International Child Art Foundation, a nonprofit organization dedicated to promoting child art and visual learning, *ChildArt* presents a broad view of the world of art. Often written from a child's perspective, the magazine looks at art history, contemporary art and artists, and the variety of forms art may assume. Children's artwork also appears in this publication. Web site: http://www.icaf.org.

Click (Ages 3–7). A *Smithsonian* magazine, *Click* is a science and discovery magazine for young children. Thirty-eight full-color pages are filled with exciting photographs, beautiful illustrations, and stories and articles that are both entertaining and thought provoking. Parents also get an online Parent's Companion with suggestions for things to do and books to read. Web site: http://www.cobblestonepub.com.

Cobblestone (Ages 8–15). American history comes alive through articles, maps, illustrations, songs, poems, puzzles, crafts, and activities. Web site: http://www.cobblestonepub.com.

Cousteau Kids (Ages 7–15). Published by the Cousteau Society, this magazine is packed with news and adventures from Cousteau expeditions and amazing stories about the wet and wild creatures of the sea. Web site: http://www.cousteaukids.org.

Creative Kids (Ages 8–14). *Creative Kids* is a forum for children's writing. Young writers' work about almost any subject may be accepted for publication. Web site: http://www.prufrock.com.

Cricket (Ages 9–14). This magazine publishes quality stories, poems, and nonfiction pieces often written by well-known names in the field of children's literature. It is nicely illustrated in full color. Web site: http://www.cricketmag.com.

Dig (Ages 9–14). *Dig,* published with the Archaeological Institute of America, lets young people share in the thrill of archaeological discovery while learning about the cultural, scientific, and architectural traits and beliefs of different societies. Recent developments in the field of archaeology form the magazine's core subject matter. Each issue focuses on one theme, providing a broad understanding of the topic. Colorful graphics, photos, puzzles, games, and hands-on projects enhance cognitive and critical thinking skills. Web site: http://www.cobblestonepub.com.

Faces (Ages 8–14). This magazine explores and celebrates human diversity. The editorial staff is aided by the Anthropology Department of the American Museum of Natural History in creating a magazine that examines the lifestyles, beliefs, and customs of world cultures. Web site: http://www.cobblestonepub.com.

Highlights for Children (Ages 2–12). *Highlights* contains fiction, nonfiction, science projects and experiments, craft projects, games, puzzles, and hidden pictures. It emphasizes "values instead of violence" and "fun with a purpose." Web site: http://www.highlightsforchildren.com.

Hopscotch (Ages 6–12). *Hopscotch* is a magazine for young girls that includes articles and features, short stories, poetry, nonfiction, games, crafts, and activities. It is one of the few magazines targeted at younger girls. Web site: http://www.hopscotchmagazine.com.

Kids Discover (Ages 6–12). Each issue is themed, focusing on a fascinating subject that is sure to stimulate young curiosity. Illustrations, diagrams, and photographs illuminate each topic, such as the construction and use of skyscrapers. Web site: http://kidsdiscover.com.

Kiki (Ages 8-14). *Kiki* is an interactive fashion magazine for tween girls that emphasizes creative self-expression over glamour and beauty. The magazine also presents articles about world culture, fine art, money management, and other interesting subjects. Parents and teachers will be pleased that there is no celebrity gossip, sexual innuendo, or other inappropriate topics.

Ladybug (Ages 2–6). Each issue includes songs, finger plays, poems, nursery rhymes, longer read-aloud stories illustrated by award-winning illustrators, and activities for preschool and primary-grade children. *Ladybug* is designed to encourage a lifetime of reading and learning in youngsters. Web site: http://www.cricketmag.com.

Muse (Ages 10+). A Smithsonian magazine for children, *Muse* is produced by the editors and publishers of *Cricket* magazine. It features articles covering the breadth and wonder of the Smithsonian's collections and research, including topics such as the latest technology, architecture, paleontology, music, physics, theater, math, visual arts, earth sciences, space travel, ancient and modern world history, and almost everything else in the universe. Web site: http://www.cobblestonepub.com.

National Geographic Kids (Ages 8–14). Designed to encourage geographic awareness in young readers, *National Geographic Kids* includes full-color pictures, short articles, far-out facts, and activities. Children who subscribe become members of the National Geographic Society. Web site: http://www.nationalgeographic.com.

Odyssey (Ages 10–16). With a focus on physical and natural science, this magazine contains full-length articles, star charts, spectacular photographs, activities, contests, puzzles, and interviews. Web site: http://www.cobblestonepub.com.

Owl (Ages 9–14). *Owl* is a beautifully illustrated nature magazine from Canada. Full-color photographs and paintings illustrate an interesting assortment of articles, stories, and experiments concerning the environment. Web site: http://www.owlkids.com.

Ranger Rick (Ages 6–12). *Ranger Rick* contains nonfiction, fiction, jokes and riddles, crafts and activities, plays, and poetry—all focused on nature and natural history. This well-illustrated magazine comes with membership in the Ranger Rick Nature Club. Web site: http://www.nwf.org/rangerrick.

Shoofly: An Audiomagazine for Children (Ages 3–7). This audiomagazine can be purchased as CDs or MP3s to offer children "catchy songs, entertaining stories, and age appropriate poetry." Web site: http://www.shooflyaudio.com.

Skipping Stones (Ages 7–16). *Skipping Stones* is a multicultural, multilingual magazine that accepts art and original writings from people of all ages and from all corners of the globe. Issues have included photos, stories, and art by children from Russia; traditional arts and crafts of East Africa; environmental games in Spanish and English; and songs from India. Web site: http://www.skippingstones.org.

Spider (Ages 6–9). *Spider* includes quality stories, poems, and nonfiction pieces. It is nicely illustrated in full color. Web site: http://www.cricketmag.com.

Sports Illustrated for Kids (Ages 8–13). This magazine focuses on sports-related subjects and introduces young readers to professional and amateur sports figures, including athletes who began their careers at young ages. Departments include sports cards, legends, puzzles, activities, and "Tips from the Pros." Web site: http://www.sikids.com.

Stone Soup (Ages 6–13). *Stone Soup* is a bimonthly literary magazine that publishes fiction, poetry, book reviews, and art produced by children. Web site: http://www.stonesoup.com.

Your Big Backyard (Ages 3–5). This magazine presents a conservation message by focusing on animals and nature. Each issue contains a "read-to-me" story and encourages language and number skills in very young children. Web site: http://www.nwf.org/yourbigbackyard.

Zoobooks (Ages 5–14). This magazine contains photographs, artwork, and scientific facts about wildlife and often focuses on a particular animal. Web site: http://www.zoobooks.com.

Appendix D

Children's Book Awards

Children's book awards have proliferated in recent years; today, over 200 different awards and prizes are presented by a variety of organizations in the United States alone. The awards may be given for books of a specific genre or simply for the best of all children's books published within a given period. An award may honor a particular book or an author or illustrator for a lifetime contribution to the world of children's literature. Most children's book awards are chosen by adults, but children's choice book awards are becoming more common. Awards help considerably to raise public awareness about the books being published for young readers. Of course, readers are wise not to put too much faith in award-winning books. Winning an award doesn't necessarily mean a book will provide a good reading experience, but it does provide a starting place when choosing books.

National Awards

United States of America

John Newbery Medal

Sponsored and administered by the Association for Library Service to Children, an arm of the American Library Association, the Newbery Medal is presented to the author of the most distinguished contribution to children's literature published in the United States during the preceding year. A variable number of Newbery Honors also may be given by the Newbery Selection Committee. Eligibility for this award is limited to U.S. citizens and residents. Named for the 18th-century British publisher, the Newbery Medal is one of the world's oldest and most prestigious children's book prizes.

Randolph Caldecott Medal

Sponsored and administered by the Association for Library Service to Children, an arm of the American Library Association, the Caldecott Medal is presented to the illustrator of the most distinguished picture book for children published in the United States during the preceding year. A variable number of Caldecott Honors also may be given by the Caldecott Selection Committee.

Eligibility for this award is limited to U.S. citizens and residents. Named for the 19th-century British illustrator, the Caldecott Medal is the United States' major picture book award.

The winners of both the Newbery and Caldecott Awards are printed on the inside of the front and back covers of this book. You may find complete lists that include Newbery Honors and Caldecott Honors at http://www.ala.org/alsc.

Canada

Governor-General's Literary Award

Administered by the Canada Council for the Arts since 1987, awards are presented to honor the finest in Canadian literature. In the children's literature category, English and French awards are presented each year. For each of the official languages, one award is given to an author and a separate award is given to an illustrator.

Canadian Library Association Book of the Year for Children Award

Sponsored and administered by the Canadian Library Association since 1947, the Canadian Library Association Book of the Year for Children Award is presented to the authors of the outstanding children's books published during the preceding year. Only Canadian citizens are eligible for this award.

Amelia Frances Howard-Gibbon Medal

Sponsored and administered by the Canadian Library Association since 1971, the Amelia Frances Howard-Gibbon Medal is presented to the illustrator of the most outstanding artwork in a children's book published in Canada during the preceding year. Eligibility for this award is limited to citizens and residents of Canada.

United Kingdom

Carnegie Medal

Sponsored and administered since 1936 by the British Library Association, the Carnegie Medal is presented to the author of a children's book of outstanding merit. The book must be written in English and first published in the United Kingdom in the preceding year.

Kate Greenaway Medal

Sponsored and administered since 1955 by the British Library Association, the Kate Greenaway Medal is presented to the illustrator of the most distinguished picture book. The book must be first published in the United Kingdom in the preceding year.

Australia

Children's Books of the Year Award

The Children's Books of the Year Awards program began in 1946 under the direction of various agencies in Australia. In 1959, the administration of the award program was taken over by the Children's Book Council of Australia. Currently, four awards are given annually: the Picture Book of the Year Award, the Children's Book for Younger Readers Award, the Children's Book of the Year for Older Readers Award, and the Eve Pownall Award for Information Books. Eligibility for the awards is limited to authors and illustrators who are Australian residents or citizens.

New Zealand

Russell Clark Award

The New Zealand Library and Information Association established the Russell Clark Award in 1975. It was first awarded in 1978 and is given for the most distinguished illustrations for a children's book. The illustrator must be a citizen or resident of New Zealand. The award is given annually to a book published in the previous year.

Esther Glen Award

Sponsored and administered by the New Zealand Library and Information Association since 1945, the Esther Glen Award is presented to the author of the most distinguished contribution to New Zealand's literature for children published in the previous year. Eligibility for the Esther Glen Award is limited to New Zealand residents and citizens.

Awards for a Body of Work

Hans Christian Andersen Award

Sponsored and administered by the International Board on Books for Young People, the Hans Christian Andersen Awards honor biennially one author (since 1956) and one illustrator (since 1966) for his or her entire body of work. This truly international award is chosen by a panel of judges representing several countries. The award must be given to a living author or illustrator who has made important and time-proven contributions to international children's literature. The Americans who have won the Hans Christian Andersen Award are Meindert DeJong (1962), Maurice Sendak (1970), Scott O'Dell (1972), Paula Fox (1978), Virginia Hamilton (1992), and Katherine Paterson (1998).

NCTE Award for Excellence in Poetry for Children

Sponsored and administered by the National Council of Teachers of English, the Excellence in Poetry for Children Award was given annually from 1977 to 1982, but beginning with the 1985 award, it has been presented every three years. The award is given to a living American poet whose body of work is considered an outstanding contribution to poetry for children ages 3 through 13. (See Chapter 8 for a list of the winners.)

Laura Ingalls Wilder Award

Sponsored and administered by the Association for Library Service to Children, an arm of the American Library Association, the Laura Ingalls Wilder Award is presented to a U.S. author or illustrator whose body of work is deemed to have made a substantial and lasting contribution to literature for children. The Wilder Award was first given in 1954. Between 1960 and 1980, it was presented every five years; from 1980 to 2001, every three years; and since 2001, every two years. Winners include Laura Ingalls Wilder (1954), Clara Ingram Judson (1960), Ruth Sawyer (1965), E. B. White (1970), Beverly Cleary (1975), Theodor S. Geisel (Dr. Seuss) (1980), Maurice Sendak

(1983), Jean Fritz (1986), Elizabeth George Speare (1989), Marcia Brown (1992), Virginia Hamilton (1995), Russell Freedman (1998), Milton Meltzer (2001), Eric Carle (2003), Laurence Yep (2005), James Marshall (2007), and Ashley Bryan (2009).

Other Selected Awards

Boston Globe/Horn Book Award

Since 1967, the *Boston Globe* and the *Horn Book Magazine*—one of the United States' oldest and most prestigious children's book review sources—have sponsored awards for children's book writing and illustration. As of 1976, three Boston Globe/Horn Book Awards have been presented annually: Fiction or Poetry, Nonfiction, and Picture Book.

Carter G. Woodson Award

Since 1974, the National Council for the Social Studies has sponsored awards for the most distinguished social science books for young readers that treat topics related to ethnic minorities and race relations within the United States with sensitivity and accuracy. The annual awards are given to books published in the United States in the preceding year, and since 1980, winners for both elementary and secondary school readers have been named.

Coretta Scott King Award

Since 1970, the Social Responsibilities Round Table, with the support of the American Library Association, has sponsored and administered the Coretta Scott King Award. This award commemorates the life and dreams of Dr. Martin Luther King Jr., as well as the work of his wife, Coretta Scott King, for peace and world brotherhood. It also recognizes the creative work of African American authors. Beginning in 1974, two awards have been presented annually: one to an African American author and one to an African American illustrator whose books for young readers published in the preceding year are deemed outstanding, educational, and inspirational.

Edgar Allan Poe Award

Since 1962, the Mystery Writers of America has presented an award for the Best Juvenile Novel in the fields of mystery, suspense, crime, and intrigue. In 1989, a second category was added: Best Young Adult Novel. A ceramic bust of Edgar Allan Poe is presented to the winner in each category, including adult fiction and filmmaking. The Edgars are the mystery writers' equivalent of Hollywood's Oscars.

International Reading Association Children's and Young Adult's Book Award

Since 1975, the International Reading Association has sponsored and administered an award presented to new authors of children's books. Publishers worldwide nominate books whose authors show special promise for a successful career in writing for young readers. Beginning in 1987, two awards were given annually: one for novels and another for picture books. In 1995, a third award

was added for informational books. In 2002, a total of six award categories were put in place: Primary–Fiction, Primary–Nonfiction, Intermediate–Fiction, Intermediate–Nonfiction, Young Adult–Fiction, and Young Adult–Nonfiction.

Jane Addams Children's Book Award

The Jane Addams Children's Book Awards are given annually to the children's books published the preceding year that effectively promote the cause of peace, social justice, world community, and the equality of the sexes and all races, as well as meet conventional standards for excellence. The Jane Addams Children's Book Awards have been presented annually since 1953 by the Women's International League for Peace and Freedom (WILPF) and the Jane Addams Peace Association. In 1993, a Picture Book category was added.

Lee Bennett Hopkins Promising Poet Award

The Lee Bennett Hopkins Promising Poet Award is sponsored by the poet Lee Bennett Hopkins and administered by the International Reading Association. It is a monetary award given every three years, starting in 1995, to a promising new author of children's poetry who has published no more than two poetry books.

The Michael L. Printz Award for Excellence in Young Adult Literature

Since 2000, the Michael L. Printz Award has been given for a book that exemplifies literary excellence in young adult literature. It is named for a Topeka, Kansas, school librarian who was a longtime active member of the Young Adult Library Services Association.

Mildred L. Batchelder Award

Since 1968, the Association for Library Service to Children, an arm of the American Library Association, has presented an award to an American publisher for the most outstanding children's book originally published in another country in a language other than English and subsequently translated and published in the United States during the previous year.

National Book Award

A consortium of book publishing groups has presented the National Book Awards since 1950. The sponsors' goal was to enhance the public's awareness of exceptional books written by Americans and to increase the popularity of reading in general. The awards are given in these categories: Fiction, Nonfiction, Poetry, and Young People's Literature.

Orbis Pictus Award for Outstanding Nonfiction for Children

The *Orbis Pictus* Award has been given annually since 1990 by the National Council of Teachers of English. Only nonfiction or informational children's books published in the United States during the preceding year are considered. The selection committee chooses the most outstanding contribution by examining each candidate's "accuracy, organization, design, writing style, and usefulness for classroom teaching in grades K–8." One winner and up to five honor books are selected each year. The award is named for the book *Orbis Pictus* ("The World in Pictures"), which is considered to be the first nonfiction book created exclusively for children. This work was written and illustrated by Johann Amos Comenius in 1657.

Phoenix Award

Since 1985, the Children's Literature Association has sponsored an award for "a book for children published twenty years earlier which did not win a major award at the time of its publication but which, from the perspective of time, is deemed worthy of special recognition for its literary quality." Consideration is limited to titles published originally in English.

Pura Belpré Award

The Pura Belpré Award is cosponsored by the Association for Library Services to Children and the National Association to Promote Library Services to the Spanish Speaking, both part of the American Library Association. First presented in 1996, this award is given biennially to a writer and an illustrator who are Latino/Latina and who have produced works that best portray, affirm, and celebrate the Latino cultural experience. The Pura Belpré Award is named after the first Latina librarian from the New York Public Library.

Robert F. Sibert Informational Book Award

The Robert F. Sibert Informational Book Award, administered by the Association for Library Services to Children and first presented in 2001, is given annually to the author of the most distinguished informational book published during the preceding year. The award is named in honor of Robert F. Sibert, the longtime president of Bound to Stay Bound Books, Inc., of Jacksonville, Illinois, and is sponsored by the company.

Scott O'Dell Award for Historical Fiction

The Scott O'Dell Award, first presented in 1984, is given to the author of a distinguished work of historical fiction written for children or adolescent readers. The winning books must be written in English, published by a U.S. publisher, and set in the New World (North, Central, or South America). The award was originated and donated by the celebrated children's author Scott O'Dell and is administered and selected by an advisory board.

Theodor Seuss Geisel Award

Since 2006, the Association for Library Services to Children has presented this award to the author(s) and illustrator(s) of beginning reader books published in the United States during the preceding year.

State Children's Choice Awards

Most U.S. states now have an organization, such as a state library or children's literature association, that sponsors a children's choice book award. Typically, schoolchildren nominate books and an adult committee narrows the list to about 10 to 20 titles. During the year, schools participating in the award process make the books available to children. To vote, the children must have read or had read to them a specified number of the titles. Only children may vote.

For an up-to-date list of the state children's choice book awards in the United States, access the following two websites:

McBookwords: State and Regional Book Awards—http://www.mcelmeel.com/curriculum/bookawards.html

State Awards for Children's and Young Adult Books—http://www.cynthialeitichsmith.com /lit_resources/awards/stateawards.html

Following is a current list as of the publication date of this textbook:

Alabama	Emphasis on Reading: Children's Choice Book Award Program, since 1980 (three categories: grades K–1, 2–3, 4–6)
Alaska	See Pacific Northwest: Library Association's Young Reader's Choice Award.
Arizona	Grand Canyon Readers' Awards (formerly Arizona Young Readers Award), since 1977 (four categories: picture books, intermediate, teen, nonfiction)
Arkansas	Charlie May Simon Children's Book Award, since 1971 (grades 4–6)
	Diamond Primary Book Award, since 1998 (grades K–3)
California	California Young Reader Medals, since 1974 (four categories: primary, intermediate, middle school/junior high, young adult)
Colorado	Colorado Children's Book Award, since 1976 (two categories: picture book, junior novel)
	Blue Spruce Award, since 1985 (young adult)
Connecticut	Nutmeg Children's Book Award, since 1993 (two categories: intermediate, teen)
Delaware	Blue Hen Book Award, since 1996 (two categories: picture book, chapter book)
	Delaware Diamonds, since 1990 (two categories: grades K–2, 3–5)
Florida	Florida Reading Association Children's Book Award, since 1989 (grades K–2)
	Sunshine State Young Reader's Award, since 1984 (grades 3–8)
	Florida Teens Read, since 2006 (high school)
Georgia	Georgia Children's Book Award, since 1969 (grades 4–8)
	Georgia Children's Picture Storybook Award, since 1977 (grades K–4)
Hawaii	Nene Award, since 1964 (grades 4–6)

Idaho	See Pacific Northwest: Library Association's Young Reader's Choice Award.
Illinois	Rebecca Caudill Young Readers' Book Award, since 1988 (grades 4–8)
	Monarch Award, since 2003 (K–3)
	Abraham Lincoln Award, since 2005 (high school)
Indiana	Young Hoosier Award, since 1975 (three categories: picture book, intermediate, middle grades)
	Eliot Rosewater Indiana High School Book Award, since 1997 (grades 9–12)
Iowa	Iowa Children's Choice Award, since 1980 (grades 3–6)
	Iowa Teen Award, since 1985 (grades 6–9)
	Iowa High School Book Award, since 2004 (high school)
Kansas	William Allen White Children's Book Award, since 1953 (two categories: grades 3–5, 6–8)
	Heartland Award, since 1997 (young adult)
Kentucky	Kentucky Bluegrass Award, since 1983 (four categories: grades K–2, 3–5, 6–8, 9–12)
Louisiana	Louisiana Young Reader's Choice Award, since 2000 (two categories: grades 3–5, 6–8)
Maine	Maine Student Book Award, since 1989 (grades 4–8)
	Lupine Award, since 1989 (two categories: picture book, juvenile/young adult)
Maryland	Maryland Children's Book Award, since 1988 (three categories: primary, intermediate, middle school)
	Black-Eyed Susan Award, since 1992 (three categories: picture book, grades 4–12, grades 6–9)
Massachusetts	Massachusetts Children's Book Award, since 1976 (grades 4–6). An award for grades 7–9 was presented during the years 1978–1983.
Michigan	Michigan Young Readers' Awards, since 1980
	Great Lakes Great Books Awards, since 2004 (five divisions: grades K–1, 2–3, 4–5, 6–8, 9–12)
Minnesota	Maud Hart Lovelace Award, since 1980 (two categories: grades 3–5, 6–8)
Missouri	Mark Twain Award, since 1972 (grades 4–8)
	Show Me Readers Award, since 1995 (grades 1–3)
	Building Block Picture Book Award, since 1997 (birth–grade K)
	Gateway Award, since 2004 (grades 9–12)

Montana	Treasure State Award, since 1994 (grades K–3)
	Also see Pacific Northwest: Library Association's Young Reader's Choice Award.
Nebraska	Golden Sower Award, since 1981 (three categories: grades K–3, 4–6, 6–9)
Nevada	Nevada Young Readers' Award, since 1988 (four categories: picture book, intermediate, young reader, young adult)
New Hampshire	Great Stone Face Award, since 1980 (grades 4–6)
	Ladybug Picture Book Award, since 2003 (picture book)
New Jersey	Garden State Children's Book Awards, since 1977 (four categories: easy to read, easy to read series, children's fiction, children's nonfiction)
	Garden State Teen Book Award, since 1995 (three categories: fiction, grades 6–8; fiction, grades 9–12; nonfiction)
New Mexico	Land of Enchantment Book Award, since 1981 (two categories: children's, young adult)
New York	Charlotte Award, since 1990 (three categories: primary, intermediate, young adult)
North Carolina	Children's Book Award, since 1992 (two categories: picture book, junior book)
North Dakota	Flicker Tale Children's Book Award, since 1978 (five categories: picture book, intermediate, juvenile, early-primary grades, upper grade level nonfiction)
Ohio	Buckeye Children's Book Awards, since 1982 (three categories: grades K–2, 3–5, 6–8)
Oklahoma	Sequoyah Children's Book Award, since 1959 (grades 3–6)
	Sequoyah Young Adult Book Award, since 1988 (grades 7–9)
Oregon	See Pacific Northwest: Library Association's Young Reader's Choice Award.
Pacific Northwest	Library Association's Young Reader's Choice Award (Alaska, Alberta, British Columbia, Idaho, Montana, Oregon, Washington), since 1940 (three categories: junior—grades 4–6, intermediate—grades 7–9, senior—grades 10–12)
Pennsylvania	Carolyn W. Field Award, since 1984 (grades K–8)
	Keystone to Reading Book Award, since 1985 (two categories: primary, intermediate)
	Pennsylvania Young Reader's Choice Award, since 1992 (grades K–12)
Rhode Island	Rhode Island Children's Book Award, since 1991 (grades 3–6)
	Rhode Island Teen Book Award, since 2002 (young adult)

South Carolina	South Carolina Children's Book Award, since 1976 (children's division)
	South Carolina Young Adult Book Award, since 1980 (young adult division)
	South Carolina Junior Book Award, since 1993 (junior division)
	South Carolina Picture Book Award, since 2003 (picture book division)
South Dakota	Prairie Bud Children's Book Award, since 1998 (grades K–3)
	Prairie Pasque Children's Book Award, since 1987 (grades 4–6)
Tennessee	Volunteer State Book Award, since 1979 (three categories: grades K–3, 4–6, 7–12)
Texas	The Texas Bluebonnet Award, since 1981 (grades 3–6)
	Lone Star Award, since 1990 (grades 6–8)
	Tayshas Award, since 1996 (high school)
	2X2 Award, since 2001 (age 2–grade 2)
Utah	Beehive Book Award, since 1980 (five categories: picture book—grades K–3, fiction—grades 3–6, informational—grades 3–6, young adult—grades 7–12, poetry—grades K–9)
Vermont	Dorothy Canfield Fisher Children's Book Award, since 1957 (grades 4–8)
	Red Clover Award, since 1996 (grades K–4)
Virginia	Virginia Readers' Choice (formerly Virginia Young Readers Program), since 1982 (four divisions: primary, elementary, middle school, high school)
Washington	Washington Children's Choice Picture Book Award, since 1982 (grades K–3)
	Sasquatch Award, since 1998 (grades 4–8)
	Evergreen Young Adult Book Award, since 1991 (middle and high school)
	Also see Pacific Northwest: Library Association's Young Reader's Choice Award.
West Virginia	West Virginia Children's Book Award, since 1985 (grades 3–6)
Wisconsin	Golden Archer Award, since 1974 (three categories: primary, intermediate, middle/junior high)
	Elizabeth Burr/Worzalla Award (for Wisconsin artists and illustrators), since 1992 (grades K–8)
Wyoming	Indian Paintbrush Book Award, since 1986 (grades 4–6)
	Soaring Eagle Young Adult Book Award, since 1989 (grades 7–12)
	Buckaroo Book Award, since 1999 (grades K–3)

Lists of the Best Books

The American Library Association

Notable Children's Books, an annual list of outstanding children's books chosen by a committee of the Association for Library Service to Children. Available at http://www.ala.org/alsc.

Best Books for Young Adults, an annual list of outstanding young adult books chosen by a committee of the Young Adult Library Services Association. Available at http://www.ala.org /yalsa. YALSA also offers two other lists: Quick Picks for Reluctant Teenage Readers and Popular Paperbacks for Young Adult Readers.

School Library Journal

School Library Journal Best Books, an annual list of the best books reviewed in *School Library Journal.* Available at http://www.slj.com.

Horn Book Magazine

Hornbook Fanfare, an annual list of recommended books chosen from among those reviewed in the *Horn Book Magazine.* Appears in the March/April issue and at http://www.hbook.com.

The Children's Book Council

Children's Choices. In cooperation with the International Reading Association, the Children's Book Council sponsors a project that produces an annual list of about 100 titles that 10,000 young readers from five project locations across the country have selected as their "best reads." Available at http://www.cbcbooks.org.

Outstanding Science Trade Books for Children. In cooperation with the National Science Teachers Association (NSTA), the CBC sponsors an annual listing of the best science trade books for young readers. Available at http://www.cbcbooks.org.

Notable Children's Trade Books in the Field of Social Studies. In cooperation with the National Council for the Social Studies (NCSS), the CBC sponsors an annual listing of the best social studies trade books (fiction and nonfiction) for young readers. Available at http://www.cbcbooks.org.

Others

A variety of organizations and individuals prepare many other annual "best books" lists. Some others of note include:

- Amelia Bloomer List, books celebrating strong women and girls (American Library Association)
- Blue Ribbons (*Bulletin of the Center for Children's Books*)
- Books for the Teen Age (New York Public Library; compiled annually)

- One Hundred Titles for Reading and Sharing (New York Public Library; compiled annually)
- Children's Books of the Year (Children's Literature Center, Library of Congress)
- Editor's Choice (*Booklist,* American Library Association)
- *New York Times* Best Illustrated Children's Books of the Year (*New York Times Book Review Supplement*)
- Notable Books for a Global Society (International Reading Association, Children's Literature and Reading Special Interest Group)
- Notable Children's Books in the Language Arts (National Council of Teachers of English, Children's Literature Assembly)
- Outstanding International Books (United States Board on Books for Young People)
- Parents' Choice Awards (Parents' Choice Foundation)
- Teachers' Choices (International Reading Association)
- VOYA Nonfiction Honor List (*Voice of Youth Advocates,* Young Adult Library Services Association, American Library Association)

For complete lists of all the awards and the award-winning books, see the latest edition of *Children's Books: Awards and Prizes* published online by the Children's Book Council (http://awardsandprizes.cbcbooks.org).

Appendix E

Publishing Children's Books

Children generally don't come to school knowing that books are written and illustrated by people. In their minds, books simply *are,* appearing magically on library and bookstore shelves. Teachers familiar with the publishing process can round out children's perceptions by helping them see how books come to be.

Reflecting a general business trend, large corporations have been buying independent publishers, so that today, most national publishing houses are owned by someone other than the company whose name appears on the book. But the business of getting a book published remains the same.

Steps in Getting a First Book Published

Because submission procedures can vary from publisher to publisher, an aspiring author benefits from checking one of the many publishing guides, such as *Children's Writer's and Illustrator's Market,* published by Writer's Digest. Some publishers announce that they are not currently accepting picture book manuscripts, for instance. Or the hopeful author may learn that a query letter is needed before submitting anything. (A query letter is a description of the manuscript sent to the publisher to see whether the publisher is interested in seeing the actual work.) Then the submission process is generally as follows:

1. *Author sends a query letter or manuscript to a publisher.* Depending on the information gleaned from a publisher's guide, the would-be author sends off a query letter or the manuscript. After the final rewriting, the author of a picture book prints out a double-spaced manuscript of the complete text, and the author of a chapter book either prints out a few chapters and prepares a detailed outline of the rest or submits the entire manuscript. A cover letter of no more than one page should accompany the manuscript. It is becoming an accepted practice for authors to submit to more than one publisher at a time. Once frowned on by publishers, their acquiescence to this practice recognizes that publishers may hold onto unsolicited manuscripts for a few months to more than a year. The manuscript will be looked at by a staff member or freelance reader. If not acceptable, it is returned to the author with a rejection notice. If the first reader finds some promise in the manuscript, it is passed to another staff member and eventually to the editor—usually, the fourth or fifth reader. An editor who likes the manuscript may be required to present it to the rest of the editorial staff for approval.

2. *Author signs contract.* When the publisher decides to accept the manuscript, a multipage contract is sent to the author. The contract states the financial conditions as well as scores of other income-producing possibilities, such as translation into other languages; adaptation into film, stage play, or CD; paperback rights; and the right to consider for publication the author's next manuscript. Half of the advance goes to the author when the contract is signed. The editor will ask the author to make some changes—usually, when the contract is signed but sometimes as a condition of signing. The changes can be small or extensive, but almost always the author has revisions to make. The author then works on the corrections suggested by the editor, and eventually, the manuscript is declared ready for publication. When the final copy is submitted, the remaining half of the advance is sent to the author.

3. *Book is produced.* The publisher sees that the manuscript is edited, proofread, and polished, laying out all the plans for printing: typeface style and size, where page numbers go, placement of text with art, weight of paper, finish of paper, color of paper, style of endpapers, and so on. Because publishers do not own printing presses (too expensive), a printer is selected to produce the book according to the publisher's specifications. Unless the printer has binding facilities, the printed sheets then go to a binder to be made into books. Finished books are delivered to the warehouse.

4. *Book is sold.* Marketing people at the publishing house decide how to feature the book in a catalog and whether to promote it with a poster, display, or advertisements in book review journals. Except for sending sample copies to book reviewers, the publisher has no say in how or even if the book is reviewed, but author and publisher alike hope for favorable reviews to appear.

Often-Asked Questions

- **Where do authors get their ideas?** This is the question asked most often of authors. Like all people, they get their ideas from living and thinking. Russell Freedman visits an exhibition of old photographs and comes away with the idea for a book about immigrant children (*Immigrant Kids,* 1980). Lloyd Alexander sees in his mind an adolescent boy running up wide steps leading to an official government building in what seems to be Europe about 200 years ago. He then has to determine who this boy is, why he is hurrying, and what is going on in the world around him. After months of asking and answering his own questions, Alexander eventually fashions the idea for *The Marvelous Misadventures of Sebastian* (1970). Eric Kimmel scours collections of folktales to locate one that strikes his fancy and can be turned into the text for a picture book. Richard Peck hears a librarian say that any book with "secret" in the title won't stay on the shelf. His next book is *The Secrets of the Shopping Mall* (1979). Where authors get their ideas is as varied as human personalities and the books that line library shelves, but the common denominator is that each seems interesting or important to the writer.

- **What are the chances that a publisher will buy an author's first book?** About 1 manuscript of every 5,000 received will be published. But as one publisher pointed out, "some people win the lottery." Every author was once a new author, and new authors must persevere. Madeleine L'Engle's *A Wrinkle in Time* (1962) was rejected by every publisher in New York, so she started at the top of the list again. This time Farrar, Straus and Giroux took it, and the book promptly won the Newbery Medal.

• **Why are most picture books 32 pages long?** Books are not printed on small pieces of paper that are then collated but on one large sheet that is folded four times by a machine and then made into pages by trimming the folds on three sides. The most economical way to produce a short book, like a picture book, is to print only one sheet—32 book pages when folded and trimmed. (Sometimes the first and last 4 pages—8 total—are used as endpapers, making the book itself 24 pages.)

• **If the author of a picture book can't draw, how is an artist chosen to do the illustrations?** The publisher chooses the artist. Traditionally, the author has no say in who is chosen to illustrate the manuscript and gets no chance to approve the artwork. If the two had to agree, people could grow old waiting for a successful compromise. So the author is in charge of the words, the artist is given authority to interpret the story visually, and the book gets printed on time.

• **When an author finishes a book, how long will it take before it is on bookstore shelves?** Time varies, but one year is customary.

• **How many copies of an author's first book are printed?** The usual number printed is around 7,500 for picture books and 5,000 for novels. Considering that the population of the United States is about 300 million, that translates into one copy of a new novel for approximately every 60,000 Americans. When an author is well known, the press run is much larger. Most initial printings for established authors are in the 20,000 to 50,000 range. A first printing of more than 100,000 copies would indicate that the author is one of a handful of the most popular writers.

• **What do *in print, out of stock,* and *out of print* mean?** *In print* means the book is currently available; the publisher has copies stacked in a warehouse ready to ship to bookstores and libraries when ordered. *Out of stock* means the books aren't in the warehouse but probably will be reprinted and available in the near future. *Out of print* means the book is no longer available and the publisher has no plans to reprint it.

• **What do *first printing, second printing,* and *third printing* mean?** The first time a book is printed is the first printing. When the first printing sells out within a reasonable time, a second lot of books is printed—a second printing. Printings are identified on the copyright page with a row of numbers, usually 1 through 10. When the book is printed again, the 1 is removed, leaving 2 as the lowest number, indicating the second printing. The next time, the 3 will be the lowest, and so on.

• **What is a royalty?** In trade book publishing, the *royalty* is a percentage paid to the author for each copy sold. The standard royalty is 10% of the retail price. Royalties are calculated and checks are mailed twice a year, so an author living solely from creative works usually needs to budget well.

• **What is an advance?** When the publisher agrees to buy a book, the author is given an advance against royalties—good faith money that will be paid back to the publisher with future earnings from the book. Only when the advance is repaid does the author receive additional money. An advance for a first-time author of a children's picture book text is in the range of $3,500 to $6,000 (with the illustrator receiving the same), and a new novelist for children will receive from $5,000 to $10,000 for a first book. Established authors, of course, receive a much larger advance. In providing an advance, the publisher is saying, in essence, "We believe your book will sell well enough to return this investment to us." If the book does not sell enough to repay the advance, however, the author still keeps the money.

• **How much money do authors make?** At a 10% royalty, a $20 picture book earns $2.00 for the author. If the press run is 7,500 copies and all of them sell, the author will make $15,000

(7,500 multiplied by $2.00). If the picture book has both an author and an illustrator, the two share the royalty, usually split 50/50: $7,500 each. If a first novel, on the other hand, sells for $18 with a print run of 5,000 copies, the total author earnings would be $9,000 if all the books sell. Production time for a book is about a year, royalties are calculated every 6 months, and the money the book first earns repays the advance, so it is not unusual for an author to wait a year or two after publication of a book before receiving money beyond the advance. Of course, the author hopes the book will go into additional printings. For instance, *Make Way for Ducklings,* first published in 1941, was in its 67th printing when Robert McCloskey died in 2003. He must have been very satisfied when a book he created more than 60 years earlier was still being bought and read, as well as continuing to produce income.

- **Why do books cost so much, particularly picture books?** The $20 a consumer pays for a picture book usually is split into the categories that follow, but the percentages vary from publisher to publisher and year to year. They depend on the general health of the publishing industry and the economy. The following ballpark figures show the approximate percentages of where a book buyer's dollar goes:

  50% discount to the bookseller (discount is slightly higher for jobbers, chain stores, and warehouse stores; slightly lower for independent bookstores) = $10.00, which leaves the publisher with $10.00

  10% of the retail price to the author and illustrator = $2.00, which leaves the publisher with $8.00

  20% for manufacturing costs (color separations, press plates, paper, printing, binding, shipping) = $4.00, which leaves the publisher with $4.00

  10% for overhead (salaries, rent, office equipment, utilities, advertising, marketing, and warehousing) = $2.00, which leaves the publisher with $2.00

  10% profit = $2.00 left after paying all expenses

Chapter books cost less than picture books because of the expense related to color printing. Producing full-color books requires a larger press so each sheet can printed on four separate times—one for each primary color plus black—which takes longer and demands more sophisticated technology and equipment, thus costing more. Chapter books, usually printed only in black and white, simply are cheaper to produce.

- **Does every book make money for the publisher?** No. Much like the movie industry, some make a profit and some don't. In children's books, about 65% of the books never pay out, which means they don't make back enough money to reimburse the publisher for expenses—author's advance, some overhead costs, preparing the manuscript for printing, and paper and ink for printing. Approximately 35% of the children's books published do pay out, and they must earn enough additional money to bear the costs of those titles that do not meet their expenses. Naturally, the publisher hopes that each title will be profitable, even though two-thirds will become financial liabilities. When a book is not selling enough to meet expenses, the additional copies remaining in the warehouse often are sold in bulk to a remainder house, which pays pennies on the dollar for each hardcover book. Those remaindered books then are resold to chain stores and bookstores, where customers can buy titles for a fraction of their list price.

References

Aardema, Verna. (1975). *Why mosquitoes buzz in people's ears.* New York: Dial.

Abbott, Tony. 2008. *The Postcard.* Boston: Little, Brown.

ACT. (2004). *ACT high school profile report, high school graduating class 2005.* Retrieved from http://www.act.org/news/data/05/pdf/data.pdf

Ada, Alma Flor. (1998). *Under the royal palms.* New York: Atheneum.

Adeney, Anne. (2010). *Monkey see, Monkey do.* Illustrated by Christina Bretschneider. Mankato, MN: Sea-to-Sea Publications.

Adler, David A. (1993). *A picture book of Anne Frank.* Illustrated by Karen Ritz. New York: Holiday House.

Adler, David A. (2000). *A picture book of Sacagawea.* Illustrated by Dan Brown. New York: Holiday House.

Adler, David, & Adler, Michael S. (2006). *A picture book of John Hancock.* Illustrated by Ronald Himler. New York: Holiday House.

Adler, David, & Adler, Michael S. (2010). *A picture book of Cesar Chavez.* Illustrated by Marie Olofsdotter. New York: Holiday House.

Ahlberg, Janet, & Ahlberg, Allan. (1979). *Each peach pear plum.* New York: Viking.

Ahlberg, Janet, & Ahlberg, Allan. (1998). *See the rabbit.* Boston: Little, Brown.

Alexander, Lloyd. (1964). *The book of three.* New York: Holt, Rinehart and Winston.

Alexander, Lloyd. (1965, April). The flat-heeled muse. *The Horn Book, 41,* 141–146.

Alexander, Lloyd. (1967). *Taran wanderer.* New York: Holt.

Alexander, Lloyd. (1968a). *The high king.* New York: Holt.

Alexander, Lloyd. (1968b, August). Wishful thinking—or hopeful dreaming. *The Horn Book, 44,* 382–390.

Alexander, Lloyd. (1970). *The marvelous misadventures of Sebastian.* New York: Dutton.

Alexander, Lloyd. (1973, February 20). Letter to Shelton L. Root Jr.

Alexander, Lloyd. (1986). *The Illyrian adventure.* New York: Dutton.

Alexander, Lloyd. (1992). *The fortune-tellers.* Illustrated by Trina Schart Hyman. New York: Dutton.

Alexander, Lloyd. (1993, March 2). Telephone conversation with James S. Jacobs.

Allington, Richard A., & Cunningham, Patricia M. (2007). *Schools that work: Where all children read and write.* Boston: Allyn & Bacon.

Allison, Linda. (1976). *Blood and guts.* Boston: Little, Brown.

Altman, A., Barovick, H., Fetini, A., Fitzpatrick, L., Haire, M., James, R., Romero, F., Stephey, M. J., & Suddath, C. (2009, June 22). Numbers. *Time, 173*(24), 15.

American Library Association. (n.d.). About banned and challenged books. Retrieved from http://www.ala.org/ala/issuesadvocacy/banned/aboutbannedbooks/index.cfm

American Library Association. (n.d.). Office for Intellectual Freedom. Retrieved from http://www.ala.org/ala/aboutala/offices/oif/index.cfm

American Textbook Council. (2006, May 23). Homepage. Retrieved from http://historytextbooks.org

Anderson, Laurie Halse. (2008). *Chains.* New York: Simon & Schuster.

Anderson, Richard C., Hiebert, Elfrieda H., Scott, Judith A., & Wilkinson, Ian A. G. (1985). *Becoming a nation of readers: The report of the Commission on Reading.* Champaign-Urbana, IL: Center for the Study of Reading.

Anderson, Richard C., Wilson, Paul T., & Fielding, Linda G. (1988). Growth in reading and how children spend their time outside of school. *Reading Research Quarterly, 23,* 285–303.

Andrews, Julie, & Hamilton, Emma Walton. (2009). *Julie Andrews' collection of poems, songs, and lullabies.* New York: Little, Brown.

Anno, Mitsumasa. (1977). *Anno's counting book.* New York: HarperCollins.

Appelt, Kathi. (2008). *The underneath.* New York: Atheneum.

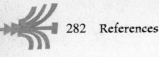

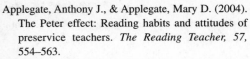

Applegate, Anthony J., & Applegate, Mary D. (2004). The Peter effect: Reading habits and attitudes of preservice teachers. *The Reading Teacher, 57,* 554–563.

Arias, Ron, & McNeil, Liz. (1989, October 23). A boy sides with Dr. Seuss, and puts a town at loggerheads. *People Weekly, 32*(17), 67–68.

Armbruster, Bonnie B., & Anderson, Thomas H. (1984). Structures for explanation in history textbooks, or what if Governor Stanford missed the spike and hit the rail? In Richard C. Anderson, Jean Osborn, & Robert J. Tierney (Eds.), *Learning to read in American schools.* Hillsdale, NJ: Erlbaum.

Armbruster, Bonnie B., Lehr, Fran, & Osborn, Jean. (2001). *Put reading first: The research building blocks for teaching children to read.* Jessup, MD: National Institute for Literacy.

Armstrong, Jennifer. (1998). *Shipwreck at the bottom of the world: The extraordinary true story of Shackleton and the Endurance.* New York: Crown.

Armstrong, William. (1969). *Sounder.* New York: Harper & Row.

Arnold, Caroline. (2007). *Giant sea reptiles of the dinosaur age.* New York: Clarion.

Ash, Russell. (1996). *Incredible comparisons.* New York: DK Publishing.

Associated Press. (1994, September 14). Students cite pregnancies as a reason to drop out. *New York Times,* p. B7.

Attenborough, Liz. (2001). *Poetry by heart.* New York: Chicken House (Scholastic).

Augarde, Steve. (2009). *Winter wood.* New York: David Fickling Books/Random House.

Avi. (1984). *The fighting ground.* Philadelphia: Lippincott.

Avi. (1992). *Blue heron.* New York: Avon.

Avi. (2008). *The seer of shadows.* New York: HarperCollins.

Azarian, Mary. (2000). *The gardener's alphabet.* Boston: Houghton Mifflin.

Babbitt, Natalie. (1975). *Tuck everlasting.* New York: Farrar, Straus & Giroux.

Babbitt, Natalie. (1987, October). Fantasy and the classic hero. *School Library Journal, 34,* 25–29.

Baker, John F. (2001, August 20). Big money for kids' mouse book. *Publishers Weekly, 248*(34), 17.

Baker, Linda, Dreher, Mariam J., & Guthrie, John T. (2000). Why teachers should promote reading engagement. In Linda Baker, Mariam J. Dreher, & John T. Guthrie (Eds.), *Engaging young readers: Promoting achievement and motivation* (pp. 1–16). New York: Guilford Press.

Balliett, Blue. (2006). *Wright 3.* New York: Scholastic.

Bandura, Albert. (1986). *Social foundations of thought and action: A social cognitive theory.* Englewood Cliffs, NJ: Prentice-Hall.

Bang, Molly. (1985). *The paper crane.* New York: Greenwillow.

Bang, Molly. (2000). *Nobody in particular: One woman's fight to save the bays.* New York: Holt.

Banks, James A., Colleary, Kevin P., Greenow, Linda, Parker, Walter C., Schell, Emily M., & Zike, Dinah. (2009). *The United States* (Vol. 1 and 2). Columbus, OH: Macmillan/McGraw-Hill.

Barrie, J. M. (1906). *Peter Pan.* New York: Scribner's.

Barrie, J. M. (2008). *Peter Pan: A pop-up adaptation of J. M. Barrie's original tale.* Illustrated by Robert Sabuda. New York: Little Simon. (Original work published 1906)

Bartoletti, Susan Campbell. (2005). *Hitler youth: Growing up in Hitler's shadow.* New York: Scholastic.

Barton, Byron. (2001). *My car.* New York: Greenwillow.

Barton, David, Hamilton, Mary, & Ivanič, Roz (Eds.). (2000). *Situated literacies: Reading and writing in context.* London, UK: Routledge.

Bates, John, & Bates, Natalie. (2004). *My first Buddhist alphabet.* Santa Monica, CA: Treasure Tower Press.

Baum, L. Frank. (1900). *The wonderful Wizard of Oz.* New York: G. M. Hill.

Baum, L. Frank. (2000). *The wonderful Wizard of Oz: A commemorative pop-up.* Illustrated by Robert Sabuda. New York: Little Simon. (Original work published 1900)

Baumann, James F., Hoffman, James V., Moon, Jennifer, & Duffy-Hester, Ann M. (1998). Where are the teachers' voices in the phonics/whole language debate? Results from a survey of U.S. elementary classroom teachers. *The Reading Teacher, 51,* 636–650.

BBC News. (2001, December 31). "Satanic" Harry Potter books burnt. Retrieved from http://news.bbc.co.uk/hi/english/entertainment/arts/newsid_1735000/1735623.stm

Berne, Emma Carlson. (2008). *Christopher Columbus: The voyage that changed the world.* New York: Sterling.

Berson, Michael J., Howard, Tyrone C., & Salinas, Cinthia. (2007). *The United States: Making a new nation.* Orlando, FL: Harcourt.

Bettelheim, Bruno. (1977). *The uses of enchantment: The meaning and importance of fairy tales.* New York: Vintage.

Bial, Raymond. (2009). *Ellis Island: Coming to the land of liberty.* Boston: Houghton Mifflin.

Biblow, Ephraim. (1973). Imaginative play and the control of aggressive behavior. In Jerome L. Singer (Ed.), *The child's world of make-believe* (pp. 104–128). New York: Academic Press.

Bierhorst, John. (1987). *Doctor Coyote: A Native American Aesop's fables.* New York: Macmillan.

Birdsal, Jeanne. (2008). *The Penderwicks on Gardham Street.* New York: Knopf.

Bishop, Rudine Sims. (1992). Multicultural literature for children: Making informed choices. In Violet J. Harris (Ed.), *Teaching multicultural literature in grades K–8* (pp. 37–53). Norwood, MA: Christopher-Gordon.

Bitton-Jackson, Livia. (1997). *I have lived a thousand years: Growing up in the Holocaust.* New York: Simon & Schuster.

Blackwood, Gary. (2002). *Year of the hangman.* New York: Dutton.

Blackwood, Gary. (2005). *Second sight.* New York: Dutton.

Blackwood, Gary. (2009). *Mysterious messages.* New York: Dutton.

Blake, Michel. (2007). *Baby's day.* Cambridge, MA: Candlewick.

Blake, William. (1993). *The tyger.* Illustrated by Neil Waldman. New York: Harcourt. (Original work published 1794)

Blos, Joan. (1979). *A gathering of days.* New York: Scribner's.

Blos, Joan. (1985, November). The overstuffed sentence and other means for assessing historical fiction for children. *School Library Journal,* 38–39.

Blumberg, Rhoda. (1985). *Commodore Perry in the land of the Shogun.* New York: Lothrop.

Blume, Judy. (1970). *Are you there God? It's me, Margaret.* New York: Bradbury.

Blume, Judy. (1975). *Forever.* New York: Bradbury.

Bogart, Dave (Ed). (1997). *The Bowker annual: Library and book trade almanac* (42nd ed). New Providence, NJ: R. R. Bowker.

Bogart, Dave (Ed). (2001). *The Bowker annual: Library and book trade almanac* (46th ed). New Providence, NJ: R. R. Bowker.

Bontemps, Arna. (1948). *Story of the Negro.* New York: Knopf.

Booth, David. (2006). *Reading doesn't matter anymore . . . : Shattering the myths of literacy.* Markham, ON, Canada: Pembroke.

Bowker, R. R. (2009). *Children's books in print 2009* (Vol. 1). New Providence, NJ: Bowker.

Boyd, Candy Dawson. (1990, June 5). Presentation given at the American Bookseller's Association Convention and Trade Exhibit [Cassette recording], Las Vegas, Nevada.

Boynton, Sandra. (2003). *Fuzzy, fuzzy, fuzzy! Touch, skritch, & tickle book.* New York: Little Simon.

Branley, Franklyn. (1996). *What makes a magnet?* New York: HarperCollins.

Brannen, Sarah S. (2008). *Uncle Bobby's wedding.* New York: Putnam.

Brassell, Danny. (2006). Inspiring young scientists with great books. *The Reading Teacher, 60,* 336–342.

Bringing ancient history back to life: An interview with Nancy Toff. (2005, November). *Curriculum Review, 45*(3), 14–15.

Broach, Elise. (2005). *Shakespeare's secret.* New York: Henry Holt.

Broach, Elise. (2008). *Masterpiece.* New York: Henry Holt.

Bronson, O. P., & Merryman, Ashley. (2009, September 14). See baby discriminate. *Newsweek, 154*(11), 53–60.

Brooke, John. (1972). *King George III.* New York: McGraw-Hill.

Brooks, Bruce. (1984). *The moves makes the man.* New York: Harper.

Brooks, G., Waterman, R., & Allington, R. (2003, Spring). A national survey of teachers' reports of children's favorite series books. *The Dragon Lode, 21*(2), 8–14.

Brooks, Walter R. (1932). *Freddy the detective.* New York: Walck. (Rereleased in 1997 by Overlook Press)

Brown, Cynthia Stokes. (1994). *Connecting with the past: History workshop in middle and high schools.* Portsmouth, NH: Heinemann.

Brown, Don. (2000). *Uncommon traveler: Mary Kingsley in Africa.* New York: Houghton.

Brown, Jonathan. (2004, September 2). Lawyer who turned to children's books £3m advance. *The Independent.* Retrieved from http://www.independent.co.uk

Brown, Marcia. (1961). *Once a mouse. . . .* New York: Scribner's.

Brown, Margaret Wise. (1947). *Goodnight moon.* Illustrated by Clement Hurd. New York: Harper & Row.

Brown, Margaret Wise. (1991). *Goodnight moon.* New York: HarperFestival. (Original work published 1947)

Bruner, J. (1996). *The culture of education.* Cambridge, MA: Harvard University Press.

Bryan, Gregory. (2009). Exploring the reading non-engagement of two grade six students during sustained silent reading. Unpublished doctoral dissertation, University of British Columbia, Vancouver, BC, Canada.

Bryan, Gregory, Tunnell, Michael O., & Jacobs, James S. (2007). A most valuable player: The place of books in teaching children to read. *Canadian Children, 32*(2), 25–33.

Bryson, Bill. (2008). *A really short history of nearly everything.* New York: Delacorte.

Buehner, Caralyn, & Buehner, Mark. (2002). *Snowmen at night.* New York: Phyllis Fogelman.

Buehner, Caralyn, & Buehner, Mark. (2004). *Snowmen at night.* Illustrated by Mark Buehner. New York: Dial.

Bunting, Eve. (1994). *Smoky night.* Illustrated by David Diaz. New York: Harcourt.

Burchard, Peter. (1995). *Charlotte Forten: A black teacher in the Civil War.* New York: Crown.

Burgess, Melvin. (2004). *Doing it.* New York: Henry Holt.

Burnford, Sheila. (1961). *The incredible journey.* Boston: Little, Brown.

Burns, Marilyn. (1994). *The greedy triangle.* New York: Scholastic.

Burstein, Joyce, & Hutton, Lisa. (2005, September/October). Planning and teaching with multiple perspectives. *Social Studies and the Young Learner, 18*(1), 15–17.

Butler, Dori Hillestad. (2003). *Sliding into home.* Atlanta, GA: Peachtree.

Byam, Michelle. (2000). *Arms and armor.* New York: Knopf.

Cairney, Trevor H. (2000). Developing parent partnerships in secondary literacy learning. In David W. Moore, Donna E. Alvermann, & Kathleen A. Hinchman (Eds.), *Struggling adolescent readers: A collection of teaching strategies* (pp. 58–65). Newark, DE: International Reading Association.

Calkins, Lucy M. (1994). *The art of teaching writing.* Portsmouth, NH: Heinemann.

Cameron, Judy, & Pierce, W. David. (1994). Reinforcement, reward, and intrinsic motivation: A meta-analysis. *Review of Educational Research, 64,* 363–423.

Campbell, Joseph. (1968). *The hero with a thousand faces* (2nd ed.). Princeton, NJ: Princeton University Press.

Canaday, John. (1980). *What is art?* New York: Knopf.

Cannon, A. E. (2002). *Charlotte's rose.* New York: Wendy Lamb Books/Random House.

Carle, Eric. (1969). *The very hungry caterpillar.* New York: Philomel.

Carle, Eric. (1990). *The very quiet cricket.* New York: Philomel.

Carle, Eric. (1997). *The very quiet cricket.* New York: Philomel.

Carroll, Lewis. (1865). *Alice's adventures in Wonderland.* London, UK: Macmillan.

Carter, Anne. (1981). *Dinnertime.* Los Angeles: Price Stern Sloan.

Catling, Patrick. (1979). *The chocolate touch.* New York: William Morrow.

Cazet, Denys. (1990). *Never spit on your shoes.* London, UK: Orchard.

Cerullo, Mary. (2009). *Shipwrecks: Exploring sunken cities beneath the sea.* New York: Dutton.

Chatton, Barbara. (1988, Spring). Apply with caution: Bibliotherapy in the library. *Journal of Youth Services in Libraries, 1*(3), 334–338.

Chevannes, Ingrid, McEvoy, Dermot, & Simson, Maria. (1997, April 4). Big names top the charts. *Publishers Weekly, 244*(14), 58–64.

Chodos-Irvine, Margaret. (2003). *Ella Sarah gets dressed.* San Diego: Harcourt.

Chodos-Irvine, Margaret. (2008). *Ella Sarah gets dressed.* New York: Red Wagon/Harcourt.

Chrisp, Peter. (2001). *Columbus: Explorer of the New World.* New York: Dorling Kindersley.

Chu, Nancy. (1982, March). Some thoughts concerning censorship. *The Dragon Lode, 3*(2), 6–10.

Chukovsky, Kornei. (1968). *From two to five.* Los Angeles: University of California Press.

Chwast, Seymour. (2006). *The miracle of Hanukkah.* Maplewood, NJ: Blue Apple Books.

Cianciolo, Patricia. (1976). *Illustrations in children's books.* Dubuque, IA: Wm. C. Brown.

Clark, Ann Nolan. (1952). *Secret of the Andes.* New York: Viking.

Cleary, Beverly. (1983). *Dear Mr. Henshaw.* New York: Morrow.

Cleary, Brian, & Gable, Brian. 2005. *How much can a bare bear bear? What are homonyms and homophones?* Minneapolis, MN: Millbrook Press.

Clément, Claude. (1989). *The voice of the wood.* Illustrated by Frédéric Clément. New York: Dial.

Clements, Andrew. (1996). *Frindle.* New York: Simon & Schuster.

Climo, Shirley. (1989). *The Egyptian Cinderella.* New York: Harper.

Cobb, Vicki. (1981). *The secret life of school supplies.* Philadelphia: Lippincott.

Cochrane, Mick. (2009). *The girl who threw butterflies.* New York: Knopf.

Codell, Esmé R. (2006). *Vive la Paris.* New York: Hyperion.

Cohen, Dorothy. (1968). The effects of literature on vocabulary and reading achievement. *Elementary English, 45,* 209–213, 217.

Coleridge, Samuel Taylor. (1992). *The rime of the ancient mariner.* Illustrated by Ed Young. New York: Atheneum. (Original work published 1798)

Coles, Robert. (1995). *The story of Ruby Bridges.* Illustrated by George Cephas Ford. New York: Scholastic.

Collard, Sneed B. (2005). *One night in the Coral Sea.* Illustrated by Robin Brickman. Watertown, MA: Charlesbridge.

Collier, Christopher. (1976, April). Johnny and Sam: Old and new approaches to the American Revolution. *The Horn Book, 52,* 132–138.

Collier, James Lincoln, & Collier, Christopher. (1974). *My brother Sam is dead.* New York: Four Winds.

Collier, James Lincoln, & Collier, Christopher. (1981). *Jump ship to freedom.* New York: Delacorte.

Collins, Suzanne. (2008). *The hunger games.* New York: Scholastic.

Collodi, Carlo. (1904). *Pinocchio.* Boston: Ginn.

Colwell, Elizabeth. (1968, January). An oral tradition and an oral art: Folk literature. *Top of the News, 24,* 174–180.

Conner, Leslie. (2008). *Waiting for normal.* New York: Katherine Tegan/HarperCollins.

Conrad, Pam. (1990). *Stonewords.* New York: HarperCollins.

Cooper, Susan. (1999). *King of shadows.* New York: McElderry.

Cope, Bill, & Kalantzis, Mary (Eds.). (2000). *Multiliteracies: Literacy learning and the design of social futures.* London, UK: Routledge.

Cottin, Menena, & Faria, Rosana. (2008). *The black book of colors.* Toronto, ON, Canada: Groundwood.

Cowley, Joy. (2005). *Mrs. Wishy-Washy's splishy-sploshy day.* New York: Philomel.

Crews, Donald. (1978). *Freight train.* New York: Greenwillow.

Crews, Donald. (1996). *Freight train.* New York: Greenwillow.

Crews, Donald. (1999). *Cloudy day, sunny day.* New York: Harcourt.

Criscoe, Betty. (1988, Summer). A pleasant reminder: There is an established criteria for writing alphabet books. *Reading Horizons, 28*(4), 232–234.

Cullinan, Bernice E. (Ed). (1996). *A jar of tiny stars: Poems by NCTE Award–winning poets.* Honesdale, PA: Wordsong/Boyds Mills.

Cullinan, Bernice. (2000). Independent reading and school achievement. *School Library Media Research, 3.*

Cunningham, Anne E., & Stanovich, Keith E. (1998). What reading does for the mind. *American Educator, 22* (1 & 2), 8–15.

Cunningham, Anne E., & Stanovich, Keith E. (2003). Reading matters: How reading engagement influences cognition. In James Flood, Diane Lapp, James R. Squire, & Julie M. Jensen (Eds.), *Handbook of research on teaching the English language arts* (pp. 666–675). Mahwah, NJ: Erlbaum.

Curlee, Lynn. (2002). *The seven wonders of the ancient world.* New York: Atheneum.

Curtis, Christopher Paul. (1999). *Bud, not Buddy.* New York: Delacorte.

Dahl, Roald. (1961). *James and the giant peach.* New York: Knopf.

Dahl, Roald. (1964). *Charlie and the chocolate factory.* New York: Knopf.

Dahl, Roald. (1975). *Danny: The champion of the world.* New York: Knopf.

Dahl, Roald. (1983). *The witches.* New York: Farrar, Straus & Giroux.

Dahl, Roald. (1988). *Matilda.* New York: Viking.

Daniels, Harvey. (2002). *Literature circles, voice and choice in book clubs and reading groups.* Honesdale, PA: Stenhouse.

Darigan, Daniel. (1991). The effects of teachers reading aloud on elementary children's attitudes toward African Americans. Dissertation, University of Oregon, Eugene.

Daugherty, James. (1972). *James Daugherty* [Videocassette]. Weston, CT: Weston Woods.

d'Aulaire, Ingri, & d'Aulaire, Edgar. (1939). *Abraham Lincoln.* New York: Doubleday.

Davis, Kenneth C. (2003). *Don't know much about American history.* New York: HarperCollins.

Davis, Kenneth C. (2005). *Don't know much about mummies.* New York: HarperCollins.

Davis, Kenneth C. (2007). *Don't know much about anything.* New York: HarperCollins.

Davis, Kenneth C., & Davis, Jenny. (2009). *Don't know much about literature: What you need to know but never learned about great books and authors.* New York: HarperCollins.

Day, Jeni P., Spiegel, Dixie L., McLellan, Janet, & Brown, Valerie B. (2002). *Moving forward with literature circles.* New York: Scholastic.

Day, Jennifer Cheeseman, & Newburger, Eric C. (2002). *The big payoff: Educational attainment and synthetic estimates of work-life earnings.* Washington, DC: U.S. Census Bureau.

DeFelice, Cynthia. (2002, July 19). Speech presented at the Brigham Young University Symposium on Books for Young Readers, Provo, Utah.

Demi. (1997). *Buddha stories.* New York: Holt.

Denega, Danielle. (2007). *Gut-eating bugs: Maggots reveal the time of death!* Danbury, CT: Children's Press.

dePaola, Tomie. (1980). *The legend of Old Befana.* New York: Harcourt.

de Vinck, Christopher. (1991, Spring). An open book. *The College Board Review, 159,* 9–12.

DiCamillo, Kate. (2000). *Because of Winn-Dixie.* Cambridge, MA: Candlewick.

DiCamillo, Kate. (2006). *The miraculous journey of Edward Tulane.* Cambridge, MA: Candlewick.

DK Publishing. (2009). *The most fantastic atlas of the whole wide world . . . By The Brainwaves.* New York: Author.

Dodson, Peter. (1995). *An alphabet of dinosaurs.* New York: Scholastic.

Donelson, K. L., & Nilsen, A. P. (1989). *Literature for today's young adults.* Glenview, IL: Scott, Foresman.

Donovan, Melanie. (2006, May 18). Telephone interview with Michael O. Tunnell.

Dosani, Sabina, & Peter Cross. (2007). *Raising young children: 52 brilliant little ideas for parenting under 5's.* Oxford, UK: Infinite Idea Publishing.

Dowell, Francie O'Roark. (2000). *Dovey Coe.* New York: Atheneum.

Dowhower, Sarah L., & Beagle, Kimberly G. (1998). The print environment in kindergartens: A study of conventional and holistic teachers and their classrooms. *Reading Research and Instruction, 37,* 161–190.

Downey, Mathew T., & Levstik, Linda S. (1988, September). Teaching and learning history: The research base. *Social Education,* 336–342.

Doyle, Robert P. (2009). Books challenged and banned in 2008–2009: Speak, read, know. Retrieved from http://www.ala.org/ala/issuesadvocacy/banned/bannedbooksweek/ideasandresources/free_downloads/ 2009banned.pdf

Duke, Nell K. (2000). 3.6 minutes per day: The scarcity of informational texts in first grade. *Reading Research Quarterly, 35,* 202–224.

Duke, Nell K., Purcell-Gates, Victoria, Hall, Leigh A., & Tower, Cathy. (2006). Authentic literacy activities for developing comprehension and writing. *The Reading Teacher, 60,* 344–355.

Dygard, Thomas. (1998). *Second stringer.* New York: Morrow.

Edmunds, Kathryn M., & Bauserman, Kathryn L. (2006). What teachers can learn about reading motivation through conversations with children. *The Reading Teacher, 59,* 414–424.

Edwards, Roberta. (2009). *Who was George Washington?* Illustrated by True Kelley. New York: Grosset & Dunlap.

Eeds, Maryann, & Peterson, Ralph. (1997, Winter). Literature studies revisited: Some thoughts on talking with children about books. *The New Advocate, 10,* 49–59.

Ehlert, Lois. (1989). *Color zoo.* New York: Lippincott.

Ehlert, Lois. (2010). *Lots of spots.* New York: Beach Lane Books.

Engdahl, Sylvia Louise. (1970). *Enchantress from the stars.* New York: Atheneum.

Engdahl, Sylvia Louise. (1971, October). The changing role of science fiction in children's literature. *The Horn Book, 47,* 449–455.

Engle, Margarita. (2008). *The surrender tree.* New York: Holt.

Esbensen, Barbara Juster. (1995). *A celebration of bees: Helping children write poetry.* New York: Holt.

Facklam, Margery. (1990, July 12). Writing nonfiction. Speech given at the Highlights Writer's Conference, Chautauqua, New York.

Fader, Daniel. (1976). *Hooked on books.* New York: Berkley Books.

Fader, Daniel, Duggins, James, Finn, Tom, & McNeil, Elton. (1976). *The new hooked on books.* New York: Berkley.

Falconer, Ian. (2000). *Olivia.* New York: Atheneum.

Falconer, Ian. (2004). *Olivia.* New York: Atheneum.

Farley, Walter. (1941). *Black stallion.* New York: Random House.

Farmer, Nancy. (2002). *The house of the scorpion.* New York: Atheneum.

Farris, Pamela J., Werderich, Donna E., Nelson, Pamela A., & Fuhler, Carol J. (2009). Male call: Fifth-grade boys' reading preferences. *The Reading Teacher, 63,* 180–188.

Fawson, Parker C., & Moore, Sharon A. (1999). Reading incentive programs: Beliefs and practices. *Reading Psychology, 20,* 325–340.

Feldman, David. (2006). *Why do pirates love parrots?* New York: Collins.

Field, Rachel. (1944). *Prayer for a child.* New York: Macmillan.

Field, Rachel. (2005). *Prayer for a child.* New York: Simon & Schuster.

Fink, Rosalie. (2006). *Why Jane and John couldn't read—and how they learned: A new look at striving readers.* Newark, DE: International Reading Association.

Fischer, B. (Ed.). (1997, November). The bottom line. *NEA Today, 16*(4), 9.

Fisher, Douglas, & Ivey, Gay. (2007). Farewell to *A Farewell to Arms:* Deemphasizing the whole-class novel. *Phi Delta Kappan, 88,* 494–497.

Fitzhugh, Louise. (1964). *Harriet the spy.* New York: Harper.

Fleischman, Paul. (1988). *Joyful noise: Poems for two voices.* New York: Harper.

Fleming, Candace. (2005). *Our Eleanor: A scrapbook look at Eleanor Roosevelt.* New York: Schwartz & Wade.

Fleming, Candace. (2008). *The Lincolns: A scrapbook look at Abraham and Mary.* New York: Schwartz & Wade.

Fleming, Candace. (2009). *The great and only Barnum: The tremendous, stupendous life of showman P. T. Barnum.* New York: Schwartz & Wade.

Fleming, Candace. (2011). *Amelia lost: The life and disappearance of Amelia Earhart.* New York: Schwartz & Wade.

Fletcher, Susan. (1989). *Dragon's milk.* New York: Atheneum.

Fletcher, Susan. (2006, March 3). Personal letter to Michael O. Tunnell.

Foertsch, Mary. (1992, May). *Reading in and out of school.* Washington, DC: U.S. Department of Education.

Forbes, Darla. (2008). "I wanted to lie about my level." A self study: How my daughter's experiences with leveled books became a lens for re-imagining myself as a literacy educator. Unpublished master's thesis, University of Manitoba, Winnipeg, MB, Canada.

Forbes, Esther. (1943). *Johnny Tremain.* New York: Houghton Mifflin.

Forbringer, Linda L. (2004). The thirteen days of Halloween: Using children's literature to differentiate instruction in the mathematics classroom. *Teaching Children Mathematics, 11,* 82–90.

Foster, Stuart, Morris, J. W., & Davis, O. L. (1996, Summer). Prospects for teaching historical analysis and interpretation: National curriculum standards for history meet current history textbooks. *Journal of Curriculum and Supervision, 11*(4), 367–385.

Fox, Mem, & Denton, Terry. (1989). *Night noises.* Orlando, FL: Harcourt.

Fox, Paula. (1973). *The slave dancer.* Scarsdale, NY: Bradbury Press.

Freedman, Russell. (1980). *Immigrant kids.* New York: Dutton.

Freedman, Russell. (1987). *Lincoln: A photobiography.* New York: Clarion.

Freedman, Russell. (1991). *The Wright Brothers: How they invented the airplane.* New York: Holiday House.

Freedman, Russell. (1993a). Bring 'em back alive. In M. O. Tunnell & R. Ammon (Eds.), *The story of ourselves: Teaching history through children's literature.* Portsmouth, NH: Heinemann.

Freedman, Russell. (1993b). *Eleanor Roosevelt: A life of discovery.* New York: Clarion.

Freedman, Russell. (2004). *The voice that challenged the nation: Marian Anderson and the struggle for equal rights.* New York: Clarion.

Fresch, Mary J. (1995). Self-selection of early literacy learners. *The Reading Teacher, 49,* 220–227.

Fritz, Jean. (1977). *Can't you make them behave, King George?* New York: Coward, McCann & Geoghegan.

Fritz, Jean. (1980). *Where do you think you're going, Christopher Columbus?* New York: Putnam.

Fritz, Jean. (1982). *Homesick: My own story.* New York: Putnam.

Fritz, Jean. (1988, November/December). Biography: Readability plus responsibility. *The Horn Book, 64*(6), 759–760.

Fritz, Jean. (1991). *Bully for you, Teddy Roosevelt!* New York: Putnam.

Fritz, Jean. (1994). *Harriet Beecher Stowe and the Beecher preachers.* New York: Putnam.

Fritz, Jean. (1999). *Why not, Lafayette?* New York: Putnam.

Frost, Robert. (1978). *Stopping by woods on a snowy evening.* Illustrated by Susan Jeffers. New York: Dutton. (Original work published 1923)

Frye, Northrop. (1964). *The educated imagination.* Bloomington: University of Indiana Press.

Gág, Wanda. (1928). *Millions of cats.* New York: Coward McCann.

Gagliano, Eugene M. (2003). *C is for cowboy: A Wyoming alphabet.* Chelsea, MI: Sleeping Bear Press.

Gaiman, Neil. (2008). *The graveyard book.* New York: HarperCollins.

Galda, Lee, Cullinan, Bernice E., & Sipe, Lawrence R. (2010). *Literature and the child.* Belmont, CA: Wadsworth.

Gambrell, Linda B., & Marinak, Barbara A. (2009, May). *Classroom practices that support reading motivation: Findings from recent investigations.* Paper presented at the 54th annual convention of the International Reading Association (North Central), Minneapolis, MN.

Gardiner, John. (1980). *Stone Fox.* New York: Crowell.

Gee, James P. (2000). The new literacy studies: From "socially situated" to the work of the social. In David Barton, Mary Hamilton, & Roz Ivani (Eds.), *Situated literacies: Reading and writing in context* (pp. 180–196). London, UK: Routledge.

Gee, James P. (2004). *Situated language and learning: A critique of traditional schooling.* New York: Routledge.

George, Jean Craighead. (1959). *My side of the mountain.* New York: Dutton.

George, Jean Craighead. (1972). *Julie of the wolves.* New York: Harper.

Gibbons, Gail. (2010). *Alligators and crocodiles.* New York: Holiday House.

Giblin, James Cross. (2002). *The life and death of Adolf Hitler.* New York: Clarion.

Giblin, James Cross. (2005). *Good brother, bad brother: The story of Edwin Booth and John Wilkes Booth.* New York: Clarion.

Giblin, James Cross. (2009). *The rise and fall of Senator Joe McCarthy.* New York: Clarion.

Gillis, Jennifer Blizen. (2002). *Candle time ABC.* Chicago: Heinemann Library.

Gipson, Fred. (1962). *Savage Sam.* New York: Harper.

Golenbock, Peter. (1990). *Teammates.* Illustrated by Paul Bacon. New York: Harcourt Brace.

Goodman, Kenneth. (1988, Fall). Look what they've done to Judy Blume! The basalization of children's literature. *The New Advocate, 1*(1), 29–41.

Grahame, Kenneth. (1908). *The wind in the willows.* London, UK: Methuen.

Greene, Carol, & Raglin, Tim. (2000). *The 13 days of Halloween.* Mahwah, NY: Troll.

Greenlee, Adele A., Monson, Dianne L., & Taylor, Barbara M. (1996, November). The lure of series books: Does it affect appreciation for recommended literature? *The Reading Teacher, 50*(3), 216–225.

Grimm Brothers. (1972). *Snow-White and the seven dwarfs.* Translated by Randall Jarrell. Illustrated by Nancy Eckholm Burkert. New York: Farrar, Straus & Giroux.

Grimm Brothers. (1975). *Thorn Rose.* Illustrated by Errol Le Cain. New York: Bradbury.

Grossman, Bill, & Hawkes, Kevin. (1996). *My little sister ate one hare.* New York: Random House.

Guthrie, John T., Schafer, William D., & Huang, Chun-Wei. (2001). Benefits of opportunity to read and balanced instruction on the NAEP. *Journal of Educational Research, 94,*145–162.

Guthrie, John T., Wigfield, Allan, Metsala, Jamie L., & Cox, Kathleen E. (1999). Motivational and cognitive predictors of text comprehension and reading amount. *Scientific Studies of Reading, 3,* 231–256.

Gutman, Dan. (2008). *Jim and me.* New York: HarperCollins.

Gutman, Dan. (2009). *Ray and me.* New York: HarperCollins.

Gutman, Dan. (2010). *Roberto and me.* New York: HarperCollins.

Haferd, Laura. (1988, April 23). Activist leads fight against "subliminals." *Akron (Ohio) Beacon Journal.*

Hahn, Mary Downing. (1985). *Wait till Helen comes: A ghost story.* New York: Houghton Mifflin.

Haley, Alex. (1976). *Roots.* New York: Doubleday.

Haley, Gail. (1970). *A story, a story.* New York: Atheneum.

Hamilton, Virginia. (1974). *M. C. Higgins, the great.* New York: Macmillan.

Hamilton, Virginia. (1988). *In the beginning: Creation stories from around the world.* New York: Harcourt.

Handford, Martin. (2006). *Where's Waldo? The great picture hunt.* Cambridge, MA: Candlewick.

Hansen, S. (2004). Fourth and fifth graders' poetry preferences before and after classroom poetry experiences: A case study. Unpublished manuscript, University of Minnesota.

Hansen-Krening, Nancy. (1992, October). Authors of color: A multicultural perspective. *Journal of Reading, 36*(2), 124–129.

Harley, Avis. (2000). *Fly with poetry: An ABC of poetry.* Honesdale, PA: Wordsong/Boyds Mills Press.

Harley, Avis. (2001). *Leap into poetry: More ABCs of poetry.* Honesdale, PA: Wordsong/Boyds Mills Press.

Harris, Robie. (2006). *It's not the stork! A book about girls, boys, babies, bodies, families, and friends.* Cambridge, MA: Candlewick.

Harvey, James S. (1971, March). *Newsletter on Intellectual Freedom,* 44–45.

Hautzig, Esther. (1968). *The endless steppe.* New York: Crowell.

Hayden, Torey. (2003). *The very worst thing.* New York: HarperCollins.

Haynes, Carol. (1988). The explanatory power of content for identifying children's literature preferences. Unpublished doctoral dissertation, Northern Illinois University, DeKalb, IL.

Hedges, Chris. (2009). *Empire of illusion.* New York: Nation Books.

Heller, Ruth. (1988). *Kites sail high: A book about verbs.* New York: Grosset & Dunlap.

Heller, Ruth. (1997). *Mine, all mine: A book about pronouns.* New York: Grosset & Dunlap.

Heller, Ruth. (1998). *Fantastic! Wow! and Unreal! A book about interjections and conjunctions.* New York: Grosset & Dunlap.

Helprin, Mark. (1989). *Swan Lake.* Boston: Houghton Mifflin.

Henderson, Douglas. (2000). *Asteroid impact.* New York: Dial.

Henkes, Kevin. (1990). *Julius, the baby of the world.* New York: Greenwillow.

Henry, Marguerite. (1945). *Justin Morgan had a horse.* Chicago: Wilcox & Follett.

Henry, Marguerite. (1947). *Misty of Chincoteague.* Chicago: Rand McNally.

Henry, Marguerite. (1948). *King of the wind.* Chicago: Rand McNally.

Hepworth, Cathi. (1992). *Antics! An alphabetical anthology.* New York: Putnam.

Hesse, Karen. (1997). *Out of the dust.* New York: Scholastic.

Hiaasen, Carl. (2002). *Hoot.* New York: Random House.

Hidi, Suzanne, Baird, William, & Hildyard, Angela. (1982). That's important but is it interesting? Two factors in text processing. In August Flammer & Walter Kintsch (Eds.), *Discourse processing.* Amsterdam, The Netherlands: Elsevier-North Holland.

Hiebert, Elfrieda H., & Martin, Leigh A. (2009). Opportunity to read: A critical but neglected construct in reading instruction. In Elfrieda H. Hiebert (Ed.), *Read more, read better* (pp. 3–29). New York: Guilford Press.

Highwater, Jamake. (1994). *Rama: A legend.* New York: Harper.

Hill, Eric. (2010). *Spot's hide and seek.* New York: Putnam.

Hillman, Ben. (2007). *How big is it?* New York: Scholastic.

Hillman, Ben. (2008). *How strong is it?* New York: Scholastic.

Hoban, Tana. (1972). *Push-pull, empty-full: A book of opposites.* New York: Macmillan.

Hoban, Tana. (1978). *Is it red? Is it yellow? Is it blue?* New York: Greenwillow.

Hoban, Tana. (1986). *Shapes, shapes, shapes.* New York: Greenwillow.

Hoban, Tana. (1990). *Exactly the opposite.* New York: Greenwillow.

Hoban, Tana. (1996). *Just look.* New York: Greenwillow.

Hoban, Tana. (1998). *So many circles, so many squares.* New York: Greenwillow.

Hoban, Tana. (2000). *Cubes, cones, cylinders & spheres.* New York: Greenwillow.

Hobbs, Will. (1992). *The big wander.* New York: Atheneum.

Hobbs, Will. (2006). *Crossing the wire.* New York: HarperCollins.

Hodges, Margaret. (1984). *Saint George and the dragon.* Illustrated by Trina Schart Hyman. Boston: Little, Brown.

Hoeye, Michael. (2002). *Time stops for no mouse.* New York: Putnam.

Holdaway, Don. (1982). Shared book experience: Teaching reading using favorite books. *Theory into Practice, 21,* 293–300.

Hollyer, Beatrice. (2008). *Our world of water: Children and water around the world.* New York: Henry Holt.

Hollyer, Belinda. (2003). *The Kingfisher book of family poems.* New York: Kingfisher.

Holman, Felice. (1974). *Slake's limbo.* New York: Scribner's.

Holmes, Betty, & Ammon, Richard. (1985, May/June). Teaching content with trade books: A strategy. *Childhood Education, 61*(5), 366–370.

Hoose, Phillip. (2001). *We were there, too! Young people in U.S. history.* New York: Farrar.

Hoose, Phillip. (2009). *Claudette Colvin: Twice toward justice.* New York: Farrar, Straus, & Giroux.

Hopkins, Lee Bennett. (1997). *Marvelous math: A book of poems.* New York: Simon & Schuster.

Hopkins, Lee Bennett. (1999). *Spectacular science: A book of poems.* New York: Simon & Schuster.

Hopkins, Lee Bennett. (2006). *Got geography! Poems.* New York: Greenwillow.

Hopkins, Lee Bennett. (2008). *America at war.* New York: McElderry.

Horn, Miriam. (1993). Imagining others' lives. *U.S. News and World Report, 114*(6), 78–81.

Horowitz, Anthony. (2004). *Eagle strike.* New York: Philomel.

Huck, Charlotte. (1982, Autumn). I give you the end of a golden string. *Theory into Practice, 12*(4), 315–325.

Hughes, Langston. (2009). *My people.* New York: Atheneum.

Hunt, Irene. (2002). *The lottery rose.* New York: Berkley/Penguin. (Original work published 1976)

Hunt, Jonathan. (1998). *Beastiary: An illuminated alphabet of medieval beasts.* New York: Simon & Schuster.

Hunt, Lyman C., Jr. (1996–1997). The effect of self-selection, interest, and motivation upon independent, instructional, and frustrational levels. *The Reading Teacher, 50,* 278–282.

Hunter, Mollie. (1974). *The stronghold.* New York: Harper.

Hunter, Mollie. (1976). *Talent is not enough.* New York: Harper & Row.

Hutchins, Pat. (1968). *Rosie's walk.* New York: Macmillan.

Hyman, Trina Schart. (1995, January 27). Telephone interview with Elena Rockmany.

Irvine, Joan. (2005). *Easy-to-make pop-ups.* New York: Dover.

Isaacson, Philip M. (2001). *Round buildings, square buildings, & buildings that wiggle like a fish.* New York: Knopf.

Isadora, Rachel. (1979). *Ben's trumpet.* New York: Greenwillow.

Ivey, Gay, & Broaddus, Karen. (2001). "Just plain reading": A survey of what makes students want to read in middle school classrooms. *Reading Research Quarterly, 36,* 350–377.

Jackson, Donna M. (2009). *Extreme scientists: Exploring nature's mysteries from perilous places.* Boston: Houghton Mifflin Harcourt.

Jackson, Ellen. (2008). *The mysterious universe: Supernovae, dark energy, and black holes.* Boston: Houghton Mifflin.

Jaeger, Elizabeth. (2006). Silencing teachers in an era of scripted reading. *Rethinking Schools Online, 20*(3). Retrieved from http://www.rethinkingschools.org/archive/20_03/sile203.shtml

Janeczko, Paul B. (2005). *A kick in the head: An everyday guide to poetic forms.* Cambridge, MA: Candlewick.

Jenkins, Emily, & Pratt, Pierre. (2008). *Skunk dog.* New York: Farrar, Straus & Giroux.

Jenkins, Steve. (2006). *Almost gone: The world's rarest animals.* New York: Collins.

Johnson, Stephen T. (1995). *Alphabet City.* New York: Viking.

Jonas, Ann. (1983). *Round trip.* New York: Greenwillow.

Jones, David. (2007). *Baboon.* Toronto, ON, Canada: Annick.

Jones, H. Jon, Coombs, William T., & McKinney, Warren C. (1994, Winter). A themed literature unit versus a textbook: A comparison of the effects on content acquisition and attitudes in elementary social studies. *Reading Research and Instruction, 34,* 85–96.

Jones, Ivan, & Jones, Mal. (2000). *Good night, sleep tight.* New York: Scholastic.

Jones, Patrick. (2005). Wrestling with reading. In John Scieszka (Ed.), *Guys write for guys read* (pp. 127–129). New York: Viking.

Jordan, Amy B., Hersey, James C., McDivitt, Judith A., & Heitzler, Carrie D. (2006). Reducing children's television viewing time: A qualitative study of parents and their children. *Pediatrics, 118,* 1303–1310.

Juel, C., Griffith, P. I., & Gough, P. B. (1986). Acquisition of literacy: A longitudinal study of children in first and second grade. *Journal of Educational Psychology, 78,* 243–255.

Kadohata, Cynthia. (2004). *Kira-Kira.* New York: Atheneum.

Kaniut, Larry. (2003). *Alaska bear tales.* Anchorage, AK: Alaska Northwest.

Kasza, Keiko. (1996). *The wolf's chicken stew.* New York: Putnam & Grosset.

Keats, Ezra Jack. (1962). *The snowy day.* New York: Viking.

Kelley, True. (2005). *Pierre-Auguste Renoir: Paintings that smile.* New York: Grosset & Dunlap.

Kelly, Cathal. (2010, January 26). U.S. school bans the dictionary. *TheStar.com.* Retrieved from http://www.thestar.com/news/world/article/755936—u-s-school-bans-the-dictionary

Kiefer, Barbara Z. (1995). *The potential of picturebooks: From visual literacy to aesthetic understanding.* Upper Saddle River, NJ: Merrill/Prentice-Hall.

Kjelgaard, Jim. (1945). *Big Red.* New York: Holiday House.

Klutz Press. (1992). *Kids shenanigans: Great things to do that Mom and Dad will just barely approve of.* Palo Alto, CA: Author.

Knight, Eric. (1940). *Lassie, come home.* Chicago: John C. Winston.

Kobrin, Beverly. (1988). *Eyeopeners!* New York: Viking.

Konigsburg, E. L. (1970, February 15). Double image. *Library Journal, 95,* 731–734.

Korman, Gordon. (1998). *The 6th grade nickname game.* New York: Scholastic.

Korman, Gordon. (2005). *Chasing the falconers.* New York: Scholastic.

Korman, Gordon. (2007). *Schooled.* New York: Hyperion.

Korman, Gordon. (2009). *Zoobreak.* New York: Scholastic.

Krashen, Stephen D. (2004). *The power of reading: Insights from the research.* Westport, CT: Libraries Unlimited.

Krathwohl, David R., Bloom, Benjamin S., & Masia, Bertram B. (1964). *Taxonomy of educational objectives, handbook II: Affective domain.* New York: David McKay.

Krementz, Jill. (1992). *How it feels to live with a physical disability.* New York: Simon & Schuster.

Krementz, Jill. (2007). *A very young writer.* New York: Dream House.

Krull, Kathleen. (1993). *Lives of the musicians: Good times, bad times (and what the neighbors thought).* Illustrated by Kathryn Hewitt. New York: Harcourt.

Krull, Kathleen. (1997). *Lives of the athletes: Thrills, spills (and what the neighbors thought).* Illustrated by Kathryn Hewitt. New York: Harcourt.

Krull, Kathleen. (1998). *Lives of the presidents: Fame, shame (and what the neighbors thought).* Illustrated by Kathryn Hewitt. New York: Harcourt.

Krull, Kathleen. (2003). *M is for music.* New York: Harcourt.

Krull, Kathleen. (2009). *The boy who invented TV: The story of Philo Farnsworth.* Illustrated by Greg Couch. New York: Knopf.

Krull, Kathleen. (2010). *Lives of the pirates: Swashbucklers, scoundrels (neighbors beware!).* Illustrated by Kathryn Hewitt. New York: Harcourt.

Krumgold, Joseph. (1953). *. . . And now Miguel.* New York: Crowell.

Kudlinski, Kathleen V. (2005). *Boy, were we wrong about dinosaurs!* New York: Dutton.

Kunhardt, Dorothy. (1940). *Pat the bunny.* Racine, WI: Western.

Kutiper, Karen, & Wilson, Patricia. (1993, September). Updating poetry preferences: A look at the poetry children really like. *The Reading Teacher, 47*(1), 28–35.

Lane, Kimberly. (2008). *Come look with me: Asian art.* Watertown, MA: Charlesbridge.

Larrick, Nancy. (1965, September 11). The all white world of children's books. *Saturday Review,* pp. 63–65, 84–85.

Lasky, Kathryn. (1983a). *Beyond the divide.* New York: Macmillan.

Lasky, Kathryn. (1983b). *Sugaring time.* New York: Macmillan.

Lasky, Kathryn. (1990, Summer). The fiction of history: Or, what did Miss Kitty really do? *The New Advocate, 3*(3), 157–166.

Lasky, Kathryn. (2000). *Vision of beauty: The story of Sarah Breedlove Walker.* Illustrated by Nneka Bennett. Cambridge, MA: Candlewick.

Lasky, Kathryn. (2009). *Georgia rises: A day in the life of Georgia O'Keeffe.* Illustrated by Ora Eitan. New York: Farrar.

Lattimore, Deborah. (1998). *I wonder what's under there? A brief history of underwear.* San Diego: Harcourt.

Lauber, Patricia. (1986). *Volcano: The eruption and healing of Mount St. Helens.* New York: Bradbury.

Lauber, Patricia. (1998). *Painters of the caves.* Washington, DC: National Geographic Society.

Lauber, Patricia. (2001). *What you never knew about tubs, toilets, and showers.* New York: Simon & Schuster.

Lear, Edward. (1863). *Book of nonsense.* Philadelphia: W. P. Hazard.

Lee, Harper. (1960). *To kill a mockingbird.* New York: Lippincott.

Lee, Melissa. (1994, July 22). When it comes to salary, it's academic. *The Washington Post,* p. D1.

Lefrancois, Guy R. (1986). *Of children.* Belmont, CA: Wadsworth.

Lemna, Don. (2008). *When the sergeant came marching home.* New York: Holiday House.

L'Engle, Madeleine. (1962). *A wrinkle in time.* New York: Farrar, Straus & Giroux.

L'Engle, Madeleine. (1980). *Walking on water: Reflections on faith and art.* Wheaton, IL: H. Shaw.

Lenski, Lois. (1946). *The little fire engine.* New York: Random House. (Rereleased in 2000)

Levstik, Linda. (1989). A gift of time: Children's historical fiction. In Janet Hickman & Bernice Cullinan (Eds.), *Children's literature in the classroom: Weaving Charlotte's web* (pp. 135–145). Needham Heights, MA: Christopher-Gordon.

Lewis, C. S. (1950). *The lion, the witch and the wardrobe.* New York: Macmillan.

Lewis, C. S. (1980). *On stories and other essays on literature.* New York: Harcourt.

Lewis, J. Patrick. (2004). *Scien-trickery: Riddles in science.* New York: Silver Whistle/Harcourt.

Lin, Grace. (2008). *The year of the rat.* New York: Little Brown.

Lithgow, John. (2000). *Marsupial Sue.* New York: Simon & Schuster.

Livingston, Myra Cohn. (1986). *Poems for Jewish holidays.* Holiday House.

Livingston, Myra Cohn. (1987a). *Cat poems.* New York: Holiday House.

Livingston, Myra Cohn. (1987b). *Valentine poems.* New York: Holiday House.

Livingston, Myra Cohn. (1988). *Poems for mothers.* New York: Holiday House.

Livingston, Myra Cohn. (1989a). *Birthday poems.* New York: Holiday House.

Livingston, Myra Cohn. (1989b). *Halloween poems.* New York: Holiday House.

Livingston, Myra Cohn. (1994). *Animal, vegetable, mineral: Poems about small things.* New York: HarperCollins.

Livingston, Myra Cohn. (1997). *Cricket never does: A collection of haiku and tanka.* New York: McElderry.

Lobel, Arnold. (1970). *Frog and Toad are friends.* New York: Harper & Row.

Lobel, Arnold. (1972). *Frog and Toad together.* New York: Harper & Row.

Lobel, Arnold. (1981). *On Market Street.* Illustrated by Anita Lobel. New York: Greenwillow.

Locke, John. (1693). *Some thoughts concerning education* (1709 ed.). London, UK: A. and J. Churchill.

Loewen, James. (1995, January). By the book. *The American School Board Journal, 182*(1), 24–27.

Longfellow, Henry Wadsworth. (2001). *The midnight ride of Paul Revere.* Illustrated by Christopher Bing. New York: Handprint. (Original work published 1860)

Lonsdale, Bernard J., & Mackintosh, Helen K. (1973). *Children experience literature.* New York: Random House.

Louie, Ai-Ling. (1990). *Yeh-Shen.* New York: Philomel.

Lowry, Lois. (1977). *A summer to die.* Boston: Houghton Mifflin.

Lowry, Lois. (1989). *Number the stars.* Boston: Houghton Mifflin.

Lowry, Lois. (1993). *The giver.* New York: Houghton Mifflin.

Lowry, Lois. (2008). A dangerous utopia. *Random House, Inc., 3*(1), 54–55.

MacDonald, Fiona. (2004). *You wouldn't want to sail with Christopher Columbus: Uncharted waters you'd rather not cross.* Canbury, CT: Franklin Watts.

MacDonald, Suse. (1986). *Alphabatics.* New York: Bradbury.

MacGillivray, Laurie, Ardell, Amy L., Curwen, Margaret S., & Palma, Jennifer. (2004). Colonized teachers: Examining the implementation of a scripted reading program. *Teaching Education, 15,* 131–144.

Madsen, Linda Lee. (1976). Fantasy in children's literature: A generic study. Unpublished master's thesis, Utah State University, Logan, UT.

Mahy, Margaret. (1987). *17 kings and 42 elephants.* Illustrated by Patricia McCarthy. New York: Dial.

Malinsky, Marci A., & McJunkin, Mark. (2008). Wondrous tales of measurement. *Teaching Children Mathematics, 14,* 410–413.

Markle, Sandra. (2000). *Outside and inside dinosaurs.* New York: Atheneum.

Marmot, Michael. (2005). Life at the top. *New York Times Weekend,* February 27, p. 13.

Marrin, Albert. (2009). *Years of dust: The story of the Dust Bowl.* New York: Dutton.

Marsalis, Wynton. (2005). *Jazz A-B-Z: An A to Z collection of jazz portraits.* Cambridge, MA: Candlewick.

Martin, Ann. (2003). *A corner of the universe.* New York: Scholastic.

Martin, Ann. (2005). *A dog's life: The autobiography of a stray.* New York: Scholastic.

Martin, Bill, Jr. (1967). *Brown bear, brown bear, what do you see?* Illustrated by Eric Carle. New York: Holt, Rinehart & Winston. (Rereleased in 1992)

Martin, Bill, Jr. (1972). *Sounds of mystery.* New York: Holt, Rinehart & Winston.

Martin, Bill, Jr. (1991). *Polar bear, polar bear, what do you hear?* Illustrated by Eric Carle. New York: Henry Holt.

Martin, Bill, Jr. (2003). *Panda bear, panda bear, what do you see?* Illustrated by Eric Carle. New York: Henry Holt.

Martin, Bill, Jr. (2007). *Baby bear, baby bear, what do you see?* Illustrated by Eric Carle. New York: Henry Holt.

Martin, Rafe. (1992). *The rough-face girl.* New York: Putnam.

Martinez, Miriam G., & McGee, Lea M. (2000). Children's literature and reading instruction: Past, present, and future. *Reading Research Quarterly, 35,* 154–169.

Mayer, Mercer. (1967). *A boy, a dog, and a frog.* New York: Dial.

Mayer, Mercer. (1974). *Frog goes to dinner.* New York: Dial.

McClintock, Barbara. (2005). *Cinderella.* New York: Scholastic.

McCloskey, Robert. (1941). *Make way for ducklings.* New York: Viking.

McCloskey, Robert. (1948). *Blueberries for Sal.* New York: Viking.

McCloskey, Robert. (1965). *The lively art of picture books* [Videocassette]. Weston, CT: Weston Woods.

McClure, Amy. (1985). Children's responses to poetry in a supportive literary context. Unpublished doctoral dissertation, Ohio State University, Columbus, OH.

McDermott, Gerald. (1974a). *Arrow to the sun.* New York: Viking.

McDermott, Gerald. (1974b, September 26). Image in film and picture book. Speech given at the University of Georgia, Athens, GA.

McDermott, Gerald. (1993). *Raven.* New York: Harcourt.

McDermott, Gerald. (1997). *Musicians of the sun.* New York: Simon & Schuster.

McDermott, Gerald. (2001). *Jabuti the tortoise: A trickster tale from the Amazon.* New York: Harcourt.

McDermott, Gerald. (2003). *Creation.* New York: Dutton.

McDermott, Gerald. (2009). *Pig-Boy: A trickster tale from Hawai'i.* New York: Harcourt.

McGowan, Tom, & Guzzetti, Barbara. (1991, January/February). Promoting social studies understanding through literature-based instruction. *The Social Studies, 82*(1), 16–21.

McKinley, Robin. (1978). *Beauty.* New York: HarperCollins.

McLimans, David. (2006). *Gone wild.* New York: Walker.

McMillan, Bruce. (1993). *Mouse views: What the class pet saw.* New York: Holiday House.

McPhail, David. (1984). *Fix-it.* New York: Dutton.

McPhail, David. (2002). *Fix-it.* New York: Dutton.

McSwigan, Marie. (1942). *Snow treasure.* New York: Dutton.

Meek, Margaret. (1991). *On being literate.* London, UK: Bodley Head.

Meltzer, Milton. (1984). *The black Americans: A history in their own words.* New York: Crowell.

Meltzer, Milton. (1990). *Columbus and the world around him.* New York: Watts.

Meltzer, Milton. (1993). *Gold: The true story of why people search for it, mine it, trade it, steal it, mint it, hoard it, shape it, wear it, fight and kill for it.* New York: HarperCollins.

Meyer, Stephenie. (2005). *Twilight.* Boston: Little, Brown.

Michaels, Anna. (2004). *Best friends.* Illustrated by G. Brian Karas. New York: Harcourt.

Micklethwait, Lucy. (2004). *I spy shapes in art.* New York: Greenwillow.

Micklethwait, Lucy. (2007). *I spy colors in art.* New York: Greenwillow.

Micklos, John, Jr. (1996, September). 30 years of minorities in children's books. *The Education Digest, 62*(1), 61–64.

Miele, Madeline, & Prakken, Sarah (Eds.). (1975). *The Bowker annual of library and book trade information* (20th ed.). New York: R. R. Bowker.

Miller, Margaret. (1998). *Big and little.* New York: Greenwillow.

Milne, A. A. (1926). *Winnie-the-Pooh.* New York: Dutton.

Minarik, Else. (1957). *Little Bear.* Illustrated by Maurice Sendak. New York: Harper.

Moje, Elizabeth B. (2000). *"All the stories that we have": Adolescents' insights about literacy and learning in secondary schools.* Newark, DE: International Reading Association.

Moje, Elizabeth B. (2009, May). Youth popular literacies and school literacies: Exploring the in-between. Paper presented at the 54th annual convention of the International Reading Association (North Central), Minneapolis, MN.

Morpurgo, Michael. (2003). *Kensuke's kingdom.* New York: Scholastic.

Morrow, Lesley M. (1992). The impact of a literature-based program on literacy achievement, use of literature, and attitudes of children from minority backgrounds. *Reading Research Quarterly, 27,* 250–275.

Morrow, Lesley M. (2003). Motivating lifelong voluntary readers. In J. Flood, D. Lapp, J. Squire, & J. M. Jensen (Eds.), *Handbook of research on teaching the English language arts* (2nd ed., pp. 857–867). Mahwah, NJ: Erlbaum.

Morrow, Lesley M. (2004). Motivation: The forgotten factor. *Reading Today, 21*(5), 6.

Morrow, Leslie M. (2005). *Literacy development in the early years: Helping children read and* write. Boston: Allyn & Bacon.

Morrow, Lesley M., Connor, Ellen M., & Smith, Jeffrey K. (1990). Effects of a story reading program on the literacy development of at-risk kindergarten children. *Journal of Reading Behavior, 22,* 255–275.

Morrow, Lesley M., Tracey, Diane H., Woo, Deborah G., & Pressley, Michael. (1999). Characteristics of exemplary first-grade literacy instruction. *The Reading Teacher, 52,* 464–476.

Moses, Will. (2003). *Will Moses Mother Goose.* New York: Philomel.

Moss, B., & Young, T. A. (2010). *Creating lifelong readers through independent reading.* Newark, DE: International Reading Association.

Moss, Elaine. (1977). What is a good book? In Margaret Meek, Aiden Warlow, & Griselda Barton (Eds.), *The cool web.* London, UK: Bodley Head.

Mowat, Farley. (1956). *Lost in the barrens.* New York: Little, Brown.

Mowat, Farley. (1961). *Owls in the family.* New York: Little, Brown.

Moyer, R., Daniel, L., Hackett, J., Prentice, B. H., Stryker, P., & Vasquez, J. (Eds.). (2002). *Science.* New York: Macmillan/McGraw-Hill.

Murphy, Jim. (1990). *The boys' war.* New York: Clarion.

Murphy, Jim. (1995). *The great fire.* New York: Scholastic.

Murphy, Jim. (2003). *An American plague: The true and terrifying story of the yellow fever epidemic of 1793.* New York: Clarion.

Murphy, Jim. (2009). *Truce: The day the soldiers stopped fighting.* New York: Scholastic.

Murray, J. (1997, December 15). "Marguerite Henry—(1902–1997)." *Publishers Weekly,* 27.

Myracle, Lauren. (2009). *Luv ya bunches.* New York: Amulet.

Nagy, William E., & Anderson, Richard C. (1984). How many words are there in printed school English? *Reading Research Quarterly, 19,* 304–330.

National Children's Book and Literary Alliance. (2008). *Our White House: Looking in, looking out.* Cambridge, MA: Candlewick.

Naylor, Phyllis Reynolds. (1991). *Shiloh.* New York: Atheneum.

Nelson, Kadir. (2008). *We are the ship: The story of Negro baseball.* New York: Jump at the Sun/ Hyperion.

Nelson, R. A. (2005). *Teach me.* New York: Razorbill.

Neuman, Susan B. (1997). *Getting books in children's hands: The book flood of '96. Final report to the William Penn Foundation.* Philadelphia: Temple University.

Neuman, Susan B. (1999). Books make a difference: A study of access to literacy. *Reading Research Quarterly, 34,* 286–311.

Neuman, Susan B., & Celano, Donna. (2001). Books Aloud: A campaign to "put books in children's hands." *The Reading Teacher, 54,* 550–557.

Nieto, Sonia. (2000). *Affirming diversity* (3rd ed.). White Plains, NY: Longman.

Norris, Michael, & Warren Pawlowski. (2009). *Children's publishing market forecast 2010.* Stamford, CT: Simba Information.

Norton, Mary. (1953). *The borrowers.* New York: Harcourt Brace.

Noyes, Deborah. (2008). *Encyclopedia of the end: Mysterious death in fact, fancy, folklore, and more.* Boston: Houghton Mifflin.

Numeroff, Laura Joffe. (1985). *If you give a mouse a cookie.* Illustrated by Felicia Bond. New York: Harper.

Numeroff, Laura Joffe. (2008). *If you give a cat a cupcake.* Illustrated by Felicia Bond. New York: Harper.

O'Dell, Scott. (1960). *Island of the blue dolphins.* Boston: Houghton Mifflin.

O'Dell, Scott. (1980). *Sarah Bishop.* New York: Houghton Mifflin.

O'Flahavan, John, Gambrell, Linda B., Guthrie, John, Stahl, Stephen, & Alvermann, Donna. (1992). Poll results guide activities of research center. *Reading Today, 10*(1), 12.

Oppenheim, Shulamith Levey. (1996). *And the Earth trembled: The creation of Adam and Eve.* New York: Harcourt.

Ormrod, Jeanne E. (1998). *Educational psychology: Developing learners* (2nd ed.). Upper Saddle River, NJ: Merrill Prentice-Hall.

Osborne, Mary Pope. (1996). *One world, many religions: The ways we worship.* New York: Knopf.

Oxenbury, Helen. (1981a). *Dressing.* New York: Wanderer Books.

Oxenbury, Helen. (1981b). *Family.* New York: Wanderer Books.

Oxenbury, Helen. (1981c). *Friends.* New York: Wanderer Books.

Oxenbury, Helen. (1981d). *Playing.* New York: Wanderer Books.

Oxenbury, Helen. (1981e). *Working.* New York: Wanderer Books.

Pachtman, Andrew B., & Wilson, Karen A. (2006). What do the kids think? *The Reading Teacher, 59,* 680–684.

Palotta, Jerry. (2001). *The boat alphabet book.* Watertown, MA: Charlesbridge.

Park, Linda Sue. (2001). *A single shard.* New York: Clarion.

Parker, Steve. (1998). *The human body: And how it works.* Illustrated by Giovanni Caselli. New York: Dorling Kindersley.

Parnell, Peter, & Richardson, Justin. (2005). *And Tango makes three.* New York: Simon & Schuster.

Parsons, Alexandra. (1990). *Amazing mammals.* New York: Dorling Kindersley.

Pate, Glenn S. (1988, April/May). Research on reducing prejudice. *Social Education, 52*(4), 287–291.

Paterson, Katherine. (1977). *Bridge to Terabithia.* New York: Crowell.

Paterson, Katherine. (1978). *The great Gilly Hopkins.* New York: Crowell.

Patron, Susan. (2006). *The higher power of lucky.* New York: Atheneum.

Pattou, Edith. (2003). *East.* New York: Harcourt.

Paulsen, Gary. (1987, January 29). Books and early reading. Speech given to Clarke County Library Association, Las Vegas, NV.

Paulsen, Gary. (1987). *Hatchet.* New York: Viking.

Paulsen, Gary. (1993). *Nightjohn.* New York: Delacorte.

Paver, Michelle. (2004). *Wolf brother.* New York: HarperCollins.

Paxton, Richard J. (1999, Fall). A deafening silence: History textbooks and the students who read them. *Review of Educational Research, 69*(3), 315–339.

Peck, Richard. (1979). *The secrets of the shopping mall.* New York: Delacorte.

Peet, Bill. (1967). *Buford the little bighorn.* Boston: Houghton Mifflin.

Peet, Bill. (1989). *Bill Peet: An autobiography.* New York: Houghton Mifflin.

Pelta, Kathy. (1991). *Discovering Christopher Columbus: How history is invented.* Minneapolis, MN: Lerner.

Perez, Samuel A. (1986). Children see, children do: Teachers as reading models. *The Reading Teacher, 40,* 8–11.

Perie, M., Moran, R., & Lutkus, A. D. (2005). *NAEP 2004 trends in academic progress: Three decades of student performance in reading and mathematics* (pp. 36–38). Washington, DC: U.S. Department of Education, National Center for Educational Studies.

Peterson, Ralph, & Eeds, Maryann. (1990). *Grand conversations: Literature groups in action.* Richmond Hill, ON, Canada: Scholastic.

Petty, Kate, & Maizels, Jennie. (2001). *The amazing pop-up geography book.* New York: Dutton.

Peyton, K. M. (2001). *Blind Beauty.* New York: Dutton.

Phineas, Sarah. (2008). *The magic thief.* New York: HarperCollins.

Piénkowski, Jan. (1979). *Haunted house.* New York: Dutton.

Piénkowski, Jan. (1993). *ABC dinosaurs.* New York: Dutton.

Piénkowski, Jan. (2004). *The first noël.* Cambridge, MA: Candlewick.

Pilkey, Dav. (1994). *Dog breath.* New York: Blue Sky.

Pinkney, Andrea. (2002). *Ella Fitzgerald: The tale of a vocal virtuoso.* Illustrated by Brian Pinkney. New York: Jump at the Sun/Hyperion.

Pinkney, Jerry. (2002). *Noah's ark.* New York: SeaStar.

Pinkney, Jerry. (2009). *The lion & the mouse.* New York: Little, Brown.

Pinkwater, Daniel. (1980). *The Wuggie Norpel story.* New York: Four Winds Press.

Pinkwater, Daniel. (2002). *Fat camp commandos.* New York: Scholastic.

Pinkwater, Daniel. (2007). *The Neddiad.* Boston: Houghton Mifflin.

Pinkwater, Daniel. (2009). *The Yggyssey.* Boston: Houghton Mifflin.

Platt, Richard. (1993). *Stephen Biesty's cross-sections: Man of War.* New York: Dorling Kindersley.

Platt, Richard, & Hawcock, David. (2008). *Moon landing.* Cambridge, MA: Candlewick.

Polacco, Patricia. (2008). *Someone for Mr. Sussman.* New York: Philomel.

Politi, Leo. (1949). *Song of the swallows.* New York: Scribner's.

Potter, Beatrix. (1902). *The tale of Peter Rabbit.* New York: Warne.

Prelutsky, Jack. (1984). *The new kid on the block.* Illustrated by James Stevenson. New York: Greenwillow.

Prelutsky, Jack (Ed). (1983). *The Random House book of poetry.* Illustrated by Arnold Lobel. New York: Random House.

Prelutsky, Jack (Ed.). (1999). *The twentieth century children's poetry treasury.* New York: Random House.

Pressley, Michael. (2001). Effective beginning reading instruction. Executive summary and paper commissioned by the National Reading Conference. Chicago: National Reading Conference.

Prévost, Guillaume. (2008). *The gate of days.* New York: Scholastic.

Pullman, Philip. (1985). *Ruby in the smoke.* New York: Random House.

Purcell-Gates, Victoria, McIntyre, Ellen, & Freppon, Penny A. (1995). Learning written storybook language in school: A comparison of low-SES children in skills-based and whole language classrooms. *American Educational Research Journal, 32,* 659–685.

Rallison, Janette. (2006). *It's a mall world after all.* New York: Walker.

Ravitch, D. (1985, Spring). The precarious state of history. *American Educator, 9*(4), 11–17.

Ravitch, Diane, & Finn, Chester. (1987). *What do our 17-year-olds know?* New York: Harper & Row.

Rawls, Wilson. (1961). *Where the red fern grows.* Garden City, NY: Doubleday.

redOrbit. (2006). TiVo KidZone launches as parents concern over children's television viewing soars. Retrieved from http://www.redorbit.com/news/technology/538959/tivo_kidzone_launches_as_parents_concern_over_childrens_television_viewing/index.html

Reinhart, Matthew, & Sabuda, Robert. (2010). *Gods and heroes.* Cambridge, MA: Candlewick.

Reutzel, D. Ray, & Cooter Jr., Robert B. (2009). *The essentials of teaching children to read: The teacher makes the difference* (2nd ed.). Boston: Allyn & Bacon.

Ritter, John. (2009). *The desperado who stole baseball.* New York: Philomel.

Roback, Diane. (2001, March 19). A year of big numbers. *Publishers Weekly, 248*(12), 43–50.

Robbins, Ruth. (1960). *Baboushka and the three kings.* New York: Parnassus.

Robinson, Barbara. (1972). *Temporary times, temporary places.* New York: Harper & Row.

Robinson, Barbara. (1972). *The best Christmas pageant ever.* New York: Harper & Row.

Robinson, Clyde C., Larsen, Jean M., & Haupt, Julie H. (1996). The influence of selecting and taking picture books home on the at-home reading behaviors of kindergarten children. *Reading Research and Instruction, 35,* 249–259.

Rockwell, Anne. (2008). *Clouds.* Illustrated by Frané Lessac. New York: HarperCollins.

Rockwell, Anne. (2009). *What's so bad about gasoline? Fossil fuels and what they do.* New York: Collins.

Roe, Mary F., Cuellar, Megan B., & Fickle, Michelle J. (2004, November 5). 49th Annual Meeting of the College Reading Association, Savannah, GA.

Roehrig, Catharine. (2008). *Fun with hieroglyphs.* New York: Simon & Schuster.

Rogasky, Barbara. (2002). *Smoke and ashes.* New York: Holiday House.

Rogot, Eugene, Sorlie, Paul D., & Johnson, Norman J. (1992, July/August). Life expectancy by employment status, income, and education in the National Longitudinal Mortality Study. *Public Health Reports, 107,* 457–461.

Rollock, Barbara. (1989). *Black experience in children's books.* New York: New York Public Library.

Roop, Connie, & Roop, Peter. (2001). *Escape from the ice: Shackleton and the Endurance.* Illustrated by Bob Doucet. New York: Scholastic.

Root, Shelton L., Jr. (1975, March 21). Lecture, University of Georgia, Athens, GA.

Rosen, Judith. (1997, July 21). They're everywhere you look. *Publishers Weekly, 244*(29), 120–123.

Rosen, Michael. (1989). *We're going on a bear hunt.* Illustrated by Helen Oxenbury. New York: Macmillan.

Rosenblatt, Louise. (1978). *The reader, the text, the poem.* Carbondale: Southern Illinois University Press.

Ross, C. S. (1995). "If They Read Nancy Drew, So What?" Series book readers talk back. *Library and Information Science Research, 17,* 201–236.

Rounds, Glen. (1992). *Three little pigs and the big bad wolf.* New York: Holiday House.

Rowling, J. K. (1998). *Harry Potter and the sorcerer's stone.* New York: Scholastic.

Rowling, J. K. (2000). *Harry Potter and the goblet of fire.* New York: Scholastic.

Rowling, J. K. (2007). *Harry Potter and the deathly hallows.* New York: Scholastic.

Rubel, David. (2009). *Scholastic encyclopedia of the presidents and their times.* New York: Scholastic.

Rutkoski, Marie. (2009). *The celestial globe.* New York: Farrar, Straus & Giroux.

Ryan, Pam Muñoz. (1999). *Amelia and Eleanor go for a ride.* New York: Scholastic.

Rylant, Cynthia. (1985). *The relatives came.* Illustrated by Stephen Gammell. New York: Bradbury.

Rylant, Cynthia. (2000). *Henry and Mudge and Annie's perfect pet.* Illustrated by Suçie Stevenson. New York: Simon & Schuster.

Rylant, Cynthia. (2005). *Henry and Mudge and the great grandpas.* New York: Simon & Schuster.

Rylant, Cynthia. (2006). *Henry and Mudge and the big sleepover.* Illustrated by Suçie Stevenson. New York: Simon & Schuster.

Rylant, Cynthia. (2007). *Little Whistle's medicine.* Illustrated by Tim Bowers. Edina, MN: Spotlight.

Rylant, Cynthia. (2010a). *Annie and Snowball and the magical house.* Illustrated by Suçie Stevenson. New York: Aladdin.

Rylant, Cynthia. (2010b). *Brownie and Pearl see the sights.* Illustrated by Brian Biggs. New York: Beach Lane Books.

Rylant, Cynthia. (2010c). *Mr. Putter and Tabby clear the decks.* Illustrated by Arthur Howard. Boston: Harcourt.

Sabine, Gordon, & Sabine, Patricia. (1983). *Books that made the difference.* Hamden, CT: Shoe String Press.

Sabuda, Robert. (1994). *The Christmas alphabet.* New York: Orchard.

Sabuda, Robert, & Reinhardt, Matthew. (2005). *Dinosaurs: Encyclopedia prehistorica.* Cambridge, MA: Candlewick.

Sabuda, Robert, & Reinhart, Matthew. (2006). *Encyclopedia prehistorica: Sharks and other sea monsters.* Cambridge, MA: Candlewick.

Sabuda, Robert, & Reinhart, Matthew. (2007). *Megabeasts.* Cambridge, MA: Candlewick.

Sabuda, Robert, with Matthew Reinhart. (2010). *Gods and heroes: Encyclopedia mythologica.* Cambridge, MA: Candlewick.

Sachar, Louis. (1998). *Holes.* New York: Farrar, Straus & Giroux.

Salomon, Stephanie. (2007). *Come look with me: American Indian art.* Watertown, MA: Charlesbridge.

Saltman, Judith. (1997, May/June). Groaning under the weight of series books. *Emergency Librarian, 24*(5), 23–25.

Sandburg, Carl. (1928). *Abe Lincoln grows up.* New York: Harcourt Brace.

Sandler, Martin W. (2009). *The Dust Bowl through the lens: How photography revealed and helped remedy a national disaster.* New York: Walker.

Sandved, Kjell. (1996). *The butterfly alphabet.* New York: Scholastic.

Sanford, Kathy. (2005–2006). Gendered literacy experiences: The effects of expectation and opportunity for boys' and girls' learning. *Journal of Adolescent & Adult Literacy, 49,* 302–315.

Santoro, Lucio, & Santoro, Meera. (2008). *Predators.* New York: Little Simon.

Saunders, Susan. (2000). *Lucky Lady.* New York: HarperCollins.

Say, Allen. (1993). *Grandfather's journey.* New York: Houghton Mifflin.

Schachner, Judy. (2008). *Skippyjon Jones shape up.* New York: Dutton.

Schlessinger, Laura. (2001). *Growing up is hard.* New York: HarperCollins.

Schmidt, Gary D. (1990). *Robert McCloskey.* Boston: Twayne.

Schuker, Lauren A. E. (2009, July 9). Harry Potter and the rival teen franchise. *The Wall Street Journal.* Retrieved from http://online.wsj.com

Schwartz, Alvin. (1974). *Cross your fingers, spit in your hat: Superstitions and other beliefs.* Philadelphia: Lippincott.

Schwartz, David M. (1985). *How much is a million?* Illustrated by Steven Kellogg. New York: Lothrop, Lee, & Shepard.

Schwartz, David M. (1999). *If you hopped like a frog.* Illustrated by James Warhola. New York: Scholastic.

Schwartz, David M., & Schy, Yael. (2009). *Where else in the wild? More camouflaged creatures concealed—and revealed.* Berkeley, CA: Tricycle Press.

Scieszka, Jon. (1989). *The true story of the 3 little pigs!* Illustrated by Lane Smith. New York: Viking.

Selznick, Brian. (2008). *The invention of Hugo Cabret.* New York: Scholastic.

Sendak, Maurice. (1963). *Where the wild things are.* New York: Harper & Row.

Seuss, Dr. (1957). *The cat in the hat.* New York: Random House.

Seuss, Dr. (1971). *The lorax.* New York: Random House.

Sewall, Gilbert T. (1988, April). American history textbooks: Where do we go from here? *Phi Delta Kappan, 69,* 553–558.

Sewall, Gilbert T. (2000). *History textbooks at the new century: A report of the American textbook council.* New York: American Textbook Council. (ERIC Document ED 441 731)

Shannon, George. (1996). *Tomorrow's alphabet.* Illustrated by Donald Crews. New York: Greenwillow.

Shannon, Patrick. (1989, Spring). Overt and covert censorship of children's books. *The New Advocate, 2*(2), 97–104.

Sharmat, Marjorie. (1972). *Nate the Great.* Illustrated by Marc Simont. New York: Coward, McCann & Geoghegan.

Sharmat, Marjorie. (2003). *Nate the Great on the Owl Express.* Illustrated by Martha Weston. New York: Delacorte.

Sharmat, Marjorie. (2009). *Nate the Great and the hungry book club.* Illustrated by Jody Wheeler. New York: Delacorte.

Shatzer, Joyce. (2008). Picture book power: Connecting children's literature and mathematics. *The Reading Teacher, 61,* 649–653.

Shaw, Nancy. (1986). *Sheep in a jeep.* Illustrated by Margot Apple. Boston: Houghton Mifflin.

Shaw, Nancy. (1992). *Sheep out to eat.* Illustrated by Margot Apple. Boston: Houghton Mifflin.

Shaw, Nancy. (1997). *Sheep trick or treat.* Illustrated by Margot Apple. Boston: Houghton Mifflin.

Shaw, Nancy. (2008). *Sheep blast off.* Illustrated by Margot Apple. Boston: Houghton Mifflin.

Shulevitz, Uri. (2005). *The travels of Benjamin of Tudela: Through three continents in the twelfth century.* New York: Farrar, Straus & Giroux.

Shulevitz, Uri. (2008). *How I learned geography.* New York: Farrar, Straus & Giroux.

Siebert, Diane. (1989). *Heartland.* Illustrated by Wendell Minor. New York: Crowell.

Siegal, Aranka. (1981). *Upon the head of the goat.* New York: Farrar, Straus & Giroux.

Sierra, Judy. (2000). *The gift of the crocodile: A Cinderella story.* New York: Simon & Schuster.

Silverstein, Shel. (1974). *Where the sidewalk ends.* New York: Harper.

Silverstein, Shel. (1981). *A light in the attic.* New York: Harper & Row.

Simon, Seymour. (1985). *Saturn.* New York: Morrow.

Simon, Seymour. (2006). *Creatures of the dark.* New York: Scholastic.

Sims, Rudine. (1982). *Shadow and substance: Afro-American experience in contemporary children's fiction.* Urbana, IL: National Council of Teachers of English.

Singer, Isaac Bashevis. (1992). *A day of pleasure and other stories for children.* New York: Galahad Books.

Slobodkina, Esphyr. (1940). *Caps for sale.* New York: W. R. Scott.

Smiley, Jane. (1994, February 15). Censorship in a world of fantasy. *The Chicago Tribune,* section 1, p. 19.

Smith, Carl B., Smith, Sharon L., & Mikulecky, Larry. (1978). *Teaching reading in secondary school content subjects: A bookthinking process.* New York: Holt, Rinehart & Winston.

Smith, Charles A. (1989). *From wonder to wisdom.* New York: New American Library.

Smith, Roland. (1995). *Thunder cave.* New York: Hyperion.

Smith, Roland. (2010, March 11). Personal letter to Michael O. Tunnell.

Sobol, Thomas. (1990, November). Understanding diversity. *Educational Leadership, 48*(3), 27–30.

Sonnenschein, Frances M. (1988). Countering prejudiced beliefs and behaviors: The role of the social studies professional. *Social Education, 52*(4), 264–266.

Spier, Peter. (1978). *Oh, were they ever happy.* New York: Doubleday.

Spinelli, Jerry. (1990). *Maniac Magee.* Boston: Little, Brown.

Spinelli, Jerry. (1996). *Crash.* New York: Knopf.

Spinelli, Jerry. (1997). *Wringer.* New York: HarperCollins.

Spinelli, Jerry. (2000). *Stargirl.* New York: Knopf.

Spinelli, Jerry. (2002). *Loser.* New York: Scholastic.

St. George, Judith. (2005). *So you want to be an explorer.* Illustrated by David Small. New York: Philomel.

Stanley, Diane. (2000). *Michelangelo.* New York: HarperCollins.

Stanley, Diane. (2002). *Saladin: Noble prince of Islam.* New York: HarperCollins.

Stanley, Diane. (2004). *The giant and the beanstalk.* New York: HarperCollins.

Stanley, Diane, & Vennema, Peter. (1993). *The bard of Avon: The story of William Shakespeare.* Illustrated by Diane Stanley. New York: William Morrow.

Stanley, Diane, & Vennema, Peter. (1994). *Cleopatra.* Illustrated by Diane Stanley. New York: William Morrow.

Stanley, Jerry. (1992). *Children of the Dust Bowl: The true story of the school at Weedpatch Camp.* New York: Crown.

Stanovich, Keith E. (1986). Matthew effects in reading: Some consequences of individual differences in the acquisition of literacy. *Reading Research Quarterly, 21,* 360–407.

Staples, Suzanne Fisher. (2005). *Under the persimmon tree.* New York: Farrar, Straus & Giroux.

Steig, William. (1969). *Sylvester and the magic pebble.* New York: Windmill.

Steig, William. (1976). *The amazing bone.* New York: Farrar, Straus & Giroux.

Stephens, Meic. (1990). *A dictionary of literary quotations.* London, UK: Routledge.

Steptoe, John. (1987). *Mufaro's beautiful daughters.* New York: Lothrop.

Stevens, Janet. (1995). *Tops and bottoms.* New York: Harcourt.

Stevenson, James. (2004). *Flying feet: A mud flat story.* New York: Greenwillow.

Stewart, Sarah. (2004). *The friend.* Illustrated by David Small. New York: Farrar, Straus & Giroux.

Stone, Jeff. (2005). *Tiger.* New York: Random House.

Street, Brian V. (1995). *Social literacies: Critical approaches to literacy in development, ethnography and education.* London, UK: Longman.

Sutcliff, Rosemary. (1959). *The lantern bearers.* New York: Walck.

Sutcliff, Rosemary. (1995). *Outcast.* New York: Farrar, Straus & Giroux.

Szabo, Corinne. (1997). *Sky pioneer: A photobiography of Amelia Earhart.* Washington, DC: National Geographic.

Taback, Simms. (1997). *There was an old lady who swallowed a fly.* New York: Viking.

Taback, Simms. (1999). *Joseph had a little overcoat.* New York: Viking.

Talwar, Kunal. (2005). Quotations. Retrieved from http://stat.www.berkeley.edu/users/shanky/quotations.html

Tan, Shaun. (2007). *The arrival.* New York: Arthur A. Levine.

Tate, Nikki. (2005). *Trouble on Tarragon Island.* Winlaw, BC, Canada: Sono Nis.

Tate, Nikki. (2007, June 27). The censor is alive and well and living in Saskatchewan. Retrieved from http://nikkitate.blogspot.com/2007/06/censor-is-alive-and-well-in.html

Taylor, Barbara M., Frye, Barbara J., & Maruyama, Geoffrey M. 1990. *American Educational Research Journal, 27*(2), 351–362.

Taylor, Mildred. (1976). *Roll of thunder, hear my cry.* New York: Dial.

Taylor, Sarah Stewart. (2010). *Amelia Earhart: This broad ocean.* New York: Hyperion.

Terry, Ann C. (1974). *Children's poetry preferences.* Urbana, IL: National Council of Teachers of English. (NCTE Research Report no. 16)

Thayer, Ernest Lawrence. (2000). *Casey at the bat: A ballad of the republic sung in the year 1888.* Illustrated by Christopher Bing. Brooklyn, NY: Handprint. (Original work published 1888)

Tilden, Thomasine E. Lewis. (2007). *Belly-busting worm invasions! Parasites that love your insides.* Danbury, CT: Children's Press.

Todd, Traci N., Gillingham, Sara, & Vance, Steve. (2007). *C is for caboose: Riding the rails from A to Z.* San Francisco: Chronicle.

Tolkien, J. R. R. (1937). *The hobbit.* London, UK: Allen & Unwin.

Tomlinson, Carl M., & Tunnell, Michael O. (1994). Children's supernatural stories: Popular but persecuted. In John S. Simmons (Ed.), *Censorship: A threat to reading, learning, thinking* (pp. 107–114). Newark, DE: International Reading Association.

Travers, P. L. (1934). *Mary Poppins.* London, UK: G. Howe.

Trease, Geoffrey. (1983, Autumn). Fifty years on: A writer looks back. *Children's Literature in Education, 14*(3), 21–28.

Trelease, Jim. (2001). *The read-aloud handbook.* New York: Penguin.

Trelease, Jim. (2006). *The read-aloud handbook* (6th ed.). New York: Penguin.

Trousdale, Ann. (1989, June). Who's afraid of the big bad wolf? *Children's Literature in Education, 20*(2), 68–79.

Tunnell, Michael O. (1994). The double-edged sword: Fantasy and censorship. *Language Arts, 71*(8), 606–612.

Tunnell, Michael O. (1999). *Halloween pie.* New York: Lothrop, Lee & Shepard.

Tunnell, Michael O., & Ammon, Richard. (1996, April/May). The story of ourselves: Fostering new perspectives. *Social Education, 60*(4), 212–215.

Tunnell, Michael O., & Jacobs, James S. (2005, September 1). Writers & readers: Series fiction and young readers. *Booklist, 102*(2), 64–65.

Turkle, Brinton. (1976). *Deep in the forest.* New York: Dutton.

Uchida, Yoshiko. (1971). *Journey to Topaz.* Berkeley, CA: Creative Arts.

Vail, Rachel. (2008). *Jibberwillies at night.* New York: Scholastic.

Van Allsburg, Chris. (1985). *The Polar Express.* Boston: Houghton Mifflin.

Van Allsburg, Chris. (1990). *Just a dream.* Boston: Houghton Mifflin.

Van Allsburg, Chris. (2002). *Zathura.* Boston: Houghton Mifflin.

Vandewater, Elizabeth A., Bickham, David S., & Lee, June H. (2006). Time well spent? Relating television use to children's free-time activities. *Pediatrics, 117,* 181–191.

Van Draanen, Wendelin. (2008). *Sammy Keyes and the cold hard cash.* New York: Random House.

Van Fleet, Matthew. (1995). *Fuzzy yellow ducklings.* New York: Dial.

Waber, Bernard. (1972). *Ira sleeps over.* Boston: Houghton Mifflin.

Wade, Suzanne E., & Moje, Elizabeth B. (2000). The role of text in classroom learning. In Michael L. Kamil, Peter B. Mosenthal, P. David Pearson, & Rebecca Barr (Eds.), *Handbook of reading research* (Vol. 3, pp. 609–627). Mahwah, NJ: Erlbaum.

Walker, Richard. (2010). *The human body Q & A.* New York: DK Publishing.

Wallace, Bill. (1988). *Beauty.* New York: Holiday House.

Wallace, Rich. 2010. *Kickers: Benched.* New York: Knopf.

Walsh, Ellen Stoll. (2007). *Mouse shapes.* New York: Harcourt.

Walt Disney Productions. (1973). *Snow White and the seven dwarfs.* New York: Random House.

Walton, Rick. (2000). *One more bunny.* New York: Lothrop.

Walton, Rick. (2001). *One more bunny.* Illustrated by Paige Miglio. New York: HarperFestival.

Wan, Guofong. (2006, Fall). Teaching diversity and tolerance in the classroom: A thematic storybook approach. *Education, 127*(1), 140–154.

Wasserman, Dale. (2001, February/March). Flipping the meat train. *American Heritage,* pp. 58–66.

Webb, Sophie. (2000). *My season with penguins: An Antarctic journal.* New York: Harper.

Wells, Deborah. (1995). Leading grand conversations. In Nancy L. Roser & Miriam G. Martinez (Eds.), *Book talk and beyond: Children and teachers respond to literature.* Newark, DE: International Reading Association.

Wells, Rosemary. (1979). *Max's first word.* New York: Dial.

Wells, Rosemary. (1999). *Bingo.* New York: Scholastic.

Wells, Rosemary. (2000). *Emily's first 100 days of school.* New York: Hyperion.

Whelan, Debra Lau. (2009). A dirty little secret: Self-censorship. *School Library Journal, 55*(2), 26–30.

White, E. B. (1952). *Charlotte's web.* New York: HarperCollins.

Whitin, David J. (2008). Learning our way to one million. *Teaching Children Mathematics, 14,* 448–453.

Whittemore, Hank. (1991, December 22). The most precious gift. *Parade Magazine,* pp. 4–6.

Wiesner, David. (1988). *Free fall.* New York: Lothrop.

Wiesner, David. (1991). *Tuesday.* New York: Clarion.

Wiesner, David. (1999). *Sector 7.* New York: Clarion.

Wiesner, David. (2003). *The three pigs.* New York: Clarion.

Wiesner, David. (2006). *Flotsam.* New York: Clarion.

Wigfield, Allan, & Guthrie, John T. (1997). Relations of children's motivation for reading to the amount and breadth of their reading. *Journal of Educational Psychology, 89,* 420–432.

Wilder, Laura Ingalls. (1932). *Little house in the big woods.* New York: Harper.

Wilder, Laura Ingalls. (1935). *Little house on the prairie.* New York: Harper.

Wiles, Deborah. (2001). *Freedom summer.* Illustrated by Jerome Lagarrigue. New York: Atheneum.

Willard, Nancy. (1981). *A visit to William Blake's inn: Poems for innocent and experienced travelers.* New York: Harcourt Brace and Jovanovich.

Williams, Carol Lynch. (2009). *The chosen one.* New York: St. Martin's Griffin.

Williams, Vera B. (1982). *A chair for my mother.* New York: Greenwillow.

Wilson, August. (1990, September 26). I want a black director. *New York Times,* p. A25.

Wilson, Robert, & Hall, Mary A. (1972). *Reading and the elementary school child.* New York: Van Nostrand Reinhold.

Winters, Kay. (2005). *And fly she did! The amazing childhood adventures of Amelia Earhart.* Washington, DC: National Geographic.

Wisniewski, David. (1996). *Golem.* New York: Clarion.

Wong, Janet S. (2010). *Me and Rolly Maloo.* Illustrated by Elizabeth Butler. Watertown, MA: Charlesbridge.

Wood, A. J., & Twist, Clinton. (2009). *Charles Darwin and the beagle adventure.* Cambridge, MA: Templar/Candlewick.

Woodard, Emory H., & Gridina, Natalia. (2000). *Media in the home 2000: The fifth annual survey of parents and children.* Philadelphia: Annenberg Public Policy Center of the University of Pennsylvania.

Woods, George. (1977, September 17). Evaluating children's books. Speech given at Brigham Young University, Provo, UT.

Wormell, Mary. (2001). *Bernard the angry rooster.* New York: Farrar, Straus & Giroux.

Worthy, Jo. (2000). "On every page someone gets killed!" Book conversations you don't hear in school. In David W. Moore, Donna E. Alvermann, & Kathleen A. Hinchman (Eds.), *Struggling adolescent readers: A collection of teaching strategies* (pp. 226–237). Newark, DE: International Reading Association.

Worthy, Jo, Moorman, Megan, & Turner, Margo. (1999). What Johnny likes to read is hard to find in school. *Reading Research Quarterly, 34,* 12–27.

Worthy, Jo, Turner, Margo, & Moorman, Megan. (1998). The precarious place of self-selected reading. *Language Arts, 75,* 296–304.

Wright, Betty Ren. (1983). *The dollhouse murders.* New York: Holiday House.

Wright, Betty Ren. (2000). *Moonlight man.* New York: Scholastic.

Wright, Betty Ren. (2003). *Crandall's castle.* New York: Holiday House.

Wright, Jessica Noelani. (2003). *Come look with me: Exploring modern art.* Watertown, MA: Charlesbridge.

Yates, Elizabeth. (1950). *Amos Fortune, free man.* New York: Dutton.

Yolen, Jane. (1988). *The devil's arithmetic.* New York: Viking Penguin.

Yolen, Jane. (1989, March). An experiential act. *Language Arts, 66*(3), 246–251.

Yolen, Jane, & Peters, Andrew Fusek. (2007). *Here's a little poem: A very first book of poetry.* Cambridge, MA: Candlewick.

Young, Ed. (1989). *Lon Po Po: A Red Riding Hood story from China.* New York: Philomel.

Young, Ed. (1992). *Seven blind mice.* New York: Philomel.

Zelinsky, Paul O. (1990). *The wheels on the bus.* New York: Dutton.

Zelinsky, Paul O. (1997). *Rapunzel.* New York: Dutton.

Index